CORPORATE FINANCE

CORPORATE FINANCE

Narender L. Ahuja
Professor of Finance
Institute of Management Technology (IMT)
Ghaziabad

Varun Dawar
Assistant Professor of Finance
Institute of Management Technology (IMT)
Ghaziabad

Rakesh Arrawatia
Assistant Professor of Finance
Institute of Rural Management (IRMA)
Anand

PHI Learning Private Limited

Delhi-110092
2016

₹ 595.00

CORPORATE FINANCE
Narender L. Ahuja, Varun Dawar and Rakesh Arrawatia

ISBN-978-81-203-5161-5

Published by Asoke K. Ghosh, PHI Learning Private Limited, Rimjhim House, 111, Patparganj Industrial Estate, Delhi-110092 and Printed by Mohan Makhijani at Rekha Printers Private Limited, New Delhi-110020.

Warmly Dedicated to
*our **families** and **students***
who have been great source
of strength and encouragement throughout

Contents

PART II CAPITAL INVESTMENT DECISION

Preface

Rule Number 1: Never lose money.
Rule Number 2: Never forget Rule Number 1.

—Warren Buffett

Many businessmen have succeeded without doing MBA, but no one has succeeded without astute management of finances. Finance is the life blood of business and its incisive management would be a pre-requisite for achieving the objectives of any organization. This book has been inspired by the long felt need to provide conceptual framework and the skills required for effective financial management in a simple yet comprehensive manner. The book has a practical bias, with emphasis on step-wise approach to financial analysis and decision making while at the same time developing a deep understanding of the theories of finance.

The pleasure of authoring this Corporate Finance textbook comes from the 60 years of our combined experiences in industry and academia. As authors, we intend to educate the readers on fundamentals of Corporate Finance carefully supplemented with real-life examples and scenarios. In the wake of fast changing economic landscape—characterized by global financial crisis, volatile equity and bond markets, rising dominance of emerging markets and increasing investor activism, the role of financial managers in an organization has assumed significant importance. This is further accentuated by the fact that financial markets across the world have become more integrated than ever before and financial decision-making needs to take into account the spate of global happenings in addition to domestic developments. For example, the Zero Interest Rate Policies (ZIRP) adopted by US and Europe in the aftermath of global financial crisis has led to extensive use of external commercial borrowings by corporates in emerging countries like India to take advantage of ultra-low interest rates while raising debt. Although financial managers have been able to lower the cost of capital using this cheaper route of financing, an impending rate hike by Federal Reserve could unwind this trade and force financial managers to change their financing strategies. Similarly, a reversal of interest rates in US and Europe could lead to significant outflow of foreign money parked in emerging markets equity and bond markets forcing financial managers to look for alternative sources of funding for financing their investment projects. In essence, the job of the corporate financial manager has become dynamic and requires a complete understanding of finance theory for implementing effective financial strategies.

This textbook aims at educating the readers on fundamentals of corporate finance and explains how various theories can be applied for efficient decision making of financial managers. To ensure that the readers imbibe the right understanding of financial theory, practical India-centric cases have been included at the end of chapters. Further, the chapters contain innumerable references to Indian companies so that readers can understand corporate financial decision making in the regional context. In addition, side-boxes have been included in major sections to facilitate memorization of important concepts and terms.

The encouragement to write this book came from the persistent appreciation of our students who continuously expressed the need for a simple, compact yet comprehensive text on this important subject. The book will be useful for both students and practitioners as it covers the course of PGDM/MBA taught in most leading business schools in the country, as well as the professional finance courses, such as the Chartered Accountancy (CA), Bank Management, CFA and Management Accounting courses.

The book is divided into 18 chapters. Chapter 1 introduces the readers to the objectives of a business firm and discusses the pros and cons of profit maximization versus wealth maximization. It further focuses on the scope of finance function and explains the three main financial decisions that a business firm must take. Chapter 2 introduces the concept of time value of money and highlight the implications of simple and compound interest along with calculation of terminal and present values using Present Value (PV) tables. Chapter 3 discusses the importance of investment decision and the need for a serious evaluation of project proposals. The chapter further identifies the information required for financial evaluations of proposals and help readers understand the computations of accounting rate of return and payback period.

Chapter 4 introduces the readers to DCF methods of project appraisal including the Net Present Value (NPV), Internal Rate of Return (IRR) and profitability index. Chapter 5 discusses the importance of risk analysis in project appraisal using various techniques, like sensitivity analysis, scenario analysis and simulation techniques. Chapter 6 talks about investment decision making under capital rationing and introduces the concept of real options for evaluating a project.

Chapter 7 discusses the meaning and significance of risk and return in the investment world and highlights how asset allocation or diversification can help in reducing portfolio risk and return. Chapter 8 introduces the readers to Capital Market Line (CML) and explains how optimal portfolios can be constructed using the efficient frontier and risk return tolerances of the investors. The chapter further focuses on determination of expected or required returns using Capital Asset Pricing Model (CAPM) and Arbitrage Pricing Theory (APT).

Chapter 9 introduces the bond valuation and various determinants of interest rates. The chapter discusses the valuation of zero coupon bonds and explain the methods of computing yield to maturity, yield to call and current yield. Chapter 10 discusses the concept and process of valuation and highlight the various valuation methodologies used by analysts globally. The chapter introduces the readers to relative valuation using various price multiples like P/E, P/B, P/S and PEG. The chapter further explains the Dividend Discount Model (DDM), Free Cash Flow to Firm (FCFF) and Free Cash Flow to Equity (FCFE) methodologies to arrive at equity value for the firm.

Chapter 11 introduces the concept of cost of capital and its constituents. The chapter help readers understand the calculation of cost of debt, equity and preference shares and discusses ways to assign weights to components of the cost of capital. Chapter 12 discusses various theories of capital structure including the Modigliani–Miller (MM) approach, net income approach, net operating income approach and the traditional approach. Chapter 13 introduces the readers to operating, financial and combined leverage and a step-wise approach to carry out the EBIT-EPS analysis. Chapter 14 talks about the relationship between dividends and financing decisions and lists out the practical aspects that companies have to consider while deciding on their dividend policy. The chapter distinguishes between bonus shares and share-splits and introduces the readers to the concept of buy-back of shares. Chapter 15 discusses the need for financial ratios analysis and covers various types of ratios such as liquidity ratios, profitability ratios, turnover ratios, capital structure ratios, return on investment ratios and their use in carrying out inter-firm and inter-period comparison of performance.

Chapters 16 and 17 discuss the meaning and importance of working capital and highlight the main factors that determine the working capital requirements. The chapter further introduces the concept of operating cycle to help readers understand the importance of efficient management of inventories, debtors, creditors and cash. Finally Chapter 18 discusses the financial management from the perspective of Non-Profit Organizations (NPOs).

We would urge our colleagues, students and readers to continue their support in future too. Any constructive suggestion to improve the book are most welcome.

Narender L. Ahuja
Varun Dawar
Rakesh Arrawatia

PEDAGOGY

The book contains a number of pedagogical aids to enable focussed learning of the students and hone their financial decision-making skills.

- Every Chapter starts with a list of learning objectives to be achieved at the end of the chapter

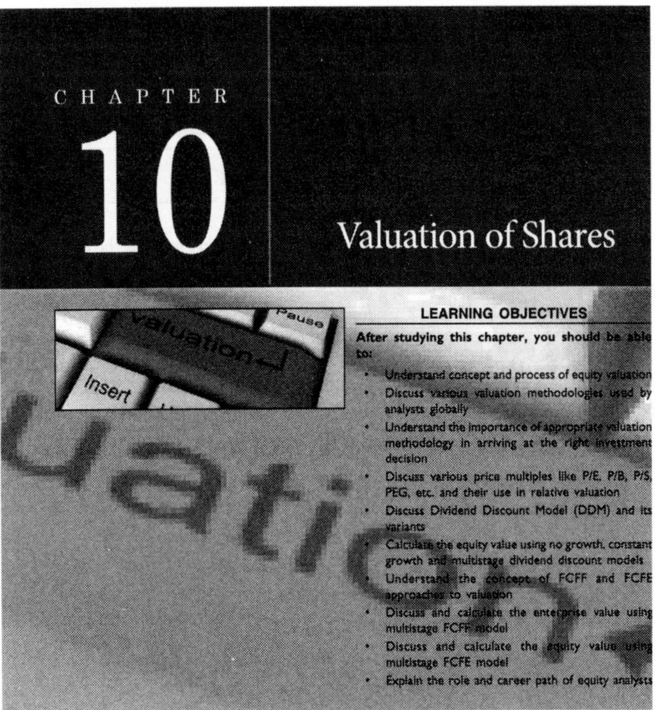

CHAPTER 10

Valuation of Shares

LEARNING OBJECTIVES

After studying this chapter, you should be able to:

- Understand concept and process of equity valuation
- Discuss various valuation methodologies used by analysts globally
- Understand the importance of appropriate valuation methodology in arriving at the right investment decision
- Discuss various price multiples like P/E, P/B, P/S, PEG, etc. and their use in relative valuation
- Discuss Dividend Discount Model (DDM) and its variants
- Calculate the equity value using no growth, constant growth and multistage dividend discount models
- Understand the concept of FCFF and FCFE approaches to valuation
- Discuss and calculate the enterprise value using multistage FCFF model
- Discuss and calculate the equity value using multistage FCFE model
- Explain the role and career path of equity analysts

- Practical relevant company references provided in various sections for better understanding of theory

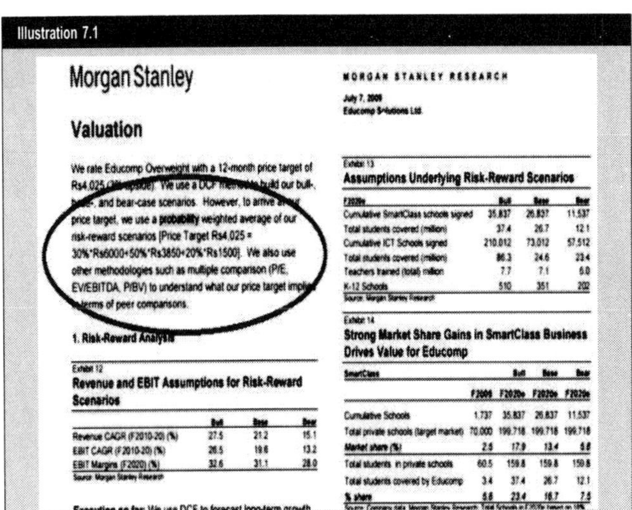

Illustration 7.1

Morgan Stanley

MORGAN STANLEY RESEARCH

Educomp Solutions Ltd.

Valuation

We rate Educomp Overweight with a 12-month price target of Rs4,025. We use a DCF method to build our bull-, base-, and bear-case scenarios. However, to arrive at our price target, we use a probability weighted average of our risk-reward scenarios [Price Target Rs4,025 = 30%*Rs6000+50%*Rs3850+20%*Rs1500]. We also use other methodologies such as multiple comparison (P/E, EV/EBITDA, P/BV) to understand what our price target implies in terms of peer comparisons.

1. Risk-Reward Analysis

Exhibit 12

Revenue and EBIT Assumptions for Risk-Reward Scenarios

	Bull	Base	Bear
Revenue CAGR (F2010-20) (%)	27.5	21.2	15.1
EBIT CAGR (F2010-20) (%)	26.5	19.6	13.2
EBIT Margins (F2020) (%)	32.6	31.1	28.0

Source: Morgan Stanley Research

Exhibit 13

Assumptions Underlying Risk-Reward Scenarios

F2020e	Bull	Base	Bear
Cumulative SmartClass schools signed	35,837	26,837	11,537
Total students covered (million)	37.4	26.7	12.1
Cumulative ICT Schools signed	210,012	73,012	57,512
Total students covered (million)	86.3	24.6	23.4
Teachers trained (total) million	7.7	7.1	6.0
K-12 Schools	510	351	202

Source: Morgan Stanley Research

Exhibit 14

Strong Market Share Gains in SmartClass Business Drives Value for Educomp

SmartClass		Bull	Base	Bear
	F2009	F2020e	F2020e	F2020e
Cumulative Schools	1,737	35,837	26,837	11,537
Total private schools (target market)	70,000	199,718	199,718	199,718
Market share (%)	2.5	17.9	13.4	5.8
Total students in private schools	60.5	159.8	159.8	159.8
Total students covered by Educomp	3.4	37.4	26.7	12.1
% share	5.6	23.4	16.7	7.5

- Excel based solved examples for deeper understanding of concepts discussed

IF =VARP(C3:C7)

	A	C	D	E
1	Year	Return	Squared deviations from the Mean	Squared deviations from the Mean
2	Mar-09			
3	Mar-10	-29.43%	[(-29.43%-(-7.36%))]^2	4.87%
4	Mar-11	-2.33%	[(-2.33%-(-7.36%))]^2	0.25%
5	Mar-12	-28.41%	[(-28.41%-(-7.36%))]^2	4.43%
6	Mar-13	2.80%	[(-2.80%-(-7.36%))]^2	1.03%
7	Mar-14	20.60%	[(-20.60%-(-7.36%))]^2	7.81%
8				
9	Mean	-7.36%		
10	Variance			3.68%
11	VAR()			=VARP(C3:C7)
12				VARP(number1, [number2], ...)

IF =STDEVP(C3:C7)

	A	C	D	E
1	Year	Return	Squared deviations from the Mean	Squared deviations from the Mean
2	Mar-09			
3	Mar-10	-29.43%	[(-29.43%-(-7.36%))]^2	4.87%
4	Mar-11	-2.33%	[(-2.33%-(-7.36%))]^2	0.25%
5	Mar-12	-28.41%	[(-28.41%-(-7.36%))]^2	4.43%
6	Mar-13	2.80%	[(-2.80%-(-7.36%))]^2	1.03%
7	Mar-14	20.60%	[(-20.60%-(-7.36%))]^2	7.81%
8				
9	Mean	-7.36%		

- Case studies have been provided at the end of the chapters for practical orientation of the theories studied

Annexure-1

Decision Case

GLOBAL SYNFUELS*

Financial and Strategic Appraisal of a Coal-to-Liquid Project

Abstract

Rapid economic growth in India during the past two decades had led to an ever-increasing demand for energy. India imported about two-third of its crude oil requirements resulting in huge outflow of precious foreign exchange. As a result, it became necessary for the country to look for alternative sources of energy. The Coal To Liquid (CTL) technology of coal gasification offered a credible alternative source of fuels as proved by Sasol of South Africa. In February 2009, the Government of India shortlisted Global Steel & Power Limited (GSPL) as one of the selected few companies to build a coal to liquid (CTL) project.

The CTL process involves extracting fossil oil from coal. GSPL set up a subsidiary named Global Synfuels and started evaluating the project viability. The project was strategically important to the company, but there were serious doubts about the commercial viability of a CTL project, particularly without Government subsidy. If the company did sink the huge investment and the project turned sour, the company could go bust and the management could earn the wrath of thousands of shareholders! While the company wanted to capitalize on the unique opportunities offered by the project, the project proposal must be subjected to rigorous financial and strategic appraisal before the company took a final call on the project.

➢ Solved numericals have been provided in major sections for student guidance

EXAMPLE 8.1 Vijay wants to determine the required return as per the CAPM Model for one of his portfolio security—ICICI Bank. He estimates that the beta (β) or systematic risk for the stock using daily returns for last 1 year as 1.14. Further, the risk-free rate in the economy currently is 7.8%. Finally, Vijay determines the equity risk premium as 5%.

Calculate the required or expected return for ICICI Bank using the above information.

Solution: Fitting the various components in the CAPM equation, we get required or expected return as:

Required return on ICICI Bank (R_i) = $R_F + (R_M - R_F) \times \beta_i$

$$R_i = 7.8\% + (5\%) \times 1.14 = 13.5\%$$

So, the CAPM determined required or expected rate of return for ICICI bank is 13.5%.

➢ Points to remember at the end of every chapter summarizes the important concepts discussed in a nutshell format

Points to Remember

- **Managers should analyze the risk profile** of the project and incorporate risk and uncertainty in the financial evaluation of the projects so that they could take rational and well informed decisions.
- **Sensitivity analysis** helps in answering 'What If' type of questions such as 'what if' the project's initial investment turns out to be X% higher than our estimates. It analyses important variables one by one to measure the impact of a change in the variable on the project NPV. Such analysis would highlight the variables, in which a small adverse change could cause the largest fall in the NPV.
- **Sensitivity analysis has only a limited use** because (i) it considers the impact of a change in only one variable at a time, (ii) it does not consider the probability of the adverse changes in variables, (ii) it ignores the interdependency between variables and (iii) it is not an optimizing or maximizing technique because it does not directly indicate the decision to be taken.
- **Scenario analysis:** Unlike sensitivity analysis which considers the impact of changing one variable at a time, scenario analysis can be used to analyze the collective effect of changing more than one variable simultaneously on the project's NPV. Scenario analysis can also take into account the interrelationship between variables.
- **The expected value** of cash flow is the probability-weighted average of all possible cash flows in different scenarios. The 'expected value' concept says that if the same types of projects are repeated again and again for a large number of times, then on an average, the expected value would be realized.

➢ Researchable issues provides students with 'food for thought' for future research

Researchable Issues

Faculty members, students and research scholars may like to consider the following selected issues for further research and case writing.

➢ Capital budgeting practices in multinationals.
➢ Financial appraisal of risky projects in Indian companies.
➢ Risk evaluation techniques and corporate governance.
➢ Corporate practices in the area of capital budgeting.
➢ Theory versus practice of risk analysis for project appraisal.
➢ Risk analysis of foreign acquisitions by Indian companies.
➢ Risk anrlysis and investment decision practices in the services sector.
➢ Risk analysis and investment decision practices in the infrastructure sector [power, water, transport projects].

➢ Various formats of *Problems*-theoretical questions, numericals and MCQs have been provided at the end of every chapter for critical thinking & practice of students

Questions

1. Explain the importance of risk analysis in project appraisal, and differentiate between risk and uncertainty.
2. Explain the meaning of sensitivity analysis, and using suitable numerical examples show its application to understand project risk.

Multiple Choice Questions

1. NMO company's current EBITDA is ₹400 crores. Market value of the company is 1,000 crores and market value of debt is 200 crores. Calculate the EV/EBITDA ratio of NMO company.
   (a) $4x$ (b) $0.33x$ (c) $6x$ (d) $3x$
2. Dividend payout ratio of company MKJ is 50%. If the required rate of return is 10% and long-term growth rate is 5%, calculate the fundamental P/E ratio for the company.
   (a) $11x$ (b) $20x$
   (c) $10x$ (d) None of the above

Self-Test Questions

1. Safex Company is evaluating an investment proposal that would require an initial investment of ₹2,50,000 in plant and equipment to produce a new product. The project is expected to generate annual sales revenue of ₹4,00,000 for a period of three years at the end of which the plant and equipment are expected to have a resale value of ₹50,000. The variable cost of the product is expected to be ₹2,40,000 per annum for the above budgeted sales revenue. The annual fixed cost of the company (other than depreciation) would increase by ₹40,000. Assume Safex Company's cost of capital is 15%. Ignore taxes.
   (a) On the basis of the information given above, calculate the project's NPV and decide if the project should be accepted.
   (b) Taking one variable at a time, calculate the percentage changes in the following estimates that would be required for the investment decision to change:
      (i) Initial investment
      (ii) Variable cost
      (iii) Fixed cost

Acknowledgements

The authors would like to express their gratitude to a number of present and former colleagues from academia, industry as well as thousands of former students for their support and encouragement. Thanks are due to CA Dipankar Chatterji, Dr. V. Panduranga Rao, Dr. A.K. Chauhan, Dr. A. Kastia, and Dr. D. Maitra, Dr. R.K. Chakraborty, Dr. S.K. Batra (IMT, Ghaziabad), Dr. L.C. Gupta, Dr. S.P. Parashar and Bhavesh Patel (XLRI Jamshedpur), Dr. Nand Dhameja (MDI, Gurgaon), Dr. Avinash Chander and Dr. Vijay Kapur (ICAI), Dr. S.K. Chakraborty, Prof. K.K. Bhattacharya and Prof. N.K. Rao (IIMC), Dr. Madhu Vij, Dr. S.K. Tuteja and Dr. Anjali Kalsie (FMS, Delhi University), Dr. Deepak Chawla, Dr. V.K. Seth and Dr. Barnali Chakladar (IMI, New Delhi), Prof. S. Sundararajan (IIMB), Dr. S.K. Ganguli (XIMB), Dr. Sweta Agarwal and Dr. Gunjan Mittal (IILM), Ms. Bhavna Ranjan Ahuja (Alliance, Bangalore), Dr. G.L. Sharma (LBSIM), Dr. Raj Agrawal (AIMA), Dr. Girish Tripathi (NTPC), Dr. S.R. Dash (IIM, Indore), Dr. Jeemol Unni and Prof. Paresh J. Bhatt and Late Prof. Shiladitya Roy (IRMA), Dr. Arun Misra (IIT, Kharagpur), Dr. Anirban Dutta (NIT, Agartala), Dr. Dipali Krishnakumar, SCMHRD, Dr. Sarita Vichore, Durgadevi Saraf Institute of Management Studies (DSIMS), Arit Chaudhury and Rohit Tandon (Max Life), Mandeep S. Manihani (JP Morgan), Hitesh Goel (Kotak), as well as academic associates, Deeksha Arora and Megha Pandey, and many others.

We are also grateful to the publishers for the unstinted support and timely execution of this textbook.

Narender L. Ahuja
Varun Dawar
Rakesh Arrawatia

PART I

INTRODUCTION TO CORPORATE FINANCE

CHAPTER

1 Objectives, Scope and the Financial Environment

LEARNING OBJECTIVES

After studying this chapter, you should be able to:

- Understand the meaning of organizational mission and how it differs from the corporate objectives.
- Discuss the pros and cons of profit maximization as the financial objective of a business firm.
- Explain the meaning of wealth maximization and how it is a better financial objective than profit maximization.
- Explain the three main financial decisions that a business firm must take.
- Describe the advantages of the company form of business over sole proprietor and partnership.
- Distinguish between (i) money and capital markets and (ii) primary and secondary markets.

1.1 Introduction

There has been a gradual, but significant change in the role and scope of the finance function over the past few decades. Initially firms were mostly managed by the persons or families who owned the business and the role of the finance manager was more confined to performing functions such as accounting and preparing financial reports, cash budgets, sales collections and dealing with banks. The focus of the finance function then was more on 'accounting' for the monies received and paid rather than 'management' of finances. After the Companies Act, 1956 came into force, the finance function was expanded to cover legal compliance related to issues such as corporate reporting and issue of shares and other matters.

The finance function is involved in all aspects of business including production, purchases, marketing, strategy formulation and implementation.

Over time, particularly since the opening up of the Indian economy in the 1990s when businesses started growing rapidly and competition from local and global companies became intense, the role of the finance manager became critical to the success of the firm. In the modern corporate set-up, finance managers are involved in all important aspects of financial decision making including strategy formulation and implementation, evaluation of new investment projects, risk management, valuing bonds and shares, deciding on the optimal financing mix to minimize the cost of capital, evaluating mergers and acquisitions, working capital management, the dividend decision and share buybacks.

Thus the finance function plays a critical role in management of businesses and ensuring that the corporate objectives are achieved.

1.2 Objectives of Business Organizations

There are several stakeholder groups in a business each of which would have their own objectives to pursue.

A number of parties or groups from within and outside the business have a stake in the success of the firm. These groups include the owners (shareholders) who provide the risk capital, lenders such as banks, creditors who supply goods and services, managers, employees, competitors, tax and regulatory authorities. Each of these groups would have their own objectives to protect their self-interest. However, the corporate objectives or the objectives of an 'organization' should be guided by the firm's mission and not the objectives of any particular stakeholder group. All the same, in practice the corporate objectives may be significantly influenced by the stakeholder group that has maximum power in the organization.

1.2.1 The Corporate Mission

The mission may be defined as the very long-term (perpetual) objective of the firm, stated in general, non-quantifiable terms, and is related to the reason for which the firm was established. The mission of a hospital may be to provide best possible healthcare to patients using latest technology. The mission of an automobile company may be to produce efficient, safe and environment friendly cars. The mission statement of Tata Steel is an excellent example of the purpose and contents of a mission statement.

ILLUSTRATION 1.1 TATA STEEL MISSION

"Consistent with the vision and values of the founder Jamsetji Tata, Tata Steel strives to strengthen India's industrial base through the effective utilization of staff and materials. The means envisaged to achieve this are high technology and productivity, consistent with modern management practices.

Tata Steel recognizes that while honesty and integrity are the essential ingredients of a strong and stable enterprise, profitability provides the main spark for economic activity.

Overall, the Company seeks to scale the heights of excellence in all that it does in an atmosphere free from fear, and thereby reaffirms its faith in democratic values."

Source: [http://www.tatasteelindia.com/corporate/vision-and-strategy.asp]

1.2.2 The Corporate Objectives

Corporate objectives should be related to the company as a whole and not a particular stakeholder group. As far as possible, the following points may be considered while deciding on the corporate objectives:

The mission of an organization is the reason for its being in existence. Mission states the long term objective of the firm in general terms.

1. The corporate objectives should be explicitly stated: Every organization should clearly determine the objectives it wishes to pursue and all executives who are expected to contribute to the achievement of the objectives should be well informed about the same. This would set a clear direction in which the firm would move and help in better planning and coordination of the activities of the firm.

2. The corporate objectives should be quantifiable: This is required so that they can be measured and used as a benchmark to evaluate actual managerial performance.

3. The corporate objectives should be realistic: Setting unrealistic objectives would de-motivate managers who are expected to achieve them and thus may not serve the purpose.

The corporate objectives should be guided by the firm's mission and not the objectives of any particular stakeholder group.

4. Objectives should relate to the key factors for business success, which may be profitability (or Return on Investment), market share, growth, cash flows, customer satisfaction and the quality of the firm's products. The objectives of an organization may be financial and non-financial.

1.2.3 Profit Maximization as the Objective

It has been observed that some firms shy away from stating profitability as their financial objective. However, the mission statement of Tata Steel given above clearly states the financial objectives, "Tata Steel recognizes that ... profitability provides the main spark for economic activity".

In general, profitability or earning a satisfactory amount of profits may be regarded as the primary financial objective of a business organization in the private sector. The short-term financial objectives of companies usually include targets for profits. For example, a firm may have the objective of earning a profit of ₹20 million per annum.

Although profits do matter, they have limitations as a measure of a company's achievements:

1. Absolute figure of profits: They do not take into account the amount of investment made to earn the profit. For example, if two firms A and B earned a profit of ₹1,00,000 each, they might appear to be equally profitable. But if the amount of investment in A was ₹5,00,000 and in B it was ₹2,00,000, then return on investment (ROI) rather than the absolute amount of profits would be a better measure of profitability (see Table 1.1):

TABLE 1.1
Profit vs ROI

	A	*B*
Profits earned	1,00,000	1,00,000
Investment	5,00,000	2,00,000
Return On Investment (ROI)	20%	50%

Going by the return on investment (profits as a percentage of investment) criteria, B is more profitable as compared to A. Thus, it would be better to express the profitability objective in terms of the return on investment. In case of companies, the Earnings Per Share (EPS) can be used instead of ROI.

Profit maximization neither considers the investment base nor the time value of money.

2. Short-term profits may be manipulated: Companies listed on the stock exchanges report annual as well as quarterly and half-yearly interim results. Such reported profits are measures of short-term performance, whereas a firm's true performance should ideally be judged over a longer term. There have been instances where, in order to show rosy short-term performance, managers avoided necessary expenditures on training, research and development or postponed replacement of equipment in order to reduce current costs and report better short-term profits, even though such actions could be disastrous for the long-term viability of the firm.

3. Time value of money: Due to the time value of money, an equal amount of profit earned today would be more valuable than the same amount of profit earned in a later year. However, the objective of profit maximization ignores this aspect.

4. The risk factor: The amount of reported profits does not state the degree of risk involved in the project. Thus, if two businesses X and Y earned the same amount of profits but X is regarded as more risky than Y, then Y company would be more valuable to the investors than X.

5. Dividend policy: Profits and return on investment objectives do not specify how the earned profits should be used. Profits earned may be used to pay dividends or may be retained by the company to finance further growth of the business.

1.2.4 The Wealth Maximization Objective

Shareholder wealth maximization takes care of all the shortcomings of the profit maximization objective.

In spite of the above conceptual limitations of the profit maximization objective, it is a common practice to include profit targets in the annual budgets and financial plans of the company. However, from a long-term point of view, the prime financial objective of a company should be to maximize the wealth of its shareholders. Shareholders are the owners of the company and their wealth can be measured by the market value of the shares that they hold in the company. For example: if X holds 10 shares of Reliance Industries and the market price (on the stock exchange) is ₹1,000 per share, then his wealth (as far as these shares are concerned) is ₹10,000.

The wealth maximization objective states that the company should take such investment, financing and dividends decisions that would lead to maximization of shareholder wealth in the long term.

How would the wealth maximization objective take care of the shortcomings of the profit-maximization objective? More and more investors would want to buy the shares of well run, profitable companies with bright prospects. As the demand for a company's shares increases, the share prices would rise thereby increasing the shareholder wealth. Brighter the future prospects of a company, greater would be the demand for its shares leading to an increase in the shareholders wealth.

Shareholder Wealth and Risk Management

However, the company should manage its operating activities without taking undue business and financial risks which are a cause of concern for the shareholders. If the risk undertaken by a company is perceived to be disproportionately high, investors may panic and start selling the shares. Such an action by a large number of investors would reduce the share prices leading to a loss of shareholder wealth. This way the wealth maximization objective can reflect the riskiness of a company's business.

Shareholder Wealth and Dividend Policy

How the earned profits are utilized can also have an impact on the share prices and shareholder wealth. A company can either use the earned profits to pay cash dividends to shareholders or retain the same for reinvestment in the business. If the company is retaining profits but not reinvesting wisely, the investors may perceive bleak future prospects and may want the company to distribute profits as cash dividends, failing which they may start selling the shares. This would have a negative effect on the market value of the shares resulting in a decline in the shareholder wealth. Once again we see that the wealth maximization objective can reflect the effect of management decisions through the market price mechanism.

Time Value of Money

The wealth maximization objective can also take care of the time value of money by discounting the future expected cash flows to find their equivalent present values using the appropriate discount rate. An example of this would be the Net Present Value (NPV) method we shall study in the chapter on investment decision.

Wealth maximization is conceptually the most accepted financial objective of a business firm. Accordingly, note that throughout this book, it is assumed that the financial objective of a firm is to maximize the shareholder wealth.

1.2.5 Corporate Versus Departmental Objectives

The ability of a firm to make profits and create wealth, in turn, would depend on its sales performance and the cost structure. Thus wealth maximization would be possible only by achieving a satisfactory sales volume, controlling costs, earning profits and utilizing them in the best possible manner to create value. In their words, while the main financial objective remains to maximize shareholders wealth, sub objectives of achieving target sales, market share and cost control would also be important.

Accordingly, in addition to corporate objectives which may be set in terms of profitability and shareholder wealth, departmental objectives are established specific to individual units or departments of an organization. The departmental objectives are often 'operational' objectives, examples of which may be as follows:

1. The sales and marketing department may target to increase the number of customers by 10%.
2. The production department may target to reduce the number of rejects by 50%.
3. The management accounting department may target to produce monthly reports more quickly, say within 4 working days at the end of each month.

1.2.6 The Non-financial Objectives

A business should have non-financial objectives too, and should strive to maintain a balance between the financial and non-financial objectives. The latter category may include employee welfare, customer satisfaction, servicing society, providing employment and environment protection.

In addition to corporate objectives, a firm should have departmental and non-financial objectives to pursue.

1.2.7 Trade-off Between Objectives

When a company is following several key objectives, it may be that some of them could be achieved only at the expense of others. For example, an objective of achieving a high rate of growth in sales and market share may force the firm to lower prices that will have an adverse effect on profit-margins. In such situations, there may be a trade-off between objectives and a choice will have to be made.

Also note that following the wealth maximization objective does not mean that the firm should ignore the legitimate interests of other stakeholders. To the extent required legally or by market forces, the legitimate interest of other stakeholders should be met. However, serving the interests or objectives of the individual stakeholders can be seen as a way of achieving the final objective of shareholder wealth maximization rather than an end in itself. For example, take the objective of employee welfare. Instead of looking at it as an end in itself, the firm should aim at maximizing the shareholder wealth while providing for the legitimate welfare of the employees.

1.3 Scope of the Finance Function

As was stated earlier, the finance function is involved in all aspects of business, chasing cash flows through the organization. The scope of the finance function is characterized by the functions performed by the finance team which may include right up to the CEO or the managing director of the company. The functions of the modern day finance manager/team may be classified into three major decision areas as follows.

1.3.1 The Investment Decision

The finance function shadows cash flows through the organization and deals with investment, financing and dividend decisions.

Given that the primary objective of a firm is to maximize shareholder wealth, it becomes imperative that managers understand the impact of their decisions on company valuation in the market. For this purpose, an in-depth understanding of how an investment decision of purchasing a new asset would change the future cash flows and the associated valuation of the business would help managers in making right choices.

Investment decision or capital budgeting is among the most important decisions made by the management. Investment decisions define the industry in which the firm would operate and the types of goods and services it would produce and sell. Investment projects undertaken today would influence the long-term profitability of the firm and involve commitment of relatively huge sums of money for a long period. A wrong investment decision could be very expensive for the firm and therefore the firm should be very careful in selecting investment projects.

The finance manager would be expected to determine the cash flows over the life of the projects being considered and evaluate the same using modern techniques such as the Net Present Value (NPV) and the Internal Rate of Return (IRR) that take into account the time value of money. Thus, the finance manager would help the top management in choosing the set of projects that meet the firm's objectives ensuring optimum utilization of financial and other resources.

Complications in the investment decision could arise due to uncertainty surrounding the future cash flows related to the projects, as well as the need for capital rationing resulting from limitation of funds available. The existence of inflation and conditional probabilities could further complicate the investment decision making. Accordingly, the finance manager would have to be adequately trained in risk analysis techniques including sensitivity analysis and simulation.

Often the investment decision may relate to acquiring another firm. Such an investment decision would require an appropriate understanding of the valuation techniques and tools to arrive at the fair enterprise valuation of the target company.

1.3.2 The Financing Decision

The investment and financing decisions are related. While the selected projects would determine the amount of funds required to implement the project, the funding limitations should also be kept in mind before selecting the projects.

As a part of the financing decision, the finance manager should identify the long-term sources that can be tapped to raise the required funds. The sources of long-term funds would broadly consist of equity capital, preference capital and debt sources. For each of these sources, the finance manager would consider the cost of capital as well as other terms and conditions while deciding on the specific sources from which to raise funds.

The financing mix decision should take into account all relevant factors including the operating earnings expected from the new projects, amounts and proportion of funds that can be raised from each source, the target financing mix of the firm, impact of the specific funding options on the earnings per share as well as the operating and financial leverage.

One of the most debated topics in corporate finance is whether or not the capital structure has any impact on the value of the firm and the overall (weighted average) cost of capital. In other words, is there an optimal capital structure that the firm could identify and use to minimize its overall cost of capital and maximize the value of the firm?

Some experts argue that no matter what proportions of debt and equity sources are mixed to finance a project, the overall cost of capital would remain the same and that any capital structure would be as good as any other. This is because any advantage of using cheaper debt in the capital structure would be exactly offset by an equivalent rise in the cost of equity.

However, an alternative (the traditional) approach suggests that the firm can increase its total market value through judicious mix of debt and equity sources, and that the firm should make efforts to identify an optimal capital structure that would minimize its overall cost of capital. The finance manager should have adequate understanding of the implications of different theories and the maturity to decide what would be the most relevant approach in the specific circumstances of the firm.

Using all the relevant information, he should also be able to advise the pecking (priority) order in which different sources should be tapped to finance new projects.

From time-to-time, the company may enter the capital market to raise additional funds by issuing new shares, either to launch new projects or to acquire other companies. For this purpose, the finance manager would need to make a sharp assessment of the relationship between market values of shares and the returns expected by the investors, so that the company can avoid over-pricing or underpricing of the new shares and make its share offerings at prices attractive enough for the investors.

Again, from time-to-time, the company would need to raise fresh debt funding to invest in long-term assets and undertake new projects. For this purpose, an understanding of the functioning of bond markets and pricing of bonds becomes imperative for the modern day corporate finance managers. A rightful insight into pricing and valuation of bonds can help managers in minimizing cost of capital by raising debt at an appropriate time at low interest rates. For example, in the past few years, a number of Indian companies have raised cheaper debt through USD or Euro denominated bonds to make use of ultra-low interest rates prevailing in these markets.

1.3.3 The Dividend Decision

Companies may use their earned profits to either pay dividends to shareholders or retain the earnings to finance new projects. Thus, the dividend and financing decisions are inter-related. In this respect, an understanding of the market valuation impact of dividend and financing decisions would be required so that the company can maintain the right balance between paying dividends and retention of earnings in a way that would maximize the shareholder wealth. Other relevant factors that have a bearing on the dividend decision including shareholder preferences, future investment opportunities and the company's liquidity position should also be considered while deciding on the dividend policy.

The three main financial decisions that confront the corporate managements are the ones discussed above, namely the investment, financing and the dividend decision. However, given the importance of the working capital management for effective financial management and shareholder wealth maximization, it deserves a separate discussion as follows.

1.3.4 Working Capital Management

The firm should pay adequate attention to working capital management which can considerably boost return on investment.

While evaluating new investment projects, the estimated net working capital required should be included in the project cost. From this perspective, the working capital may be regarded as a part of the investment decision. However, liquidity and working capital also influence the dividend and financing decisions of the company.

The working capital requirements should be estimated keeping in mind the operating cycle of the firm and other practical aspects. Part of the working capital requirements may be met with bank financing while the remaining portion is financed from long-term sources, suppliers' credit or other short-term funding avenues. A proactive and prudent management of debtors, inventories, creditors and cash management can considerably improve the return of investment and add to shareholder wealth.

The financial managers and the companies they represent must function within the legal and regulatory framework operating in the country. For this purpose, it is important to be familiar with certain important aspects of the Indian financial and regulatory environment discussed below. In particular, the areas relevant to financial management would be the forms of business organization, selected provisions of the Companies Act, corporate governance, stock markets and their regulation.

1.4 The Financial Environment

The financial environment refers to the set of rules governing different forms of organization, financial markets, securities, institutions and the regulatory environment that exists to facilitate and ensure fair business practices. These are briefly discussed below.

1.4.1 Forms of Business Organization

The forms of business organization have evolved from sole proprietorship to the modern conglomerates. From the perspective of business ownership, we can distinguish between sole trader, partnership and the company forms of business organization. The following discussion would also bring out their respective pros and cons.

Sole Trader or Sole Proprietor

The sole proprietor is liable for all the business debts. Even his personal assets may be acquired to pay up liabilities.

In this form of business, a single person called the proprietor owns the business. The proprietor brings in the required ownership capital and may run the business with the help of his family or some employees. Small businesses, such as a grocery store, a chemist shop, vegetable and fruit mart or a furniture store may be examples of sole proprietorship.

In such a business, the profits or losses made by the business belong to the proprietor. He is liable for all the business debts up to the full extent of his business as well as his personal assets. For example, if the business runs into losses and has total assets of the value of ₹2,00,000 while the money owed to outsiders (lenders and creditors) is ₹3,00,000, the sole proprietor would be required to make up for the shortfall of ₹1,00,000 from his personal properties.

Financial decision-making including evaluation of investment projects and financing decisions in small businesses run as sole proprietorships would be similar to companies except that sole proprietors cannot issue shares and bonds like companies to raise funds. On the plus side, such businesses would not be subjected to detailed corporate governance provisions applicable to companies because the proprietor himself owns and manages the business and does not have external financing.

Partnership

Partnership is a form of business where two or more persons agree to jointly own and run a business with the objective of sharing the profits and losses in an agreed proportion. Suppose John wants to start a business which requires a larger amount of ownership capital than he can afford. He may take a partner so that they can jointly provide the ownership capital and share the profits and losses of the business. A partnership could also happen for another reason. Suppose Raj is an engineer who wants to set up a business, but has little funds to invest, while Dilip has funds to invest, but no technical skills. They may form a partnership, whereby Dilip provides most of the required capital while Raj provides technical skills to run the business, and they agree to share the profits/losses in an agreed manner.

In India, partnership enterprises are regulated as per the provisions of the Indian Partnership Act, 1932, according to which a partnership firm can have up to a maximum of 20 partners. In partnership, the business belongs to the partners and they are individually and jointly liable for the amounts owed by the partnership business to outsiders. Since each partner can bind other partners by his business decisions, a partnership can last only as long as partners have full faith in one another.

A good transparent system of financial management would be a must for every partnership business so that all business transactions are properly recorded and known to partners, reducing the chances of any misunderstanding between them. Profits of the partnership firm are split among the partners according to the terms of their agreement. Thus, if X, Y and Z are in a partnership business which earned a profit of ₹1,00,000 during a period and there exists an agreement between them to share it in the ratio of X: 50%, Y: 30% and Z: 20%, then they would get ₹50,000, ₹30,000 and ₹20,000 respectively as their part of the profits. If there is no formal agreement on the sharing of profits, it is assumed that they have agreed to share the profits equally.

A common shortcoming of the sole proprietorship and partnership is the *unlimited* liability of the owners. What it means is that even the personal wealth of the proprietor or partners can be taken over to meet the business obligations to outsiders if the business runs into losses and does not have adequate resources to meet its obligations. For example, suppose the Raj & Dilip's partnership business runs into losses and owes ₹1,00,000 to outsiders while the value of all resources left with the business is only ₹50,000. The partners would have to pay up the balance from their personal wealth.

A major disadvantage of sole proprietor and partnership is the unlimited liability of the owners.

Limited Liability Partnership (LLP)

A Limited Liability Partnership (LLP) is a form of business organization in which some or all partners (as permissible by applicable laws) have a limited liability, similar to the shareholders of a company. This is a relatively new form of organization that aims to combine the advantage of limited liability with partnership. In a simple partnership, all partners have a right to take active part in managing business and partners are individually and jointly responsible for the decisions taken by any partner. This greatly increases the risk or possible liability of partners because at times, the wrongful decisions or misconduct of one partner could lead to huge business losses and all other partners would be held jointly responsible for the liabilities of the business.

In contrast, in an LLP some partners may have a limited liability similar to shareholders of a company. Such partners with limited liability will normally be the ones who have chosen to be passive investors and are not directly involved in the management of the partnership business. In several countries, the LLP law requires that at least one of the partners must have unlimited liability.

In India, LLPs are governed by the Limited Liability Partnership Act, 2008 which provides that in an LLP, "no partner would be liable on account of the independent or unauthorized actions of other partners". Thus, in an LLP, individual partners may

In LLP, passive partners may be shielded from the joint liability arising from misconduct of other partners.

be shielded from the joint liability arising from the wrongful business decisions or misconduct of another partner. An LLP is treated as a legal entity separate from its partners, similar to a registered company. There is no upper limit on the number of partners to an LLP, while a normal unlimited-liability partnership cannot have more than 20 partners.

In India, LLPs are controlled by the registrar of companies and at least one of the partners to an LLP should be an Indian. LLPs are becoming popular as the preferred form of organizing small and medium businesses particularly in the service industry and among professionals.

Company Form of Business

Shareholders appoint the Board to run the company on their behalf, thus separating ownership from management.

The growth of the company form of business since the 19th century has brought about a radical transformation in the way businesses are owned and managed. There was a time when most businesses were small in size and would be owned and managed either by a single person or a few persons called partners. When businesses grow to a size that would require huge sums of ownership capital, sometimes running into millions and billions, it may not be possible for a single or a few persons to provide all the ownership capital required. In such cases, the company form of business may be the best way because in this form of business, a large number of investors can subscribe to the ownership capital.

Shareholders (also called members) put in the ownership capital needed to operate the business, but the management is in the hands of the Board of Directors of the company. Thus, the company form involves separation of ownership from management whereby shareholders appoint directors to run the company on their behalf. Companies in India are set up under the Indian Companies Act, 2013 (previously 1956). Examples of some large companies in India include Reliance Industries Limited, ITC Limited, Tata Motors Limited, ONGC Limited and Wipro Limited.

Note that the names of all these companies end with the word 'limited'. This word emphasizes an important feature of the company form of organization that the liability of the shareholders of the company is *limited* to the amount they have invested in the share capital of the company and their personal wealth cannot be touched to pay up the company's liabilities to outsiders. To illustrate, if Ravi invested ₹20,000 in the ownership capital of a company and the company runs into losses, the maximum amount he can lose is his investment as above, and is not liable to pay any more money to meet the losses of the company.

The company's share capital is divided into small parts or shares of equal value to facilitate wider ownership base.

The ownership capital in a company is known as 'share capital'. The total amount of ownership capital required in a company is divided into small parts or shares of equal value, and investors are invited to subscribe for a number of shares according to their investment needs.

Assume a company wishes to raise an ownership capital of ₹10,00,000. This total amount can be divided into 1,00,000 parts or shares of ₹10 each and public can be invited to subscribe to these shares according to their investment requirements. So, Anil a small investor may apply for 100 shares of ₹10 each, or a total value of ₹1,000, while Brij a large investor may apply for ₹10,000 shares of ₹10 each, total value of applied shares being ₹1,00,000. The persons who buy the shares of a company like Anil and Brij are known as its shareholders.

A company is considered a completely separate legal entity and the shareholders' possible liability for the company's debts is limited to the amount invested in the shares of the company.

1.4.2 Types of Shares

A Company can normally issue two types of shares: preference shares and equity (ordinary) shares.

Preference Shares

Preference shares are those on which the company pays a fixed rate of dividend on a preferential basis. The holders of these shares are entitled to priority treatment in payment of dividends and also in refund of capital (if the company is wound up). The law provides that dividend on preference shares should be paid before any dividend is paid on the ordinary share capital. Similarly, if the company is wound up, the preference share capital should be repaid in full before any part of the ordinary share capital is repaid.

Preference shareholders get a fixed rate of dividend and have priority in payment of dividends and refund of capital.

Due to this privilege of preferential treatment, investment in preference shares may be regarded as less risky than investment in ordinary shares. However, a disadvantage of investment in such shares is that preference shareholders would get a fixed rate of dividend even when the company makes huge profits. Another disadvantage is that preference shareholders normally do not have 'voting rights' to participate in the selection of directors and other management decisions.

Equity (Ordinary) Shares

The holders of ordinary shares are the providers of the ownership risk capital, and as such, are not entitled to any preferential treatment in payment of dividends or in refunding the capital if the company is wound up. But if the company is profitable, the balance of profits remaining after paying taxes and the preference dividends belong to the ordinary shareholders. They have voting rights and as the legal owners of the company, all net surplus generated by the business belongs to them.

Equity holders have voting rights and all net surplus generated by the business belongs to them.

1.4.3 Private and Public Limited Companies

How many equity shareholders can a company have? Companies may be classified into Private Limited and Public Limited companies:

1. Private Limited Companies: In India, Private Limited Companies should have at least two shareholders, and the maximum permissible number under the Companies Act, 2013 is 200 shareholders (previously maximum number was 50 under the 1956 Act). Such companies are not allowed to invite the general public to subscribe to any shares. Private limited companies may often be closely-held companies where the majority of shares are held by a family or friends.

2. Public Limited Companies: A public limited company must have at least seven shareholders and there is no upper limit of members/shareholders. Thus, Reliance Industries has several million shareholders. ITC and many other companies also have a large number of shareholders running into thousands or even millions.

As a large number of persons from the general public might invest in the shares of a company, the Governments are obliged to prescribe strict rules for regulating the affairs of companies, and also have elaborate corporate governance requirements for protecting the interests of the investing public. For obvious reasons, such regulatory requirements are more rigid for public limited companies than for private limited companies.

The public limited companies can get their shares 'listed' on the stock exchanges such as the National Stock Exchange and the Bombay Stock Exchange. As a part of the listing agreements, the stock exchanges would also mandate companies to disclose

Listed companies must provide required financial and other information at regular intervals to the stock exchange.

certain financial and other information about their business activities at regular intervals.

Note that unless specifically mentioned otherwise, the discussion of topics in this book would be assumed to relate to public limited companies.

1.4.4 Methods of Issue of Shares

The Companies Act, 2013 provides that a Public Limited Company can issue securities (such as shares) by the following methods:

- Public offer through prospectus
- Private placement
- Rights or bonus issues

The public offer by prospectus can include the following types of issues: Initial Public Offer (IPO), Further Public Offer (FPO) or offer for sale by an existing shareholder through prospectus. In case of public offers, it would be necessary to list the shares on the stock exchange. Either the company should be already listed at the time of making the public offer of shares, or should have the intention to have its shares listed.

1.4.5 The Issue of Shares by Prospectus

As noted above, public limited companies can make a public offer to issue securities (such as shares) through the prospectus. The prospectus is a detailed document that provides relevant information about the shares (or other securities) offered and the company making the offer for information of the prospective investors. The information to be provided in the prospectus is governed by the Companies (Prospectus and Allotment of Securities) Rules, 2014.

Among other details, the "prospectus to be issued shall contain the following particulars, namely:

(a) the objects of the issue;
(b) the purpose for which there is a requirement of funds;
(c) the funding plan (means of finance);
(d) the summary of the project appraisal report (if any);
(e) the schedule of implementation of the project;
(f) the interim use of funds, if any." [Rule 3]

Public limited companies can issue securities by (a) Public offer through prospectus, (b) Private placement or (c) Rights and bonus issues.

In addition, the prospectus should provide last five years' profit and loss statements and other financial information about the company's operations as required. Further, information about the company and its business, promoters and directors, auditors, any litigation going on and other relevant information as provided in the said rules has to be provided so that prospective buyers of the shares are well-informed.

Red Herring Prospectus

A red herring prospectus is a preliminary prospectus which contains most of the information required except some key details about either the price or the total amount of the issue. When the issue is being made by the book-building process, the final price cannot be determined until the bidding process is complete. Accordingly, the company making the issue initially files a red herring prospectus and later after the bidding process is over and the final issue price has been determined, it would file a final prospectus with the Registrar of Companies (ROC).

1.4.6 Listing of Shares on the Stock Exchange

The listing of a company's shares on the stock exchange means that these shares can be traded on the stock exchange. Trading facility enables investors to buy and sell the shares easily, and thus, listing imparts liquidity to the investment in shares.

A company intending to get its shares listed on the stock exchange has to apply for the same. Only such companies can get listed that fulfill the eligibility criteria. For example, the National Stock exchange has prescribed detailed eligibility criteria for permitting listing of shares and other securities. The National Stock Exchange allows two types of listing of securities as given in Box 1.1:

BOX 1.1 NATIONAL STOCK EXCHANGE

IPO & NEW LISTING

Initial Public Offering (IPO)

Initial Public Offer (IPO) is a process through which an unlisted Company can be listed on the stock exchange by offering its securities to the public in the primary market. The object of an IPO may be relating to expansion of existing activities of the Company or setting up of new projects or any other object as may be specified by the Company in its offer document or just to get its existing equity shares listed by diluting the stake of existing equity shareholders through offer for sale.

New Listing

New Listing is a process through which a company which is already listed on other stock exchange/s approaches the Exchange for listing of its equity shares. The companies fulfilling the eligibility criteria prescribed by the Exchange; from time to time; are listed on the Exchange.

Eligibility of any company for listing on NSE will be examined on the following six criteria:

(a) Paid up Capital, Market Capitalisation and Net Worth
(b) Three year track record
(c) Dividend/Distributable Profit Track Record
(d) Fulfilment of listing requirements on other Exchanges, where the company is listed
(e) Conditions Precedent to Listing on the Exchange
(f) Disciplinary Action Track Record

[Adapted: http://www.nseindia.com/corporates/content/ipo_listing.htm]

Companies seeking listing of securities should have a 'paid up equity capital of not less than ₹10 crores' post issue and meet other eligibility conditions.

1.4.7 Agency Theory and the Corporate Greed

A possible disadvantage of the company form of organization is the separation of ownership from management. The agency theory deals with the relationship between shareholders as the principals (owners) and company managers as their agents. Shareholders, who are the owners or principals of the company, delegate the task of running the business to the directors and managers, who are the shareholders' agents. Being the shareholders' agents, the managers should work to maximize the shareholders' wealth.

However, it may not work this way in practice. Often the managers could get greedy and exploit the company's wealth for their own benefit. In other words, there is a conflict between the interests of the two groups and there is a need to develop rules and incentives to avoid or minimize the conflict. A possible solution to this problem is to devise such incentive systems (such as variable remuneration and employee stock options) so that when managers work hard to get higher benefits, shareholder wealth would also be maximized.

1.4.8 The Securities and Exchange Board of India

The Securities and Exchange Board of India was established in 1992 with a view to develop and regulate the securities markets and to protect the interests of the investors in securities. The main functions of the Board are given in Box 1.2:

BOX 1.2 MAIN FUNCTIONS OF SEBI

(a) Protect the interests of investors in securities
(b) Promote the development of the securities market and to regulate the same.
(c) Regulating the business in stock exchanges and other securities markets;
(d) Registering and regulating the working of intermediaries such as stock brokers, bankers to an issue, merchant bankers and underwriters.
(e) Registering and regulating the working of the depositories, foreign institutional investors, credit rating agencies, mutual funds and venture funds.
(f) Promoting investors' education and training of intermediaries of securities markets;
(g) Prohibiting insider trading.
(h) Performing such other functions as may be prescribed."

[Adapted, www.sebi.gov.in]

1.4.9 Corporate Governance and Clause 49 of the Listing Agreement

The (revised) Clause 49 of the Listing Agreement issued by SEBI has been implemented with effect from October, 2014. It aims to strengthen corporate governance in listed companies with the objective of balancing the interest of the individuals, companies and the society.

Among other things, it mandates that listed companies must honour the rights of the shareholders. These include the right to be adequately informed about—and participate in deciding—any important changes taking place in the company.

Further the shareholders must get the opportunity to participate and vote in general shareholder's meetings, and have a right to place items on the agenda of the meeting and propose resolutions. In general, the management must allow the shareholders an opportunity to exercise ownership rights.

Further, it requires that the listed companies must take effective steps to avoid 'insider trading' and abusive exploitation of the minority shareholder by the majority. Companies must ensure equitable treatment of all shareholders.

The clause 49 also deals with a number of other important aspects of corporate governance including the duties and responsibilities of the Board of Directors, independent directors, directors' remuneration, auditors committee and whistle blower policy.

1.4.10 The Securities Markets

Securities are financial instruments such as shares, debentures, commercial paper and treasury bonds that can be traded in the market. The securities market may be classified as follows:

1. Money and capital markets: Securities may be of long-term or short-term duration. The market which deals in short-term securities, such as treasury bonds and commercial paper is known as the money market. In comparison, the market where long-term financial securities are traded is called the capital market. Thus, market for equity shares, preference shares and long-term debentures/bonds would be called the capital market.

2. Primary and secondary markets: Issue of new shares by a company to the investors is known as a primary market activity. In a primary market transaction, new shares are issued by the company to the investors and the investors pay the consideration amount to the company. The stock exchanges like NSE and BSE are called secondary markets because they facilitate buying and selling of existing shares that were already issued by the companies to investors. Thus, if X subscribed to the initial public offer of shares made by Tata Motors, it would be a primary market transaction in which X makes the payment to the issuing company Tata Motors and the company issues him the shares. Later if X wants to sell off his Tata Motors shares, he would not go back to the company to return the shares. Instead he can easily sell the shares held by him on the stock exchanges.

References

Ansoff, H. Igor., *Strategic Management*, Palgrave Macmillan, 2007

Argenti, John, *Strategic Corporate Planning*, Nelson, 1974.

www.tatasteelindia.com/corporate/vision-and-strategy.asp]

www.nseindia.com/corporates/content/ipo_listing.htm

www.sebi.gov.in/cms/sebi_data/about_us/act15ac.html

www.nseindia.com/getting_listed/content/eligibility_criteria.htm

http://taxguru.in/company-law/comparison-private-public-limited-company-companies-act-2013.html

www.sebi.gov.in/commreport/clause49.html

Solomon Ezra, *The Theory of Financial Management*, Columbia University Press, 1963.

Points to Remember

- **Corporate objectives:** Several parties or groups from within and outside the firm would want to push their own objectives, but the corporate objectives should be guided by the firm's mission and not the objectives of any particular stakeholder group.
- **Deciding the Corporate objectives:** Corporate objectives (i) should be explicitly stated and shared with managers, (ii) should be quantifiable so that they can be measured, (iii) should be realistic and (iv) should relate to the key factors for business success.
- **Profit maximization:** This, as an objective, has the following shortcomings: (a) profits do not take into account the amount of investment made, (b) short-term profits may be manipulated, (c) do not consider time value of money, (d) profits do not state the degree of risk involved in the project and (e) from the figure of earned profits it is not clear how they should be utilized for value creation.
- **Wealth maximization:** Wealth maximization is accepted as the financial objective of business as it takes care of all the shortcomings of the profit maximization objective. The firm should thus aim at increasing the wealth of the shareholders who are the owners of a company. For this purpose, their wealth can be measured by the market value of the shares that they hold.
- **Scope of the finance function:** The finance function is involved in all aspects of business including manufacturing, purchases and marketing. The functions of the modern day finance manager may be classified into three major decision areas (i) investment decision, (ii) financing decision and (iii) the dividend decision. In addition, the firm should pay adequate attention to working capital management.
- **Company form of business:** When businesses grow to a size that would require huge sums of ownership capital, the company form of business may be the best way because in this form of business, a large number of investors can subscribe to the ownership capital. The limited liability and liquidity features are added advantages that account for the popularity of the company form of business.

- **Share capital:** A Company can normally issue two types of shares: preference shares and equity shares. Preference shareholders get a fixed rate of dividend *and* are entitled to priority treatment in payment of dividends and in refund of capital if the company is wound up. No such privileges are available to equity shareholders.
- **Private and public limited companies:** Private Limited Companies should have at least two shareholders and the maximum permissible under the Companies Act, 2013 is 200 shareholders. Such companies are not allowed to invite the general public to subscribe to any shares. A public limited company must have at least 7 shareholders and there is no upper limit of members/shareholders.
- **Issue and listing of shares:** The Companies Act, 2013 provides that a public limited company can issue securities through (a) Public offer through prospectus, (b) Private placement or (c) Rights or bonus issues. The securities can be listed on the stock exchanges as per rules.

Questions

1. What do you understand by the organizational mission? How is it different from corporate objectives?
2. Discuss the main shortcomings of the profit maximization as the financial objective of a business firm. Support your answer with suitable examples.
3. Explain the meaning of wealth maximization as the financial objective of business. How does wealth maximization score over profit maximization?
4. "Finance is the life blood of business". In the light of this statement, discuss the scope of the finance function highlighting the main financial decisions that management must take.
5. Explain why the company form of business organization has become more popular over the past few decades?
6. Distinguish between (i) money and capital markets and (ii) primary and secondary markets.
7. Explain the meaning of listing of shares and discuss its advantages to the investors. Briefly discuss the factors that a stock exchange would consider to decide on the eligibility of a company for listing.

Multiple Choice Questions

1. Limited liability is a feature of which of the following forms of business?
   (a) Sole trader (b) Partnership
   (c) Company (d) None of the above
2. Ramu's Farm earned a profit of ₹60,000 in a year. If Ramu's investment in the farm amounted to ₹2,00,000, what would be his Return on Investment (ROI)?
   (a) 15% (b) 20%
   (c) 30% (d) None of the above
3. The minimum number of shareholders in a public limited company is:
   (a) 2 (b) 7
   (c) 20 (d) None of the above
4. Preference shareholders are those who:
   (a) Get dividends at a fixed rate
   (b) Are the personal friends of the Finance Minister
   (c) Take away most of the profits of the business
   (d) None of the above
5. What is the management objective on which the theory of corporate finance is based?
   (a) Profit maximization (b) Shareholder wealth maximization
   (c) Cost minimization (d) None of the above

CHAPTER

2

Time Value of Money

Compound interest is the eighth wonder of the world. He who understands it, earns it ... he who doesn't ... pays it.

—Albert Einstein

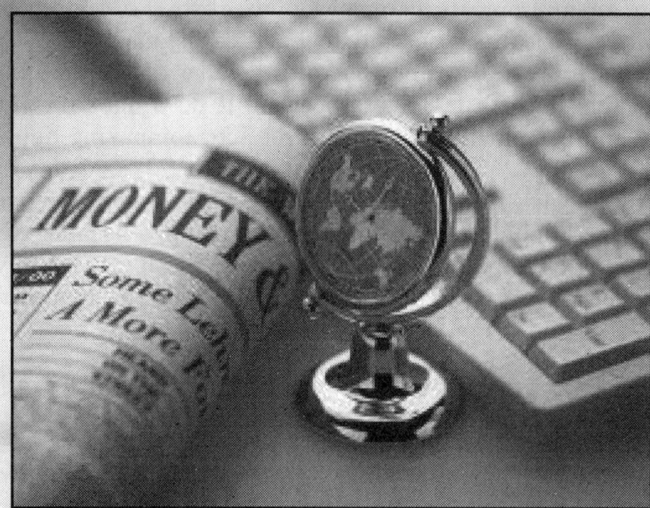

LEARNING OBJECTIVES

After studying this chapter, you should be able to:

- Understand the importance of time value of money.
- Distinguish between simple and compound interest.
- Explain the meaning of discounting and present values.
- Calculate the terminal and present values using formulas.
- Compute the present values of future single sums and annuities using PV tables.
- Determine the Equated Annual Installments (EAI) to repay loans.
- Explain the effect of compounding more than once a year.
- Determine the present value of perpetuity.

2.1 Introduction

Corporate managers would be required to consider the time value of money in a number of situations, particularly when cash flows are expected to be spread across a number of future periods. One such common situation arises when a firm is evaluating an investment project that would require an initial cash outflow in current period and promise returns in several future years. Assume a firm has to invest an amount of ₹5.00 million now to undertake a new project that promises cash returns of ₹1.00 million in each of the subsequent six years. Is the project acceptable? A simple but naïve way to evaluate the project would be to compare the total of future cash inflows with the initial investment and conclude that the project is acceptable since the total of future cash returns ₹6 million exceeds the initial project investment.

However, that would not be an appropriate comparison because the cash flows taking place at different points of time cannot be said to have the same value. The ₹1.00 million cash inflow receivable in year 6 cannot be said to have the same value as an equal sum of money receivable in year 1. This is because it does not take into account the time value of money and comparing them would be like comparing apples with oranges.

When cash flows are spread over a number of future periods, time value of money becomes an important consideration in decision making.

Take another example. A company is issuing ₹100 bond at par now and promises to redeem it at ₹110 in ten years. Should investors lap it up simply because the amount to be returned by the company is higher than the amount it takes initially? This simple rule would be wrong because it does not take into account the investor's time value of money.

2.2 Reasons for the Time Preference

What then is the time value of money? The time value of money refers to the time preference for receiving the same amount of money sooner rather than later, for the simple reason that one can invest the sum of money to earn a return (or interest) during the intervening period. For example, if a person has a choice to receive ₹1,000 either now or after 5 years, quite obviously he would prefer to receive it now because he can invest the amount for the intervening period of five years to earn a return, and thus, increase his wealth. Applying the same logic to cash outflows, there would be a time preference for paying a sum of money later rather than sooner.

Of course there could be other reasons for the time preference in addition to the possibility of earning a return during the intervening period. Two other common reasons may be: (i) consumption preference and (ii) the risk avoidance. The consumption preference says that a person would prefer to spend the same money on consumption now rather than at a future point of time. Again, the purchasing power of money may decline due to inflation in future periods, which could be another reason for preferring to receive an equal sum of money now rather than in future. The risk avoidance reason means that future investments have an element of risk involved, so it would be safer to get the same amount of money sooner rather than later.

There is time preference to receive a sum of money sooner rather than later due to the possibility of earning a return.

Among the reasons for the time preference, the ability to invest and earn a return would be more relevant for our discussion here, because it gives us a way to measure the time value in monetary terms. For example, if a person can earn a return of 8% per annum by investing the amount in a bank term deposit, we can say that his time value of money is 8% per annum.

2.3 Terminal Values Versus Present Values

The essence of the time value is that sums of money receivable or payable at different future dates are not comparable, and therefore, cannot be added or subtracted without first transforming them into equivalent comparable sums of money.

To make such cash flows comparable, we can use either of the two processes:

1. Terminal values: Find out the terminal values of the cash flows related to two competing projects as at a future point of time. For example, if a firm is considering investing in one of the two projects, both requiring the same initial investment and having the same life of ten years, then we could find out what each one of them would be worth after ten years and choose the one that promises maximum terminal value at that point of time. However, such a comparison of the terminal values would look so unreal and distant. The firm is investing now and would want to know the result in terms of today's money rather than as at a distant future point of time.

2. Present values: In this method, all future cash flows related to competing projects are transformed into their equivalent present values using the time value of money relevant to the firm. This process is called discounting and is regarded as a more acceptable alternative as compared to comparing the terminal values. Once all future cash flows are converted into their present value equivalents, it would be easier for the firm to compare the initial project investment with the present value of the expected cash flows from the project because they would both be expressed in terms of the same time value.

'Discounting' is thus, used as a method of converting the future sums of money into their present value equivalents. By discounting future sums back to the present, we can place all sums to be received (or paid) in the future on a comparable basis so that they can be added and subtracted.

Discounting is reverse of compounding, and is based on the same principles as the compound interest. Therefore, let us briefly revise our understanding of compound interest before we discuss discounting to find the present values of future cash flows.

2.4 Compound Versus Simple Interest

Interest is the price or cost the borrower pays to the lender for letting him use his (lender's) money. Interest could be classified as simple interest or compound interest. Understanding the different implications of simple and compound interest is absolutely essential before one could become a good manager.

Discounting future cash flows to their present value equivalents makes them comparable so that they can be added and subtracted.

2.4.1 Simple Interest

Simple interest is calculated on the principal amount of the loan. The assumption here is that the interest accruing to the lender would be paid to him by the borrower each period as it becomes due, and would NOT be added to the principal amount of the loan for calculating interest in future periods. Thus, if a firm has taken a loan of ₹10,000 from ICICI bank at simple interest rate of 12% per annum, the interest amounting to ₹1,200 would be paid by the firm to the bank each year. This interest amount would then not be added to the principal loan amount and interest payable in future years would also be calculated only on the principal of ₹10,000.

2.4.2 Compound Interest

In the above example of a loan of ₹10,000 at 12% interest rate, assume the agreed terms of the loan are such that the firm would not have to pay interest annually as it accrues; rather the firm would repay the principal loan amount along with the accumulated interest at the end of five years. Thus, the interest amount of ₹1,200 accrued at the end of the first year would not be paid by the firm, but would instead be added to the loan principal amount. As a result, the second year's interest would be calculated not only on the principal amount of ₹10,000 but also on the accrued interest of ₹1,200. The second year interest calculation would thus be = 11,200 × 12% = ₹1,344 (and not ₹1,200). Similarly, the interest for subsequent years would be calculated on the aggregate amount of principal loan plus accumulated accrued interest. This process is called compounding.

Compound interest means that accrued interest is added to the loan amount and subsequent interest would be calculated on the total of principal plus accrued interest.

In general terms, compounding refers to a process where previous earnings from an asset are reinvested to generate future earnings. Thus, in relation to a loan situation it would mean that the interest earned is redeployed by the lender to earn more interest income in future. In other words, the accrued interest is added to the outstanding loan amount and subsequent interest would be calculated on the revised balance. Similarly, in relation to any other investment, compounding would refer to generating further income on the previously earned income.

EXAMPLE 2.1 Terminal or Future Values

Krish deposits ₹1,000 in a bank term deposit earning 6% compound interest per annum. What would be the amount (terminal value) that would have accumulated (a) at the end of one year, (b) at the end of two years, (c) at the end of three years, and (d) at the end of five years?

Solution: The future value or terminal value based on compound interest can be calculated by the following formula:

$$\text{TV} = P(1 + r)^n$$

where,

TV = Terminal value or the amount accumulated

P = Principal amount initially deposited

r = Interest rate per annum (expressed as a decimal)

n = Number of years of the term deposit.

Substituting the values:

(a) Terminal value at the end of one year:

= ₹1,000 × (1.06) = ₹1,060

(b) Terminal value at the end of two years:

= ₹1,000 × 1.06 × 1.06

= ₹1,000 × 1.1236 = ₹1,123.6

(c) Terminal value at the end of three years:

= ₹1,000 × 1.06 × 1.06 × 1.06

= ₹1,000 × $(1.06)^3$

= ₹1,000 × 1.191016 = ₹1,191.02

(d) Terminal value at the end of five years:

= ₹1,000 × $(1.06)^5$

= ₹1,000 × 1.338226 = ₹1,338.23

EXAMPLE 2.2 Present Values

Jay wants to accumulate a sum of ₹5,000. If the bank allows a compound interest rate of 8% per annum on the term deposit, how much should Jay deposit now so that

₹5,000 would be accumulated (a) at the end of one year, (b) at the end of two years, (c) at the end of three years and (d) at the end of five years?

Solution: In the given situation, the future or terminal value (TV) is known and we have to find out the principal (*P*) or initial amount of deposit to be made. The initial amount of deposit would be the present value of the terminal value using the given compound rate of interest. This can be computed by rearranging the above formula to calculate the principal amount (*P*):

$$P = \frac{TV}{(1+r)^n}$$

Substituting the values:

(a) If a terminal value of ₹5,000 is required at the end of one year, the principal amount (*P*) of deposit now should be:

$$P = \frac{5000}{1.08} = ₹4,629.63 \text{ (approximately)}$$

(b) If a terminal value of ₹5,000 is required at the end of two years, the principal amount (*P*) of deposit now should be:

$$P = \frac{5,000}{1.08 \times 1.08} = ₹4,286.69$$

(c) If a terminal value of ₹5,000 is required at the end of three years, the principal amount (*P*) of deposit now should be:

$$P = \frac{5,000}{(1.08)^3} = ₹3,969.16$$

(d) If a terminal value of ₹5,000 is required at the end of five years, the principal amount (*P*) of deposit now should be:

$$P = \frac{5,000}{(1.08)^5} = ₹3,402.92$$

2.5 The Purpose of Discounting

In the previous example, we computed the initial deposit that one would have to make now to get the desired sums (terminal values) at a future point of time. This is the process of discounting the future sums of money to calculate their present values. For example, in part (a) above, ₹4,629.63 is the present value of ₹5,000 receivable at the end of one year if the discount rate (compound interest or time value of money) is 8%. What it signifies is that if the time value (interest rate or discount rate) is 8%, one would be equally happy or indifferent between receiving ₹5,000 at the end of one year or ₹4,629.63 now. Thus the purpose of discounting is to calculate an equivalent present value of a future cash flow that would make one equally happy or indifferent between the two amounts—the present value now or the sum of money at a future point of time.

Given the applicable rate of interest, the present value would make one indifferent between the present value now or the sum of money at a future point of time.

2.6 Present Value Formula for Single Sums

The present value of a single sum of money receivable (or payable) at the end of 'n' years from now, at the given compound interest (discount) rate 'r' can be calculated as follows:

$$PV = \frac{FV}{(1+r)^n}$$

where,

PV = Present Value
FV = Future Value (future cash flow)
r = Interest rate (expressed as a decimal)
n = Number of years

Present value formula: $PV = FV \div (1 + r)^n$

The future value (FV) in the above equation may be called by various names such as the terminal value, accumulated amount, cash flow or simply the sum of money.

EXAMPLE 2.3 Calculate the present values of the following single sums of money receivable in future:

(a) ₹10,000 receivable at the end of 1 year from now if rate of discount (interest) is 12%.
(b) ₹8,000 receivable at the end of 2 years from now if rate of discount (interest) is 10%.
(c) ₹15,000 receivable at the end of 3 years from now if rate of discount (interest) is 8%.
(d) ₹20,000 receivable at the end of 4 years from now if rate of discount (interest) is 6%.

Solution: Present values are found by discounting the future sums of money using the following formula:

$$PV = \frac{FV}{(1+r)^n}$$

Substituting the values:

(a) Present value of ₹10,000 receivable at the end of 1 year, r = 12%:

$$PV = \frac{10,000}{1.12} = ₹8,928.57$$

(b) Present value of ₹8,000 receivable at the end of 2 years, r = 10%;

$$PV = \frac{8,000}{(1.10)^2} = \frac{8,000}{1.21} = ₹6,611.57$$

(c) Present value of ₹15,000 receivable at the end of 3 years, r = 8%.

$$PV = \frac{15,000}{(1.08)^3} = \frac{15,000}{1.259712} = ₹11,907.48$$

(d) Present value of ₹20,000 receivable at the end of 4 years, $r = 6\%$:

$$\text{PV} = \frac{20{,}000}{(1.06)^4}$$

$$= \frac{20{,}000}{1.262477} = ₹15{,}841.87$$

2.6.1 Formula to Find Present Values of Annuities

When an equal amount of money is received (or paid) for a number of periods at regular intervals, it is referred to as an annuity. Examples of annuities may be: a student getting a scholarship of ₹24,000 per annum for three years, or a person paying back the car loan in 10 equal annual instalments of ₹50,000 each.

EXAMPLE 2.4 A student has been selected to get a scholarship of ₹24,000 per annum at the end of each of the next three years. What would be the present value of the scholarship if the relevant discount (interest) rate is 9% per annum?

Solution: There is a series of three equal sums of money included in this annuity. There can be two approaches to find the present value in this situation: (a) we can first find out the present values of three single scholarship instalments and then add them up to calculate the present value of the annuity, or (b) use a formula that would save us some time and effort. Let us try both ways.

Approach 1 Adding together separate PVs:

$$\text{PV} = \left(\frac{24{,}000}{1.09}\right) + \left(\frac{24{,}000}{(1.09)^2}\right) + \left(\frac{24{,}000}{(1.09)^3}\right)$$

$$= \left(\frac{24{,}000}{1.09}\right) + \left(\frac{24{,}000}{1.1881}\right) + \left(\frac{24{,}000}{1.295029}\right)$$

$$= 22{,}018.35 + 20{,}200.32 + 18{,}532.40$$

$$= 60{,}751.07$$

Approach 2 Using the present value formula for annuities:
The following formula may be used to calculate the present value of an annuity:

$$\text{PV} = \frac{A}{r}\left[1 - \left(\frac{1}{(1+r)^n}\right)\right]$$

where, A = Annuity amount receivable at the end of each year

Substituting the values:

$$\text{PV} = \frac{24{,}000}{0.09}\left(1 - \frac{1}{(1.09)^3}\right)$$

$$= \frac{24{,}000}{0.09}(1 - 0.772183)$$

$$= 2{,}66{,}666.67(0.227817)$$

$$= 60{,}751.20\,*$$

*The small difference is due to rounding.

Note that for this formula to work, the annual cash flows should be receivable in arrears, that is, should be received at the end of each of the years covered by the annuity.

2.7 Present Value Factor (PVF) Tables

Formula to calculate the present value of annuity: PV = $A/r\,[1 - (1 \div (1+r)^n)]$

Using the above given formulas to calculate present values may be okay for simple situations involving just a few future values. However, working with the formulas may become time consuming when there are a large number of future values. The availability of present value tables makes the task easy.

The present value tables readily provide the Present Value Factors (PVF) for different combinations of r (rate of discount) and n (periods). The present value factor (PVF) is also referred to as present value interest factor (PVIF).

Present value Table (given in Appendix A at the end of the book) gives the present value of ₹1 (or one Dollar) due at the end of n periods if the relevant compound interest rate is r% per period. The interest rate (r) chosen represents the rate at which funds can be borrowed or loaned out by the firm.

2.7.1 Using the PV Tables

To find the present value, get PVF (for the given 'r' and 'n') from PV tables and multiply the same with the future value.

To calculate the present value of a sum of money (future value) receivable or payable at the end of 'n' periods when 'r' is the discount rate, multiply the future value with the PVF given in the PV table at the combination of the specific 'n' and 'r'.

For example, assume a firm has to receive ₹12,100 at the end of 2 years and 10% is the relevant interest rate. Its present value can be found as follows:

PV = Future Value × [PV factor for r = 10%, n = 2]
= ₹12,100 × PV factor for r = 10%, n = 2
= ₹12,100 × 0.82645
= ₹10,000 (approx.)

2.7.2 Assumptions on Which PV Tables are Based

For the PV tables to serve their purpose, following assumptions must be satisfied: (i) compound interest and (ii) all cash flows take place at the end of a period.

Note that the present value tables are based on the following assumptions and would provide reliable results only when these assumptions are fulfilled:

1. Compound interest: The present value tables are based on compound interest and not simple interest principles. Therefore they should be used only when compound interest rates are applicable.

2. Timing of receipts/payments: It is assumed that all sums of money are received or paid in arrears; that is, all cash flows take place at the end a period.

EXAMPLE 2.5 Using the present value tables (given in Appendix A at the end of the book), calculate the present values of the following single sums of money receivable in future:

(a) ₹10,000 receivable at the end of 1 year from now if rate of discount (interest) is 12%.
(b) ₹8,000 receivable at the end of 2 years from now if rate of discount (interest) is 10%.
(c) ₹15,000 receivable at the end of 3 years from now if rate of discount (interest) is 8%.
(d) ₹20,000 receivable at the end of 4 years from now if rate of discount (interest) is 6%.

Solution. To calculate the present values using the PV tables, it would be helpful to draw a table with columns as shown below:

Finding Present Values Using PV Tables					
S.No.	*Future Value*	*Years 'n'*	*Rate 'r'*	*PVF (for given 'n' and 'r')*	*Present Value*
1	10,000	1	0.12	0.89286	8,928.6
2	8,000	2	0.1	0.82645	6,611.6
3	15,000	3	0.08	0.79383	1,19,07.45
4	20,000	4	0.06	0.79209	15,841.8

The present values in the last column are obtained by multiplying the amounts receivable (future values) by the respective 'PVF'. You are encouraged to re-do the question yourself to get familiar with using the present value tables.

Note that in a previous section we had solved the same question by using the formula instead of the PV tables. Comparing the present values obtained by the two methods, we find that both provide similar approximate results. The slight difference if any may arise due to rounding.

2.7.3 Present Value Factors (PVF) for Annuities

Annuities are a series of equally spaced payments of equal amounts. Present value Table (given in Appendix A at the end of the book) shows the present value of one Rupee (or one Dollar) due per period for '*n*' periods at *r*%.

The present value tables for single values and annuities are given in Appendix at the end of the book.

For example, to find the present value of ₹10,000 receivable annually for 5 years at 10% interest rate, we first use the annuities table (Annuity Present Values Table given in Appendix A at the end of the book) to find out the 'present value factor' for $n = 5$ and $r = 10\%$ which would be equal to 3.7908. Check for yourself from Table 2. Then, PV = ₹10,000 × 3.7908 = ₹37,908.

EXAMPLE 2.6 A student has been selected to get a scholarship of ₹24,000 per annum at the end of each of the next three years. What would be the present value of the scholarship if the relevant discount (interest) rate is 9% per annum?

Solution:

Step 1 Find the relevant PVF from the Annuity Present Values Table (in Appendix A)

$$\text{PVF for } n = 3,\ r = 9\% = 2.5313$$

Step 2 Present Value = ₹24,000 × 2.5313 = ₹60,751.20

Again, you would recall that in a previous section we had solved the same question by using the formula instead of the PV tables. Comparing the present values obtained by the two methods, we find that both provide similar approximate results. The slight difference if any may arise due to rounding.

2.8 Finding Equal Annual Installment (EAI)

If a firm has taken a loan that has to be repaid in '*n*' number of annual equal installments including interest, the present value tables can help in finding the amount of the annual installment.

Assume a firm borrows ₹10,000 at 15% interest per annum and must pay back the loan (including interest) in two annual equal installments. What would be the annual installment?

To find the annual installment, we should take the following steps:

Step 1 Find the relevant PVF from the Annuity Present Values (Table 2 in Appendix) for 2 years @15%:

$$\text{PVF for } n = 2,\ r = 15\% = 1.6257$$

Step 2 Let x be the amount of annuity. Since PV (Table 2 in Appendix) gives PV factor for 2 years at 15% = 1.6257, x must satisfy the following relationship:

$$1.6257x = ₹10{,}000$$

$$x = ₹10{,}000 \div 1.6257$$

$$= ₹6{,}151.20 \text{ per annum (approx.)}$$

What the above calculation means is that by paying two annual installments of ₹6,151.20 each (at the end of first and second years), the firm can settle the loan principal amount as well as the interest accrued thereon. Let us check it out from Table 2.1.

TABLE 2.1 Repaying Loan in Annual Installments

Amount in (₹)

Year	*Opening balance*	*Interest @ 15%*	*Total owed*	*Annual Installment*	*Closing Balance*
1	10,000	1,500	11,500	6,151.20	5,348.80
2	5348.80	802.32	6,151.12	6,151.12*	Nil

*Slight difference due to rounding.

2.9 Perpetual Annuities

An amount receivable each year for the foreseeable future is called perpetuity. PV of a perpetuity = A/r

If an amount is receivable (or payable) per annum for a very long time or forever, it is called a perpetual annuity or perpetuity. Perpetuities create a problem because the present value tables provide PV Factors (PVF) for only limited or finite number of years. Hence, we would have to manage with the present value formula instead of the PV tables.

You would recall the formula for finding the present value of annuities:

$$\text{PV} = \frac{A}{r}\left[1 - \left(\frac{1}{(1+r)^n}\right)\right]$$

In the above equation, when the number of years 'n' becomes very large and approaches infinity, $(1 + r)^n$ would also tend to approach infinity. As a result, $1 \div (1 + r)^n$ would become zero, and the formula for present value of a perpetuity would thus become:

$$\text{Perpetuity PV} = \frac{A}{r}$$

where A = Annual cash flow in perpetuity

Accordingly, when the interest rate is r, the cumulative present value of ₹1 (or one Dollar) per annum in perpetuity is = $1/r$.

Examples: PV of ₹1 in perpetuity at 10% $= \dfrac{1}{0.1} = 10$

$$\text{PV of ₹1 in perpetuity at 15\%} = \frac{1}{0.15} = 6.67$$

$$\text{PV of ₹1 in perpetuity at 20\%} = \frac{1}{0.20} = 5$$

2.10 Compounding Interest More Than Once a Year

In our discussion so far, we have assumed that interest on a loan or bank deposit would be receivable (or payable) once annually at the end of each year. If interest is paid or accrues more frequently, say every quarter, then we would have to adjust the present value formula. Assuming interest is compounded on quarterly basis, each quarter would be defined as one period. Accordingly, the annual interest rate would be divided by four and there would be four periods each year. For example, if the annual rate of compound interest was 12%, the revised interest would be 3% per quarter. The present value formula would then be:

If compounding is done more than once a year, the formula will change to:

$$PV = \frac{FV}{\left(1+\frac{r}{t}\right)^{nt}}$$

$$PV = \frac{FV}{\left(1+\frac{r}{t}\right)^{nt}}$$

where,

FV = Future value (cash flow)

n = Number of years

r = Compound interest rate per annum

t = Times interest is compounded per year

Assume a firm has to receive ₹1,00,000 at the end of 3rd year. What would be its present value if the discount rate is 24% per annum, compounded quarterly? Note that in this situation, 'n' would be = 3 × 4 = 12, and 'r' = 24 ÷ 4 = 6%.

Then,

$$PV = \frac{1,00,000}{\left(1+\frac{0.24}{4}\right)^{4\times3}}$$

$$= \frac{1,00,000}{(1.06)^{12}}$$

$$= 1,00,000 \times 0.496969364$$

$$= ₹49,696.94$$

What would have been the present value if the interest was compounded on annual basis? If compounded on annual basis:

$$PV = \frac{1,00,000}{(1+0.24)^3}$$

$$= \frac{1,00,000}{(1.24)^3}$$

$$= 1,00,000 \times 0.524487261$$

$$= ₹52,448.73$$

Comparing the results of annual compounding versus quarterly compounding, it is obvious that more times the compounding is done each year, smaller would be the present value of a future cash flow.

2.10.1 Infinite or Continuous Compounding

In the above equation, if 't' continues to increase and approaches infinity leading to continuous compounding, the term $(1 + r/t)^{nt}$ approaches e^{rn} where 'e' is approximately equal to 2.71828.

When interest is compounded continuously, the present value of a cash flow at the end of year 'n' would be PV = $\frac{FV}{e^{rn}}$ where e is approx 2.71828, r = rate of interest per annum (in decimal) and n is number of years.

Solving the previous example assuming continuous compounding,

$$PV = \frac{FV}{e^{rn}}$$

$$= \frac{1,00,000}{2.71828^{(0.24)(3)}}$$

$$= \frac{1,00,000}{2.054432216}$$

$$= ₹48,675.25$$

As expected, the present value has further declined due to continuous compounding that would discount the future cash flow more deeply than quarterly compounding.

Points to Remember

- **Time value of money:** In a number of financial decision-making situations, such as evaluating investment projects, when cash flows are expected to be spread across a number of future periods it would be necessary to consider the time value of money in arriving at a decision.
- **Time preference:** There are three main reasons for the time preference: (i) the possibility of earning a return, (ii) consumption preference and (iii) risk avoidance. The first one is more relevant because it gives us a way to measure the time value in monetary terms.
- **Compounding** in relation to a loan situation would mean that the interest earned is reinvested by the lender to earn more interest income in future. As a result, the interest for subsequent years would be calculated on the aggregate of principal loan amount plus accumulated accrued interest.
- **Discounting:** Finding the equivalent present values of future cash flows using the relevant interest rate. This way cash flows receivable at different points of time are made comparable so that they may be added or subtracted.
- **Present value formula:** If the Future Value (FV), period 'n' and the interest rate 'r' are known, the present value can be computed by the formula: $PV = FV \div (1 + r)^n$.
- **Annuity:** It refers to an equal amount of money receivable or payable for a number of periods at regular intervals. The formula to calculate the present value of an annuity is: PV of annuity $= A \times 1/r[1 - (1 \div (1 + r)^n)]$.
- **Present value tables:** The calculation of present values is facilitated by PV tables that provide the present value factors (PVF) for different combinations of 'r' and 'n'. The present value can be computed by multiplying the future value with the PVF given in the PV tables.

- **Assumptions:** The present value tables are based on two important assumptions: (i) Compound interest and (ii) Timing of receipts/payments: it is assumed that all sums of money are received or paid at the end of the respective periods.
- **Compounding more than once a year**: If compounding is done more than once a year, the present value of future cash flows would be reduced as compared to annual compounding.

Questions

1. Explain the importance of time value of money with particular reference to investment decision of a firm.
2. Distinguish between simple and compound interest and illustrate your answer with the help of a suitable numerical example.
3. Explain the meaning and significance of discounting and present values. Using a suitable numerical example, show how to compute the present value of a future sum using the formula.
4. Explain the effect of compounding more than once a year and using a numerical example show how it would impact the present value of a future value.
5. Explain the meaning of perpetuity and using a suitable numerical example show how to determine the present value of perpetuity.

Multiple Choice Questions

[*Note:* Answer the MCQs by using the formula and not PV tables.]

1. If a deposit of ₹2,500 is made in a bank deposit earning 5% compound interest per annum, the terminal value at the end of two years would be closest to:
(a) ₹2,456.35 (b) ₹2,675.80 (c) ₹2,756.25 (d) None of these

2. If the bank allows a compound interest rate of 8% per annum on the term deposit, how much should be deposited now so that ₹10,000 would be accumulated at the end of three years?
(a) ₹8,450.25 (b) ₹7,938.32 (c) ₹7,315.76 (d) None of these

3. What would be the present value of ₹18,000 receivable at the end of 2 years, if the rate of compound interest is 10%?
(a) ₹19,800.00 (b) ₹16,754.35 (c) ₹14,876.03 (d) None of these

4. Assume you are given the choice of either receiving ₹10,000 after two years or receiving some amount now. If your discount rate is 12%, what amount now will make you indifferent between the two choices?
(a) ₹7,972 (b) ₹8,234 (c) ₹8,912 (d) None of these

Self-Test Questions

1. Leo deposits ₹40,000 in a bank term deposit earning 7% compound interest per annum. What would be the amount (terminal value) that would have accumulated (i) at the end of one year, (ii) at the end of two years, (iii) at the end of three years and (iv) at the end of five years?

2. Ronnie wants to buy a new car in a few years for which he needs to accumulate a sum of ₹5,00,000. If the bank allows a compound interest rate of 7% per annum on the term deposit, how much should he deposit now so that ₹5,00,000 would be accumulated (i) at the end of three years, (ii) at the end of four years and (iii) at the end of five years.

3. Using the PV tables, calculate the present values of the following single sums of money receivable in future:
   (a) ₹25,000 receivable at the end of 1 year from now if rate of discount (interest) is 11%.
   (b) ₹30,000 receivable at the end of 3 years from now if rate of discount (interest) is 10%.
   (c) ₹35,000 receivable at the end of 5 years from now if rate of discount (interest) is 9%.
   (d) ₹40,000 receivable at the end of 10 years from now if rate of discount (interest) is 8%.

Problems

1. Adi deposits ₹50,000 in a bank term deposit earning 9% compound interest per annum. What would be the amount (terminal value) that would have accumulated (i) at the end of one year, (ii) at the end of two years, (iii) at the end of three years and (iv) at the end of five years?
2. Robin wants to send his daughter for higher studies in a few years for which he needs to accumulate a sum of ₹8,00,000. If the bank allows a compound interest rate of 7.5% per annum on the term deposit, how much should he deposit now so that ₹6,00,000 would be accumulated (i) at the end of two years, (ii) at the end of three years and (iii) at the end of four years.

   [*Note:* Answer the following question by using the formula and not with the help of PV tables.]
3. Annie is sending her child to a boarding high school that would cost ₹50,000 per annum payable at the end of each of the next three years. What would be the present value of the three years' schooling cost if the relevant discount (interest) rate is 10% per annum?
4. A person will receive a pension of ₹60,000 per annum at the end of each of the next eight years. What would be the present value of the pension if the relevant discount (interest) rate is 11% per annum?
5. A firm has borrowed ₹94,770 from a bank at an annual compound interest rate of 10%. The loan including interest is to be paid back in five equal installments at the end of each of the following five years. Find the annual installment.
6. Use the PV tables to calculate the present value of ₹1,000 assuming a 10% per year time value of money:
   (i) Received one year from now
   (ii) Received at the end of five years
   (iii) Received at the beginning of sixth year
   (iv) Received immediately
   (v) Received a the end of 50 years
   (vi) Received at the end of each of the ten years
   (vii) Received continuously for 5 years beginning with the end of 6th year.
7. Assume a 15% time value of money. A loan of ₹1,00,000 received now is equal to what amount paid in ten equal annual payments, if the first payment is to be made one year from now. What would be the annual amount if the first payment was made immediately?

PART II

CAPITAL INVESTMENT DECISION

CHAPTER

3 Principles of Investment Decision

LEARNING OBJECTIVES

After studying this chapter, you should be able to:

- Understand the importance of investment decision and the need for a serious evaluation of project proposals.
- Discuss the main types of projects and how new project ideas could originate in an organization.
- Explain the meaning and contents of the feasibility study.
- Identify the information required for financial evaluation of proposals.
- Calculate the accounting rate of return and list its pros and cons.
- Calculate the payback period and list its pros and cons.
- Take investment decisions on the basis of information available and acceptance criteria of the firm.

3.1 Introduction

As the Indian economy aims to accelerate the development process to become an economy of US$ 5 Trillion, by 2020, thousands and millions of new large and small projects are likely to be taken up in the next few years. The infrastructure sector alone would require investments of an equivalent of several trillion dollars, and then think of all those new projects being planned in sector such as energy, information technology, telecom, automobile, steel, mining, cement, and others. However, the desired results would be obtained only if the limited capital resources are invested wisely. To ensure that the proposed projects yield expected results, they would need to undergo intensive appraisal process so that only the most promising projects are undertaken, while projects that seem less profitable or too risky get rejected.

To ensure that the proposed projects yield expected results, they would need to undergo intensive appraisal process so that only the most promising projects are undertaken.

3.2 Nature of Investment Decision

Investment may mean different things to different persons. Investment of money to acquire an educational qualification (such as MBA or BTech), buying of financial assets, such as shares or bonds, or building of a factory to produce goods, are all examples of investments. Again, investments may be short-term or long-term. However, our focus here is on making long-term capital investments in business projects with the objective of earning positive returns in future.

The focus here is on making long-term capital investments in business projects with the objective of earning positive returns in future.

Investment projects typically involve an investment (cash outflow) in the current period or initial periods from which benefits are expected to be received beyond one year in the future. Examples may include setting up of a factory to produce goods, an expansion project, investment in plant, equipment and buildings, etc.

Box 3.1 provides information on some big-ticket projects announced by select companies in India during 2014–15; the projects would be executed in the next few years.

BOX 3.1
Big-Ticket Investment Projects

PROJECT ANNOUNCED BY SELECT COMPANIES* IN 2014–15 To be executed over next few years		
Company	**Nature of Project**	**Investment (₹ in crores)**
ITC Ltd.	Various projects in the country	25,000
Reliance Industries	Energy projects in Jamnagar	78,000
NTPC	Building renewable projects	60,000
Sesa Sterlite	Zinc mining project in Africa	4,700
GSFC	Capacity expansion	15,000
**Source:* Data compiled from www.itcportal; dnaindia; *Economic Times;* Reuters and Projects Today		

Investment decision, also called capital budgeting, is one of the most important decisions made by the management. Investment decisions determine the long-term profitability of the firm, and might often mean commitment of huge sums of money for a long period. A wrong investment decision may be very expensive for the firm, adversely affect its profitability, and may even make its survival difficult. Hence, all possible aspects of the proposed project should be carefully analyzed before accepting the proposal.

3.3 Project Returns Compared to Cost of Funding

From a financial viewpoint, an investment proposal should be evaluated in relation to whether it provides a return equal to, or greater than, what is required by the investors. A business enterprise wanting to invest in a project would have to raise funds from some sources, whether by debt or equity, and would have to incur the associated costs of interest on loans and cost of equity. Accordingly, it would obviously expect the planned projects to yield returns greater than or at least equal to the cost of funding incurred.

As you can imagine, there is a correlation between the type of the project being undertaken, and the cost of funds. For example, if the planned project is perceived to be very risky, the suppliers of funds (lenders and equity providers) would demand a risk-premium, corresponding to the riskiness of the proposed project, thus raising the cost of funding. However, in order to simplify the presentation of the basics of project appraisal and investment decision, we assume that (i) the risk profile of the firm, as perceived by the suppliers of capital, would not change as a result of the acceptance of any project(s) being considered; and (ii) the required rate of return on investment projects is known or given.

These assumptions are necessary so that we can focus on the impact of investment decisions on the value of the firm. Project appraisal under risk and uncertainty would be considered in a separate chapter.

3.4 New Investment Projects: Planning and Ideas

Ideas for new investment projects might originate from marketing, production and engineering, personnel, finance or any other part of the organization.

Many new successful projects were started in response to a careful study of customers' needs. Ratan Tata, then Chairman of the Tata group, saw a family of four—the man, wife with two small kids—riding a two wheeler on a rainy day, and felt the need for producing an affordable small car, that resulted into origination of the Nano car, which has been branded as the world's cheapest car. Similarly, Maruti-Suzuki car project started in early 1980s to fulfill a long-felt need for a technologically superior, and yet affordable car. Products like laptops, i-pads, walk-man, water-purifiers and the services like e-commerce have all been developed to meet the customers' requirements. Indeed, many companies use the services of market-research firms to study the changing customer needs and preferences to get some new product ideas.

Ideas for new investment projects might originate from marketing, production and engineering, personnel, finance or any other part of the organization.

Proposals for adding new products or expansion of existing product lines may often originate from the marketing department, while proposals for replacement of old equipment or buildings might come from production department. Other sources of ideas for new investment projects could be import-substitution, automation of processes for greater efficiency and savings in labour cost, export markets and technological up-gradation of products, and so on.

3.4.1 Types of Investment Projects

Investment projects could be classified in a number of ways, but the following classification shall be particularly helpful in understanding the concepts:

Profit-Oriented vs. Legally Binding Projects

While most projects would be taken up for the profit motive, some socially-oriented projects may be mandatory and must be executed even if not profitable; for example, pollution control equipment to be installed as per Government rules. Even if a project is undertaken to meet with legal requirements, it must be subjected to due diligence and appraisal to ensure maximum value from the capital expenditure.

New Products, Expansion and Replacement Projects

A project might involve setting up a new cement factory or expand its existing capacity and replace old worn-out plant and equipment. While most concepts we discuss in this chapter would be relevant to all such situations, the replacement type of investment decisions have been specifically illustrated in a separate section.

Mutually Exclusive and Accept-Reject Proposals

Projects are called mutually exclusive when only one of the proposals can be accepted. But in an accept-reject situation, each investment proposal is independently evaluated against the acceptance criteria (say, financial viability).

Projects are called mutually exclusive when only one of the proposals can be accepted, so that acceptance of one of the proposals under consideration would automatically mean that the others are rejected. If two proposals are mutually exclusive, they compete against each other so that both of them cannot be undertaken. For example, if a company is evaluating whether it should go for technology-X or technology-Y, acceptance of technology-X would automatically mean rejection of technology-Y proposal.

In contrast, when projects are evaluated in an **accept-reject or standalone situation**, each investment proposal is independently evaluated against the acceptance criteria (say, financial viability) rather than competing against each other. As a result, any or all proposals being considered can be accepted provided they meet the acceptance criteria of financial viability.

The concept of mutually exclusive proposals will be useful to us at a later stage where we compare the pros and cons of two methods of evaluating investment proposals: the Net Present Value and the Internal Rate of Return.

Contingent vs Independent Proposals

A contingent investment proposal is one whose acceptance depends on the acceptance of one or more other proposals. For example, the proposal on constructing a sales warehouse could be contingent upon acceptance of the proposal to expand production capacity. Investment proposals that are not contingent are called independent proposals.

Research and not-for-profit Projects

In industries, such as pharmaceutical, some research projects might be undertaken for the general purpose of better understanding various ailments, their causes and possible cures. Such projects may not be aimed at introducing new products that would generate future revenues to cover costs and yield profits. Similarly, governments may take up socially-oriented projects that are not aimed at generating profits or surpluses. Such projects should be evaluated on the basis of capital expenditures involved and appropriate measureable achievements projected against those expenditures.

Investment proposals aimed at profitability and wealth creation, as well as others, must be thoroughly analyzed and appraised as per appropriate criteria before they are accepted.

3.4.2 Feasibility Study of Investment Proposals

Most firms screen investment proposals at multiple levels of hierarchy, depending on the amount of investment required and importance of the proposed project to the firm. While small budget projects might be decided at the level of product or plant managers, proposals requiring significant outlays would be progressively evaluated at higher management levels. For large projects, a detailed feasibility study should be conducted before a final decision is reached.

A feasibility study involves intensive investigation and research into all aspects of a proposed project to evaluate the project's potential for success and value to the organization. A feasibility study should cover the following aspects:

1. Economic feasibility: The economic feasibility examines the long-term prospects of the economy, the state of industry, and determines the positive economic benefits of the proposed project to the organization and the society.

2. Commercial feasibility: The purpose of the commercial feasibility is to analyze demand of the product over the lifespan of the project, and check availability of various inputs, including raw materials, infrastructure, water, power, etc.

3. Technical feasibility: It analyzes aspects concerning the location, scale of the project and choice of technology.

4. Legal and environmental feasibility: Aims to determine whether the proposed project would meet with legal requirements of the country's corporate laws, business laws and environmental clearances required.

5. Organizational and manpower feasibility: It analyzes requirements of skilled manpower and cost of initial training.

6. Strategic synergy analysis: To ensure that the new investment project would go well with the overall long-term strategy of the firm.

7. Financial appraisal: Financial appraisal would require determination of the initial capital expenditure, future year-wise sales, operating expenses, profits and cash flows for the proposed project, financing alternatives, cost of capital and target rate of return on the investment. The methods of financial appraisal are discussed in a later section.

A feasibility study involves intensive investigation and research into all aspects of a proposed project to evaluate the project's potential for success and value to the organization.

3.5 Relevant Information for Project Appraisal

For appropriate financial evaluation of investment proposals, information should be carefully selected keeping in mind the following principles.

3.5.1 Consider Cash Flows, Not Accounting Profits

An investment project requires cash outflow in the beginning, and therefore, to evaluate its value, we would need information on expected future net 'cash flows' (on an after-tax basis if taxes are applicable) to make an equitable comparison. Some methods evaluate investment proposals on the basis of accounting profits, but such methods are not considered scientific. Accounting profits are determined on accrual basis, and do not represent cash flows or cash profits, while for project appraisal we need to compare cash coming into the firm against the cash outflow required initially to start the project.

The importance of cash flows can be easily understood when we consider the implications of new projects on the firm's liquidity position. Any investment project is likely to affect the liquidity of the firm, since projects typically require significant amounts of money for a long time. Also, if the firm has no cash, it would not be able to pay dividends to shareholders and interest on loans taken to finance the project. Hence, it is important to consider the size and timing of cash flows while evaluating investment projects.

It is important to consider the size and timing of cash flows while evaluating investment projects.

3.5.2 Consider 'Incremental' Costs and Benefits

Information related to the investment proposal should be provided on a differential or incremental basis, so that we could analyze the difference between the cash flows of the firm with, and without the project. In a new project, all expenditures and incomes would be incremental, because there were no existing operations before the project under consideration. However, if the proposed project involves replacement of existing plant and equipment, expected incomes and expenditures related to the project should be carefully calculated.

To illustrate, assume a firm is considering replacing its old plant with an improved automatic plant. The new plant can be installed at a cost of ₹50 million, and the old plant can be sold to fetch ₹10 million. With the new plant, the firm's annual profit would increase to ₹17 million from the existing ₹5 million per annum with the old plant. For the purpose of evaluating the proposal, the incremental or additional annual profit of ₹(17 – 5) million = 12 million will be related to the additional investment of ₹(50 – 10) million = 40 million, and the firm would accept the project if an annual return of ₹12 million on an investment of ₹40 million is considered satisfactory.

3.5.3 Consider Total Investment

Total investment in a project includes investment in fixed assets (plant and equipment, land and buildings, etc.) as well as increase in working capital (inventories, receivables, etc.) caused by the project. Thus, the working capital investment in the beginning of the project should be taken as a cash outflow. By their nature, funds invested in working capital remain circulating in business in the form of cash, inventories and receivables. Unlike fixed assets, working capital is not depreciated, and normally, the same is assumed to be recovered as cash inflow at the end of a project's useful life.

3.5.4 Depreciation

As we know, fixed assets are depreciated over their useful life. Depreciation being a business expense has to be considered for calculation of taxable income and income tax liability. But depreciation is a 'non-cash' expense and different from other business expenses, such as raw materials, salaries and rent for which cash outflow is required. Being a non-cash expense, depreciation provided in accounts would not impact the cash flows from the project. Accordingly, if a firm uses cash flow methods for project appraisal, the annual depreciation (considered for calculation of income tax liability) should be added back to the profits after taxes to determine the period's cash inflows.

In other words, depreciation expense by itself is irrelevant for project appraisal, but if it helps in reducing tax liability for the firm, the tax benefits would augment cash inflows and should be considered. (This is illustrated later.) If there are any other non-cash expenses related to the project (such as amortization of goodwill), they would also be treated in a similar manner.

3.5.5 Interest Exclusion Principle

If a project is financed by a mix of debt and equity sources, the firm would have to incur an interest expense on the debt funded portion of the project. Often, one may be tempted to include the interest expense in the operating cash outflows (along with other operating expenses) associated with the project, but that would not be appropriate.

Unless stated otherwise, you can assume that the cost of debt as well as equity financing would be taken care by the given overall cost of capital (weighted average cost of capital, covered in a separate chapter) or the minimum required rate of return to accept or reject investment projects. Therefore, we must not include interest expense on debt financing as a separate cost in computing the cash outflows, otherwise there will be double-counting of the interest cost.

3.5.6 Consider Opportunity Costs

Where relevant, opportunity costs/benefits should be included in project appraisal. To illustrate, suppose a company has an unutilized piece of land with a current market value of ₹20 million. Now the company is considering a new project that requires investment in plant and equipment of ₹60 million, and will come up on the piece of land that has been unutilized so far. In this case, the market value of the land (being an opportunity cost) should be added to the initial outlay required to start the project; thus, the project cost in this case would amount to ₹(60 + 20) million = 80 million and not 60 million.

The above principles would be consistently applied and illustrated as we proceed in the rest of this chapter.

3.6 Methods of Evaluating Investment Proposals

We are now ready to discuss the main methods of evaluating financial viability of investment proposals. For this purpose, we would use the following data of the Progressive Company.

EXAMPLE 3.1 The Progressive Company wants to invest in new productive machinery and is considering two proposals for this purpose. The two proposals have several similarities, but differ in the timing of expected returns.

	Proposals X	*Proposals Y*
Investment required (₹)	1,00,000	1,00,000
Expected life of the machine	5 years	5 years
Depreciation per year (₹)	20,000	20,000
Income tax rate	30%	30%
Scrap value at the end of 5 years	Nil	Nil

Expected profits before depreciation and taxes from the two proposals are as follows:

Years	1	2	3	4	5
X: Profits (₹'000)	90	30	30	30	30
Y: Profits (₹'000)	30	30	90	30	30

The cost of capital of the Progressive Company is 12%, and the company uses this as the minimum acceptable rate of return for screening investment proposals.

The main methods of evaluating investment proposals are discussed and illustrated in the next section using the above data.

3.6.1 Accounting Rate of Return (ARR)

The Accounting Rate of Return (also called the average rate of return or return on investment method) represents the ratio of the average annual profits after taxes to the investment in the project. However, investment can be defined either as 'initial' investment or 'average' investment. So, we have two variants of this method:

1. Accounting rate of return on initial investment:

$$\text{ARR} = \frac{\text{Average annual PAT}}{\text{Initial investment}} \times 100$$

where PAT is Profit After Taxes

2. Accounting rate of return on average investment:

$$\text{ARR} = \frac{\text{Average annual PAT}}{\text{Average investment}} \times 100$$

where,

$$\text{Average investment} = \frac{\text{Initial investment + Closing balance}}{2}$$

If a project involves investing in machinery or other fixed assets that are depreciated, and there is no expected salvage value (discussed in a later section), then the average investment may be taken as equal to half of the initial investment on the logic that as the fixed assets are depreciated, the net investment (after depreciation) in the project would go on reducing year after year until the fixed assets are fully depreciated. For example, assume a firm invests ₹1,00,000 in machinery that is depreciated over its useful life of five years using straight line method. So, as we charge off ₹20,000 depreciation at the end of each year, the balance net investment in the machinery would decline to ₹80,000 at the end of first year, ₹60,000 at the end of second year and so on, ending with a balance of nil (or zero) investment at the end of fifth year. The average investment would then be the arithmetic mean of investment balances at the start (year 0) and close (year 5) of the project as follows:

$$\text{Average investment} = \frac{\text{Initial investment + Closing balance}}{2}$$

$$= \frac{₹[1,00,000 + 0]}{2} = ₹50,000$$

Using this method, an investment proposal would be acceptable if it provides an ARR equal to or higher than the minimum required rate of return. Using this method, the two proposals X and Y would be evaluated as given in Table 3.1 and Table 3.2.

Calculation of ARR—Proposal X

TABLE 3.1
ARR—Proposal X

(₹'000)

Years	1	2	3	4	5
Profit before depreciation and taxes	90	30	30	30	30
Depreciation	–20	–20	–20	–20	–20
Earnings Before Tax (EBT)	70	10	10	10	10
Income Tax (30% × EBT)	–21	–3	–3	–3	–3
Profit After Taxes (PAT)	49	7	7	7	7

Accounting rate of return in initial investment:

$$\frac{\text{Average Annual PAT}}{\text{Average investment}} \times 100$$

$$\text{Average annual profit after taxes} = \frac{49+7+7+7+7}{5} (₹'000) = \frac{77,000}{5}$$

$$= 15,400$$

(a) ARR (X) on initial investment = $\frac{15,400}{1,00,000} \times 100 = 15.4\%$

(b) ARR (X) on average investment = $\frac{15,400}{50,000} \times 100 = 30.8\%$

where,

$$\text{Average investment} = \frac{\text{Initial Investment}}{2} = \frac{1,00,000}{2} = 50,000$$

Accounting rate of return on avergae investment:

$$\frac{\text{Average Annual PAT}}{\text{Average investment}} \times 100$$

Calculation of ARR—Proposal Y

TABLE 3.2 ARR—Proposal Y

(₹'000)

Years	1	2	3	4	5
Profit before depreciation and taxes	30	30	90	30	30
Depreciation	–20	–20	–20	–20	–20
Earnings Before Taxes (EBT)	10	10	70	10	10
Income tax (30% × EBT)	–3	–3	–21	–3	–3
Profit After Taxes (PAT)	7	7	49	7	7

Average annual profit after taxes = $\frac{77}{5}$ (₹'000) = 15,400

(a) ARR (Y) on initial investment = $\frac{15,400}{1,00,000} \times 100 = 15.4\%$

(b) ARR (Y) on average investment = $\frac{15,400}{50,000} \times 100 = 30.8\%$

To decide on the acceptance or rejection of a project proposal, the calculated ARR is compared with the required or cut-off rate of return. Thus, in Example 3.1, both proposals X and Y would be acceptable, since their calculated ARR is higher than the 12% minimum required rate of return.

Thus, according to this method, both proposals are equally profitable as their ARRs are the same. However, even a layman can make out that proposal X is better than Y, because it offers greater returns earlier than proposal Y. Funds received earlier have more value (time value of money is discussed later) as they can be reinvested for the interim period to earn a return.

Effect of Salvage Value and Working Capital on ARR

Often an investment project would involve aspects related to the salvage (resale) value of fixed assets and working capital changes caused by the project under consideration. The treatment of these items in calculation of the ARR is as follows.

1. Salvage value: Salvage value (also called scrap or residual value) refers to the resale value of a fixed asset at the end of its useful life. If the expected salvage value of a fixed asset is known in advance (or given in the exam questions) and the firm uses straight line method of depreciation, the expected salvage value should be deducted from the cost of the fixed asset before calculating the yearly depreciation on the asset. For example, if the cost of a fixed asset was ₹60,000, and its useful life was ten years, at the end of which the expected salvage value would be ₹10,000, using straight line method of depreciation, the annual depreciation would amount to ₹5,000 per annum

$$\frac{60,000 - 10,000}{10 \text{ years}}$$

In straight line method of depreciation, the expected salvage value should be deducted from the cost of the fixed asset before calculating the yearly depreciation on the asset.

The depreciation, so calculated, would be charged against the project's annual profit before proceeding to compute ARR (as shown above).

If the firm uses 'accounting rate of return on average investment' method, then scrap value should be considered for calculating the 'average investment'. Hence,

$$\text{Average investment} = \frac{\text{Initial investment} + \text{Salvage value}}{2}$$

2. Working capital requirements: Any additional (incremental) investment in working capital caused by a project would increase the total investment in the project, and should therefore, be added to the capital expenditure in the project. Thus, the project's initial investment would increase by the amount of additional investment in working capital.

Investment in working capital can be normally assumed to be fully recovered (except when specifically stated otherwise) at the end of the project, and would constitute part of the closing book value of the investment. To illustrate, suppose project-X (discussed earlier in the chapter) required an investment of ₹25,000 in the beginning of the project in addition to the investment in machinery. This amount of ₹25,000 invested in working capital, would thus increase the total initial investment, and assumed to be fully recoverable at the end of year 5, the last year of the project.

Additions or reductions in working capital investment not only might happen at the beginning and end of the project respectively, but might happen any time during the life of a project. What is important to note is that any changes in working capital would affect the project investment and should be considered in ARR calculations.

3. Income taxes: At times, we may come across firms or projects that are exempted from income taxes; indeed, often exam questions may ask you to 'ignore taxes' to keep calculations simple. In such cases, proceed as usual without considering the income taxes.

Following example would illustrate calculation of ARR when salvage value and working capital investment are involved.

ILLUSTRATION: ARR with Salvage Value and Working Capital

Munjal Company is considering a new project that will require investing ₹1,00,000 in machinery and ₹25,000 in working capital. The project will increase the earnings before depreciation and taxes by ₹35,000 per year for five years. The machinery will have a resale value of ₹10,000 at the end of year 5. The working capital invested in the project would be recovered at the end of year 5. The company's required rate of return is 12% and its applicable income tax rate is 25%.

Calculate the Accounting rate of return on average investment. Should the company undertake the project?

Solution: We proceed as usual to calculate profit after taxes and then calculate the ratio of 'average annual profit after taxes' to the 'average investment' during the life of the project.

	Annual Profit (₹)
Profit before depreciation and taxes	35,000
Less: Depreciation (100 – 10)/5	18,000
Earnings Before Taxes (EBT)	17,000
Less: Income tax (25% x EBT)	4,250
Profit After Taxes (PAT) per annum	12,750

Average investment

$$= \frac{\text{Initial investment} + \text{Resale value} + \text{Recovered working capital}}{2}$$

$$= \frac{1,25,000 + 10,000 + 25,000}{2} = \frac{1,60,000}{2} = 80,000$$

Then, ARR would be

$$\frac{\text{Average annual profit after taxes}}{\text{Average investment in the project}} \times 100 = \frac{12,750}{80,000} \times 100 = 15.94\%$$

The company can accept the investment proposal as the calculated ARR is higher than the minimum required return of 12%.

Cross-checking the 'Average' Investment

At times, you might wonder whether the average investment, as calculated above, is correct and if there is a way to cross-check our finding. There are two ways you can cross-check, as follows.

Method 1: The average investment can be calculated as the average of the net book values at the end of Year 0 (start year) to last year of the project's life.

$$\text{Average investment} = \frac{\text{Initial investment} + \text{NBVYr1} + \text{NBVYr2} + \cdots + \text{NBVYrN}}{\text{N} + 1}$$

where, NBVYr1, NBVYr2 = Net book value of investment at the end of years 1, 2, etc. Net book value means investment 'after depreciation'. Calculations are shown in Table 3.3.

TABLE 3.3 Method 1

Year	Opening Net Book Value	Annual Depreciation	Year-end Net Book Value
0	1,25,000	0	1,25,000
1	1,25,000	18,000	1,07,000
2	1,07,000	18,000	89,000
3	89,000	18,000	71,000
4	71,000	18,000	53,000
5	53,000	18,000	35,000
		TOTAL	4,80,000
Average investment = 4,80,000/(5 + 1) = 80,000			

Method 2: The average investment can be calculated as the average of the mid-year net book values from year-1 to last year of the project's life. The mid-year net book value is the average of the beginning and year-end balances. Calculations are shown in Table 3.4.

TABLE 3.4 Method 2

Year	Opening balance	Annual depreciation	Closing balance	Mid-year balance
1	1,25,000	18,000	1,07,000	1,16,000*
2	1,07,000	18,000	89,000	98,000
3	89,000	18,000	71,000	80,000
4	71,000	18,000	53,000	62,000
5	53,000	18,000	35,000	44,000
		Total		4,00,000
Average Investment = 4,00,000/5				80,000
*(1,25,000+1,07,000)/2 = 1,16,000.				

Merits of the ARR method:

1. Simple to understand and use: The Accounting Rate of Return is a simple ratio that every businessman understands, and can use even without any special training in finance.

2. Makes use of accounting information: The information on profits earned by the firm is readily available from its accounting statement (profit and loss account). That again makes the method easy to use.

Shortcomings of the ARR Method

1. **ARR** is based on accounting income rather than cash flows. You would recall from our discussion in a previous section that investment projects require cash outflow in the beginning and to evaluate their value we would need information on 'cash flows' basis rather than accounting profits. Accounting profits are determined on the accrual basis, while our focus here is on cash flows.
2. It fails to take into account the 'timing' of future costs and benefits. As per this method, a rupee received in 5th year has same value as the one received in first year. Differences in the timing of receiving future sums are ignored in the process of calculating the 'average' annual profits. In other words, this method ignores the 'time value of money'.
3. For the purpose of calculating ARR, investment can be interpreted in several ways (such as initial investment and average investment) which may be confusing. The firms using this method should specify whether the 'required rate of return' or cut-off rate is based on the 'initial' investment or 'average investment', and use the same method consistently.

In spite of its limitations, the method continues to be in use, particularly for smaller investments that are not so crucial for the firm and where an approximate understanding of its value is enough to decide on its acceptance or rejection. Small entrepreneurs without adequate financial training may also find the method useful.

3.6.2 The Payback Period Method

As the name suggests, the payback period is the period over which the project would payback or return the initial investment. Thus, the payback period tells us the time period required to recover the initial cash investment in the project.

In industries where technology or market conditions change very fast (such as computers or fashion goods), a firm might prefer those projects which promise to return the initial investment faster than others, in order to minimize the risk. Often a firm might also decide on the maximum acceptable payback period, which would mean that project proposals with longer payback periods than the maximum acceptable period would not be taken up. Using this method, an investment proposal would be acceptable if its payback period is less than the maximum acceptable payback period.

To calculate the payback period, we would first need to determine the project's year-wise net cash flows. Each successive year's net cash inflow is applied to recover a part of the initial investment, until the initial investment is completely recovered. Payback period, is thus, the number of years required to fully recover the initial cash investment in the project.

How to Calculate a Period's Net Cash Flow

To determine a period's net cash flow, first compute the profit after taxes in a similar manner as in the ARR method, and then add-back depreciation that was charged for determining the taxable income. Depreciation charged is added back to the amount of profit after taxes, because it is a non-cash expense and no cash outflow is involved when we provide for depreciation. Depreciation is a way of spreading the original cost of a fixed asset over its useful life and, in that sense, you could say it is just a book entry. The calculation of cash flows and the payback period for proposals X and Y is illustrated in Tables 3.5, 3.6 and 3.7.

TABLE 3.5 Payback period—Proposal X

(₹'000)

Years	1	2	3	4	5
Profit before depreciation and taxes	90	30	30	30	30
Depreciation	–20	–20	–20	–20	–20
Earnings Before Taxes (EBT)	70	10	10	10	10
Income tax (30% × EBT)	–21	–3	–3	–3	–3
Profit After Taxes (PAT)	49	7	7	7	7
Add-back depreciation	20	20	20	20	20
Net cash flow	69	27	27	27	27

To calculate the payback period, go on deducting each year's net cash inflow from the initial investment until the initial investment is fully recovered. Thus, first year brought in cash flow of ₹69,000, leaving a balance of ₹1,00,000 – 69,000 = 31,000. Second year brought in ₹27,000, leaving a balance of ₹31,000 – 27,000 = 4,000 to be covered in the third year. Recovery of project investment in the form of cash inflows may be clearly presented in Table 3.6.

TABLE 3.6 Recovery of Project

Year	Beginning balance of investment	Annual net cash inflow	Yer-end unrecovered investment
1	1,00,000	69,000	31,000
2	31,000	27,000	4,000
3	4,000	27,000	0

Since third year's cash inflow amounted to ₹27,000, only a fraction of the year (4/27) would be adequate to cover the initial investment. Thus,

$$\text{Payback period (X)} = 2 \text{ years} + \frac{4}{27}$$
$$= 2.15 \text{ years}$$

Table 3.6 determines the payback, which may be modified as required. You are advised to calculate the payback period of Proposal–Y (see Table 3.7) yourself before reading further.

TABLE 3.7 Payback period—Proposal Y

(₹'000)

Years	1	2	3	4	5
Profit before depreciation and taxes	30	30	90	30	30
Depreciation	–20	–20	–20	–20	–20
Earnings Before Taxes (EBT)	10	10	70	10	10
Income tax (30% × EBT)	–3	–3	–21	–3	–3
Profit After Taxes (PAT)	7	7	49	7	7
+ Depreciation added back	20	20	20	20	20
Net cash flow	27	27	69	27	27

$$\text{Payback period (Y)} = 2 \text{ years} + \frac{46}{69}$$
$$= 2.67 \text{ years}$$

According to this method, proposal X is better than proposal Y, because it returns the initial investment faster than proposal Y.

Payback period in case of constant annual cash inflows

In case of a conventional investment project involving an initial investment followed by constant (even) annual cash inflows, the payback period may be calculated as follows:

$$\text{Payback period} = \frac{\text{Initial project investment}}{\text{Annual net cash inflow}}$$

For example, if a firm is considering investing in new machinery that would require an initial investment of ₹60,000 and gives annual net cash inflows of ₹15,000 for a period of 7 years, then the project's payback period would be equal to 60,000/15,000 = 4 years.

Effect of salvage value and working capital on payback period

The treatment of these items in calculation of the payback period is explained as follows:

1. Salvage value: The effect of salvage value on annual depreciation would remain as discussed in a previous section. In addition, the salvage value received at the end of the project would be added as an additional cash inflow in the project's last operating year.

2. Working capital requirements: Any additional (incremental) investment in working capital caused by a project would be taken as a cash outflow. When the working capital investment is recovered at the end of the project, it would be taken as a cash inflow of the last year of the project. Even during the life of the project, if there are any changes in working capital investment, their impact on cash flows should be considered in calculation of the payback period.

EXAMPLE 3.2 Payback Period with Salvage Value and Working Capital

Question: Continuing with the example of Munjal Company discussed:

(i) Calculate the payback period of the project
(ii) Should the company undertake the project if its maximum acceptable payback period is 3 years?

Solution: We proceed as usual to calculate the project's operating cash flows and then compute the payback period.

	Annual profit (₹)
Profit before depreciation and taxes	35,000
Less: Depreciation (100 – 10)/5	18,000
Earnings Before Taxes (EBT)	17,000
Less: Income tax (25% × EBT)	4,250
Profit After Taxes (PAT) per annum	12,750
Add back depreciation	+18,000
Annual net cash inflow	30,750

Note that in the fifth year, additional cash inflows of ₹10,000 of resale value and ₹25,000 of recovered working capital would also be added to the operating cash flow as shown in the table above; so the year 5 net cash inflow would be

$$30{,}750 + 10{,}000 + 25{,}000 = 65{,}750$$

The payback period then would be determined as follows:

Initial investment	₹1,25,000
Investment recovered in first 4 years [30,750 × 4 = 1,23,000]	1,23,000
Balance investment to be recovered in fifth year	2,000

Proportion of fifth year's cash inflow required to payback investment

$$= \frac{2{,}000}{65{,}750} = 0.03 \text{ year}$$

Hence, payback period of the project = 4.03 years.

As the calculated payback period is more than the maximum acceptable payback period of 3 years, the company would not undertake the project.

Contradiction: It is quite possible that, as in the above example of Munjal Company, the ARR and the payback period methods might give contradictory results. The company management would then have to exercise judgment to decide acceptance or rejection of such a project. In the above case, if the project's risk factor is considered significant and the company does not want to accept projects with payback periods exceeding three years, the company might as well decide to sacrifice the project opportunity even if it is otherwise an acceptable proposal.

Merits of the Payback Period Method

1. It is a cash flow method, which is an improvement over the accounting rate of return method.
2. Another plus point of the payback method is that it gives a limited insight into the risk and liquidity of a project. Projects with shorter payback period would be considered less risky than projects with longer payback periods. Projects with a long payback period would be considered more risky, because there would be a high probability that factors affecting the viability of the project could change over a longer term, thus increasing the project's risk profile. For example, if a firm is investing in machinery and considers that the technology could change in three years, it could decide on a target payback period of three years for the recovery of its initial investment to reduce the risk factor. Also, early recovery of project investment would be crucial to firms facing liquidity issues.

Shortcomings of the Payback Period Method

1. A serious shortcoming of this method is that it fails to consider cash flows beyond the payback period. This method pays attention to only such cash flows that occur up to the time of recovery of the initial investment. If Project-X has a payback period of 3 years, and Project-Y of 4 years, this method would recommend taking up Project-X even if Project-Y has much

longer useful life and promised much higher cash flows after year 4 as compared to Project-X. In this process, the firm could unwisely reject some really good projects simply because they might take longer to reach a stage of full potential, but otherwise would be extremely profitable for the firm in the long run.

2. It does not take account of the magnitude or timing of cash flows during the payback period. As per this method, a rupee received in third or fifth year has same value as the one received in first year. In other words, it does not consider the time value of money.

In spite of its limitations, the payback period method continues to be in use as a supplement to other more sophisticated methods.

Since both the ARR and Payback period fail to consider the time value of money, we now turn our attention to the discounted cash flow methods in the next chapter.

Researchable Issues

Faculty members, students and research scholars may like to consider the following selected issues for further research and case writing.

- The capital budgeting decisions in small businesses.
- Capital budgeting process: theoretical aspects.
- Corporate mission, strategic planning and capital budgeting.
- Investment Appraisal of CSR projects.
- Social cost-benefit analysis versus capital budgeting techniques

References

Bierman, H. Jr. and S. Smidt., *The Capital Budgeting Decision: Economic Analysis of Investment Projects*, 9th ed. Routledge, New York, 2006.

Dion, L.G. Robertson, and S.B. Hughes, 'What a university can teach you about choosing capital projects,' *Strategic Finance* (January): USA, 2009, pp. 38–45.

Gordon, L.A. and M.D. Myers, 'Post auditing capital projects, *Management Accounting,* (January): USA, 1991, pp. 39–42.

Seitz, N. and M. Ellison. *Capital Budgeting and Long-Term Financing Decisions*, 4th ed. South-Western Educational Publishing, Kentucky, 2004.

Shapiro, A.C., *Capital Budgeting and Investment Analysis*, Prentice-Hall, London, 2004.

Websiteresources

http://www.projectstoday.com/News/GSFC-to-invest-₹-15,000-cr

http://www.itcportal.com/media-centre/press-reports- C&news

http://www.dnaindia.com/money/report-reliance-industries

http://articles.economictimes.indiatimes.com/2015-02-17/news

http://in.reuters.com/article/2014/11/13/sesa-sterlite-africa

Points to Remember

- **Investment decision**, also called capital budgeting, is one of the most important decisions made by the management. Investment decisions determine the long-term profitability of the firm, and might often mean commitment of huge sums of money for a long period. A wrong investment decision may be very expensive for the firm; hence all care should be exercised in selecting investment projects.
- **Investment projects typically involve** an investment (cash outflow) in the current period from which benefits are expected to be received beyond one year in the future. Examples may include setting up of a factory to produce goods, an expansion project, investment in plant, equipment and buildings, etc.
- **From a financial viewpoint**, an investment proposal should be evaluated in relation to whether it provides a return equal to, or greater than, that required by the investors. There would normally be a correlation between the type of the project being undertaken and the cost of funds. For example, if the planned project is perceived to be very risky, the suppliers of funds (lenders and equity providers) would demand a risk-premium corresponding to the riskiness of the proposed project, thus raising the cost of funding.
- **The ideas for new investment** projects might originate from marketing, production and engineering, personnel, finance or any other part of the organization. Many new successful projects were started in response to a careful study of customers' needs.
- **Projects are called mutually exclusive** when only one of the proposals can be accepted, so that acceptance of one of the proposals under consideration would automatically mean that others are rejected. If two proposals are mutually exclusive, they compete against each other so that both of them cannot be accepted.
- **Information required** for the financial evaluation of investment proposals is based on incremental cash flows. Total investment in a project includes investment in fixed assets (plant and equipment, land, and buildings, etc.) as well as working capital (inventories, receivables, etc.). Depreciation and other 'non-cash' expenses should be excluded in calculation of cash flows. Opportunity costs where relevant should be considered.
- **The accounting rate of return** (also called the average rate of return) represents the ratio of the average annual profits after taxes to the investment in the project. However, investment can be defined either as 'initial' investment or 'average' investment.
- **The payback period** is the period over which the project would payback or return the initial investment. Thus, the payback period tells us the time period required to recover the initial cash investment in the project. Both the ARR and Payback period fail to consider the time value of money and have other limitations.

Questions

1. Explain the importance of capital budgeting or investment decision for a business firm.
2. Discuss the main types of investment proposals. Using suitable examples, distinguish between independent, mutually exclusive and contingent projects.
3. Discuss how can a firm get ideas for new investment projects.
4. Explain the meaning and relevance of the project feasibility study. Briefly explain the main aspects of project feasibility that a firm should consider before deciding on a large new project.
5. Discuss the nature of relevant information that would be required for financial evaluation of proposals. In this connection, discuss why depreciation and interest expenses are excluded in calculation of cash flows related to an investment proposal.
6. Explain the meaning of the accounting rate of return, and using suitable numerical examples, show its calculation with respect to (i) initial investment and (ii) average investment. Discuss its main advantages and disadvantages as a method of project appraisal as compared to other methods.
7. Explain the meaning of payback period and using suitable numerical examples, show its calculation. Discuss its main advantages and disadvantages as a method of project appraisal as compared to other methods.

Multiple Choice Questions

1. Two projects are called mutually exclusive when:
   (a) Only one of the proposals under consideration can be accepted
   (b) They are made for each other so that both must be accepted or rejected
   (c) Acceptance of one project is contingent upon acceptance of the other.
   (d) None of the above
2. If a project is financed by a mix of debt and equity sources, the interest expense on the debt funded portion:
   (a) Should be included in the operating cash outflows along with other operating expenses associated with the project.
   (b) Should be covered in the project cost of capital rather than the project operating cash outflows.
   (c) Should be included both in the project operating cash outflows and in the cost of capital.
   (d) None of the above
3. A project would cost ₹45,000 now, and would earn the following cash inflows:

1st year	₹15,000	3rd year	₹20,000
2nd year	₹20,000	4th year	₹6,000

   The plant and equipment purchased at the start of the project would have a resale value of ₹5,000 at the end of the fourth year. What would be the payback period of the project?
   (a) 3.5 years (b) 3.0 years
   (c) 2.5 years (d) None of these

4. A company is evaluating an investment proposal, which requires an initial investment of ₹2,50,000 in plant and machinery. The estimated profit before depreciation and taxes from the project are estimated at ₹1,75,000 per annum for five years starting from the end of the first year. The plant and machinery is to be depreciated on straight line basis, and the income tax rate applicable to the company is 40%. The ARR on initial investment for the project would be:
   (a) 20% (b) 25%
   (c) 30% (d) None of these
5. ABC Company is considering an investment proposal, which would involve a cash outflow of ₹40,000 now and a further cash outflow of ₹40,000 after one year. Cash inflows thereafter would be as follows.

2nd year	₹30,000	3rd year	₹25,000	4th to 6th years	₹20,000

   The payback period for the project would be closest to:
   (a) 4.25 years (b) 5.50 years
   (c) 6.00 years (d) None of these

Data given for MCQs 6 and 7

ABC Company is considering two capital expenditure proposals. Both proposals are for similar products, and both are expected to operate for four years. Only one proposal can be accepted.

	Proposal A ₹	Proposal B ₹
Initial investment	45,000	45,000
Profit/(loss) after depreciation and taxes:		
Year 1	7,000	4,000
Year 2	6,000	5,000
Year 3	14,000	6,000
Year 4	2,000	10,000
Scrap value at end of year 4	5,000	5,000

Depreciation has been charged on the straight line basis.

6. The payback period for Proposal A will be closest to:
   (a) 3.00 years (b) 2.75 years
   (c) 2.50 years (d) None of these
7. The payback period for Proposal B will be closest to:
   (a) 3.00 years (b) 2.75 years
   (c) 2.50 years (d) None of these

Self-Test Questions

1. Accounting Rate of Return and Payback

Ronny Company is considering investing in a project for which the following information is provided.

Initial capital expenditure	₹ 60,000
Profits/(losses) after depreciation and taxes:	
Year 1	20,000
Year 2	20,000
Year 3	10,000
Year 4	–5,000
Year 5	–5,000

The project will have an operating life of five years, at the end of which there is not expected to be any salvage value. Depreciation has been provided on straight line basis. The company uses 15% as the required rate of return from capital investments. Also, to be acceptable, a project's payback period should be within 2.5 years.

Calculate the following:

(a) The accounting rate of return based on 'average' investment
(b) The payback period in years.

Should the company undertake the project?

2. Arrow Company is considering investing ₹1,20,000 in new machinery, which will reduce operating costs by ₹40,000 a year for five years, and which will have a resale value of ₹20,000 at the end of year 5. The company's cost of capital (to be used as the required rate of return) is 12%, and its applicable income tax rate is 25%. Calculate the Accounting Rate of Return on average investment. Assume straight line depreciation.

Problems

1. Gems Company is considering investing in a project for which the following information is provided.

Initial capital expenditure	₹ 1,50,000
Profits/(losses) after depreciation and taxes:	
Year 1	60,000
Year 2	50,000
Year 3	40,000
Year 4	–30,000
Year 5	–20,000

The project will be operational for five years, at the end of which time there is not expected to be any scrap value. Depreciation has been provided on straight line basis. The company uses 16% as the required rate of return from capital investments.

Calculate the following.

(a) The accounting rate of return based on 'average' investment
(b) The payback period in years.

2. CGL Company is considering the manufacture of a new product, which would involve the use of both a new machine and an existing machine. The new machine would cost ₹14,00,000. The existing machine was purchased at ₹7,00,000 two years ago, and has a current net book value of ₹5,00,000. There is sufficient under-utilized capacity on the existing machine to produce the new product.

The sales of the new product would be 5,000 units per annum and its sales price would be ₹320 per unit. Per unit costs would be as follows:

Direct Labour (2 Hours @ ₹50 per hour)	100
Direct materials	50
Fixed costs including depreciation	90
Total per unit cost	240

The project would have a five-year life, after which the new machine would have a resale value of ₹1,00,000. Because direct labour is continuously in short supply, labour resources would have to be diverted from other work, which currently earns a contribution of ₹30 per direct labour hour. The fixed overhead absorption rate would be ₹45 per hour (₹90 per unit) but the actual expenditure on fixed overhead would not change because of the new product.

Working capital requirements for the new product would be ₹1,00,000 in the first year, rise to ₹1,50,000 in the second year, and will remain at this level until the end of the project. Working capital will be recovered at the end of the project.

The company's cost of capital of 16% is used as the required rate of return. Ignore taxation.

Calculate the project's payback period and suggest whether the project is worthwhile assuming the maximum acceptable payback period is 3 years.

3. **Feisty Treats**, a fast food restaurant, is planning to invest in installing a drive-through window (with a suitable driveway and speaker system) that will allow customers to order from their cars, collect their order and drive-out in a seamless manner. The project would cost ₹5,00,000 and as a result of considerable increase in sales, it is estimated that the firm's operating profits (before depreciation and taxes) would increase by ₹2,00,000 per annum. Assume the project would have a useful life of five years, after which there would be no salvage value of the project. The firm's applicable tax rate is 30%, and the company needs 16% as the minimum rate of return on new investments. The company would like to avoid investment projects with a payback period exceeding 3 years.

(a) Calculate the project's accounting rate of return on initial investment.

(b) Determine the project's payback period and comment on its suitability as a method of project appraisal.

(c) Advise the company whether to accept or reject the project proposal.

4. **Joy company** is considering an investment proposal to install new machinery at a cost of ₹60,000. The machinery has a life expectancy of 5 years with no salvage value. The income tax rate is 25%. Assume the firm uses straight line depreciation and the same is allowed for tax purposes. The estimated Cash Flows Before Depreciation and Tax (CFBDT) from the investment proposal are as follows:

Year	1	2	3	4	5
CFBDT (₹)	10,000	12,000	14,000	20,000	16,000

The company needs 16% as the minimum rate of return on new investments. The company would like to avoid investment projects with a payback period exceeding 4 years.

(a) Calculate the project's accounting rate of return on initial investment.

(b) Determine the project's payback period, and comment on its suitability as a method of project appraisal.

(c) Advise the company whether to accept or reject the project proposal.

CASE

Nano Technologics

Haresh did not believe in a slow and steady career progression, "slow and steady game is only for the tortoise, not for me," he would tell his friends. He wanted to rise in life and rise fast! After doing his MBA, he had job offers from several large companies but the position they offered did not satisfy him. Instead he joined a small company Nano Technologics, which gave him a middle level managerial position.

The company had recently raised an amount of ₹48 million (₹4.8 crore) which it wanted to invest in one of the three mutually exclusive projects that had been shortlisted. The CEO asked Haresh to evaluate the three projects and suggest which one should be undertaken, indicating that he would take charge of the selected project.

The following summary had been prepared of the initial cost and other details of the three projects:

	Proposal X	*Proposal Y*	*Proposal Z*
Investment required ₹'000	48,000	48,000	48,000
Expected life of plant and equipment (and the project)	6 years	5 years	4 years
Annual depreciation (using straight line method) ₹'000	8,000	9,600	12,000

Expected net cash flows from the three proposals are as follows:

Project	*Year-wise net cash flows [₹'000]*					
	1	*2*	*3*	*4*	*5*	*6*
X: Net cash flow	15,000	20,000	26,000	22,000	20,000	18,000
Y: Net cash flow	10,000	14,000	16,000	32,000	32,000	0
Z: Net cash flow	20,000	28,000	20,000	16,000	0	0

Though Haresh joined the small firm, he had no intention of working there for long. His plan was to stay with the company for a period of about 2–3 years, prove his mettle and move on to join a larger company at a senior position. He wanted to undertake such a project that would provide highest returns as soon as possible so that he could put his plan into action. Therefore, he recommended project Z to the CEO, emphasizing that it had the shortest payback period and would help the company recover its initial investment in the least possible time. He added, "Once you recover your investment, you can always look for new projects to invest in."

The CEO agreed with him about the importance of the payback period but was not sure whether payback period could be the sole criteria for accepting or rejecting a project. He decided to seek advice from an independent consultant before making a final choice of the project to undertake.

Question for Discussion

The CEO has asked you to evaluate the three projects using (i) the accounting rate of return, and (ii) the payback period. Ignore income taxes and assume the company's cost of capital is 18%. What would you advise the CEO and why?

CHAPTER 4

Investment Decision—DCF Methods of Appraising Projects

LEARNING OBJECTIVES

After studying this chapter, you should be able to:

- Identify the information that is relevant for financial evaluation of investment proposals.
- Calculate cash flows after taxes for project appraisal taking into account the residual value and working capital.
- Discuss why DCF methods are considered superior to non-DCF methods.
- Determine the Net Present Value and Profitability Index, and decide on whether to accept or reject a project proposal.
- Determine the internal rate of return and decide on whether to accept or reject a project proposal.
- Find discounted payback period and identify its pros and cons.
- Discuss and illustrate the merits and demerits of NPV and IRR as methods of project appraisal.

4.1 Introduction

In the previous chapter, we discussed two methods of appraising investment proposals: the accounting rate of return and the payback period. Both these methods have some merits but also have some serious shortcomings due to which they are not considered scientific and reliable. The Accounting Rate of Return (ARR) is simple to understand and use, and is based on accounting information related to profits earned by the firm, which is readily available in firms. But this feature is more of a limitation of the method, rather than an advantage, because investment projects involve cash outflows in the beginning, and to evaluate their worth we would need information on 'cash flows' rather than accounting profits. Accounting profits are determined on the accrual basis, while our focus here is on cash flows. In addition, the fact that 'investment' can be interpreted in several ways (such as initial investment and average investment) makes the accounting rate of return more confusing and less reliable.

The second method discussed in the previous chapter, the payback period, is simple as well as a cash flow method, but has serious handicaps that it neither considers the cash flows beyond the payback period nor the time value of money. Also, it only measures the time required for the return of the project investment and is not really a measure of profitability of the project.

Since both the ARR and payback period fail to consider the time value of money, we now turn our attention to the discounted cash flow methods. For this purpose, we would continue to work with the Progressive company example we discussed in the previous chapter, so that we can compare the results of our analysis using Discounted Cash Flow (DCF) methods with those we obtained using ARR and the payback period methods.

The Progressive Company example is repeated below for your ready reference.

EXAMPLE 4.1 The Progressive Company wants to invest in new productive machinery and is considering two proposals for this purpose. The two proposals have several similarities but differ in the timing of expected profits.

	Proposals X	*Proposals Y*
Investment required (in ₹)	1,00,000	1,00,000
Expected life of the machine	5 years	5 years
Depreciation per year (in ₹)	20,000	20,000
Income tax rate	30%	30%
Scrap value at the end of 5 years	Nil	Nil

Expected profits before depreciation and taxes from the two proposals are as follows:

Year	1	2	3	4	5
X: Profits (₹000)	90	30	30	30	30
Y: Profits (₹000)	30	30	90	30	30

The cost of capital of the Progressive company is 12%, and the company uses this as the minimum acceptable rate of return for screening investment proposals.

The main Discounted Cash Flow (DCF) methods of evaluating investment proposals are discussed now using the illustrative data of Progressive company given in Example 4.1.

4.2 Discounted Cash Flow (DCF) Methods

Discounted cash flow methods provide a more objective basis for evaluating and selecting investment proposals, as these methods take into account both the magnitude and the timing of expected cash flows in each period of a project's life.

To apply the DCF methods, we should understand the concept of time value of money, and be familiar with using the discounting tables. The concepts of discounting and time value of money were explained in detail in an earlier chapter, but for your ready reference, they have been briefly reviewed below before we discuss the main DCF methods, such as the Net Present Value and Internal Rate of Return. However, you are advised to carefully read the chapter on time value of money, if not already done.

4.2.1 Time Value of Money and Discounting of Future Values

The concept of time value of money simply says that a rupee or dollar available now has more value than a rupee or dollar receivable after some time. Thus, an amount of ₹100 in hand now would be more valuable as compared to the same amount of money to be received after say one year. This is because of the earning capacity of money; for example, ₹100 available now could be invested in a bank fixed deposit and earn interest income so that it grows to more than ₹100 by the end of the year.

Managers evaluating investment proposals have to deal with the problem of time value of money. A typical investment decision involves cash outflow in the beginning (let us call it Year-0) followed by a series of cash inflows in the future periods (years 1, 2, 3, etc). Cash flows occurring at different points of time cannot be simply added or subtracted at their face values (nominal values) because of their different time value of money. Adding or subtracting them without first bringing them to their comparable equivalents in terms of time value of money would be as illogical as comparing apples with oranges.

Discounting of future sums of money to their present values offers a solution to the time value problem. Discounting is reverse of compounding, and involves computing the present equivalent of future sums of money. By 'discounting' future sums back to the present, we can place all sums to be received (or paid) in the future on a comparable basis so that they can be added and subtracted.

Thus, discounting involves transformation of future sums into present equivalents which is achieved by using the present value tables. Two types of discounting tables would be relevant here as follows:

Single Value Discounting Tables

Table 1 (given in Appendix A at the end of the book) gives the present value of ₹1 due at the end of 'n' periods if the relevant interest rate is r% per period. The interest rate (r) chosen represents the rate at which funds can be lent and borrowed by the firm.

For example, if a firm has to receive ₹12,100 at the end of 2 years, and 10% is the relevant interest rate, what is its present value?

The mathematical formula for Present Value (PV) is:

$$\text{PV} = \text{Future value} \times \left[\frac{1}{(1+r)^n}\right]$$

Solving the equation, we get

$$\text{PV} = 12{,}100 \times \left[\frac{1}{(1.10)^2}\right] = 12{,}100 \times \left[\frac{1}{1.21}\right] = ₹10{,}000$$

As compared to computing present values mathematically, it is easier to compute the same by using the present value tables. To find out the present value of ₹12,100 receivable at the end of two years if interest rate is 10% per annum, we would first use the single values discounting table (Table 1 Appendix A) to find out the 'present value factor' for $n = 2$ and $r = 10\%$ which would be equal to 0.8264. Check for yourself from Table 1. Then,

PV = Future Value × PV factor for $r = 10\%$, $n = 2$

= 12,100 × PV factor for $r = 10\%$, $n = 2$

= 12,100 × 0.8264

= 10,000 (approx.)

Annuities

Annuities are a series of equally spaced receipts or payments of equal amounts. Consider the following examples of annuities: a student has been awarded a scholarship of ₹50,000 per annum for the next five years, or a person entitled to get annual pension of ₹1,20,000 for ten years. Table 2 (given in Appendix A at the end of the book) shows the present value of ₹1 due per period for n periods at r%.

For example, to find out the present value of ₹10,000 receivable annually for 5 years at 10% interest rate, we would first use the annuities table to find out the present value factor (or annuity factor) for $n = 5$ and $r = 10\%$ which would be equal to 3.7908. Check for yourself from Table 2. Then,

PV = Annuity amount × PV factor for $n = 5$ $r = 10\%$ from Table 2

PV = 10,000 × 3.7908 = 37,908.

When we are dealing with a large number of future values, using the discounting tables would save a lot of time and effort. However, we should remember the assumptions which form the basis of preparing the discounting tables.

Assumptions

Discounting tables are based on the following assumptions:

1. Compound interest: It is assumed that present values are to be calculated using the principle of compound interest (and not simple interest). Suppose you borrow from bank a sum of ₹1,000 at 10% annual interest rate and must repay the loan with interest at the end of 2nd year. At the end of year-1, interest of ₹1,000 × 10% = ₹100 would accrue, increasing the total outstanding loan amount to ₹1,000 + 100 = 1,100 at end of year 1. Now, following the compound interest principle, interest payable for the second year would be charged not only on the principal loan amount but also on the interest that has accrued up to the end of year 1. Thus, second year interest would amount to ₹1,100 × 10% = ₹110, raising the total loan amount to ₹1,100 + 110 = ₹1,210.
2. Cash flows occur at end of a period: It is assumed that all sums of money are received or paid at the end of a period, such as end of year 1, year 2, etc. This assumption simplifies the computation of present values in a standardized manner.

4.3 Net Present Value Method (NPV)

Net Present Value (NPV) is the excess of the present value of cash inflows over the present value of cash outflows relating to a project, when all future cash flows have been discounted at the required rate of return. The required rate of return would be the cost of capital or the minimum acceptable return from the project.

Mathematically, Net Present Value (NPV) would be presented as follows:

$$\text{NPV} = \sum_{t=0}^{n} \frac{C_t}{(1+k)^t}$$

Where, C_t is the net cash flow for period t whether it is a net cash outflow or inflow, $t = 0$ to n periods and n is the last period in which cash flow is expected; and k is the required rate of return. Net cash flow of period t_0 would usually be a cash outflow representing the initial project investment, while in other periods, the net cash flow would be equal to project related operating cash inflows (from sales collections and other incomes) less operating cash expenses as well as any further investments made in to the project in that period.

However, in practice we would be using the discounting tables to compute the NPV. Steps involved for using the NPV method are:

1. Determine net cash flow for each year of the project's life.
2. Using the cost of capital (or the minimum acceptable return from the project) as the discount rate, compute the Present Value of net cash flows determined under (1) above.
3. NPV = PV of cash inflows – PV of cash outflows.

Accept/Reject Rule

Using NPV approach, an investment proposal would be acceptable if its NPV is positive (that is, equal to zero or more than zero); and rejected if the NPV is negative. While comparing two proposals, the one with maximum NPV should be preferred over others. Let us compute the NPV of proposals X and Y given above to find out whether either of them would be acceptable to the firm. To compute the NPV, we need to first calculate X and Y proposals' cash flows as shown in Tables 4.1 and 4.2.

TABLE 4.1
NPV—Proposal X

₹

Year	1	2	3	4	5
Profit before depreciation and taxes	90,000	30,000	30,000	30,000	30,000
Depreciation	–20,000	–20,000	–20,000	–20,000	**–20,000**
Earnings Before Taxes (EBT)	70,000	10,000	10,000	10,000	10,000
Income Tax (30% × EBT)	–21,000	–3,000	–3,000	–3,000	**–3,000**
Profit After Taxes (PAT)	49,000	7,000	7,000	7,000	7,000
+ Depreciation added back	20,000	20,000	20,000	20,000	**20,000**
Net cash flow	69,000	27,000	27,000	27,000	27,000
PV factor at 12%	0.8929	0.7972	0.7118	0.6355	0.5674
PV	61,610.1	21,524.4	19,218.6	17,158.5	15,319.8

Total PV of future cash flow from project (X) = 1,34,831.4
Less: Initial Investment = **–1,00,000.0**
Net Present Value (X) = 34,831.4

TABLE 4.2
NPV—Proposal Y

₹

Year	1	2	3	4	5
Profit before depreciation and taxes	30,000	30,000	90,000	30,000	30,000
Depreciation	–20,000	–20,000	–20,000	–20,000	**–20,000**
Earnings Before Taxes (EBT)	10,000	10,000	70,000	10,000	10,000
Income tax (30% × EBT)	–3,000	–3,000	–21,000	–3,000	**–3,000**
Profit After Taxes (PAT)	7,000	7,000	49,000	7,000	7,000
+ Depreciation added back	20,000	20,000	20,000	20,000	**20,000**
Net cash flow	27,000	27,000	69,000	27,000	27,000
PV factor at 12%	0.8929	0.7972	0.7118	0.6355	0.5674
PV	24,108.3	21,524.4	49,114.2	17,158.5	15,319.8

Total PV of future cash flows from project (Y) = 1,27,225.2
Less: Initial Investment = –100,000.0
Net Present Value (Y) = 27,225.2

The use of NPV method clearly shows that proposal X is better than proposal Y and that the firm will be better off by a NPV of over ₹7,606 by selecting X as compared to Y.

4.3.1 Short-cut to Calculate NPV in Situation of Constant Annual Cash Inflows

In case of conventional projects involving an initial investment followed by constant or even annual cash inflows, we can use Annuity present value tables (PV Table 2) to reduce the calculations involved. For example, assume a firm is considering investing in a new project that would require an initial investment of ₹60,000, gives future annual net cash inflows of ₹15,000 for a period of 7 years (starting from the end of year 1), and the company's cost of capital is 14% per annum. In such a situation we can calculate NPV by taking following simple steps:

1. Since the future cash inflows form an annuity, we can use the annuities PV table. From the annuities PV table, find the annuity PV factor for n = Useful life of the project (7 years in our example) and r = cost of capital (14% in our example).
2. Multiply the annual cash inflow by the annuity PV factor identified in step-1 above to calculate the present value of the future net cash flows from the project.
3. Calculate NPV = PV of future net cash inflows – Initial Investment.

Applying the steps to our example:

NPV = PV of future net cash inflows – Initial Investment

NPV = (Annuity PV factor t =7@14% × 15,000) – 60,000

NPV = (4.2883 × 15,000) – 60,000

NPV = 64,324.5 – 60,000 = 4,324.5

The NPV method is regarded as more reliable than other methods. This is because it has several desirable features: considers cash flows during the entire life of the project and takes into account the time value of money. However, to use this method, the firm must decide on a target rate of return that would be used as the cut-off discounting rate.

4.4 Internal Rate of Return (IRR)

The Internal Rate of Return (IRR) may be simply defined as the discount rate which, when applied to the cash flows of an investment project, produces a Net Present Value (NPV) equal to zero. Thus, the Internal Rate of Return (IRR) is the discount rate that equates the present value of expected cash outflows for a project with the present value of the expected inflows. In other words, when all cash flows related to a project are discounted at a rate equal to IRR, the NPV = 0.

Mathematically, IRR is the rate of interest r, that satisfies the following equation:

$$\sum_{t=0}^{N}\left[\frac{C_t}{(1+r)^t}\right]=0 \tag{4.1}$$

Where C_t is the net cash flow in period t whether it is a net cash outflow or inflow, r is the rate of interest used for discounting and n is the last period in which cash flow is expected. If the initial cash outflow or project cost occurs at time 0, Eq. (4.1) can be expressed as:

$$C_0=\frac{C_1}{(1+r)}+\frac{C_2}{(1+r)^2}+\cdots+\frac{C_n}{(1+r)^n}$$

where

C_0, C_1, C_2... are the net cash flows in period 0, 1, 2, etc.

r = Internal Rate of Return (IRR)

Acceptance Criterion

The calculated Internal Rate of Return (IRR) is compared with the target rate or the required rate of return (k) and a proposal would be acceptable if IRR is equal to or greater than the required rate of return (k). Otherwise, the proposal would be rejected. Thus,

- Accept the proposal if IRR $\geq k$
- Reject the proposal if IRR $< k$

4.4.1 Graphical Presentation of the Relationship Between Discount Rates, NPV and IRR

To graphically show the relationship, let us take a simple example. Assume a project would require investment in year 0 = 10,000; and gives a cash inflow in year 1 = 11,500 as shown in Table 4.3.

TABLE 4.3 Project Cash Flows

Year	*CF*
0	–10,000
1	11,500

Using a range of discount rates between 0% to 25%, we find the corresponding NPVs as given in Table 4.4.

TABLE 4.4 NPVs at different Discount Rates

Discount Rate	*NPV*
0%	1,500.0
5%	948.0
10%	453.5
15%	0.0
20%	–420.5
25%	–800.0

Presenting the discount rates and related NPVs on a graph, we get Figure 4.1.

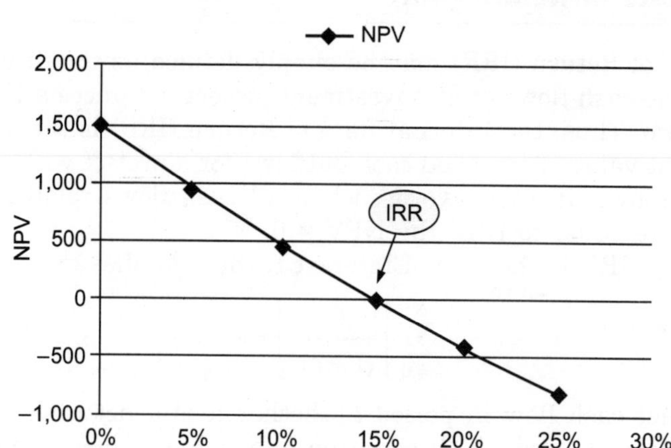

FIGURE 4.1 Graphical representation of discount rates and related NPVs

IRR is shown at the intersection of NPV line and the X-axis when NPV would be equal to zero at a discount rate of 15%.

4.4.2 Computation of the IRR

As a basic rule, be prepared to calculate the IRR by trial and error method. Remember that we are trying to determine that discount rate (IRR) which would give NPV = 0. Therefore, using the trial and error method, if we get a positive NPV when discounting cash flows at X% discount rate, it would mean that future cash flows need to be discounted at a rate higher than X% to make NPV equal to zero, and therefore, the actual IRR would be higher than X%, and vice-versa. After a few trials, we may get close to the IRR that would give a NPV = 0.

Let us continue with the example of projects X and Y to illustrate the calculation of IRR.

Calculation of IRR for Project X

If we tried discounting future cash flows from project X at interest rates of 20% and then 25%, we would get significantly positive NPVs, indicating that actual IRR was higher than 25% and that we should increase the discount rate. Then using interest rates of 28% and 29% to discount the future cash flows, we would get Table 4.5.

TABLE 4.5 Project-X: Calculating NPV at 28%

Year	1	2	3	4	5
Cash flows (from previous section)	69,000	27,000	27,000	27,000	27,000
PV Factor@28%	0.7812	0.6104	0.4768	0.3725	0.291
Present Value	53,902.8	16,480.8	12,873.6	10,057.5	7,857

Total Present Value = 53,902.8 + 16,480.8 + 12,873.6 + 10,057.5 + 7,857
= 1,01,171.7

Net Present Value = 1,01,171.7 – 1,00,000 = 1,171.7

Since we are getting a positive NPV, we need to raise the discount rate further, (although by a small margin) to make NPV = 0. So, we try 29% discount rate as given in Table 4.6.

Year	1	2	3	4	5
Cash flows	69,000	27,000	27,000	27,000	27,000
Present Value factor@29%	0.7752	0.6009	0.4658	0.3611	0.2799
Present Value	53,488.8	16,224.3	12,576.6	9,749.7	7,557.3

TABLE 4.6
Project X: Calculating NPV at 29%

Total PV = 53,488.8 + 16,224.3 + 12,576.6 + 9,749.7 + 7,557.3
= 99,596.7

Net Present Value = 99,596.7 – 1,00,000 = –403.3

Since we are getting a negative NPV using 29% rate of discount, it indicates that actual IRR would be lower than 29%. But when we discounted cash flows at lower rate of 28%, we got a positive NPV. Putting the two results together, that is when a lower rate gives positive NPV and a higher rate gives a negative NPV, it is certain that the IRR lies between these two discount rates. In some situations, a manager would be satisfied by saying that the IRR is between 28–29%. However, for very large projects competing with each other as well as for exam purposes, it might be necessary to compute the exact IRR.

In such situations, we can approximately calculate the IRR by the process of interpolation as follows:

1. IRR by Interpolation—for Project X

$$\text{IRR} = \text{LR} + \frac{(\text{NPV by LR})}{(\text{PV by LR} - \text{PV by HR})} \times (\text{HR} - \text{LR})$$

where,
LR = Lower Rate
HR = Higher Rate

Using the above formula:

$$\text{IRR (X)} = 28\% + \frac{(1{,}01{,}171.7 - 1{,}00{,}000)}{(1{,}01{,}171.7 - 99{,}596.7)} \times 1$$
$$= 28.74\%$$

Similar to how we proceeded to calculate IRR for project X, let us determine the IRR for project Y. To begin with, let us check project Y's NPV at 28% discount rate as given in Table 4.7.

Year	1	2	3	4	5
Cash flows as above	27,000	27,000	69,000	27,000	27,000
PV factor at 28%	0.7812	0.6104	0.4768	0.3725	0.2910
PV	21,092.4	16,480.8	32,899.2	10,057.5	7,857.0

TABLE 4.7
Project Y: Calculating NPV at 28%

Total Present Value (PV) = 21,092.4 + 16,480.8 + 32,899.2 + 10,057.5 + 7,857.0
= 88,386.90

NPV = 88,386.90 – 1,00,000 = –11,613.10

Since we are getting a significantly negative NPV at 28% rate of discount, it indicates that actual IRR would be lower than 28%, and that we need to reduce the discount rate by a good margin. Let us try 24% interest rate as shown in Table 4.8.

TABLE 4.8
Project Y: Calculating NPV at 24%

Year	1	2	3	4	5
Cash flows as above	27,000	27,000	69,000	27,000	27,000
PV factor at 24%	0.8065	0.6504	0.5245	0.4230	0.3411
Present Value	21,775.5	17,560.8	36,190.5	11,421.0	9,209.7

Total Present Value (PV) = 21,775.5 + 17,560.8 + 36,190.5 + 11,421.0 + 9,209.7
= 96,157.50.
NPV = 96,157.50 − 1,00,000 = −3,842.50

Again we are getting a negative NPV at 24% rate of discount; it indicates that actual IRR would be lower than 24%, and that we need to reduce the discount rate. Let us try 20% interest rate as shown in Table 4.9.

TABLE 4.9
Project Y: Calculating NPV at 20%

Year	1	2	3	4	5
Cash flow as above	27,000	27,000	69,000	27,000	27,000
PV factor at 20%	0.8333	0.6944	0.5787	0.4823	0.4019
Present Value	22,499.1	18,748.8	39,930.3	13,022.1	10,851.3

Total Present Value (PV) = 22,499.1 + 18,748.8 + 39,930.3 + 13,022.1 + 10,851.3
= 1,05,051.6
NPV @ 20% = PV at 20% − Initial Investement = +5,051.6

As we have noted above, when a lower rate gives positive NPV and a higher rate gives a negative NPV, it is certain that the IRR lies between these two discount rates. In such a situation, IRR can be calculated by interpolation.

2. IRR by Interpolation—for Project Y

$$\text{IRR} = \text{LR} + \frac{(\text{NPV by LR})}{(\text{PV by LR} - \text{PV by HR})} \times (\text{HR} - \text{LR})$$

where
LR = Lower Rate, HR = Higher Rate

Using the above formula:

$$\text{IRR (Y)} = 20\% + \frac{(1{,}05{,}051.6 - 1{,}00{,}000)}{(1{,}05{,}051.6 - 96{,}157.5)} \times 4$$
$$= 22.27\%$$

Similar to the results we obtained by using the Net Present Value, IRR method also recommends taking up project X as its IRR is higher than that of project Y.

Short-cut to Calculate IRR in Case of Constant Annual Cash Inflows

Although IRR is normally calculated by trial and error method, you can use a short-cut to estimate IRR in case of conventional projects involving an initial investment followed by constant or even annual cash inflows. For example, assume a firm is considering investing in new project that would require an initial investment of ₹60,000 and gives annual net cash inflows of ₹15,000 for a period of 7 years. In such situations, we can estimate (or get close to) IRR by taking following simple steps:

Step 1 Determine the payback period.

$$\frac{60,000}{15,000} = 4 \text{ years payback}$$

Step 2 Using the Annuities PV table, find the PV factor for n = Useful life of the project (7 years in our example) that comes closest to the payback period (4.00 in our example).

Step 3 Use the interest rate (16%) identified with this PV factor to discount the future annual cash flows.

Step 4 Adjust the rate, as necessary until IRR found (i.e. until NPV becomes = 0).

Using the annuities present value tables for $n = 7$, we find that the PV factor closest to 4.00 is 4.0386 against interest rate 16%. Therefore, 16% can be taken as the starting point to calculate IRR.

Project NPV @ 16% = Present Value of future net cash inflows – Initial investment
= (15,000 × 4.0386) – 60,000 = 579

We have got a quick starting point, and know that actual IRR would be slightly above 16% because we need to discount the future cash inflows by a further ₹579 to make NPV = 0. Now, we can proceed to calculate the exact IRR by interpolation. For this purpose, we should take a higher discount rate that would give a negative NPV. Raising the discount rate to 18%, taking n = 7 years, annuity present value table (Table 2) gives 3.8115 as the annuity PV factor. Then,

Project NPV @ 18% = Present value of future net cash inflows – Initial Investment
= (15,000 × 3.8115) – 60,000 = –2827.5

Using interpolation, IRR would be estimated as follows:

$$\text{IRR} = \text{LR} + \frac{(\text{NPV by LR})}{(\text{PV by LR} - \text{PV by HR})} \times (\text{HR} - \text{LR})$$

Where, LR = Lower Rate, HR = Higher Rate

Using the above formula:

$$\text{IRR} = 16\% + \left(\frac{579}{60{,}579 - 57{,}172.5}\right) \times 2$$

$$= 16.17\%$$

Explanation of the Short-cut

In case of even or constant cash inflows each year, we can utilize the annuities present value tables (Table 2, Appendix A) to quickly estimate IRR or get close to the IRR. Note that for computing IRR, we are looking for such a discount rate that would make the NPV equal to zero. In other words, IRR is that discount rate which would satisfy the following equation:

Present Value of future net cash inflows – Initial investment = 0

Since we are assuming constant net cash inflows per year (equal amount each year), the above equation may be written as:

(Annuity PV factor $t = n@r\%$ × annual net cash inflow) – Initial investment = 0 where $t = n$ is the life time of the project (in years) during which constant annual cash inflows would be expected, and r is the discount rate that would give NPV = 0. The above equation may be re-written as follows:

$$\text{Initial investment} = \text{Annuity PV factor } t = n@r\% \times \text{Annual net cash inflow}$$

Applying the formula to our example, we get:

$$60{,}000 = \text{Annuity PV factor } t = 7@r\% \times 15{,}000, \text{ or}$$

$$\frac{60{,}000}{15{,}000} = \text{Annuity PV factor } t = 7@r\%, \text{ or}$$

$$4.00 = \text{Annuity PV factor } t = 7@r\%,$$

Looking at Annuity present value table (Table 2, Appendix A) for an annuity present value factor closest to 4.00 for $n = 7$, we find that a discount rate of 16% gives 4.0386 as the annuity PV factor closest to the desired value of 4.00, indicating that IRR is expected to be close to 16%.

4.5 Discounted Payback Period Method

In the previous chapter, we explained the simple payback period, and noted that one of its main limitations was that it did not take into account the time value of money. An improvement in this respect may be to calculate the discounted payback period instead of a simple payback period.

The discounted payback period indicates the number of years it would take the project to return the initial capital expenditure (project cost) while taking into account the time value of money. The procedure required to compute the discounted payback period is similar to a simple payback period, except that instead of using gross future cash inflows, here we would first discount the gross future cash inflows to get their equivalent present values in year-zero (beginning of the project) and then proceed to calculate the payback period.

Like the NPV method, the firm would have to decide its cost of capital that is used to discount the gross future cash inflows.

Continuing with our examples of projects X and Y, and assuming the discounting rate is the same as we used in NPV method, their discounted payback periods are calculated in Tables 4.10 and 4.11.

TABLE 4.10
Discounted Payback Period: Project X

Year	1	2	3	4	5
Cash flows (as calculated above)	69,000	27,000	27,000	27,000	27,000
PV factor at 12%	0.8929	0.7972	0.7118	0.6355	0.5674
PV	61,610.1	21,524.4	19,218.6	17,158.5	15,319.8

Cumulative discounted cash inflow recovered in first two years

$$= 61{,}610.1 + 21{,}524.4 = 82{,}134.5$$

Balance of un-recovered initial investment at the end of second year

$$= 1{,}00{,}000 - 82{,}134.5 = 17{,}865.5$$

Since the discounted cash inflow in the third year is more than the balance unrecovered amount, it would approximately take 17,865.5/19,218.6 or about 0.93 portion of third year to fully recover the initial investment, while also taking care of the time value of money.

Hence, the payback period of Project X = 2.93 years.

TABLE 4.11 Discounted Payback Period: Project Y

Year	1	2	3	4	5
Cash flows (as calculated above)	27,000	27,000	69,000	27,000	27,000
PV factor at 12%	0.8929	0.7972	0.7118	0.6355	0.5674
PV	24,108.3	21,524.4	49,114.2	17,158.5	15,319.8

Cumulative discounted cash inflow recovered in first three years

$$= 24{,}108.3 + 21{,}524.4 + 49{,}114.2 = 94{,}746.9$$

Balance of un-recovered initial investment at the end of third year

$$= 1{,}00{,}000 - 94{,}746.9 = 5{,}253.1$$

Since the discounted cash inflow in the fourth year is more than the balance unrecovered amount, it would approximately take 5,253.1/17,158.5 or about 0.31 portion of fourth year to fully recover the initial investment while also taking care of the time value of money.

Hence, the payback period of project X = 3.31 years.

Accept/Reject Rules

For appraising individual projects (called an accept–reject situation), the calculated discounted payback period is compared with the maximum tolerable payback period. If a project has a payback period equal to or less than the maximum tolerable payback period, it would be accepted; otherwise rejected. If a firm is considering two mutually exclusive projects, the project with shorter discounted payback period would be preferred. Comparing projects X and Y, since the discounted payback period of project X is lesser than that of project Y, project X would be preferred as compared to Y.

NPV vs Discounted Payback Period

Since both methods use discounted future cash flows, it is natural to ask: is discounted payback period as good as the NPV, and can it replace NPV? The answer is no, because in spite of taking the time value of money, the discounted payback period still suffers from one major drawback that it does not consider cash flows beyond the payback period while the Net Present Value method takes into account cash flows during the full life of the projects under consideration.

Also note that discounted payback period cannot be calculated if a project has negative Net Present Value; this is because the initial investment would never be fully recovered. Due to these reasons, NPV remains a superior method as compared to the discounted payback period method.

4.6 Profitability Index or Benefits—Cost Ratio

The Profitability Index, also called the benefit–cost ratio, is the ratio of the present value of future net cash flows of a project to the initial cash investment in the project. Mathematically, it can be expressed as follows:

$$\text{Profitability Index} = \frac{\sum_{t=1}^{n} \frac{C_t}{(1+k)^t}}{C_0}$$

$$= \frac{\text{Present Value of future net cashflows}}{\text{Initial investment}}$$

While the Net Present Value (NPV) is an excess of the Present Value of cash inflows from a project over the cash outflows and expresses the result in an absolute sum of money, the Profitability Index is a 'ratio' of the Present Value of cash inflows from a project over the initial investment.

For the projects X and Y taken up above, the profitability index would be computed as follows:

$$\text{PI of Project X} = \frac{\text{Present Value of future net cashflows}}{\text{Initial investment}}$$

$$= \frac{1,34,831.4}{1,00,000} = 1.35 \text{ Approx.}$$

$$\text{PI of Project Y} = \frac{1,27,225.2}{1,00,000} = 1.27 \text{ (Approx.)}$$

Accept/Reject Rules

Using the Profitability Index, a project would be acceptable if its Profitability Index is equal to or greater than one (that is PI ≥ 1), and rejected if its Profitability Index is less than one (that is PI < 1). Projects X and Y evaluated above both have a Profitability Index greater than one, and hence, each of these projects is acceptable on a standalone basis (accept–reject situation). However, if they are mutually exclusive projects so that only one of them can be taken up, then project X would be preferable than project Y since X project's PI is greater than Y.

Net Present Value vs. Profitability Index

As illustrated above, both Net Present Value and Profitability Index would normally give similar results, particularly in accept–reject situations. However, Profitability Index being only a 'ratio' suffers from some limitations. One major limitation of Profitability Index as a method of evaluating projects is that it ignores the scale of investment. Consider the situation given in Table 4.12.

TABLE 4.12
NPV vs IPR

Project	*Initial investment*	*Present Value of future cash flows*	*NPV*	*PI*
A	10,000	14,000	4,000	1.40
B	1,00,000	1,30,000	30,000	1.30

Assuming projects A and B are mutually exclusive, NPV method would suggest taking up project B (due to higher NPV) while Profitability Index would recommend accepting project A (due to greater PI). Profitability Index expresses only the relative profitability of projects under consideration, and ignores the scale of investment. For example, if we accept project A, the net value addition to the firm would be only ₹4,000 while project B would yield a net value addition of ₹30,000. Therefore, while choosing between mutually exclusive proposals, results of PI should be viewed cautiously. In general, NPV is considered a better method of evaluating projects because it gives the result in terms of absolute sums of money.

In spite of its limitations, Profitability Index is a useful tool, particularly in dealing with situations of capital rationing, which requires 'ranking' of available projects in terms of their importance to the firm. Investment appraisal in times of capital rationing is explained later.

4.7 Effect of Salvage Value, Working Capital and Taxes

In our discussion so far, we have not considered the salvage (resale) value of fixed assets and working capital requirements in order to keep the discussion simple and focused on the methods of evaluating investment proposals. Now, we can briefly deal with the effect of these items on cash flows and evaluation of proposals.

4.7.1 Salvage Value

Salvage value or scrap value refers to the resale value of a fixed asset at the end of its useful life. If some plant, machinery or other fixed assets have a salvage value at the end of their useful life, it would increase the cash inflow of the year when they are disposed of (usually the last year of the project). The net increase in cash inflow would amount to the net resale price (gross resale price less any selling expenses incurred in the process of disposing off the asset) minus any taxes payable. The tax liability on the salvage value might arise if the fixed asset has already been fully depreciated in the books of accounts of the firm, so that the net salvage value realized would be treated as taxable income. To illustrate, suppose the fixed assets in project X (discussed earlier in the chapter) had an estimated resale value of ₹20,000 at the end of the project, but the firm had to incur a sales commission of ₹1,000 to dispose of the assets. Also, assume that the fixed asset under consideration had already been fully depreciated, and that the income tax rate applicable to the firm is 30%. The net increase in the cash inflow would then be calculated as follows:

Gross sales proceeds from sale of the asset = ₹20,000

Less: Sales commission = ₹1,000

Net sales proceeds = ₹19,000

Less: Income taxes @30% = ₹5,700

Net increase in cash inflow of the year = ₹13,300

If the expected salvage value of an asset is known in advance (or given in the exam questions) and the firm uses straight line method of depreciation, the expected salvage value should be deducted from the cost of the fixed asset before calculating the yearly depreciation on the asset. For example, if the cost of a fixed asset was ₹60,000 and its useful life was ten years at the end of which the expected salvage value would be ₹10,000, using straight line method of depreciation, the annual depreciation would amount to ₹5,000 per annum [(60,000–10,000)/10 years]. Assuming the fixed asset is actually sold for ₹10,000 at the end of ten years, there would not be any taxable income or tax liability as shown below:

Cost of the fixed asset= ₹60,000

Less: Depreciation in ten year (5,000 × 10 years) = ₹50,000

Balance un-depreciated cost at end of ten years = ₹10,000

Resale value realized = ₹10,000

Taxable income from sale of asset = Nil

While using the DCF methods, the additional net cash inflow from salvage value would be discounted as usual along with the project's operating cash flows.

4.7.2 Working Capital Requirements

A new project typically would require some investment in working capital items, such as inventories and trade receivables in addition to the investment in fixed assets including plant, machinery and equipment. Projects involving replacement of existing plant and equipment might also require some additional (incremental) investment in working capital. For calculating cash flows related to a project, investment made in working capital should be taken as a cash outflow in the year in which such investment is made. Any investment in working capital can be normally assumed to be fully recovered (except when specifically stated otherwise) as cash inflow at the end of the project, and thus added to the net cash inflow of the last year of the project.

To illustrate, suppose project X (discussed earlier in the chapter) required an investment of ₹25,000 in the beginning of the project in addition to the investment in machinery. This amount of ₹25,000 invested in working capital would be taken as additional cash 'outflow' in year 0 of the project (thus increasing the total initial investment), and assumed to be fully recovered as a cash 'inflow' at the end of year 5, the last year of the project. Note that normally there would not be any tax liability on the recovery of the working capital at the end of the project because it is just return of the original investment and does not involve any gains. While using the DCF methods, the additional net cash inflow from recovery of working capital would be discounted as usual along with the project's other operating cash flows.

Additions or reductions in working capital investment might not only happen at the beginning and end of a project, respectively, but might happen any time during the life of a project. What is important to note is that whenever additional (incremental) investment is made in working capital, it should be taken as a cash outflow, and when there is a reduction in working capital, the same would be considered as a cash inflow.

4.7.3 Depreciation and Taxes

Dealing with depreciation in capital budgeting might often be perplexing. Depreciation is known to be a 'non-cash' expense, whereas we want to focus only on cash flows while evaluating investment proposals; yet we did include depreciation in our calculation of cash flows related to project X and project Y in this chapter. Why?

Of course, when a firm buys a fixed asset, there is a cash outflow that is duly accounted for as investment. Since a fixed asset would have a long life, the (depreciable) cost of the fixed asset is spread over its useful life through the accounting process called depreciation. Depreciation is rightly called a non-cash expense, because it is merely an accounting entry, and there is no cash flow involved when a firm depreciates a fixed asset. So why did we include depreciation in our calculation of cash flows related to project X and project Y in this chapter?

The answer lies in the fact that when a firm provides for depreciation on its fixed assets, its taxable income would reduce to the extent of depreciation provided (as permissible under the applicable tax laws), and the firm would save on tax liability which helps in conservation of cash flows. The cash flow saved by way of tax-savings (often referred to as tax-shield) is taken as additional cash inflow resulting from the project. In other words, cash inflow does not result from depreciation itself, but due to income taxes saved on the amount of depreciation provided in accounts. That is why the amount of annual depreciation deducted in calculating 'taxable income' is added back to 'profits after taxes' for calculating net cash inflow for a period.

EXAMPLE 4.2 **Residual Value, Depreciation and Taxes**

Grace company is considering investing ₹1,00,000 in new machinery which will reduce costs to save ₹30,000 annually for five years and which will have a resale value of ₹10,000 at the end of year 5. The company's cost of capital (to be used as the required rate of return) is 12% and its applicable income tax rate is 25%. Calculate (a) The accounting rate of return on average investment, and (b) NPV of the proposal. Should the company undertake the project?

Solution: In this situation, benefits from the investment will arise in the form of cost savings (and hence increase in profits). We proceed as usual to calculate profit after taxes and cash flows.

ARR and NPV—Grace Company

Year	0	1	2	3	4	5
Initial investment	–1,00,000					
Savings or profit before depreciation & taxes	0	30,000	30,000	30,000	30,000	30,000
Less: Depreciation [(100–10)/5	0	18,000	18,000	18,000	18,000	18,000
Earnings Before Taxes (EBT)	0	12,000	12,000	12,000	12,000	12,000
Less: Income Tax (25% × EBT)	0	3,000	3,000	3,000	3,000	3,000
Profit After Taxes (PAT)	0	9,000	9,000	9,000	9,000	9,000
Add back depreciation	0	18,000	18,000	18,000	18,000	18,000
Cash flow from operations	0	27,000	27,000	27,000	27,000	27,000
Add salvage value	0	0	0	0	0	10,000
Net cash flow	–1,00,000	27,000	27,000	27,000	27,000	37,000
PV factor @ 12%	1.0000	0.8929	0.7972	0.7118	0.6355	0.5674
Present Value of cash flows	–1,00,000	24,108.3	21,524.4	19,218.6	17,158.5	20,993.8

$$\text{The ARR would be} = \frac{\text{Average annual profit after taxes}}{\frac{1}{2}\text{ of } (1{,}00{,}000 + 10{,}000)} = \frac{9{,}000}{55{,}000} = 16.37\%$$

Net Present Value = Total PV of future cash flows – Initial Investment

= ₹3,003.6

Conclusion: Both ARR and NPV signal acceptance of the proposal even though between ARR and NPV methods, NPV is certainly more reliable. Since the NPV of the proposed project is positive, it is acceptable. However, the margin of error is very thin due to a small amount of NPV. Hence the project should be undertaken carefully to avoid risk.

4.8 Investment Decision Involving Asset Replacement

Cash flows in a replacement investment decision often arise in the form of cash savings from greater efficiency of the new plant and machinery. Therefore, in such situations, first calculate the 'incremental' net cash savings, and then proceed to compute the NPV.

The relevant costs and benefits of replacement type investment decisions would be:

- Future cash flows related to the project,
- Cash flows should be incremental or differential between the alternatives courses of action, and
- Ignore sunk costs.

Sunk costs represent costs already incurred that cannot be recovered, or resources already committed that cannot be changed by our future decisions. Remember that sunk costs (such as depreciation on old equipment) are always irrelevant in future decision making. Consider the following interesting question.

EXAMPLE 4.3 Replacement Decision

Rocket company manufactures product XL which it sells for ₹100 per unit. The variable cost of production is currently ₹70 per unit, and fixed costs are ₹10 per unit. The company is considering replacing its existing machinery with more efficient new machinery that would cost ₹12,00,000. Purchase of the new machinery would result in reducing the variable cost to ₹50 only per unit. However, the purchase of the new machinery would increase the company's fixed costs by ₹1,00,000 per annum. The new machinery would have a useful life of five years, after which it would have a resale value of ₹50,000 at the end of 5th year. The firm sells 25,000 units of the product per year and it would remain unaffected by the machinery replacement. If the minimum required rate of return from new investments is 15% per year, should the company purchase the new machinery? (Ignore taxation).

Solution: As stated above, cash flows in a replacement investment decision such as this may often arise in the form of cash savings from higher efficiency of the new plant and machinery. Therefore, in such situations, first calculate the 'incremental' net cash savings and then proceed to compute the NPV.

Calculation of Annual Incremental Cash Savings

Annual savings due to new machinery = 25,000 units × ₹(70 – 50)	₹5,00,000
Less: Annual increase in fixed cost due to new machinery	₹1,00,000
Annual incremental net cash savings due to new machinery	₹4,00,000

Using the net cash savings as the cash flow from the replacement project, we can proceed to calculate the present values and NPV.

Calculation of NPV

Year	*Cash flow* (₹)	*PV factor* @15%	*PV of Cash Flow* (₹)
0	–12,00,000	1.000	–12,00,000
1	4,00,000	0.8696	3,47,840
2	4,00,000	0.7561	3,02,440
3	4,00,000	0.6575	2,63,000
4	4,00,000	0.5718	2,28,720
5	4,50,000*	0.4972	2,23,740
* Including salvage value			**NPV = 1,65,740**

The NPV is positive @15% discount rate; therefore, the project is acceptable.

Explanation: If you are wondering why we did not consider the existing fixed cost given in the question or the total revenue from the sales of product XL in our analysis, it is because only the incremental or differential information would be relevant for future decision making. Items of costs or revenues that would not change due to the decision situation at hand need not be considered simply because they would not change our decision one way or the other.

To illustrate, let us re-work the analysis of relevant cash flows for the above machinery replacement situation. What we wish to find out is the 'difference' in net cash flows (i) without new machinery and (ii) with new machinery, as presented below:

Product-XL Annual Operating Costs and Revenue

Items of cost and revenue	*Without new machine*	*With new machine*	*Differential cash flows*
Total sales revenue	25,00,000	25,00,000	0
Variable cost	17,50,000	12,50,000	5,00,000
Existing fixed cost [25,000 × 10]	2,50,000	2,50,000	0
Increase in fixed cost	Nil	1,00,000	–1,00,000
Incremental cash flows			4,00,000

Once again, as you can see, even when we included all details of revenues and costs, the incremental cash flows would remain the same as in our previous simplified calculation. Incidentally, the existing fixed cost of ₹2,50,000 is an example of a sunk cost.

4.9 Net Present Value Versus Internal Rate of Return

Both NPV and IRR methods of project appraisal are regarded as superior to the accounting rate of return and the payback period method. This is because NPV and IRR take into account the time value of money, consider full life span of the project and most importantly, they are based on cash flows rather than accounting profits which are affected by non-cash items and may be manipulated by the management's subjective choice of accounting policies related to depreciation, inventory valuation and provision for bad debts.

An important question here is whether NPV and IRR would both provide same conclusion regarding acceptance or rejection of a project. In other words, if the calculated NPV for a project suggests the project is acceptable, would IRR also give the same conclusion or provide an opposite signal as compared to the NPV?

In the previous chapter, we distinguished between **mutually exclusive and standalone proposals.** Two projects are called mutually exclusive when only one of the proposals under consideration can be accepted, so that the acceptance of one proposal would automatically mean that the other proposal is rejected. For example, if a company is evaluating whether it should go for technology X or technology Y, acceptance of technology X would automatically mean rejection of technology Y proposal. In contrast, when projects are evaluated in an **accept–reject or standalone situation**, each investment proposal is independently evaluated against the acceptance criteria (such as target rate of return) rather than competing against each other.

In an accept–reject situation (when a project is evaluated on a standalone basis), both NPV and IRR would tend to provide the same conclusion regarding acceptance or rejection of a project. However, in a mutually-exclusive situation, when two investment proposals compete against each other so that only one of the proposals under consideration can be accepted, the two methods of NPV and IRR might provide different signals regarding acceptance or rejection of a project. When two mutually-exclusive projects are under consideration, then we must 'rank' them on the basis of their attractiveness to the firm: the IRR will rank the projects on the 'percentage' of (discounted) return, while NPV would rank the projects on the basis of 'absolute' amount of (discounted) net value created for the firm.

Thus, in a mutually-exclusive situation, the two methods of NPV and IRR might provide contradictive signals: one of them indicating that the project is acceptable while the other method indicating the project should be rejected. Obviously, a manager confronted with such contradictory results would be confused regarding the action he should take. The nature of contradictory results between the NPV and IRR methods can be explained with reference to two types of situations: (a) Scale difference: where the scale of initial investment required by the two projects is significantly different from each other and (b) Timing difference: where the initial investment is same, but the 'timing' of future cash flows generated by the two competing projects is significantly different from each other. These are discussed in the following sections:

4.9.1 Different Scale of Initial Investment

If the initial cash investment required in two mutually exclusive projects is significantly different from each other, the two methods NPV and IRR could provide different conclusions. Consider the following example:

EXAMPLE 4.4 Assume a company is considering two mutually exclusive investment proposals 'A' and 'B'. The initial investment required for Proposal A is ₹10,000 and proposal B ₹50,000. The expected cash inflow at the end of one year for proposal A is ₹14,000 and that of proposal B is ₹60,000. Assume both have a project-life of 1 year and the target rate of return is 12%:

	Cash flows (₹)				*Rank by IRR*	*Rank by NPV*
Project	*Year 0*	*Year 1*	*IRR*	*NPV@12%*		
A	–10,000	13,000	30%	+1,608	1	2
B	–50,000	60,000	20%	+3,574	2	1

Had it been an accept–reject situation, both projects would be acceptable on a stand-alone basis since each one gives a positive NPV as well as an IRR higher than the target rate of return. However, since we have to choose only one of the two mutually exclusive proposals, we must rank them to determine priority. When we rank the two proposals by IRR method, we would choose proposal A because its IRR of 30% is higher than B's IRR of 20%. But if we go by NPV method, proposal B would be preferable because its NPV of ₹3,574 is higher than A's 1,608. Which one is more reliable and how to resolve the conflict?

To resolve the issue, let us find the 'differential' cash flows between the two proposals and calculate the NPV and IRR of such differential cash flows, as follows:

	Cash flows (₹)			
Project	*Year 0*	*Year 1*	*IRR*	*NPV@12%*
A	–10,000	13,000	30%	+1,608
B	**–50,000**	**60,000**	**20%**	**+3,574**
Differential	**–40,000**	**47,000**	**17.5**	**+1,966**

The differential cash flows indicate that proposal B would require additional investment of ₹40,000 now (year zero or the start of year 1) against which it would offer additional cash inflow of ₹47,000 at the end of year 1. Since the IRR of the differential cash flows (17.5%) is higher than the target rate of return (12%), the additional investment required by proposal B is a good investment and thus proposal B is the one we should choose. But is this not what the NPV method was recommending anyway? The NPV of the differential cash flows is also positive when cash flows are discounted at the discount rate of 12%. Even logically, between the two proposals, proposal B is superior because its scale of investment is larger which would yield a greater Net Present Value.

4.9.2 Different Timing of Cash Flows

Even if the initial cash investment required in two mutually exclusive projects is the same, the two methods NPV and IRR could provide conflicting conclusions if the timing of future cash flows from one project are significantly different from the other. Consider the following example.

EXAMPLE 4.5 Assume a firm was considering two mutually exclusive investment proposals A and B that were expected to generate the following cash flows:

	Cash flow for year (₹)					
Proposal	**0**	**1**	**2**	**3**	***NPV @10%***	***IRR***
A	–25,000	13,000	13,000	13,000	7,303	26.06%
B	–25,000	0	0	45,000	8,809	21.71%

When we rank the two proposals by IRR method, we would choose proposal A because its IRR of 26.06% is higher than B's IRR of 21.71%. However, if the required rate of return is 10%, and we use this rate to discount cash flows to calculate the NPV, proposal B would be preferable because its NPV of ₹8,809 is higher than A's NPV of ₹7,303. What could be the reason for this conflicting conclusion and how to resolve the conflict?

Solution: The main reason for the conflicting results provided by the two methods is the difference in their implicit compound interest rates. The IRR method implies that cash flows are compounded at a rate equal to the internal rate of return, while the NPV method implies compounding at the required rate of return. Since in our example the IRR is higher than the required rate of return, future cash flows would be more heavily discounted in IRR method than they would be under the NPV method.

To resolve the conflict and decide which one of the two proposals should be accepted, let us find the 'differential' cash flows between the two proposals and calculate the NPV and IRR of such differential cash flows, as follows:

	Cash flow for year (₹)					
Proposal	**0**	**1**	**2**	**3**	***NPV* @10%**	***IRR***
A	–25,000	13,000	13,000	13,000	7,303	26.06%
B	–25,000	**0**	**0**	**45,000**	**8,809**	**21.71%**
Differential:		–13,000	–13,000	32,000	+1,452	14.67%

The differential cash flows indicate that proposal B would mean sacrificing a cash flow of ₹13,000 each in year 1 and 2, against which it would offer additional cash inflow of ₹32,000 at the end of year 3. Since the IRR of the differential cash flows (14.67%) is higher than the required rate of return (10%), proposal B is the one the firm should choose. The NPV of the differential cash flows is also positive when cash flows are discounted at the discount rate of 10%.

In both the above situations of conflicting conclusions, it was found that NPV provided more reliable conclusions. It is for this reason that NPV is conceptually regarded as the superior method as compared to IRR.

4.9.3 Multiple IRRs

In the previous section, we considered two situations when the IRR may not provide consistent results as compared to NPV. In addition, at times, we may not get a unique or single IRR. There may be multiple IRRs; in other words, more than one rates of discount may be able to get NPV equal to zero. When to expect such a situation?

In a conventional investment proposal, where an initial cash outflow is followed by future cash inflows, we should expect a unique or single IRR. However, when there are multiple sign changes in the cash flows (for example, –10,000 + 15,000 – 4,000 + 13,000 – 9,000 in years 0, 1, 2, 3 and 4, respectively) resulting from a project, there are chances of getting multiple IRR, that is, more than one rates of discount are able to equate the present value of cash inflows with the total present value of cash outflows.

ILLUSTRATION: More Than One IRR

To illustrate how a project could have more than one IRR, assume the following cash flows have been estimated for a proposed project with two year life:

Year	Cash Flow (₹)
0	–1,00,000
1	2,50,000
2	–1,53,000

Projects in some industries, such as mining or oil exploration could have unconventional pattern of cash flows such as the above. In mining or oil exploration projects, an initial investment is followed by positive cash flows (from sales and profits) but significant reparation cost could be required at the end of the project resulting in huge cash outflows.

Using discount rates ranging from 0% to 50% for the above proposal, we have the corresponding NPVs as follows:

Discount Rate	NPV
0%	–3,000
5%	–771
10%	872
15%	1,832
20%	2,068
25%	2,080
30%	1,674
35%	1,253
40%	470
45%	–328
50%	–1,182

Presenting the discount rates and related NPVs on a graph, we have:

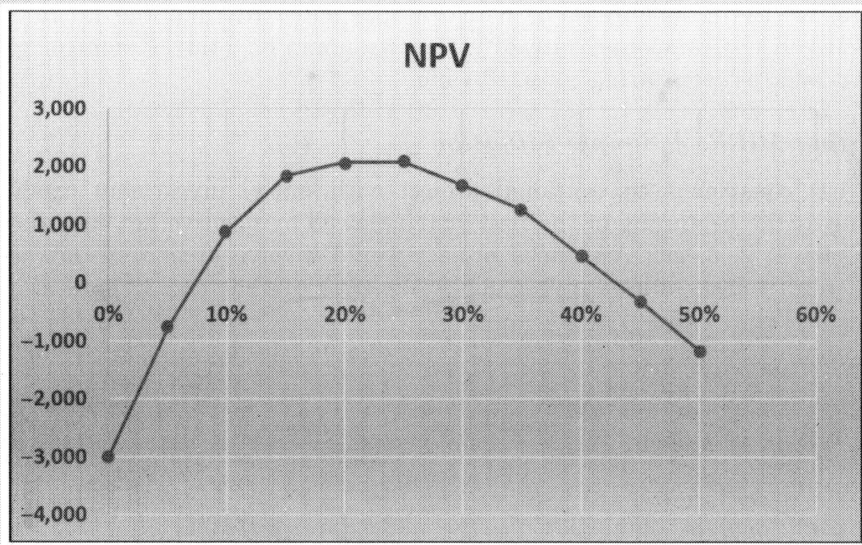

As the above graphical presentation shows, the NPV line crosses the horizontal axis (showing discount rates) twice indicating the existence of two IRRs or two rates of discount that would make NPV equal to zero.

Clearly, it would be confusing and difficult for managers to use the IRR method under such circumstances. Though efforts can be made to modify the cash flows (by discounting some cash flows by one or two years until a negative cash flow turns into positive) to reduce the number of sign changes until a single IRR could be found, the option of using NPV method would become even more attractive.

The above discussion proves that NPV method is superior to the IRR method for consistently reliable results for appraisal of investment projects. However, if a firm still wants to use IRR method for some reasons and wants to avoid the difficulties outlined above, an alternative could be use the Modified Internal Rate of Return (MIRR) explained below.

4.10 Modified Internal Rate of Return (MIRR)

The internal rate of return, as discussed above, has been criticized for a number of shortcomings, which include the difficulty to compute, conflicting results as compared to the NPV method and possibility of getting multiple IRRs. Several of these problems might be taken care of by the Modified Internal Rate of Return (MIRR).

The simple IRR method assumes that the intermediate cash flows arising during the life of a project get reinvested at the same rate of return as the IRR itself. For example, assume that a firm is considering a project with a useful life of four years for which the calculated IRR is 18%; further assume that the firm's cost of capital is 10%. In this example, the IRR calculation of 18% is based on an in-built assumption that the firm would be able to continuously reinvest all cash flows arising at the end of years 1, 2 and 3 at a compound rate of 18% itself. This forms a major limitation of the IRR method because the firm may not always find opportunities to reinvest its funds (emerging from the project) at a rate of return equal to the IRR.

In comparison, it would be more reasonable to assume that if the firm's cost of capital is 10%, it would not re-invest any funds below this rate. In the modified IRR method, it is feasible to assume that a project's intermediate cash flows are reinvested at a rate equal to the firm's cost of capital or any other rate that is regarded as more realistic. This feature makes the modified IRR not only closer to reality, but also easier to calculate.

Therefore, the main difference between the plain IRR and the Modified IRR is with regard to the compound rate of return assumed on reinvestment of cash flows generated by a project during its useful life.

Calculating MIRR: A Simple Situation

Let us first consider a conventional project with initial investment (cash outflow) happening at the beginning of the first year followed by positive net cash flows at the end of years 1, 2, 3, etc. Assume a project would involve a cash outflow of ₹25,000 now and return cash inflows of ₹16,000 at the end of year one as well as year two, as shown in Table 4.13.

TABLE 4.13
MIRR Example

	Initial investment	*Positive returns*	
	Year 0	*Year 1*	*Year 2*
Project cash flows	–25,000	16,000	16,000

The traditional or plain IRR for the above project would be 18%. Now let us compute MIRR.

Steps involved in the MIRR method are as follows:

1. Assume the positive cash flows generated by the project are reinvested until the end of the project at a rate equal to the cost of capital (or another suitable rate of return). In our example, we assume this rate is 10%.
2. For each positive cash flow generated by the project, find the equivalent 'terminal cash flow' (future value as at the end of the project), by compounding each cash flow forward to the end of the last year of the project using the firm's cost of capital (or a reinvestment rate given specifically for this purpose). Thus, the positive cash flow of ₹16,000 at the end of year-1 will be compounded forward at rate of return of 10% to get a terminal cash flow = 16,000 (1.10) = ₹17,600 as at the end of 2nd year.
   The cash flow of ₹16,000 generated by the project at the end of 2nd year would not be reinvested, so its terminal value would be at par value of ₹16,000 itself. Then, Total terminal cash flow at the end of 2nd year = 17,600 + 16,000 = 33,600.
3. Now the investment proposal to be analyzed can be simply stated like this: what would be the (modified) IRR if the firm has to invest ₹25,000 now and get cash inflow of ₹33,600 at the end of 2nd year?
   Apply formulae for calculating MIRR:

$$\text{MIRR} = \sqrt[n]{\frac{\text{Terminal cash flow}}{\text{Initial investment}}} - 1$$

$$= \sqrt[2]{\frac{33{,}600}{25{,}000}} - 1 = \sqrt[2]{1.344} - 1$$

$$= 1.1593 - 1 = 15.93\%$$

As we can see, the MIRR is considerably lower than the plain vanilla IRR. By assuming that all intermediate cash flows would be necessarily reinvested at the IRR itself, the plain vanilla IRR reports an inflated result.

Complex Situations

Let us now move on to discuss more complex situations. Often the initial investment in a project might not be confined to the beginning of the first year (time zero), but may spill over to one or more future periods before the project would start giving positive cash flows. In such situations, it would be advisable to divide the cash flows into two phases: 'investment phase' and 'returns phase'. Then, take the following steps:

1. Identify cash flows in the investment phase and discount all such cash flows at the firm's cost of capital to find their Present Value.
2. Identify cash flows in the returns phase and compound forward all such cash flows at the firm's reinvestment rate (or cost of capital if no specific reinvestment rate is given) to find their equivalent terminal cash flows as at the end of the project.
3. Find total present value of the investment phase cash flows and total terminal value of the cash flows in the returns phase.
4. Apply the MIRR formula:

$$\text{MIRR} = \sqrt[n]{\frac{\text{Terminal cash flow}}{\text{PV of investment cash flows}}} - 1$$

Where 'PV of investment cash flow' = the present value of cash flows in the investment phase. Ignore the minus (–) sign of the Present Value of investment phase cash flows.

EXAMPLE 4.6 A firm is considering a project with following expected cash flows:

Year	0	1	2	3
Cash flows	–5,000	–10,000	14,000	7,000

The firm's cost of capital is 10%.

(a) Calculate the IRR.

(b) Calculate MIRR assuming that any intermediate cash flows from the project can be reinvested at the same rate as the cost of capital.

Solution: (a) Plain or traditional IRR of the project = 22.36%

(b) Calculating MIRR:

Year	0	1	2	3
Cash flows	–5,000	–10,000	14,000	7,000
PVF @10%	1	0.9091		
PV of year 0 and 1 cash flow	–5,000	–9,091		
Total PV of investment phase	**–14,091**			
TV of positive CF of year 2, 3			15,680	7,000
Total terminal cash flows				**22,680**

Applying the MIRR formulae (note that n = 3):

$$\text{MIRR} = \sqrt[n]{\frac{\text{Terminal cash flow}}{\text{PV of investment cash flows}}} - 1$$

$$= \sqrt[3]{\frac{22{,}680}{14{,}091}} - 1$$

$$= 0.1719 = 17.19\%.$$

EXAMPLE 4.7 Emerald Company Limited (ECL) is considering the manufacture of a new product, which would involve the use of both a new machine and an existing machine. The new machine would cost ₹1,80,000. The existing machine was purchased at ₹5,60,000 two years ago and has a current net book value of ₹4,00,000. There is sufficient under-utilized capacity on the existing machine to produce the new product.

The sales of the new product would be 400 units per annum and its sales price would be ₹500 per unit. Per unit costs would be as follows:

Direct labour (2 hours @ ₹80 per hour)	160
Direct materials	90
Fixed costs including depreciation	100
Total per unit cost	350

The project would have a five-year life, after which the new machine would have a resale value of ₹20,000. There is shortage of direct labour (skilled workers) and if this project is undertaken, labour resources would have to be diverted from other work, which earns the firm a contribution of ₹40 per direct labour hour. The fixed overhead absorption rate would be ₹50 per hour (₹100 per unit) but the actual expenditure on fixed overhead would not change because of the new product.

Working capital requirements for the new product would be ₹15,000 in the first year which will increase to ₹25,000 in the second year and will remain at this level until the end of the project. Working capital will be recovered at the end of the project.

The company's cost of capital of 20% is used as the required rate of return. Ignore taxation.

Calculate NPV and suggest whether the project is acceptable.

Solution: Make the tabular presentation of relevant information to calculate cash flows and calculate NPV.

Year	0	1	2	3	4	5
Initial investment	–1,80,000	0	0	0	0	
Sales revenue	0	2,00,000	2,00,000	2,00,000	2,00,000	2,00,000
Variable cost	0	–1,00,000	–1,00,000	–1,00,000	–1,00,000	–1,00,000
Contribution loss due to labour shift	0	–32,000	–32,000	–32,000	–32,000	–32,000
Cash flow	0	68,000	68,000	68,000	68,000	68,000
Residual value	0	0	0	0	0	20,000
Working capital	–15,000	–10,000	0	0		25,000
Net cash flow	–1,95,000	58,000	68,000	68,000	68,000	1,13,000
PV factor @20%	1	0.8333	0.6944	0.5787	0.4826	0.4019
PV of CFs	–1,95,000	48,331.4	47,219.2	39,351.6	32,816.8	45,414.7
NPV	18,134					

The project has a positive NPV, and is thus acceptable.

Researchable Issues

Faculty members, students and research scholars may like to consider the following selected issues for further research and case writing.

- Capital budgeting practices and value of shares in listed companies.
- Corporate practices in the area of capital budgeting.
- Theory versus practice of capital budgeting.
- Impact investing and capital budgeting.
- Investment Appraisal of CSR projects.
- Social cost-benefit analysis versus capital budgeting techniques.
- Investment decision practices in the services sector.
- Investment decision process and practices in the infrastructure sector [power, water, transport projects].
- Capital budgeting in MNCs.

References

Arya, A., Fellingham, J.C., and Glover, J.C., Capital budgeting: Some exceptions to the net present value rule. *Issues In Accounting Education* (August): 1998, pp. 499–508.

Bavishi, V.B., Capital budgeting practices at multinationals. *Management Accounting* (August): 1981, pp. 32–35. (Survey of Fortune 500 multinationals)

Bierman, H. Jr. and Smidt, S., *The Capital Budgeting Decision: Economic Analysis of Investment Projects*, 9th ed., Routledge, 2006.

Dion, L., Robertson, G., and Hughes, S.B., What a university can teach you about choosing capital projects, *Strategic Finance* (January): 2009, pp. 38–45.

Gordon, L.A. and Myers, M.D. Post auditing capital projects, *Management Accounting* (January): 1991, pp. 39–42.

Lawson, G.H. and Windle, D.W., "Capital Budgeting and the Use of DCF Criteria in the Corporation Tax Regime". Oliver and Boyd, 1967, California.

Seitz, N. and Ellison, M., *Capital Budgeting and Long-Term Financing Decisions*, 4th ed., South-Western Educational Publishing, Kentucky, 2004.

Shapiro, A.C., *Capital Budgeting and Investment Analysis*, Prentice-Hall, 2004.

Points to Remember

- **Investment decision**, also called capital budgeting, is one of the most important decisions made by the management. Investment decisions determine the long-term profitability of the firm, and might often mean commitment of huge sums of money for a long period. A wrong investment decision may be very expensive for the firm; hence all care should be exercised in selecting investment projects.
- **Investment projects typically involve** an investment (cash outflow) in the current period in which benefits are expected to be received beyond one year in the future. Examples may include setting up of a factory to produce goods, an expansion project, investment in plant, equipment and buildings, etc.
- **Projects are called mutually exclusive** when only one of the proposals can be accepted, so that acceptance of one of the proposals under consideration would automatically mean that others are rejected. If two proposals are mutually exclusive, they compete against each other so that both of them cannot be accepted.
- **Information required** for the financial evaluation of investment proposals is based on incremental cash flows. Total investment in a project includes investment in fixed assets (plant and equipment, land and buildings, etc.) as

well as working capital (inventories, receivables, etc.). Depreciation and other 'non-cash' expenses should be excluded in calculation of cash flows. Opportunity costs where relevant should be considered.

- **Discounted cash flow methods** provide a more objective basis for evaluating and selecting investment proposals, as these methods take into account both the magnitude and the timing of expected cash flows in each period of a project's life. Discounting is reverse of compounding, and involves computing the present equivalent of future sums of money. By 'discounting', future sums back to the present, we can place all sums to be received (or paid) in the future on a comparable basis so that they can be added and subtracted.
- **Net Present Value** is the excess of the Present Value of cash inflows over the Present Value of cash outflows relating to a project, when all future cash flows have been discounted at the required rate of return. The required rate of return would be the cost of capital or the minimum acceptable return from the project. Investment proposals with a positive NPV are acceptable.
- **The Internal Rate of Return** (IRR) may be simply defined as the discount rate which, when applied to the cash flows of an investment project, produces a net present value (NPV) of zero or nil. A project is acceptable if its IRR is greater than the required or target rate of return.
- **The Profitability Index (PI)**, also called the benefit cost ratio, is the ratio of the present value of future net cash flows of a project to the initial cash investment in the project. A project is acceptable if its PI is greater than one.

Questions

1. Explain the importance of capital budgeting or investment decision for a business firm.
2. Discuss the main types of investment proposals. Using suitable examples, distinguish between independent, mutually exclusive and contingent projects.
3. Discuss the nature of relevant information that would be required for financial evaluation of proposals. In this connection, discuss why depreciation and interest expenses are excluded in calculation of cash flows related to an investment proposal.
4. Explain why discounted cash flow methods (NPV and IRR) are considered superior to Non-DCF methods (accounting rate of return and payback period) of project appraisal.
5. Explain the Net Present Value (NPV) method, and using suitable numerical examples show its calculation. Discuss why the NPV method of project appraisal is regarded superior to other methods.
6. Explain the Internal Rate of Return (IRR) method and using suitable numerical examples show its calculation. Discuss its main advantages and disadvantages as compared to NPV method of project appraisal.
7. Explain the meaning of Profitability Index and using suitable numerical examples show its calculation. Discuss its main advantages and disadvantages as compared to NPV method of project appraisal.
8. Discuss why the NPV method of project appraisal is regarded superior to IRR method, even though both these methods are based on discounted cash flows. Illustrate your answer with reference to (i) scale difference and (ii) cash flows timing difference.
9. Discuss the reasons why NPV and IRR could give conflicting signals about acceptability of an investment proposal. How can these conflicts be resolved? Use a numerical example to support your answer.
10. What are the circumstances when a project could have more than one IRR?

Multiple Choice Questions

1. Present Value of ₹80,000 receivable after 10 years, assuming a 16% per year time value of money, will approximately be:
(a) ₹18,136 (b) ₹36,043 (c) ₹45,361 (d) None of these

2. Present Value of ₹25,000 per annum receivable for 5 years beginning with the end of first year, assuming a 15% per year time value of money, will approximately be:
(a) ₹63,404 (b) ₹78,762 (c) ₹83,805 (d) None of these

3. A project would cost ₹90,000 now, and would earn the following cash inflows (cash profits).

1st year	₹25,000	3rd year	₹60,000
2nd year	₹35,000	4th year	₹30,000

The machinery purchased at the start of the project would be resold for ₹10,000 at the end of the fourth year. What would be the payback period of the project?
(a) 4.0 years (b) 2.5 years (c) 1.5 years (d) None of these

4. A company is evaluating an investment proposal which requires an initial investment of ₹2,00,000 in plant & machinery and ₹60,000 in working capital. The estimated profit before depreciation and taxes from the project are estimated at ₹1,80,000 p.a. for four years starting from the end of the first year. The plant & machinery is to be depreciated on straight line basis, and the working capital would be recovered at the end of the fourth year. The income tax rate applicable to the company is 40%. If the company's WACC is 10% p.a., the NPV from the project would approximately be:
(a) ₹1,86,727 (b) ₹1,98,763 (c) ₹2,83,805 (d) None of these

5. A project would cost ₹90,000 now, and would earn the following cash inflows (cash profits).

1st year	₹25,000	3rd year	₹60,000
2nd year	₹35,000	4th year	₹30,000

The machinery purchased at the start of the project would be resold for ₹10,000 at the end of the fourth year. If the cost of capital is 12%, the NPV of the project would be closest to:
(a) 32,223 (b) 30,450 (c) 28,353 (d) None of these

6. Project 2G would involve an outlay of ₹30,000 now and a further outlay of ₹30,000 after one year. Cash profits (cash inflows) thereafter would be as follows.

2nd year	₹20,000
3rd year	₹25,000
4th to 10th years	₹10,000 per annum

The payback period for Project 2G will be closest to:
(a) 5.50 years (a) 4.50 years (a) 3.50 years (a) None of these

7. Project Ipex is a long-term project that would require an immediate investment of ₹32,000 and return annual cash profits of ₹4,500 in perpetuity. Ignore income taxes. Assuming a cost of capital of 15%, the IRR for the project will be closest to:
(a) 12% (b) 14% (c) 16% (d) 20%

Self-Test Questions

1. Net Present Value Method

A company is considering investing in a project for which the following information is provided.

Initial capital expenditure	₹ 75,000
Profits/(losses) after depreciation and taxes:	
Year 1	30,000
Year 2	30,000
Year 3	20,000
Year 4	(10,000)
Year 5	(10,000)

The project will be operational for five years, at the end of which time there is not expected to be any scrap value. Depreciation has been provided on straight line basis. The company uses 15% as the required rate of return from capital investments.

Calculate the net present value and recommend whether the firm should undertake the project.

2. NPV With Working Capital Involved

Saaz company is considering investing in a project for which the following information is available.

Initial project cost:	₹
Cost of machinery	1,40,000
Working capital	60,000
Total initial investment	**2,00,000**
Profits/(losses) 'after' depreciation and taxes:	
Year 1	40,000
Year 2	40,000
Year 3	40,000
Year 4	–20,000

The project will be operational for four years, at the end of which there is not expected to be any scrap value of machinery. Depreciation on machinery has been provided on straight line basis in calculating the profit given above. The entire working capital investment would be recovered at the end of the project. The company's cost of capital is 16%.

Calculate the Net Present Value of the investment proposal and recommend whether the proposal should be accepted.

3. Grace company is considering investing ₹1,00,000 in a machine which will save ₹30,000 a year for five years and which will have a resale value of ₹10,000 at the end of year 5. The company's cost of capital (to be used as the required rate of return) is 12% and its applicable income tax rate is 25%. Calculate (a) The Accounting rate of return on average investment, and (b) NPV of the proposal. Should the company undertake the project? Assume straight line depreciation.

Problems

1. Gems company is considering investing in a project for which the following information is provided.

Initial capital expenditure	₹1,50,000
Profits/(losses) after depreciation and taxes:	
Year 1	60,000
Year 2	50,000
Year 3	40,000
Year 4	(30,000)
Year 5	(20,000)

The project will be operational for five years, at the end of which time there is not expected to be any scrap value. Depreciation has been provided on straight line basis. The company uses 16% as the required rate of return from capital investments.

Calculate the project's net present value and advise the company whether to undertake the project.

2. Using the same data as in question 1, calculate the IRR for Gems Company's investment proposal.
3. ***Consider the same data as in self-correction problem 2 (Saaz company).*** Calculate the internal rate of return (IRR) and recommend whether the proposal should be accepted.
4. **Computer Games Limited (CGL)—Project Appraisal**
   CGL is considering the manufacture of a new product which would involve the use of both a new machine and an existing machine. The new machine would cost ₹14,00,000. The existing machine was purchased at ₹7,00,000 two years ago and has a current net book value of ₹5,00,000. There is sufficient under-utilized capacity on the existing machine to produce the new product.

   The sales of the new product would be 5,000 units per annum and its sales price would be ₹320 per unit. Per unit costs would be as follows:

Direct Labour (2 hours @ ₹50 per hour)	100
Direct materials	50
Fixed costs including depreciation	90
Total per unit cost	₹240

   The project would have a five-year life, after which the new machine would have a resale value of ₹1,00,000. Because direct labour is continuously in short supply, labour resources would have to be diverted from other work which currently earns a contribution of ₹30 per direct labour hour. The fixed overhead absorption rate would be ₹45 per hour (₹90 per unit) but the actual expenditure on fixed overhead would not change because of the new product.

   Working capital requirements for the new product would be ₹1,00,000 in the first year, rise to ₹1,50,000 in the second year and will remain at this level until the end of the project. Working capital will be recovered at the end of the project.

   The company's cost of capital of 16% is used as the required rate of return. Ignore taxation.

   Calculate NPV and suggest whether the project is worthwhile.
5. **Velvet company** manufactures product VXL which it sells for ₹250 per unit. The variable cost of production is currently ₹200 per unit, and fixed costs are ₹1,20,000 per annum. The company is considering replacing its existing machinery with more efficient new machinery that would cost ₹18,00,000. Purchase of the new machinery would result in reducing the variable cost to ₹140 only per unit. However, the purchase of the new machinery would increase the company's fixed costs by ₹2,00,000 per annum. The new machinery would have a useful life of

five years, after which it would have a resale value of ₹1,80,000 at the end of 5th year. Sales of product VXL are estimated to be 12,000 units a year. If the minimum required rate of return from new investments is 15% per year, should the company purchase the new machinery? (Ignore taxation).

6. **Short-case**

WINSUM ELECTRONICS

Mukesh had never been so worried in his fifteen years as an entrepreneur. His firm Winsum Electronics manufactured Integrated Circuits that were extensively used in a variety of electronic equipment. He had recently come to know of a patent for new technology on production of superior quality integrated circuits that would reduce power consumption, improve durability and ensure flawless performance. If his competitors acquired the patents for the new technology, his firm's sales and profits could be seriously affected.

The new technology patent could be acquired at a cost of ₹12,50,000. An additional investment of ₹7,50,000 would be required to modify the existing equipment to incorporate the new technology features. The existing equipment has a remaining useful life of five years and a salvage value of ₹2,00,000; these would remain unaffected and would not change irrespective of the modifications required to produce the new product. Once the equipment has been modified, the existing models of the integrated circuits cannot be produced.

The current profit and loss statement related to circuits manufacturing is as follows.

Item	*Details*	₹
Sales	15,000 units @ ₹100	15,00,000
Less: Variable costs	15,000 units @ ₹40	6,00,000
Contribution		9,00,000
Fixed costs	Depreciation on existing equipment ₹1,00,000 + Other fixed costs of 4,00,000	5,00,000
Net income before taxes		4,00,000
Taxes @ 30%		1,20,000
Net income after taxes		2,80,000

Fixed costs given in the above profit and loss account include a depreciation charge of ₹1,00,000 on existing equipment, calculated on the straight-line basis with a useful life of 10 years. Fixed costs would remain constant, except for the amortization of the cost of patents. Due to the fast changing technology, the patent acquired now would be useless in five years; hence the patents should be amortized over a five year period.

Variable cost consists of direct material, direct labour and variable overheads. If the firm buys the patent and shifts to the new product, the variable cost would increase by ₹4 per unit.

Market research has indicated that if the firm goes for the new technology and does not increase the product price, its sales would soar to 25,000 units per annum. However, if the firm does not buy the patent, its sales would fall to 10,000 units per year.

If the firm goes for the patent, the expected increase in sales would also warrant an additional investment in working capital amounting to ₹2,50,000.

Mukesh was wondering as to which alternative should be preferred. The firm's cost of capital is 15%.

Analyze the investment situation using NPV method. Would you advise the firm to acquire the patent, and why?

CHAPTER

5

Risk Analysis for Investment Decisions

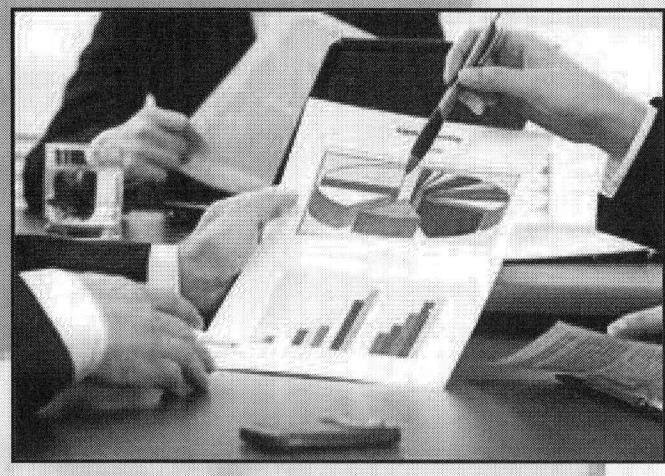

LEARNING OBJECTIVES

After studying this chapter, you should be able to:

- Understand the importance of risk analysis in project appraisal, and differentiate between risk and uncertainty.
- Explain the meaning of sensitivity analysis, and apply the same to determine the impact of adverse changes in a variable on the NPV.
- Discuss the pros and cons of scenario analysis vis-à-vis sensitivity analysis.
- Compute a project's NPVs under different scenarios and interpret results.
- Calculate the expected NPV, standard deviation and coefficient of variation to evaluate the riskiness of the project.
- Explain how simulation is an improvement over scenario analysis and discuss the steps required to run the simulation analysis.

5.1 Introduction

As per a report presented to the Parliament, in December 2014, "out of 720 central infrastructure-sector projects costing ₹150 crore and above, 295 projects were delayed. The original cost of the 295 delayed projects was ₹5.49 lakh crore and anticipated (revised) cost is ₹6.50 lakh crore, thus leading to a total cost overrun of ₹1.01 lakh crore (18.4%)" [*Economic Times*]. As this example shows, often the time and cash flow estimates used to appraise long-term investment projects may have to be revised, and this phenomenon is not limited only to the public sector projects.

In our discussion of the project appraisal techniques (NPV, IRR, etc.) in the previous chapter, we assumed a state of certainty regarding the future. We assumed that our estimates of the project cost, life span of the project and year-wise operating cash inflows from the project would definitely occur, and there is no risk of any variability in these factors or the NPV that we calculated. This was done to keep our discussion simple, but we are aware that in real life no one could forecast the future outcomes with certainty, and all forecasts are subject to varying degrees of uncertainty.

All long-term capital investment decisions are based on a number of forecasts regarding the time required to execute the project, initial investment, project life as well as the future cash flows. Any calculation of the Net Present Value (NPV) or Internal Rate of Return (IRR) could only be as reliable as the quality of time and cash flow estimates. Accurate estimation of future cash flows of particularly long life projects (such as projects having a useful life of 10–20 years or more) could indeed be very difficult and is a great problem.

Risk and uncertainty, are thus, inherent in the very nature of investment decisions; indeed, longer the future time-span for which forecasts have been made, the greater would be the risk and uncertainty. Much as managers would want to be certain about all elements affecting the success of a project, risk and uncertainty are the necessary evils they must embrace. What the managers can do to deal with such situations is not to shy away from accepting the risk and uncertainty; rather they should analyze the risk profile of the project and incorporate risk and uncertainty in the financial evaluation of the projects so that they could take rational and well-informed decisions. A number of techniques that managers can use in this context are discussed in this chapter.

5.2 Difference Between Risk and Uncertainty

Before we take up the techniques of dealing with risk and uncertainty in project evaluation, a basic question here could be: are risk and uncertainty one and the same thing? While in practice, these two terms might be used interchangeably, in the field of finance they can be differentiated according to whether the future outcome is quantifiable or not:

- **Risk** is mathematically quantifiable. In project appraisal, the firm could attach probabilities to the future possible outcomes (such as cash flows) and the mathematical concept of *expected value* could be used to quantify the risk.
- **Uncertainty** is mathematically not quantifiable. Uncertainty signifies that future outcomes cannot be predicted from the available data, and hence, the outcome is not quantifiable. If the future returns from a project are neither predictable nor quantifiable, then we would say the future returns are uncertain.

5.3 Types of Risks and Project Appraisal

There are three types of risks: the standalone risk of an individual project, the corporate risk consisting of the combined risk of all the projects undertaken by a firm, and the market risk that would be related to the performance of the financial markets and economy, in general.

In a way, all three risks are correlated to each other. For example, in boom conditions when the economy is doing well, the firm and its projects would also do well, and vice-versa. However, our concern here is primarily with the standalone risk of the project under consideration.

Fortunately, among the three types of risks, it is easier to measure the standalone risk than the corporate or the market risk. In most of the situations of project appraisal, it is possible to attach probabilities to the possible outcomes of a proposed project, and the riskiness of a project can be analyzed with the help of techniques discussed below to enable managers to incorporate the risk factor in financial evaluation of projects.

5.4 Sensitivity Analysis

In this commonly used technique of risk analysis, an attempt is made to analyze how an adverse change in any of the important variables would impact the project's NPV (or IRR). Major variables that could impact the NPV of the project (such as the product selling price, cost and life of the project, operating cash flows and resale value) are identified and then, changing a single variable at a time—while keeping others constant—the effect of an adverse possible change in the variable on the NPV is analyzed. The process is repeated for all variables one by one to study the impact of an adverse change in each variable on the NPV.

Net Present Value (NPV) is said to be sensitive to a variable if a given adverse change in the variable brings about a more than proportionate change in the NPV. The variables in which a small adverse change could make a relatively big dent in the NPV would be identified as the most crucial factors that would need to be carefully watched and managed to ensure the project's success.

Thus, the sensitivity analysis is very helpful in identifying the key variables. It helps in answering 'What If' type of questions, such as: what if the project's initial investment turns out to be X% higher than our estimates; or what if the actual annual cash flows are X% lower than our estimates; or what if the actual resale value turns out to be X% lower than expected, etc. Such analysis would highlight the variables in which a small adverse change could cause the largest fall in the NPV. Consider Example 5.1.

EXAMPLE 5.1 The expected initial investment and cash inflows related to a proposed project are given below:

Year	*Variables*	₹
0	Initial investment	–1,00,000
1	Operating cash inflow	70,000
2	Operating cash inflow	70,000
2	Resale value	10,000

Assuming the firm's cost of capital is 12%:

(a) Calculate the project's NPV using the estimated cash flows as above.

(b) What would be the impact on the NPV if there was a 10% increase in the initial investment, assuming no change in future cash inflows?

(c) What would be the impact on the NPV if the future cash inflows were lower by 10%, assuming no change in the initial investment?

(d) What would be the impact on the NPV if the resale value at the end of 2nd year was lower by 10%, assuming no change in other variables?

(e) Rank the three variables (initial investment, operating cash inflows and resale value) in terms of the NPV's sensitivity to adverse changes in these variables.

Solution:

(a) Calculation of NPV using original estimates

Year	*Variables*	*Original estimates*	*PVF @ 12%*	*Present Value (PV)*
0	Initial investment	–1,00,000	1.0000	–1,00,000
1	Operating cash flow	70,000	0.8929	62,503
2	Operating cash flow	70,000	0.7972	55,804
2	Resale value	10,000	0.7972	7,972
				NPV = 26,279

(b) NPV if initial investment goes up by 10%

Year	*Variables*	*Cash flows*	*PVF @12%*	*Present Value*
0	Initial investment	–1,10,000	1.0000	–1,10,000
1	Operating cash flow	70,000	0.8929	62,503
2	Operating cash flow	70,000	0.7972	55,804
2	Resale value	10,000	0.7972	7,972
				NPV = 16,279

% Reduction in NPV as compared to original estimates = 38.05%

(c) NPV if operating cash Inflows fall by 10%

Year	*Variables*	*Cash flows*	*PVF @12%*	*Present Value*
0	Initial investment	–1,00,000	1.0000	–1,00,000
1	Operating cash flow	63,000	0.8929	56,252.7
2	Operating cash flow	63,000	0.7972	50,223.6
2	Resale value	10,000	0.7972	7,972
				NPV = 14,448.3

% Reduction in NPV as compared to original estimates = 45.02%

(d) NPV if Resale Value Falls by 10%

Year	*Variables*	*Cash flows*	*PVF @ 12%*	*Present Value*
0	Initial investment	–1,00,000	1.0000	–1,00,000
1	Operating cash flow	70,000	0.8929	62,503
2	Operating cash flow	70,000	0.7972	55,804
2	Resale value	9,000	0.7972	7,174.8
				NPV = 25,481.8

% Reduction in NPV as compared to original estimates = 3.03%.

(e) Ranking of the variables

The above results indicate that the project's NPV is most vulnerable to adverse changes in future cash inflows, followed by initial investment, and least sensitive to changes in the resale value of the project at the end of its useful life. Such information is used by the firms to draw up a priority list of crucial factors that would require close monitoring to ensure the project's success.

5.4.1 Sensitivity Analysis and the Margin of Safety

We have seen above how sensitivity analysis can be used to measure the impact of a given change in a variable on the project's NPV. An alternative and perhaps more interesting form of sensitivity analysis could be to ask: what is the maximum percentage downside in a variable that can be tolerated without having to change the investment decision? The maximum tolerable 'percentage downside' would act as a 'margin of safety' by which the variable could be adversely affected, and yet, the project would remain acceptable.

In this form of analysis, we can calculate the percentage change in each major variable that would be required to turn a positive NPV into a negative NPV to make the project unacceptable, and hence, change our investment decision. Such analysis would not only help identify the most crucial variables to watch, but would also make the risk profile of the project much clearer and help management take a final decision whether to go ahead with the project. Consider the following example.

EXAMPLE 5.2 Orange company is evaluating an investment proposal that would require an initial investment of ₹3,25,000 in plant and equipment to produce a new electric instant coffee maker. The project is expected to generate annual sales revenue of ₹5,00,000 for a period of three years at the end of which the plant and equipment are expected to have a resale value of ₹40,000. The variable cost of the product is expected to be ₹3,00,000 per annum for the above budgeted sales revenue. The annual fixed cost of the company (other than depreciation) would increase by ₹50,000. Assume Orange Company's cost of capital is 16%. Ignore taxes.

(a) On the basis of the information given above, calculate the project's NPV and decide if the project should be accepted.

(b) Taking one variable at a time, calculate the percentage changes in the following estimates that would be required for the investment decision to change:
 (i) Initial investment
 (ii) Sales revenue
 (iii) Variable cost
 (iv) Annual fixed cost

Solution:

(a) Calculation of the Project's NPV (Base case)

Note: Since there are no income taxes involved, there is no need to consider the depreciation. Therefore, we can use the cash flows as given to calculate the NPV as follows:

Years	*Item*	*Cash flow (₹)*	*PVF @ 16%*	*Present value (PV) (₹)*
0	Plant and equipment	–3,25,000	1.0000	–3,25,000
1 to 3	Sales revenue	5,00,000	2.2459	11,22,950
1 to 3	Variable cost	–3,00,000	2.2459	–6,73,770
1 to 3	Fixed cost	–50,000	2.2459	–1,12,295
3	Scrap value	40,000	0.6407	25,628
				NPV = 37,513

(b) *(i) Percentage change required in the initial investment for the investment decision to change*

In order to change the investment decision, the entire NPV should be eroded. That will happen when the initial investment increases by an amount greater than ₹37,513. In percentage, therefore, the initial investment would need to increase by more than:

$$\% \text{ Increase in initial investment} = \frac{\text{NPV}}{\text{Initial investment}} \times 100$$

$$= \frac{37,513}{3,25,000} \times 100 = 11.54\%$$

Thus, an increase of more than 11.54% in the initial investment would make the project unacceptable.

(ii) Percentage change required in sales revenue for the investment decision to change

In order to change the investment decision, the entire NPV should be eroded. That will happen when the 'present value' of sales revenue declines by an amount greater than ₹37,513. In percentage terms, therefore, the 'present value' of sales revenue would need to fall by

$$\frac{\text{NPV}}{\text{Present value of sales revenue}} \times 100$$

$$= \frac{37,513}{11,22,950} \times 100 = 3.34\%$$

Explanation: Note that sales revenue figures given in the question are gross and have not been discounted for the time value of money, while NPV is in terms of the 'present value'. To make them comparable, we should take the 'present value' of sales revenues of the three years and not the gross figures given. We can generalize the formula to calculate the percentage change in an estimate required to change the investment decision as follows:

$$\% \text{ Change required} = \frac{\text{Net Present Value}}{\text{PV of the relevant estimate}} \times 100$$

(iii) Percentage change required in variable cost for the investment decision to change

In order to change the investment decision, the NPV should decline by 37,513. That will happen when the 'present value' of variable cost increases by an amount greater than ₹37,513. In percentage terms, therefore, the 'present value' of variable cost increase would need to rise by:

$$\frac{\text{NPV}}{\text{Present value of annual variable cost}} \times 100$$

$$= \frac{37,513}{6,73,770} \times 100 = 5.57\%$$

Thus, an increase of more than 5.57% in variable cost would make the project unacceptable.

(iv) Percentage change required in fixed cost for the investment decision to change

In order to change the investment decision, the NPV should decline by 37,513. That will happen when the 'present value' of fixed cost increases by an amount greater than ₹37,513. In percentage terms, therefore, the 'present value' of fixed cost would need to rise by:

$$\frac{\text{NPV}}{\text{Present value of annual fix cost}} \times 100$$

$$= \frac{37,513}{1,12,295} \times 100 = 33.41\%$$

Conclusion: Presenting the percentage changes in the four estimates that would be required for the investment decision to change:

S. No.	*Variable*	*% Change in estimate needed to change decision*
1	Initial investment	11.54%
2	Sales revenue	3.34%
3	Variable cost	5.57%
4	Fixed cost	33.41%

From above, it is clear that the calculated NPV is most vulnerable to changes in the sales revenue; the margin of safety being just 3.34%. Similarly, variable cost is also a crucial factor, which again has a low margin of safety. The management should manage these variables carefully, and take precautions to ensure minimum variability in these items.

5.4.2 Advantages and Disadvantages of Sensitivity Analysis

Advantages

The main advantages of sensitivity analysis are:

1. Sensitivity analysis is **easy to understand and apply**. It does not involve any complicated theories or formulas.
2. It is **helpful in identifying the key variables** that would be crucial to the success of the project. Given this analysis, management is able to better understand the risk profile of the project, and take well-informed decisions.
3. The analysis provided by this technique can be **immensely helpful in strategy formulation**. Once a few variables crucial to the success of the project have been identified as per the sensitivity analysis, the management's maximum focus would be on tying up all loose ends related to these chosen variables and keep contingent plans ready to make up for any deficiency concerning these variables.

Disadvantages

The main disadvantages of sensitivity analysis include:

1. The technique has only a limited use because it **does not consider the probability** of the adverse changes in variables. For example, in the previous illustration, sensitivity analysis indicated that the NPV will be completely wiped out, if there is a rise of more than 11.54% in the initial investment required; but what is the probability of this escalation in the initial investment was not considered in this technique.
2. It considers the impact of a change in **only one variable** at a time, while often there are occasions when managers would want to simultaneously analyze the collective impact of a change in several variables.
3. Another serious drawback of the technique is that it assumes changes in one variable would not affect other variables. In other words, it **ignores the interdependency between variables**. For example, while considering how

a change in product prices would affect the NPV of the project, it ignores the fact that a change in the price of a product could also have an effect on the volume of sales.

4. Sensitivity analysis is **not an optimizing or maximizing technique** because it does not directly indicate the decision to be taken. Thus, subjective judgment would be required to utilize the findings of sensitivity analysis to arrive at decisions.

In spite of these limitations, sensitivity analysis is a popular technique and commonly used to understand the risk profile of investment projects. Its importance can be better visualized if we consider long-term investment projects that would be impacted by a large number of variables (a steel company undertaking a large expansion project identified as many as forty two such variables); in such cases, often managers could spend all their energy on relatively unimportant matters, and fail to focus on the crucial ones. In order to avoid being 'penny wise pound foolish', managers should focus more on the few crucial factors identified by sensitivity analysis.

5.5 Three Level Estimates

Investment decision necessarily involves dealing with future. To evaluate an investment proposition, the management would try to make as reliable estimates as possible of the initial project cost, product prices and related demand, variable and fixed costs and resale value, etc. However, often it would be easier to make a 'range' of estimates rather than a single value estimate for each variable impacting the project. A range of estimates would be more realistic, because often business cycles can bring about favourable or adverse changes in the business environment. Always be prepared for the pleasant and nasty surprises in business!

Accordingly, one way to deal with risky situations would be to evaluate an investment proposal under three sets of assumptions: optimistic (reflecting favourable business conditions), most likely (reflecting normal business conditions) and pessimistic (reflecting unfavourable business conditions). Thus, three level estimates would be made for the project cost, cash inflows and other key variables, and NPVs (or IRRs) would be calculated separately for each series of the estimates made. The optimistic, most likely and pessimistic levels are also referred to as the best-case, base-case and the worst-case estimates, respectively.

Consider the following example on working with three level estimates.

EXAMPLE 5.3 Mayo Company is considering a risky project for which it has made three levels of cash flow estimates as follows:

Three Level Estimates of Cash Flows

Year	*Optimistic*	*Most likely*	*Pessimistic*
0	–1,25,000	–1,50,000	–1,75,000
1	1,00,000	90,000	80,000
2	80,000	70,000	60,000
3	60,000	50,000	40,000

The company's cost of capital is 12%, and the same is used to calculate NPV for each series of cash flows to understand risk before deciding on the project.

Calculation of NPV for the three level estimates

Year	PVF @12%	*Optimistic*		*Most likely*		*Pessimistic*	
		Cash flow	*PV**	*Cash flow*	*PV*	*Cash flow*	*PV*
0	1.0000	–1,25,000	–1,25,000	–1,50,000	–1,50,000	–1,75,000	–1,75,000
1	0.8929	1,00,000	89,290	90,000	80,361	80,000	71,432
2	0.7972	80,000	63,776	70,000	55,804	60,000	47,832
3	0.7118	60,000	42,708	50,000	35,590	40,000	28,472
			NPV = 70,774		**NPV = 21,755**		**NPV = –27,264**

PV* = Present values using 12% discount rate

Summary of the results

Type of estimate	*NPV*
Optimistic	70,774
Most likely	21,755
Pessimistic	–27,264

The range of NPVs obtained would give the management a better understanding of the project risk involved than the NPV based on single-value (most likely) estimates. In the above illustration, if the management had used only the 'most likely' estimates for calculation of a single NPV, it would get the impression that all is well with the project, but considering the range of NPVs makes it clear that a downside is also possible in the pessimistic scenario. Given this additional information, the management would proceed with the project only if it is not risk-averse.

Advantages

Similar to the sensitivity analysis, this method is also simple to understand and apply, and might appeal to the practising managers because it is more realistic to consider a range of possible outcomes, and the NPVs provided by the three level estimates would throw more light on the risk involved.

Disadvantages

The major limitation of this method is that similar to the sensitivity analysis, this method does not consider the probability of occurrence of pessimistic or optimistic conditions. Another limitation of this method is the implicit assumption that the three levels can be clearly demarcated, and it ignores the interrelationship between variables. Thus, while considering the optimistic scenario, we presume that all variables would take their optimistic values, and similarly, in pessimistic situation, we assume that all variables would take their pessimistic values.

5.6 Scenario Analysis

Scenario analysis might be regarded as an extension of sensitivity analysis and three level estimates. At times, the project being considered may be so large and complex that management may like to analyze risk with respect to more than three levels of estimates, and may include several more different scenarios in the analysis.

Also, unlike sensitivity analysis, which considers the impact of changing one variable at a time, scenario analysis can be used to analyze the collective effect of changing more than one variable simultaneously on the project's NPV. For example, a firm undertaking the project could be interested in analyzing 'what if' the variable cost rises by 5% simultaneously with a 3% fall in the sales revenue. Scenario analysis is most suitable to answer this type of specific 'what if' questions.

Whereas sensitivity analysis assumes that a change in one variable would not affect other variables, and thus, ignores the interrelationship between variables, scenario analysis takes into account the interrelationship between variables. For example, it is well-known that for most products, there would usually be an interrelationship between price and quantity demanded. Accordingly, a firm may define several possible scenarios of price–demand combinations, such as the following: (i) high price–low demand, (ii) medium price–moderate demand, and (iii) low price–high demand.

Once the relevant scenarios to be analyzed have been identified, the related cash flows should be estimated, and probabilities should be assigned to each scenario to facilitate computation of the expected values. The expected values would then be used to compute the corresponding NPVs. Probability and expected values are discussed below:

5.6.1 Expected Values and Project Risk Analysis

As we discussed above in scenario analysis, in most situations of project appraisal it may be possible to make several estimates of different future outcomes and to assign probabilities to them. For example, success of a new spa and fitness project may depend on whether another competitor decides to start a similar venture in the neighbourhood. Considering the possibility, suppose the firm makes estimates of different future outcomes and assigns probabilities as given in Table 5.1.

TABLE 5.1
Risk Analysis

Possible outcome	*Probability*	*Project NPV (₹)*
Competing spa comes up in area	0.40	–50,000
No competing spa in area	0.60	2,00,000

Taking into account the possible outcomes and their probabilities, the expected net present value of the proposed project would be:

$$E[\text{NPV}] = [(-50{,}000 \times 0.40) + (2{,}00{,}000 \times 0.60)]$$
$$= 1{,}00{,}000$$

where E[NPV] is the 'expected NPV' (or 'expected value' of the NPV) from the project.

Accept/reject rules using expected values

Using the expected value approach as above to calculate the NPV, we follow the following rules to accept or reject investment proposals:

1. Rule for accept/reject situations (single independent projects):
   Accept the proposal with +ve expected NPV
   Reject the proposal with –ve expected NPV
2. Rule for mutually exclusive projects (where only one of the alternative proposals can be accepted): Accept the proposal with the highest expected NPV.

The meaning of 'expected value' should be carefully understood so that we know when to use this concept and how to interpret the results. An 'expected' NPV (or expected value of NPV) of ₹1,00,000 in the above example means that if same type of projects are repeated again and again for a large number of times, 40% of such projects were likely to face competition from neighbourhood spas while 60% of such projects were expected not to face neighbourhood competition, so that 'on an average', the firm would be expected to get a positive NPV per project in the long run.

Thus, the concept is likely to apply more directly in situations where similar projects are often taken up. If we look around, we may find several interesting examples of this type: the branch offices started by Domino Pizzas, Café Coffee Day, McDonald's, Bata stores and NIIT educational centers, which are all examples of a chain of similar projects of relatively smaller size, where the companies could use the expected value concept to analyze risk.

Consider Example 5.4 of using expected values to understand the risk involved in a project.

EXAMPLE 5.4 Shepherd Company is considering a new project for which it has made three levels of cash flow estimates with probabilities as follows:

Net Cash Flows After Tax

Year	*Worst case*	*Most likely*	*Best case*
	P = 0.25	P = 0.50	P = 0.25
0	–1,50,000	–1,50,000	–1,50,000
1	40,000	50,000	60,000
2	40,000	50,000	60,000
3	40,000	50,000	60,000
4	40,000	50,000	60,000
4*	20,000	30,000	40,000

*The last cash flow is for the resale value of equipment.

The company's required rate of return for projects with similar risk profile is 12%.

(a) Using the above scenario-wise cash flows with corresponding probabilities, calculate the expected values of each year's cash flows.
(b) Compute the project's expected net present value.
(c) Compute the project's best-case net present value.
(d) Compute the project's worst-case net present value.
(e) Compute the project's most-likely net present value.

Solution:

(a) Determining the Expected Values of Cash Flows: For each year of the project's life, first multiply the scenario-wise cash flows with their respective probability of occurrence; then add up the resulting figures to calculate the expected value of the cash flow. Thus, the expected value of cash flow is the probability-weighted average of all possible cash flows in different scenarios.

Year	*Worst case*	*Most likely*	*Best case*	*Expected value of CF*
	Probability × Scenario cash flow			
0	0.25 (–1,50,000)	0.5 (–1,50,000)	0.25 (–1,50,000)	–1,50,000
1	0.25 (40,000)	0.5 (50,000)	0.25 (60,000)	50,000
2	0.25 (40,000)	0.5 (50,000)	0.25 (60,000)	50,000
3	0.25 (40,000)	0.5 (50,000)	0.25 (60,000)	50,000
4	0.25 (40,000)	0.5 (50,000)	0.25 (60,000)	50,000
4	0.25 (20,000)	0.5 (30,000)	0.25 (40,000)	30,000

(b) Calculation of Expected Net Present Value

Year	*Expected CF value**	*PVF @12%*	*Present value*
0	–1,50,000	1.0000	–1,50,000
1	50,000	0.8929	44,645
2	50,000	0.7972	39,860
3	50,000	0.7118	35,590
4	50,000	0.6355	31,775
4	30,000	0.6355	19,065
			NPV = 20,935

Note: *Expected Values As Per Table In Part (a) Above.

The positive expected NPV indicates that the project is acceptable

(c) Calculation of Best Case NPV

Year	*Cash flow*	*PVF @12%*	*Present Value*
0	–1,50,000	1.0000	–1,50,000
1	60,000	0.8929	53,574
2	60,000	0.7972	47,832
3	60,000	0.7118	42,708
4	60,000	0.6355	38,130
4	40,000	0.6355	25,420
			NPV = 57,664

(d) Calculation of Worst Case NPV

Year	*Cash flow*	*PVF @12%*	*Present Value*
0	–1,50,000	1.0000	–1,50,000
1	40,000	0.8929	35,716
2	40,000	0.7972	31,888
3	40,000	0.7118	28,472
4	40,000	0.6355	25,420
4	20,000	0.6355	12,710
			NPV = –15,794

(e) NPV in Most Likely Scenario

Year	*Cash flow*	*PVF @12%*	*Present Value*
0	–1,50,000	1.0000	–1,50,000
1	50,000	0.8929	44,645
2	50,000	0.7972	39,860
3	50,000	0.7118	35,590
4	50,000	0.6355	31,775
4	30,000	0.6355	19,065
			NPV = 20,935

Statistical Calculation of Expected NPV

One way to compute the expected NPV was explained in part (b) above. An alternative way could be to use the statistical formula as follows:

$$\text{EV of NPV} = \sum_{i=1}^{n} P_i(\text{NPV}_i)$$

where 'EV' is the expected value, Σ is the summation sign, 'P' is the probability of occurrence of scenario-i, 'i' is the number of scenarios from 1 to 'n', and NPV_i is the NPV of scenario-i.

To use the formula, we should first calculate the NPVs of possible scenarios as we did in parts (c), (d) and (e) in Example 5.4. The range of NPVs computed, along with scenario-probabilities are presented in Table 5.2.

TABLE 5.2 Range of NPV and Scenario Probabilities

Scenario	*NPV*	*Probability*
Best case	57,664	0.25
Most likely	20,935	0.50
Worst case	–15,794	0.25

Then, applying the formula:

$$\begin{aligned}\text{EV of NPV} &= 57{,}664 \times 0.25 + 20{,}935 \times 0.5 + -15{,}794 \times 0.25\\ &= 20{,}935\end{aligned}$$

Alternatively, you could extend Table 5.2 to first multiply scenario NPVs with their respective probabilities and then add up the resulting (product) figures in Table 5.3.

TABLE 5.3 Alternative Method to Find Expected NPV

Scenario	*NPV*	*Probability*	*Product [NPV × Prob]*
Best	57,664	0.25	14,416
Likely	20,935	0.5	10,467.5
Worst	–15,794	0.25	–3,948.5
Expected NPV			20,935

Conclusion: Although the positive expected NPV indicates acceptance of the project, the spread of possible NPVs in different scenarios shows that the project is considerably risky, because in the worst-case scenario, there is a possibility of a negative NPV by a substantial amount.

As we discussed earlier, the concept of expected values is likely to apply more directly in situations where similar projects are often taken up by an organization. In such a situation, the firm would like to compare the riskiness of the proposed project with other projects that the firm has taken up. To facilitate the inter-project comparison of risk, we would need to consider not only the expected value of NPV, but also the relative riskiness of the proposed investment project. The relative riskiness of projects can be understood with the help of standard deviation and coefficient of variation.

Probability Distribution, Standard Deviation and Co-efficient of Variation

The standard deviation and coefficient of variation are statistical measures that indicate the risk associated with the proposed investment project. While standard deviation is reported in the same units as the expected cash flows (such as Rupees, USD, etc.), the coefficient of variation is a relative measure and reported as a ratio of the standard deviation of NPV to the expected value of NPV.

Standard deviation of the NPV: The following statistical formula can be used to compute the standard deviation of the NPV:

$$\sigma NPV = \sqrt{\sum_{i=1}^{n} P_i(NPV_i - \text{Expected NPV})^2}$$

Using the scenario NPVs and their probabilities given in Table 5.3, and the expected NPV of ₹20,935, we have:

$$\sigma NPV = \sqrt{[0.25(57{,}664 - 20{,}935)^2 + 0.50(20{,}935 - 20{,}935)^2 + 0.25(-15{,}794 - 20{,}935)^2}$$
$$= 25{,}971$$

A high standard deviation of ₹25,971, along with a wide range of possible results ranging from a high positive NPV of ₹57,664 to a negative NPV of ₹–15,794, indicates that the proposed project is risky.

Measuring relative riskiness: Relative riskiness is better measured by the **Coefficient of Variation** which can be calculated as follows:

$$\text{CV of NPV} = \frac{\sigma NPV}{\text{EV of NPV}} = \frac{25{,}971}{20{,}935} = 1.24$$

To evaluate the relative riskiness of the proposed project, the calculated coefficient of variation of 1.24 for the proposed project would be compared with the average coefficient of variation of other projects undertaken by the firm. Assuming other projects have an average coefficient of variation of 1.0, the coefficient of variation of 1.24 would mean the proposed project is relatively risky, but the degree of risk perceived may not be regarded as very high. Such analysis would help the management take a final view on the proposed project. In the above example, motivated by the prospects of making a high positive NPV of ₹57,664 in the best-case scenario, the management may decide to embrace the somewhat higher risk and undertake the project. It should also put in place the strategies required to avoid the worst-case scenario as far as possible.

Hillier Model and Dependence of Cash Flows Over Time

Frederic S. Hillier [Hillier, 1963] was the first to propound that the standard deviation of the proposed project's NPV would be different depending on whether the cash flows from the project were 'perfectly correlated' over time, or 'mutually independent' over time.

Mutual independence of cash flows over time means that cash flows in any period would not be dependent on the performance of cash flows in any other periods. In other words, even if the cash flows achieved in first year of the project were low (worst-case), still the subsequent year's cash flows could be low (worstcase), most likely or high (bestcase) type.

On the other hand, perfect correlation of cash flows over time means that cash flows in any subsequent period would be perfectly dependent over the cash flows' performance in the previous periods, implying that if the cash flows achieved in the first year of the project were low (worstcase type), then subsequent year's cash flows would also tend to be low or worstcase scenario. Perfect correlation of cash flows, would thus, increase the risk of the proposed project and its standard deviation would be greater than if cash flows were mutually independent over time.

Dependence of Cash Flows Over Time and the Probability of Getting the Worst Cash Flows

If the proposed project is considered risky, one thing that the firm would want to know is: what is the probability of getting the worstcase cash flows?

EXAMPLE 5.5 Continuing with the previous example of Shepherds Company: what is the probability of getting the worstcase cash flows (a) If the cash flows are perfectly correlated over time, and (b) If the cash flows are mutually independent over time?

Solution

(a) If the cash flows are **perfectly correlated over time**, the probability of getting the worst case is 0.25 itself, because if the first year cash flows are low, the subsequent years' cash flows would also be low.

(b) If the cash flows are **independent over time**, if the first year cash flows are low, still the subsequent years' cash flows could be low or high. Then the probability of getting low cash flows in all years or getting the worst case is $= 0.25 \times 0.25 \times 0.25 \times 0.25 = 0.0039$.

Conclusion: This analysis throws further light on the riskiness of the proposed project. To conclude, assuming the cash flows of the Shepherd Company's proposed project are independent over time, the project may be acceptable, because the probability of getting the worst case scenario is less than 1%, while the project is clearly acceptable in both other scenarios.

Pros and Cons of Expected Values

Advantages of expected values are as follows:

1. Expected value concept is simple to understand and apply.
2. As compared to single value estimates of cash flows, expected values are more realistic, because they recognize that several outcomes are possible.
3. Expected value considers the probability of occurrence of variables affecting the success of the project.
4. Unlike sensitivity analysis, which is not a maximizing or optimizing technique and does not directly tell us what decision should be taken, expected values analysis directly indicates the decision to be taken, and thus, helps in the decision-making.

Limitations of expected values are as follows:

1. The results of 'expected value' analysis, such as an expected NPV, would be valid only if same types of projects are repeated again and again for a large number of times. However, in many organizations, the investment project would be undertaken only once and if it results in a heavy loss to the organization, the survival of the organization itself would be questionable, and there may not be any second chance to make up for the losses incurred.
2. The probabilities used in the expected value analysis are mostly 'subjective' probabilities that are not based on any quantifiable objective data. Subjective probabilities would reduce the accuracy or reliability of the results.

Conclusion: Expected value analysis is a popular technique to analyze the riskiness of a project. However, in view of its limitations, it should be used only when (i) the firm takes up such projects repeatedly, (ii) the standalone project under consideration is relatively of small magnitude so that the risk would also be limited, and (iii) probabilities are based on some reliable and rational data analysis and not completely subjective.

5.6.2 Decision Trees and Project Risk Analysis

The decision tree technique involves application of expected value principles to situations which require a number of decisions to be made sequentially. To illustrate, assume a pharmaceutical firm is evaluating a proposal to invest ₹1,00,000 in a research project to develop a new medicine. The research could either succeed or fail to develop a saleable product: probabilities being 0.6 for success and 0.4 for failure. If the research fails, the firm would drop the project and accept the loss. If the research succeeds, the firm could decide to either market the product or drop the project. If it decides to market the product, the product sales could be high (probability 0.7) or low (probability 0.3). If sales are high, the present value of cash inflow would be ₹4,00,000 and if sales are low, the present value of cash inflow would be ₹2,00,000.

As we can see from the above situation, the decision to market the product [decision number 2] depends on the outcome of the first decision [whether to invest in research], and each of the decisions have alternative possible outcomes with their own probabilities. In situations like this involving a chain of decision-making, the decision tree approach helps in systematic presentation of all decisions, and their possible outcomes in the form of a graph, which looks like a tree with several branches; hence the name decision-tree.

Before we proceed, let us familiarize with the main symbols used in the decision tree. A decision tree would consist of the following symbols:

1. Decision box: A decision box (or node) is used to represent a situation when management must decide between alternative courses of action. A decision box is typically shown as a square-box and the alternative courses of action are shown as branches of the square box (See Figure 5.1).

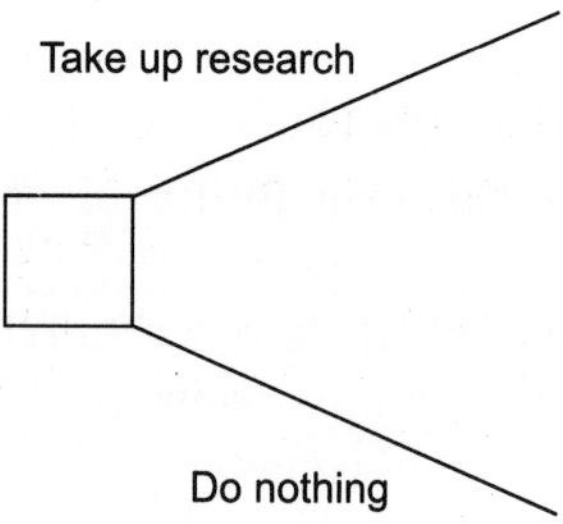

FIGURE 5.1
Decision box.

2. Outcome box: An outcome box (or node) is used to represent the possible outcomes (of a decision) with their probabilities. An outcome box is typically shown as a circle and the possible outcomes with their probabilities are shown as branches of the outcome box (Figure 5.2).

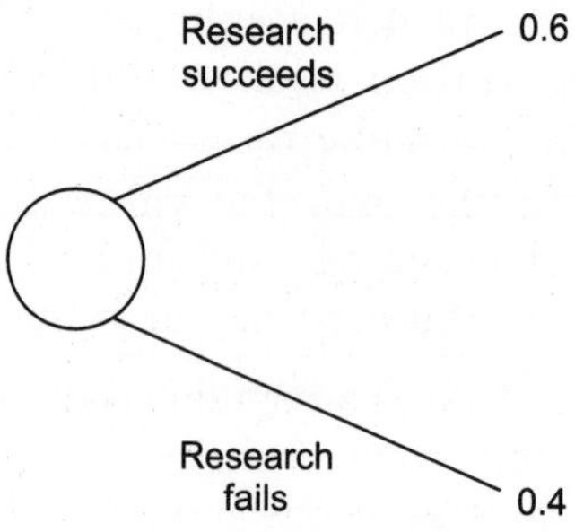

FIGURE 5.2
Outcome box.

The decision boxes and outcomes boxes are put together to prepare a decision tree. The decision tree for the pharmaceutical firm's research project mentioned above may appear as follows:

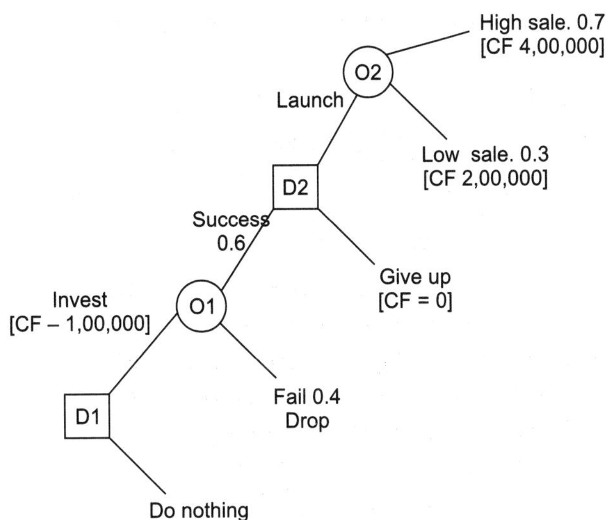

FIGURE 5.3
Decision Tree.

Explanation: (See Figure 5.3).

1. Decision box 'D1' shows that the firm at this point can either decide to invest in research or do nothing.
2. Outcome box 'O1' shows that 'D1' can have two outcomes: success in product development with a probability of 0.6, or failure with a probability of 0.4. [*Note:* Probabilities should always add up to 1.0, that is 0.6 + 0.4 = 1.0]
3. Decision box 'D2' shows that the firm at this point can either decide to launch the product or give up the project.
4. Outcome box 'O2' shows that 'D2' can have two possible outcomes: the product launch could either result in high sales (cash flow of ₹4,00,000) with a probability of 0.7, or low sales (cash flow of ₹2,00,000) with a probability of 0.3.

The Roll-back Technique

Note that the decision tree (Figure 5.3) includes the present values of cash inflows with each possible outcome, and its probability. We can now take steps to analyze the investment decision using the expected values of possible outcomes. For this purpose, we use the roll-back technique, starting calculations from right side, of the tree and moving to the left side until we find the NPV of the proposal at decision point 'D1'. The step-wise process is explained as follows:

(a) Find the expected value at outcome point O2 as follows:

TABLE 5.4
Finding, the Expected Value.

Outcome	*Cash flow*	*Probability*	*Product [CF × Prob]*
High sales	4,00,000	0.7	2,80,000
Low sales	2,00,000	0.3	60,000
		Expected Value	**3,40,000**

(b) At decision point D2, the firm should decide as follows:

Expected value, if product launched = ₹3,40,000
Expected value, if product dropped = ₹Nil
Gain by launching the product = ₹3,40,000

Hence, if the initial research is successful, the firm should launch the product because the expected value of launching (₹3,40,000) far exceeds the expected value of not launching (cash flow = Nil).

(c) Find the expected value at outcome point 'O1' as follows:

TABLE 5.5
Expected Value at Outcome Point 'O1'

Outcome	*Expected Value of Cash Flow*	*Probability Prob.*	*Product [EV of CF × Prob.]*
Reseach Successful	3,40,000	0.6	2,04,000
Research Failed	0	0.4	0
Expected Value			2,04,000

(d) The expected NPV at decision point D1 would then be calculated as follows:
Present value of the expected cash inflows = ₹2,04,000
Less initial investment in research = ₹1,00,000
Expected Net Present value = ₹1,04.000.

Conclusion: The sequence of decisions should be to invest in the research project. If the research is successful, the firm should launch the product. If research fails, the project should be abandoned.

You may like to try the following question yourself before checking with the answer.

EXAMPLE 5.6 Paragliding Company is evaluating a proposal to take up a Research and Development (R&D) project to develop and launch a new product. The R&D will require an investment of ₹5,00,000, and there is a 60% probability that the R&D and product launch will be successful, and a 40% chance that it will fail. However, the company is not certain about the level of returns from the product launch, and has made the following estimates of the present value of cash inflows during the life of the project:

Sales	*Probability*	*PV of Cash Flow (₹)*
High	0.3	9,00,000
Medium	0.5	8,00,000
Low	0.2	7,00,000

If the R&D is not successful, the company would drop the project and dispose of the R&D equipment; there is 80% probability that the R&D equipment will have a resale value of ₹60,000, and 20% probability that the resale value will be nil.

Draw a decision tree to graphically present the investment decision of the company. Determine the project's expected NPV, and suggest, whether the company should take up the R&D project.

Solution: The decision tree is as follows: [₹ in '000]

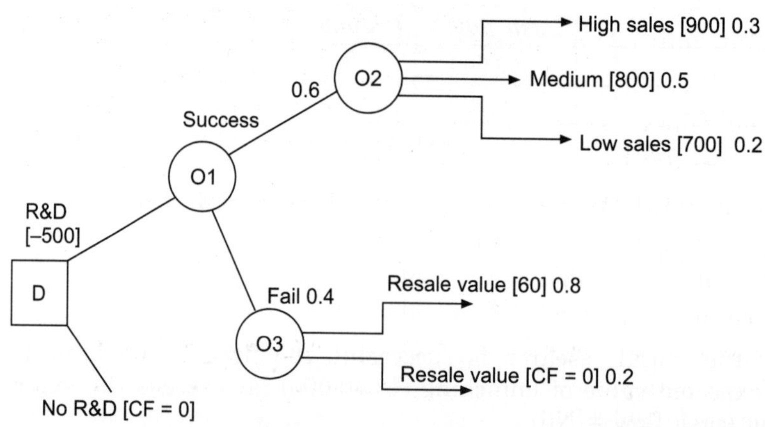

Explanation:

- Decision box 'D' shows the point at which the firm has to decide whether to undertake R&D or not.
- Outcome boxes 'O1 to O3' show the possible outcomes of the decisions taken along with probabilities.
- The (present values of) cash inflows have also been inserted with each possible outcome and its probability.

Now, we can take steps to analyze the investment decision using the expected values of possible outcomes. For this purpose, we use the roll-back technique starting calculations from right side of the tree and moving to the left side, until we find the expected NPV at decision point D.

Steps to evoluate the project

(a) Expected value at outcome point 'O2'

Outcome	*Cash flow (₹)*	*Probability (Prob.)*	*Product [CF × Prob.]*
High sales	9,00,000	0.3	2,70,000
Medium	8,00,000	0.5	4,00,000
Low sales	7,00,000	0.2	1,40,000
		Expected Value	**8,10,000**

(b) Expected value at outcome point 'O3'

Outcome of Failed R&D	*Cash flow*	*Probability*	*Product [EV of CF × Prob.]*
High Resale	60,000	0.8	48,000
Low Resale	0	0.2	0
		Expected Value	**48,000**

(c) Expected value at outcome point 'O1'

Outcome of R&D	*Cash flow (₹)*	*Probability*	*Product [CF × Prob.]*
Sucess	8,10,000	0.6	486,000
Failure	48,000	0.4	19,200
		Expected Value	**505,200**

(d) At decision point D, the firm should decide as follows:

Expected value if R&D launched = ₹5,05,200

Expected value if R&D NOT launched = ₹Nil

Net cash inflow if R&D launched = ₹5,05,200

Less: Investment required to start R&D = ₹–5,00,000

Net Present Value of the project = ₹5,200

Conclusion: Since the NPV is positive, the R&D project is acceptable. However, the NPV is positive by a small amount, which indicates that the margin of error is very thin. Hence, the firm should carefully evaluate the cash flow estimates to ensure that they are reliable. Also, it would be advisable that the firm puts in place contingency plans to make up for error in cash flow estimates.

5.7 Monte Carlo Simulation

We have discussed in the previous section that scenario analysis does away with limitations of the sensitivity analysis, which considers the effect of changing only one variable at a time. Scenario analysis can be used to analyze risk with respect to several discrete scenarios. However, from a practical point-of-view, we know that scenario analysis would be limited to analyze the effect of just a few combinations of variables out of an infinite number of possible combinations. Monte Carlo simulation can be used to consider the effect of all possible combinations of variables that have an impact on the success or failure of a project, including the sales volume, selling price, input costs, fixed costs, rate of inflation, salvage value, cost of capital and change in foreign exchange rates, etc.

In relation to project evaluation, simulation would involve building a mathematical model to recreate a potential investment project by combining a random value for each of the relevant variables. The following steps would be required to apply simulation for analysis of project risk:

1. **Identify main variables that affect the project's success.** Such variables might include the following:

   (a) **Related to product and market**
   - Selling price
   - Market size and target market share
   - Market growth rate
   - Inter-relationship between product price and sales volume

   (b) **Related to operating costs**
   - Variable input costs
   - Rate of inflation in relation to input costs
   - Fixed production and marketing costs

   (c) **Related to investment and financing cost**
   - Amount of initial investment required
   - Working capital investment
   - Project useful life
   - Cost of capital

   (d) **Related to depreciation and taxes**
   - Depreciation method and amount
   - Rates of income tax
   - Government subsidy if any, etc.

2. **Define the probability distribution for each variable.** In this step, probabilities are attached to estimates of each variable. For example, the firm may have the following probability distribution for sales volume:

Sales per annum (units):	1,000	1,500	2,000
Probability:	0.3	0.5	0.2

3. **Assign a random number range to each variable.** Random numbers (usually one digit or two digits) are assigned to variables in a way that reflects the underlying

probability distribution of the variable. For example, assuming one digit random numbers ranging from 0 to 9 are to be assigned, the following numbers would be assigned to the above probability distribution of sales units:

Sales per annum (units):	1,000	1,500	2,000
Probability:	0.3	0.5	0.2
Random numbers assigned:	0–2	3–7	8–9

4. Run the simulation: In a simulation analysis,

(a) A random value is drawn for each variable (either manually or by using the computer),

(b) The value of each variable corresponding to the random number drawn is identified;

(c) Calculate the project NPV using the values identified in (b).

(d) The above process is repeated a large number of times to get a probability distribution of NPVs.

5. Interpret the simulation results: The probability distribution and range of NPVs obtained from simulation would indicate the riskiness of the project.

Simulations are facilitated by using the computers. However, to get a flavour of the process of simulation, consider the following interesting illustration.

EXAMPLE 5.7 Simone Company is considering a new project which will require an initial investment of ₹50,000. The company is not certain about the future returns and has made cash flow estimates with probabilities as follows:

Annual net cash flows after taxes

Year 1		*Year 2*		*Year 3*	
CF	*Prob.*	*CF*	*Prob.*	*CF*	*Prob.*
15,000	0.3	20,000	0.2	15,000	0.1
20,000	0.5	25,000	0.4	20,000	0.5
25,000	0.2	30,000	0.3	25,000	0.2
		35,000	0.1	30,000	0.2

The company has decided to analyze the project risk by simulating the NPV calculation. For this purpose, the following random numbers have been generated that will be used to simulate five sets of cash flows.

Year	*Random numbers*				
	Set 1	*Set 2*	*Set 3*	*Set 4*	*Set 5*
1	5	0	3	4	9
2	7	1	1	4	6
3	8	6	5	2	3

Assuming the company's cost of capital is 12%, calculate the following:

(a) Assign a value ranging from 0 to 9 (in digits) to each year's cash flows in such a way that the number of digits assigned is proportionate to the probability of cash flow.

(b) For each set of random numbers given above, identify the corresponding cash flows. Present the 5 sets of relevant cash flows of the three years in a suitable tabular form.

(c) Calculate the present value of 5 sets of cash flows identified in 'b', and compute the project's NPV for each set.

(d) Using the simulation results (as per 'c' above), calculate the average NPV.

(e) Determine the probability of the project giving a negative NPV, and comment on the riskiness of the project.

Solution.

(a) Assigning digit values to cash flows

Year 1			*Year 2*			*Year 3*		
CF	*Prob.*	*Digits*	*CF*	*Prob.*	*Digits*	*CF*	*Prob.*	*Digits*
15,000	0.3	0–2	20,000	0.2	0–1	15,000	0.1	0
20,000	0.5	3–7	25,000	0.4	2–5	20,000	0.5	1–5
25,000	0.2	8–9	30,000	0.3	6–8	25,000	0.2	6–7
			35,000	0.1	9	30,000	0.2	8–9

(b) Indentifying cash flows matching random numbers

	Year 1		*Year 2*		*Year 3*	
Set	*R No.*	*CF*	*R No.*	*CF*	*R No.*	*CF*
1	5	20,000	7	30,000	8	30,000
2	0	15,000	1	20,000	6	25,000
3	3	20,000	1	20,000	5	20,000
4	4	20,000	4	25,000	2	20,000
5	9	25,000	6	30,000	3	20,000

(c) Calculating simulated NPVs

	Year 1		*Year 2*		*Year 3*			
	PVF = 0.8929*		*PVF = 0.7972*		*PVF = 0.7118*			
Set	*CF*	*PV*	*CF*	*PV*	*CF*	*PV*	*Initial outflow*	*NPV***
1	20,000	17,858	30,000	23,916	30,000	21,354	–50,000	13,128.0
2	15,000	13,393.5	20,000	15,944	25,000	17,795	–50,000	–2,867.5
3	20,000	17,858	20,000	15,944	20,000	14,236	–50,000	–1,962.0
4	20,000	17,858	25,000	19,930	20,000	14,236	–50,000	2,024.0
5	25,000	22,322.5	30,000	23,916	20,000	14,236	–50,000	10,474.5
								20,797.0
							Average NPV	**4,159.4**

*PVF (Present Value Factor) at 12% discount rate. **NPV computed by adding together the PV of cash flows for the three years less initial outflow.

(d) The average NPV: As shown in the above simulated calculations, the average NPV is likely to be ₹4,159.4.

(e) The project risk and possibility of negative NPV: On the basis of the above simulated results, there is 2/5 or 40% chance that the NPV would be negative. Let us see this pictorially:

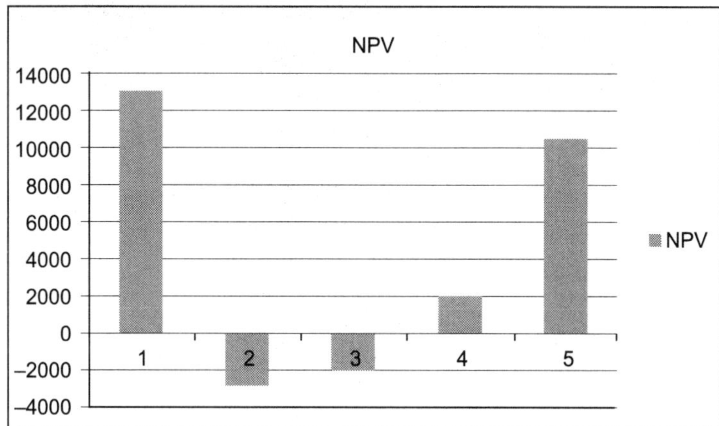

The possibility of negative NPVs makes the project risky, but each time the negative NPV has been reported, the negative value of NPV is not as significant as the positive NPVs reported in other simulated sets. That should give some confidence to the management, and it may decide to accept the proposal if the company is not risk averse.

Note that to provide any reliable understanding of the risk profile of the proposal, a large number of simulations (may be several hundred) would be required which is facilitated by computer-based simulations such as the Monte Carlo simulations.

Note: You are encouraged to try the Monte Carlo simulation for the 'Global Synfuels' case given in the Annexure at the end of the chapter, and compare the results with the Teaching note of the case.

5.7.1 Pros and Cons of Simulation

The major advantage of simulation is that it can cover all possible outcomes of variables that have an impact on the success of a project. However, the mathematical simulation models can become highly complex and time consuming, particularly when variables are inter-dependent, such as product price and sales volume. Simulation should be adopted only when likely benefits from a detailed risk analysis exceed the cost and time invested in simulation.

5.8 Risk Adjusted Discount Rates

One of the simplest methods theoretically might be to raise the rate of discount according to the degree of risk perceived in an investment project. For example, a firm might decide to use three types of discount rates: 10%, 14% and 18% for the low risk, moderate risk and high risk projects. While the method seems to have a logical appeal, its main limitation is that all such risk-adjusted rates are decided by subjective judgment. Also, if the quality of cash flows forecasts is poor, no risk adjustment of discount rates would be of much use. Note that while using other methods of risk analysis such as scenario analysis, a risk-free discount rate and not a risk-adjusted discount rate should be used to calculate the NPVs, otherwise the risk premium would be counted twice: once included in the risk-adjusted discount rate and secondly again in the course of scenario analysis, such as Worst case-Most Likely-Best case scenarios.

To conclude, several techniques of analyzing project risk have been discussed in this chapter. Choice of a suitable technique would depend on the objectives of analysis, size and complexity of the project as well as the cost-benefit of using specific techniques. If applied appropriately, these techniques can go a long way in helping the management in understanding the project risk, and make better and more informed decisions.

Researchable Issues

Faculty members, students and research scholars may like to consider the following selected issues for further research and case writing.

- Capital budgeting practices in multinationals.
- Financial appraisal of risky projects in Indian companies.
- Risk evaluation techniques and corporate governance.
- Corporate practices in the area of capital budgeting.
- Theory versus practice of risk analysis for project appraisal.
- Risk analysis of foreign acquisitions by Indian companies.
- Risk analysis and investment decision practices in the services sector.
- Risk analysis and investment decision practices in the infrastructure sector [power, water, transport projects].

References

Bavishi, V.B., Capital budgeting practices at multinationals, *Management Accounting,* pp. 32–35, August, 1981.

Bierman, H. Jr. and Smidt, S., *The Capital Budgeting Decision: Economic Analysis of Investment Projects*, 9th ed., Routledge, New York, 2006.

David J. Oblak and Roy J. Helm, Jr., 'Survey and Analysis of Capital Budgeting Methods Used by Multinationals', *Financial Management,* Vol. 9, No. 4, pp. 37–41, Winter, 1980.

Eugene, F. Fama, 'Risk-adjusted discount rates and capital budgeting under uncertainty', *Journal of Financial Economics*, Vol. 5, Issue 1, , pp. 3–24, August, 1977.

Frederic S. Hillier, "The Derivative of Probabilistic Information for the evaluation of Risky Investments", *Management Science*, 9, pp. 443–57, April, 1963.

Lawson, G.H. and Windle, D.W., "Capital Budgeting and the Use of DCF Criteria in the Corporation Tax Regime", Oliver and Boyd, California, 1967.

Pike, R.H., The University of Bradford Management Centre, UK

Schall, L.D., Sundem, G.L., and Geijsbeek, W.R., 'Survey And Analysis of Capital Budgeting Methods, *The Journal of Finance*, 33, pp. 281–287, 1978.

Seitz, N. and Ellison, M., Capital Budgeting and Long-Term Financing Decisions, 4th ed. South-Western Educational Publishing, 2004.

Shapiro, A.C., *Capital Budgeting and Investment Analysis*, Prentice Hall, 2004.

SSM Ho, 'Risk analysis in capital budgeting: Barriers and benefits', Omega, Vol. 19, Issue 4, pp. 235–245, 1991.

Economic Times: http://articles.economictimes.indiatimes.com/2014-12-04/news/56723426_1_cost-overrun-62-projects-rs-1-lakh-crore

Points to Remember

- **Managers should analyze the risk profile** of the project and incorporate risk and uncertainty in the financial evaluation of the projects so that they could take rational and well informed decisions.
- **Sensitivity analysis** helps in answering 'What If' type of questions such as 'what if' the project's initial investment turns out to be X% higher than our estimates. It analyses important variables one by one to measure the impact of a change in the variable on the project NPV. Such analysis would highlight the variables, in which a small adverse change could cause the largest fall in the NPV.
- **Sensitivity analysis has only a limited use** because (i) it considers the impact of a change in only one variable at a time, (ii) it does not consider the probability of the adverse changes in variables, (ii) it ignores the interdependency between variables and (iii) it is not an optimizing or maximizing technique because it does not directly indicate the decision to be taken.
- **Scenario analysis:** Unlike sensitivity analysis which considers the impact of changing one variable at a time, scenario analysis can be used to analyze the collective effect of changing more than one variable simultaneously on the project's NPV. Scenario analysis can also take into account the interrelationship between variables.
- **The expected value** of cash flow is the probability-weighted average of all possible cash flows in different scenarios. The 'expected value' concept says that if the same types of projects are repeated again and again for a large number of times, then on an average, the expected value would be realized.
- **The standard deviation and coefficient of variation** are statistical measures that are used to understand the risk associated with the proposed investment project. While standard deviation is reported in the same units as the expected cash flows, the coefficient of variation is a relative measure and reported as a ratio of the standard deviation of NPV to the expected value of NPV.
- **Perfect correlation of cash flows over time** would increase the risk of the proposed project and its standard deviation would be greater than if cash flows were mutually independent over time.
- **The decision tree technique** involves application of expected value principles to situations which require a number of decisions to be made sequentially. In decision tree approach, we use the roll-back technique, starting calculations from right side of the tree and moving to the left side until we find the NPV of the proposal.
- **Monte Carlo simulation** can be used to consider the effect of all possible combinations of variables that have an impact on the success or failure of a project. Simulation involves building a mathematical model to recreate a potential investment project by combining a random value for each of the relevant variables.

Questions

1. Explain the importance of risk analysis in project appraisal, and differentiate between risk and uncertainty.
2. Explain the meaning of sensitivity analysis, and using suitable numerical examples show its application to understand project risk.

3. Explain the difference between scenario analysis and sensitivity analysis. In the context of project appraisal, what are the advantages of scenario analysis over the sensitivity analysis?
4. How can you use sensitivity analysis to reduce risk? Using suitable numerical examples show how to calculate the sensitivity of a project NPV to changes in (i) initial investment and (ii) cost of capital.
5. Explain the meaning and significance of the project's expected NPV, standard deviation and coefficient of variation. Using suitable numerical examples show how to calculate each of them.
6. Explain the meaning of the decision tree and the basic principles involved in preparing the same. Using suitable numerical examples show how to prepare and use the decision tree for project appraisal.
7. Explain how simulation is an improvement over scenario analysis and discuss the steps required to run the simulation analysis.
8. Distinguish between perfect correlation and mutual independence of cash flows over time? What are their implications for the project risk?
9. In the context of project appraisal, explain the meaning of expected value and using suitable numerical examples show its calculation. Discuss its main advantages and disadvantages as compared to (i) sensitivity analysis and (ii) simulation.
10. Explain the meaning of risk-adjusted discount rates in the context of reducing project risk, and discuss their advantages and limitations.

Multiple Choice Questions

1. The difference between risk and uncertainty is that:
   (a) Risk is quantifiable while uncertainty is not quantifiable
   (b) Risk is not quantifiable while uncertainty is quantifiable
   (c) When risk rises, uncertainty declines but when uncertainty rises, risk also rises
   (d) None of the above

2. If a project requires an initial investment of ₹1,20,000 and promises a NPV of ₹40,000, what would be the impact on the NPV if there was a 10% increase in the initial investment?
   (a) NPV would rise by 10%
   (b) NPV would decline by 20%
   (c) NPV would decline by 30%
   (d) None of the above

3. If a project requires an initial investment of ₹1,50,000 and promises a NPV of ₹29,990, what would be the approximate percentage change in the initial investment that would be required for the investment decision to change?
   (a) Increase of 10% in initial investment
   (b) Increase of 15% in initial investment
   (c) Increase of 20% in initial investment
   (d) None of the above

4. A firm is considering an investment project for which it has made the following estimates of different future outcomes with probabilities and NPV:

Possible Outcome	*Probability*	*Project NPV (₹)*
Low sales	0.40	–80,000
High sales	0.60	2,50,000

Taking into account the possible outcomes and their probabilities, the expected net present value of the proposed project would be:
(a) ₹1,02,000
(b) ₹1,18,000
(c) ₹1,32,000
(d) None of the above

5. A firm wishes to measure the relative riskiness of a project under consideration. If the project's expected NPV is ₹21,000 and the standard deviation of the NPV (σ NPV) is ₹26,000, then what is the project's Coefficient of variation?
(a) 1.24
(b) 1.13
(c) 0.81
(d) None of the above

6. The major limitation(s) of sensitivity analysis are that:
(a) It does not consider the probability of the adverse changes in variables
(b) It ignores the interdependency between variables
(c) Both of the above
(d) None of the above

7. Perfect correlation of cash flows over time is likely to:
(a) Decrease the risk of the proposed project
(b) Increase the risk of the proposed project
(c) Make no difference to the risk of the proposed project
(d) None of the above

Self-Test Questions

1. Safex Company is evaluating an investment proposal that would require an initial investment of ₹2,50,000 in plant and equipment to produce a new product. The project is expected to generate annual sales revenue of ₹4,00,000 for a period of three years at the end of which the plant and equipment are expected to have a resale value of ₹50,000. The variable cost of the product is expected to be ₹2,40,000 per annum for the above budgeted sales revenue. The annual fixed cost of the company (other than depreciation) would increase by ₹40,000. Assume Safex Company's cost of capital is 15%. Ignore taxes.
(a) On the basis of the information given above, calculate the project's NPV and decide if the project should be accepted.
(b) Taking one variable at a time, calculate the percentage changes in the following estimates that would be required for the investment decision to change:
(i) Initial investment
(ii) Variable cost
(iii) Fixed cost

2. Gardenia Company is considering a project for which it has made three levels of cash flow estimates as follows:

Three level estimates of cash flows

Year	*Optimistic*	*Most Likely*	*Pessimistic*
0	–2,25,000	–2,50,000	–2,75,000
1	1,40,000	1,30,000	1,20,000
2	1,30,000	1,20,000	1,10,000
3	1,10,000	1,00,000	90,000

The company's cost of capital is 12% and the same is used as the required rate of return on project investments.

Calculate NPV for each series of the cash flows. Comment on the riskiness of the project and advise whether the project should be undertaken.

3. Rose Company is considering a new project for which it has made three levels of cash flow estimates with probabilities as follows:

Net cash flows after tax

Year	*Worst case*	*Most likely*	*Best case*
	P = 0.25	**P = 0.50**	**P = 0.25**
0	–2,50,000	–2,50,000	–2,50,000
1	60,000	80,000	1,00,000
2	60,000	80,000	1,00,000
3	60,000	80,000	1,00,000
4	60,000	80,000	1,00,000
4*	40,000	60,000	80,000

The last cash flow is for the resale value of equipment. The company's requried rate of return for projects with a risk profile as this project is 12%.

(a) Using the above scenario-wise cash flows with corresponding probabilities, calculate the expected values of each year's cash flows.
(b) Compute the project's expected net present value.
(c) Compute the project's best-case net present value.
(d) Compute the project's worst-case net present value.
(e) Compute the project's most-likely net present value.
(f) What is the probability of occurrence of the worst-case scenario if cash flows are perfectly correlated over time?
(g) What is the probability of occurrence of the worst-case scenario if cash flows are mutually independent over time?

4. Prohealth Company is considering a proposal to invest ₹6,00,000 on a one year R&D project for the development of a herbal anti-aging product. There is a 70% probability of R&D success by the end of one year period, after which the product could be sold for a period of five years. The company has made the following estimates of the present value of cash inflows during the life of the project:

Sales	*Probability*	*PV of cash flow*
		₹000
High	0.6	2,000
Moderate	0.4	1,000

If the R&D does not succeed in developing a marketable product in one year's time, the company can decide to either abandon the project or extend the period of R&D by one more year for which it would have to invest a further ₹4,00,000. There is a 50% probability that the R&D would succeed in the extended period. If the R&D succeeds in the extended period, the company could decide to introduce the product into the market from the end of second year, or abandon the project. In the situation of late introduction of the product, the project life would be reduced to four years and the company has estimated the present value of cash inflows from the project as follows:

Sales	*Probability*	*PV of cash flow*
		₹'000
High	0.2	1,200
Moderate	0.8	600

Draw a decision tree to graphically present the investment decision facing the company. Determine the project's expected NPV and suggest whether the company should take up the R&D project.

Problems

1. The expected initial investment and cash inflows related to a proposed project are given below:

Year	*Estimated cash flows*
0	–1,80,000
1	1,30,000
2	1,30,000

Assuming the firm's cost of capital is 14%:

(a) Calculate the project's NPV using the estimated cash flows as above.
(b) What would be the impact on the NPV if there was a 10% increase in the initial investment, assuming no change in future cash inflows?
(c) What would be the impact on the NPV if there was a 10% decrease in future cash inflows, assuming no change in the initial investment?
(d) Rank the two variables (initial investment and cash inflows) in terms of the NPV's vulnerability to adverse changes in these variables.

2. ELTA Enterprises is considering an investment proposal which has the expected initial investment and operating cash inflows as given below:

Year	*Variables*	(₹)
0	Initial Investment	–1,70,000
1	Operating cash inflow	1,20,000
2	Operating cash inflow	1,20,000

Assuming the firm's cost of capital is 10%:

(a) Calculate the project's NPV using the estimated cash flows as above.
(b) What would be the impact on the NPV if there was a 10% increase in the initial investment, assuming no change in future operating cash inflows?
(c) What would be the impact on the NPV if the future operating cash inflows were lower by 10%, assuming no change in the initial investment?

(d) What would be the impact on the NPV if the cost of capital increased to 11%, assuming no change in other variables?

(e) Rank the three variables (initial investment, operating cash inflows and cost of capital) in terms of the NPV's vulnerability to adverse changes in these variables.

3. Mahe Company is evaluating an investment proposal that would require an initial investment of ₹2,00,000 in plant and equipment to produce a new product. The project is expected to generate annual sales revenue of ₹3,30,000 for a period of three years at the end of which the plant and equipment are expected to have a resale value of ₹50,000. The variable cost of the product is expected to be ₹2,10,000 per annum for the above budgeted sales revenue. The annual fixed cost of the company (other than depreciation) would increase by ₹40,000. Assume Mahe Company's cost of capital is 14%. Ignore taxes.

(a) On the basis of the information given above, calculate the project's NPV and decide if the project should be accepted.

(b) Taking one variable at a time, calculate the percentage changes in the following estimates that would be required for the investment decision to change:

(i) Initial cost
(ii) Sales revenue
(iii) Variable cost
(iv) Resale value
(v) Cost of capital

4. Charlie is a first time entrepreneur who wants to tread cautiously, avoiding risk completely as far as possible. He is considering a project for which he has made three levels of cash flow estimates as follows:

Three level estimates of cash flows

Year	*Optimistic*	*Most likely*	*Pessimistic*
0	–4,20,000	–4,50,000	–4,80,000
1	3,10,000	2,80,000	2,50,000
2	2,40,000	2,20,000	2,00,000
3	1,80,000	1,70,000	1,60,000

The company's cost of capital is 12%, and the same is used as the required rate of return on investments.

Calculate NPV for each series of the cash flows. Comment on the riskiness of the project, and advise whether the project should be undertaken.

5. Apex Company is considering a new project for which it has made three levels of cash flow estimates with probabilities as follows:

Net cash flows after tax

	Worst case	*Most likely*	*Best case*
Year	*P* = 0.20	*P* = 0.60	*P* = 0.20
0	–4,00,000	–4,00,000	–4,00,000
1	80,000	1,20,000	1,60,000
2	80,000	1,20,000	1,60,000
3	80,000	1,20,000	1,60,000
4	80,000	1,20,000	1,60,000
4*	70,000	80,000	90,000

*The last cash flow is for the resale value of equipment.

The company's required rate of return for projects with a risk profile as this project is 12%.

(a) Using the above scenario-wise cash flows with corresponding probabilities, calculate the expected values of each year's cash flows.
(b) Compute the project's expected net present value.
(c) Compute the project's best-case net present value.
(d) Compute the project's worst-case net present value.
(e) Compute the project's most-likely net present value.
(f) Calculate the project's standard deviation and coefficient of variation, and comment on whether the project should be undertaken, assuming the Company has a maximum acceptable coefficient of variation limit of 2.0.

SHORT-CASE

John Computer Accessories

John looked at the papers concerning the new project and asked his accountant, "Are you sure you have included all details and not missed out on anything important?" He was disappointed that the expansion project he was so excited about did not seem to promise high returns.

John's computer accessories business had been doing fairly well, and now he was considering expanding his product range by adding a new product for which the following details had been prepared:

An initial investment of ₹2 million would be required to acquire the plant and equipment to manufacture the product. The product life had been estimated at four years during which sales of the product were estimated at 1,000 units per annum. The selling price and the cost of manufacturing and marketing the product had been estimated as follows:

TABLE CS (1)

Items	*Details*	(₹)
Selling price per unit		1,500
Cost per unit:		
Material cost [4 kg @ ₹50 per kg]	200	
Direct labour [3.5 hours @ ₹100 per hour]	350	
Variable overhead	150	
Depreciation [Note-1]	500	
Fixed costs [Note-2]	100	1,300
Profit margin per unit		200
Total profit from 1,000 units per annum = 1,000 × 200		2,00,000
Cost of capital on investment = ₹20,00,000 × 10%		2,00,000
Net profit		Nil

Note: (1) Annual depreciation using straight line method= ₹20,00,000 ÷ 4 years = ₹5,00,000 per annum. Depreciation per unit = ₹5,00,000 ÷ 1000 units = ₹500 per unit. (2) Annual fixed cost of ₹1,00,000 (rent and other cash expenses) caused by the new product spread over 1,000 units = ₹1,00,000 ÷ 1000 units = ₹100 per unit.

John looked worried and said, "If there is no net profit, why should we undertake the project? Also, you have not considered the risk factor. Although we have estimated the project cash flows carefully to make them as reliable as possible, the business environment remains uncertain and so we must be prepared for some possible margin of error, particularly with regard to our estimates of the annual sales volume, direct material price and cost of capital."

The firm's cost of capital is estimated at 10% per annum. Assume the plant and equipment would not have any resale value at the end of the project, and ignore income taxes.

Required:

1. Using the estimates given above, calculate the Net Present Value (NPV) and decide whether the investment proposal is acceptable.
2. Carry out a sensitivity analysis to show how sensitive is the NPV to errors of estimates in each of the following: (i) Annual sales volume, (ii) per unit material price, and (iii) the cost of capital.

Annexure-1

Decision Case

GLOBAL SYNFUELS*

Financial and Strategic Appraisal of a Coal-to-Liquid Project

Abstract

Rapid economic growth in India during the past two decades had led to an ever-increasing demand for energy. India imported about two-third of its crude oil requirements resulting in huge outflow of precious foreign exchange. As a result, it became necessary for the country to look for alternative sources of energy. The Coal To Liquid (CTL) technology of coal gasification offered a credible alternative source of fuels as proved by Sasol of South Africa. In February 2009, the Government of India shortlisted Global Steel & Power Limited (GSPL) as one of the selected few companies to build a coal to liquid (CTL) project.

The CTL process involves extracting fossil oil from coal. GSPL set up a subsidiary named Global Synfuels and started evaluating the project viability. The project was strategically important to the company, but there were serious doubts about the commercial viability of a CTL project, particularly without Government subsidy. If the company did sink the huge investment and the project turned sour, the company could go bust and the management could earn the wrath of thousands of shareholders! While the company wanted to capitalize on the unique opportunities offered by the project, the project proposal must be subjected to rigorous financial and strategic appraisal before the company took a final call on the project.

Keywords: Coal liquefaction, syngas, CO_2 emissions, carbon capture and storage (CCS) technologies, CO_2 emissions, Carbon Credits, economic feasibility.

Case

Jai was a nervous wreck. He had been involved in several large investment projects in the past, but this one would beat them all in terms of size, risk and complexity. He and his team had worked for weeks to gather tons of information, made all types of projections, but at the end of all that, you had limited choices: you could say "Yes, I do" or "No, I won't". As the Vice-President—CTL project of Global Steel and Power Limited (GSPL), Jai was to present his project appraisal in a Board meeting that was just a week away, and he was still undecided whether to recommend the project or not! Technology-wise, he was very excited by the project and would love to recommend to the Board that the company should take it up. But in his heart, he knew the project was more risky than anything else he had seen in his career of over two decades.

If the company did sink the huge investment, and the project turned sour, the company could go bust and you could earn the wrath of thousands of shareholders! On the other hand, if the company did not take up the investment—and the challenge—it could mean foregoing an opportunity that might never arise again and the company would lose billions of dollars of money that the project could possibly generate if it became successful. But that was a very big 'IF'.

---

* This case has been authored by Dr. Narender Ahuja and Dr. Sweta Agarwal.

Global Steel and Power

Global Steel and Power Limited was a major player in Steel, Power, Mining, Oil & Gas and Infrastructure. With an annual turnover of US $2.3 billion, in 2010, GSPL produced steel and power most economically through backward integration with its own captive coal and iron-ore mines. Belonging to the US$ 15 billion Global Group, it had been able to achieve remarkable growth during the past decade, expanding its businesses to several parts of the world in Asia, Africa, South America and Australia. Renowned for an enterprising spirit and willingness to explore new technologies, it had won accolades for its environment-friendly, efficient operations, and was recently rated by an international Consulting Group as the second highest value creator in the world. It had a skilled workforce of 15,000 persons, and was constantly on the lookout for opportunities to venture into new businesses, with current investment commitments running at about US$ 30 billion.

New Opportunity

A new investment opportunity arose in February 2009, when the Government shortlisted GSPL as one of the chosen few companies to build a Coal To Liquid (CTL) project. The CTL process involves extracting fossil oil from coal. India imported about two-third of its crude oil requirements resulting in huge outflow of precious foreign exchange. A coal-to-liquid project would provide an alternative to crude oil, exploit abundantly available coal reserves in the country (estimated to be the fifth largest in the world), insulate the country from volatile crude prices and create employment for thousands.

Jai Patil was born and brought up in South Africa where he studied chemical engineering, and then worked in industries ranging from oil exploration to mining for two decades before joining GSPL recently as Vice-President—CTL. Jai had worked with Sasol CTL project in South Africa for a number of years, and had deep knowledge of all technological aspects of the CTL project.

While shortlisting the company to build a Coal to Liquid project in Orissa, an eastern state of India, the Government also awarded it coal blocks for securing raw material for the plant. GSPL formed a subsidiary named Global Synfuels for setting up the Coal to Liquid plant with a capacity of 80,000 barrels per day equivalent of key oil products, such as Diesel and Naphtha. GSPL was one of the country's largest coal producers and diversifying into the coal-to-liquid business would add strategic value to the company. The CTL Project envisaged an investment of US$ 9.34 billion, including mining operations. Once completed, this would be first such project in the country that would meet 10% of India's current crude oil requirements and provide employment to approximately 30,000 persons while allowing the company to benefit from the strong and rising demand for liquid fuels in one of the fastest growing economies of the world.

However, there were doubts about the commercial viability of a CTL project as long as crude oil was available at prices lower than the cost of producing fuels from coal. GSPL had no previous experience in CTL projects, and the big question was whether such a project would be financially viable, particularly without any Government subsidy? In South Africa, where such projects first came up, they were set up and survived for a long time with liberal Government funding. No such Government financial support was assured for the GSPL-CTL project. It would be impossible to raise the huge equity and debt funding required by the project without proving its financial viability beyond doubt.

Was the project doomed even before it was launched?

CTL: History

A CTL project involves converting coal into liquid fuel. The process, called coal liquefaction, allows coal to be utilized as an alternative to oil. The CTL technology was first developed by two German chemists Franz Fischer and Hans Tropsch in the 1920s. During the Nazi reign, when Germany lacked adequate supplies of crude oil, the CTL process was used to convert coal into synthetic fuels for the war effort.

Companies in oil and energy fields from several countries experimented with the process, but did not find it commercially viable because crude oil was cheaper at that time. During the apartheid-era isolation, when South Africa did not have sufficient crude oil, this technology was perfected by Sasol to build its first CTL plant in Sasolburg in 1955. In the 1970s, when crude oil prices shot up excessively, Sasol built two more plants in Secunda with a $6-billion government loan. In 1979, the company was privatised, but the Government maintained a 23.5% stake. The heavy subsidisation pattern continued in South Africa for a long time. In China too, the CTL projects received substantial Government support to make them viable. In several other countries where the CTL technology was attempted, companies found the technology too expensive and asked for Government incentives and loan guarantees to make the project commercially viable.

As a rough estimate, the capital investment required by a CTL project was about three-times that of a traditional crude oil refinery project of similar capacity. As a result, the CTL technology was shunned for a long time mainly because crude oil was available at a lower cost. But with the crude oil prices rising in recent years, the CTL technology was being considered more favourably and in 2011–12, about 30 CTL projects were at different stages of development in the world. However, doubts still persisted about the CTL viability.

Technology and Environmental Issues

Two alternative methods are available for converting coal into liquid fuels: direct liquefaction and indirect liquefaction. In the direct liquefaction method, coal is dissolved in a solvent at very high temperatures to produce the desired products. This process is claimed to be more efficient but the final operational cost is higher because it requires further refining of the products that would involve additional cost.

Under the indirect liquefaction process, coal is first gasified to produce syngas, which is a mixture of hydrogen and carbon monoxide. The syngas is then condensed over a catalyst to produce high quality, ultra-clean products. The second process is based on the German technology, for which the main supplier Lurgi has a virtual monopoly over the technology. GSPL was negotiating with Lurgi as a strategic partner to supply the required plant and technology, but with 30 CTL projects simultaneously being developed in various parts of the world, doubts were raised about the timely supply of technology to avoid time and cost over-runs. The GSPL management was confident that this aspect would be taken care of.

Using the German Lurgi CTL technology, it would be possible to make a number of products including ultra-clean petroleum and diesel, gasoline, naphtha, synthetic waxes, lubricants, and alternative liquid fuels such as methanol and dimethyl ether. As of now, the plan was to use 60–70% plant capacity for diesel production, and the remaining for other products. The actual product mix would be varied from time to time in tune with changing market requirements to maximize revenue.

The basic CTL technology is known to be a major environment pollutant, involving large quantity of CO_2 emissions. According to some estimates, liquid coal would emit 10% more global warming pollution than gasoline. It is also said to be extremely wasteful, requiring 3.5 gallons of water for making each gallon of fuel.

Replying to concerns regarding the CTL effect on environment, GSPL senior executives claimed in a media conference that the Coal-to-Liquid (CTL) project of GSPL was environment friendly and would cause no pollution. While the coal to liquids process generated more CO_2 emissions than conventional oil refining, there were ways to reduce such emissions. The CO_2 emissions from the CTL process could be almost completely (99%) reduced by using the carbon capture and storage (CCS) technologies. However, this was only possible with additional costs and significant reduction in the efficiency of the process. GSPL had carried out CO_2 management feasibility and the project cost covered the investment required to take care of the environment issues.

The management felt confident that the quality of products would be far superior to crude oil products and take care of the environmental issues. The product quality would not only satisfy Euro-VI quality standards but also be able to fetch a price premium of 10% as compared to crude oil. The company also hoped to earn considerable carbon credits on account of the clean technology used by the project.

India's Energy Security

Rapid economic growth in India during the past two decades had led to an ever-increasing energy demand and tremendous rise in vehicle ownership. Due to this, it became necessary for the country to look for alternative sources of energy. An important aspect of fuel consumption in India was that the consumption of diesel was several times more than that of petrol. The CTL technology of coal gasification, followed by Fischer–Tropsch synthesis offered a credible alternative source of diesel as proved by Sasol of South Africa. India had large coal reserves which could be exploited to build four-five Sasol type CTL projects to generate coal liquids, adequate to meet 20–25% of the expected diesel demand in year 2012. India had about 256 billion tonnes of coal reserves, of which presently only around 455 million tonnes was mined annually. An additional consideration was that Indian coal had a high ash content which made it unsuitable for other technologies but would have no problem with CTL process; hence it was a strategic fit to Indian requirements.

Coal-to-liquid projects based on Fischer–Tropsch technology had a number of benefits. These included proven technology, affordable and easy availability of domestic coal supplies, reduced dependence on oil imports, thereby, improving the economy's energy security as well as saving precious foreign exchange. Ultra-clean coal liquid fuels can be used for transport, cooking as well as for power generation at less cost. For vehicle owners, the advantage of CTL technology is that car engines would not require any modification to use the coal fuels. CTL technology can also be used to produce jet fuels. Also, coal liquid fuels are sulphur-free and low in nitrogen oxides. In addition, the project could offer employment opportunities to about 30,000 persons.

However, coal supply and transportation could pose problems and the CTL process would increase India's CO2 emissions. That was why, from an environmental point-of-view, biomass fuels were considered more environment-friendly as compared to the CTL technology. But growing biomass for fuels would require much larger land resources, and the related capital investment cost per barrel of daily capacity would be much more, almost double, as compared to the CTL process. In any case, a large emerging economy like India could not depend on one or two sources of fuels for its ever-increasing requirements; it would have to continue efforts on developing several alternative sources of fuels for sustainable economic growth.

It was this pursuit of diversifying the country's energy sources that had led the Government of India to shortlist GSPL and a few other companies in February 2009 for setting up CTL projects. While another shortlisted company had already roped in South African Sasol as a strategic partner, GSPL was yet to take a call though steps were being taken to finalize the technology partner. A detailed project report was also being prepared by a professional group of consultants, and financing alternatives were being explored.

Capacity and Product Mix

As estimated by the company, the CTL project with a capacity to produce 80,000 bbl/day of coal liquids—consisting of the CTL main plant, coal mining and power plants —would have a total project cost of US$ 9.34 billion. The estimated cost details are given in Case Table 5.1.

Project	*Capacity*	*Project Investment in US$ (Million)*
CTL plant	80,000 bbl/day	7111
Coal mining	50 MTPA	556
Power plant	1350 MW	1678
Total		9344

CS TABLE 5.1: Facilities Requirements and Estimated Cost of a CTL Project

A silver lining with regard to the project cost was that lots of research was currently going on in a number of countries including the USA, to refine the CTL technology and reduce project cost. Since setting up of the CTL project was still a few years away, it was being optimistically hoped that a major breakthrough could take place in the meantime and possibly the project cost could reduce by up to 20%.

Project Time Planning

The different phases of the CTL project and time required were estimated as follows:

Year	***Development***	***Project Investment (%) and Cash flows***
2009–11	Conception	
2012	Pre-feasibility phase	3%
2013	Feasibility phase	3%
2014	Feasibility phase	4%
2015	EPC (Equipment, Procurement & Construction)	60%
2016	EPC (Equipment, Procurement & Construction)	10%
2017	EPC (Equipment, Procurement & Construction)	10%
2018	Commissioning/Start up	10%
2019–2048	Normal operations	Cash flows

CS TABLE 5.2: Phases of CTL Project

The capital costs at the EPC level included equipment, materials, labour, construction costs and engineering.

The Economic Feasibility

While a team of experts was working with detailed project feasibility analysis, Jai thought it wise to benefit from the feasibility analyses performed internationally. In particular, he found two feasibility reports relevant to the GSPL project, both from the USA. First one was a 2008 'Recommended Project Finance Structures for the Economic Analysis of Fossil-Based Energy Projects' developed by the National Energy Technology Laboratory (NETL), and second was a 2009 report titled 'Economic Feasibility of Coal to Liquids Development in Alaska's Interior' prepared for Northern Alaska Environmental Center, USA. Since the CTL output had to be competitively priced to match with global crude oil prices, it was important that the project's cost structure should also remain competitive and well within the internationally set norms.

After a careful study of the two feasibility reports as above, and in consultation with technical experts, he noted the following points that would be helpful in developing an initial financial feasibility of the GSPL-CTL project:

(a) Working capital investment: Investment outlay will have to be increased to account for working capital investment of about $1.156 billion at the end of 2018, raising the total project cost to $10.5 billion.

(b) Operating cost: Operating cost was estimated at $45.00/bbl for the first year of operations in 2019.

(c) Plant operating factor: Though efforts would be made to operate the plant at 100% efficiency, a conservative 90% plant efficiency factor would be used as the basis for analysing financial viability. The 100% efficiency would of course be ideal, but considering that the project was likely to face teething problems in the initial period and production might be periodically affected for maintenance and technology up-gradation, 90% plant utilization would be a reasonable minimum estimate.

(d) Other assumptions: It was decided to make the following additional assumptions: an income tax rate of 30%, a 30-year plant life, a 3% annual price escalation on all plant outputs, and a 2% annual escalation in the operating cost. Most of these assumptions were the same as made in the above quoted reports except the one about income tax rate which was estimated at 40% in these reports. The assumption had been changed in view of the lower income tax rates in India in recent years.

    Initially he was not comfortable with the assumption of 2% annual escalation in the operating cost in view of the higher inflation rate that had been seen in India for the past several years. But considering that once the project matured after the initial trial period, it should benefit from the 'learning curve' effect to reduce cost, he retained the assumption. Another factor that could have a positive effect on the operating cost was that, as in other countries, the Government could be persuaded to provide some financial support, such as a long tax-holiday or operating cost subsidy in view of the high potential to save precious foreign exchange and huge employment generation. Again, the benefits expected from carbon credits would also help in reducing the operating costs. All considered, the company felt confident that given these positives, the net rise in operating cost could be contained. However, it was clear that the company would have to continuously strive hard for operational efficiencies to keep the net annual rise within this limit.

(e) All project cash flows would be assumed to occur at the end of the respective periods. Working capital investment would be recovered at the end of the project.

Estimating yearly net cash flows for the period 2019 to 2048 presented different challenges. While the plant capacity was decided at 80,000 barrels of fuel liquid per day, the price that the product could fetch per barrel would depend on the market crude oil price, adjusted for the premium or discount for the differential product quality. The crude oil prices had been highly volatile in the past few years, ranging from US$35/bbl to over US$140/bbl. The crude oil price volatility was the most critical risk factor in the financial viability of CTL projects.

Currently, in January 2012, the crude oil price was approximately $111 per barrel and, given the fact that oil demand from developed as well as emerging markets was peaking while oil reserves in the world were getting depleted with time, management found it reasonable to assume a 3% annual compound increase in crude prices over the next three decades. With this assumption, CS Table 3 presents the crude oil forecasts for next three decades. The management felt that future cash flows could be based on the forecast of crude oil prices given in CS Table 3 along with an average of 10% price premium that the CTL output would command due to superior quality.

Of course, a sense of high risk prevailed because forecasts were after all forecasts and the actual crude prices would depend on several factors impacting on global demand and supply of crude oil in future. However, with India currently importing nearly 70% of its oil requirements and the economy marching ahead at a relatively high GDP growth rate that should further boost the demand for oil products, management felt there was adequate ground to believe that the domestic demand for the CTL output would remain strong, and even if the crude oil prices plummeted on account of a world-wide recession or some other major factors, they would bounce back soon enough.

A major attraction of the CTL project was that once the plant got going, as noted above, the operating cost per US$ of revenue was expected to be much lower than that of a conventional oil refinery project. This was due to the fact that the major raw material coal came from captive mines. Thus, using an illustrative price of US$ 111 per barrel of output, the operating margin (before depreciation, interest and income taxes) would be around US$ 111 – US$ 45 = US$ 66 per barrel. That surely sounded impressive though the actual price of output would be determined by market forces, and the net return from the project would also depend on the cost of capital and taxes. The CTL Project would require about 30 MMT Run of Mine (ROM) Coal per annum. The company controlled adequate coal reserves to last 30 years.

Depreciation and amortization on the capital cost of US$9.34 billion would be charged by straight line method over the useful life of 30 years.

Financing and Cost of Capital

Jai reckoned that from lenders' point of view, the CTL would be considered a high risk project. It was the first such project in the country, it suffered from a long gestation period, future revenues would virtually depend on the highly volatile crude oil prices, and serious doubts prevailed the world over on whether the CTL projects could survive on their own merit without the Governmental support. In addition, domestic banks and lenders had no prior experience of financing such projects, and hence, in all probability would hesitate from risking their funds to the new technology.

Due to these factors, as well as considering the large size of investment required, Jai knew that they would have to look for global sources of debt capital. As an alternative, the entire project could be equity funded, but given the size of the GSPL group, it was not considered feasible. With its high goodwill in the domestic market, GSPL could launch a successful public issue of equity of a moderate size, but the amount of US$ 10 billion was regarded as too big for the Indian capital market, particularly with the 'high risk' tag attached to the project.

Hence it would be more practical to look for international sources of funding. Already there were examples of how in recent years some Indian companies had successfully raised huge capital resources from global markets. For example, when Tata Steel acquired Corus of Britain for a whopping US$ 13 billion in 2007–08, Tata Steel had embarked upon perhaps the biggest fund-raising exercise till then by an Indian company. Tata Steel had raised funds through a number of sources, including internal generation, a rights issue of equity shares, rights issue of convertible preference shares and long-term debt including foreign currency structured issues. Majority of the required funding to finance the Corus buy was raised from global capital markets, and that's what GSPL might also have to do.

The NETL (2008) report referred to above, had projected an overall or weighted average cost of capital (WACC) of 14.75% for a similar project in the USA. This calculation was based on following assumptions: a debt-equity 50:50 financing mix, cost of debt (before tax) of 9.5% (made up of LIBOR 3.5% + 6% premium for higher risk), and a 20% cost of equity, so that the WACC would be = (0.5 × 9.5%) + (0.5 × 20%) = 14.75.

In the Indian scenario, Jai knew that the cost of debt as well as equity would have to be budgeted at a higher level due to greater risk factors listed above. Preliminary enquiries with market experts revealed that it would be reasonable to assume a before tax cost of debt of 10% per annum, and given the risk factors, equity investors would expect a return of 25% to compensate them for the higher risk. He also noted that the WACC should be based on the 'after-tax' cost of debt, and not the 'before-tax' cost of debt as assumed in the NETL calculation given above, because interest paid on loans was a tax-deductible expense just like any other business expenses. As a result, the after-tax cost of debt would be lower than the before-tax cost. The debt-equity ratio could be assumed to remain 50:50. If the resulting WACC was a fraction, it would be rounded-off to the next whole number.

Jai was at his nerves end and could not wait to put together his projections and financially evaluate the project using NPV technique. He decided to first make a base level analysis even though he was aware that going by a single estimate of costs and incomes in investment planning was always risky. Therefore, he also decided to carry out a scenario analysis by changing important assumptions made in the base level calculations of NPV to check how far the viability would be affected by changes in important variables.

Note: Names of the company and persons used in the case have been changed and are not real. The case is based on secondary sources and certain assumptions. It has been prepared for the sole academic purpose of facilitating class-room discussion and interactive learning.

CS TABLE 5.3
Crude price forecast assuming 3% annual rise

Year	*Forecast Crude price*	*Year*	*Forecast Crude price*
2012	111	2031	195
2013	114	2032	200
2014	118	2033	206
2015	121	2034	213
2016	125	2035	219
2017	129	2036	226
2018	133	2037	232
2019	137	2038	239
2020	141	2039	247
2021	145	2040	254
2022	149	2041	262
2023	154	2042	269
2024	158	2043	278
2025	163	2044	286
2026	168	2045	294
2027	173	2046	303
2028	178	2047	312
2029	183	2048	322
2030	189		

Case Questions for Discussion

1. How would the CTL project be a strategic fit for GSPL and how would it enhance India's energy security?
2. According to you, what are the main opportunities, strengths, weaknesses and threats related to the project?
3. Briefly outline the relevant information that is normally required for the financial evaluation of investment proposals, and discuss how the same would be determined for the CTL project under consideration.
4. Using relevant data for the CTL project:
   (a) Calculate the annual net cash flows over the life of the project;
   (b) Determine a Weighted Average Cost of Capital (WACC);
   (c) Calculate the NPV and IRR for the project.
5. [Advanced question] Carry out single variable Monte Carlo simulation to analyze the impact of variability in 'price premium' on NPV by using data table function of excel. Generate 1000 iterations for price premium assuming a mean value of 10%, a normal distribution and a standard deviation of 1%.
6. [Advanced question] Carry out multiple variable Monte Carlo simulation or analysis on NPV by using data table function of excel. Generate 1000 iterations for the price premium, annual operating cost escalation and plant efficiency. Assume mean values to be 10%, 2% and 90% for price premium, annual operating cost escalation and plant efficiency.
7. Carry out the Scenario Analysis for the project by re-calculating the NPV under the following set of changed assumptions: (The scenarios are indicative, the participants are encouraged to create more scenarios to test the robustness of the project)

Item	*Current*	*Scenario A*	*Scenario B*	*Scenario C*	*Scenario D*
Price premium	10%	Higher by 10%	Higher by 10%	Lower by 10%	Lower by 20%
Operating cost escalation p.a.	2%	Higher by 10%	Higher by 10%	Lower by 10%	Lower by 20%
Plant efficiency	90%	Higher by 10%	Lower by 10%	Higher by 10%	Lower by 20%

8. Overall, would you recommend that the company should go ahead with the project? Why?

References

Feasibility Reports

Northern Alaska Environmental Center, USA, Center for Sustainable Economy, "Economic Feasibility of Coal to Liquid Development in Alaska's Interior", Feb. 2009. Alaska, USA. www.sustainable-economy.org.

National Energy Technology Laboratory (NETL), "Recommended Project Finance Structures for the Economic Analysis of Fossil-Based Energy Projects", USA 2009.

National Energy Technology Laboratory, Baseline Technical and Economic Assessment of a Commercial Scale Fischer-Tropsch Liquids Facility, April 2007. www.netl.doe.gov.

Online Newspaper Articles

Bhaskar, U., 2009, India fears lower crude prices could hurt coal-to-liquid plans. *Live Mint* [online] 6 Jan Available at: <http://www.livemint.com/2009/01/06212610/India-fears-lower-crude-prices.html> [Accessed on 16 April 2011].

Dash, J., 2010, India: Global Steel MoU soon for coal-to-liquid plant. *Reuters* [online] 23 March Available at: <http://uk.reuters.com/article/2010/03/23/Global-coal-india-idUKSGE62M07Q20100323> [Accessed on 14 April 2011].

Jog, A., 2008, Lurgi offers coal to liquid technology – FE. *Financial Express* [online] 14 August Available at: <http://www.financialexpress.com/news/lurgi-offers-coal-to-liquid-technology/348582/1> [Accessed on 14 April 2011].

Mjunction. Sasol keen to promote Coal-to-Liquid technology in India. [online] Available at:http://www.mjunction.in/market_news/coal_1/sasol_keen_to_promote_coaltoli.php> [Accessed on 22 April 2011].

Mukherjee, P., 2011, Global Steel scouting tech partner for coal–to-liquid foray. *DNA* [online] 29 Jan Available at: <http://www.dnaindia.com/money/report_Global-steel-scouting-tech-partner-for-coal-to-liquid-foray_1500317 > [Accessed on 22 April 2011].

Nilles, B., 2008, China Drops Coal-To-Liquid. *Sierra Club* [online] 16 Oct Available at: <http://sierraclub.typepad.com/compass/2008/10/china-drops-coa.html>[Accessed on 11 May 2011].

Shah, A., 2010, Is the Global ₹42,000 crore Coal to Liquid project in Orissa wasteful just like the Tata-Sasol CTL plant? *Green World Investor* **[online] 13 July Available at:** <http://greenworldinvestor.com/2010/07/13/is-the-Global-rs-42000-crore-coal-to-liquild-project-in-orissa-wasteful-just-like-the-tata-sasol-ctl-plant/> [Accessed on 14 April 2011].

Schutze, E. Liquid fuel from coal. [online] Available at:< http://www.mediaclubsouthafrica.com/index.php?option=com_content&view=article&catid=38:innovation_bg&id=123:liquid-fuel-from-coal>[Accessed on 28 April 2011].

Times New Network, 2009, Tata JV, GSPL bag $18bn coal-to-liquid projects. *Times of India* [online] 4 March Available at: <http://articles.timesofindia.indiatimes.com/2009-03-04/india-business/28000056_1_coal-block-coal-ministry-liquid-project> [Accessed on 16 April 2011].

Newspaper Articles

Khandari, R., 2008, Economics of coal-to-liquid fuel conversion. *The Economic Times*, 11 Aug. p. 12.

Nageshwar, P., 2011, GSPL proposes Rs 45,000 crore CTL Project in Orissa. *Economic Times,* 9 Jun. p. 8.

Tripathy, V., 2011, CTL Project: GSPL allays pollution fears. *The New Indian Express,* 9 Jun. p. 5.

Website Articles

Alliance for Synthetic Fuels in Europe, 2010. Emissions Reductions from Synthetic Fuels (Europe). *ETSAP* [online] Available at:< http://www.worldcoal.org/coal/uses-of-coal/coal-to-liquids/>[Accessed on 16 July 2011].

Global Steel and Power. Coal to Liquid Petroleum Project. [online] Available at:< http://www.Globalsteelpower.com/about-us/future-outlook.aspx > [Accessed on 22 April 2011].

Research Papers

Bharadwaj, A., Tongia, R., Arunachalam, V.S., 2007. Scoping technology options for India's oil security: Part II – Coal to liquids and bio-diesel. *Current Science.* 92(9).

CHAPTER

6

Investment Decision: Capital Rationing, Inflation and Real Options

LEARNING OBJECTIVES

After studying this chapter, you should be able to:

- Rank and evaluate projects in situations of capital rationing.
- Explain the meaning of inflation, and how it affects project evaluation.
- Differentiate between real and money rates of interest.
- Evaluate projects with unequal lives using the equivalent annual cost method.
- Explain the meaning of abandonment value and compute the NPV of projects with abandonment option.
- Differentiate between NPV and APV approaches
- Discuss the additional complications that might arise while evaluating a foreign project.

6.1 Introduction

The techniques of evaluating investment proposals discussed in the previous two chapters would be applicable to almost all situations involving capital investment in long-term projects. However, there are certain situations where additional considerations might be required in deciding on the best investment options available.

In this chapter, we take up several interesting aspects related to investment decision including project appraisal involving capital rationing and inflation, asset replacement decision, appraisal of projects involving abandonment option, adjusted present value method, appraisal of overseas projects, Indian income tax and depreciation rates, and project implementation and post-audit.

6.2 Capital Rationing

Capital rationing refers to a situation in which a firm has an upper limit on the amount of funds that can be invested in new projects during a period. Such a budget ceiling might be induced by external factors or result from self-imposed internal strategies. Government departments and public utilities must make investment decisions within the approved budget ceilings. Organizations dependent on funding by international organizations (such as the international development agencies) as well as foreign divisions of MNCs must also keep their investment initiatives within the limits of funds sanctioned.

However, often companies might self-impose certain investment ceilings as a part of their strategy, due to reasons as follows:

1. **Internal funding:** Firms relying mostly on internally generated funds would limit the capital budget in order to avoid external funding such as issuing more equity or raising more debt.
2. **Difficulty of raising new equity:** When capital markets are down and the company would not get the right price for additional shares it could issue.
3. **Uncertain environment:** When the business environment is uncertain or perceived as hostile, the firm might decide to go slow on new investments until the government policy becomes clear and supportive.
4. **Complacency:** The top management might not like to place too large an amount of funds in the hands of divisional managers lest they become complacent due to over-abundance of funds and be less rigorous in their investment decisions.
5. **Management focus:** The management might choose to focus on a few selected projects at a time rather than scatter limited managerial and technical resources over too many projects at the same time.

Capital rationing refers to a budget ceiling on the amount of funds that can be invested in new projects during a period.

In theory, it would be easy to suggest ways to resolve all the above concerns, but in practice it is often seen that companies would like to go slow and steady in making capital investments, and decide on a ceiling of investible funds available during a period such as a year.

6.2.1 Selection Criteria in Capital Rationing

A capital rationing situation implies that the firm would have more number of acceptable projects than it can undertake in a period due to the ceiling on investible funds. Suppose a firm has identified a total of 15 project proposals with a positive NPV, that would require an initial investment of ₹30 million in a period, but the amount available for funding new projects is limited to ₹20 million for the period. Going by the 'wealth maximization' objective, the firm should take up all investment proposals with a positive NPV, but given the capital rationing constraint, the firm would have to 'rank' the available investment proposals in terms of their relative profitability and actually undertake such a combination of projects that maximizes the combined NPV within the funding budget available. A method called Profitability Index that we studied earlier, can be very useful in ranking the available projects before the firm chooses the best combination of projects that would not only exhaust the budget ceiling but also yield maximum possible Net Present Value.

6.2.2 Review of Profitability Index

The Profitability Index (PI), also called the benefit-cost ratio, is the ratio of the present value of future net cash flows of a project to the initial cash investment in the project. Mathematically, it can be expressed as:

$$\text{Profitability Index (PI)} = \frac{\sum_{t=1}^{n} \frac{C_t}{(1+k)^t}}{C_o} = \frac{\text{Present Value of future net cash flows}}{\text{Initial Investment}}$$

Comparing Net Present Value (NPV) and Profitability Index (PI), the latter is particularly helpful in ranking investment proposals in situations of capital rationing. This is because the NPV method expresses the result in an absolute sum of money, and does not reflect the investment base, while PI is a ratio that clearly expresses the project's profitability in relation to its initial investment.

As compared to NPV, Profitability Index is more helpful in ranking projects, because PI expresses the project's profitability in relation to its initial investment.

If adequate information is not available to calculate the Profitability Index, the Internal Rate of Return (IRR) may be used to rank the projects in capital rationing situations, because the internal rate of return is also a measure of relative profitability of projects. However, wherever possible, the profitability index is preferred due to limitations of IRR as a method of evaluating projects as discussed in the previous chapter.

6.2.3 Divisible and Indivisible Projects

The investment projects may be classified into divisible and indivisible categories:

1. The indivisible projects: Indivisible projects are those that must be taken up in entirety; you can either take the whole project or leave it. For example, if the project relates to introducing a new product, one may either introduce the new product or not introduce. Similarly, if the firm is considering acquiring certain machinery, it can either acquire the whole machinery or leave it: you cannot acquire the machinery in parts or a fraction of the machinery.

2. The divisible projects: Divisible projects are those which may be undertaken either in entirety or any fraction of the project. Where the firm decides to undertake only a fraction of such a project, the initial project cost as well as future benefits would both be reduced proportionately.

When a project is divisible, the firm may undertake even a fraction of the project. This is not possible when projects are indivisible.

It must be acknowledged here that most projects one would come across might be of the indivisible types. However, the assumption of divisibility is important in situations of capital rationing because it would help the firm fully utilize the funding budget available. If projects are all indivisible, a part of the funding budget might not be utilized because the remaining funds fall short of the required investment to undertake the project in entirety and the firm cannot take up a fraction of the project.

Assumptions

In all situations of capital rationing, we assume projects cannot be repeated. Also, unless stated otherwise, projects are assumed to be independent of each other.

Consider the following Example 6.1.

EXAMPLE 6.1 A firm with an investible amount ceiling of ₹1,00,000 in Year 0 is considering the following six proposals with positive NPVs:

Proposal	*Initial investment*	*Net Present Value*
1	60,000	13,200
2	10,000	3,600
3	50,000	20,000
4	30,000	7,500
5	20,000	5,600
6	40,000	12,800

Assuming all projects are independent and cannot be repeated:

(a) Calculate the profitability index of the proposals.
(b) Rank the proposals in descending order of the profitability index.
(c) Select the combination of projects that would maximize the NPV within the investment ceiling given.
(d) Comment on whether your investment decision would lead to shareholders' wealth maximization.

Solution: (a) **Calculating the profitability index of the proposals**

Proposal	*Initial investment*	*Net Present Value (NPV)*	*Profitability Index (PI)*
1	60,000	13,200	1.22
2	10,000	3,600	1.36
3	50,000	20,000	1.40
4	30,000	7,500	1.25
5	20,000	5,600	1.28
6	40,000	12,800	1.32

Note: PI is calculated as a ratio of the present value of future net cash flows over the initial investment. For Proposal 1, NPV of ₹13,200 means the total present value of future net cash flows would be 60,000 + 13,200 = 73,200. Then, PI = 73,200/60,000 = 1.22. PI for other proposals has been computed in a similar manner.

(b) **Rank the proposals in descending order of the profitability index**

A careful look at the PIs of the six proposals shows that proposal number 3 with initial investment outlay of ₹50,000 has the highest PI among all proposals. This would be ranked as number 1 or most preferred proposal, followed by proposal numbers 2, 6, 5, 4 and 1, as presented in the table.

Proposal	*Initial investment*	*Net Present Value (NPV)*	*PI*	*Rank*
1	60,000	13,200	1.22	6
2	10,000	3,600	1.36	2
3	50,000	20,000	1.40	1
4	30,000	7,500	1.25	5
5	20,000	5,600	1.28	4
6	40,000	12,800	1.32	3

(c) **Select the combination of projects that would maximize the NPV within the investment ceiling given:** Based on the ranking of proposals as above, the selected combination of proposals would be as follows:

Proposal	*Initial investment*	*Net Present Value (NPV)*	*PI*	*Rank*
3	50,000	20,000	1.40	1
2	10,000	3,600	1.36	2
6	40,000	12,800	1.32	3
Total	1,00,000	36,400		

The investment amount of ₹1,00,000 would be utilized to undertake proposals 3, 2 and 6 which together would provide the firm with a net present value of ₹36,400. The NPV from this combination of proposals would be higher than any other combination of the proposals given.

(d) **Would this investment decision lead to shareholders' wealth maximization?**

The wealth maximization objective would require that the firm should take up all available investment proposals with a positive NPV. However, it is a fact that businesses all over the world have to function within the constraints of available resources, be it financial or other types of resources. Therefore, the choice of investment proposals, as above, should be regarded as wealth maximizing within the budget constraints. Over time, pro-active firms should be able to overcome the ceiling constraints and improve their performance.

In Example 6.1, the firm was able to fully utilize the investment budget without having to worry about whether the projects are divisible or not. If the projects can be assumed to be divisible, it is easier for the firm to fully utilize the investment budget. Consider Example 6.2.

EXAMPLE 6.2 A company with an initial investible amount ceiling of ₹1,00,000 in Year 0 is considering the five proposals given in the table below.

Proposal	*Initial investment*	*Cash inflow per annum to perpetuity*
1	60,000	7,500
2	20,000	2,600
3	50,000	6,750
4	30,000	3,450
5	40,000	5,800

The company's cost of capital is 10%. All projects are divisible.

Assuming all projects are independent and cannot be repeated:

(a) Calculate the NPV and profitability index of each proposal.
(b) Rank the proposals in descending order of the profitability index.
(c) Select the combination of projects that would maximize the NPV within the investment ceiling given.

Solution: (a) **Calculate the NPV and profitability index of the proposals.**

S. No.	*Initial investment*	*Cash inflow per annum for perpetuity*	*Present value* @ 10%*	*NPV*	*PI*
1	60,000	7,500	75,000	15,000	1.25
2	20,000	2,600	26,000	6,000	1.30
3	50,000	6,750	67,500	17,500	1.35
4	30,000	3,450	34,500	4,500	1.15
5	40,000	5,800	58,000	18,000	1.45

Note: Present value of an amount receivable in perpetuity = [Amount receivable per annum ÷ Discount rate expressed as a proportion]. Thus, for project 1, present value of cash inflows = 7,500 ÷ 0.10 = 75,000.

(b) **Rank the proposals in descending order of the profitability index.**

S. No.	*Initial investment*	*NPV*	*PI*	*Project rank*
1	60,000	15,000	1.25	4
2	20,000	6,000	1.30	3
3	50,000	17,500	1.35	2
4	30,000	4,500	1.15	5
5	40,000	18,000	1.45	1

(c) **Select the combination of projects that would maximize the NPV within the investment ceiling given (note that the projects are divisible):**

S. No.	*Initial investment*	*NPV*	*PI*	*Project rank*
5	40,000	18,000	1.45	1
3	50,000	17,500	1.35	2

So far the company has allocated a total of ₹90,000 of investment funds, leaving a balance of ₹10,000. As the projects are assumed to be divisible (the firm can undertake a fraction of the project), the balance ₹10,000 would be invested to undertake 50% of proposal number 2 that was ranked number 3 as per the profitability index. The final combination of projects and the collective NPV from them would be as follows:

Project	*Initial investment*	*NPV*	*PI*	*Project rank*
5 [Full]	40,000	18,000	1.45	1
3 [Full]	50,000	17,500	1.35	2
2 [50%]	10,000	3,000	1.30	3
Total	1,00,000	38,500		

Note: As only 50% of project number 2 would be undertaken, both the initial investment and NPV of the project have been reduced by half.

You may be wondering how the investment decision would be different in the above illustration if the projects had been indivisible rather than divisible as assumed. Let us analyze.

EXAMPLE 6.3 Assume the same data as in the previous question, except that **the projects are indivisible**; you could either undertake the full project or give it up.

Select the combination of projects that would maximize the NPV within the investment ceiling, given that projects are indivisible.

Solution: Knowing that the projects are indivisible, the company would try out different combinations to exhaust the investment limit as well as maximize the collective NPV. Since the company can either take a project in entirety or leave it, the available combinations of full projects would be:

Projects combined	*Combined investment*	*Combined NPV*
5 + 3	90,000	35,500
2 + 3 + 4	1,00,000	28,000
1 + 5	1,00,000	33,000

If the company is determined to exhaust the investment budget, it could go for combining projects 1 and 5. However, such a combination would not yield the maximum NPV. If the objective is to maximize the NPV, the company would invest only ₹90,000 for getting a NPV of ₹35,500. Thus, when projects are indivisible, the company may have to live with sub-optimal investment decisions.

In this section, we have considered a single period (year 0) capital rationing situations. The ceiling on capital budget might last a single year or could extend to two or more years. When capital rationing lasts for several periods, the situation could become complex and would need the help of computer programming or other techniques. However, the main principles remain the same.

6.3 Inflation and Project Evaluation

Inflation refers to a general rise in the prices of goods and services in an economy, during a period (usually a year). Inflation results in a decline in the purchasing power of money. Suppose the rate of inflation in the economy has been 6% per annum. As a result, the basket of goods and services that could be purchased for ₹100 now would cost ₹(100 × 1.06) = 106 next year.

Inflation affects the households and businesses alike. Just as inflation results in an increase in the kitchen expenses and cost of living for the household sector, inflation can increase the cost of inputs (such as cost of materials, labour and utilities) for business firms. However, unlike the household sector, business firms are often able to pass on the rise in input costs to the consumers by raising the selling prices of their products.

Business firms may therefore be affected by inflation both on the revenue side as well as the cost of inputs.

Effect of Inflation on Revenue

How far a firm can raise the product prices to cover its rising cost of inputs would depend on the competition and market situation. The increase in product prices may be less than, equal to or at times even more than the rise in input costs. When an economy is witnessing inflationary trends, people may develop a mind-set of 'expecting' the prices to rise; business firms may often take advantage of this inflationary preparedness of the customers to raise prices of their products.

Effect of Inflation on Input Costs

Inflation would usually be expected to increase the cost of raw materials and other inputs of a business. However, the cost of raw materials and other inputs may not rise or fall at the same rate as the general rate of inflation in the economy. For example, it may be that while the general rate of inflation in the economy is 6% per annum, the prices of iron ore (used as a raw material by steel making companies) could rise by over 10% per annum. Depending on the demand–supply situation in the specific materials (and other inputs) used by a firm, the increase in inputs costs may be less than, equal to or more than the general rate of inflation in the economy.

6.3.1 Inflation and the Cost of Capital

Inflation refers to a general rise in the prices of goods and services in an economy during a period and results in a decline in the purchasing power of money.

An important element in the appraisal of investment projects is the cost of capital or the discount rate used to calculate the project's Net Present Value. Do you think the cost of capital would be affected by inflation?

To answer the question, let us put ourselves in the shoes of a lender. Banks and other money lenders are as affected by inflation as the rest of us. Suppose a lender wants to earn a 'real' interest of 10% per annum (for letting you use his money for one year) in addition to being compensated for the effect of inflation. Assuming the inflation rate to be 6% per annum, what would be the 'money' or nominal rate of interest charged by him?

From the above example, it should be clear that 'real' interest rates exclude the effect of inflation, while the 'money' (or nominal) rates of interest are inclusive of the effect of inflation. The relationship between the real interest rate, money interest rate and inflation may be expressed as follows:

$$(1+r)=\frac{(1+m)}{(1+i)}$$

where,

r = Real interest rate,
m = Money or nominal rate of interest, and
i = Inflation rate

Note that all three (r, m and i) should be expressed as a proportion.

Then, the money rate of interest 'm' could be calculated as follows:

$$(1 + m) = (1 + r) \times (1 + i)$$
$$= (1 + 0.10) \times (1 + 0.06) = 1.166$$
$$m = 0.166 \text{ or } 16.6\%$$

To cross-check, if we are given that the money rate of interest is 16.6% and inflation rate is 6%, what would be the real rate of interest?

$$(1+r)=\frac{(1+m)}{(1+i)}$$
$$(1 + r) = (1 + 0.166) \div (1 + 0.06)$$
$$= 1.10$$

Then, $r = 0.10$ or 10%.

EXAMPLE 6.4 The money or nominal rate of interest on a loan is 14% per annum. If the rate of inflation is 6% per annum, what is the real rate of interest?

$$(1+r)=\frac{(1+m)}{(1+i)}$$
$$(1 + \text{r}) = (1 + 0.14) \div (1 + 0.06)$$
$$= 1.0755$$

Then real rate of interest (r) = 0.0755 or 7.55% per annum.

6.3.2 Approaches to Deal with Inflation

We can use one of the following two approaches to deal with inflation in investment decision:

1. Use the money (nominal) cash flows as well as the money (nominal) cost of capital related to the project being considered. In this approach, the project cash flows as well as the cost of capital should include the effect of inflation.
2. Use the 'real' (unadjusted for inflation) cash flows as well as the cost of capital related to the project being considered. In this approach, the project cash flows as well as the cost of capital should exclude the effect of inflation.

The relationship between the real interest rate (r), money interest rate (m) and inflation (i) is expressed by:

$$(1 + r) = \frac{(1 + m)}{(1 + i)}$$

To conclude, the project cash flows and cost of capital should either both be estimated on 'real' basis or both of them can be taken on nominal basis. Other things being equal, either of these approaches should lead to the same conclusion regarding acceptability of the project. Consider the following example.

EXAMPLE 6.5 The cash flows related to a project before considering the effect of inflation are given below:

Year	*Cash flow*
0	–50,000
1	16,000
2	16,000
3	16,000
4	16,000

The money (nominal) cost of capital of the company is 15% per annum, which includes the effect of inflation that is estimated to be 6.48% per annum.

(a) Calculate the NPV of the project using real cash flows and cost of capital.

(b) Calculate the NPV of the project using money (nominal) cash flows and cost of capital.

***Solution*: (a) Calculating the NPV of the project using real cash flows and cost of capital.** The cash flows are already given in real terms without the effect of inflation. The given cost of capital is in money terms that can be converted into real cost of capital as follows:

$$(1+r) = \frac{(1+m)}{(1+i)}$$

$$(1 + r) = (1 + 0.15) \div (1 + 0.0648)$$

$$= 1.08$$

Then, $r = 0.08$ or 8% approximately.

Using the real cost of capital of 8%, we calculate the project's NPV as follows:

Year	*Cash flow*	*PVF@8%*	*PV*
0	–50,000	1.0000	–50,000
1	16,000	0.9259	14,814
2	16,000	0.8573	13,717
3	16,000	0.7938	12,702
4	16,000	0.7350	11,760
			NPV = 2,993

(b) **Calculating the NPV of the project using money (nominal) cash flows and cost of capital.** In order to evaluate the project in terms of money (nominal) cash flows and cost of capital, the given 'real' cash flows will have to be first converted into nominal cash flows by increasing them at 6.48% annual compound rate to include the effect of inflation. Allowing for some approximation (due to rounding off), the Net Present Value would be calculated as follows:

Year	*Cash flow*	*Nominal cash flows (increased @6.48% p.a.*	*PVF @15%*	*PV*
0	–50,000	–50,000	1.0000	–50,000
1	16,000	17,037	0.8696	14,815
2	16,000	18,141	0.7561	13,717
3	16,000	19,317	0.6575	12,701
4	16,000	20,568	0.5718	11,760
				NPV* = 2,993

Note * There may be a small difference due to rounding off.

To deal with inflation, the project cash flows and cost of capital should either both be estimated on 'real' basis or both of them can be taken on nominal basis.

As Example 6.5 shows the two approaches should give the same results provided the same rate of inflation is applied to all variables. Therefore, if the adjustment for inflation is made, it should be made for the cash flows as well the cost of capital. Otherwise, both these elements can be taken on 'real' terms for project evaluation.

As was mentioned in a previous section, it is not necessary that the sales revenue or the cost of raw materials and other inputs may rise or fall at the same rate as the general rate of inflation in the economy. Where relevant information is available, the rates of inflation specifically applicable to different variables should be taken into account. Consider the following example.

EXAMPLE 6.6 Kinderjoy Company is considering a project to replace its existing machinery with more sophisticated machinery that would cost ₹80,000 in Year 0. Due to greater efficiency, the machinery would result in a material cost saving of ₹30,000 per annum and savings in labour and variable overhead of ₹10,000 per annum. The machine will have a useful life of four years, after which there will be no resale value. The estimates of savings in material and labour costs have been made at current (year 0) prices without including the effect of inflation.

The cost of capital is 16% in nominal terms. It is estimated that the following rates of inflation would prevail in next four years:

Variable	*Inflation per annum*
General inflation in economy	7%
Material cost	4%
Labour cost	8%

Calculate the project's NPV and decide if it should be accepted.

Solution:

Step 1: Convert real (current prices) savings into nominal values for four years.

Note: The rates of inflation estimated specifically for material cost (4%) and labour (8%) would be used, and not the general inflation rate which is not relevant in this situation:

	Material cost savings			*Labour cost and overheads*			*Total*
Year	*CF as given*	*Inflation adjustment*	*CF in nominal terms*	*CF as given*	*Inflation*	*Nominal*	*(₹)*
1	30,000	(1.04)	31,200	10,000	(1.08)	10,800	42,000
2	30,000	$(1.04)^2$	32,448	10,000	$(1.08)^2$	11,664	44,112
3	30,000	$(1.04)^3$	33,746	10,000	$(1.08)^3$	12,597	46,343
4	30,000	$(1.04)^4$	35,096	10,000	$(1.08)^4$	13,605	48,701

Step 2: Calculating the project's NPV using the total cash savings in nominal terms (note that the cost of capital is also stated in nominal terms):

Year	*Cash flow (₹)*	*PVF @16%*	*Present value*
0	–80,000	1	–80,000
1	42,000	0.8621	36,208
2	44,112	0.7432	32,784
3	46,343	0.6407	29,692
4	48,701	0.5523	26,898
			NPV = 45,582

The project has a positive NPV and is therefore acceptable.

6.4 Projects Involving Assets of Unequal Lives

Managers may often be confronted with a situation where they must choose between two mutually exclusive assets that would essentially perform the same function: one of them with longer useful life being more expensive, while the other being less expensive but having shorter useful life. Suppose a power company chooses between two transformers: the costly one having a useful life of 10 years and cheaper one with a useful life of 5 years. Some other differences between them might also exist: the maintenance and operating costs related to the expensive equipment would be typically lower than the cheaper one throughout their respective lives. What should the manager do?

When two mutually exclusive assets have significantly different lives, it would not be appropriate to evaluate them by conventional methods such as the payback or the NPV. For example, comparing the NPV of costs attached to an equipment with a useful life of 5-year with the NPV of costs attached to an equipment with a useful life of 10 years would not be like comparing apples with apples. Other things being equal, the present value of the costs related to the 5-year proposal might most likely be lower and that would apparently seem to be the right choice. However, such a choice would be wrong because it does not include the cost of providing the asset for years 6–10, when again the firm would require the services of a similar asset.

The important point to note is that two mutually exclusive projects with unequal lives can be compared only when we cover their respective costs and benefits for a 'common' period. In the above example, we should compare the cost-benefits of the two proposals over a 'common period' of ten years.

Two mutually exclusive projects with unequal lives can be compared only when we cover their respective costs and benefits for a 'common' period.

However, an alternative and better way is to use the Equivalent Annual Cost (EAC) method described as follows:

6.4.1 The Equivalent Annual Cost (EAC) Method

To compute equivalent annual cost (EAC), calculate the PV of the costs over full life-cycle of the asset, and then convert it into EAC by using the annuity present value factor.

The Equivalent Annual Cost (EAC) method calculates the equivalent cost of owning and using an asset over a common period of one year. The EAC method has been developed to overcome the problem of different time-scales involved in mutually exclusive projects.

For each proposal, we calculate the present value of the estimated costs over a full life-cycle of the asset, and then convert it into Equivalent Annual Cost (EAC) by using the annuity present value factor. The result would provide us with the equivalent cost of owning and operating each of the competing equipment for a common period of one year, and thus facilitate their comparative evaluation. Consider the following example.

EXAMPLE 6.7 The management of Crona Company is considering two mutually exclusive machines code named X and Y. X would cost ₹2,00,000 and have a useful life of 10 years, while Y would cost ₹1,40,000 and have a useful life of 5 years. Relevant data including the maintenance and operating costs during their respective useful lives is provided as follows:

Items	*Machine X cash flow*	*Machine Y cash flow*
Machine price [Year 0]	2,00,000	1,40,000
Annual repairs cost	10,000	14,000
Annual operating cost	20,000	25,000
Trade-in value*	20,000	10,000

Note: *The trade-in value at the end of the machine's life.

Assume the cost of capital of the company is 12%.

Using the Equivalent Annual Cost (EAC) method, evaluate the two machines and recommend which one should be purchased.

Solution: For each machine, first calculate the present value of costs during the life-cycle of the machine and then divide the result by the appropriate annuity PV factor.

Machine X
[Useful Life = 10 Years]

Items	*Years*	*Cash flow (₹)*	*PVF @ 12 %*	*Present value (₹)*
Machine price	0	2,00,000	1.0000	2,00,000
Annual repairs	1–10	10,000	5.6502	56,502
Operating cost	1–10	20,000	5.6502	1,13,004
Trade-in value*	10	–20,000	0.3220	–6,440
			Total PV	3,63,066
Annuity PV factor [n = 10, r = 12%]				5.6502
Annualized equivalent = 3,63,066/5.6502 =				64,257

*The trade-in value represents the exchange value or resale value of the asset and being a cash inflow, would be deducted to calculate the net cost of using the asset.

Machine Y
[Useful Life = 5 Years]

Item	*Years*	*Cash flow (₹)*	*PVF @12%*	*Present value (₹)*
Machine price	0	1,40,000	1.0000	1,40,000
Annual repairs	1–5	14,000	3.6048	50,467
Operating cost	1–5	25,000	3.6048	90,120
Trade-in value	5	–10,000	0.5674	–5,674
			Total PV	2,74,913
Annuity PV Factor [n = 5, r = 12%]				3.6048
Annualized Equivalent = 2,74,913/3.6048 =				76,263

Machine X should be preferred, because it has lower equivalent annual cost of owning and running the machine.

6.4.2 Asset Replacement and Equivalent Annual Cost

Some fixed assets may be providing such essential services that would be perpetually required by the firm for all times into the future. Therefore, when one such asset runs out of its economic useful life, it would be replaced with a similar new asset, and so on. Examples of such fixed assets would be transformers (required by power companies), computers, delivery vans, air-conditioners, certain types of machinery and equipment. Due to the perpetual need for their services, such assets need to be replaced at regular intervals, because with time, their efficiency declines, and the cost of maintaining and operating them goes on increasing.

Assume your firm is currently having a computer for which you wish to determine the optimal replacement cycle, that is, how frequently should the computer be replaced? Should the firm replace it after every 1, 2 or 3 years?

The equivalent annual cost method can be used to determine the optimal replacement cycle for assets that would be continuously required by the firm for the foreseeable future. All relevant information pertaining to the equipment including its purchase price, annual repairs and maintenance, other operating costs, exchange (trade-in) value at the time of replacement, and taxes, if applicable, can be considered to calculate the equivalent annual cost for each of the replacement cycle before taking a final decision. Consider the following example.

The EAC method can be used to decide the optimal replacement cycle for assets that would always be needed by the firm for the foreseeable future.

EXAMPLE 6.8 Chris Company wants to decide the replacement policy for computers. The relevant information has been provided as follows:

Purchase cost of computer: ₹50,000
Cost of annual maintenance contract: ₹5,000
Trade-in value at the end of Year 1 = ₹35,000
Year 2 = ₹25,000
Year 3 = ₹6,000

Assume the cost of capital is 10%. Annual maintenance cost is to be paid even in the year of replacement. Ignore taxes and inflation.

Using the equivalent annual cost method, calculate the optimal replacement cycle of computers.

Solution: For each replacement cycle, first calculate the present value of costs during a single cycle and then divide the result by the appropriate annuity PV factor, explained as follows:

- **Replace every year:** If the computer is replaced at the end of every year, cash flows and present values would be as follows:

	Year 0	*Year 1*
Price	–50,000	
Maintenance		–5,000
Trade-in value		**35,000**
Net cash flows	–50,000	30,000
PV Factor @ 10%	1.0000	0.9091
Present Value	–50,000	27,273

NPV = –50,000 + 27,273 = –22,727
Annuity PV factor (APVF) [n = 1, r = 10%] 0.9091
Equivalent Annual Cost = NPV ÷ APVF = –22,727 ÷ 0.9091= –24,999

Thus, to replace the computer every year the company would have to set aside a sum of ₹24,999 per year.

- **Replace every two years:** If the computer is replaced at the end of every 2nd year, cash flows and present values would be as follows:

	Year 0	*Year 1*	*Year 2*
Price	–50,000		
Maintenance		–5,000	–5,000
Trade-in value			**25,000**
Net cash flows	–50,000	–5,000	20,000
Pv factor @ 10%	1	0.9091	0.8264
Present value	–50,000	–4545	16,528
NPV = (–50,000 – 4,545 + 16,528) = –38,018			
Annuity PV factor (APVF) [n = 2, r = 10%] 1.7355			
Equivalent annual cost = NPV ÷ APVF = –38,018 ÷ 1.7355= –21,906			

To replace the computer every two years, the company would have to set aside a sum of ₹21,906 per year. Thus, replacing the computers every two years is more economical than replacing them every year.

- **Replace every three years**

	Year 0	*Year 1*	*Year 2*	*Year 3*
Price	–50,000			
Maintenance		–5,000	–5,000	–5,000
Trade-in value				**6,000**
Net cash flows	–50,000	–5,000	–5,000	1,000
Pv factor @ 10%	1	0.9091	0.8264	0.7513
Present value	–50,000	–4,545.5	–4,132	751
NPV =				–57,926
Annuity PV Factor (APVF) [n = 3, r = 10%] 2.4869				
Equivalent annual cost = NPV/APVF = –57,926 ÷ 2.4869 = –23,293				

To replace the computer every three years, the company would have to set aside a sum of ₹23,293 per year. Thus, replacing the computers every three years is more expensive than replacing them every two years. Therefore, the optimal replacement period for computers would be every two years as this replacement cycle gives the company least equivalent annual cost.

6.4.3 Assessment of the Equivalent Annual Cost Method

The equivalent annual cost method has been criticized for the following limitations:

1. Risk differences: The method assumes that the alternative proposals being considered have the same risk profile. If one alternative is more risky than the other, then the equivalent annual cost would not be meaningful, because it does not take into account the risk differences between proposals.

2. Technology: The method assumes there would be no technological changes in future periods and the same type of equipment would be continuously purchased again and again.

3. Inflation: The impact of inflation in future periods may alter all calculations. The purchase prices of the equipment under consideration might rise with inflation and so would the cost of repairs and maintenance.

Most of the above concerns can be built into the calculation of equivalent annual cost, if relevant and reliable information is available. Therefore, these are not serious limitations of the method. However, the method should not be used for evaluating independent proposals. It is mainly useful while comparing two mutually exclusive proposals when there is a significant difference in the project lives of proposals being considered.

6.5 Real Options in Project Investments

The concept of 'options' was first developed with reference to investments in financial securities, such as shares and bonds, and later got extended to project investments. To differentiate between the two, the options embedded in project investments are called 'real' options as distinct from 'financial' options related to investments in financial securities, such as shares and bonds. Thus, the application of options theory for project evaluation is a relatively new concept.

The options embedded in project investments are called 'real' options as distinct from 'financial' options related to investments in shares and bonds.

Real options involve situations where a firm is evaluating a project that would give it an option to exploit certain further opportunities in future, beyond the initial phase of the project being considered. In other words, real options give the firm a choice to decide on further follow-on action sometime in the future. The option to take further follow-on action in future could relate to the following choices: (a) option to expand, (b) option to abandon the project or (c) option to 'wait' (buy time) before undertaking the project. These options are discussed in the following sections.

6.5.1 The Option to Expand

Often you may come across news items talking about a foreign company entering the Indian market, and introducing its first products in a few key cities before deciding on whether to launch the product on a national scale. When the firm is introducing a new product or entering a new market, it may look at the project in two phases: the initial phase of testing the market, and learning the tricks of the trade before deciding on launching the full-scale operations in the second phase. Such an option to expand would minimize losses if the new product did not succeed, and yet the company would keep its options open to expand if the product meets with initial success.

To evaluate the option to expand (in terms of its value to the firm), the firm would need to consider relevant variables, such as (i) the time when the option can be exercised, (ii) investment (cash outflow) needed for the expansion, (iii) the present values of the future net cash flows resulting from the expansion, (iv) probability distribution of the cash flows and (v) the required rate of return.

With the option to expand, the project evaluation would involve three steps: (a) calculate the NPV of the project's initial phase (without expansion), (b) calculate the standalone NPV of the expansion phase, and (c) finally calculate the overall NPV of the project including the expansion, compare the results and decide. Consider Example 6.9.

To evaluate the option to expand, compare the project's NPV with and without the option to expand.

EXAMPLE 6.9 The Spark Company is considering a proposal to launch a new product that will be initially introduced in a few select cities as a pilot project. The company has estimated a negative Net Present Value of ₹12,500 on the basis of first four years' estimated production and sales of the product. If the product launch is successful during this period, the company would have the option to expand its operations at an additional investment of ₹50,000. There is an 80% probability that the product launch will be successful. If the product launch is not successful, the company would not invest the additional ₹50,000.

The production and sales of the product are likely to be much higher during the expansion phase and company has made the following estimates of the additional cash inflows from the expansion project:

Years	*Sales*	*Cash inflow per annum*	*Probability*
5–10	High	32,000	0.6
5–10	Low	24,000	0.4

The company's required rate of return is 10%.

Calculate the NPV of the expansion option as well as the whole project including the expansion. Should the company accept the project?

Solution: The negative NPV indicates that the project is not acceptable on the basis of the expected performance during the initial phase. However, the company is looking at the long-term prospects and would like to include the expansion phase in the project evaluation.

To evaluate the investment proposal, we should first calculate the NPV of the expansion option as given in the table below:

		Expansion Phase			
		High cash flow		*Low cash flow*	
Year	*PVF @10%*	*P = 0.6*	*PV @10%*	*P = 0.4*	*PV @10%*
4	0.6830	–50,000	–34,150	–50,000	–34,150
5	0.6209	32,000	19,869	24,000	14,902
6	0.5645	32,000	18,064	24,000	13,548
7	0.5132	32,000	16,422	24,000	12,317
8	0.4665	32,000	14,928	24,000	11,196
9	0.4241	32,000	13,571	24,000	10,178
10	0.3855	32,000	12,336	24,000	9,252
			PV = 61,040		PV = 37,243

Expected value of NPV from expansion phase = 61,040*0.6 + 37,243*0.4
= ₹51,521.2

However, note that the expansion project can be undertaken only if the initial product launch is successful which has a probability of 0.80 for success, and a probability of 0.20 for failure. Hence, the value of the expansion option would be:

= 0.8[51,521.2] + 0.2[0] = 41,217

Now we can compute the NPV of the full project

= NPV of initial phase + NPV of the expansion phase
= ₹–12,500 + 41,217 = 28,717.

Conclusion: The NPV of the initial project was negative (₹–12,500) and the project would have been rejected on a standalone basis, but the option to expand has added substantial value (₹41,217) to the project so that overall it has become acceptable.

6.5.2 The Option to Abandon

An important feature of the investment decision is that once a project is undertaken, the funds would remain committed for a long time, and it is very difficult to reverse the decision. As a result, if the investment decision turns out to be a bad one, the future prospects of the company might be severely damaged. However, things could be different and the company might get a chance to cash out of a bad project if the company has an option to abandon the project after it has been undertaken. Options have the advantage of limiting the possible losses, while allowing the company to benefit if good times prevail.

Abandonment means divesting from a project, and the abandonment value might come in several possible ways. At times, the supplier of plant and equipment might give the buying firm an option to abandon and return the plant and equipment within a stipulated time period against a pre-determined abandonment value. In other situations, the firm could sell the project in the market to realize the abandonment or resale value. Another way of abandonment could be to re-employ the asset in some other project within the firm where the firm would have to buy another similar asset, if this one was not shifted.

To evaluate the option to abandon, we would have to compare the value of the project with and without the abandonment value. In general, it would make sense to abandon a project when the present value of all future cash flows from the project is less than its current abandonment value. If the company has a wide flexibility of time when to abandon (for example, the company could have the option to abandon any time between years 1 to 3), then the project should be abandoned at a point of time that maximizes the project NPV.

With the option to abandon, total value of the project would equal NPV of the project without abandonment option plus the value of the abandonment option.

When a project being considered has an embedded option to abandon, the total value of the project would equal the NPV of the project without the abandonment option, plus the value of the abandonment option. The abandonment option can, at times, substantially increase the NPV of a project. Consider the following example.

EXAMPLE 6.10 Roadies Company is considering a new project which will require an initial investment of ₹50,000. The company is not certain about the future returns and has made cash flow estimates with probabilities as follows:

Annual Net Cash Flows after Taxes

Year 1		*Year 2*		*Joint probability [Year 1 × Year 2]*
Year 1 CF	*Prob*	*Year 2 CF*	*Prob*	
25,000	0.25	15,000	0.6	0.150
		35,000	0.4	0.100
35,000	0.50	30,000	0.6	0.300
		50,000	0.4	0.200
45,000	0.25	35,000	0.6	0.150
		55,000	0.4	0.100

The company has the option to abandon the project at the end of year 1 for an abandonment value of ₹30,000. Assume the company's cost of capital is 12%.

(a) Calculate the expected value of the project cash flows and the project NPV without the abandonment option.

(b) For each level of year 1 cash flow, compare the discounted value of the year 2 cash flows with the abandonment value as at the end of year 1. Should the company abandon? Why?

(c) Calculate the expected NPV of the project with the abandonment option.

Solution:

(a) Calculate the expected value of the project cash flows and the project NPV without the abandonment option.

Year 1 CF	*PVF @12%*	*PV*	*Prob*	*EV*	*Year 2 CF*	*PVF*	*PV*	*Cond. Prob*	*E(PV) PV(P)*
25,000	0.8929	22,322.5	0.25	5,581	15,000	0.7972	11,958	0.150	1,794
			0.25		35,000	0.7972	27,902	0.100	2,790
35,000	0.8929	31,251.5	0.5	15,626	30,000	0.7972	23,916	0.300	7,175
			0.5		50,000	0.7972	39,860	0.200	7,972
45,000	0.8929	40,180.5	0.25	10,045	35,000	0.7972	27,902	0.150	4,185
			0.25		55,000	0.7972	43,846	0.100	4,385
				31,252					28,301
	NPV = 31,252 + 28,301 – 50,000 = 9,553								

NPV = Expected value of year 1 cash flows + Expected value of year 2 cash flows – Initial investment

= ₹31,252 + 28,301 – 50,000 = ₹9,553

(b) To compare the discounted value of Year 2 cash flows and the abandonment value as at the end of Year 1.

For each level of year 1 cash flow, we should compare the discounted value of the year 2 cash flows and the abandonment value 'as at the end of year 1'. Note that the comparison should be made as at the end of year 1; therefore, year 2 cash flows would be discounted only for one year at the given cost of capital of 12%. This is shown as follows:

(i) If the first year cash flow is ₹25,000, then the comparison of abandonment value with discounted value of year 2 cash flow as at end of year 1 would be as follows:

Year 2 cash flow	*Prob.*	*Expected value of cash flow*	*PVF @ 12%*	*PV at end of Year 1*
15,000	0.6	9,000	0.8929	8,036.1
35,000	0.4	14,000	0.8929	12,500.6
Total PV of 2nd year cash flow				20,536.7
Abandonment value				30,000
Discounted cash flow less abandonment value				–9,463.3

If the year 1 cash flow is ₹25,000, then the year 2 cash flows multiplied by the respective probabilities and discounted for one year (at the cost of capital of 12%) give a discounted value lesser than the abandonment value at the same time. Since the abandonment value is higher, it would be advisable to abandon the project at the end of Year 1.

(ii) If the first year cash flow is ₹35,000, then the comparison of abandonment value with discounted value of year 2 cash flow as at the end of year 1 would be as follows:

Year 2 cash flow	*Prob.*	*Expected value of cash flow*	*PVF@12%*	*PV at end of Year 1*
30,000	0.6	18,000	0.8929	16,072.2
50,000	0.4	20,000	0.8929	17,858.0
Total PV of 2nd year cash flow				33,930.2
Abandonment value				30,000
Discounted cash flow less abandonment value				3,930.2

If the year 1 cash flow is ₹35,000, then the year 2 cash flows multiplied by the respective probabilities and discounted for one year (at the cost of capital of 12%) give a discounted value of more than the abandonment value at the same time, and therefore, it would be advisable not to abandon the project at the end of year.

(iii) If the first year cash flow is ₹45,000, then the comparison of abandonment value with discounted value of year 2 cash flow as at the end of year 1 would be as follows:

Year 2 cash flow	*Prob.*	*Expected value of cash flow*	*PVF @12%*	*PV at the end of Year 1*
35,000	0.6	21,000	0.8929	18,750.9
55,000	0.4	22,000	0.8929	19,643.8
Total PV of 2nd year cash flow				38,394.7
Abandonment value				30,000
Discounted cash flow less abandonment value				8,394.7

If the year 1 cash flow is ₹45,000, then the year 2 cash flows multiplied by the respective probabilities, and discounted for one year (at the cost of capital of 12%) give a discounted value of more than the abandonment value at the same time, and therefore, it would be advisable not to abandon the project at the end of Year 1.

To conclude, if the first year cash flow is ₹25,000 then it is advisable to abandon the project. In other two given scenarios (first year cash flows of ₹35,000 and ₹45,000, respectively), the project should not be abandoned.

(c) Calculate the expected NPV of the project with the abandonment option:

In the first scenario, since the firm would abandon the project, total first year cash flow would become 25,000 + 30,000 = 55,000 while the year 2 cash flow in that situation would be nil. Substituting these values we get:

Year 1 CF	*PVF @12%*	*PV*	*Prob*	*E(PV)** of CF*	*Year 2 CF*	*PVF*	*PV*	*Joint Prob*	*E(PV) of CF*
55,000*	0.8929	49,109.5	0.25	12,277	0				0
35,000	0.8929	31,251.5	0.5	15,626	30,000	0.7972	23,916	0.300	7,175
			0.5		50,000	0.7972	39,860	0.200	7,972
45,000	0.8929	40,180.5	0.25	10,045	35,000	0.7972	27,902	0.150	4,185
			0.25		55,000	0.7972	43,846	0.100	4,385
				37,948					**23,717**

Note *Cash flow inclusive of abandonment value = 25,000 + 30,000 = 55,000.
**E(PV) = Expected Present Value

NPV = Expected value of year 1 cash flows + Expected value of year 2 cash flows – Initial investment

= 37,948 + 23,717 – 50,000 = ₹11,665

Conclusion: The expected NPV of the project without abandonment value was ₹9,553 while it is ₹11,665 with the abandonment value. Thus, the expected NPV of the project has enhanced because of the option to abandon at the end of year 1. Therefore, it would be advisable to undertake the project and if the first year cash flow is ₹25,000 then it is advisable to abandon the project; if the first year witnesses better cash flow (say ₹35,000), then there is no need to abandon and the project should be continued.

6.5.3 The Option to 'Wait' or Postpone

There are occasions when a decision must be made to either undertake the project 'now or never', that is, if the project is not undertaken immediately, the opportunity might be lost forever and the project proposal would have to be dropped. One such time in India was before the Commonwealth Games of 2010; a large number of infrastructure and other projects were in a state that if not completed in time for the Commonwealth games, they would lose their relevance and a great market opportunity. However, in most of the other situations, the company considering a project might have the option to either undertake the project now or postpone it to a future period.

There might be several reasons why a firm would consider postponing the project, including the need for more information about product demand, interest rates or Government policy. If there is an uncertainty about certain critical factors that could affect the success of the project, the company should consider waiting until more information becomes available to give it the confidence to undertake the project. Faced with uncertainty, a company would better wait and tread cautiously rather than act in haste and repent in leisure!

The evaluation of the option to postpone the project should be based on a cost-benefit analysis and its possible impact on the project's future cash flows. The 'waiting' period would be used to get more certain information on the emerging business environment as well as tying up reliable sources of plant and equipment, raw materials and other critical inputs that would go a long way in improving the quality of estimated future cash flows. On the negative side, postponement could result in loss of cash flows in the intervening period as well as the loss of the first-mover advantage to capture the market before competition set in. To the extent possible, the impact of both quantifiable and subjective factors should be carefully analyzed before deciding on whether to postpone the project.

6.6 The Adjusted Present Value (APV) Method

We have discussed in a previous chapter that the Net Present Value (NPV) approach based on discounted cash flow method is a scientific way of appraising projects. In certain situations of project evaluation, a modification of NPV called the Adjusted Present Value (APV) method would be more suitable. Before we explain the APV, it would be appropriate to review the NPV method.

Review of NPV Method

Net Present Value is the excess of the present value of cash inflows over the present value of cash outflows relating to a project, when all future cash flows have been discounted at the required rate of return. The required rate of return would be the weighted average cost of capital that represents the minimum acceptable return from the project.

Mathematically, Net Present Value (NPV) can be presented as follows:

$$\text{NPV} = \sum_{t=0}^{n} \frac{C_t}{(1+k)^t}$$

where:

- C_t is the net cash flow for period 't' whether it is a net cash outflow or inflow, 't' = 0 to 'n' periods and 'n' is the last period in which cash flow is expected. Net cash flow of period 't_0' would usually be a cash outflow representing the initial project investment, while in other periods, the net cash flow would be equal to operating cash inflows (sales revenue and other incomes) less operating cash expenses as well as any further investments made in to the project at that period.
- Each cash flow C_t is discounted by the discount factor $(1 + k)^t$ where 'k' is the weighted average cost of capital defined as:

$$k = aK_e + (1 - a)(1 - T)K_d$$

where 'K_e' is the cost of equity capital, 'K_d' is the pre-tax cost of debt, 'T' is the corporate tax rate and 'a' is the proportion of equity finance for the project.

You would recall that the decision rules using the NPV method are: accept a project if it has a positive NPV; reject the project with a negative NPV. Now let us turn our attention to the APV method.

6.6.1 The APV Approach: Rationale and Steps

The APV approach separates the effects of any specific financing sources used from the NPV of the project. A project is initially evaluated as if it was an all-equity funded investment, and then the resulting NPV is adjusted for any benefits that debt financing (or other special funding method used) could bring in as 'add-on' benefits.

Thus, APV involves the following steps:

1. **Evaluate the project as if it is entirely funded by equity**. Accordingly, the unlevered cost of equity would be used as the rate of discount to compute the NPV.
2. **Now add the present value of all cash benefits (after taxes) that would arise from any special financing features** of the project, such as debt financing and special Government subsidies, etc.

   Note that the **discount rate used** to determine the present value of such cash flows **should reflect the risk associated** with such cash flows. For example, if the company intends to use debt funding to part-finance the project, the main benefits of debt financing would relate to the tax-shield on interest expenses. Such benefits (cash flows) should be discounted at a rate equal to the company's cost of debt itself because the cash inflows related to tax-shield benefits would carry the same degree of risk as the debt funding.
3. **The issue expenses (floatation costs),** if any, incurred in issuing new equity shares or raising debt (including the cost of advertisements, printing of prospectus and investment bankers' fees) should be deducted from the total of the above two components.

The APV approach separates the effects of any specific financing sources from the NPV of the project. APV = Unlevered all equity NPV + PV of benefits from special financing features.

6.6.2 WACC Versus Cost of Equity

According to the APV approach, unlevered cost of equity (and not WACC) should be taken as the base required rate of return for project evaluation. This is due to the following reasons:

- In many situations, particularly for risky projects, the NPV approach using WACC (Weighted Average Cost of Capital of equity and debt sources) as the discount rate may not be appropriate if the debt sources are not reliable. Banks and other lenders may often act as 'fair weather friends' wanting to extend credit facilities as long as the company is doing well, but withdraw financial support in difficult times when you need them the most.
- Second, the Weighted Average Cost of Capital (WACC) assumes a constant proportion of debt funding throughout the life of the project while in practice a firm may repay loans as it earns. This will affect interest payments as well as the tax-shield on the interest cost (both will reduce as debt is repaid, say, in annual installments).
- Third, as Modigliani–Miller (MM) theory suggests, debt has explicit and implicit costs so that as a firm uses more and more of debt, the cost of equity may rise to offset any advantage of cheaper debt.

Thus, APV of a project would be:

APV = Unlevered all equity NPV + PV of benefits from special financing features. Consider the following example

EXAMPLE 6.11 A project requires an initial investment of ₹2,00,000 that would be funded by perpetual debt and equity sources in equal proportions. The project would yield after-tax cash inflows of ₹38,000 per annum in perpetuity. If the project was an all equity funded project, the appropriate cost of equity would be 20%. The company's cost of perpetual debt is 14% per annum and the corporate tax rate is 30%. Compute the APV of the project.

Solution:

(a) **Calculate the NPV assuming it is an all equity funded project**

Annual cash inflow in perpetuity = ₹38,000

Cost of equity = 0.20

Present value of the cash inflows = ₹38,000 ÷ 0.20 = 1,90,000.

Net present value = ₹1,90,000 – 2,00,000

= ₹–10,000.

The project would be rejected if it was an all equity funded project due to a negative NPV. The high cost of equity is used as the discount rate that has heavily discounted the cash flows resulting in a negative NPV. However, let us not forget that the company plans to finance 50% of the initial investment by debt funding which will bring in some benefits as follows:

(b) **Calculate the present value of tax-shield on interest expense:**

Amount of debt funding in the project = ₹1,00,000

Rate of interest per annum = 14%

Annual interest payable = ₹14,000

Tax-shield on interest expense @30% = ₹14,000 × 30% = 4,200

Present value of tax-shield in perpetuity = 4,200 ÷ 0.14 = 30,000.

(c) **Adjusted Present Value (APV)**

= All equity NPV + PV of tax-shield

= ₹–10,000 + 30,000

= ₹20,000.

Since the adjusted present value is positive, the project is acceptable.

Conclusion: The adjusted present value approach might be a better alternative in certain circumstances (involving risky projects or uncertain sources of debt funding) than the WACC based NPV method, but it is more complicated than the latter. That could be the reason why NPV method is more popular among practising managers.

6.7 International Project Appraisal

There has been a phenomenal growth in the global trade and investments during the past few decades. A firm can acquire a global presence in a number of ways: exports, joint ventures and wholly-owned foreign subsidiaries. Our discussion here will be in the context of a fully-owned subsidiary incorporated under the 'host' country's laws.

Appraisal of international projects is a critical aspect of the MNC operations. When a company undertakes a project in another country, it would have to abide by the laws and rules of the 'host' country where the project is located. The company would like to repatriate profits to its shareholders back in the 'home' country, and might also wish to use the local (host country) capital markets to raise funds. In this context, it would be relevant to consider the following issues while evaluating a foreign project.

6.7.1 NPV Versus APV Method for Foreign Projects

In the previous section, we compared the NPV and APV methods of project appraisal. It is felt that the Adjusted Present Value (APV) approach might be more suitable for evaluation of foreign projects due to the higher degree of risk and uncertainty attached to such projects. The APV uses the cost of equity as the discount rate to compute the base case NPV of the project, and then adds on any benefits of debt financing if it becomes available. Thus, when a firm uses the APV method, it would be prepared both ways: with or without the debt financing.

A number of additional complications (including double taxation and withholding tax) may arise in evaluation of foreign projects.

Such an approach would be particularly relevant in the context of foreign projects, where raising debt capital in the host country may not be as easy and economical as in the MNC's home country. For example, suppose an Indian company is considering a mining project in Australia. The company might be well-known in India, but may not be equally reputed in Australia; so raising debt funding there to finance the project might be more difficult and should not be taken for granted. Therefore, the initial evaluation of the project should be done on the assumption that the project would be fully-financed out of the company's equity capital. Then, using the APV approach, the present value of any special financing strategy (such as debt financing if it becomes available) can be used as an added sweetener in project appraisal.

6.7.2 Other Issues Concerning Foreign Projects

In addition to the issue of choosing a suitable method for financial appraisal of projects, a number of other issues often come up that would need to be given due consideration while evaluating foreign projects. These are discussed below.

Project Cash Flows vs. Parent Cash Flows

The host country may have restrictions on the amount of profits that can be repatriated to foreign shareholders. There may also be a withholding tax on any remittances made to foreign shareholders. Again, different rates of taxes may be applicable to various cash flows remitted such as interest, royalties, license fees and dividends. In such situations, the parent company should focus more on 'remittable' cash flows rather than all cash flows from the project. In other words, for the purpose of project evaluation, the MNC would do well to focus only on such proportion of the project cash flows that can be remitted back to its home country.

International Taxation

The problem of double taxation on the foreign subsidiary's profits often complicates project evaluation. The host country as well as the MNC's home country may both want to tax the profits repatriated, unless there is a double-tax-avoidance treaty between the two countries. The issue must be investigated before undertaking a foreign project.

Blocked Funds

Sometimes a foreign project may become attractive because the MNC has accumulated funds (from previous projects) in the host country, which cannot be taken out (or can be taken out only with heavy taxes) but may be fully utilized for a project in the host country.

Effect on Exports

Often, setting up of a foreign project might mean a loss of export sales to the host country. This must be accounted for in appraising a foreign project as an opportunity cost.

Foreign Exchange and Political Risk

The political risk and frequently changing Government policies in the host country increase the uncertainty of future cash flows. On top of that, the ever fluctuating foreign exchange rates only complicate the issue of foreign project evaluation. The company may have to resort to foreign exchange derivatives for hedging the risk and the cost implications of such measures should be covered in the project appraisal.

6.8 Project Evaluation and Income Taxes

As we have discussed earlier, the cash flows used for financial evaluation of projects should be determined on an after-tax basis. The income tax rates and related rules might have a significant impact on project viability and should be taken into account while appraising a project.

In order to encourage more investments in certain industries (for example power, infrastructure and exports) or geographic areas (for example, the notified industrially backwards regions of the country), the Government might announce certain tax incentives by way of a tax-holiday, reduced rates of taxes or Government subsidies. In addition, accelerated depreciation and investment allowance allowable under the Income Tax Act might help in reducing the tax outflow. Depending on the type of projects being considered, the provisions of the Income Tax Act should be carefully studied and their implications should be incorporated in estimation of the project's net cash flows.

Incidentally, to keep our discussions simple, we have mostly assumed straight line method of depreciation in our examples. For the purpose of calculating the income tax liability, the Income Tax Act, 1961 allows depreciation according to the Written Down Value (WDV) method at the depreciation rates prescribed for different types of fixed assets. The prescribed rates of depreciation (as at the time of writing) are given in Annexure-1 at the end of the chapter.

6.9 Project Implementation and Post-Audit

Before closing our discussion on investment decision, it is important to highlight the importance of timely and meticulous implementation of the project. Some of the main aspects of project implementation may be briefly outlined here as follows:

To begin with, the entire project should be divided into an exhaustive check list of activities that would need to be carried out starting from scratch and ending with successful completion of the trial production runs. Second, a Critical Path Method (CPM) approach would help in sequencing activities in terms of their priority or criticality to complete the project. Third, a detailed time-table should be drawn up for timely execution of various activities and a 'reverse' time-clock started to continuously inform the execution team how much time is left to complete each activity (reportedly, this step was a major contributor to the successful implementation of the Delhi Metro project). Fourth, some well defined parts of the project (such as development of the project site and construction of buildings) can be outsourced on turnkey basis, with penalty clauses for late completion to keep the contractors under pressure to deliver on time. Fifth, the company's execution team should comprise of qualified and experienced managers, and equally important is that the team should remain stable until the project is fully-executed. There is a significant correlation between frequent changes in the execution team (particularly the chief executive officer) and delayed completion of the project. Each single day's delay in project execution leads to time and cost overruns. Sixth, a seamless flow of funds to finance each stage of the project is extremely important. Therefore, funding sources should be tied up in a way that the work on the project should never be interrupted due to funds shortage. Finally, when the project is complete and fully-implemented, a post-audit team headed by a senior manager should review the project planning and execution by the company and document the lessons learnt for improving the future performance in execution of similar projects.

References

Bierman, H. Jr., and S. Smidt, *The Capital Budgeting Decision: Economic Analysis of Investment Projects*, 9th ed., Routledge, New York, 2006.

David, J., Oblak, and Roy, J., Helm, Jr., 'Survey and Analysis of Capital Budgeting Methods Used by Multinationals', *Financial Management,* Wiley., Vol. 9, No. 4 (Winter, 1980), pp. 37–41.

Government of India, *Income Tax Act*, 1961, Section 32.

Lawson, G.H. and Windle, D.W., "Capital Budgeting and the Use of DCF Criteria in the Corporation Tax Regime", Oliver and Boyd, California, 1967.

Seitz, N. and Ellison, M., *Capital Budgeting and Long-term Financing Decisions*, 4th ed., South-Western Educational Publishing, Kentucky, 2004.

Shapiro, A.C., *Capital Budgeting and Investment Analysis*, Prentice-Hall, London, 2004.

Points to Remember

- **Capital rationing** refers to a situation in which a firm has an upper cap on the amount of funds that can be invested in new projects during a period. Such a budget ceiling might be induced by external factors or result from self imposed internal strategies.
- **Comparing** Net Present Value (NPV) and Profitability Index (PI), the latter is particularly helpful in ranking investment proposals in situations of capital rationing because PI is a ratio that clearly expresses the project's profitability in relation to its initial investment.
- **Inflation** refers to a general rise in the prices of goods and services in an economy during a period and results in a decline in the purchasing power of money. In inflationary conditions, the project cash flows and cost of capital

should either both be estimated on 'real' basis or both of them can be taken on nominal basis.

- **The Equivalent Annual Cost** (EAC) method calculates the equivalent cost of owning and using an asset over a common period of one year. The EAC method overcomes the problem of different time-scales involved in mutually exclusive projects.
- **The equivalent annual cost** method can also be used to decide the optimal replacement cycle for assets that would always be needed by the firm for the foreseeable future.
- **The concept of 'options'** was first developed with reference to investments in financial securities such as shares and bonds and later got extended to project investments. To differentiate between the two, the options embedded in project investments are called 'real' options as distinct from 'financial' options.
- **With the option to expand**, the project evaluation would involve three steps: (a) calculate the NPV of the project's initial phase, (b) calculate the standalone NPV of the expansion phase, and (c) Finally calculate the overall NPV of the project including the expansion, compare the results and decide.
- To evaluate **the option to abandon**, compare the value of the project with and without the abandonment value. In general, it would make sense to abandon a project when the present value of all possible future cash flows from the project is less than its current abandonment value.
- If there is **uncertainty about certain critical factors** that could affect the success of the project, the company should consider waiting until more information becomes available to give the company confidence to undertake the project.
- **The APV approach** separates the effects of any specific financing sources used from the NPV of the project. A project is initially evaluated as if it was an all-equity funded investment, and the resulting NPV is adjusted for any benefits of debt financing.
- **Appraisal of international projects** is a critical aspect of the MNC operations. A number of additional complications may arise in evaluation of foreign projects as the company would have to abide by the laws and rules of the 'host' country where the project is located.

Questions

1. Explain the meaning of capital rationing and discuss the main reasons why a situation of capital rationing could arise in a company.
2. Discuss the pros and cons of using NPV and PI methods for evaluating projects in situations of capital rationing. Which of the two methods would be most suitable and why?
3. Explain the meaning of inflation and how it affects project evaluation.
4. Differentiate between real and money rates of interest, and using suitable numerical examples, show how to estimate the real interest rate when money rate of interest is given and vice versa.
5. Explain the equivalent annual cost method. Under what types of situations it might be considered a better method for evaluating projects as compared to other methods such as the NPV?
6. Using suitable numerical examples, explain how to evaluate projects with unequal lives using the equivalent annual cost method.

7. Explain the meaning of real options, and using suitable examples, discuss three types of real options.
8. Explain the meaning of abandonment value and using a suitable numerical example show how to compute the NPV of a project with abandonment option.
9. Differentiate between NPV and APV approaches. What is the rationale of the APV method?
10. Discuss the additional complications that might arise while evaluating foreign projects.

Multiple Choice Questions

1. Which of the following methods of project evaluation would be most suitable in situations of capital rationing?
(a) The payback period method
(b) The net present value method
(c) The profitability index
(d) All of the above

2. If a project requires an initial investment of ₹1,20,000 and promises a NPV of ₹40,000, the profitability index would equal to:
(a) 1.40
(b) 1.33
(c) 1.20
(d) None of the above

3. If a company has an investment budget of ₹1,00,000 and is considering five proposals as follows, what combination of projects would maximize the NPV if projects are divisible?

S. No.	*Initial investment*	*NPV*	*PI*	*Project rank*
1	60,000	15,000	1.25	4
2	20,000	6,000	1.30	3
3	50,000	17,500	1.35	2
4	30,000	4,500	1.15	5
5	40,000	18,000	1.45	1

(a) Project 1 (full) + 2 (full) + 3 (full)
(b) Project 5 (full) + project 3 (full) + project 2 (50%)
(c) Project 4 (full) + project 2 (full) + project 5 (50%)
(d) None of the above

4. If a company has an investment budget of ₹1,00,000, and is considering five proposals as follows, what would be the maximum NPV that can be generated by an optimum combination of projects if projects are divisible?

S. No.	*Initial investment*	*NPV*	*PI*	*Project rank*
1	60,000	15,000	1.25	4
2	20,000	6,000	1.30	3
3	50,000	17,500	1.35	2
4	30,000	4,500	1.15	5
5	40,000	18,000	1.45	1

(a) ₹38,500
(b) ₹43,500
(c) ₹46,500
(d) None of the above.

5. If the real rate of interest is 10% and inflation rate is 5%, what would be the money (nominal) rate of interest?
   (a) 10.5% (b) 12.5%
   (c) 15.5% (d) None of the above
6. If the money (nominal) rate of interest is 14% and inflation rate is 5%, what would be the real rate of interest?
   (a) 9.52% (b) 8.57%
   (c) 7.89% (d) None of the above
7. A project would yield a NPV of ₹20,000 if it is completely funded by equity capital. If the project could be part-financed by debt sources, the present value of the tax-shield on interest expenses would amount to ₹50,000. What would be the Adjusted Present Value (APV) of the project?
   (a) ₹30,000 (b) ₹50,000
   (c) ₹70,000 (d) None of the above

Self-Test Questions

1. Grand Company has an investment budget of ₹1,20,000 in Year 0, for which it has shortlisted the following proposals:

Proposal	*Initial investment*	*Year 1 cash inflow*	*Year 2 cash inflow*
1	80,000	59,000	59,000
2	50,000	40,600	40,600
3	60,000	53,500	53,500
4	70,000	64,600	64,600
5	40,000	32,000	32,000
6	20,000	17,000	17,000

   The company's cost of capital is 15%.
   Assuming all projects are independent and cannot be repeated:
   (a) Calculate the NPV and profitability index of the proposals.
   (b) Rank the proposals in descending order of the profitability index.
   (c) Select the combination of projects that would maximize the NPV assuming all projects are divisible.
   (d) Select the combination of projects that would maximize the NPV assuming all projects are indivisible.
2. Ascent Company is considering a new project. The cash flows at current (real) prices related to a project are given below:

Year	*Cash flow*
0	–60,000
1	20,000
2	20,000
3	20,000
4	20,000

The money (nominal) cost of capital of the company is 14% per annum which includes the effect of inflation that is estimated to be 5.555% per annum.

1. Calculate the NPV of the project using real cash flows and cost of capital.
2. Calculate the NPV of the project using money (nominal) cash flows and cost of capital.

3. The management of Roland Company is considering two mutually exclusive machines code named Alpha and Gamma. Alpha would cost ₹1,00,000 and have a useful life of 10 years, while Gamma would cost ₹60,000 and have a useful life of 5 years. Relevant data including the maintenance and operating costs during their respective useful lives is provided as follows:

Items	*Machine-Alpha cash flow*	*Machine-Gamma cash flow*
Machine Price [Year 0]	1,00,000	60,000
Annual Repairs Cost	8,000	12,000
Annual Operating Cost	10,000	16,000
Trade-In Value*	15,000	8,000

Note: *The trade-in value at the end of the machine's life.

Assume the cost of capital of the company is 12%.
Using the Equivalent Annual Cost (EAC) method, evaluate the two machines and recommend which one should be purchased.

4. Pixel Company wants to decide its replacement policy for air-conditioners and is considering three alternative replacement periods: 2 years, 3 years or 4 years. The relevant information has been provided as follows:

Purchase cost of air-conditioner: ₹80,000
Cost of annual maintenance contract: ₹10,000
Trade-in value at the end of Year 2 = ₹40,000,
Year 3 = ₹30,000,
Year 4 = ₹10,000.

If the air-conditioners are not replaced by the end of third year, an additional expense of ₹20,000 for major overhaul/servicing would be required in fourth year. Assume the cost of capital is 10%. Annual maintenance cost is to be paid even in the year of replacement. Ignore taxes and inflation.

Using the equivalent annual cost method, calculate the optimal replacement cycle of air-conditioners.

5. A project requires an initial investment of ₹3,00,000 that would be funded by 50% perpetual debt and 50% equity capital. The project would yield after-tax cash inflows of ₹59,000 per annum in perpetuity. If the project was an all equity funded project, the appropriate cost of equity would be 20%. The company's cost of perpetual debt is 13% per annum and the corporate tax rate is 30%. Compute the APV of the project.

Numerical Problems

1. Hilltop Company with an investible amount ceiling of ₹90,000 is considering the following five proposals:

Proposal	*Initial investment*	*Year 1 cash inflow*	*Year 2 cash inflow*
1	60,000	40,000	40,000
2	20,000	26,000	26,000
3	50,000	35,000	35,000
4	30,000	24,000	24,000
5	40,000	23,000	23,000

The company's cost of capital is 12%.

Assuming all projects are independent and cannot be repeated:

(a) Calculate the NPV and profitability index of the proposals.

(b) Rank the proposals in descending order of the profitability index.

(c) Select the combination of projects that would maximize the NPV assuming all projects are divisible.

(d) Select the combination of projects that would maximize the NPV assuming all projects are indivisible.

2. Lucky Company is considering a project to replace its existing machinery with more sophisticated machinery that would cost ₹75,000 in Year 0. Due to greater efficiency, the machinery would result in a material cost saving of ₹20,000 per annum and savings in labour and variable overhead of ₹12,000 per annum. The machine will have a useful life of four years after which there will be no resale value. The estimates of savings in material and labour costs have been made at current (Year 0) prices without including the effect of inflation.

   The cost of capital is 15% in nominal terms. It is estimated that the following rates of inflation would prevail in next four years:

Variable	*Inflation per annum*
General inflation in economy	6%
Material cost	5%
Labour cost	9%

Calculate the project NPV and decide if it should be accepted.

3. The management of Prime Company is considering two mutually exclusive machines, code named Rose and Lily. Rose would cost ₹5,00,000 and have a useful life of 10 years, while Lily would cost ₹3,00,000 and have a useful life of 5 years. Relevant data including the maintenance and operating costs during their respective useful lives is provided as follows:

Items	*Machine-Rose cash flow*	*Machine-Lily cash flow*
Machine Price [Year 0]	5,00,000	3,00,000
Annual Repairs Cost	20,000	40,000
Annual Operating Cost	30,000	60,000
Trade-In Value*	50,000	10,000

Note: *The trade-in value at the end of the machine's life.

Assume the cost of capital of the company is 12%.

   Using the Equivalent Annual Cost (EAC) method, evaluate the two machines and recommend which one should be purchased.

4. Mango Company wants to decide its replacement policy for delivery vans and is considering three alternative replacement periods: 2 years, 3 years or 4 years. The relevant information has been provided as follows:

Purchase cost of van: ₹4,50,000
Cost of annual maintenance: ₹50,000
Trade-in value at the end of Year 2 = ₹3,40,000,
Year 3 = ₹2,00,000,
Year 4 = ₹1,00,000.

If the vans are not replaced by the end of third year, an additional expense of ₹80,000 for major overhaul/servicing would be required in fourth year. Assume the cost of capital is 10%. Annual maintenance cost is to be paid even in the year of replacement. Ignore taxes and inflation.

Using the equivalent annual cost method, calculate the optimal replacement cycle of vans.

5. The Progressive Company is considering investing in a foreign project X as follows:

	Proposal X
Investment required [USD]	1,00,000
Expected life of the machine	5 years
Depreciation per year [USD]	20,000
Income tax rate assumed	30%
Scrap value at the end of 5 years	Nil

Expected *profits before depreciation and taxes* from the investment are as follows:

Years	1	2	3	4	5
X: PBDT ([USD'000]	90	30	30	30	30

The cost of equity capital of the Progressive Company is 18%.

(a) Compute the project's NPV assuming the company uses cost of equity as the minimum acceptable rate of return for screening investment proposals.

(b) Now assume the company can use perpetual debt funding of ₹40,000 at a (pre-tax) interest rate of 10% per annum to part-finance the project. Calculate the APV of the project.

6. A project requires an initial investment of ₹4,00,000 that would be funded by 50% perpetual debt and 50% equity capital. The project would yield after-tax cash inflows of ₹90,000 per annum in perpetuity. If the project was an all equity funded project, the appropriate cost of equity would be 22%. The company's cost of perpetual debt is 12% per annum and the corporate tax rate is 30%. Compute the APV of the project.

7. Short-Case

SMARTEX FOREIGN PROJECT

The management of Smartex India Limited is considering setting up their first overseas plant in Zimbabwe to manufacture and market smart phones there. The manager in charge of the project has spent sleepless nights collecting the relevant information as presented below:

The project would require an initial investment in plant and machinery: ZWD 100 million. In addition, a working capital investment of ZWD 10 million would be made at the same time as initial investment. The company has accumulated an amount of ZWD 5 million in a local bank from its earlier export sales. This can be repatriated to India after paying 50% tax or freely utilized for any project within Zimbabwe. The investment in plant and machinery will be depreciated over 5 years by the straight line method. The working capital investment will be recovered at the end of 5th year. The company has decided to take a 5-year horizon starting now for appraisal of the investment proposal. The plant will produce 1 million units of the product per year. Comparable phones imported from China are being sold there at a price of ZWD 400 per phone.

The operating costs are estimated as follows:

(a) Direct materials : ZWD 180 per phone.
(b) Direct labour : ZWD 30 per phone.
(c) Selling expenses : ZWD 10 per phone.

The current spot rate is INR 5.00/ZWD. Currently, the parent company exports 1,00,000 phones per year to Zimbabwe. These will be replaced by sales from the new plant. A crucial component for manufacturing phones will be supplied by the parent company. This component accounts for ZWD 80 per phone at world prices (included in the materials cost of ZWD 180 per phone). Its variable cost of manufacturing is ZWD 40 at the current exchange rate. No extra capacity needs to be installed to meet the requirements of the new plant. The corporate income tax rate in Zimbabwe is 50%, while it is 40% in India. There is a double tax avoidance treaty between the two countries under which full credit is given to Indian companies for taxes paid in Zimbabwe provided the rate does not exceed the Indian rate of 40%. The Zimbabwe authorities impose a 10% withholding tax on dividends remitted to the parent company by the subsidiary. The company discounts the operating cash flows from the project at the required real rate of return on equity on similar projects in Zimbabwe, which is 10%. However, the additional cash flows earned by the parent company on supply of the crucial component to the new plant are discounted at a lower rate of 8% per annum since the risk associated with these cash flows is less than the risk of the entire project cash flows. There is a possibility of obtaining external local financing of about ZWD 20 million at a pre-tax interest rate of 12% per annum. Any tax-shield from this interest payment should be discounted at the same rate as the operating cash flows.

It may be possible to work out a technology licensing agreement between the parent and subsidiary company under which the latter can pay royalties to the parent company. The Zimbabwean Government can allow upto 5% of sales as tax deductible royalty expense. The Indian government will treat this royalty income in the hands of the parent company as export income and tax it at a lower income tax rate of 25%. Any cash flows related to this are considered the lower risk class to be discounted at 8%.

(a) List and discuss the main factors that should be considered while evaluating a foreign investment project.
(b) Calculate the relevant cash flows during the life of the project.
(c) Calculate the Adjusted Present Value (APV) of the project, and decide whether the project should be undertaken.

Annexure-1

DEPRECIATION RATES AS PER THE INCOME TAX ACT, 1961

Some of the main provisions of Section 32 of the Income Tax Act, 1961 are reproduced below:

Basis of Depreciation

- Depreciation is allowable as expense in Income Tax Act, 1961 on the basis of block of assets. Block of assets means group of assets falling within a class of assets for which same rate of depreciation is prescribed.
- Depreciation is allowable only to the owner of the asset.
- Asset must be used for the purpose of business or profession.
- Depreciation under Income Tax Act is different from that of Companies Act, 1956. Therefore depreciation rates prescribed under income tax is only allowable whatever the depreciation is charged in books of accounts.

Depreciation in the Year of Purchase

- Depreciation is allowed only if the asset is put to use in the year of purchase.
- Degree of utilization of assets will not be considered while determining whether the asset is put to use or not. For example, if the asset is used for trial run then it is considered the asset is put to use.
- If asset is put to use for less than 180 days then an amount equal to 50% of the amount calculated using normal depreciating rates is allowed as depreciation.
- Depreciation will be allowed on the basis of block of asset method.

Additional Depreciation U/S 32(1)(IIA)

Additional depreciation shall be allowed if following conditions are fulfilled by the assessee:

1. Additional depreciation is allowed only on new machinery or plant excluding ships and aircraft which has been purchased and installed after 31-03-2005.
2. The assessee shall be engaged in the business of manufacturing and production of any article or thing.
3. Depreciation @20% of actual cost of assets is allowed as additional depreciation. However if the asset is put to use for less than 180 days then additional depreciation will be allowed @10% of actual cost of assets.

Depreciation Rates as per the Income Tax Act for Most Commonly Used Assets:

Annexure Table 1 Depreciation Rates

S No.	*Asset class*	*Asset type*	*Rate of depreciation*
1.	Building	Residential buildings except hotels and boarding houses	5%
2.	Building	Hotels and boarding houses	10%
3.	Building	Purely temporary erections such as wooden structures	100%

(Contd.)

Annexure Table 1
(Contd.)

S No.	*Asset class*	*Asset type*	*Rate of depreciation*
4.	Furniture	Furniture – Any furniture/fittings including electrical fittings	10%
5.	Plant and Machinery	Motor cars other than those used in a business of running them on hire	15%
6.	Plant and Machinery	Motor buses/taxies/lorries used in a business of running them on hire	30%
7.	Plant and Machinery	Computers and computer software	60%
8.	Plant and Machinery	Books owned by assessee, carrying on profession being annual publications	100%
9.	Plant and Machinery	Books owned by assessee, carrying on profession not being annual publications	60%
10.	Plant and Machinery	Books owned by assessee, carrying on business in running lending libraries	100%
11.	Intangible Assets	Know-how, patents, copyright, trademark, license, franchise or any other business or commercial rights of similar nature	25%

PART III

RISK, RETURN AND VALUATION

CHAPTER

7

Market Risk and Return

LEARNING OBJECTIVES

After studying this chapter, you should be able to:

- Understand the meaning and significance of risk and return in the investment world
- Understand difference between holding period return and expected rate of return and their calculations thereof
- Understand the concept of multiple holding period return
- Discuss various measures of risk and their calculations thereof
- Discuss Portfolio return and risk and significance of diversification.
- Determine how asset allocation or diversification affects portfolio risk and return.

7.1 Introduction to Risk and Return

Holding Period return measures the total return earned on an investment for the time period it is held upon

BSE Sensex has delivered a compounded annual growth rate (CAGR) of 16.6% since 1980 (Year of Inception) till 2014. Looking at the BSE Sensex chart (Figure 7.1), the trajectory and the return looks picture perfect and every investor would have loved to be part of this uni-directional (upwardly rising) line (and wealth!!). However, what misses the eye is showcased in the second chart (Figure 7.2 BSE Sensex Annual return). This eye-popping CAGR return comes with a huge underlying risk as evident from the volatility of annual returns. As they say **"There ain't no such thing as a free lunch."** Similarly return always comes hand-in-hand with risk. Higher risk...higher return, lower risk...lower return!

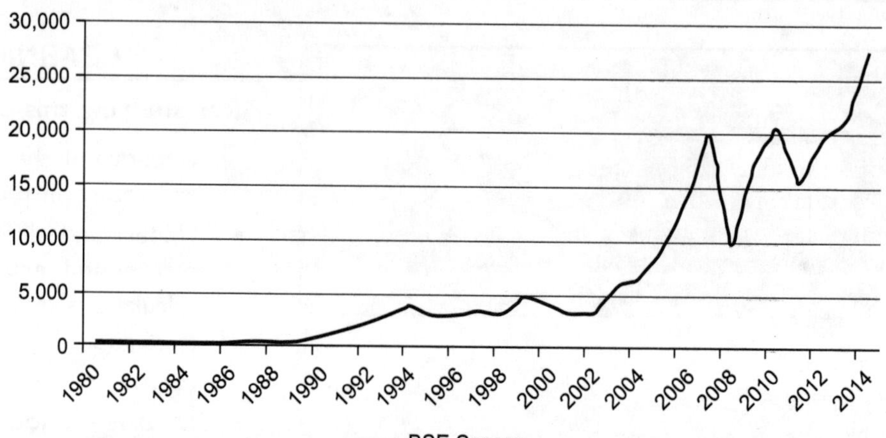

FIGURE 7.1
BSE Sensex.

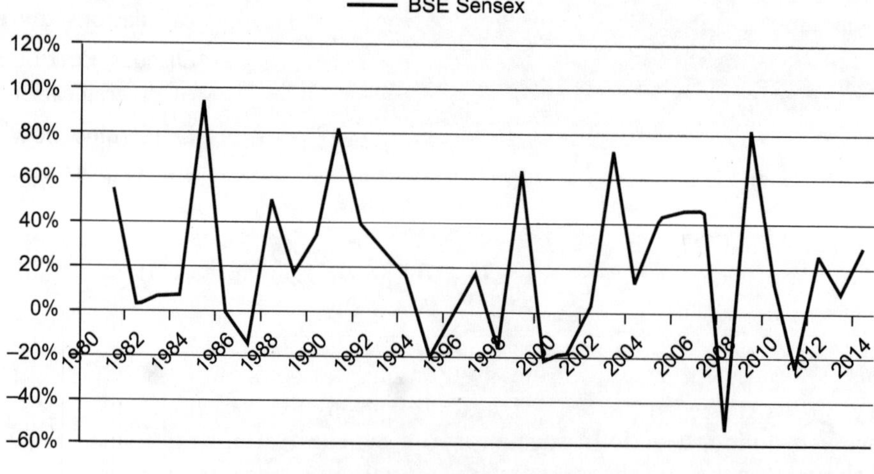

FIGURE 7.2
BSE Sensex: Annual Returns

Every investor on this planet always dreams to find an investment which provides high returns and carries no risk. While this is not theoretically impossible, realistically the probability of this happening is extremely low. Generally, higher the expected rate of return demanded by the investor, higher shall be the risk attached to it. Before we explore this fascinating interaction between risk and return, and its effect on investment decisions, we must first discuss the concept of risk and return in detail and determine ways to measure the same.

7.2 Return

In the financial world, the term 'return' is always used in conjunction with the term 'investment'. In literal sense, return refers to something earned over and above the base (initial) investment made. Now, this return may accrue one time or periodically depending upon the nature of investment made. For example investment in five years Fixed Deposit (FD) of Bank of Baroda would yield periodic returns (for 5 years) in form of interest credited annually (or at any other frequency). On the other hand, investment made in equity stock of Tata Steel would yield both periodic returns (in form of dividends) and capital gain/loss, when the stock is disposed off in the market.

Summarizing the above discussion, the term return thus can be categorized into two components—the first being the accrual income (interest/dividends) that are received by investors on a periodical basis and the second component being the capital gain/loss which gets crystallized when the investment is sold off.

Return = Periodic Return (Interest/Dividend) + Capital Gain/Loss

While the above definition presents a simplified way of determining returns, actual measurement of return may entail certain complications. For example, while past performance of an investment made using historical data is easy, calculating expected return for a current investment can present some challenges, such as uncertainty about the future selling price, exit date, timing, etc.

Measurement of returns can be looked in from two dimensions—first from the historical period perspective also popularly known as Holding Period Return or ex-post return or realized return, and secondly from future period perspective referred to as expected return or ex-ante return.

7.2.1 Holding Period Return

As the name suggests, holding period return or ex-post returns attempts to measure the return over the holding period of an investment made. Basically, it represents the total return (Accrual Income + Capital Gain/Loss) earned on an investment for the time period it is held upon.

Holding Period Return (HPR) = (Ending price of an Investment – Beginning price of an Investment + Periodical accruals)/Beginning price of an Investment

EXAMPLE 7.1 Suppose Ravi buys 100 shares of Axis bank @ INR 500 each on 1st January 2014. At the end of the year, Ravi sold off his entire shares 520 each. Ravi also received dividend of INR 50 during the year. His Holding Period Return at the end of the year is calculated as follows:

$$\text{Holding Period Return (HPR)} = \frac{(100 \text{ shares} \times 520) - (100 \text{ shares} \times 500) + 50}{(100 \text{ shares} \times 500) = 0.041 \text{ or } 4.1\%}$$

In the above calculation of Holding Period Return, we have assumed that dividends were paid at the end of the year and consequently there was no reinvestment income.

In case of stock investment (as shown in above example), the HPR equation can be rewritten as

$$\text{HPR} = \frac{\text{Dividends}}{\text{Beginning price on an Investment}} + \frac{\text{Ending price} - \text{Beginning price}}{\text{Beginning price on an Investment}}$$

HPR = Dividend Yield + Capital Gain

EXAMPLE 7.2 Arun bought 100 shares of ICICI on 31 March 2008, at ₹642. In February 2013, he sold them at ₹1,139. In between, he received 4 dividend payouts. The price of ICICI bank on 31 March 2009, 2010, 2011 and 2012 was 385, 955, 1,006 and 915, respectively. The corresponding dividend yield at those dates was 2.8%, 1.3%, 1.1% and 1.6%. Calculate the Holding Period Returns.

Spreadsheet Analysis

Period	*Price*	*Dividend Yield*	*Dividends*
31-Mar-09	385	2.80%	10.78
31-Mar-10	955	1.30%	12.41
31-Mar-11	1,006	1.10%	11.06
31-Mar-12	915	1.60%	14.64
Periodical Payments/Dividends	48.9		
Beginning price	642		
Ending price	1,139		
Holding Period Return	**85%**		

Holding Period Returns in Indian Stock Market

Since 1992, when Foreign Institutional Investors (FII) started investing in India, their cumulative equity investment has reached to around $167 billion, till date. As this investment nears the $200 billion mark over next few years, we present year by year historical Holding period returns for the Indian market since 1992 by using BSE (Bombay Stock Exchange) Sensex Index as the benchmark. Table 7.1 lists the year-on-year returns of BSE Sensex Index in the 32-year period from 1992 to 2014. Figure 7.3 shows the CAGR (Compounded Annual Growth Rate) for every INR 1 invested at the beginning of each decade since 1980 to 2014. Interestingly, an investment of INR 1 in BSE Sensex at the start of every decade would have yielded double digit compounded returns in all decades except for 4 decades (1991–2001; 1992–2002; 1993–2003; 1994–2004).

TABLE 7.1 Annual (Year-on-Year) Returns of BSE Sensex Index

Year	*BSE Sensex Annual Return*	*Year*	*BSE Sensex Annual Return*
1992	37%	2004	13%
1993	28%	2005	42%
1994	17%	2006	47%
1995	–21%	2007	47%
1996	–1%	2008	–52%
1997	19%	2009	81%
1998	–16%	2010	17%
1999	64%	2011	–25%
2000	–21%	2012	26%
2001	–18%	2013	9%
2002	4%	2014	30%
2003	73%	**Average (1992–2014)**	**17%**

Source: http://www.bseindia.com/

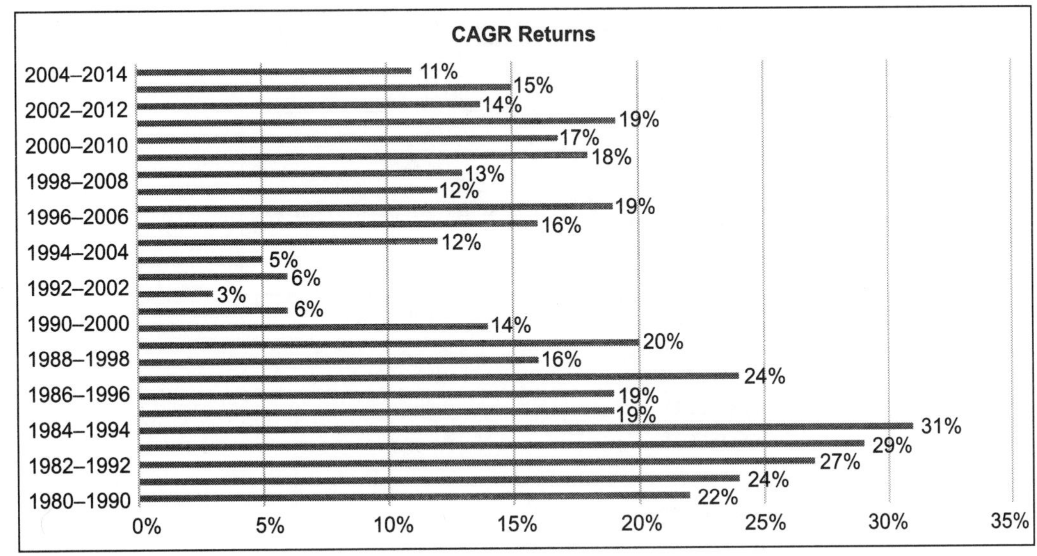

FIGURE 7.3 CAGR Returns for Every INR 1 Invested at the Beginning of Each Decade.

Multiple Holding Period Returns

When holding period for investments involves multi-years, it becomes necessary to combine returns for all periods to arrive at a single consolidated figure of return. There are two ways in which returns for multi-period can be aggregated to arrive at a single return figure.

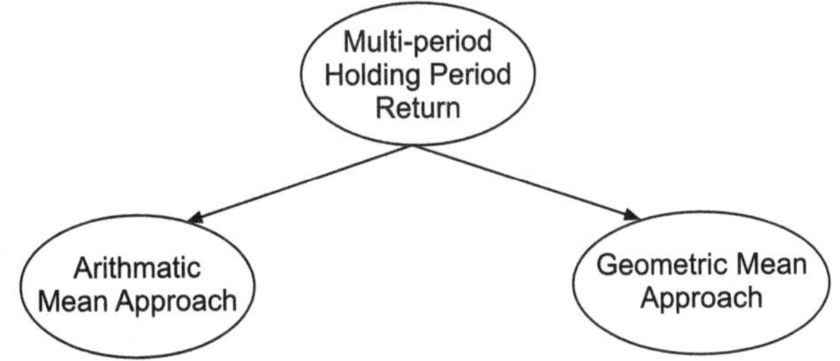

FIGURE 7.4 Multiple Holding Period Return

Arithmetic mean approach simply involves averaging of all Holding Period Returns to arrive at a single figure:

$$\text{AMHPR} = \frac{\text{HPR}_1 + \text{HPR}_2 + \cdots + \text{HPR}_n}{n}$$

AMHPR = Arithmetic Mean Holding Period Return

Geometric mean approach involves compounding of past returns for arriving at a single figure

$$\text{GMHPR} = \sqrt[n]{(1+\text{HPR}_1)\times(1+\text{HPR}_2)\times\cdots\times(1+\text{HPR}_n)} - 1$$

GMHPR = Geometric Mean Holding Period Return

EXAMPLE 7.3 Anoop bought 200 shares of TTK Prestige in 2010 @ ₹1,624 each. Annual returns for the stock for past 4 years are given below. Using Arithmetic Mean and Geometric Mean approaches calculate the multi-period holding return for Anoop's holding.

Year	TTK Prestige Annual return
2011	55%
2012	34%
2013	3%
2014	3%

Year	TTK Prestige Annual return
2010	–
2011	55%
2012	34%
2013	3%
2014	3%
AMHPR	24%
GMHPR	21.97%

7.2.2 Expected Rate of Return

In the words of Warren Buffett, "*In the business world, the rear-view mirror is always clearer than the windshield*". In other words life is easy looking in the rear-view mirror, as we already know what did not worked out or what mistakes we did. Similarly, holding period or realized return is easy to determine and calculate as historical data is readily available. The problem arises when returns are to be calculated for future periods as there is uncertainty about the future price of the share as well as periodical accruals.

Expected return can be calculated in terms of probability weighted average of the rates of return in each scenario.

One of the ways to deal with the above problem is to assign probabilities to the future scenarios so that expected rate of return can be calculated in terms of probability weighted average of the rates of return in each scenario. For example, while calculating target prices for stocks, most brokerage houses assign probabilities to three kinds of scenarios namely optimistic scenario, pessimistic scenario and most likely scenario. Target prices are then calculated under each scenario and final price is arrived at by summing up the probability weighted average of the rates of return in each scenario.

Below provided is an excerpt from the brokerage report prepared by Morgan Stanley on Educomp in year 2009. Probabilities have been assigned to three scenarios namely *"Bull Case", "Bear Case" and "Base Case".* To arrive at final price target, probability weighted average of 3 scenarios have been used.

ILLUSTRATION 7.1

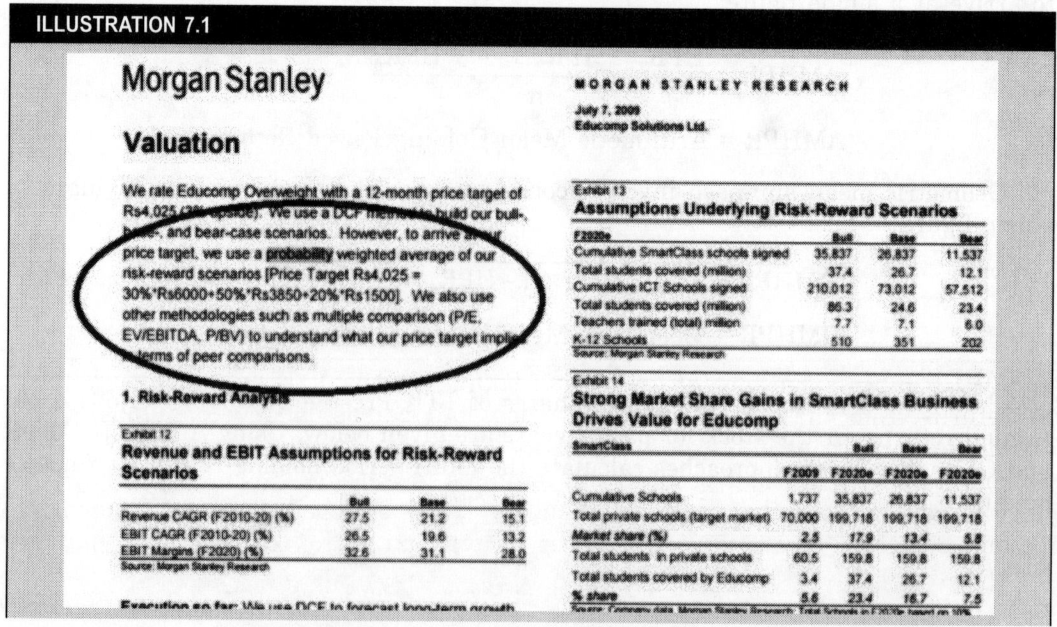

Morgan Stanley

MORGAN STANLEY RESEARCH
July 7, 2009
Educomp Solutions Ltd.

Valuation

We rate Educomp Overweight with a 12-month price target of Rs4,025 (3% upside). We use a DCF method to build our bull-, base-, and bear-case scenarios. However, to arrive at our price target, we use a probability weighted average of our risk-reward scenarios [Price Target Rs4,025 = 30%*Rs6000+50%*Rs3850+20%*Rs1500]. We also use other methodologies such as multiple comparison (P/E, EV/EBITDA, P/BV) to understand what our price target implies in terms of peer comparisons.

1. Risk-Reward Analysis

Exhibit 12

Revenue and EBIT Assumptions for Risk-Reward Scenarios

	Bull	Base	Bear
Revenue CAGR (F2010-20) (%)	27.5	21.2	15.1
EBIT CAGR (F2010-20) (%)	26.5	19.6	13.2
EBIT Margins (F2020) (%)	32.6	31.1	28.0

Source: Morgan Stanley Research

Execution so far: We use DCF to forecast long-term growth [illegible]

Exhibit 13

Assumptions Underlying Risk-Reward Scenarios

F2020e	Bull	Base	Bear
Cumulative SmartClass schools signed	35,837	26,837	11,537
Total students covered (million)	37.4	26.7	12.1
Cumulative ICT Schools signed	210,012	73,012	57,512
Total students covered (million)	86.3	24.6	23.4
Teachers trained (total) million	7.7	7.1	6.0
K-12 Schools	510	351	202

Source: Morgan Stanley Research

Exhibit 14

Strong Market Share Gains in SmartClass Business Drives Value for Educomp

SmartClass		Bull	Base	Bear
	F2009	F2020e	F2020e	F2020e
Cumulative Schools	1,737	35,837	26,837	11,537
Total private schools (target market)	70,000	199,718	199,718	199,718
Market share (%)	2.5	17.9	13.4	5.8
Total students in private schools	60.5	159.8	159.8	159.8
Total students covered by Educomp	3.4	37.4	26.7	12.1
% share	5.6	23.4	16.7	7.5

Source: Company data, Morgan Stanley Research; [illegible]

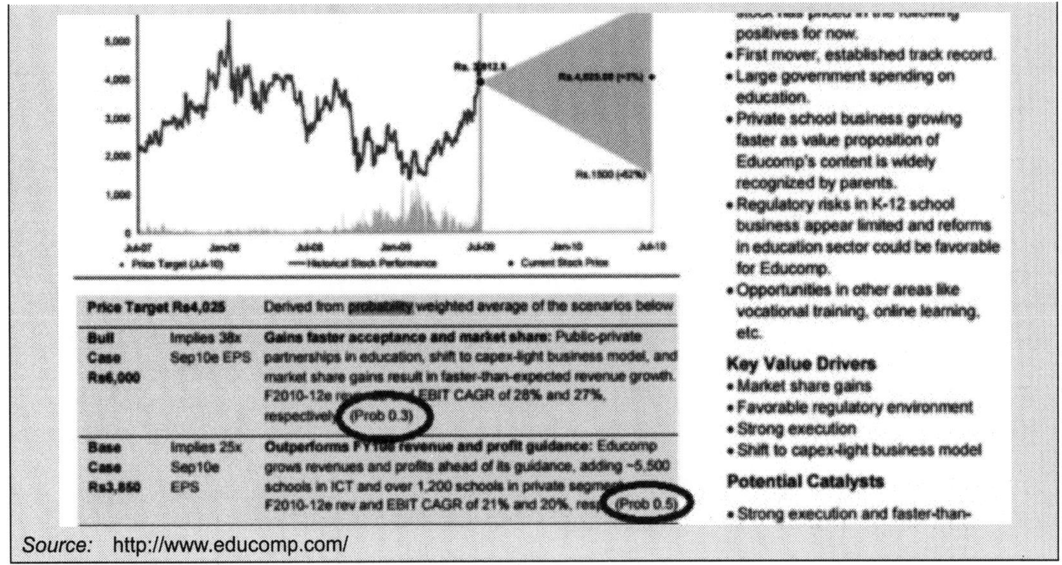

Source: http://www.educomp.com/

Calculation of Expected Return

To calculate expected return, basically two inputs are needed—first being estimated returns under various scenarios and second being the probabilities associated with those expected scenarios. Mathematically,

$$E(R_i) = \sum_{i=1}^{n} (\text{Probability of Return under each scenario}) \times (\text{Estimated Return under each scenario})$$

EXAMPLE 7.4 Ajay has bought 150 shares of Hindalco @ ₹120 each. He predicts two scenarios—'optimistic' and 'pessimistic' for calculating expected returns. The probability assigned to both the scenarios is 0.5 each. Ajay predicts that under optimistic scenario, price of Hindalco shares would rise to ₹200 each. Under pessimistic scenario, he predicts the price to touch ₹150. Calculate the expected return of Hindalco stock using the given data:

	A	B	C	D	E
1					
2	Expected Return on Hindalco Shares				((200/120)-1)*100
3	Scenarios	Price	Probability	Return	
4	Optimistic	200	0.5	67%	
5	Pessimistic	150	0.5	25%	
6					
7	Probability Weighted Return = (0.5×67% + 0.5×25%) = 45.8%				

EXAMPLE 7.5 Vishesh plans to invest ₹1 lakh in Axis bank. However, he estimates that returns from these stocks are dependent on macroeconomic conditions. The probability distributions and expected returns are enumerated in the table. For every 1% change in GDP growth, deposit growth improves by a factor of 3 and for every +1% change in deposits, Axis bank returns change by +50bps. Deposit growth is currently 15%, and Base case return for Axis bank is 5% for next year.

Scenario-Axis Bank	*GDP*	*Probability*
Flat GDP growth	5%	50%
GDP growth is 2% points above last year	7%	30%
GDP growth is 1% points below last year	4%	20%

	A	B	C	D	E	F	G	H	I	J
1	**Scenario-Axis Bank**	**GDP**	**Probability**							
2	Flat GDP Growth	5%	50%							
3	GDP Growth is 2% Points above last year	7%	30%							
4	GDP Growth is 1% Points below last year	4%	20%							
5										
6										
7										
8	**Scenario**	**GDP**	**Deposits**	**Axis Bank Estimate Return**	**Probability**					
9	Flat GDP Growth	5%	15%	5%	50%			Sumproduct		
10	GDP Growth is 2% Points above last year	7%	21%	8%	30%			(D9:D11, E9:E11)		
11	GDP Growth is 1% Points below last year	4%	12%	3.50%	20%					
12										
13	Expected Returns (Probability Weighted Return)				5.60%					

7.3 Risk

Risk refers to dispersion or variability of actual returns from the expected returns

Let us start this section by first accepting the reality that nobody likes uncertainty. In the financial world, this uncertainty takes the name of risk and is generally associated with an investment that guarantees no fixed returns. For example, let us say that you have 10 million in your bank account to invest and two investment options available are—10-year Fixed Deposit with a bank, which would pay annually 9% rate of interest and guarantees payback of principal after 10 years. As against this, the second option involves investing in BSE Sensex (India's Benchmark Index) for a similar period, but with no guaranteed returns (even payback of principal is not guaranteed!).

Now the first option involves *zero uncertainty or zero deviation* or *zero dispersion* of actual returns from the promised return over the investment horizon. Compared to this, in the second option, actual returns are uncertain and unknown. It may happen that equity investment of 10 million may get doubled to 20 million (in a bullish scenario) or investment may get reduced to half in a bearish scenario. There might be many other scenarios possible like these. However, the bottom-line that drives the above argument is that the second option (equity investment) involves considerable *uncertainty* or *considerable deviation* or *considerable dispersion* of actual returns from the expected returns. This deviation or dispersion or variability of actual returns from the expected returns is technically referred to as risk. The greater this deviation or dispersion or variability of actual returns from the expected returns, higher shall be the risk of the investment undertaken. In Example 7.5, Option 1 is a zero risk investment, whereas Option 2 involves a considerable degree of risk.

Now that we have discussed the concept of risk, let us try to understand the measures by which we can assess this risk. In the financial world, two popular measures to assess risk are Standard Deviation and Variance.

7.3.1 Standard Deviation

Standard Deviation, represented by greek letter sigma (σ) is the square root of Variance (σ^2) and measures the relative dispersion of data from its mean. In statistics, variance and Standard Deviation can be calculated for past series and future series. In case of past data, variance is the average of squared deviations from the mean of the data. On the other hand, for future series, where probabilities are associated with the variables, variance is the expected value of the squared deviations from the expected value.

Now the question is, how does the above discussion on variance of past and future data relates to measuring risk in the financial world. Similar to measurement of returns (Holding Period Returns and Expected Return), measurement of risk can also be looked into from two dimensions—first from the historical period perspective, and secondly from future period perspective. From the historical period perspective, risk (or variance) can be calculated by averaging the squared deviations of the actual past returns from the average returns over the entire period.

$$\sigma^2 = \left[\frac{1}{n}\sum_{i=1}^{n}[\text{HPR}_i - \overline{\text{HPR}}]^2\right] \tag{7.1}$$

$$\sigma = \sqrt{\frac{1}{n}\sum_{i=1}^{n}[\text{HPR}_i - \overline{\text{HPR}}]^2} \tag{7.2}$$

In Eq. 7.1, HPR represents the Holding period returns, and n represents the number of years.

EXAMPLE 7.6 Ashish invested in shares of Reliance Industries on 31st March 2009 at ₹1,522. He sold of his investment on 31st March 2014 at ₹931. The closing price of Reliance shares at the end of every year is given in below table. Calculate the variance and standard deviation of Ashish's investment over the investment horizon

Year	*Reliance share price (₹)*
Mar-09	1,522
Mar-10	1,074
Mar-11	1,049
Mar-12	751
Mar-13	772
Mar-14	931

Steps to Calculate Standard Deviation and Variance of Reliance Investment

Step 1 Calculate the annual Holding period return from the prices given.

Year	*Reliance stock price*	*Return*
Mar-09	1,522	
Mar-10	1,074	–29.43%
Mar-11	1,049	–2.33%
Mar-12	751	–28.41%
Mar-13	772	2.80%
Mar-14	931	20.60%

Step 2 Calculate the mean return of the annual returns from March 2010–14. Further calculate the squared deviations of annual returns from mean returns.

Year	*Return*	*Squared deviations from the mean*	*Squared deviations from the mean*
Mar-09			
Mar-10	–29.43%	[(–29.43% – (–7.36%))]^2	4.87%
Mar-11	–2.33%	[(–2.33% – (–7.36%))]^2	0.25%
Mar-12	–28.41%	[(–28.41% – (–7.36%))]^2	4.43%
Mar-13	–2.80%	[(–2.80% – (–7.36%))]^2	1.03%
Mar-14	–20.60%	[(–20.60% – (–7.36%))]^2	7.81%
Mean	–7.36%		

Step 3 Calculate the Variance–Find the sum of squared deviations from the mean and average it.

IF =SUM(E3:E7)/5

	A	C	D	E
1	**Year**	**Return**	**Squared deviations from the Mean**	**Squared deviations from the Mean**
2	Mar-09			
3	Mar-10	-29.43%	[(-29.43%-(-7.36%))]^2	4.87%
4	Mar-11	-2.33%	[(-2.33%-(-7.36%))]^2	0.25%
5	Mar-12	-28.41%	[(-28.41%-(-7.36%))]^2	4.43%
6	Mar-13	2.80%	[(-2.80%-(-7.36%))]^2	1.03%
7	Mar-14	20.60%	[(-20.60%-(-7.36%))]^2	7.81%
8				
9	**Mean**	-7.36%		
10	**Variance**			=SUM(E3:E7)/5
11	**VAR()**			SUM(number1, [number2], ...
12				
13	**Standard Deviation**			19.19%

Step 4 Calculate the Standard Deviation—Find the square root of Variance to calculate Standard deviation.

E13 =(E11)^(0.5)

	A	C	D	E
1	**Year**	**Return**	**Squared deviations from the Mean**	**Squared deviations from the Mean**
2	Mar-09			
3	Mar-10	-29.43%	[(-29.43%-(-7.36%))]^2	4.87%
4	Mar-11	-2.33%	[(-2.33%-(-7.36%))]^2	0.25%
5	Mar-12	-28.41%	[(-28.41%-(-7.36%))]^2	4.43%
6	Mar-13	2.80%	[(-2.80%-(-7.36%))]^2	1.03%
7	Mar-14	20.60%	[(-20.60%-(-7.36%))]^2	7.81%
8				
9	**Mean**	-7.36%		
10	**Variance**			3.68%
12				
13	**Standard Deviation**			19.19%
14	**STDEV()**			19.19%

Note: In excel spreadsheet, Variance and Standard deviation can also be directly calculated using function VARP() and STDEVP(), respectively.

IF =VARP(C3:C7)

	A	C	D	E
1	Year	Return	Squared deviations from the Mean	Squared deviations from the Mean
2	Mar-09			
3	Mar-10	-29.43%	[(-29.43%-(-7.36%))]^2	4.87%
4	Mar-11	-2.33%	[(-2.33%-(-7.36%))]^2	0.25%
5	Mar-12	-28.41%	[(-28.41%-(-7.36%))]^2	4.43%
6	Mar-13	2.80%	[(-2.80%-(-7.36%))]^2	1.03%
7	Mar-14	20.60%	[(-20.60%-(-7.36%))]^2	7.81%
8				
9	Mean	-7.36%		
10	Variance			3.68%
11	VAR()			=VARP(C3:C7)
12				VARP(number1, [number2], ...)

IF =STDEVP(C3:C7)

	A	C	D	E
1	Year	Return	Squared deviations from the Mean	Squared deviations from the Mean
2	Mar-09			
3	Mar-10	-29.43%	[(-29.43%-(-7.36%))]^2	4.87%
4	Mar-11	-2.33%	[(-2.33%-(-7.36%))]^2	0.25%
5	Mar-12	-28.41%	[(-28.41%-(-7.36%))]^2	4.43%
6	Mar-13	2.80%	[(-2.80%-(-7.36%))]^2	1.03%
7	Mar-14	20.60%	[(-20.60%-(-7.36%))]^2	7.81%
8				
9	Mean	-7.36%		
10	Variance			3.68%
11	VAR()			3.68%
12				
13	Standard Deviation			19.19%
14	STDEV()			=STDEVP(C3:C7)

7.3.2 Variance for Expected Return

As we discussed earlier, for future data, where probabilities are associated with the variables, variance is the expected value of the squared deviations from the expected value.

$$\sigma^2 = \sum_{i=1}^{n} [R_i - E(R_i)]^2 P_i \qquad (7.3)$$

$$\sigma = \sqrt{\sum_{i=1}^{n} [R_i - E(R_i)]^2 P_i} \qquad (7.3)$$

In Eqs. (7.3) and (7.4), R represents the return, and P the probability associated with those returns.

EXAMPLE 7.7 Nilesh, a private wealth manager, is in the process of preparing the presentation for advising his clients to buy shares of Tata Steel Limited. Nilesh had forecasted three scenarios for the economy on the basis of which he has arrived at three target returns for Tata Steel. Further, Nilesh has assigned probabilities to various scenarios to arrive at expected price. With the help of information given below, calculate the Standard Deviation and Variance of Tata Steel stock.

Economic scenarios	*Tata steel returns*	*Probability*
Optimistic	15%	30%
Base Case	8%	50%
Pessimistic	–2%	20%

Steps to Calculate Standard Deviation and Variance of Tata Steel

Step 1 Calculate the expected rate of return for Tata steel by multiplying returns for each scenario with probability associated with that scenario and adding them all up. Alternatively, in excel, students can use the sum product function to arrive at the expected return.

IF =SUMPRODUCT(E3:E5,F3:F5)

	B	E	F
2	**Economic Scenarios**	**Tata Steel Estimate Return**	**Probability**
3	Optimistic	15%	30%
4	Base Case	8%	50%
5	Pessimistic	-2.0%	20%
6			
7	**Expected Returns**	=SUMPRODUCT(E3:E5,F3:F5)	
8	**Variance**		
9	**Standard Deviation**		

Step 2 Further calculate the squared deviations under each scenario by subtracting respective returns from expected return calculated in Step 1 and squaring them up.

Coefficient of Variation (CV) refers to the risk per unit of return generated by the investment

IF =(E3-F7)^2

	B	E	F	G
2	**Economic Scenarios**	**Tata Steel Estimate Return**	**Probability**	**Squared deviations from Expected Return**
3	Optimistic	15%	30%	=(E3-F7)^2
4	Base Case	8%	50%	0.000%
5	Pessimistic	-2.0%	20%	1.020%
6				
7	**Expected Returns**		**8.1%**	
8	**Variance**			
9	**Standard Deviation**			

Step 3 Multiply the squared deviation from expected returns calculated under each scenario with probability assigned to that scenario. Sum it up and the result is Variance. Square root it to arrive at Standard Deviation.

New Microsoft Excel Worksheet - Microsoft Excel

IF =F3*G3

	A	B	E	F	G	H
1						
2		Economic Scenarios	Tata Steel Estimate Return	Probability	Squared deviations from Expected Return	Probability*Squared Deviations
3		Optimistic	15%	30%	0.476%	=F3*G3
4		Base Case	8%	50%	0.000%	0.000%
5		Pessimistic	-2.0%	20%	1.020%	0.204%
6						
7		Expected Returns		8.1%		

New Microsoft Excel Worksheet - Microsoft Excel

IF =SUM(H3:H5)

	A	B	E	F	G	H
1						
2		Economic Scenarios	Tata Steel Estimate Return	Probability	Squared deviations from Expected Return	Probability*Squared Deviations
3		Optimistic	15%	30%	0.476%	0.143%
4		Base Case	8%	50%	0.000%	0.000%
5		Pessimistic	-2.0%	20%	1.020%	0.204%
6						
7		Expected Returns		8.1%		
8		Variance				=SUM(H3:H5)
9		Standard Deviation				SUM(number1, [number2], ...

New Microsoft Excel Worksheet - Microsoft Excel

H8 =SUM(H3:H5)

	A	B	E	F	G	H
1						
2		Economic Scenarios	Tata Steel Estimate Return	Probability	Squared deviations from Expected Return	Probability*Squared Deviations
3		Optimistic	15%	30%	0.476%	0.143%
4		Base Case	8%	50%	0.000%	0.000%
5		Pessimistic	-2.0%	20%	1.020%	0.204%
6						
7		Expected Returns		8.1%		
8		Variance				0.347%
9		Standard Deviation				5.890%
10						

7.4 Coefficient of Variation

Let us say that you have two investment options to choose—both having different returns (or expected returns) and different standard deviations (or risk). Which investment option will you choose? Confused? Merely looking at returns and standard deviation at standalone basis does not aid in arriving at rationale investment decisions. However, when we combine the both (return and risk) in form of a ratio, the resultant number will immediately tell us about the superiority of one investment over the other.

Coefficient of Variation (CV), a relative measure of risk, primarily serves the above purpose by combining risk and return, and letting us know which investment to choose from. Coefficient of Variation (CV) measures the risk per unit of expected return, and is arrived at by dividing standard deviation of return by expected return.

$$\text{CV} = \text{Standard deviation of return/Expected return} = \sigma/E(R_i)$$

Lower the Coefficient of Variation (CV), lower the risk per unit of return generated by the investment. So when we are comparing multiple investments on the basis of Coefficient of Variation (CV), choose the one with the lowest CV.

EXAMPLE 7.8 Vishesh plans to choose between investing ₹1 lakh in Axis bank and ICICI bank. However, he estimates that returns from these stocks are dependent on macroeconomic conditions. The probability distributions and expected returns are enumerated as follows:

Axis Bank

For every 1% change in GDP growth, deposit growth improves by a factor of 3 and for every +1% change in deposits, Axis bank returns change by +50 bps. Deposit growth is currently 15% and Base case return for Axis bank is 5% for next year.

ICICI Bank

For every 1% change in GDP growth, deposit growth improves by a factor of 3 and for every +1% change in deposits. ICICI bank returns change by +75 bps. Deposit growth is currently 15% and Base case return for ICICI bank is 7% for next year.

Which stock should he invest in on the basis of coefficient of variation (CV)?

Calculation of Coefficient of Variation (CV)

Scenario-Axis bank	*GDP*	*Deposits*	*Axis bank estimate return*	*Prob.*	*Squared deviations*	*Prob. * Squared deviations*
Flat GDP growth	5%	15%	5.0%	50%	0.004%	0.002%
GDP growth is 2% Points above last year	7%	21%	8.0%	30%	0.058%	0.017%
GDP growth is 1% points below last year	4%	12%	3.5%	20%	0.044%	0.009%
Expected returns				**5.6%**		
Variance						**0.028%**
Standard deviation						**1.67%**
CV						**29.83%**

Scenario-ICICI bank	*GDP*	*Deposits*	*ICICI bank estimate return*	*Prob.*	*Squared deviations*	*Prob. * Squared deviations*
Flat GDP growth	5%	15%	7.0%	50%	0.008%	0.004%
GDP growth is 2% points above last year	7%	21%	11.5%	30%	0.130%	0.039%
GDP growth is 1% points below last year	4%	12%	4.75%	20%	0.099%	0.020%
Expected returns				**7.9%**		
Variance						**0.063%**
Standard deviation						**2.51%**
CV						**31.72%**

It is clear from the above analysis that Axis Bank (29.83%) has the lower Coefficient of Variation (CV) as compared to ICICI Bank (31.72%). Consequently, Vishesh should choose Axis Bank over ICICI Bank.

7.5 Portfolio Return and Risk

Till now, we have been talking about return and risk from the point-of-view of standalone assets. In real world, however, it rarely happens that people invest their entire wealth in a single asset or security. Generally, the tendency is to diversify the investment over various assets, such as equity, debt, real estate, commodities, gold, etc. so as to reduce the risk of concentrated bets. This brings us to the concept of a portfolio or a combination of assets. In the financial world, a portfolio basically represents an investment spread over more than one asset or security. Now since a portfolio contains more than one asset/security, the return and risk of a portfolio would be very different from the return and risk of an individual asset. In this section, we will learn to compute risk and return from the portfolio perspective and show how it is different from the risk/return computation of standalone assets.

7.5.1 Portfolio Return

Portfolio return is simply the weighted average of the returns of the individual assets that comprise the portfolio.

Mathematically, in case of a two assets (Asset A and B) portfolio, portfolio return shall be calculated as:

$$R_p = w_A \times R_A + w_B \times R_B$$

where,

R_P = Portfolio return
w_A = Weight of asset A
w_b = Weight of asset B
R_A = Return on asset A
R_B = Return on asset B

Similarly, for a three asset portfolio (Asset A, B, C), portfolio return shall be calculated as:

$$R_p = w_A \times R_A + w_B \times R_B + w_C \times R_C$$

where,

R_P = Portfolio return
w_A = Weight of asset A
w_B = Weight of asset B
w_C = Weight of asset C
R_A = Return on asset A
R_B = Return on asset B
R_C = Return on asset C

Portfolio return is the weighted average of the returns of the individual assets that comprise the portfolio

EXAMPLE 7.9 Naresh, a retail investor, has invested his wealth in three securities—Tata Motors, DLF and Nestle in the ratio of 40:50:10. One year returns for the three securities are provided as follows:

Calculate the portfolio return for Naresh over past one year.

Security	*1 year return*
Tata Motors	17%
DLF	5%
Nestle	21%

Calculation of Portfolio Return

$$R_P = w_A \times R_A + w_B \times R_B + w_C \times R_C$$

$$R_P = 40\% \times 17\% + 5\% \times 50\% + 21\% \times 10\% = 11.4\%$$

Alternatively, students can arrange the data, and use sum product function in excel to arrive at portfolio return.

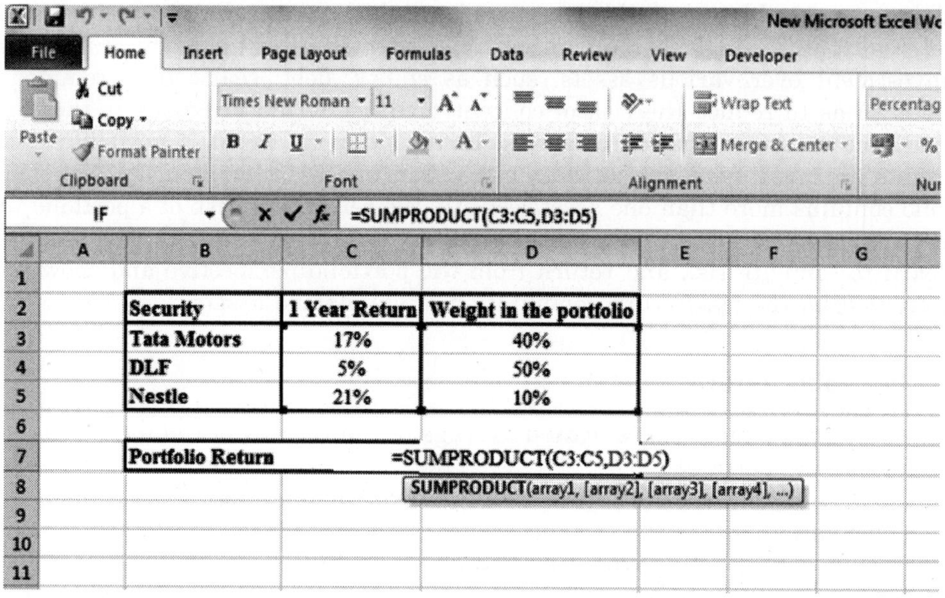

=SUMPRODUCT(C3:C5,D3:D5)

Security	1 Year Return	Weight in the portfolio
Tata Motors	17%	40%
DLF	5%	50%
Nestle	21%	10%

Portfolio Return	=SUMPRODUCT(C3:C5,D3:D5)

SUMPRODUCT(array1, [array2], [array3], [array4], ...)

7.5.2 Portfolio Risk

Assume that you have ₹10 million in your bank account available for investment. You choose to equally divide your investment in stocks of Nestle India and JSW Steel. Now, as we discussed in the preceding section, if respective securities returns are provided, portfolio return simply becomes a weighted average number. Now the question is, whether portfolio risk can also be calculated in a similar manner. Would portfolio risk of your 10 million investment be a linear sum of individual risks of securities comprising it, weighted by their respective proportionate holdings in the portfolio? If the answer, to this question was yes, then the popular axiom **"Don't put all your eggs in one basket"** would have never existed!!

The unequivocal answer to the above question is a clear No. Portfolio risk is simply not a weighted average of individual risks of securities comprising it. In this section, we will discuss as to how portfolio risk can be entirely different from the risk of individual securities comprising it on account of correlation (or covariance) between their returns.

Portfolio Risk–Two Asset Portfolio

To understand the portfolio risk, let us start with a classic two asset portfolio. From our original example, let us assume that you have invested ₹10 million equally between the stocks of Nestle India and JSW Steel (both are listed securities on BSE and NSE). Now Nestle India is a consumer staple company whereas JSW Steel is a commodity company. Given the nature of their respective businesses, demand for JSW Steel will be more volatile compared to the demand for Nestle India. This is because irrespective of the economic conditions and income levels, people will continue to consume basic necessity such as food whereas demand for steel will go up and down in congruity with the economic cycle. The essence of the argument is that given the differences in inherent business characteristics of two companies (Nestle and JSW Steel), their returns would behave very differently in different economic cycles. This difference in movement of returns would make calculation of portfolio risk very different from simply being the weighted average of individual returns of securities comprising the portfolio.

Now the question is how do we capture this co-movement of returns for securities comprising the portfolio. One of the ways in which it can be captured is by calculating covariance between the returns of two securities. Covariance measures the degree to which two assets move together relative to their individual mean values over time. These movements may be positive or negative. For two assets A and B, covariance of rates of return is defined as

$$\text{Cov}(R_{A,} R_B) = [(R_A - \bar{R}_A)]\ [(R_B - \bar{R}_B)]$$

where, R_A and R_B are the actual returns and $\bar{R}_A$ and $\bar{R}_B$ are the mean returns for assets A and B

Another way of measuring co-movement of returns for securities is through a measure called correlation. Correlation basically standardize the covariance by dividing it with individual standard deviation of securities comprising the portfolio

$$r_{AB} = \frac{\text{Cov}_{AB}}{\sigma_A \sigma_B}$$

where,

r_{AB} = Correlation coefficient between returns of asset A and asset B
Cov_{AB} = Covariance between returns of asset A and asset B
σ_A = Standard deviation of asset A
σ_B = Standard deviation of asset B

Now that we have learnt to measure Covariance and Correlation, we can define portfolio risk in case of two assets. Mathematically Portfolio Variance for a 2 asset portfolio equals

$$\sigma_P^2 = w_A^2 \times \sigma_A^2 + w_B^2 \times \sigma_B^2 + 2 \times w_A \times w_B \times \rho_{AB} \times \sigma_A \times \sigma_B$$

where,

σ_P^2 = Portfolio variance
w_A = weight of asset A
w_b = weight of asset B
σ_A^2 = Variance of asset A
σ_B^2 = Variance of asset B
$\rho_{A,B}$ = Correlation coefficient between asset A and B
σ_A = Standard deviation of asset A
σ_B = Standard deviation of asset B

Also,

$$\text{Portfolio standard deviation } (\sigma_P) = \sqrt{\sigma_P^2}$$

Can Diversification Reduce Portfolio Risk

As evident from the description of Portfolio Variance, if an investor can diversify his investment in assets, which have a correlation coefficient of less than 1, portfolio risk can be brought down. If the assets returns are perfectly positively correlated (+1), it essentially means that they would go up and down together resulting in no risk reduction. However, if an investor can find assets or securities where returns are perfectly negatively correlated (–1), all risk can be diversified away.

While the above discussion looks good on paper, but realistically is it possible to find investments (or stocks) which have a perfect negative correlation? Although it is a rarity to find such investments (or stocks) which have a perfect negative correlation for a prolonged period of time, it is certainly possible to identify investment (or stocks) which have negative correlations (near perfect if not perfect).

During my good old days as a Fund manager, I came across a lot of such investments (or stocks) which had a near perfect negative correlation and which helped me reduce portfolio risk by a considerable extent. Some examples of such kind of investments are enumerated as follows:

1. **Equity and gold:** Investment in gold generally serves as a hedge or outperforms during periods of global deflation/depression and/or macroeconomic shocks. Investment in equity generally underperforms during the above-mentioned scenarios. The opposite is also generally true. Gold underperforms when economy tend to do well as people shift towards equity investment. So, a portfolio comprising of investment in equity and gold would generally have a negative correlation leading to diversification of risk.

2. **Equity and bonds:** Bonds generally tend to do well during periods of economic weakness and deflation/depression. This is because as economy crumbles, inflation starts to go down which feeds into lowering of benchmark interest rates, and hence, increase in bond prices. Consequently, you would generally see a flight of safety being taken by investors towards bonds during global deflation/depression and/or macroeconomic shocks. The opposite is also true. During periods of economic boom and recovery, as inflation starts to go up, benchmark rates rise and bonds tend to underperform. Investment in equity generally underperforms during periods of global deflation/depression and/or macroeconomic shocks and outperforms as economy starts to recover. So, a portfolio comprising of investment in equity and bonds would generally have a negative correlation leading to diversification of risk.

3. **INR (Indian Rupee) and Crude Oil (Commodity):** Specifically talking about India, Indian currency and crude oil, generally tend to exhibit negative correlation. This is because around 75% of India's crude oil requirements are met through imports. A rise in price of crude oil leads to widening of current account deficit (exports–imports), which further feeds into weakening of the Indian currency (₹). The opposite is also generally true. So, a portfolio comprising investment in crude oil (Commodity) and currency (₹) would generally have a negative correlation leading to diversification of risk.

Specifically talking of individual stocks (in case of Indian investor), following combinations generally tends to exhibit negative correlation:

4. **Cairn India and Infosys:** Cairn India, being an oil exploration company, generally tends to benefit from higher prices of crude oil. As crude oil price rises, it provides a positive fillip to Cairn India's profitability and stock price. Similarly, Cairn India will be negatively impacted by lower crude oil prices. Lower crude oil prices acts as a panacea to India's current account balance given that 75% of India's crude oil requirements are met through imports. So while lower crude prices negatively affects Cairn India, it tends to positively affect FMCG companies like Hindustan Unilever, Colgate Palmolive, Dabur, etc. who imports most of their raw materials. So, an appreciating rupee on account of falling crude prices would lower the input cost of above FMCG companies and increase their profit margins. This would give a positive fillip to their stock prices. So a portfolio comprising of investment in Cairn India (a proxy for crude oil) and Hindustan Unilever (or Colgate Palmolive, Dabur, etc.) would generally have a negative correlation leading to diversification of risk.

5. **Cairn India and Apollo tyres:** As discussed above, Cairn India is generally negatively impacted by falling crude prices. However, tyre companies like Apollo tyres

stands to benefit with falling crude price as a substantial portion of their raw material cost is linked to crude oil price. Falling crude reduces the raw material cost, leading to improvement in margins and profitability, and hence, higher stock prices. So, a portfolio comprising of investment in Cairn India (a proxy for crude oil) and Apollo tyres would generally have a negative correlation leading to diversification of risk.

Extending the above argument, falling crude also positively impacts paint companies such as Asian Paints, Kansai Nerolac, etc. as raw materials for paint companies include a lot of crude derivatives (titanium dioxide, solvents, etc.). Similarly, Airlines stock tend to benefit with falling crude on account of falling ATF (Aviation Turbine Fuel) whose price is directly linked to international crude prices. So, a combination of Oil Exploration Company with any of the above stocks can produce a negative correlation leading to diversification of risk.

6. Hindustan Unilever Ltd. (HINDUNILVR) and Indian Hotels (INDHOTEL): During periods of global deflation/depression and/or macroeconomic shocks, Hindustan Unilever generally tends to outperform. This is because being a consumer staples company; demand for its product is generally stable. During periods of recession and falling incomes, while people tend to cut down on discretionary products (cars, air-conditioners, vacation, etc.), demand for staples (wheat, rice, salt, spices, etc.) generally remains unaffected. Consequently, consumer staples companies, like Hindustan Unilever acts as defensives during periods of deflation/depression and/ or macroeconomic shocks. On the other hand, as people cut down on discretionary products, such as vacation travel, demand for hotel rooms go down which dents profitability of hotel companies such as Indian hotels. Resultantly, investors shift from cyclical sectors like hotels (Indian Hotels) to defensives like FMCG (Hindustan Lever) during periods of deflation/depression leading to negative correlation between returns of stocks of above 2 sectors/companies. The opposite is also generally true. During periods of economic recovery, investors shun defensives like Hindustan Lever and flock towards cyclical companies like Indian Hotels as demand for discretionary product rises. So, a portfolio comprising investment in Consumer Staple Company (Hindustan Unilever) and Hotel Company (Indian hotels) would generally have a negative correlation leading to diversification of risk.

7. Sun Pharmaceuticals (SUNPHARMA) and ICICI bank (ICICI BANK): Similar to consumer staple companies, demand for products of pharma companies is generally, perpetual. During periods of recession and falling incomes, while people would generally desist from taking loans (credit) from banks, they would not cut down on healthcare cost. Consequently, while profitability and stock prices of banking stocks like ICICI bank goes for a toss during periods of recession on account of falling topline (loans) and rising non-performing assets (NPA's), profitability and stock prices of pharma companies remain stable. Consequently, there is negative correlation between returns of stocks of above 2 sectors/companies as investors move from cyclical to defensive sectors. The opposite is also generally true. So, a portfolio comprising of investment in pharma Company (Sun Pharmaceutical) and bank (ICICI Bank) would generally have a negative correlation leading to diversification of risk.

In congruence with above discussion, many more such negatively correlated asset combinations can be created for diversification of risk in the portfolio.

EXAMPLE 7.10 Two-Asset Portfolio

Rakesh, an HNI investor has been running a portfolio since March 2003 comprising 2 securities—ICICI Bank and Maruti Ltd.—ICICI Bank comprising 60% of the portfolio and Maruti comprising 40% of the portfolio. In the year 2014, Rakesh decided to calculate the risk his portfolio he has been running over all these years. Yearly returns for both the stocks over last 12 years are given in the following table. Compute the portfolio risk for Rakesh's investment using the concepts discussed in above section.

Year	*ICICI Annual Returns*	*Maruti Annual Returns*
Mar-03	–3.62%	4.05%
Mar-04	122.56%	176.11%
Mar-05	32.43%	–15.29%
Mar-06	50.26%	107.60%
Mar-07	44.82%	–6.18%
Mar-08	–9.85%	–0.37%
Mar-09	–56.70%	–4.65%
Mar-10	185.89%	81.90%
Mar-11	17.23%	–10.94%
Mar-12	–20.25%	6.97%
Mar-13	17.42%	–5.11%
Mar-14	19.14%	53.86%

Calculation of Portfolio Risk

Step 1 Start with calculating the mean or average returns over the period using the above data. The mean returns over the last 12 years for ICICI Bank and Maruti are 33.28% and 32.33%, respectively.

Step 2 Next calculate the deviations of annual returns from the mean returns calculated above for each year for both the stocks.

Step 3 Calculate the covariance by multiplying the deviations of both the stocks for each year and averaging it up. Alternatively covariance can also be found out by using the COVAR() function in excel.

Step 4 Find out the Variance of ICICI bank and Maruti

Year	*ICICI annual returns*	*Maruti annual returns*	*Deviations for ICICI bank from mean return*	*Deviations for Maruti from mean return*	*Covariance*	*Squared deviations for ICICI bank from mean return*	*Squared deviations for Maruti from mean return*
Mar-03	–3.62%	4.05%	–36.90%	–28.28%	10.44%	13.62%	8.00%
Mar-04	122.56%	176.11%	89.28%	143.78%	128.37%	79.71%	206.73%
Mar-05	32.43%	–15.29%	–0.84%	–47.62%	0.40%	0.01%	22.68%
Mar-06	50.26%	107.60%	16.98%	75.27%	12.78%	2.88%	56.66%
Mar-07	44.82%	–6.18%	11.55%	–38.51%	–4.45%	1.33%	14.83%
Mar-08	–9.85%	–0.37%	–43.12%	–32.70%	14.10%	18.60%	10.69%
Mar-09	–56.70%	–4.65%	–89.97%	–36.98%	33.27%	80.95%	13.68%
Mar-10	185.89%	81.90%	152.61%	49.57%	75.65%	232.90%	24.57%
Mar-11	17.23%	–10.94%	–16.05%	–43.27%	6.94%	2.58%	18.72%
Mar-12	–20.25%	6.97%	–53.53%	–25.36%	13.57%	28.65%	6.43%
Mar-13	17.42%	–5.11%	–15.86%	–37.44%	5.94%	2.52%	14.02%
Mar-14	19.14%	53.86%	–14.14%	21.53%	–3.04%	2.00%	4.64%
Mean	**33.28%**	**32.33%**					
Covariance					**24.50%**		
Variance						**38.81%**	**33.47%**
Standard Deviation						**62.30%**	**57.85%**

Step 5 Calculate the correlation coefficient using the formula

$$r_{AB} = \frac{\text{Cov}_{AB}}{\sigma_A \sigma_B}$$

$$= 0.2450/(0.6230 \times 0.5785) = 0.68$$

Now, we have all the figures to fit in the formula for Portfolio Variance (risk)

$$\sigma_P^2 = w_A^2 \times \sigma_A^2 + w_B^2 \times \sigma_B^2 + 2 \times w_A \times w_B \times \rho_{A,B} \times \sigma_A \times \sigma_B$$

$$\sigma_P^2 = (0.6)^2 \times 0.3881 + (0.4)^2 \times 0.3347 + 2 \times 0.6 \times 0.4 \times 0.68 \times 0.6230 \times 0.5785$$

$$= 0.3109 \text{ or } 31.09\%$$

Similarly, Portfolio standard deviation (σ) = $\sqrt{31.09\%}$ = 55.8%

Portfolio Risk—Three Asset Portfolio

Now that we have learnt the calculation of portfolio risk for two asset portfolio, it is easy to extrapolate the same to three asset portfolio. Mathematically Portfolio Variance for a 3 asset portfolio equals

$$\sigma_P^2 = w_A^2 \times \sigma_A^2 + w_B^2 \times \sigma_B^2 + w_C^2 \times \sigma_C^2 + 2 \times w_A \times w_B \times \rho_{A,B} \times \sigma_A \times \sigma_B$$
$$+ 2 \times w_B \times w_C \times \rho_{B,C} \times \sigma_B \times \sigma_C + 2 \times w_C \times w_A \times \rho_{C,A} \times \sigma_C \times \sigma_A$$

where,

σ_P^2 = Portfolio Variance
w_A = Weight of asset A
w_B = Weight of asset B
w_C = Weight of asset C
σ_A^2 = Variance of asset A
σ_B^2 = Variance of asset B
σ_C^2 = Variance of asset C
$\rho_{A,B}$ = Correlation coefficient between asset A and B
$\rho_{B,C}$ = Correlation coefficient between asset B and C
$\rho_{C,A}$ = Correlation coefficient between asset A and C
σ_A = Standard deviation of asset A
σ_B = Standard deviation of asset B
σ_C = Standard deviation of asset C

Similar to the two asset formula, the three asset variance calculation captures the contribution of individual variances (the first three terms of the equation) as well as the cross correlations of the assets comprising the portfolio (last three terms of the equation).

Finally, the portfolio standard deviation can be shown as (σ_P) = $\sqrt{\sigma_P^2}$

EXAMPLE 7.11 Three-Asset Portfolio

Sunil, an analyst with an insurance fund is evaluating the portfolio risk of 3 asset classes he is invested in. Yearly returns for the asset classes over the last 10 years are given below. Compute the portfolio risk for Sunil's investment using the concepts discussed in above section. The weights of 3 asset classes in Sunil's portfolio are—equity (50%); debt (30%) and commodity (20%)

	Equity returns	Debt returns	Commodity returns
Mar-01	–10.0%	4.0%	12.0%
Mar-02	12.5%	0.5%	–10.0%
Mar-03	8.0%	–1.0%	15.0%
Mar-04	6.0%	3.0%	6.0%
Mar-05	–14.0%	7.0%	8.0%
Mar-06	20.0%	–3.0%	–2.0%
Mar-07	4.0%	9.0%	–10.5%
Mar-08	–9.0%	10.0%	5.0%
Mar-09	9.0%	–4.0%	8.0%
Mar-10	9.0%	–7.0%	4.0%
Mar-11	1.0%	–0.7%	–20.0%
Mar-12	7.5%	–1.8%	5.0%

Calculation of Portfolio Risk

Step 1 Start with calculating the mean or average returns over the period using the above data. The mean returns over the last 12 years for equity, debt and commodity are 3.67%, 1.33% and 1.71%, respectively.

Step 2 Next calculate the deviations of annual returns from the mean returns calculated above for each year for the 3 asset classes.

Step 3 Calculate the correlation for 3 asset classes taking two at a time—equity and debt; debt and commodity; commodity and equity (CORREL() function in excel can be used).

Step 4 Find out the variance and standard deviation of 3 asset classes (students can use VAR() and STDEV() function in excel for the same)

	Equity returns	Debt returns	Commodity returns
Mar-01	–10.0%	4.0%	12.0%
Mar-02	12.5%	0.5%	–10.0%
Mar-03	8.0%	–1.0%	15.0%
Mar-04	6.0%	3.0%	6.0%
Mar-05	–14.0%	7.0%	8.0%
Mar-06	20.0%	–3.0%	–2.0%
Mar-07	4.0%	9.0%	–10.5%
Mar-08	–9.0%	10.0%	5.0%
Mar-09	9.0%	–4.0%	8.0%
Mar-10	9.0%	–7.0%	4.0%
Mar-11	1.0%	–0.7%	–20.0%
Mar-12	7.5%	–1.8%	5.0%
Sum			
Mean	**3.67%**	**1.33%**	**1.71%**
Variance of equity	1.01%		
Variance of debt	0.28%		
Variance of commodity	1.07%		
Standard deviation of equity	10.03%		
Standard deviation of debt	5.33%		
Standard deviation of commodity	10.35%		
Correlation between equity and debt	–0.69		
Correlation between debt and commodity	–0.03		
Correlation between equity and commodity	–0.24		

Now, we have all the figures to fit in the formula for Portfolio Variance (risk)

$$\sigma_P^2 = w_A^2 \times \sigma_A^2 + w_B^2 \times \sigma_B^2 + w_C^2 \times \sigma_C^2 + 2 \times w_A \times w_B \times \rho_{A,B} \times \sigma_A \times \sigma_B + 2 \times w_B \times w_C \times \rho_{B,C} \times \sigma_B \times \sigma_C + 2 \times w_C \times w_A \times \rho_{C,A} \times \sigma_C \times \sigma_A$$

$$\sigma_P^2 = (0.5)^2 \times 1.01\% + (0.3)^2 \times 0.28\% + (0.2)^2 \times 1.07\% + 2 \times 0.5 \times 0.3 \times (-0.69) \times 10.03\% \times 5.33\% + 2 \times 0.3 \times 0.2 \times (-0.03) \times 5.33\% \times 10.35\% + 2 \times 0.2 \times 0.5 \times (-0.24) \times 10.03\% \times 10.35\% = 0.16\%$$

Similarly Portfolio standard deviation (σ) = $\sqrt{0.16\%}$ = 3.95%

Researchable Issues

Faculty members, students and research scholars may like to consider the following selected issues for further research and case writing.

- Holding period Returns of Indian Mutual funds vs BSE Sensex
- Comparison of Portfolio Risk in Indian Mutual funds vs BSE Sensex
- Comparison of Portfolio Risk and Return for Indian Mutual funds vs Insurance Funds
- Holding period Return and Risk for BSE Sensex vs Gold vs Brent Crude over historical period
- Comparison of Holding period Return and Risk between Large-Cap, Mid-Cap and Small-Cap stocks in India

References

Dawar, V., "Portfolio Diversification Enigma", Product Number–9B14N031, Ivey Publishing, 2014.

Li, J.C. and Mei, D.C., "The returns and risks of investment portfolio in a financial market" *Physica A: Statistical Mechanics and its Applications*, 406, 67–72, 2014.

Li, J.C., Long, C., and Chen, X.D., "The returns and risks of investment portfolio in stock market crashes. Physica A: *Statistical Mechanics and Its Applications*, 427, pp. 282–288, 2015.

Meade, N., "Forecasting the return and risk on a portfolio of assets", *International Journal of Forecasting*, 9(3), pp. 373–386, 1993.

Points to Remember

- Holding period return or ex-post returns attempts to measure the return over the holding period of an investment made. Basically it represents the total return (Accrual Income + Capital Gain/Loss) earned on an investment for the time period it is held upon. Expected rate of return can be calculated in terms of probability weighted average of the rates of return in each scenario.
- Deviation or dispersion or variability of actual returns from the expected returns is technically referred to as risk. In the financial world, two popular measures to assess risk are *standard deviation and variance.*
- Coefficient of Variation (CV), a relative measure of risk, primarily serves the above purpose by combining risk and return and letting us know which investment to choose from. Coefficient of Variation (CV) measures the risk per unit of expected return and is arrived at by dividing standard deviation by expected return.

- Portfolio return is simply the weighted average of the returns of the individual assets that comprise the portfolio.
- Portfolio risk can be entirely different from the risk of individual securities comprising it on account of correlation (or covariance) between their returns. Portfolio risk captures the contribution of individual variances as well as the cross-correlations of the assets comprising the portfolio.
- Covariance measures the degree to which two assets move together relative to their individual mean values over time. Correlation basically standardize the covariance by dividing it with individual standard deviation of securities comprising the portfolio.
- If the assets' returns are perfectly positively correlated (+1), it essentially means that they would go up and down together resulting in no risk reduction. However if an investor can find assets where returns are perfectly negatively correlated (–1), all risk can be diversified away.

Questions

1. Discuss the concept of holding period return in the investment world. How is it different from expected rate of return? Give examples.
2. Discuss various measures of calculation of risk. Explain how Coefficient of Variation (CV) can be used for making investment decisions.
3. Explain and illustrate the concept and formula for portfolio risk and return in case of a two asset portfolio. Discuss the significance of diversification in reducing portfolio risk.
4. Discuss how correlation is different from covariance. In this connection, give examples of financial assets which tend to exhibit (a) negative correlation (b) positive correlation.

Multiple Choice Questions

1. Ashish, a retail investor bought 1,000 shares of L&T finance for INR 1,605, in 2014. He received dividends of ₹ 150 during the year. Currently L&T Finance is priced at INR 1,779. Calculate the holding period returns for Ashish.

(a) 12.5% (b) 20.1%
(c) 15.6% (d) None of the above

2. Ravi bought 100 shares of Axis bank for ₹565. Ravi expects a dividend of ₹60 during the next year. If Ravi wants an expected holding period return of 15%, at what price should Ravi sell the shares?

(a) 632.25 (b) 589.75
(c) 527.50 (d) None of the above

3. Skyline 5-year returns are provided below. Calculate the multi-period holding period return using geometric mean approach.

Year	*Skyline return*
2009	25%
2010	70%
2011	5%
2012	20%
2013	28%

(a) 19.50% (b) 27.93%
(c) 32.43% (d) 21.80%

4. Anil, an HNI investor expects his portfolio to yield expected return of 15% for next year. He further expects variance of his expected return to be 10%. Calculate the Coefficient of Variation (CV) for Anil's portfolio.
(a) 0.27 (b) 0.36
(c) 0.47 (d) 0.45

5. Mahesh's portfolio consists of 2 stocks–Oriental Bank and Nestle Ltd. in the ratio of 70:30. Standard deviation of Oriental Bank returns for past 1 year is 15% and that of Nestle Ltd. is 10%. Correlation between the returns of two stocks is 0.6. What is the portfolio risk (standard deviation) for Mahesh's investment?
(a) 0.172% (b) 0.453%
(c) 0.381% (d) 0.125%

6. Arit has invested his wealth in four securities- Godrej Ltd, Unitech, Powergrid and Britannia in the ratio of 20:30:40:10. One year returns for Godrej Ltd, Unitech, Powergrid and Britannia are 9%, 12%, 6% and 3%, respectively. Calculate the portfolio return for Arit.
(a) 7.5% (b) 8.1%
(c) 5.6% (d) None of the above

7. Asset A has an expected return of 17% and standard deviation of 12%. Asset B has an expected return of 11% and standard deviation of 6%. Which investment would be better as per Coefficient of Variation (CV).
(a) Asset A
(b) Asset B
(c) Both are equivalent in terms of risk and return

8. Sreesh's portfolio, which consists of 2 assets, has an expected return of 14%. If individual assets expected returns are 10% and 15%, calculate the weights of the assets comprising the portfolio (assume positive weights).
(a) 20% and 80% (b) 15% and 85%
(c) 30% and 70% (d) 25% and 75%

9. Nishant bought 500 shares of NMDC Ltd. for ₹160 in 2014. He received dividends of ₹15 during the year. Currently, NMDC trades at ₹118. Calculate the holding period returns for Nishant's investment.
(a) 10.5% (b) –20.6%
(c) –16.8% (d) None of the above

10. Shreya's investment expected return for next year is 29% and standard deviation of expected returns is 16%. Calculate the Coefficient of Variation (CV) for the investment.
(a) 0.34 (b) 0.55
(c) 0.16 (d) 0.45

Self-Test Questions

1. Vijay, an individual investor has predicted 3 scenarios for the Indian economy in the next year—normal, boom and recession. The probabilities assigned by him to the three mentioned scenarios are 50%, 40% and 10% respectively. After formulating these scenarios, Vijay plans to buy 1,000 shares of Tata Steel, which are trading at ₹300 each. Vijay believes that while normal scenario for Indian

economy next year would lead to appreciation of 10% in stock of Tata Steel, a boom scenario could lead to an appreciation of 50% in the stock price. However, in case of a recession scenario, Tata Steel price could tank down by 40%. Using all the above information, calculate the expected return for Vijay's investment in Tata Steel stock for next year.

2. Angad, a second year MBA student is a part of endowment fund run by his university for investing in various asset classes. Angad wanted to compare the holding period return of the endowment portfolio vis-à-vis the return of the benchmark index. To compare the same, he collects the following data for the past 5 years for both endowment fund as well as the benchmark index.

Year	*Endowment portfolio yearly returns*	*Benchmark index yearly returns*
2011	14%	10%
2012	21%	25%
2013	–17%	–24%
2014	4%	1%
2015	–6%	–3%

Using the above-mentioned data, calculate the Holding Period Return for Endowment Portfolio and Benchmark Index using (a) Arithmetic Mean Approach (b) Geometric Mean Approach.

3. Hitesh, an HNI investor is planning to invest his money in equities. For this he has been able to shortlist 2 stocks for his planned investment namely ITC and Vijaya Bank. He now wants to assess the risk of these 2 investments using historical data over the last 5 years using the metrics of variance and standard deviation. For this, he collects the following data for the two stocks for the past 5 years:

Year	*ITC Ltd.*	*Vijaya bank*
2007	23%	–24%
2008	22%	40%
2009	–20%	–52%
2010	46%	59%
2011	23%	76%

Using the above data, calculate the risk of two investments individually using metrics of variance and standard deviation.

4. Rohan portfolio consists of 2 stocks–VKL Ltd. and SMJ Ltd. in the ratio of 40% and 60%, respectively. Annual returns of two stocks for last 4 years (2004–07) are given below:

Year	*VKL*	*SMJ*
2004	23%	40%
2005	12%	10%
2006	–5%	–24%
2007	16%	12%

Using the above data, calculate the portfolio risk for Rohan's investment.

5. Prashant, a retail investor is trying to choose between 2 investments—Investment A and Investment B for investment of his funds. To decide the same, he plans to use the metric of Coefficient of Variation (CV), a relative measure of risk. For this he has collected the following data

Scenarios	*Investment A yearly return*	*Investment B yearly return*	*Probabilities of yearly return for both investments*
Scenario 1	41%	13%	0.2
Scenario 2	23%	11%	0.1
Scenario 3	–10%	–10%	0.3
Scenario 4	–6%	–4%	0.1
Scenario 5	28%	17%	0.3

Using the above data, calculate the Coefficient of Variation (CV) for both investments and decide, which is better suited for Prashant.

6. Asim holds 2 stocks in his portfolio, namely SKS Ltd. and SGH Ltd. in the ratio of 30% and 70%, respectively. The historical yearly returns of the two stocks are given as follows:

Year	*SKS Ltd.*	*SGH Ltd.*
2001	50%	34%
2002	24%	42%
2003	–60%	–67%
2004	11%	–23%
2005	5%	17%

Using the above historical data, calculate the Portfolio return and risk for Asim's investment.

7. Neha plans to invest her money in DLF stock. However, she estimates that return on DLF stock is very much dependent on macroeconomic condition. She estimates that for every +/–1% change in GDP growth DLF stock returns change by +/–250 bps. Base case return for DLF stock for next year is 10%. GDP growth is currently 7%. The probability distribution and for GDP growth is enumerated below

Scenario	*GDP*	*Probability*
Flat GDP Growth	7%	25%
GDP Growth is 3% Points above last year	10%	35%
GDP Growth is 2% Points below last year	5%	40%

Using the above data, calculate the expected return for DLF stock for the next year.

8. Sachin wants to calculate the risk of his 3 stock portfolio he is invested in. Yearly returns for the asset classes over the last 5 years are given below. Compute the portfolio risk for Sachin's investment. The weights of 3 asset classes in Sunil's portfolio are

BHEL: 40%
Bharti Airtel: 35%
Lupin: 25%

Year	*BHEL*	*Airtel*	*Lupin*
Year 1	14.00%	8.00%	6.00%
Year 2	–12.00%	10.00%	8.00%
Year 3	16.00%	–11.00%	–2.00%
Year 4	2.00%	4.00%	–10.50%
Year 5	–10.00%	2.00%	5.00%

CASE

Portfolio Investment Analysis

In the year 2014, it was a late evening for Saumik Banerjee, senior private wealth manager at one of the prominent banks operating out of Manhattan, New York. Saumik, who generally handled High Net Worth (HNI) clients for the bank was particularly analyzing the portfolio for one of his esteemed client Ramesh Kumar who had recently approached Saumik for financial advice. Ramesh's portfolio in the past consisted primarily of large-cap equities. However, with his changing view on the economic growth, Ramesh was interested in adding mid-cap and small-cap stocks to his portfolio. Before adding the mid-cap and small-cap stocks to his existing portfolio, Ramesh wanted to assess the risk that he will be undertaking by including this category of stocks. Ramesh approached Saumik for the same who decided to carry out this exercise of assessing risk for the client's proposed portfolio.

For carrying out the above analysis, Saumik decided to test the backdated data by including the mid-cap and small-cap stocks to the large-cap portfolio of his client. Saumik basically constructed two backdated portfolios—one consisting of only large-cap equity (100% invested in large-cap stocks) and the other consisting of large-cap equity (50%), mid-cap equity (25%) and small-cap equity (25%) stocks. He further collected the yearly returns of large-cap, mid-cap and small-cap stocks for the last 12 years. The backdated yearly data for the same is provided in CS Table 7.1.

Assuming yourself as Saumik, calculate the portfolio risk and return for both scenarios (with and without mid-cap and small-cap stocks) along with the coefficient of variation and advice Ramesh whether he should go for adding mid-cap and small-cap stocks to his existing large-cap portfolio.

CS TABLE 7.1
Annual Returns for Large-Cap, Mid-Cap and Small-Cap Stocks.

	% Annual returns		
Year	*Large-cap stocks return*	*Mid-cap stocks return*	*Small-cap stocks return*
2002	23%	55%	46%
2003	–12%	–22%	–15%
2004	14%	38%	42%
2005	19%	17%	31%
2006	–14%	–20%	–40%
2007	–21%	–26%	–30%
2008	4%	7%	20%
2009	8%	30%	9%
2010	–7%	–4%	–3%
2011	15%	25%	34%
2012	–19%	–17%	–21%
2013	24%	29%	48%

CHAPTER

8

Portfolio Theory and Asset Pricing Models

LEARNING OBJECTIVES

After studying this chapter, you should be able to:

- Understand the construction of efficient frontier with portfolios comprising of risky assets.
- Understand how risk return tolerances of the investor can be mapped through utility functions or indifference curves.
- Discuss the concept of Capital Market Line (CML) and identification of optimal portfolios.
- Discuss the Capital Asset Pricing Model (CAPM) and determination of expected or required returns.
- Understand the construction and significance of Security Market Line (SML).
- Discuss the relevance of CAPM framework in real world and its extensions such as Arbitrage Pricing Theory (APT).

8.1 Introduction

In the previous chapter we learnt the calculation of portfolio risk and return and discussed how diversification (or correlation) between assets can go on reducing the portfolio risk. Further, in most of our discussions, the weights of assets/securities comprising the portfolio were assumed to be given or provided beforehand. However in the real world, determination of weights of assets/securities comprising the portfolio is as much an important task for the fund manager as the calculation of portfolio risk and return. So the important question that arises is how do the fund managers/portfolio managers determine the appropriate weight of assets/securities to be included in the portfolio? In this section, we shall determine the methodology to arrive at the weights of assets/securities that comprise the portfolio using the concept of efficient frontier.

8.2 Efficient Frontier—Two Asset Portfolios

Let us start our discussion with a simple two asset portfolio and then the same may be extended to multi-asset portfolio. Assume that a portfolio consists of two assets—equity and commodity. The individual returns and standard deviations for both these assets are given in Table 8.1.

TABLE 8.1
Return and Risk for Two-Asset portfolio

	Expected return	*Standard deviation*	*Correlation coefficient between equity and commodity*
Equity	30.0%	40.0%	–0.6
Commodity	7.0%	15.0%	

Now the above two assets may be combined in an umpteen number of ways (in terms of different weights) to comprise portfolios with varied return and risk. For example, if we combine the above two assets in ratio of 25% and 75%, respectively, the portfolio return and risk would be:

Portfolio return (R_P) = $w_A \times R_A + w_B \times R_B = 0.25 \times 30\% + 0.75 \times 7\% = 12.75\%$

Portfolio risk = $\sigma_P^2 = w_A^2 \times \sigma_A^2 + w_B^2 \times \sigma_B^2 + 2 \times w_A \times w_B \times \rho_{A,B} \times \sigma_A \times \sigma_B$

Markowitz efficient portfolio represents portfolios for which there is maximum rate of return for each unit of risk undertaken.

$\sigma_P^2 = (0.25)^2 \times (0.40)^2 + (0.75)^2 \times (0.15)^2 + 2 \times 0.25 \times 0.75 \times (-0.6) \times 0.40 \times 0.15 = 0.92\%$

Portfolio standard deviation (σ) = $\sqrt{0.92\%} = 9.59\%$

Similarly, there can be other multiple combinations of weights to comprise portfolios with different return and risk estimates.

Now, if we were to plot various combinations of these assets in a risk-return space, we would get various data points representing the investment opportunity set. An example of investment opportunity set is shown in Figure 8.1, where the area within the curve **SAVMZ** is the feasible opportunity set representing all the possible portfolio combinations. Further, if we were to draw a line along the upper edge of this region (investment opportunity set), we would get a curve (**AVMZ**) enveloping the data points representing the best of all the possible combinations. This envelope curve (**AVMZ**), which represents the best possible combinations of two assets is known as **Markowitz efficient portfolio** named after the American economist Harry Markowitz. Every asset combination on this efficient frontier represents portfolios for which there is maximum rate of return for each unit of risk undertaken. Conversely, each point on the efficient portfolio represents minimum risk for a given level of return.

The point A on the efficient portfolio represents the point of minimum global variance or the portfolio with minimum possible variance for any combination of assets. There is no other portfolio in the investment opportunity set with a variance (or standard deviation) less than the minimum global variance portfolio.

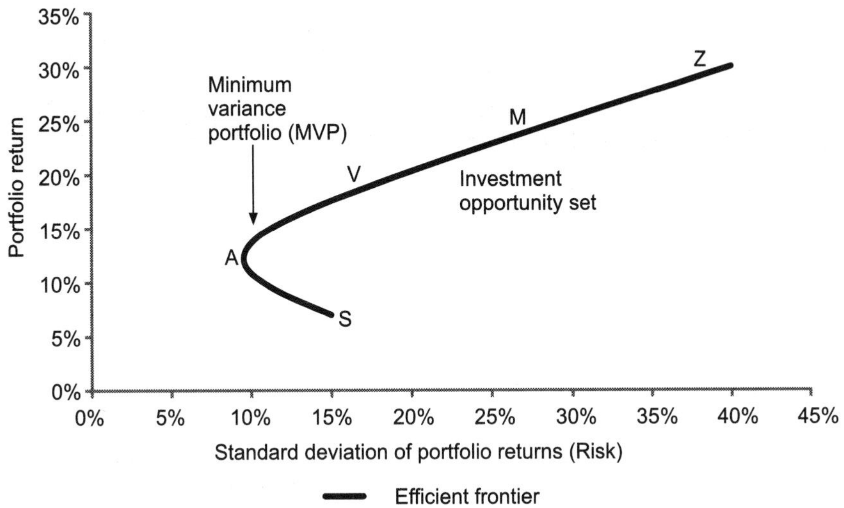

FIGURE 8.1 Investment Opportunity Set and Efficient Frontier.

Any rational investor contemplating an investment in the above portfolio comprising of equity and commodity would want to choose weights in such a manner so that he is able to achieve a point on the efficient frontier. This is because any portfolio in the investment opportunity set, which is below the efficient frontier **AVMZ**, is considered sub-optimal (as it provides lower return per unit of risk undertaken). Now determination of optimal portfolio for an investor on the efficient frontier would depend on his risk preference. An investor looking to minimize his risk would want to choose point A, which represents the portfolio with minimum global variance. Similarly, an investor who is more tolerant of risk would go further up on the efficient frontier and would want to achieve higher points.

The risk return tolerances of the investor can be mapped through utility functions or a set of curves called indifference curves. Indifference curves, which represent the trade-off between risk and return are generally used to portray investor's tolerance towards risk. To draw indifference curves, utility scores of investors' are first assessed by using risk tolerance questionnaires to determine the level of risk they are comfortable with. These risk tolerance estimates are then converted to risk aversion indexes and utility scores are then obtained using the following function (used by CFA Institute, USA)

$$U = E(r) - \frac{1}{2}A\sigma^2$$

where

$E(r)$ = Expected return

U = Utility value

A = Investor's risk aversion index

σ^2 = Variance or risk

For highly risk averse investors, the risk aversion index A would be higher and they would require more compensation for taking on additional risk so as to achieve same utility as compared to a less risk averse investor. With the help of utility scores generated, indifference curves can now be drawn to reflect investor's risk return tolerances (Figure 8.2). All the points on the same indifference curve represent the same utility for the investor i.e. an investor would be indifferent between points on the same indifference curve. However, indifference curve 1 (IC_1) has a steeper slope compared to indifference curve 2 (IC_2) which signifies that an investor lying on IC_1

Indifference curves represent the trade-off between risk and return, are generally used to portray investor's tolerance towards risk.

would require a higher incremental return for every unit of risk undertaken compared to an investor lying on IC_2. In other words, for risk averse investors (with higher risk aversion index), indifference curves tends to be steeper as compared to less risk averse investors.

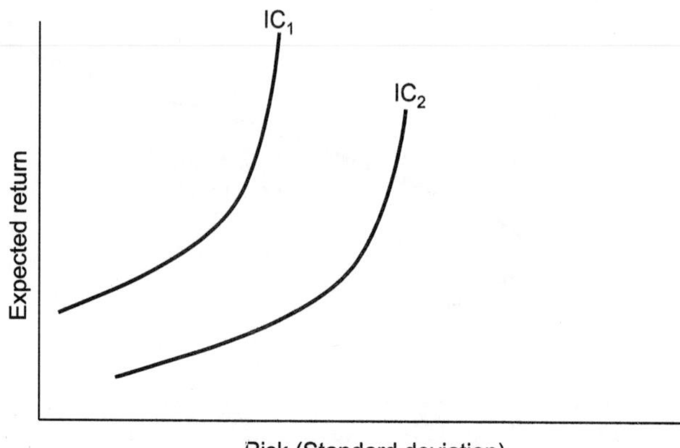

FIGURE 8.2 Investor indifference curves.

8.3 Efficent Frontier—Multiple Asset Portfolios

While the discussion in the previous section covered the case of two asset portfolio, in reality the investors generally tend to hold more than two assets or securities in their desired portfolios. Figure 8.3 specifies the investment opportunity set when many assets or securities are available to investors for forming the portfolio. All possible combinations of portfolio of assets or securities achievable by the investor given the desirable risk and return would lie within the investment opportunity set. As in the case of two asset portfolio, the efficient frontier (dark line) is indicated by the envelope curve along the upper edge of the investment opportunity set, the starting point being the minimum variance portfolio. All points on the efficient frontier would reflect portfolios for which there is maximum rate of return for each unit of risk undertaken (or lowest risk for a given level of return).

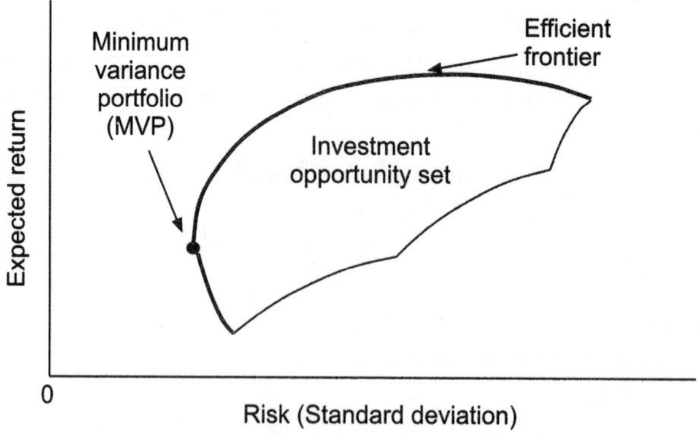

FIGURE 8.3 Investment opportunity set and efficient frontier with many assets.

8.4 Introduction of a Risk-Free Asset

Till now our discussion was confined to the construction of efficient frontier with portfolios comprising of only risky assets (or securities). However, in the real world an investor may form his portfolio by combining risky assets with a risk-free asset. In this case, the portfolio return would simply be a weighted average of the return on the risky assets and the risk-free rate.

Portfolio return = Weight of the risky assets × Return of the risky assets + Weight of the risk-free asset × Return of the risk-free asset

Similarly, the portfolio risk on combining the risky assets, with a risk-free asset can be determined as:

$$\sigma^2_{P(\text{Risky, Risk-free})} = w^2_{\text{Risky}} \times \sigma^2_{\text{Risky}} + w^2_{\text{Risk-free}} \times \sigma^2_{\text{Risk-free}} + 2 \times w_{\text{Risky}} \times w_{\text{Risk-free}} \times \rho_{\text{Risky, Risk-free}} \times \sigma_{\text{Risky}} \times \sigma_{\text{Risk-free}}$$

Given the fact that variance (or standard deviation) for a risk-free security is zero, the above equation of portfolio risk (or portfolio variance) can be reduced to a simple linear function of weight of risky asset and standard deviation of risky asset.

$$\sigma^2_{P(\text{Risky, Risk-free})} = w^2_{\text{Risky}} \times \sigma^2_{\text{Risky}}$$

$$\text{Portfolio standard deviation} = \sigma_{P(\text{Risky, Risk-free})} = w_{\text{Risky}} \times \sigma_{\text{Risky}}$$

Now given that both the return and risk for a portfolio consisting of risky assets and a risk-free asset moves in a linear fashion, the investment opportunity set (or possible portfolio combinations) becomes a straight line connecting the risk-free rate and the risky assets portfolio. Figure 8.4 depicts portfolio combinations when a risk-free asset is combined with risky assets on the Markowitz efficient frontier. While one can construct various lines from risk-free rate (R_F) to the Markowitz efficient frontier, such as R_FN, R_FO etc., the line R_FM would dominate all other lines below it. The portfolios lying on the line R_FM would have superior risk adjusted returns compared to all other portfolios lying on any lines below it. This line R_FM which is tangential to the market portfolio of risky assets (represented by Portfolio M) is thus the new efficient frontier and is known as the Capital Market Line (CML). All the portfolios lying on the left of M would represent certain proportion being lent at risk-free rate and the balance being invested in risky portfolio of assets. To achieve a point beyond M, the investor would have to borrow at the risk-free rate and invest it in the risky asset portfolio.

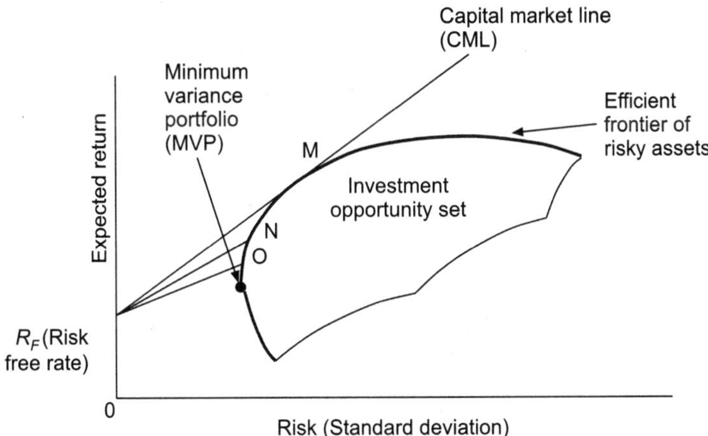

FIGURE 8.4 Introduction of risk-free asset and capital market line (CML).

Market Portfolio M which lies at the tangency of the Markowitz efficient frontier and Capital Market Line (CML) dominates all other risky portfolios and has the highest ***Sharpe Ratio*** (reward to risk ratio). Assuming that all investors have homogenous expectations or beliefs, all investors would want to hold the market portfolio M as a proxy for risky assets.

Separation Theoremz

The above analysis establishes that the portfolio selection problem involves two independent decisions—first decision being the determination of optimal portfolio of risky assets and second decision being the determination of allocation between the risk-free asset and risky portfolio of assets. While the first decision is purely technical as the CML (Capital Market Line) may lead all investors to invest in same market portfolio of risky assets, the second decision involves personal preferences and risk aversion of individual investors, and is completely independent of the first decision.

For example while all investors may choose the most optimal portfolio of risky assets (Portfolio M) and lie on the CML as a part of their first decision, their positioning on the CML might differ based on their risk preferences or the ability to tolerate risk (represented by different indifference curves) as shown in Figure 8.5.

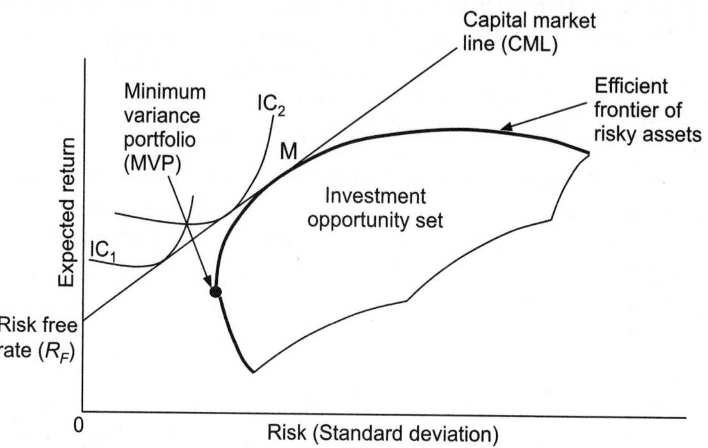

FIGURE 8.5
Determination of optimal portfolios.

8.5 Capital Asset Pricing Model (CAPM)

So far we have been discussing how investors make their portfolio investment decisions given the universe of risky assets (represented by market portfolio). We also discussed how introduction of a risk-free asset can result in the emergence of Capital Market Line (CML) which eventually becomes the relevant efficient frontier. Now given that all investors would want their portfolios to lie on CML, the appropriate risk measure for any asset shall be a function of its covariance with the market portfolio of risky assets. This understanding of this relevant measure of risk can be used for determining the required or expected rate of return on any risky asset using a popular model namely Capital Asset Pricing Model (CAPM).

CAPM provides a framework to establish the relationship between the risk and the expected return for any risky asset.

CAPM, developed in 1960's, provides a framework to establish the relationship between the risk and the expected return for any risky asset. In other words, given the relevant risk for any asset or security, CAPM model helps investors in ascertaining as to what should be the expected or required rate of return. This expected or required rate of return is generally used as a discount rate during the process of equity valuation. Although various alternative models exist in the market to determine the required rate of return, CAPM is the most widely used on account of its simplicity and practicability.

CAPM is built on the insight that the market rewards the investors only for systematic risk (which affects all assets) undertaken and ignores the unsystematic risk (unique risk) component. In effect, since the unsystematic risk can be completely diversified away by the investors, required or expected rate of return for a risky asset should be a function of only systematic risk.

Systematic Risk affects all risky securities and is attributable to macro events such as change in interest rates, inflation, exchange rates etc.

$$\text{Total risk} = \text{Systematic risk} + \text{Unsystematic risk}$$

Systematic risk, also known as market risk, affects all risky assets or securities and cannot be diversified away by the investors. This type of risk is generally attributable to macro events, such as change in interest rates, inflation, exchange rates, etc. and affects the entire universe of assets or securities, although in varying degrees. For example, while an increase in interest rates would affect all securities to a certain extent, impact on rate sensitives sectors such as banks, auto and infrastructure would be more compared to that of FMCG (Fast Moving Consumer Goods), pharma and IT (Information technology) sectors. Similarly impact of an increase in Consumer Price Inflation (CPI) would be more on FMCG and Banking sectors compared to that of other sectors.

Unsystematic risk, also known as idiosyncratic risk or specific risk, is generally unique to the industry or a particular company, and can be diversified away completely by the investors. For example, labour strikes or unrests, product recalls, management change or regulatory upheavals are prime examples of unsystematic risk as they generally affect a particular company or industry. For better understanding of the students, some recent examples of systematic and unsystematic risks are enumerated below in Table 8.2.

TABLE 8.2 Recent Examples of Systematic and Unsystematic Risk

Event	*Risk*
Federal Reserve Changes Interest Rates	Systematic
Consumer Price Inflation Increase/ decrease	Systematic
US FDA raid on a Pharma Company	Unsystematic
Change in Infosys Leadership	Unsystematic
Merger news of Kotak with ING	Unsystematic
Grexit (Greece Exit from Euro)	Systematic
Nestle Maggi issue	Unsystematic

So in essence, CAPM framework assumes that unsystematic risk being unique to a company or industry can be easily diversified away by the investors. So the leftover risk—systematic risk should only be compensated for.

8.5.1 CAPM Equation

To determine the expected or required rate of return on any risky asset, CAPM specifies the following equation:

Required return on asset$_i$ = Risk-free rate + (Equity risk premium) × Beta$_i$

$$R_i = R_F + (R_M - R_F) \times \beta_i$$

where, R_M refers to market returns, and R_F refers to risk-free rate

The above equation specifies that the required rate of return on a risky asset is equal to the return available on a risk-free or riskless investment plus a compensation for risk premium as measured by the product of Equity risk premium ($R_M - R_F$) and beta (β).

Equity risk premium refers to the premium investors at a large demand for shifting their investments from risk-free to risky assets. Higher the risk aversion of the investors, higher shall be the premium or compensation required for making this shift in allocation (from risk-free to risky assets). Similarly, beta (β) in the above equation, serves as a measure of systematic risk. So higher the beta, higher shall be the required return on the risky asset and vice-versa.

Equity risk premium refers to the premium investors at a large demand for shifting their investments from risk-free to risky assets.

8.5.2 Modalities of CAPM Equation Components

While CAPM looks easy to implement given the above equation, in reality investors tend to make errors while arriving at the required or expected rate of return on risky assets. In this section, we will look at individual components of CAPM in a detailed manner and arrive at the right understanding of the same from the market perspective.

Risk-free Rate

The choice of the risk-free rate in CAPM equation can significantly affect the required rate of return on the risky asset. While investors generally tend to use nominal treasury rates as a proxy for risk-free rate in the economy, estimates differ on account of different maturity treasury security being used. For example, an investor using 1 year treasury rate as a proxy for risk-free rate would find his CAPM determined return much different from the investor using the 10 year treasury rate. This is because long-term treasury rates would be generally higher than short term rates (assuming upward sloping yield curve). So the question arises as to what maturity treasury security is to be used given that treasury rates are readily available for maturities ranging between 3 months to 30 years (see Table 8.3).

TABLE 8.3
Treasury Security Yields in India

	Treasury security	*Maturity*	*Current rate/Yield*
3 months treasury bill	091 DTB 10092015	3 months	7.25%
1 year treasury bond	07.59 GS 2016	1 year	7.94%
3 year treasury bond	07.83 GS 2018	3 year	7.79%
5 year treasury bond	08.27 GS 2020	5 year	7.85%
7 year treasury bond	08.08 GS 2022	7 year	7.95%
10 year treasury bond	07.72 GS 2025	10 year	7.73%
30 year treasury bond	08.17 GS 2044	30 year	7.97%

Source: Adapted from Reserve Bank of India.

The Way Out

CAPM determined returns are generally used for discounting the future cash flows related to a capital investment project or for discounting the free cash flows forecasted during the process of equity valuation. Ideally, the investor should discount each year's cash flows at a CAPM determined rate that matches the maturity of the cash flows. In effect, this means that year 1 cash flows should be discounted at a CAPM rate based on 1-year treasury rate as a proxy for risk-free rate. Similarly, year 5 cash flows should be discounted at a CAPM rate containing 5-year treasury rate as a proxy for risk-free rate and so on. While this method is theoretically possible, practically it may be difficult to implement. This is because on account of illiquidity of bond markets (especially in emerging markets like India), current rates on certain maturities of treasury securities may not be available. As a result, most investors and analysts in the market tend to use a single CAPM rate (and consequently the single risk-free rate) for discounting the future cash flows. In this case, it is important that the maturity of the risk-free rate being used should be matched with the maturity of the farthest forecasted cash flow. For example, if the cash flows (that are required to be discounted) have been forecasted till 10 years, then the 10 year treasury rate should be used as a proxy for risk-free rate in CAPM determined return for discounting the entire years cash flows.

Some investors make a mistake of using a shorter tenure risk-free rate (such as 3 months Treasury bill) as an input in CAPM determined returns for discounting the longer term cash flows. This is incorrect as the short-end rates do not reflect in entirety long term real rates and expected inflation and can lead to overestimation of equity value or wrong capital budgeting decisions.

Equity Risk Premium (R_M – R_F)

As discussed earlier, equity risk premium refers to the compensation required by the investors for a shift from risk-free asset to a risky security. In other words, investors would want to invest in risky assets only if they are offered an incremental return over and above the risk-free rate. So higher the risk aversion of the investors, higher shall be the equity risk premium demanded and vice versa. Given that equity risk premium is an important input in calculation of CAPM determined return, right estimation of the same is important.

The Way Out

Generally investors tend to use historical or realized equity risk premiums as a proxy for current equity risk premiums for determination of CAPM required returns. This standard approach, also known as historical risk premium approach calculates the difference, on an annual basis, between the equity market returns (using benchmark index) and risk-free returns over a period of time. This average difference represents the historical equity risk premium investors have demanded over and above the risk-free rate over a period of time and can be used as an input in CAPM assuming that the investors will expect the same risk premium in the future. For example, in Indian context, the average annual arithmetic mean between the equity market returns (using BSE Sensex as the proxy) and risk-free returns (using 10 year treasury security returns) for last 35 years of data comes out to be around 7–8%.

While this historical risk premium approach looks simple and easy to calculate, there are inherent gaps in this approach which needs to be taken into account. First, using of historical risk premium approach, assume that risk aversion of investors continues to be same in the future as in the past. However, risk aversion could be time varying depending on the future wealth levels, age, consumption, habits, etc. of the investors. So assuming a constant risk aversion for the future as in the past could lead to erroneous equity risk premium estimates. Secondly, there is no standardization with regards to the length of the historical period to be used for equity risk premium estimation purpose. For example, using the average annual arithmetic mean between the equity market returns and risk-free returns for last 20 years to arrive at the historical risk premium would be different from the arithmetic mean of the difference for the last 10 years. Generally, it has been observed that historical equity risk premiums across markets have come down in recent periods compared to that of in the past on account of development of equity markets and falling risk aversion. Lastly, under historical risk premium approach, there is no consensus on the benchmarks to be used for market returns as well as for the risk-free rates. Different investors tend to use different proxies or benchmarks for equity market returns and risk-free returns leading to wide difference in estimation of historical risk premiums.

Given the above problems associated with the historical risk premium approach, sophisticated investors and analysts have started using implied risk premium approach to estimate the risk premiums. Implied risk premium approach attempts to capture the future consensus equity risk premiums that have been priced in the benchmark indexes using forward estimates of cash flows or dividends. Under this method, the forward consensus estimates of cash flows/dividend for the benchmark index are first obtained from data sources, such as Bloomberg, Factset or Reuters. Implied CAPM determined return is then found out by equating the present value of all these future cash flows/ dividends with the current index value. From this implied CAPM determined return, risk-free rate is then deducted to arrive at implied equity risk premiums embedded in the market. As per this method, implied equity risk premium for India is currently hovering at around 4–5% which is significantly lower than what we obtained through historical premium approach. However, these equity risk premiums are time varying and continuously change depending upon the forward consensus risk aversion of the market participants.

Beta

Beta, a measure of the systematic risk, refers to the sensitivity or responsiveness of asset (or security) returns relative to that of the market portfolio or index. Conversely, it reflects the asset's relative volatility to the market as a whole. Generally, higher the beta of an asset, higher the systematic risk for that asset relative to the market as a whole. An asset with a beta of 1 tends to move up and down in line with the market index or portfolio. An asset having a beta greater than 1 would tend to move up and down much more than the market index or portfolio. For example, a beta of 1.5 indicates that if market returns change by 1%, the asset's return would change by 1.5%. Similarly, a beta of 0.5 indicates if market returns change by 1%, the asset's return would change by only 0.5%.

With reference to the above discussion, assets having beta greater than 1 are considered to be more risky than the market and assets having beta less than 1 are considered less risky relative to the market.

Beta refers to sensitivity or responsiveness of asset (or security) returns relative to that of the market portfolio or index.

Beta	**Riskiness**
$\beta > 1$	More riskier than the market
$\beta < 1$	Less riskier than the market
$\beta = 1$	Same risk as the market

In the above context, market index or portfolio is generally referred to as the benchmark index of the country (having a beta of 1). For example, in case of India market portfolio or market index can be represented by BSE Sensex or NSE Nifty.

1. Measurement of Beta: Beta can be measured using the regression approach, wherein asset's returns are regressed against the market returns over a period of time to obtain the sensitivity or responsiveness of the same. In other words, in a linear regression equation ($Y = a + bX$), where Y represents the asset returns and X represents the market returns, beta simply would be the slope of this regression line. Table 8.4 calculates the beta of DLF India using the regression approach on the daily returns for the last six months using NSE Nifty as the market benchmark. Beta for DLF is measured by the slope function – Slope (DLF daily returns, Nifty daily returns).

TABLE 8.4
Beta Estimation for DLF

Date	*DLF daily returns*	*Nifty daily returns*
31-07-2015	4.88%	1.32%
30-07-2015	8.03%	0.56%
29-07-2015	6.45%	0.46%
28-07-2015	–5.73%	–0.29%
27-07-2015	–1.94%	–1.88%
24-07-2015	–4.27%	–0.79%
23-07-2015	1.13%	–0.51%
22-07-2015	0.00%	1.22%
21-07-2015	–1.93%	–0.86%
20-07-2015	–4.82%	–0.07%
17-07-2015	–1.59%	0.02%
16-07-2015	–0.56%	0.99%
		(Contd.)

Date	*DLF daily returns*	*Nifty daily returns*
15-07-2015	2.01%	0.82%
14-07-2015	–0.87%	–0.07%
13-07-2015	0.65%	1.19%
10-07-2015	–1.88%	0.38%
09-07-2015	0.30%	–0.41%
08-07-2015	–2.27%	–1.74%
07-07-2015	1.36%	–0.13%
06-07-2015	1.38%	0.44%
03-07-2015	–0.68%	0.47%
02-07-2015	–0.51%	–0.10%
01-07-2015	0.43%	1.01%
30-06-2015	–0.09%	0.60%
29-06-2015	–2.50%	–0.75%
26-06-2015	1.52%	–0.20%
25-06-2015	3.28%	0.44%
24-06-2015	–2.60%	–0.25%
23-06-2015	2.53%	0.34%
22-06-2015	7.61%	1.56%
19-06-2015	–0.37%	0.62%
18-06-2015	–1.52%	1.03%
17-06-2015	0.60%	0.55%
16-06-2015	–0.23%	0.42%
15-06-2015	0.56%	0.39%
12-06-2015	–0.32%	0.22%
11-06-2015	–3.66%	–1.96%
10-06-2015	1.08%	1.27%
09-06-2015	0.82%	–0.27%
08-06-2015	2.47%	–0.87%
05-06-2015	–3.51%	–0.20%
04-06-2015	0.54%	–0.05%
03-06-2015	–2.25%	–1.23%
02-06-2015	–4.27%	–2.34%
01-06-2015	0.34%	0.00%
29-05-2015	–1.38%	1.38%
28-05-2015	0.00%	–0.19%
27-05-2015	2.14%	–0.06%
26-05-2015	–3.63%	–0.37%
25-05-2015	–1.54%	–1.05%
22-05-2015	–0.77%	0.45%
		(Contd.)

Date	*DLF daily returns*	*Nifty daily returns*
21-05-2015	0.73%	–0.03%
20-05-2015	–0.76%	0.69%
19-05-2015	1.14%	–0.10%
18-05-2015	–1.76%	1.35%
15-05-2015	–1.54%	0.46%
14-05-2015	1.56%	–0.14%
13-05-2015	–0.40%	1.34%
12-05-2015	–3.65%	–2.38%
11-05-2015	–2.03%	1.63%
08-05-2015	3.06%	1.67%
07-05-2015	–1.98%	–0.49%
06-05-2015	–5.53%	–2.74%
05-05-2015	0.72%	–0.09%
04-05-2015	1.36%	1.84%
30-04-2015	2.02%	–0.71%
29-04-2015	4.41%	–0.55%
28-04-2015	3.35%	0.87%
27-04-2015	–5.42%	–1.10%
24-04-2015	–3.78%	–1.11%
23-04-2015	–0.44%	–0.37%
22-04-2015	–1.51%	0.62%
21-04-2015	–5.03%	–0.83%
20-04-2015	–0.61%	–1.83%
17-04-2015	–1.97%	–1.16%
16-04-2015	–4.27%	–1.44%
13-04-2015	–1.01%	0.61%
10-04-2015	–0.56%	0.02%
09-04-2015	–0.99%	0.73%
08-04-2015	–0.65%	0.62%
07-04-2015	–3.28%	0.00%
06-04-2015	4.85%	0.86%
01-04-2015	0.92%	1.12%
31-03-2015	–0.78%	–0.02%
30-03-2015	2.94%	1.81%
27-03-2015	–2.73%	–0.01%
26-03-2015	–3.48%	–2.21%
25-03-2015	3.09%	–0.14%
24-03-2015	0.47%	–0.09%
23-03-2015	–0.34%	–0.23%
20-03-2015	–2.47%	–0.74%
19-03-2015	–0.33%	–0.59%
		(Contd.)

Date	*DLF daily returns*	*Nifty daily returns*
18-03-2015	–0.30%	–0.43%
17-03-2015	0.43%	1.04%
16-03-2015	4.38%	–0.17%
13-03-2015	5.32%	–1.46%
12-03-2015	3.03%	0.87%
11-03-2015	0.10%	–0.14%
10-03-2015	–4.04%	–0.51%
09-03-2015	–2.04%	–2.03%
05-03-2015	0.03%	0.17%
04-03-2015	1.85%	–0.82%
03-03-2015	–2.10%	0.44%
02-03-2015	–0.90%	1.27%
27-02-2015	3.62%	1.85%
26-02-2015	2.07%	–0.95%
25-02-2015	0.55%	0.06%
24-02-2015	0.07%	0.08%
23-02-2015	–3.17%	–0.89%
20-02-2015	0.73%	–0.69%
19-02-2015	0.20%	0.30%
18-02-2015	–3.57%	0.68%
16-02-2015	0.19%	0.04%
13-02-2015	–2.24%	1.08%
12-02-2015	0.22%	0.98%
11-02-2015	0.54%	0.72%
10-02-2015	0.29%	0.46%
09-02-2015	–3.88%	–1.56%
06-02-2015	–3.51%	–0.58%
05-02-2015	–2.28%	–0.14%
Beta	**1.22**	

Source: Adapted from http://www.nseindia.com/

Beta for DLF using the slope function comes out to be 1.22 using daily returns data for the last 6 months. This implies that DLF stock is riskier than market (NSE Nifty) and would move more than the market both in up-cycle as well as down-cycle.

Another way in which we can calculate beta, is through use of the following statistical formula

Beta (β) = Covariance (Stock daily returns, Market daily returns)/Variance (Market daily returns)

This measure of beta would also give the same result as to what was obtained through the slope function. Table 8.5 provides the beta values for BSE Sensex companies for daily returns during the period July 2014–June 2015.

TABLE 8.5
Calculated Betas for BSE Sensex Constituents

Scrip code	*Company*	*Beta values*
500010	Housing Development Finance Corp. Ltd.	1.35
500087	Cipla Ltd.	0.93
500103	Bharat Heavy Electricals Ltd.	1.38
500112	State Bank of India	1.28
500124	Dr. Reddy's Laboratories Ltd.	0.62
500180	HDFC Bank Ltd	0.93
500182	Hero Motocorp Ltd.	0.67
500209	Infosys Ltd.	0.69
500295	Vedanta Ltd.	1.28
500312	Oil and Natural Gas Corporation Ltd.	1.18
500325	Reliance Industries Ltd.	1.12
500400	Tata Power Co. Ltd.	1.34
500440	Hindalco Industries Ltd.	1.44
500470	Tata Steel Ltd.	1.36
500510	Larsen & Toubro Ltd.	1.38
500520	Mahindra & Mahindra Ltd.	0.87
500570	Tata Motors Ltd.	1.41
500696	Hindustan Unilever Ltd.	0.4
500875	ITC Ltd.	0.64
507685	Wipro Ltd.	0.53
524715	Sun Pharmaceutical Industries Ltd.	0.63
532155	Gail (India) Ltd.	0.93
532174	ICICI Bank Ltd.	1.14
532215	Axis Bank Ltd.	1.83
532454	Bharti Airtel Ltd.	0.55
532500	Maruti Suzuki India Ltd.	0.81
532540	Tata Consultancy Services Ltd.	0.58
532555	NTPC Ltd.	0.95
532977	Bajaj Auto Ltd.	0.63
533278	Coal India Ltd.	0.85

Source: Adapted from http://www.bseindia.com/

Adjusted beta: Certain data providers, such as Bloomberg smoothen or adjust the observed or regressed beta of the individual assets to arrive at an adjusted beta. This adjustment is done under the assumption that in the long term regressed or observed betas of individual assets tend to revert back to the market beta of 1. Under this method, a weighted average of the regressed beta and market beta is taken to arrive at final adjusted beta for determination of CAPM required returns.

$$\text{Adjusted beta} = \text{Regressed beta} \times 0.67 + \text{Market beta} \times 0.33$$

In the above formula, a weight of 2/3 is being given to actual regressed beta and remaining weight (1/3) is given to market beta to arrive at final adjusted beta.

For example, while regressed or observed beta of Tata Steel is 1.36 (as per BSE), as per Bloomberg adjusted beta approach, it is calculated as:

$$\text{Adjusted beta for Tata Steel} = 1.36 \times 0.67 + 1 \times 0.33 = 1.24$$

Table 8.6 lists out the adjusted betas for BSE Sensex constituents in comparison to the regressed or observed betas.

TABLE 8.6
Adjusted Betas for BSE Sensex Constituents

Scrip code	*Company*	*Beta values*	*Adjusted beta values*
500010	Housing Development Finance Corp. Ltd.	1.35	1.23
500087	Cipla Ltd.	0.93	0.95
500103	Bharat Heavy Electricals Ltd.	1.38	1.25
500112	State Bank of India	1.28	1.19
500124	Dr. Reddy's Laboratories Ltd.	0.62	0.75
500180	HDFC Bank Ltd.	0.93	0.95
500182	Hero Motocorp Ltd.	0.67	0.78
500209	Infosys Ltd.	0.69	0.79
500295	Vedanta Ltd.	1.28	1.19
500312	Oil and Natural Gas Corporation Ltd.	1.18	1.12
500325	Reliance Industries Ltd.	1.12	1.08
500400	Tata Power Co. Ltd.	1.34	1.23
500440	Hindalco Industries Ltd.	1.44	1.29
500470	Tata Steel Ltd.	1.36	1.24
500510	Larsen & Toubro Ltd.	1.38	1.25
500520	Mahindra & Mahindra Ltd.	0.87	0.91
500570	Tata Motors Ltd.	1.41	1.27
500696	Hindustan Unilever Ltd.	0.4	0.60
500875	ITC Ltd.	0.64	0.76
507685	Wipro Ltd.	0.53	0.69
524715	Sun Pharmaceutical Industries Ltd.	0.63	0.75
532155	GAIL (India) Ltd.	0.93	0.95
532174	ICICI Bank Ltd.	1.14	1.09
532215	Axis Bank Ltd.	1.83	1.56
532454	Bharti Airtel Ltd.	0.55	0.70
532500	Maruti Suzuki India Ltd.	0.81	0.87
532540	Tata Consultancy Services Ltd.	0.58	0.72
532555	NTPC Ltd.	0.95	0.97
532977	Bajaj Auto Ltd.	0.63	0.75
533278	Coal India Ltd.	0.85	0.90

Now that we have looked at various components of CAPM in detail, we can calculate the required or expected return for any asset or security using the below equation:

$$\text{Required return on asset}_i = \text{Risk-free rate} + (\text{Equity risk premium}) \times \text{Beta}_i$$

or

$$R_i = R_F + (R_M - R_F) \times \beta_i$$

EXAMPLE 8.1 Vijay wants to determine the required return as per the CAPM Model for one of his portfolio security—ICICI Bank. He estimates that the beta (β) or systematic risk for the stock using daily returns for last 1 year as 1.14. Further, the risk-free rate in the economy currently is 7.8%. Finally, Vijay determines the equity risk premium as 5%.

Calculate the required or expected return for ICICI Bank using the above information.

Solution: Fitting the various components in the CAPM equation, we get required or expected return as:

Required return on ICICI Bank $(R_i) = R_F + (R_M - R_F) \times \beta_i$

$$R_i = 7.8\% + (5\%) \times 1.14 = 13.5\%$$

So, the CAPM determined required or expected rate of return for ICICI bank is 13.5%.

8.6 Security Market Line (SML)

Security Market Line (SML) is the graphical representation of the Capital Asset Pricing Model (CAPM) and specifies the linear relationship between individual asset's required or expected return and its systematic risk (represented by beta measure). Figure 8.6 illustrates the construction of SML where on the x-axis we have the systematic risk or beta (β) and on the y-axis we have the expected or required rate of return. The slope of SML is the reward to risk ratio required by all the investors or the market. However, given that the beta of market is 1, the slope of the SML is the market risk premium.

$$\text{Slope of SML} = [E(R_M) - R_F)/\beta_M] = E(R_M) - R_F$$

given that $\beta_M = 1$

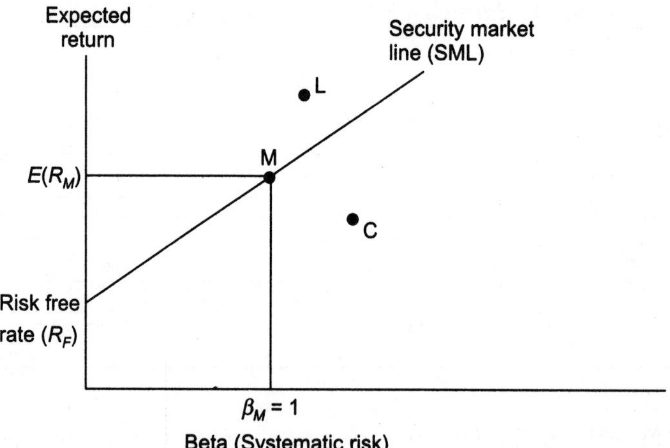

FIGURE 8.6
The Security Market Line (SML).

SML, a graphical representation of CAPM, specifies the linear relationship between individual asset's required or expected return and its systematic risk.

Under conditions of market equilibrium, all risky assets or securities should lie on SML to reflect the appropriate expected return-beta relationship. Consequently, if any asset or security departs from this equilibrium or appropriate expected return-beta relationship, it may not be correctly priced. Consequently, all assets or securities lying above the SML are underpriced or undervalued, whereas those lying below it are overpriced or overvalued. For example, in Figure 8.6, security C would be considered overpriced or overvalued and security L would be considered underpriced or undervalued.

8.7 CAPM and Its Extension—Arbitrage Pricing Theory (APT)

While a lot many finance theories have failed to take off beyond the academic textbooks into the real world, CAPM framework has gained significant prominence among the investors and analysts globally. CAPM, being a single factor model, continues to be widely used metric for determination of expected or required returns on account of its simplicity, easy availability of data for its components and minimal assumptions.

Over a period of time, researchers have attempted to extend the CAPM framework to include multiple factors resulting in emergence of models such as **Arbitrage Pricing Theory (APT)**. APT assumes that the expected return of an asset is a function of multiple factors, which have different sensitivities or betas as against a single beta estimate for CAPM. For example, under APT, there will be a host of systematic risk factors (such as interest rates, GDP, inflation, industrial production, etc.) and each will have a separate beta (such as inflation beta, GDP beta, etc.) associated with it. Expected return under APT for an r number of systematic risk factors can be written as:

$$E(R_i) = R_F + \beta_1 F_1 + \beta_2 F_2 + \beta_3 F_3 + \ldots + \beta_r F_r + \epsilon$$

where β_1, β_2, ... β_r represents the factor betas or sensitivities and F_1, F_2, ... F_r represents the surprise in the above factors.

APT assumes that the expected return of an asset is a function of multiple factors which have different sensitivities or betas as against a single beta estimate for CAPM.

The APT model is intuitively appealing given the fact that different systematic factors might affect asset's return differently and single factor model like CAPM may not be able to capture their effects in entirety. However, the APT model is still not a popular method for estimation of an asset's expected return given the challenges with regards to identification of factors and multiple assumptions involved.

Researchable Issues

Faculty members, students and research scholars may like to consider the following selected issues for further research and case writing.

- Indian Investor Risk preferences (Utility Functions) and Efficient Frontier
- Comparison of Equity Risk Premium in India vs Developed Markets
- Systematic Risk in India vs Developed Markets
- Price Return Comparisons between Diversified and Concentrated Indian Mutual Fund Portfolios
- Determinants of Factors for Arbitrage Pricing Theory (APT) in India

References

Fama, E.F. and French, K.R., The capital asset pricing model: Theory and evidence. *Journal of Economic Perspectives*, **18**, 2004, pp. 25–46.

Roll, R. and Ross, S.A., An empirical investigation of the arbitrage pricing theory. *Journal of Finance*, 1980, pp. 1073–1103.

Sharpe, W.F., Capital asset prices: A theory of market equilibrium under conditions of risk. *Journal of Finance*, **19**(3), 1964, pp. 425–442.

Sharpe, W.F., Factor models, CAPMs, and the ABT. *The Journal of Portfolio Management*, **11**(1), 1984, pp. 21–25.

Points to Remember

- Efficient frontier represents portfolios for which there is maximum rate of return for each unit of risk undertaken. Conversely, each point on the efficient portfolio represents minimum risk for a given level of return.
- Indifference curves, which represent the trade-off between risk and return, are generally used to portray investor's tolerance towards risk.
- Separation theorem establishes that the portfolio selection problem involves two independent decisions—first decision being the determination of optimal portfolio of risky assets and second decision being the determination of allocation between the risk-free asset and risky portfolio of assets.
- CAPM provides a framework to establish the relationship between the risk and the expected return for any risky asset. CAPM is built on the insight that the market rewards the investors only for systematic risk (which affects all assets) undertaken and ignores the unsystematic risk (unique risk) component.
- Equity risk premium refers to the compensation required by the investors for a shift from risk-free asset to a risky security. In other words, investors would want to invest in risky assets only if they are offered an incremental return over and above the risk-free rate.
- Beta, a measure of the systematic risk, refers to the sensitivity or responsiveness of asset (or security) returns relative to that of the market portfolio or index. Conversely it reflects the asset's relative volatility to the market as a whole.
- Security Market Line (SML) is the graphical representation of the Capital Asset Pricing Model (CAPM) and specifies the linear relationship between individual asset's required or expected return and its systematic risk (represented by beta measure).
- Arbitrage Pricing Theory (APT) assumes that expected return of an asset is a function of multiple factors, which have different sensitivities or betas as against a single beta estimate for CAPM.

Questions

1. Explain and illustrate the creation of Markowitz efficient frontier in a two asset portfolio. What happens when a risk-free asset is introduced in the portfolio?
2. Differentiate between systematic and unsystematic risk. Give examples.
3. Discuss how expected or required returns can be determined through Capital Asset Pricing Model (CAPM).
4. Discuss the issues surrounding the use of risk-free rate and equity risk premium for determination of Capital Asset pricing Model (CAPM).

Multiple Choice Questions

1. Which of the following events would classify as an example of systematic risk?
   (a) Change in the management of a company
   (b) Product recall by the company
   (c) Ban on product of a particular company
   (d) Raising of interest rates by central bank

2. Neha determines the beta of a security to be 1.1. Risk-free rate in the economy is 7% and average equity risk premium is 5%. Calculate the required return of the security using Capital Asset Pricing Model (CAPM).
   (a) 11.5% (b) 9.6%
   (c) 12.5% (d) None of the above
3. Assets or securities which lie below the Security Market Line (SML) are generally considered:
   (a) Fairly valued (b) Undervalued
   (c) Overvalued (d) None of the above
4. Anil wanted to determine the beta of one of the stocks of his portfolio. For this he collects the following information:

Variance of the market index returns	0.020%
Covariance between the stock and market returns	0.015%

   (a) 0.75 (b) 1.15
   (c) 1.33 (d) 0.97
5. Manik has estimated the CAPM determined return for one of his stocks as 11%. If the risk-free rate in the economy is 8% and equity risk premium has been taken as 5%, calculate the beta of the stock.
   (a) 0.45 (b) 0.60
   (c) 1.66 (d) None of the above
6. If the observed (or regressed) beta of Sunanda steel stock is 1.4, calculate the adjusted beta for the company
   (a) 1.56 (b) 1.19
   (c) 1.26 (d) 0.98
7. Rohit estimates the adjusted beta for Polo Company to be 1.134. Calculate the observed (or regressed) beta for the company using the adjusted beta approach.
   (a) 1.34 (b) 1.20
   (c) 0.78 (d) None of the above
8. Which of the following events would classify as an example of unsystematic risk?
   (a) Devaluation of the currency (b) Labour unrest
   (c) Increase in inflation (d) Debt default by the country

Self-Test Questions

1. Ajay, an individual investor has a portfolio of risky securities. He now plans to add a risk-free asset to his existing portfolio of risky securities. The returns as well as standard deviations of portfolio of risky securities and risk-free asset are given below. Calculate the combined portfolio return and standard deviation, assuming that Ajay has 70% of his funds invested in portfolio of risky securities and 30% in risk-free asset.

Portfolio	*Returns*	*Standard deviation*
Risky securities portfolio	10%	8%
Risk-free asset	7%	–

2. Sanjeev collects the following data points for the past 5 months for one of his stock and the benchmark index. He wants to assess the responsiveness or sensitivity of his stock returns relative to market index over the past 5 months. Using statistical measures of covariance and variances, calculate the beta for Sanjeev's stock.

Month	*Stock returns*	*Benchmark index returns*
1	18%	12%
2	27%	12%
3	–12%	–28%
4	–4%	–1%
5	16%	5%

3. Jitesh, an analyst with a brokerage firm estimates that ANG stock would deliver a return of 18% over the next year using the fundamental valuation technique. He further estimates that the beta of stock ANG is 1.2 and risk-free rate in the economy is 7%. Further, historical equity risk premium has been estimated to be around 5%.

   Using the above information, determine whether the stock is undervalued or overvalued according to Security Market Line (SML).

4. Suresh wants to assess the adjusted beta for BGS stock. The monthly returns for BGS stock along with market index returns are given below. Calculate the beta for BGS stock using the adjusted beta approach.

Month	*BGS stock returns*	*Benchmark index returns*
1	12%	15%
2	17%	18%
3	32%	19%
4	–41%	–19%
5	–14%	–5%

CASE

Beta Investing Strategy

In January 2014, Rahul, a portfolio manager for India with a hedge fund based out of Chicago, United States, was analyzing his beta investment strategy for the next year. His assessment of the economic indicators had suggested that the macro economy was on the cusp of a cyclical upturn. If the impending recovery of the economy happens, there would be a jump in stock markets and prices of stocks would rise.

Given the above analysis, Rahul was particularly analyzing the high beta stocks (stocks whose returns are more sensitive or responsive relative to that of the market index) which he can invest in to take advantage of the above macroeconomic upturn. Rahul had collected the weekly return data for five stocks for determining their sensitivity or responsiveness to market index returns during the historical period. Assuming yourself as Rahul, determine on the basis of below data, the high beta stocks that should be invested in on the basis of past data. Further calculate the CAPM required return for each of the stocks using the following estimates (Table CS 1.1):

Risk-free rate: 8%

Equity risk premium: 4%

TABLE CS 1.1

Weekly Data	Apollo Tyres	Voltas	Tata Motors	Oriental Bank	Cummins	BSE Sensex (Market Index)
30-12-2013	4.08%	0.77%	1.01%	0.46%	0.70%	–0.25%
23-12-2013	8.85%	1.87%	–0.51%	3.79%	–1.70%	0.54%
16-12-2013	12.94%	1.01%	0.76%	5.04%	11.53%	1.76%
09-12-2013	3.21%	–2.28%	–5.31%	–0.74%	–4.77%	–1.34%
02-12-2013	–1.30%	4.97%	–1.91%	13.78%	4.08%	0.98%
25-11-2013	5.30%	22.65%	6.79%	4.42%	0.78%	2.84%
18-11-2013	5.81%	1.13%	–3.29%	–1.77%	7.10%	–0.89%
11-11-2013	0.85%	2.29%	0.25%	–0.38%	–1.15%	–1.29%
04-11-2013	–3.05%	–4.43%	0.14%	–6.57%	1.35%	–2.50%
28-10-2013	6.71%	8.42%	2.23%	22.17%	–1.25%	2.48%
21-10-2013	3.36%	2.19%	–0.70%	4.58%	–2.01%	–0.95%
14-10-2013	0.00%	–2.31%	–1.67%	–5.24%	2.32%	1.73%
07-10-2013	0.69%	5.36%	10.12%	5.39%	–0.55%	3.08%
30-09-2013	–0.38%	7.96%	2.91%	1.40%	–0.77%	0.96%
23-09-2013	–8.06%	–0.93%	0.34%	–11.48%	–0.21%	–2.65%
16-09-2013	12.12%	–2.42%	1.60%	–1.54%	0.10%	2.69%
09-09-2013	–0.39%	15.50%	4.89%	18.68%	5.89%	2.40%
02-09-2013	3.27%	–0.89%	6.39%	14.16%	–1.70%	3.49%
26-08-2013	1.44%	–1.39%	–0.73%	–6.51%	3.14%	0.54%
19-08-2013	–4.60%	–3.07%	–3.99%	4.86%	–1.64%	–0.42%
12-08-2013	5.51%	–8.61%	12.45%	–7.82%	–0.36%	–1.02%
05-08-2013	–6.30%	3.02%	–4.05%	2.48%	–1.84%	–1.96%
29-07-2013	–3.67%	–8.75%	0.90%	–12.58%	–5.07%	–2.96%
22-07-2013	–3.19%	3.41%	–1.65%	–9.61%	–6.12%	–1.99%
15-07-2013	8.14%	–3.87%	0.94%	–11.67%	–0.41%	0.96%
08-07-2013	7.00%	5.53%	–1.43%	–1.30%	2.48%	2.37%
01-07-2013	8.68%	–1.79%	5.24%	–3.54%	–2.62%	0.52%
24-06-2013	–1.32%	–5.43%	–1.99%	–3.55%	–0.59%	3.31%
17-06-2013	–11.58%	4.57%	–3.28%	–9.28%	0.45%	–2.10%
10-06-2013	–28.81%	0.06%	–1.62%	0.36%	–2.39%	–1.29%
03-06-2013	2.19%	–2.27%	-3.72%	0.17%	2.55%	–1.68%
27-05-2013	3.61%	–2.78%	8.80%	–5.76%	–2.00%	0.28%
20-05-2013	–5.97%	–8.90%	–5.03%	–2.76%	–5.60%	–2.87%
13-05-2013	–3.23%	6.25%	–1.68%	2.94%	–5.73%	1.01%
06-05-2013	–4.54%	3.79%	8.15%	1.04%	1.50%	2.59%
29-04-2013	8.67%	2.02%	–3.70%	–3.78%	1.22%	1.50%
22-04-2013	1.34%	3.38%	4.94%	–0.27%	1.91%	1.42%
15-04-2013	7.73%	3.05%	2.51%	11.34%	1.10%	4.24%
08-04-2013	–0.41%	3.13%	7.87%	–3.51%	–1.09%	–1.13%
01-04-2013	0.36%	1.33%	–5.20%	–0.90%	0.40%	–2.05%
25-03-2013	1.34%	–0.93%	–0.41%	3.75%	3.68%	0.53%

(Contd.)

Weekly Data	*Apollo Tyres*	*Voltas*	*Tata Motors*	*Oriental Bank*	*Cummins*	*BSE Sensex (Market Index)*
18-03-2013	–5.40%	–10.14%	–7.11%	–12.54%	–3.29%	–3.56%
11-03-2013	–4.55%	3.42%	–4.16%	–1.87%	–1.62%	–1.30%
04-03-2013	6.67%	0.30%	5.23%	1.42%	1.33%	4.04%
25-02-2013	–4.05%	–6.09%	–1.48%	–4.69%	0.72%	–2.06%
18-02-2013	3.67%	–0.46%	–3.63%	–1.27%	2.54%	–0.78%
11-02-2013	–0.52%	–8.48%	6.48%	–2.80%	–4.28%	–0.09%
04-02-2013	–0.75%	–2.76%	0.19%	–5.78%	1.13%	–1.50%
28-01-2013	3.51%	0.72%	–5.33%	–2.65%	1.97%	–1.60%
21-01-2013	–4.17%	–3.23%	–8.24%	–2.75%	0.18%	0.32%
14-01-2013	0.69%	–3.12%	–0.62%	3.08%	–4.54%	1.91%
07-01-2013	–2.74%	–2.72%	4.71%	–6.84%	–4.12%	–0.61%
31-12-2012	3.65%	1.67%	1.82%	2.49%	2.99%	1.74%
24-12-2012	–0.69%	0.66%	3.42%	3.80%	3.31%	1.05%
17-12-2012	0.46%	–0.14%	2.57%	–5.27%	0.25%	–0.39%
10-12-2012	0.40%	–7.23%	3.58%	1.42%	0.12%	–0.55%
03-12-2012	2.14%	4.21%	2.75%	2.78%	4.14%	0.44%
26-11-2012	2.86%	5.82%	5.20%	6.83%	3.90%	4.50%
19-11-2012	2.30%	–3.99%	–1.64%	–0.58%	1.05%	1.08%
12-11-2012	0.26%	–5.50%	–5.56%	0.13%	–4.42%	–2.00%
05-11-2012	–7.41%	–2.76%	3.93%	–3.31%	0.54%	–0.38%
29-10-2012	2.18%	1.84%	3.29%	6.11%	–1.72%	0.70%
22-10-2012	0.06%	–3.72%	–2.77%	4.89%	–2.91%	–0.30%
15-10-2012	–3.20%	–4.71%	–0.61%	0.73%	3.22%	0.04%
08-10-2012	–2.62%	2.64%	–3.50%	0.79%	–4.59%	–1.39%
01-10-2012	–2.98%	–3.00%	4.82%	–3.86%	0.40%	0.94%
24-09-2012	–4.88%	–0.48%	–2.87%	3.27%	5.48%	0.05%
17-09-2012	–2.61%	7.93%	1.87%	25.45%	6.15%	1.56%
10-09-2012	6.74%	4.18%	11.10%	1.40%	–1.89%	4.41%
03-09-2012	–0.58%	0.77%	4.09%	3.58%	1.28%	1.74%
27-08-2012	–1.21%	–2.60%	–4.98%	–4.11%	–0.56%	–2.26%
20-08-2012	4.33%	0.85%	2.31%	–0.90%	–2.86%	0.52%
13-08-2012	6.34%	6.74%	3.64%	3.09%	–0.54%	0.76%
06-08-2012	8.13%	0.29%	5.03%	–3.12%	2.33%	2.09%
30-07-2012	0.50%	6.44%	3.81%	9.60%	8.30%	2.13%
23-07-2012	–4.33%	–12.02%	–4.72%	–10.69%	–0.45%	–1.86%
16-07-2012	0.36%	0.79%	–3.43%	–6.78%	0.91%	–0.32%
09-07-2012	1.22%	–1.00%	–2.10%	–1.78%	–4.31%	–1.75%
02-07-2012	3.49%	9.12%	–0.62%	3.04%	–0.75%	0.52%
25-06-2012	0.00%	2.65%	–2.00%	3.27%	5.15%	2.70%
18-06-2012	–2.29%	0.00%	2.90%	1.08%	2.23%	0.13%
11-06-2012	–1.94%	–2.11%	0.48%	2.65%	–1.61%	1.38%
						(Contd.)

Weekly Data	*Apollo Tyres*	*Voltas*	*Tata Motors*	*Oriental Bank*	*Cummins*	*BSE Sensex (Market Index)*
04-06-2012	1.54%	7.09%	6.41%	7.18%	2.54%	4.72%
28-05-2012	–7.36%	–4.14%	–16.65%	1.85%	–1.72%	–1.56%
21-05-2012	3.61%	5.36%	3.56%	3.66%	–0.73%	0.40%
14-05-2012	2.24%	–10.22%	–12.54%	–1.19%	–4.36%	–0.86%
07-05-2012	2.73%	0.61%	–1.33%	–4.12%	–5.56%	–3.20%
30-04-2012	–14.12%	–2.02%	–3.52%	–4.08%	–1.06%	–1.77%
23-04-2012	2.23%	–5.63%	–1.36%	–8.41%	–0.73%	–1.38%
16-04-2012	6.76%	–0.73%	9.55%	–0.52%	1.47%	1.63%
09-04-2012	2.99%	–4.21%	3.94%	0.60%	–1.33%	–2.24%
02-04-2012	5.17%	8.21%	0.89%	2.85%	–2.47%	0.47%
26-03-2012	–1.49%	–3.69%	1.01%	–5.70%	7.84%	0.24%
19-03-2012	–0.67%	–9.84%	–4.80%	–4.11%	–2.60%	–0.60%
12-03-2012	–0.13%	11.49%	2.69%	–2.63%	0.42%	–0.21%
05-03-2012	1.75%	–0.56%	4.39%	–0.38%	2.49%	–0.76%
27-02-2012	5.34%	7.38%	0.77%	2.70%	0.36%	–1.60%
20-02-2012	–9.39%	0.00%	–3.10%	–8.90%	–1.81%	–2.00%
13-02-2012	10.66%	8.51%	6.53%	1.47%	2.71%	3.05%
06-02-2012	7.31%	7.01%	3.69%	5.10%	4.08%	0.82%
30-01-2012	2.18%	–1.78%	3.36%	11.68%	3.94%	2.15%
23-01-2012	6.99%	3.37%	9.59%	12.61%	3.72%	2.96%
16-01-2012	–4.80%	5.99%	4.84%	1.66%	4.54%	3.62%
09-01-2012	8.33%	13.70%	2.78%	4.26%	15.63%	1.81%
02-01-2012	6.02%	3.81%	13.87%	9.91%	–3.02%	2.67%
26-12-2011	–2.48%	–8.53%	–3.38%	–9.98%	1.14%	–1.80%
19-12-2011	–0.41%	0.69%	7.20%	–9.61%	3.26%	1.60%
12-12-2011	–7.33%	–9.26%	–5.85%	–9.61%	–0.60%	–4.45%
05-12-2011	–1.21%	–4.50%	–4.34%	–2.64%	–6.08%	–3.76%
28-11-2011	4.74%	2.56%	11.32%	1.59%	–0.08%	7.34%
21-11-2011	4.53%	3.17%	0.88%	–0.91%	6.64%	–4.13%
14-11-2011	–0.89%	–8.85%	–6.27%	–7.32%	–5.41%	–4.78%
08-11-2011	7.39%	–9.44%	–3.35%	–3.81%	–5.57%	–2.11%
31-10-2011	–0.36%	4.56%	–8.83%	0.53%	–2.59%	–1.36%
24-10-2011	5.85%	4.30%	15.88%	2.91%	–1.78%	6.07%
17-10-2011	–5.12%	–8.39%	–1.08%	–1.65%	–3.48%	–1.74%
10-10-2011	4.05%	0.81%	13.29%	3.19%	0.22%	5.24%
03-10-2011	–1.28%	–6.02%	1.73%	–0.25%	–1.67%	–1.34%
26-09-2011	–4.49%	–4.67%	5.90%	4.21%	–2.80%	1.80%
19-09-2011	–1.61%	–4.76%	–8.84%	–4.33%	–0.08%	–4.56%
12-09-2011	–2.65%	0.36%	5.88%	–3.66%	–3.26%	0.40%
05-09-2011	1.26%	1.25%	1.13%	0.43%	0.11%	0.27%
29-08-2011	10.56%	9.42%	7.99%	1.05%	4.68%	6.14%
22-08-2011	2.38%	–5.52%	–1.99%	0.22%	–0.01%	–1.81%

(Contd.)

Weekly Data	*Apollo Tyres*	*Voltas*	*Tata Motors*	*Oriental Bank*	*Cummins*	*BSE Sensex (Market Index)*
16-08-2011	–15.20%	–12.51%	–10.95%	–9.29%	–2.89%	–4.14%
08-08-2011	–10.76%	1.60%	–9.94%	1.98%	–1.42%	–2.69%
01-08-2011	–4.72%	–4.64%	–6.11%	–7.79%	–4.02%	–4.90%
25-07-2011	–1.68%	–6.35%	–4.96%	0.00%	–3.78%	–2.80%
18-07-2011	–7.36%	–6.92%	6.83%	2.35%	–2.12%	0.86%
11-07-2011	2.21%	–2.91%	–1.63%	3.36%	1.15%	–1.57%
04-07-2011	–0.69%	3.84%	5.91%	–0.72%	0.66%	0.51%
27-06-2011	6.34%	0.54%	3.09%	0.97%	2.71%	2.86%
20-06-2011	–0.73%	–4.59%	–1.65%	3.75%	–4.31%	2.07%
13-06-2011	4.50%	2.22%	–3.82%	–4.23%	1.77%	–2.18%
06-06-2011	3.59%	–1.49%	–0.52%	–0.78%	–0.21%	–0.59%
30-05-2011	–0.93%	–0.09%	–5.84%	–0.58%	–3.35%	0.60%
23-05-2011	6.83%	1.45%	–6.86%	2.64%	–0.80%	–0.33%
16-05-2011	–5.59%	–1.57%	–3.48%	2.82%	–0.48%	–1.11%
09-05-2011	–1.07%	–1.93%	0.83%	–2.18%	3.46%	0.07%
02-05-2011	1.67%	1.91%	–2.29%	–2.49%	–2.31%	–3.23%
25-04-2011	–5.14%	–5.58%	–1.19%	–5.03%	–1.29%	–2.38%
18-04-2011	8.29%	–0.28%	0.72%	–2.65%	4.86%	1.11%
11-04-2011	1.51%	–3.42%	–1.59%	–0.76%	–0.64%	–0.33%
04-04-2011	–3.83%	1.88%	0.97%	–2.17%	–1.52%	0.16%
28-03-2011	1.17%	3.85%	5.17%	3.10%	6.55%	3.21%
21-03-2011	5.32%	8.86%	5.72%	1.68%	0.45%	5.24%
14-03-2011	–1.97%	4.54%	–3.41%	4.05%	–4.92%	–1.62%
07-03-2011	11.63%	–4.20%	–1.06%	0.99%	2.28%	–1.69%
28-02-2011	9.81%	–1.32%	5.85%	10.44%	2.14%	4.44%
21-02-2011	–3.81%	–6.15%	–8.06%	–3.99%	–2.17%	–2.80%
14-02-2011	10.19%	–0.12%	5.01%	–1.18%	8.03%	2.72%
07-02-2011	–4.05%	–1.17%	–0.43%	1.12%	–3.08%	–1.55%
31-01-2011	3.72%	–13.80%	0.34%	2.57%	–10.47%	–2.11%
24-01-2011	–9.70%	–5.06%	–3.58%	–10.52%	–1.27%	–3.22%
17-01-2011	–4.06%	1.67%	0.81%	3.23%	1.99%	0.78%
10-01-2011	–8.15%	–3.32%	–0.92%	–4.94%	–3.43%	–4.22%

Source: Adapted from http://www.bseindia.com/

CHAPTER

9

Valuation of Bonds

LEARNING OBJECTIVES

After studying this chapter, you should be able to:

- Understand bond valuation and interest rates.
- Differentiate between different types of bonds and their features.
- Understand and calculate the yield to maturity, yield to call and current yield for a bond.
- Understand the valuation of zero coupon bonds.
- Discuss various determinants of interest rates.
- Understand the concept of reinvestment risk and interest rate risk.

9.1 Introduction

Globally, bond markets serve as a major source of finance for the companies as well as for the governments. While firms raise money through debt market for funding long term assets and investments, governments generally issues bonds for financing their fiscal deficits. On the basis of types of issuances, bond markets can be primarily divided into corporate bond markets and government bond markets. Corporate bond markets cater mainly to the companies who are looking to raise money via debt financing through issue of short-term and long-term bonds. Government bond market caters to the trading of sovereign backed securities (considered risk free instruments) which serve as a benchmark for arriving at expected returns for various other investments. In this chapter, we would discuss various types of bonds that can be issued and determine their valuation.

9.2 Understanding Bonds

Bond legal document stating that the borrower owes a specified sum of money which will be paid as coupons every period and a principal at the end of the period.

A bond can be issued by a firm or the government. It is a legal document stating that the borrower owes a specified sum of money, which will be paid as coupons every period and a principal at the end of the period to the holder of the bond certificate. The firm utilizes the funds generated from bond subscription for expansion and other activities, which will create future cash flow. A standard bond would have interest payments for a specified period and a principal payment at the end of the period. Thus, a bond is like a loan. Investors can also invest in firms' shares to get future returns. The difference between an investment in shares and bonds is that shares give ownership to the investors and hence the investors actually get a share of the profits earned by the firm whereas bond is a debt obligation is repaid as per the terms of the bond certificate.

9.2.1 Bonds: Features

To understand bonds, it is important to understand the various terminologies associated with bonds characteristics. Some of the terms associated with bonds are as follows:

1. **Par value:** Face value or par value is the stated value of the bond. It is the amount borrowed which will be paid like a principal at the end of the period or on maturity. Par values can be smaller values or larger values. Private placements have large face values. For example the bond issued as private placement by Axis bank in December 2012 had a face value of ₹10 lakh. Most of the issues as private placements have face value of ₹10 lakh. In case of public issue, the values are lower. For example, Britania Industries Limiteds' public issue of March 2010 bond had face value of ₹170.

Face value or par value is the stated value of the bond.

2. **Coupon interest rate:** Firms need to pay a fixed amount of interest payments every period. This interest payment period can be monthly, quarterly, half yearly or yearly. For example a 6 year ₹100 bond with 10% coupon interest rate with yearly payments will have to pay ₹10 as coupon every year to the bond holder. In case the bond has half yearly interest payments, the coupon payment would ₹5 every 6 months.

There can be variations in types of bonds based on conditions related to coupon interest rates. When the coupon interest rates vary over time, they are known as floating rate bonds. A firm can issue bonds which do not have coupon payment but only a principal payment or face value payment at the end of the period. These are called as zero coupon bonds.

3. **Maturity date:** The bond agreement has a specified maturity date. On this day, the bond matures and the firm needs to pay the par value to the bondholder. For example, Axis Bank's bond issued on December 2012 has a maturity date of 31 December 2022. Most bonds have maturity periods varying between 5 years and 40 years. Corporate bonds can also have a call provision and are known as callable bonds. These bonds can be called for redemption. The terms and conditions of the bond states that the bond become callable after a particular date or on a particular date, and the firm can buy back the bond by paying a premium over the face value. A call provision has an effect on the valuation of the bond as it creates an uncertainty in cash flow for the investor. Thus, if there are two bonds with same features and issued by the same firm with one being callable and the other being a normal bond, the expected return would be higher on callable bond.

9.2.2 Types of Bonds

Bonds can generally be classified either on the basis of degree of risk or on the basis of characteristics. On the basis of degree of risk, bonds can be majorly grouped into government bonds and corporate bonds.

Government Bonds

Government bonds are also referred as treasury bonds. These are the bonds issued by the government and we can be reasonably certain the government will pay back its obligations. Thus, these kinds of bonds are of negligible default risk. Treasury bonds are the bonds mainly issued by the central banks and hence represent the central government. Bonds can also be issued by the state and local governments, and are known as municipal bonds. Short term bonds, of time period less than 1 year, issued by government are known as treasury bills or T-bills. Ratings agencies apart from rating corporations also rate countries, which ascertain their default risk and hence affect the expected returns. A government can also issue bond in some other country and are called foreign government bonds. This brings in another additional risk, i.e., exchange rate risk. If you buy a bond denominated in another currency, with the change in exchange rates, your return would also change.

Government bonds are the bonds issued by the government and are considered risk free.

Corporate Bonds

Corporate bonds are bonds issued by corporations. These bonds are exposed to default risk and are issued credit ratings depending upon the characteristics and risk profile of the firms. Generally, higher the credit rating, lower is the probability of default. Companies having higher credit ratings are able to raise finance at lower cost compared to companies with low credit ratings. For example, in India companies with highest credit ratings (AAA) are generally able to raise funds from the bond market at rates which are 20–30 bps lower than the rates at which lower rated companies (such as AA+) companies are able to raise.

Corporate bonds are issued by the corporations and are exposed to default risk.

Average Traded Spreads of corporate bonds over corresponding government bonds are published daily by fixed income money market and derivatives association of India (FIMMDA). For example traded corporate bond spreads as on 30th April, 2014 are listed in Table 9.1.

TABLE 9.1 Average Traded Spreads of Corporate Bonds Over FIMMDA-PDAI Gilt Curve

To be used only for Valuation of Outstanding Position in Corporate Bond as on 30th April 2014												
For Evaluation Purposes												
Banks												
	0.5	1	2	3	4	5	6	7	8	9	10	15
AAA	52	63	70	71	56	49	41	32	36	46	40	16
AA+	68	79	88	89	74	66	57	48	50	59	52	33
AA	83	94	103	103	87	78	68	58	60	69	62	59
PSU & FIs												
	0.5	1	2	3	4	5	6	7	8	9	10	15
AAA	54	65	73	75	61	55	48	42	47	59	54	32
AA+	70	81	90	93	78	72	65	58	62	73	67	49
AA	85	96	105	107	92	84	76	68	72	83	78	76
NBFCs												
	0.5	1	2	3	4	5	6	7	8	9	10	15
AAA	74	85	93	95	81	75	68	62	66	78	73	51
AA+	90	102	111	113	99	93	85	78	81	92	86	69
AA	101	113	124	126	112	105	97	88	92	102	97	96
Corporates												
	0.5	1	2	3	4	5	6	7	8	9	10	15
AAA	64	75	84	86	72	66	59	52	56	67	61	37
AA+	80	91	102	104	90	84	76	68	71	81	74	55
AA	95	107	117	119	104	96	87	78	81	91	85	82

Based on the characteristics of the bonds, the different types of bonds can be grouped as follows:

Zero Coupon Bonds

Zero coupon bonds that do not pay coupons or interest payment and have only principal payment at the end of the period.

Zero coupon bonds are bonds that do not pay coupons or interest payment and have only principal payment at the end of the period. They are also known as the pure discount bonds. NABARD issued zero coupon bonds in January 2012. They were called NABARD ZCB and face value of these bonds was ₹20,000. The maturity date of these bonds is 1st January 2019 and at the time of subscription, they were offered at ₹11,980. This means that you invest ₹11,980 and after 7 years, you would receive ₹20,000, giving a return of 8.25% per annum. The short-term government bonds, known as treasury bills, are zero coupon bonds as they do not have coupons but only principal payment at the end of the period and are issued at a discount. Reserve Bank of India currently offers three kinds of treasury bills: 91 day, 182 day and 364 day treasury bills.

Perpetual Bonds

Perpetual bonds do not have any maturity date and have only coupon payments which run till perpetuity. For example, Canara Bank issued ₹1,500 crores of perpetual bonds by private placements in February 2015 with a coupon rate of 10.25%.

Convertible bonds

Convertible bonds provide an option of converting it to shares of common stock at a fixed price. This option can be exercised by the bondholder. Bonds issued with warrants are similar to convertible bonds; they give the bondholder the option to buy shares at a pre-determined price.

Income bonds

Income bonds pay coupons only when the issuing firms have enough earnings to pay the investors. However, the investors are assured of the principal payment and as the risk in cash flows is higher, a higher return is expected from these bonds.

Inflation indexed bonds

Inflation indexed bonds became popular in countries with high inflation, like Brazil. These bonds are generally issued by the government to protect the common public from inflation and the coupon interest is linked to the inflation rates in the country. Thus, higher inflation would lead to higher coupon payments. These bonds have lost steam in India with fall in inflation and perception of lower inflation in future in India.

9.3 Bond Valuation

The value of any financial asset is the present value of all future cash flows. In case of bonds, there are two kinds of cash flow the investors would get: regular coupon payments and final principal or par value payment. The present value of these cash flows is the value, which an investor should be willing to pay to buy a bond. The cash flows are brought to the present at a rate which is known as the bond's market rate of interest. This interest rate is not the same as the coupon interest rate.

9.3.1 Basics of Bond Valuation

A bond has following features: Face value of bond is FV, coupon value is C, market rate of return on the bond is k_d and the bond matures after n years.

If a person buys this bond, he will receive two basic cash flows: a coupon payment every period till n years, and face value will be paid at the time of maturity. Thus, the expression for the value of a bond is as follows:

$$V_B = \frac{C}{(1+k_d)^1} + \frac{C}{(1+k_d)^2} + \cdots + \frac{C}{(1+k_d)^n} + \frac{\text{FV}}{(1+k_d)^n}$$

The generalized equation for this would be:

$$V_B = \sum_{i=1}^{n} \frac{C}{(1+k_d)^n} + \frac{\text{FV}}{(1+k_d)^n}$$

Recall the expression in the time value tables' format. You have an annuity payment of coupons and a single cash flow of the face value at the end of the period which can be expressed as:

$$V_B = C \times \text{PVIF}(k_d,\ n) + \text{FV} \times \text{PV}(k_d,\ n)$$

where $\text{PVIF}(k_d,\ n)$ is the present value of annuity factor for discount rate k_d and period n and $\text{PV}(k_d,\ n)$ is present value for discount rate k_d and period n.

Let us understand the concept of bond valuation with the help of an example:

EXAMPLE 9.1 Suppose a firm issues a bond whose maturity period is 3 years. Face value is ₹1000 and coupon interest rate is 10% with annual coupon payment. An investor willing to invest in this bond expects a return of 8%. What is the value the investor would be willing to pay for this bond?

Solution: Let us first understand the terms in this question. Let us take the following notations:

FV = Face value or par value = ₹1,000

n = Maturity period = 3 years

Coupon interest rate = I = 10%

Coupon = C = 10% of ₹1000 = ₹100

Bond's market rate of interest = k_d = 8%

If we draw a time line for this, we would have ₹100 as cash inflows at the end of the first year, second year and third year. These are the coupon payments. There also be a cash flow of the final principal payment or par value payment at the time of maturity which will be the third year.

Thus, the timeline would be as given as follows:

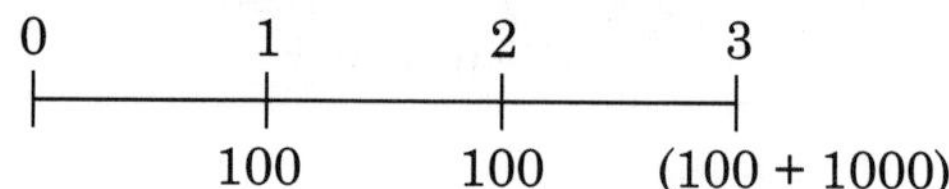

The value of the bond will be the present value of these future cash flows. Thus, bringing these future cash flows to the present, we get

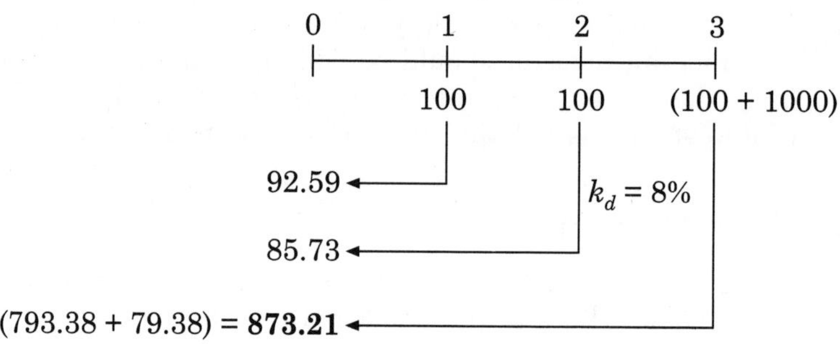

$$V_B = \mathbf{1051.54}$$

Thus, the value of the bond, V_B = ₹1051.54

The general equation for the above given method would be:

$$V_B = \frac{C}{(1+k_d)^1} + \frac{C}{(1+k_d)^2} + \ldots + \frac{C}{(1+k_d)^n} + \frac{FV}{(1+k_d)^n}$$

$$V_B = \frac{100}{(1.08)^1} + \frac{100}{(1.08)^2} + \frac{100}{(1.08)^3} + \frac{1000}{(1.08)^3}$$

$$= ₹\mathbf{1,051.54}$$

It can also be expressed in time value table form as:

$$V_B = 100 * \text{PVIF}(8\%,3) + 1000 * \text{PV}(8\%,3)$$
$$= 100 * 2.577 + 1000 * 0.794 = ₹1,051.7$$

In excel, the present value of an investment function can be used for finding the bond value (Figure 9.1).

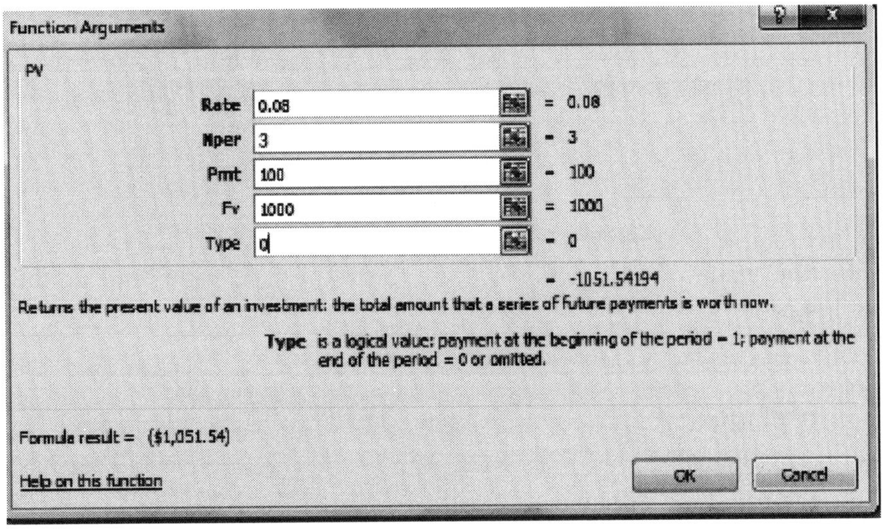

FIGURE 9.1 Snapshot of bond valuation function in excel.

In Figure 9.1 rate is bond's market rate of interest, NPER is maturity period, Pmt is Coupon amount and FV is face value. It can also be solved by entering the following function in the formula bar which is:

PV(0.08,3,100,1000,0) = ₹1,051.54

Thus, this bond with face value of ₹1,000 should sell at ₹1,051.54. As the value of the bond is greater than the face value, it is a **premium bond**. When coupon interest rate is greater than the bond's market rate of interest, the bond would sell at a premium.

In the previous example, if k_d is 12%, value of bond will be:

$$V_B = 100 * \text{PVIF}(12\%,3) + 1000 * \text{PV}(12\%,3)$$
$$= ₹951.96$$

Thus, in this case the value of the bond is less than the face value, and hence, it is selling at a discount. Thus, it would be called as a **discount bond**.

If k_d is 10%, the value of the bond would be ₹1,000 and would be know as **par value bond**.

Thus, it can be summarized as in Table 9.2:

TABLE 9.2 Relation between Face Value and Bond Value

Premium bond	$I > k_d$	Value of the bond > Face value of the bond
Discount bond	$I < k_d$	Value of the bond < Face value of the bond
Par value bond	$I = k_d$	Value of the bond = Face value of the bond

In the original problem, suppose the expected return remains 8% after 1 year, what would be the value of bond?

The time to maturity will be 2 years and other things would remain the same. Thus, the expression for value of bond would be:

$$V_B = \frac{100}{(1.08)^1} + \frac{100}{(1.08)^2} + \frac{1000}{(1.08)^2} = ₹1,035.6$$

The value of the bond has gone down and from ₹1,051.5 to ₹1,035.6. Thus, we can see the following bond values with combinations of expected return and time to maturity as in Table 9.3:

TABLE 9.3
Time to maturity versus bond value at different discount rates

Time to maturity	$k_d = 8\%$	$k_d = 10\%$	$k_d = 12\%$
3	₹1,051.54	₹1,000	₹951.96
2	₹1,035.67	₹1,000	₹966.20
1	₹1,018.52	₹1,000	₹982.14
0	₹1,000	₹1,000	₹1,000

Thus, we can see from the graph (Figure 9.2) that as the time to maturity approaches, the value of the bond moves towards the face value and at the time of maturity, the value of the bond is equal to the face value.

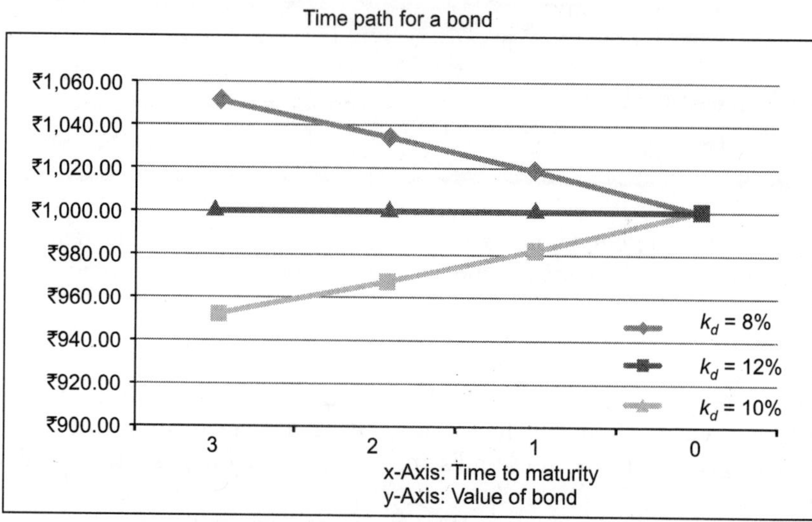

FIGURE 9.2
Time path for a bond

Figure 9.2 illustrates the following important points:

1. Whenever the market rate of interest of bond, k_d is the same as the coupon interest rate, the bond will sell at the par value. The value of the bond does not change with the change in the time to maturity if k_d = Coupon interest rate. This can be seen in row 3 of Table 9.2.
2. Due to various factors, there might be a change in the market interest rates of a bond and it affects the value of the bond. When k_d increased from 8% to 12%, the value of the bond decreased from ₹1051.54 to ₹951.56. Thus, you are able to buy the bond at a lower price, and hence, get more return. It is important to note here that the coupon interest rate remains the same as it is stated in the contract.
3. The value of a bond moves towards the face value as its maturity date approaches. As we can see from the figure above, it happens in both the cases, i.e., when $k_d <$ Coupon interest rate and when $k_d >$ Coupon interest rate.

The above given points provide valuable insights on how a bond holder may suffer loss or gain based on the changes in the expected returns of a bond. An increase in general interest rates would lead to an increase in expected returns by the investors and hence the value of the bonds would fall in the market.

9.3.2 Valuation of Semi-annual Coupon Bonds

Most bonds available in the market pay semi-annual coupons and very few bonds pay annual coupons. To evaluate bonds with semi-annual coupons, there will be changes in the valuation equation.

The generalized equation for this would be:

$$V_B = \sum_{i=1}^{2n} \frac{C/2}{(1+k_d/2)^{2n}} + \frac{\text{FV}}{(1+k_d/2)^{2n}}$$

Let us understand this with the help of an example.

EXAMPLE 9.2 A bond with ₹1000 face value and 5 years to maturity pays semi-annual coupons. The coupon interest rate is 10%. An investor expects a return of 12% on this bond. What should be the value the investor would be willing to pay for this bond?

Solution: As the coupon payment would be happening semi-annually, the yearly coupon payment would be ₹100 (10% of ₹1,000). Thus, semi-annual payment would be ₹50. There will be a cash flow of ₹50 every 6 months for a period of 5 years. The period would be twice of the time to maturity and k_d would become half. The value of the bond can be expressed as given below:

$$V_B = \frac{50}{(1.06)^1} + \frac{50}{(1.06)^2} + \cdots + \frac{50}{(1.06)^{10}} + \frac{1000}{(1.06)^{10}}$$

$$= ₹1,294.40$$

9.3.3 Valuation of Zero Coupon Bonds

As explained in the earlier sections, zero coupon bonds have only the principal payment at the end of the period. Treasury bills or T-bills are the most common zero coupon bonds. The generalized expression for a zero coupon bond is as given below:

$$V_{ZCB} = \frac{\text{FV}}{(1+k_d)^n}$$

9.4 Bond Yields

Bond dealers report bond yields of each bond along with other information, like maturity date, price, and coupon interest rate. Bond yields vary from day-to-day, and depend on the markets and general interest rates. There are three kinds of bond yields which are described as given below:

9.4.1 Yield to Maturity

Yield to Maturity (YTM) is the percentage returns that an investor would get on a bond if he holds the bond till maturity. In other words, it is the rates of return that an investor would get when he buys a bond at a market determined price. It is generally the same as the market rate of return, k_d. A simplified formula for YTM is as given below:

Yield to maturity is the percentage returns that an investor would get on a bond if he holds the bond till maturity.

$$\text{YTM} = \frac{C + (\text{FV} - V_B)/n}{(\text{FV} + 2 * V_B)/3}$$

EXAMPLE 9.3 An investor is offered a 10-year ₹1,000 bond with annual coupon interest rate of 8% at INR 728.69. What is the yield to maturity on this bond?

Solution: Here,

FV = ₹1,000

C = ₹80

n = 10 years

V_B = ₹728.69

The solution for this would be:

$$728.69 = \frac{80}{(1+\text{YTM})^1} + \frac{80}{(1+\text{YTM})^2} + \cdots + \frac{80}{(1+\text{YTM})^{10}} + \frac{1000}{(1+\text{YTM})^{10}}$$

The system of equation can be solved to find YTM. Hit and trial method can be used to solve for YTM. Applying the simplified formula to solve this problem, which will give an approximate answer is given as follows:

$$\text{YTM} = \frac{80 + (1000 - 728.69)/10}{(1000 + 2 * 728.69)/3} \approx 13\%$$

the investor buys this bond at ₹728.69, he will get a return of 13%.

9.4.2 Current Yield

Current yield is the annual interest payment divided by the current price of the bond. This represents the cash income that a bond would generate in a given year and does not give information on the return that an investor would get for holding a bond.

The expression for current yield (CY) is as follows:

$$\text{Current Yield} = \frac{C}{V_B}$$

Current yield represents the cash income that a bond would generate in a given year.

Thus, the current yield of the bond in the previous example would be:

$$\text{Current Yield} = \frac{80}{728.69} = 10.97\%$$

9.4.3 Yield to Call

Some of the bonds have a special feature in which the bond can be called back or bought back by the firm at a specific price after a specific period of time. Such bonds are known as callable bonds. If the general interest rates in the market fall, firms would call back the bonds and re-issue with the lower coupon rates. This would reduce the cash outflow for the firm. Thus, if a bond is called back by a firm, the return that an investor would get in such a case would be known as yield to call (YTC). The expression for a YTC is as follows:

$$V_B = \sum_{i=1}^{n} \frac{C}{(1+\text{YTC})^n} + \frac{\text{Call Price}}{(1+\text{YTC})^n}$$

EXAMPLE 9.4 A 10-year, 10% semi-annual coupon bond selling for ₹1,135.90 can be called in 4 years for ₹1,050, what is its Yield to Call (YTC)? What is the yield to maturity and if the firms calls back the bond is it a loss or benefit for the investor?

Solution: Here, the coupon value will be ₹50. It can be called in 4 years and coupon payment will be paid every 6 months, so n = 8. Value of bond is ₹1135.90 and Call price is ₹1,050.

$$1135.90 = \frac{50}{(1+\text{YTC}/2)^1} + \frac{50}{(1+\text{YTC}/2)^2} + \cdots + \frac{50}{(1+\text{YTC}/2)^8} + \frac{1050}{(1+\text{YTC}/2)^8}$$

Solving this, we get

$$\text{YTC}/2 = 3.6\%, \text{ YTC} = 7.2\%$$

Solving for yield to maturity, we get YTM = 8%.

Thus, it is a loss for the investor if the bond is called back as his returns fall from 8% to 7.2%.

9.5 Determinants of Market Interest Rates

We have seen that different bonds have different market interest rates. The components of the market interest rate can be expressed in the form of following equation:

$$k_d = r_{rf} + \text{IP} + \text{DRP} + \text{LP} + \text{MRP}$$

where

$$r_{rf} = r^* + \text{IP}$$

k_d = Market interest rate, r_{rf} = Nominal risk-free rate, r^* = real risk-free rate, IP = Inflation Premium, DRP = Default Risk Premium, LP = Liquidity Premium and MRP = Maturity Risk Premium.

The variables can be explained as given below:

k_d = Quoted or market interest rates. Different bonds have different market interest rates based on various risk profiles.

r^* = Real risk-free interest rate. This is the risk that would be expected on a riskless security with no inflation

IP = Inflation premium. It is the average inflation over the life of a security and may not be equal to the current inflation rate. Inflation has an effect on our real earnings. Suppose there is 10% inflation in the system today and your bond gives a return of 8%. Suppose you can buy two litres of petrol today for ₹100. Due to inflation, after one year, you would be able to buy the same two litres for ₹110. If you had invested ₹100 in the bond, you would have ₹108 and hence by selling this bond you would not be able to buy the commodity. Hence, you would rather invest the money in the commodity instead of the bond. Investors include inflation in their returns so that they can cover the effect of inflation.

r_{rf} = Nominal risk-free rate. It is the interest rate on a risk-free bond like government treasury bill as these have almost zero risk and are highly liquid.

DRP = Default risk premium. It is the premium charged for the possibility of default by the bond issuer. It is zero for a government bond and rises with the riskiness of a bond. Bond ratings by various rating agencies, like CRISIL, ICRA, FITCH, etc. determine the default risk premium.

LP = Liquidity premium. Some bonds can be bought and sold more easily than others. This premium captures the convertibility to cash by bonds and is very low for government bonds and might be very high for bonds issued by small firms.

---

* The factors on which default risk premium depend are:

- Financial Ratios: Ratios like return on assets, debt ratio, and interest coverage ratios are taken into consideration for rating the bond of a firm.
- Bond contract terms: If the bonds are backed by an asset, the probability of default would be lower. Such information is covered in the bond contract term and affects the ratings of a bond.
- Qualitative factors: Factors like the composition of the board, management of the firm, industry growth prospects and sensitivity to economic growth effects the ratings of the bond.

MRP = Maturity Risk Premium. It is the net effect of interest rate risk and reinvestment risk. Interest rate risk and reinvestment risk will be discussed in detail in the next section.

Illustration 9.1 Rating Scale for Long-term Instruments

CRISIL AAA (Highest Safety)	Instruments with this rating are considered to have the highest degree of safety regarding timely servicing of financial obligations. Such instruments carry lowest credit risk.
CRISIL AA (High Safety)	Instruments with this rating are considered to have high degree of safety regarding timely servicing of financial obligations. Such instruments carry very low credit risk.
CRISIL A (Adequate Safety)	Instruments with this rating are considered to have adequate degree of safety regarding timely servicing of financial obligations. Such instruments carry low credit risk.
CRISIL BBB (Moderate Safety)	Instruments with this rating are considered to have moderate degree of safety regarding timely servicing of financial obligations. Such instruments carry moderate credit risk.
CRISIL BB (Moderate Risk)	Instruments with this rating are considered to have moderate risk of default regarding timely servicing of financial obligations.
CRISIL B (High Risk)	Instruments with this rating are considered to have high risk of default regarding timely servicing of financial obligations.
CRISIL C (Very High Risk)	Instruments with this rating are considered to have very high risk of default regarding timely servicing of financial obligations.
CRISIL D Default	Instruments with this rating are in default or are expected to be in default soon.
Note:	*1) CRISIL may apply '+' (plus) or '-' (minus) signs for ratings from 'CRISIL AA' to 'CRISIL C' to reflect comparative standing within the category.* *2) CRISIL may assign rating outlooks for ratings from 'CRISIL AAA' to 'CRISIL B'. Ratings on Rating Watch will not carry outlooks. A rating outlook indicates the direction in which a rating may move over a medium-term horizon of one to two years. A rating outlook can be 'Positive', 'Stable', or 'Negative'. A 'Positive' or 'Negative' rating outlook is not necessarily a precursor of a rating change.* *3) A suffix of 'r' indicates investments carrying non-credit risk. The 'r' suffix indicates that payments on the rated instrument have significant risks other than credit risk. The terms of the instrument specify that the payments to investors will not be fixed, and could be linked to one or more external variables such as commodity prices, equity indices, or foreign exchange rates. This could result in variability in payments, including possible material loss of principal, because of adverse movement in value of the external variables. The risk of such adverse movement in price/value is not addressed by the rating.* *4) CRISIL may assign a rating of 'NM' (Not Meaningful) to instruments that have factors present in them, which render the outstanding rating meaningless. These include reorganisation or liquidation of the issuer, the obligation being under dispute in a court of law or before a statutory authority.* *5) A prefix of 'PP-MLD' indicates that the instrument is a principal-protected market-linked debenture. The terms of such instruments indicate that while the issuer promises to pay back the face value/principal of the instrument, the coupon rates of these instruments will not be fixed, and could be linked to one or more external variables such as commodity prices, equity share prices, indices, or foreign exchange rates.* *6) A prefix of 'Provisional' indicates that the rating centrally factors in the completion of certain critical steps/documentation by the issuer for the instrument, without these the rating would either have been different or not assigned ab initio.*

Source: www.crisil.com

Summarizing market interest rates for various types of bonds, we have Table 9.4:

	r_{rf}	*IP*	*DRP*	*LP*	*MRP*
Short-term government bond	✓	✓			
Long-term government bond	✓	✓			✓
Short-term corporate bond	✓	✓	✓	✓	
Long-term corporate bond	✓	✓	✓	✓	✓

TABLE 9.4 Determinants of Market interest rates for various types of bonds

EXAMPLE 9.5 The real risk-free rate of interest is 4%. Inflation is expected to be 2% this year and 4% during the next 2 years. Assume that the maturity risk premium is zero. What is the Market interest rate on two year government bonds and three year government bonds?

Solution: In this problem,

$$r^* = 4\%$$

$$I_1 = 2\%,\ I_2 = 4\% \text{ and } I_3 = 4\%$$

$$\text{MRP} = 0\%$$

Inflation premium is given by the expression:

$$\text{Inflation premium } (n \text{ year bond}) = \frac{I_1 + I_2 + \cdots + I_n}{n}$$

Thus, in this problem
Inflation premium for a 2 year bond will be

$$\text{Inflation premium}\left(2 \text{ year bond}\right) = \frac{4\% + 2\%}{3} = 3\%$$

Similarly, inflation premium for a 3 year bond will be

$$\text{Inflation premium}\left(3 \text{ year bond}\right) = \frac{4\% + 2\% + 2\%}{3} = 2.67\%$$

Thus, Market interest rate for a government bond will be,

$$k_d(\text{Long-term government bond}) = r^* + \text{IP} + \text{MRP}$$

$$k_d\left(2 \text{ year government bond}\right) = 3\% + 2\% = 5\%$$

$$k_d(2 \text{ year government bond}) = 3\% + 2.67\% = 5.67\%$$

9.6 Interest Rate Risk and Reinvestment Risk

Market interest rates for a bond can change for a variety of reasons. Increase in global oil prices might lead to increase in inflation. As a result, the expected returns by an investor would go up. This would lead to an increase in market interest rates for a bond and hence the value of the bond would fall. There may be various other reasons, which may affect the interest rates and this would affect the value of the bond. Thus, rising k_d would lead to fall in bond prices. This is termed as interest rate risk.

Consider two bonds, one with a time to maturity of 2 years and other with a time to maturity of 10 years. Both have a face value of INR 100 and coupon interest rate of 10%. The given below table shows the bond value at different Market Interest rates. Table 9.5 shows that the effect of change in interest rate is higher on the long-term bond compared to the short term. Thus, long-term bonds have higher interest rate risk compared to short-term bonds.

TABLE 9.5
Effect of Change in Interest Rates

Market Interest Rates (k_d)	*Value of bond (2 year)*	*Value of bond (10 year)*
5%	109.30	138.61
6%	107.33	129.44
7%	105.42	121.07
8%	103.57	113.42
9%	101.76	106.42
10%	100.00	100.00
11%	98.29	94.11
12%	96.62	88.70
13%	95.00	83.72
14%	93.41	79.14
15%	91.87	74.91
16%	90.37	71.00
17%	88.90	67.39
18%	87.47	64.05

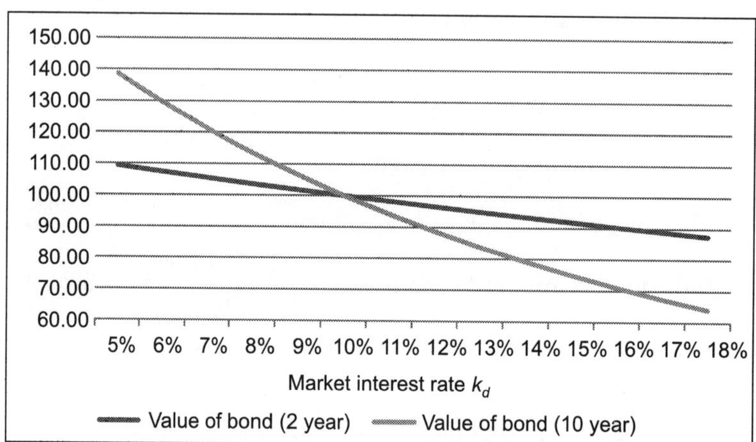

FIGURE 9.3
Effect of Interest Rate risk on a short-term versus long-term bond

Thus, we can see that an increase in interest rates lead to a loss for the bond holders as the value of the bond falls in the market. This loss shall be higher for a long-term bond as the interest rate risk is higher for a long-term bond. To reduce this risk, an investor might want to invest in short-term bonds. However, this investment in short-term bonds would lead to higher reinvestment risk. Reinvestment rate risk is the concern that market interest rates will fall, and future CFs will have to be reinvested at lower rates, hence reducing income. This can be explained with the help of the following example:

You have two options:

- **Option 1:** Invest in a 20 year bond.
- **Option 2:** Series of Ten 2 year bonds: This means that you would invest in a 2 year bond today and after two year with the cash flows received, you would invest in other two year bond and this would continue till 20 years.

If you go for option 2, you would have reduced your interest rate risk. However, if the interest rates fall, your reinvestment will give you lesser returns as the coupon rates would fall and a long-term investment would give a better return. If you go for option 1, you have higher interest rate risk as a small increase in market interest rates would lead to a fall in the bond value. Thus, if you invest in a long-term bond, you will have to bear interest rate risk and if you invest in a short-term bond, you will have to bear reinvestment risk. A callable bond also has reinvestment risk because the firm would call back the bond and reissue the bond if the interest rates fall. Both these risks are factored in maturity risk premium. It is important to note here that risk is dependent on how long the investor wishes to hold the instrument. This is called the investment horizon. Risk and investment horizon are related and affects the maturity risk premium. An investor with short investment horizon would want to invest in bond with short-term maturity as his reinvestment risk would be minimal. For an investor with long-term horizon, holding a long-term bond will lead to interest rate risk and holding short-term bond will lead to reinvestment risk.

Researchable Issues

Faculty members, students and research scholars may like to consider the following selected issues for further research and case writing.

- Bond market development in developing markets: Issues and Challenges
- Municipal Bond Markets and Infrastructure Development
- Liquidity in Government Bond Markets
- Corporate bond market and its effects on bank lending
- Factors affecting pricing of government bonds
- Monetary policy transmission and Bond markets

References

Duffee, G.R., The relation between treasury yields and corporate bond yield spreads. *The Journal of Finance*, 53(6), 1998, pp. 2225–2241.

Goodfriend, M., Interest rates and the conduct of monetary policy, *Carnegie–Rochester conference series on public policy*, Vol. 34, North-Holland. 1991, pp. 7–30.

Heath, D., Jarrow, R., and Morton, A., Bond pricing and the term structure of interest rates: A new methodology for contingent claims valuation. *Econometrica*, 60(1), 1992, pp. 77–105.

Sharpe, W.F., Alexander, G.J., and Bailey, J.V. *Investments* (Vol. 6). Upper Saddle River, NJ: Prentice-Hall, 1999.

Vasicek, O., An equilibrium characterization of the term structure, *Journal of Financial Economics*, 5(2), 1977, pp. 177–188.

Points to Remember

- A bond is an instrument issued by corporates and government for raising capital. Investors receive returns in terms of regular coupon payment and principal payment at the end of the period.
- Some special bond types were discussed. A zero coupon bond does not have coupon payment but only a principal payment whereas a perpetual bond has only coupon payment and no time to maturity.
- Value of a bond is present value of coupon payments (present value of annuity) and present value of the principal payment which is made at the time of maturity. The discount rate depends on the risk of the bond.

- The value of bond is given by the expression:

$$V_B = \sum_{i=1}^{n} \frac{C}{(1+k_d)^n} + \frac{FV}{(1+k_d)^n}$$

- The value of a semi-annual bond is given by the expression:

$$V_B = \sum_{i=1}^{2n} \frac{C/2}{(1+k_d/2)^{2n}} + \frac{FV}{(1+k_d/2)^{2n}}$$

- The return an investor would get if the bond is held to maturity is called as Yield To Maturity (YTM)
- A change in interest rates move the value of bond and this effect is more pronounced on bonds with longer maturity. This is known as interest rate risk. However, investment in short-term bonds with cash flows reinvested again in short-term bonds may lead to lower cash flows due to probable fall in interest rates. This is known as reinvestment risk.
- Corporate bonds have higher default risks compared to government bonds. This risk is indicated by the ratings assigned by the rating agencies. A AAA rated bond will have very low default risk, and hence default premium will be almost negligible, whereas a junk bond with a B- rating would have very high probability of default, and hence, high default premium.

Questions

1. Explain the following terms: Government bonds, Corporate bonds, Face value, Perpetual bonds, Yield To Maturity, Zero Coupon Bonds, Indexed Bonds.
2. Which is more volatile to changes in interest rates: short-term bonds or long-term bonds? Explain.
3. A callable bond has higher reinvestment risk than a normal bond. Explain.
4. An investor expects lower inflation in the coming years, would he invest in inflation indexed bonds? Elaborate.
5. Discuss the factors affecting bond ratings.

Multiple Choice Questions

1. A person owns a bond that has coupon payment of ₹75 for each period and ₹1,000 principal payment at maturity. What is the ₹1,000 called?

(a) Coupon (b) Face value
(c) Yield (d) Discount

2. A bond that can be paid off at the discretion of the issuer earlier than the maturity date is called:

(a) Zero coupon bond (b) Perpetual bond
(c) Callable bond (d) Municipal bond

3. A bond that has only one payment, which occurs at maturity, defines which one of the following?

(a) Zero coupon bond (b) Perpetual bond
(c) Callable bond (d) Municipal bond

4. A bond with a face value of ₹100 is selling at ₹95. Which of the following is true in this case:
   (a) Bond is selling at par
   (b) Bond is selling at a discount
   (c) Bond is selling at premium
   (d) None of the above
5. A corporate bond is selling for ₹100 and has coupon interest rate of 8%. Which of the following statement is correct?
   (a) The YTM of the bond is 8%.
   (b) The price of the bond will remain at par if YTM remains constant.
   (c) If the interest rate in the market increases, the bond price will fall below ₹100.
   (d) Both a and b are correct
   (e) All of the above are correct
6. A firm would most likely recall its bond in which of the following conditions:
   (a) A reduction in market interest rates
   (b) An increase in market interest rates
   (c) Bond ratings are upgraded
   (d) Both a and b are correct
7. Which of the following statement is most correct?
   (a) Junk bonds have lower YTM compared to government bonds
   (b) Government bonds have lower risk compared to a callable corporate bond
   (c) Both a and b are correct
   (d) All of the above are correct
8. Assume that interest rates in the economy fall from 10% to 9%. Which of the following bonds will have the largest percentage increase in price?
   (a) A 9-year bond with a 10% coupon interest rate
   (b) A 5-year bond with a 9% coupon interest rate
   (c) A 10-year zero coupon bond
   (d) A 1-year bond with a 15% coupon interest rate
9. Which of the following have the highest interest rate risk:
   (a) A 10-year semi-annual bond with coupon interest of 12%
   (b) A 10-year annual bond with coupon interest of 10%
   (c) A 10-year zero coupon bond
   (d) All will have the same risk as the maturity is 10 years for all
10. Real rates are defined as nominal rates that have been adjusted for which of the following?
   (a) Inflation
   (b) Default risk
   (c) Reinvestment risk
   (d) None of the above

Self-Test Questions

1. A company has 14% coupon bonds with 3 years maturity and face value of ₹100. If the bond's yield were 12%, what is the price of the bond?
2. A bond with maturing in 8 years has a face value of ₹1,000 and coupon rate of 8%. The bond is selling for ₹970. Find the Yield To Maturity for the bond.
3. Suppose you buy a one year zero coupon bond that has a face value of ₹1,000. The market interest rate is 8%. How much will you pay for the bond? If you purchased the bond for ₹904.4, what interest will you earn on your investment?

4. XYZ limited has a ten-year debenture that pays ₹140 annual interest. ₹1,000 will be paid on maturity. What will be the value of debenture if required rate of interest is (a) 12% (b) 14%.
5. Three bonds have face value of ₹1,000, coupon rate of 12% and maturity of 5 years. One pays interest annually, one semi-annually and one quarterly. Calculate the value of bond if the required rate of return is 10%.
6. If the par values of bonds are ₹100 with coupon rate of 5% and if they are currently selling for ₹95, ₹100 and ₹110. Find the annual yields of the bonds.
7. A 20 year, 10% ₹1,000 bond that pays interest half yearly is redeemable in twelve years at a buy back call price of ₹1150. The bond's current yield to maturity is 9.50% annually. What is the yield to call for this bond?
8. The risk-free rate on T-bills was 1.23%. If the real rate of interest is estimated to be 0.80%, what was the level of inflation?

CASE STUDY

Bond Portfolio Pricing

On 25th November, 2013, Anil Shah, fixed income fund manager with one of the leading Investment management companies was contemplating change in his bond portfolio in view of the impending rate increase by the central bank. Currently his bond portfolio comprised four bonds of varied maturities. Anil wants to determine the prices for all his bonds in the portfolio in order to form a strategy in light of the possible rate increase by the central bank. Anil's bond portfolio along with coupon, maturity and YTM (Yield To Maturity) is provided below.

Maturity	*Security*	*Coupon*	*YTM*
25-Dec-16	8.30 GS 2016	8.30%	8.15%
26-Jul-17	9.15 GS 2017	9.15%	8.25%
27-Nov-15	7.80 GS 2015	7.80%	7.90%
28-Sep-18	8.50 GS 2018	8.50%	8.60%

1. Using the above data, calculate the price for each bond portfolio security assuming the settlement date as 25th November 2013 (Assume coupon interest is paid semi-annually).
2. Calculate the new price for each bond portfolio security assuming coupon interest is paid annually.

CHAPTER

10

Valuation of Shares

LEARNING OBJECTIVES

After studying this chapter, you should be able to:

- Understand the concept and process of equity valuation
- Discuss various valuation methodologies used by analysts globally
- Understand the importance of appropriate valuation methodology in arriving at the right investment decision
- Discuss various price multiples like P/E, P/B, P/S, PEG, etc. and their use in relative valuation
- Discuss Dividend Discount Model (DDM) and its variants
- Calculate the equity value using no growth, constant growth and multistage dividend discount models
- Understand the concept of FCFF and FCFE approaches to valuation
- Discuss and calculate the enterprise value using multistage FCFF model
- Discuss and calculate the equity value using multistage FCFE model
- Explain the role and career path of equity analysts

10.1 Introduction

During my good old days as an equity analyst, besides decoding financial information, one of the important question or task that was daily encountered related to the right valuation of an asset or for that matter equity with respect to a particular stock. The objective of arriving at the right valuation was important to discover stocks which are under-priced in terms of market value relative to their true intrinsic value or worth. While finding such stocks (where there is a mispricing between the market value and true intrinsic value) is an interesting as well as a profitable task, it involves a comprehensive understanding of the various techniques needed to arrive at right valuation of shares. In this chapter, we would determine the various approaches used for the fundamental valuation of equity shares by financial analysts globally.

10.2 Valuation Process

Everyday thousands of assets (equity, debt, commodity, etc.) gets traded on the financial markets or exchanges worldwide at various price points. Have you ever wondered as to why a particular asset trades at a particular value or price or in other words, what do these prices represent for each of the assets being traded in the markets? Prices for the assets basically represent the worth or intrinsic value of the underlying businesses based on the payoffs expected to be received in the future. The process of valuation, thereby, involves assessment of right worth or intrinsic value of the business so as to determine their appropriate prices, which gets finally traded in the financial markets.

Specifically, in the context of equity, valuation of a company involves determining the payoffs expected to be received by shareholders in the future and finding out its present value (in time value terms) using an appropriate risk adjusted rate. To determine these payoffs and appropriate valuation technique, financial analysts generally follow the three-step top down approach, which begins with the macro analysis of the economy percolating down to the industry (in which the company operates) and then to the target company (see Figure 10.1). After that the appropriate valuation methodology or technique is decided to arrive at the target price for the stock and basis that the investment decision is made.

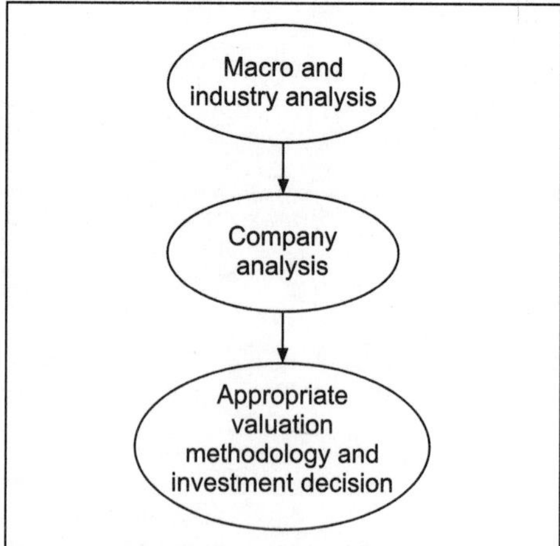

FIGURE 10.1
Top Down 3-step Process for Equity Valuation.

10.2.1 Macro and Industry Analysis

Most of the financial analysts begin the valuation process by first understanding the macroeconomic environment, in which the target company operates. This is done by assessing the stage of the business cycle in terms of fluctuations in aggregate economic activity. Analyst usually study a host of leading, coincident and lagging indicators to understand the stage of the business activity, as it would finally affect the overall demand and supply dynamics for the industry and company in context. For example, a falling business activity levels in terms of business cycle would imply softening of commodity prices such as iron ore, coal, rubber, etc. Consequently, the industries which consume some or all of these above commodities as inputs for final products could see a significant fall in their cost of production. In essence, a deep understanding of the macroeconomic scenario can have a significant impact on the estimates for the industry and company in context.

Post understanding of the macroeconomic scenario, analysts conduct the industry analysis (of which target the company is a part of) wherein they attempt to assess the sensitivity of the particular industry to the state of the economy. Generally, industries based on their operating characteristics can be broadly divided into two types: (a) cyclical industries—refers to industries with above average sensitivity to the state of the economy and (b) defensive industries—with below average (or insensitive) sensitivity to the state of the economy. This sensitivity or cyclicity of industries is generally a function of type of products produced (whether necessities or luxuries), operating leverage and financial leverage. Industries which produce products which are necessities (e.g. food, medicines), have low to medium operating and financial leverage would normally get classified into defensive industries. Conversely, companies with products which are more discretionary in nature (e.g. air-conditioners, watches, cars) and have high operating and financial leverage would get classified as cyclical industries. For example, a list of sample industries (in Indian context) with classification into defensives and cyclicals is given in Table 10.1.

TABLE 10.1 Classification of cyclical and defensive industries

Cyclical industries	*Defensive industries*
Financials	Utilities
Consumer discretionary	Healthcare
Auto	Consumer staples
Commodity companies	Education
IT	
Energy	

The above industry analysis is generally studied in conjunction with macroeconomic analysis. For example, during periods of falling aggregate economic activity (recessions), investors tend to accord higher valuation to defensive industries. Similarly, during periods of rising aggregate economic activity (expansion), cyclical industries tend to acquire higher valuations compared to defensive industries on account of faster rising profits and sales.

10.2.2 Company Analysis

The second step in the top-down approach driven valuation process pertains to the detailed analysis of the target company in light of the macroeconomic and industry analysis done above. Analysts generally try to determine the relative positioning and competitive strategy of the company in terms of market share, sales, profitability, customers, etc. through techniques like Porter's five forces analysis, Ansoff Matrix, etc.

In light of the above analysis, the analysts prepare detailed forecasts models for the company by projecting sales, profits, and assets, etc. to determine the expected payoffs (cash flows and/or dividends) available for the shareholders in future.

10.2.3 Appropriate Valuation Methodology and Investment Decision

Top down approach begins with the macro analysis of the economy percolating down to the industry and then to the target company.

The last step in the valuation process involves determination of right valuation methodology. Given the expected payoffs and nature of the industry in which company operates, analysts choose the appropriate valuation model to value the company and arrive at an expected price for the target company. Once the price has been arrived at through the appropriate valuation technique, investment decision is made with regards to buying or selling of equity for the target company.

10.3 Valuation Models

Globally, various valuation techniques for estimating the value of an equity stock can be grouped into the following two approaches or categories:

- Relative Valuation Approach
- Discounted Valuation Approach

As the name suggests, relative valuation approach arrives at a target company's valuation using relative or comparable valuation of peer companies. It basically uses the assumption that similar assets should be priced at similar valuations, and any mispricing would suggest a buy or sell investment decision. Contrary to relative valuation, discounted valuation approach attempts to discover the intrinsic value of the company using its future dividends or cash flows and then compares it with the trading market price to arrive at investment decision.

10.3.1 Relative Valuation Approach

Relative Valuation values a particular security relative to its peers or similar group of companies.

Among the two valuation approaches, relative valuation is generally more widely used among the research analysts worldwide for security valuation. This approach basically values a particular security relative to its peers or similar group of companies. This valuation approach assumes that comparable companies should be priced at similar valuations, and any deviation or mispricing would trigger an investment decision. The relative comparison is generally done through price-based multiples, such as Price to Earnings (P/E), Price to Book (P/B) value, Price to Sales (P/S), Price to Cash Flow (P/CF), etc.

Price to Earnings (P/E)

Price to Earnings (P/E) ratio is a measure of how expensive the stock is relative to its earnings. This ratio helps in assessing whether the price investors are ready to pay for each rupee of earnings generated. For example, if the P/E ratio of Infosys is 16, it implies that investors are ready to pay ₹16 for every one rupee of earnings being generated by Infosys. Price to earnings (P/E) ratio can be estimated in two ways—(a) Trailing P/E ratio and (b) Forward P/E ratio.

Trailing P/E ratio is estimated by dividing the current market price per share of the company with the Earnings Per Share (EPS) of the immediate preceding four quarters or past year. Many financial databases, like Bloomberg, Reuters, etc. refer to these past earnings as Trailing Twelve Months (TTM) Earnings Per Share (EPS).

Trailing P/E ratio ⇒ Current Market Price per Share/Trailing twelve months EPS

Forward P/E ratio is estimated by dividing market price per share of the company with the expected Earnings Per Share (EPS) of the next four quarters or next year.

Forward P/E ratio ⇒ Current Market Price per Share/Estimated EPS for next year

(***Note:*** EPS = Net profit/Number of outstanding shares)

While both trailing and forward P/E tend to capture the price being paid by investors for each rupee of earnings, forward multiples are more relevant for investors as they take into account the future profitability or earnings of the business. For a growing company, forward P/E ratio shall always be lower than the trailing P/E ratio because future earnings would be greater than the current or historical earnings. If trailing P/E is less than forward P/E ratio, it signifies that the company is facing a decline in profitability or earnings.

Price to earnings (P/E) ratio helps in assessing the price investors are ready to pay for each rupee of earnings generated.

EXAMPLE 10.1 Ajay wants to estimate the Trailing and Forward P/E multiple for Britannia Industries. For this he collects the following data:

Current market price of Britannia: ₹3,283.

Past four quarters EPS:

Quarter	*EPS*
Jun-14	9.476
Sep-14	22.55
Dec-14	11.44
Mar-15	13.94

He further estimates next fiscal year (FY 2016) EPS to be ₹65.

Solution:

Trailing P/E ratio ⇒ Current market price per share/Trailing twelve months EPS

Trailing P/E ratio ⇒ 3,283/(9.476 + 22.55 + 11.44 + 13.94) = 57.18x

Forward P/E ratio ⇒ Current market price per share/Estimated EPS for next year

Forward P/E ratio ⇒ 3,283/65 = 50.5x

While P/E ratio is easy to calculate, it suffers from certain drawbacks. The ratio cannot be used for companies with negative earnings or profits. Secondly, P/E ratio can be highly variable for cyclical companies where earnings are volatile and tend to rise and fall in line with global commodity cycles. Lastly, P/E ratio may not be comparable for companies which follow different depreciation policies or where debt levels are significantly different. Table 10.2 lists out the recent trailing P/E ratio for a sample of NSE (National Stock Exchange) companies.

TABLE 10.2 Trailing P/E ratios for NSE Companies

S.No.	*Company name*	*Trailing P/E ratio*
1	ACC Ltd.	22.61
2	Ambuja Cements Ltd.	23.84
3	Asian Paints Ltd.	55.60
4	Axis Bank Ltd.	17.84
5	Bajaj Auto Ltd.	19.29
6	Bank of Baroda	9.23
7	Bharat Heavy Electricals Ltd.	13.75
8	Bharat Petroleum Corporation Ltd.	12.18
9	Bharti Airtel Ltd.	29.94
10	Cairn India Ltd.	8.95
11	Cipla Ltd.	48.36
		(Contd.)

S.No.	Company name	Trailing P/E ratio
12	Coal India Ltd.	16.68
13	Dr. Reddy's Laboratories Ltd.	25.43
14	GAIL (India) Ltd.	15.61
15	Grasim Industries Ltd.	12.80
16	HCL Technologies Ltd.	16.09
17	HDFC Bank Ltd.	23.99
18	Hero MotoCorp Ltd.	22.32
19	Hindalco Industries Ltd.	13.45
20	Hindustan Unilever Ltd.	43.28
21	Housing Development Finance Corporation Ltd.	23.56
22	ICICI Bank Ltd.	14.93
23	Idea Cellular Ltd.	45.24
24	Infosys Ltd.	20.50
25	ITC Ltd.	27.00
26	Kotak Mahindra Bank Ltd.	33.30
27	Larsen & Toubro Ltd.	33.54
28	Lupin Ltd.	37.54
29	Mahindra & Mahindra Ltd.	22.38
30	Maruti Suzuki India Ltd.	29.34
31	NMDC Ltd.	8.68
32	NTPC Ltd.	8.67
33	Oil & Natural Gas Corporation Ltd.	14.32
34	Power Grid Corporation of India Ltd.	12.09
35	Punjab National Bank	7.88
36	Reliance Industries Ltd.	10.30
37	State Bank of India	11.73
38	Sun Pharmaceutical Industries Ltd.	37.78
39	Tata Consultancy Services Ltd.	25.13
40	Tata Motors Ltd.	12.66
41	Tech Mahindra Ltd.	23.02
42	Ultratech Cement Ltd.	37.60
43	Wipro Ltd.	17.89
44	Yes Bank Ltd.	17.08
45	Zee Entertainment Enterprises Ltd.	38.30

Source: Ace Equity

Price-to-Book (P/B)

Price-to-book (P/B) ratio compares the stock's traded market price to its reported book value per share. Reported book value refers to the shareholder's equity or the difference between assets and liabilities on the balance sheet. The ratio basically indicates as to how much price investors are ready to pay for book value (assets–liabilities) existing on the balance sheet of the company. Unlike P/E ratio, where the denominator (Earnings Per Share) is taken from the income statement, the denominator for P/B ratio (Book Value Per Share) is taken from the balance sheet.

P/B ratio can be estimated in two ways—Trailing P/B ratio and Forward P/B ratio. While trailing P/B ratio is estimated by dividing the current market price per share of the company with the Book Value Per Share (BVPS) of the past year, forward P/B ratio divides the current market price per share of the company by the Book Value Per Share (BVPS) estimated for the next year.

Price to book (P/B) ratio indicates as to how much price investors are ready to pay for book value of the company.

Trailing P/B ratio ⇒ Current market price per share/BVPS of past year

Forward P/B ratio ⇒ Current market price per share/Estimated BVPS for next year

(***Note:*** BVPS = Shareholder's equity/Number of outstanding shares)

Companies having P/B ratio equal to 1 are generally considered fairly valued. Companies with P/B ratio greater than 1 are considered overvalued, and those with P/B ratio less than 1 are considered undervalued.

Unlike P/E ratio, P/B ratio can be used for companies with negative earnings or profits as book value is an accumulated balance sheet number, and is generally not negative. Further, book value is much more stable compared to earnings, which can be highly volatile for cyclical companies. Analysts generally prefer to use P/B ratio for companies (such as banks and non-banking financial companies) where book value of assets on the balance sheet is closer to the fair market values. In case of banks and non-banking financial companies, the assets are the loans which are recorded at their fair market values in the balance sheet and consequently book value of assets is same as their fair market values. For companies where there is a mismatch between the recorded or book value of assets and their actual market value, P/B ratio would tend to be understated or overstated resulting in erroneous valuation. For example, the asset "Buildings" purchased ten years ago would have been recorded at the historical cost price in the balance sheet of the company. The market price of this building today would be very different from the historical cost price at which it is recorded in the balance sheet. Consequently, the book value (assets–liabilities) would be under/overstated and P/B ratio would not reflect the fair valuation. Table 10.3 lists out the recent trailing P/B ratio for a sample of NSE companies.

TABLE 10.3
Trailing P/B ratios for NSE Companies.

S.No.	*Company name*	*Trailing P/B ratio*
1	ACC Ltd.	3.20
2	Ambuja Cements Ltd.	3.52
3	Asian Paints Ltd.	16.36
4	Axis Bank Ltd.	2.96
5	Bajaj Auto Ltd.	5.26
6	Bank of Baroda	0.88
7	Bharat Heavy Electricals Ltd.	1.45
8	Bharat Petroleum Corporation Ltd.	2.61
9	Bharti Airtel Ltd.	2.53
10	Cairn India Ltd.	0.68
11	Cipla Ltd.	5.33
12	Coal India Ltd.	5.67
13	Dr. Reddys Laboratories Ltd.	6.09
		(Contd.)

S.No.	Company name	Trailing P/B ratio
14	GAIL (India) Ltd.	1.45
15	Grasim Industries Ltd.	1.23
16	HCL Technologies Ltd.	5.53
17	HDFC Bank Ltd.	4.06
18	Hero MotoCorp Ltd.	8.07
19	Hindalco Industries Ltd.	0.72
20	Hindustan Unilever Ltd.	47.47
21	Housing Development Finance Corporation Ltd.	4.58
22	ICICI Bank Ltd.	2.16
23	Idea Cellular Ltd.	2.51
24	Infosys Ltd.	5.00
25	ITC Ltd.	8.23
26	Kotak Mahindra Bank Ltd.	4.58
27	Larsen & Toubro Ltd.	3.95
28	Lupin Ltd.	10.23
29	Mahindra & Mahindra Ltd.	2.73
30	Maruti Suzuki India Ltd.	4.59
31	NMDC Ltd.	1.85
32	NTPC Ltd.	1.13
33	Oil & Natural Gas Corporation Ltd.	1.46
34	Power Grid Corporation of India Ltd.	1.58
35	Punjab National Bank	0.66
36	Reliance Industries Ltd.	1.12
37	State Bank of India	1.24
38	Sun Pharmaceutical Industries Ltd.	6.41
39	Tata Consultancy Services Ltd.	9.85
40	Tata Motors Ltd.	3.15
41	Tata Power Company Ltd.	1.48
42	Tata Steel Ltd.	1.02
43	Tech Mahindra Ltd.	5.11
44	Ultratech Cement Ltd.	4.15
45	Vedanta Ltd.	1.05
46	Wipro Ltd.	4.19
47	Yes Bank Ltd.	2.92

Source: Ace Equity

Price-to-Sales (P/S)

Price-to-Sales (P/S) ratio compares the stock's traded market price per share to its reported sales or revenue per share.

P/S ratio = Current market price per share/Per share revenue or sales

Generally, P/S ratio is used for early stage companies or companies where operating profitability (EBIT) is negative. For example, in India, e-commerce start-ups like Flipkart, Snapdeal, etc. are being valued at P/S or Price to Gross Merchandise Value

(P/GMV). While P/S or P/GMV ratios are easy to calculate, they do not take into account the margins, operating and financial leverage of the company concerned. So, a company may have high sales but negative profitability on account of lower margins and high financial leverage.

EV/EBITDA ratio compares the enterprise value (EV) of the company with its operating profit or EBITDA.

Enterprise Value-to-EBITDA (EV/EBITDA): Enterprise Value-to-EBITDA (EV/EBITDA) ratio compares the enterprise value (EV) of the company with its operating profit or EBITDA (Earnings before interest, tax, depreciation and amortization).

$$\text{EV/EBITDA} = \text{Enterprise Value/EBITDA}$$

where,

$$\text{Enterprise Value} = \text{Market Value of Equity} + \text{Market Value of Preferred Equity} + \text{Market Value of Debt} - \text{Cash \& Cash Equivalents}$$

EV/EBITDA ratio is generally used when the analyst wants to control for differences in depreciation and interest (debt) levels across companies. For example, EV/EBITDA ratio is primarily used for capital intensive businesses like steel, coal, infrastructure, etc. where depreciation is a big component of income statement. Similarly, for high debt companies (where earnings may be negative on account of high interest cost), EV/EBITDA ratio is an appropriate measure as it reflects the operating profitability of the business before interest has been paid out to debt holders.

Table 10.4 lists out the recent trailing EV/EBITDA ratio for a sample of NSE companies.

TABLE 10.4 Trailing EV/EBITDA ratios for NSE Companies.

S.No.	*Company name*	*Trailing EV/EBITDA ratio*
1	ACC Ltd.	14.67
2	Ambuja Cements Ltd.	14.03
3	Asian Paints Ltd.	32.24
4	Axis Bank Ltd.	15.96
5	Bajaj Auto Ltd.	12.33
6	Bank of Baroda	6.39
7	Bharat Heavy Electricals Ltd.	6.59
8	Bharat Petroleum Corporation Ltd.	6.78
9	Bharti Airtel Ltd.	8.32
10	Cairn India Ltd.	3.80
11	Cipla Ltd.	25.03
12	Coal India Ltd.	7.37
13	Dr. Reddys Laboratories Ltd.	16.42
14	GAIL (India) Ltd.	10.14
15	Grasim Industries Ltd.	6.52
16	HCL Technologies Ltd.	11.13
17	HDFC Bank Ltd.	17.22
18	Hero MotoCorp Ltd.	13.20
19	Hindalco Industries Ltd.	9.53
20	Hindustan Unilever Ltd.	31.14
21	Housing Development Finance Corporation Ltd.	14.53
22	ICICI Bank Ltd.	17.23
23	Idea Cellular Ltd.	8.92
24	Infosys Ltd.	12.19
		(Contd.)

S.No.	Company name	Trailing EV/EBITDA ratio
25	ITC Ltd.	16.36
26	Kotak Mahindra Bank Ltd.	27.93
27	Larsen & Toubro Ltd.	14.77
28	Lupin Ltd.	23.39
29	Mahindra & Mahindra Ltd.	11.08
30	Maruti Suzuki India Ltd.	14.57
31	NMDC Ltd.	3.71
32	NTPC Ltd.	7.29
33	Oil & Natural Gas Corporation Ltd.	6.22
34	Power Grid Corporation of India Ltd.	8.67
35	Punjab National Bank	6.75
36	Reliance Industries Ltd.	8.50
37	State Bank of India	8.83
38	Sun Pharmaceutical Industries Ltd.	15.05
39	Tata Consultancy Services Ltd.	17.35
40	Tata Motors Ltd.	5.44
41	Tata Power Company Ltd.	8.18
42	Tata Steel Ltd.	7.71
43	Tech Mahindra Ltd.	13.82
44	Ultratech Cement Ltd.	18.50
45	Vedanta Ltd.	5.12
46	Wipro Ltd.	11.47
47	Yes Bank Ltd.	18.61
48	Zee Entertainment Enterprises Ltd.	23.01

Source: Ace Equity

PEG ratio compares the P/E multiple of the company with its expected growth rate in earnings.

Price-Earnings-to-Growth (PEG): Price Earnings to Growth (PEG) ratio compares the P/E multiple of the company with its expected growth rate in earnings.

PEG ⇒ (P/E)/Expected Earnings Growth Rate

For example, if 1 year forward P/E ratio of HCL Technologies is 17 and expected growth rate of earnings in future is 20%, then PEG ratio is

PEG ⇒ (P/E)/Expected Earnings Growth Rate

PEG ⇒ 17/20 = 0.85

Generally, stocks with PEG = 1 are considered fairly valued. Similarly, stocks with PEG > 1 are considered overvalued, and those with PEG < 1 are considered undervalued.

Relative Valuation: How It Is To Be Used

Relative valuation is primarily used by analysts as a first filter for identifying mispriced securities. To apply this method for determining whether the target company is under/overvalued, analysts generally follow these steps:

Step 1 Identify or select the peer or comparison companies.

Step 2 Decide upon the relevant price multiple to be used for peer comparison (P/E or P/B or EV/EBITDA, etc.)

Step 3 Calculate the price multiple for each of the peer companies identified.
Step 4 Calculate the mean or median value for the price multiples calculated for the peer companies.
Step 5 Compare the mean or median value calculated above with the target company's price multiple.

If there is a significant difference between the target company's price multiple and mean/median value obtained for peer companies, assuming all other things equal, it signifies that the target company may be mispriced (under/overvalued) relative to the sector.

As mentioned earlier, relative valuation acts a first filter for determining under/overvaluation and further assessment is done by the analysts using fundamental research to make the investment decision.

EXAMPLE 10.2 Neeraj, an analyst with a retail brokerage firm wants to assess Britannia Industries using relative valuation technique. He decided to use the price multiple of Price to Earnings (P/E) and identifies the following peer or comparison companies:

Company	*Price*	*EPS for past year*	*EPS for next year*
Hindustan Unilever	600	17	19
Nestle	4,000	92	117
Dabur	260	6	7
Marico	330	9	11
Colgate	1,400	39	51
P&G	5,000	100	120

Britannia is currently trading at a price of ₹2,000. Its previous year EPS was ₹63 and the next year expected EPS is ₹70.

Using the above information:

(a) Calculate the mean and median multiple for peer companies using P/E price multiple.

(b) Determine whether Britannia is under/overvalued on the basis of relative valuation methodology.

Solution:

Trailing P/E ratio ⇒ Current Market Price per Share/Trailing twelve months EPS

Forward P/E ratio ⇒ Current Market Price per Share/Estimated EPS for next year

Company	*Price*	*EPS for past year*	*EPS for next year*	*Trailing P/E ratio*	*Forward P/E ratio*
Hindustan Unilever	600	17	19	35.29*x*	31.58*x*
Nestle	4,000	92	117	43.48*x*	34.19*x*
Dabur	260	6	7	43.33*x*	37.14*x*
Marico	330	9	11	36.67*x*	30.00*x*
Colgate	1,400	39	51	35.90*x*	27.45*x*
P&G	5,000	100	120	50.00*x*	41.67*x*
Mean P/E multiple				**40.78*x***	**33.67*x***
Median P/E multiple				**40.00*x***	**32.88*x***
Britannia	2,000	63	70	31.75*x*	28.57*x*

As evident from the above table, Britannia's trailing and forward P/E ratio is less than the peerset companies or the sector. Assuming other things equal, Britannia may be undervalued relative to the sector. Neeraj should further evaluate this by doing a fundamental analysis of the company.

Comparison with Historical Price Multiples

As an alternative to peer companies comparison, many analysts often compare the current price multiple of the target company with its historical averages to determine under/overvaluation. For example, if Britannia's historical median forward P/E ratio for the last 10 years is 35x and its current forward P/E ratio is 28.57x, it signifies that Britannia is undervalued relative to its historic price earning multiple. Assuming other things same in terms of fundamentals, the idea behind the comparison is that in the long run, the price multiple would revert back to its historical averages. Such historical price multiple comparisons can also be done on an index level (BSE Sensex or NSE Nifty) so as to determine whether the overall market is under/overvalued relative to its historical average.

Table 10.5 lists out the historical monthly P/E and P/B ratios of BSE Sensex from April-2011 to Dec-2014:

TABLE 10.5 Historical monthly P/E and P/B ratios of BSE Sensex.

Year	*P/E ratios*	*P/B ratios*
Dec-14	18.84	2.96
Nov-14	19.21	3.04
Oct-14	18.31	2.93
Sep-14	18.52	2.97
Aug-14	18.17	2.9
Jul-14	18.52	2.88
Jun-14	18.58	2.83
May-14	17.94	2.79
Apr-14	18.26	2.71
Mar-14	17.87	2.65
Feb-14	16.79	2.49
Jan-14	17.78	2.59
Dec-13	17.78	2.62
Nov-13	17.53	2.62
Oct-13	17.77	2.75
Sep-13	17.27	2.75
Aug-13	16.81	2.89
Jul-13	17.47	3.03
Jun-13	16.97	2.93
May-13	17.43	3.05
Apr-13	16.85	2.9
Mar-13	17.19	2.95
Feb-13	17.43	3
Jan-13	17.88	3.05
Dec-12	17.43	2.95
Nov-12	16.9	2.87
		(Contd.)

Year	P/E ratios	P/B ratios
Oct-12	17.31	2.89
Sep-12	17.04	2.83
Aug-12	16.68	2.76
Jul-12	16.71	2.89
Jun-12	16.37	3.09
May-12	16.49	3.01
Apr-12	17.63	3.32
Mar-12	17.85	3.46
Feb-12	18.32	3.55
Jan-12	17.09	3.30
Dec-11	16.92	3.22
Nov-11	17.61	3.34
Oct-11	18.2	3.36
Sep-11	18.35	3.36
Aug-11	18.36	3.34
Jul-11	19.6	3.44
Jun-11	19.37	3.55
May-11	19.59	3.45
Apr-11	21.05	3.65

Source: http://www.bseindia.com/

10.3.2 Discounted Valuation Approach

While relative valuation methodology arrives at a target company's valuation using relative or comparable valuation of peer companies, discounted valuation approach attempts to discover the intrinsic value of the company by forecasting its future earnings, cash flows or dividends. This approach, also popularly known as the fundamental approach to equity valuation, compares the intrinsic value of the company with its traded market price to arrive at the investment decision. Discounted valuation approach can be grouped into two types of models frequently used by the financial analysts:

Discounted valuation approach compares the intrinsic value of the company with its traded market price to arrive at the investment decision.

- Dividend Discount Models (DDM)
- Free Cash Flow Models

Dividend Discount Model

When an investor purchases the stock of a company, he expects two kinds of payouts – first being the expected dividends over the holding period and second being the market price of the share on its sale at the end of the holding period. Accordingly, the intrinsic value of the stock can be expressed as a present value of the future dividends over the holding period plus the present value of the expected market price at the end of the holding period discounted at the required rate of return. If the holding period is one year, intrinsic value of the stock can thus be expressed as:

$$P_0 = \frac{D_1}{(1+k)^1} + \frac{P_1}{(1+k)^1}$$

Intrinsic value of the stock can be expressed as the present value of an infinite stream of dividends discounted at the required rate of return.

where,

P_0 = the present or intrinsic value of the stock
D_1 = expected dividends per share over the holding period
P_1 = the expected price at the end of holding period
k = the required rate of return on the stock

Now if we extend the holding period of the stock to n periods, the above expression of present or intrinsic value of the stock can be rewritten as:

$$P_0 = \frac{D_1}{(1+k)^1} + \frac{D_2}{(1+k)^2} + \dots + \frac{D_n}{(1+k)^n} + \frac{P_n}{(1+k)^n}$$

Generally, when an investor purchases a stock, he buys it with an intention of holding it for an infinite period of time or forever. In this case, the intrinsic value of a stock simply becomes a function of present value of an infinite stream of dividends discounted at the required rate of return.

$$P_0 = \frac{D_1}{(1+k)^1} + \frac{D_2}{(1+k)^2} + \dots + \frac{D_\infty}{(1+k)^\infty}$$

where k is the required rate of return on the stock and can be estimated using the Capital Asset Pricing Model (CAPM) discussed under portfolio theory. To determine the required rate of return on any risky asset, CAPM specifies the following equation:

Required Rate of Return = Risk Free Rate + (Equity Risk Premium) × Beta

or

$$R_i = R_F + (R_M - R_F) \times \beta_i$$

The above required rate of return (k) determined through CAPM model is also popularly known as the **cost of equity**.

10.4 Valuing a No Growth Stock

P/E ratio can be expressed as a function of dividend payout, required returns and constant growth rate in dividends.

In the above section, we discussed the case of the intrinsic value of a stock for an infinite stream of dividends. Now if we assume no growth in dividends, i.e. the dividends remain the same for an infinite period, it simply becomes the case of perpetual annuity or perpetuity. In this case, value of a stock can be expressed as:

$$P_0 = \frac{D}{k}$$

where,

P_0 = The present or intrinsic value of the stock
D = Dividends per share
k = The required rate of return on the stock

EXAMPLE 10.3 Suraj, a retail investor is looking to invest in the stock of TNA Ltd. The stock is currently trading at a market price of INR 100. Suraj decides to value the stock using dividend discount model assuming his holding period as infinite. He further assumes no growth in the dividends for TNA Ltd. The current dividend of TNA Ltd. is ₹10. Calculate the intrinsic value of the stock and determine whether Suraj should purchase the stock given that the required return on the stock is 8%.

Solution: Value of a stock for an infinite stream of dividends with no growth can be expressed as:

$$P_0 = \frac{D}{k}$$

$$P_0 = \frac{10}{8\%} = 125$$

Given that intrinsic value of TNA is more than the current market price of the stock, Suraj should purchase the stock.

10.5 Valuing a Constant Growth Stock

Instead of no growth in dividends, if we assume a constant growth in the stream of dividends for an infinite period, the general dividend discount model can be expressed as:

$$P_0 = \frac{D_0(1+g)^1}{(1+k)^1} + \frac{D_0(1+g)^2}{(1+k)^2} + \dots + \frac{D_0(1+g)^\infty}{(1+k)^\infty}$$

The above equation can be rewritten as:

$$P_0 = \frac{D_0(1+g)}{(k-g)} \text{ or } \frac{D_1}{(k-g)}$$

where,

P_0 = The present or intrinsic value of the stock
D = Dividends per share
g = Constant growth rate in dividends
k = The required rate of return on the stock

The above model is also popularly known as **Gordon growth model**, named after the economist Myron J. Gordon. A necessary condition for the expression to be valid is that required rate of return (k) is greater than the rate of growth in dividends (g). In case $k = g$, the stock price would approach infinity.

EXAMPLE 10.4 Anand, a retail investor plans to invest in stock of Nida Ltd. which is currently trading at ₹750. Anand decides to value the stock using constant growth dividend discount model assuming his holding period as infinite. He further estimates a constant growth of 10% in the dividends for Nida Ltd. The current dividend of Nida Ltd. is ₹15. Calculate the intrinsic value of the stock, and determine, whether Anand should purchase the stock given that the required return on the stock is 12%.

Solution: Value of a stock for an infinite stream of dividends with constant growth in dividends can be expressed as:

$$P_0 = \frac{D_0(1+g)}{(k-g)}$$

$$P_0 = \frac{15 * (1.1)}{12\% - 10\%} = 825$$

Given that the intrinsic value of Nida Ltd. is more than the current market price of the stock, Anand should purchase the stock.

10.6 Fundamental Determinants of P/E and P/BV Ratio

P/E and P/BV ratio discussed earlier in the relative valuation, can be fundamentally determined using Gordon growth model. According to Gordon growth model, price of a stock can be expressed as:

$$P_0 = \frac{D_1}{(k-g)}$$

Dividing both sides by Earnings Per Share (EPS), we get

$$\frac{P_0}{\text{EPS}} = \frac{D_1/\text{EPS}}{(k-g)}$$

where,

D = Dividend per share
EPS = Earnings Per Share
g = Constant growth rate in dividends
k = The required rate of return on the stock

P/B ratio can be expressed as a function of dividend payout, required returns, return on equity and constant growth rate in dividends.

Fundamentally, Price to earnings ratio, can thus, be expressed as a function of dividend payout ratio (dividends per share/earnings per share), required returns (k) and constant growth rate in dividends (g). P/E ratio, is thus, directly related to dividend payout ratio, and growth in dividends whereas it is inversely related to the required rate of return.

To obtain fundamental determinants of P/B ratio, we again start with Gordon growth model.

$$P_0 = \frac{D_1}{(k-g)}$$

Dividing both sides by book value per share (B), we get

$$\frac{P_0}{B} = \frac{\text{ROE} * (D_1/\text{EPS})}{(k-g)}$$

where,

ROE = Return on equity defined as a ratio of earnings per share by book value per share
D = dividend per share
EPS = Earnings per share
B = Book value per share
g = Constant growth rate in dividends
k = The required rate of return on the stock

As evident from the above expression, Price to book (P/B) ratio can be expressed as a function of dividend payout ratio (dividends per share/earnings per share), return on equity (ROE), required returns (k) and constant growth rate (g) in dividends. P/B ratio is thus directly related to dividend payout ratio, return on equity and growth in dividends whereas it is inversely related to the required rate of return.

10.7 Multi-Stage Dividend Growth Models

Till now we have been assuming no growth or constant growth rate in dividends for valuation of a company's stock. However in reality, the dividends instead of growing at an assumed constant rate, generally grow at an uneven rate depending on the company's profitability and reinvestment needs in the future. For example, a high growth company like Voltas may have substantial reinvestment needs leading to low dividend payouts as most of the earnings get ploughed back into the business. On the other hand, a mature company like Nestle with stable cash flows may distribute most of the earnings as dividends on account of low reinvestment needs. Using an assumption of constant growth rate in dividends thus may not be a correct method for valuing companies in different phases of growth as it leads to under/overestimation of earnings being distributed as dividends.

Multi-stage dividend models divide the total investment horizon into two periods —explicit forecast period and terminal growth period. In the explicit forecast period, analysts forecasts the sales, expenses, profitability and reinvestment needs of the company to arrive at expected dividends for the future years. Although there is no thumb rule regarding the number of years for which explicit forecasting is to be done, analysts (especially in Indian context) often forecast the company's financials up to a maximum of ten years.

Investment Horizon under multistage dividend models can be divided into explicit forecast period and terminal growth period.

Total investment horizon = Explicit forecast period + Terminal period

After the explicit forecast period has been determined, analysts assume the remaining period as terminal period, which extends into the infinite. Analysts generally assume that dividends will continue to grow at a constant rate during the terminal period. To determine the terminal value, analysts make use of the Gordon growth model discussed above.

$$\text{Terminal value} = \frac{D(1+g_{\text{Terminal}})}{(k-g_{\text{Terminal}})}$$

where,

D = Dividends per share at the start of the terminal period

k = Required rate of return on the stock

g_{Terminal} = Long-term constant growth rate in dividends

Although there are several ways to determine long-term constant growth rate (g_{Terminal}) in dividends, theoretically it can be estimated based on profitability and retention rate, i.e.

g_{Terminal} = Return on Equity (ROE) × Retention ratio

While finding the long-term constant growth rate in dividends, ROE and Retention ratio forecasted at the start of the terminal period should be used. In addition to the above, long-term constant growth rate may also be determined based on the sector or industry growth rates to which the company belongs to.

Intrinsic or present value of the stock under multi-stage dividend growth model can then be expressed as the present value of all dividends during the explicit forecast period plus the present value of the dividends for terminal period.

Intrinsic value of the stock = Present value of dividends for explicit forecast period + Present value of dividends for terminal period

or

$$P_0 = \frac{D_1}{(1+k)^1} + \frac{D_2}{(1+k)^2} + \dots + \frac{D_n}{(1+k)^n} + \frac{D_n(1+g_{\text{Terminal}})/(k-g_{\text{Terminal}})}{(1+k)^n}$$

where, n represents the length of the explicit forecast period.

10.7.1 Summary of Steps under Multi-stage Dividend Growth Model

To apply the method of multi-stage dividend growth model, the analyst should thus follow the following steps:

Step 1 Identify the period for which explicit forecasting is to be done

Step 2 Forecasts the company financials to arrive at expected dividends for the explicit period identified above

Step 3 Find the terminal value of dividends using the Gordon growth model

Step 4 Find out the present value of dividends during the explicit forecast period, plus the present value of the dividends for terminal period to arrive at the intrinsic value of the stock.

Step 5 Compare the intrinsic value obtained above with the current market price of the stock to arrive at the investment decision.

EXAMPLE 10.5 Arun, a retail investor, is planning to invest in SKO Limited which is trading at a price of INR 124 as on March 2012. He decides to fundamentally value the company using the multistage dividend discount model. He divides his investment horizon into two periods—explicit forecast period (where he forecasts the company dividends for each year) and terminal period for which he decides to use Gordon growth model. To estimate the required return, Arun decides to use the Capital Asset Pricing Model (CAPM). Arun's forecast of dividends per share for SKO Limited (for next 10 years) and inputs for CAPM model are provided below:

Year	*SKO Limited Forecasted Dividends per share*
2013E*	8
2014E*	10
2015E*	13
2016E*	14.5
2017E*	16.5
2018E*	19
2019E*	17
2020E*	17.5
2021E*	18
2022E*	20

*E refers to expected

Arun further forecasts Return on Equity (ROE) and Retention ratio for SKO in year 2022 to be 10% and 50% respectively.

Risk free rate in the economy is 8%. Equity risk premium for last 5 years is 5% and beta of SKO Limited is 1.2.

Using the above information, calculate the intrinsic value per share for SKO Ltd. Should Arun purchase the stock based on multistage dividend valuation?

Solution: Explicit forecast period identified by Arun is 10 years.

Intrinsic or present value of the stock under multistage dividend growth model can be expressed as the present value of all dividends during the explicit forecast period plus the present value of the dividends for terminal period.

Intrinsic value of the stock = Present value of dividends for explicit forecast period + Present value of dividends for terminal period

or

$$P_0 = \frac{D_1}{(1+k)^1} + \frac{D_2}{(1+k)^2} + \cdots + \frac{D_n}{(1+k)^n} + \frac{D_n(1+g_{\text{Terminal}})/(k-g_{\text{Terminal}})}{(1+k)^n}$$

where, $n = 10$

Required rate of return or cost of equity (k) = Risk free rate + (Equity risk premium) × Beta or

$$R_i = R_F + (R_M - R_F) \times \beta_i$$

$$R_i = 8\% + (5\%) \times 1.2 = 14\%$$

Long-term constant growth rate (g_{Terminal}) in dividends can be estimated theoretically based on profitability and retention rate, i.e.

$$g_{\text{Terminal}} = \text{Return On Equity (ROE)} \times \text{Retention ratio}$$

$$g_{\text{Terminal}} = 10\% \times 50\% = 5\%$$

Intrinsic value of the SKO = 81.48 + 88.12 = 169.59.

E19 =SUM(E17:E18)

	A	B	C	D	E	F	G
2							
3	Inputs			Year	Dividends per Share	Dividend Growth	Present Value of Dividends
4	beta	1.2		2013E	8.00		7.02
5	Equity Risk Premium	5.0%		2014E	10.00	25.00%	7.69
6	Risk Free	8.0%		2015E	13.00	30.00%	8.77
7	k (CAPM)	14.0%		2016E	14.50	11.54%	8.59
8	Retention ratio	50%		2017E	16.50	13.79%	8.57
9	ROE	10%		2018E	19.00	15.15%	8.66
10	g (for terminal growth)	5.00%		2019E	21.00	10.53%	8.39
11				2020E	23.50	11.90%	8.24
12				2021E	26.00	10.64%	8.00
13				2022E	28.00	7.69%	7.55
14							
15		Explicit Forecast					
16		Period		Terminal Value	326.67		
17				Present Value of Terminal value	88.12		
18				Present Value of Explicit Forecast period	81.48	28 * (1+0.05)/(14% - 5%)	
19				Intrinsic Value of SKO Ltd	169.59		

Investment decision: Given that Fundamental intrinsic price per share of SKO Ltd. (169.59) is more than the traded price (124), Arun should purchase the stock.

10.8 Free Cash Flow Model

In the dividend discount models discussed above, we arrived at the value of stock or equity using dividends paid out by the firm to its shareholders. However, in case of most firms, dividends represent only a fraction of total cash flows available for distribution to shareholders. So in effect dividends distributed may be very different from cash flows available for distribution for a firm for its shareholders. In such a case, dividend discount models may not be able to capture the intrinsic value for a stock in entirety as dividends constitute only a part of equity value. Further, if a company does not have any dividend paying history, applying dividend discount model may become a challenging proposition. To do away with the above issues, analysts make often use of free cash flow models which take into consideration the entire cash flows available for distribution to shareholders. According to free cash flow valuation approach, intrinsic value of a stock can be expressed as a present value of its expected cash flows in the future discounted at an appropriate rate of return.

Under free cash flow models, intrinsic value of a stock can be expressed as a present value of its expected cash flows in the future discounted at an appropriate rate of return.

Analysts generally arrive at equity value under free cash flow approach using one of the below methods:

1. **Free Cash Flow to Firm Method (FCFF):** Under this method, enterprise value is first arrived at by computing the present value of free cash flows available for the firm, i.e. for both equityholders and debtholders. Implied value of equity is then derived by deducting the value of net debt from the value of firm.

2. **Free Cash Flow to Equity Method (FCFE):** Under this method, value of equity is directly arrived at by computing the present value of future free cash flows available only for equityholders.

10.8.1 Free Cash Flow to Firm Method (FCFF)

Free Cash Flow to the Firm (FCFF) primarily represents the profit or cash available for all investors of the firm—debtholders as well as equityholders after operating expenses have been incurred and investments related to working capital and long-term assets have been made. Under FCFF model, enterprise value is first arrived at by computing the present value of future free cash flows available for the firm by discounting at the Weighted-Average Cost of Capital (WACC). Implied value of equity is then derived by deducting the value of net debt (total debt-cash) from the enterprise value.

$$\text{Enterprise Value (EV)} = \frac{\text{FCFF}_1}{(1+\text{WACC})^1} + \frac{\text{FCFF}_2}{(1+\text{WACC})^2} + \dots + \frac{\text{FCFF}_\infty}{(1+\text{WACC})^\infty}$$

$$\text{Equity Value} = \text{Enterprise value} - \text{Net debt}$$

Under FCFF, enterprise value is first arrived at by computing the present value of future free cash flows available for the firm by discounting at the weighted-average cost of capital.

Unlike dividend discount model where we used the required rate of return (k) for discounting the dividends, we have used weighted-average cost of capital (WACC) for discounting the FCFF. WACC denotes the required rate of return demanded by all investors of the firm—debtholders as well as equityholders. To estimate the WACC, inputs related to cost of debt (required rate of return for debtholders) and cost of equity (required rate of return for equityholders) are needed. Cost of equity estimates (k_e) can be obtained using the Capital Asset Pricing Model (CAPM) as discussed under dividend discount model. Cost of debt (k_d) represents the interest payable on the total debt of the firm. Given that interest cost is a tax deductible expense, while calculating WACC, analysts usually take after tax cost of debt into account.

$$\text{WACC} = (\text{Cost of equity} \times w_e) + (\text{After-tax cost of debt} \times w_d)$$

or

$$\text{WACC} = (\text{Cost of equity} \times w_e) + [\text{Pre-tax cost of debt} \times (1 - \text{tax rate}) \times w_d]$$

where,

w_e = Proportion of equity in the capital structure
w_d = Proportion of debt in the capital structure

Computation of FCFF

Free Cash Flow to the Firm (FCFF) can be computed using the following expression:

FCFF = EBIT (Earnings before Interest and Taxes) × (1 – Tax rate)
+ Depreciation and amortization (non-cash charges)
–/+ Investment in non-cash working capital
– Capital expenditure (Investment in long-term assets)

EBIT represents the operating profitability of the business before deductions related to interest expense and taxes have been made. To arrive at FCFF, non-cash expenses such as depreciation/amortization are added back to EBIT as they do not involve any cash outflow. Non-cash working capital represents the excess of current assets (excluding cash) over current liabilities for a particular year. Any increase/decrease in non-cash working capital from previous year to next year is treated as a cash outflow/inflow and accordingly adjusted. Investment in long-term assets or capital expenditure such as purchase of plant and machinery, buildings, etc. represents a cash outflow and is deducted to arrive at FCFF.

Similar to multistage dividend model, FCFF model also divides the total investment horizon into two periods–explicit forecast period and terminal growth period. In the explicit forecast period, analysts forecast the company's financials to arrive at expected free cash flows to the firm for the future years. After the explicit forecast period has been determined, remaining period is assumed as terminal period which extends into the infinite. To determine the terminal value, analysts make use of the Gordon growth model.

$$\text{Terminal value} = \frac{\text{FCFF}(1+g_{\text{Terminal}})}{(\text{WACC}-g_{\text{Terminal}})}$$

where,

FCFF = Free Cash Flow to the Firm at the start of the terminal period

WACC = Weighted Average Cost of Capital

g_{Terminal} = Long-term constant growth rate in FCFF

Long-term constant growth rate may be determined based on the sector or industry growth rates to which the company belongs to. Some analysts also tend to take the long-term nominal growth rate of GDP for the country to which the company belongs to as a proxy for g_{Terminal}.

Enterprise Value (EV) under FCFF model can be expressed as the present value of FCFF during the explicit forecast period plus the present value of the FCFF for the terminal period.

Enterprise Value = Present value of free cash flows for explicit forecast period + Present value of free cash flows for terminal period

or

$$\text{Enterprise Value (EV)} = [\{(\text{FCFF}_1/(1 + \text{WACC})^1\} + \{\text{FCFF}_2/(1+ \text{WACC})^2\} + \cdots + \{\text{FCFF}_n /(1 + \text{WACC})^n\}] + [\{\text{FCFF}_n (1 + g_{\text{Terminal}})/(\text{WACC} - g_{\text{Terminal}})\}/(1 + \text{WACC})^n\}]$$

where, n represents the length of the explicit forecast period.

To arrive at equity value, Net debt (Total debt – Cash) has to be deducted from the enterprise value

Equity value = Enterprise value (EV) – Net debt

EXAMPLE 10.6 Saumik wants to calculate the fundamental value of one of his stock Times Ltd. using free cash to firm (FCFF) valuation approach. He estimates that current FCFF for the company is 80 crores. Saumik estimates that FCFF of the company will grow at the rate of 12% for the next 5 years (year 1 to year 5) and then will continue to grow at lower rate of 8% from year 6 to year 10. He decides to consider the period beyond year 10 as terminal period and decides to value it using Gordon growth model using a g_{Terminal} of 5%. For estimating the discounting rate or weighted average cost of capital (WACC), Saumik decides to use the debt/equity ratio of 1:1 as target capital structure for the company. Additional information for calculation of WACC is given in below table.

Incremental cost of debt	11%
Tax rate	30%
Risk free rate	9%
Beta	0.93
Equity risk premium	4.00%
Net debt of Times Ltd. (Total debt – Cash)	1,000 crores
Number of shares	8 crores

Using the above information, calculate the intrinsic value per share for Times Ltd.

Solution: In the above question, explicit forecast period identified is 10 years.

Enterprise Value (EV) under FCFF model can be expressed as the present value of FCFF during the explicit forecast period, plus the present value of the FCFF for the terminal period.

Enterprise value = Present value of free cash flows for explicit forecast period + Present value of free cash flows for terminal period

Equity value = Enterprise value – Net debt

WACC = (Cost of equity × w_e) + [Cost of debt × (1 – tax rate) × w_d]

Cost of equity = Risk free rate + (Equity risk premium) × Beta

Cost of equity = 9% + (4%) × 0.93 = 12.72%

Cost of debt = 11%

Target D/E ratio = 1:1

Tax rate = 30%

WACC = 0.5 × 12.72% + 0.5 × 11% × (1 – 0.30) = 10.21%

Enterprise value of Times Ltd. = 828 + 1,579 = 2,329

Equity value = 2,329 – 1,000 = 1,329

Per share value = Equity value/Number of shares = 1,329/8 = 166.

Clipboard | Font | Alignment | Number | Styles | Cells | Editing

D20 | Net Debt

	A	B	C	D	E	F	G
1							
2							
3	Inputs			Year	FCFF	FCFF Growth	Present Value of FCFF
4	beta	0.93		Year 0	80		
5	Equity Risk Premium	4.0%		Year 1	90	12.00%	81.30
6	Risk Free Rate	9.0%		Year 2	100	12.00%	82.62
7	Cost of Equity	12.72%		Year 3	112	12.00%	83.96
8	Cost of Debt	11.00%		Year 4	126	12.00%	85.33
9	Tax Rate	30%		Year 5	141	12.00%	86.71
10	Target Debt/Equity Ratio	1:1		Year 6	152	8.00%	84.97
11	WACC	10.21%		Year 7	164	8.00%	83.27
12	g (for terminal growth)	5.00%		Year 8	178	8.00%	81.60
13				Year 9	192	8.00%	79.96
14				Year 10	207	8.00%	78.36
15		Explicit Forecast					
16		Period		Terminal Value	4,175		
17				Present Value of Terminal value	1,579		
18				Present Value of Explicit Forecast period	828	207 * (1+0.05)/(10.21% - 5%)	
19				Enterprise Value of Times Ltd	2,329		
20				Net Debt	1,000		
21				Equity Value (Enterprise Value-Net Debt)	1,329		
22				Intrinsic Value per Share	166		

Under FCFE, value of equity is determined by computing the present value of future free cash flows available for equityholders.

10.8.2 Free Cash Flow to Equity (FCFE) Valuation

Under Free Cash Flow to Equity (FCFE) method, value of equity is directly determined by computing the present value of future free cash flows available only for equityholders. Free Cash Flow to Equity (FCFE) can be computed using the following expression:

FCFE = Net profit or net income + Depreciation and amortization (non-cash charges) –/+ Investment in non-cash working capital – Capital expenditure (Investment in Long-term assets) + Increase in net debt (Issue of new debt-repayment of older debt)

To arrive at FCFE, we start with net profits, which basically represents the cash flows for equityholders after payments related to interest expense and taxes have been made. Similar to FCFF calculation, non-cash expenses, such as depreciation/amortization are added back and increase in investments in non-cash working capital and long-term assets are deducted. Finally, while calculating FCFE, effect of new debt issuances and repayment of older debts also needs to be taken into consideration. Repayment of older debt represents a cash outflow whereas issuance of new debt represents a cash inflow for equityholders. Consequently increase in net debt (issue of new debt-repayment of older debt) is added back to net profit to arrive at FCFE.

While under FCFF approach, we discounted the future cash flows using WACC as the required rate of return, in case of FCFE, the relevant discount rate or required rate of return shall be the cost of equity (k). This is because FCFE represents the cash flows available only for equityholders, and therefore, the discount rate should also reflect the required rate of return for equityholders. To determine the terminal value under FCFE approach, Gordon growth model can be used.

$$\text{Terminal value} = \frac{\text{FCFE}\,(1 + g_{\text{Terminal}})}{(k - g_{\text{Terminal}})}$$

where,

FCFE = Free Cash Flow to Equity at the start of the terminal period

k = Required rate of return on the stock

g_{Terminal} = Long-term constant growth rate in FCFE

Intrinsic or present value of the stock under FCFE model can then be expressed as the present value of FCFE during the explicit forecast period plus the present value of FCFE for terminal period.

Intrinsic value of the stock = Present value of FCFE for explicit forecast period + Present value of FCFE for terminal period

or

$$V_0 = \frac{\text{FCFE}_1}{(1+k)^1} + \frac{\text{FCFE}_2}{(1+k)^2} + \cdots + \frac{\text{FCFE}_n}{(1+k)^n} + \frac{\text{FCFE}_n(1+g_{\text{Terminal}})/(k - g_{\text{Terminal}})}{(1+k)^n}$$

where, n represents the length of the explicit forecast period.

EXAMPLE 10.7 Anand wants to estimate the value of Maharashtra Rubber Company using Free Cash Flow to Equity (FCFE) valuation approach. To estimate the current FCFE, he collects the following data for the current year 2012:

***Particulars* (Year 2012)**	***Amount* (in crores)**
Net profit for the year	500
Depreciation	50
Capital expenditure	150
Increase in working capital for the year	75
Debt repayments for the year	30
New debt issued during the year	40

Anand further estimates that FCFE of the company will grow at the rate of 10% for each of the next 7 years and then this rate will decline to 7% for subsequent 3 years. He decides to consider the period beyond year 10 as terminal period and decides to value it using Gordon growth model using a g_{Terminal} of 4%. For estimating the required rate of return, Saumik decides to use the Capital Asset Pricing Model (CAPM).

Risk free rate	7.5%
Beta	0.76
Equity risk premium	6.00%

Using the above information, calculate the intrinsic value per share for Maharashtra Rubber assuming that the company has 10 crores shares outstanding at present. The stock is currently trading a price of INR 800. Should Anand purchase the stock based on FCFE valuation?

Solution:

Calculation of FCFE

FCFE = Net profit or net income + Depreciation and amortization (non-cash charges) –/+ Investment in non-cash working capital – Capital expenditure (investment in long-term assets) + Increase in net debt (Issue of new debt – repayment of older debt)

FCFE for year 2012 = 500 + 50 – 75 – 150 + 40 – 30 = 335

	A	B	C	D	E	F	G
2							
3	Inputs			Year	FCFE	FCFE Growth	Present Value of FCFE
4	beta	0.76		2012	335		
5	Equity Risk Premium	6.0%		2013	369	10.00%	328.84
6	Risk Free Rate	7.5%		2014	405	10.00%	322.80
7	Cost of Equity	12.06%		2015	446	10.00%	316.86
8	g (for terminal growth)	5.00%		2016	490	10.00%	311.04
9				2017	540	10.00%	305.32
10				2018	593	10.00%	299.71
11				2019	653	10.00%	294.20
12				2020	699	7.00%	280.91
13				2021	747	7.00%	268.23
14				2022	800	7.00%	256.12
15		Explicit Forecast					
16		Period		Terminal Value	11,894		
17				Present Value of Terminal value	3,809		
18				Present Value of Explicit Forecast period	2,984	800 * (1+0.05)/(12.06% - 5%)	
19				Equity Value of the Company	6,537		
20				Number of Shares	10		
21				Intrinsic Value per Share	654		

In the above question, explicit forecast period identified by Arun is 10 years.

Intrinsic or present value of the stock under FCFE model can then be expressed as the present value of FCFE during the explicit forecast period plus the present value of FCFE for terminal period.

Intrinsic value of the stock = Present value of FCFE for explicit forecast period + Present value of FCFE for terminal period

or

$$P_0 = \frac{\text{FCFE}_1}{(1+k)^1} + \frac{\text{FCFE}_2}{(1+k)^2} + \dots + \frac{\text{FCFE}_n}{(1+k)^n} + \frac{\text{FCFE}_n(1+g_{\text{Terminal}})/(k-g_{\text{Terminal}})}{(1+k)^n}$$

where, n =10

Required rate of return or cost of equity (k) = Risk free rate + (Equity risk premium) × Beta

Required rate of return = 7.5% + (6%) × 0.76 = 12.06%

$g_{\text{Terminal}} = 5\%$

Intrinsic value of Maharashtra rubber company = 3,809 + 2,984 = 6,537

Intrinsic value per share = 6,537/10 = 653.7

Investment decision: Given that the Intrinsic Value of Maharashtra Rubber Company is less than its traded market price, Anand should not purchase the stock.

10.9 Career as An Equity Analyst

The primary job of an equity analyst is to conduct valuation of a company using various techniques, such as relative valuation, DDM valuation, DCF valuation, etc. so as to arrive at the intrinsic value and issue investment recommendations to investor clientele. The requirement of equity analysts, basically comes from two types of firms:

1. Sell side firms or brokerages: These firms prepare equity research reports and issue investment recommendations for various companies and trade stocks on behalf of their clientele. Examples of brokerage firms operating in India include Motilal Oswal Financial Services, Edelweiss Securities, JP Morgan, Morgan Stanley, Goldman Sachs, Nomura Securities, etc. among others.

2. Buy side firms or asset management companies: These firms manage the money of their investor clientele in return for a fee. Examples of buy side firms include mutual funds, insurance companies, sovereign funds, wealth funds, etc.

10.9.1 Sell Side Firms Structure

In sell side firms, there are various lead equity analysts who cover various sectors in detail and issue investment recommendations such as "Buy", "Sell and "Hold". Each lead equity analyst is responsible for a particular sector and has a team of 1–3 junior analysts depending on the type and number of companies covered. In addition to equity analysts, sell side firms also employ sales persons who market equity research reports of its analysts to investor clientele. As a student of finance, one can directly join as a junior equity analyst and support the lead analyst in financial analysis of companies under coverage. Junior analysts usually get promoted to lead analyst after 9–10 years of experience depending upon the performance and opportunities available. Analysts can also switch to equity sales role where they are required to market equity research reports of its analysts to investor clientele. Salaries of equity research analysts are generally competitive and involve substantial bonus payouts at the end of the year. For high performers, bonuses can range up to 100% of annual fixed salaries.

10.9.2 Buy Side Firms Structure

Buy side firms typically have fewer equity analysts compared to sell side firms. In buy side firms, each equity analyst cover multiple sectors (atleast two) compared to sell side analysts who generally cover a single sector. Equity analysts in buy side firms report to the fund manager who is generally responsible for overall investing of the money based on analysts' recommendations and equity research reports issued by sell side analysts. Equity analyst job in a buy side firm is a highly specialized role and require deep understanding of various sectors and markets. Buy side firms typically recruit sell side analysts with substantial experience in markets for equity analysts positions and it is generally difficult for students of finance to get a direct entry into such roles. Students of finance typically start from sell side firms and then move on to buy side roles after years of experience. Salaries of equity analysts in buy side generally have a high variable payout based on the fund's outperformance relative to the benchmark.

Researchable Issues

Faculty members, students and research scholars may like to consider the following selected issues for further research and case writing.

- Historical Relative Valuation of Indian markets vs Developed country markets
- Historical Relative Valuation of Indian Large Capitalization companies vs Mid and Small Capitalization companies
- Use of Valuation methods by Indian financial analysts
- Appropriate Valuation methodology for e-commerce companies
- Stock Price Movement and Fundamental Valuation in Emerging markets like India
- Sell side research coverage and corporate governance of firms
- Best Practices followed by Sell Side Analysts in Developed market vs Emerging markets

References

Asquith, P., Mikhail, M.B., and Au, A.S., Information content of equity analyst reports", *Journal of Financial Economics*, Vol. 75, No. 2, 2005, pp. 245–282.

Bradshaw, M.T., "The use of target prices to justify sell-side analysts' stock recommendations", *Accounting Horizons*, Vol. 16, No. 1, 2002, pp. 27–41,

Dawar, V. and Arrawatia, R., "Apollo Tyres: Investment Decision Dilemma" Product Number - 9B14N032 - *Ivey Publishing.*

Dawar, V., "Earnings persistence and stock prices: empirical evidence from an emerging market," *Journal of Financial Reporting and Accounting*, Vol. 12, No. 2, 2014, pp. 117–134.

Dawar, V., "The relative predictive ability of earnings and cash flows: Evidence from Shariah compliant companies in India," *Management Research Review*, Vol. 38, No. 4, 2015, pp. 367–380.

Demirakos, E.G., Strong, N.C., and Walker, M., "What valuation models do analysts use?" *Accounting Horizons*, Vol. 18, No. 4, 2004, pp. 221–240.

Imam, S., Barker, R., and Clubb, C., "The use of valuation models by UK investment analysts", *European Accounting Review*, Vol. 17, No. 3, 2008, pp. 503–535.

Points to Remember

- Valuation of a company involves determining the payoffs expected to be received by shareholders in the future and finding out its present value (in time value terms) using an appropriate risk adjusted rate.
- Valuation involves a three step top down approach beginning with the macro analysis of the economy percolating down to the industry (in which the company

operates) and then to the target company. Appropriate valuation methodology is then used to arrive at the investment decision.

- Relative valuation approach arrives at a target company's valuation using relative or comparable valuation of peer companies. It basically uses the assumption that similar assets should be priced at similar valuations and any mispricing would suggest a buy or sell investment decision.
- Relative comparison is generally done through price-based multiples such as Price to Earnings (P/E), price to book value (P/B), price to sales (P/S), price to cash flow (P/CF), etc.
- Price to Earnings (P/E) ratio is a measure of how expensive the stock is relative to its earnings. Price to book (P/B) ratio compares the stock's traded market price to its reported book value per share. Price to Sales (P/S) ratio compares the stock's traded market price to its reported sales or revenue per share.
- Relative valuation acts a first filter for determining under/overvaluation and further assessment is done by the analysts using fundamental research to make the investment decision.
- Discounted valuation approach attempts to discover the intrinsic value of the company by forecasting its future earnings, cash flows or dividends. Also, popularly known as the fundamental approach to equity valuation, it compares the intrinsic value of the company with its traded market price to arrive at the investment decision.
- According to Dividend Discount Model (DDM), the present value of the stock can be expressed as a present value of the future dividends over the holding period plus the present value of the expected market price at the end of the holding period discounted at the required rate of return.
- Free Cash Flow to the Firm (FCFF) primarily represents the profit or cash available for all investors of the firm-debtholders as well as equityholders after operating expenses have been incurred and investments related to working capital and long-term assets have been made.
- Under FCFF model, enterprise value is first arrived at by computing the present value of future free cash flows available for the firm by discounting at the Weighted-Average Cost of Capital (WACC). Implied value of equity is then derived by deducting the value of net debt from the enterprise value.
- Enterprise Value (EV) under FCFF model can be expressed as the present value of FCFF during the explicit forecast period plus the present value of the FCFF for the terminal period.
- Under Free Cash Flow to Equity (FCFE) method, value of equity is directly determined by computing the present value of future free cash flows available only for equityholders.

Questions

1. Discuss the top down 3-step process of equity valuation followed by financial analysts.
2. Discuss various valuation techniques used by analysts for estimating the value of an equity stock.
3. Discuss the relative valuation technique and the steps analysts generally follow for determining whether the target company is under/overvalued.
4. Discuss how dividend discount model can be used for valuing (a) no growth stock and (b) constant growth stock

5. Explain the process of determining the terminal value in a multistage dividend discount model.
6. Differentiate between FCFF and FCFE approach to equity valuation. Determine how FCFF and FCFE can be computed using company's financial statements.

Multiple Choice Questions

1. NMO company's current EBITDA is ₹400 crores. Market value of the company is 1,000 crores and market value of debt is 200 crores. Calculate the EV/EBITDA ratio of NMO company.
   (a) $4x$ (b) $0.33x$ (c) $6x$ (d) $3x$
2. Dividend payout ratio of company MKJ is 50%. If the required rate of return is 10% and long-term growth rate is 5%, calculate the fundamental P/E ratio for the company.
   (a) $11x$ (b) $20x$
   (c) $10x$ (d) None of the above
3. 1 year forward P/E ratio for a particular company is $10x$. If the expected growth rate in earnings for the future is 20%, calculate the Price Earnings to Growth (PEG) ratio.
   (a) 2 (b) 0.5
   (c) 5 (d) None of the above
4. The current dividend of MSO company is ₹20. Assuming no growth in dividends, calculate the intrinsic value of the stock if the required return on the stock is 15%.
   (a) 75 (b) 50
   (c) 133 (d) None of the above
5. Arup expects dividends of ₹50 for the next year on one of his stocks. If the required rate of return is 10% and long-term growth rate is 6%, calculate the intrinsic value of the stock as per Gordon growth model.
   (a) 600 (b) 1,250
   (c) 500 (d) None of the above
6. Price to book value ratio should generally go up when the following increases:
   (a) Required rate of return (b) Return on equity
   (c) Book value (d) None of the above
7. Which of the following is generally deducted from enterprise value to arrive at equity value:
   (a) Cash (b) Debtors
   (c) Net debt (d) Reserves and surplus
8. Price to Earnings (P/E) ratio should generally go down when the following increases:
   (a) Required rate of return
   (b) Dividends
   (c) Long-term growth (g)
   (d) None of the above
9. Neeraj wants to estimate the Trailing P/E multiple for Supra Ltd. For this he collects the following data:

Current Market price of Supra: ₹500
Past four quarters EPS:

Quarter	*EPS*
June	7.6
Sep.	4.5
Dec.	5.2
Mar.	6.4

Trailing P/E multiple for Supra Ltd. is

(a) 11.19x (b) 21.09x
(c) 16.80x (d) None of the above

10. Dividend payout ratio of company Safari Ltd. is 50% and return on equity (ROE) is 15%. If the required rate of return is 10%, calculate the fundamental P/B ratio for the company.

(a) 2x (b) 3x
(c) 5x (d) None of the above

Self-Test Questions

1. Sanjay, a retail investor wants to estimate the value of ICICI bank using Gordon growth model. He collects the following data for ICICI bank to arrive at the equity valuation

EPS (Earnings Per share)	15
BVPS (Book Value Per share)	120
Beta	1.2
Risk Free Rate	9%
Equity Risk Premium	7%
Payout Ratio	30%

On the basis of above information, calculate the intrinsic price of ICICI bank.

2. Ajay wants to calculate the Free Cash Flow to Equity (FCFE) for the company PTR Ltd. For this he collects the following financial information.

	in ₹crores
Net Profit for the current year	2,000
Capital expenditure for the year	400
Increase in working capital	100
Debt issue	200
Debt repayment	100
Depreciation expense	50

Using the above information, compute the FCFE for the above company.

3. Shipra, an analyst with an institutional brokerage firm wants to assess Raj Software Company using relative valuation technique. She decided to use the price multiple of Price to Earnings (P/E) and identifies the following peer or comparison companies.

Company	*Price*	*EPS for past year*	*EPS for next year*
Zylo Software	100	10	12
Nita Tech	290	80	95
Super Tech Solutions	12	1.5	2
Jeet Software	1,000	260	250
Amba Tech	650	120	150
Alfa Tech	24	5	8

Raj software is currently trading at a price of ₹150. Its previous year EPS was ₹22 and the next year expected EPS is ₹25

Using the above information

1. Calculate the mean and median multiple for peer companies using P/E price multiple
2. Determine whether Raj Software is under/overvalued on the basis of relative valuation methodology

4. Rita, a retail investor plans to invest in the stock of Alok Industries which is currently trading at a price of ₹20. Rita decides to value the stock using constant growth dividend discount model assuming her holding period as infinite. She further estimates a constant growth of 5% in the dividends for Alok Industries. The current dividend of Alok Industries is ₹2.50. Calculate the intrinsic value of the stock and determine whether Rita should purchase the stock given that the required return on the stock is 15%.
5. Saumya is looking to invest his money in Hindustan Systems. Hindustan Systems is expected to pay a dividend of ₹100 next year. The dividend is expected to grow at an annual rate of 15% for years 2, 3 and 4. For years 5 and 6, dividends are expected to grow at 10%. Beyond year 6 dividends will grow at 6% annually. If required rate of return for Saumya is 12%, calculate the intrinsic value of the stock using multistage dividend discount model.
6. Sahil decides to fundamentally value Quickheal Company using the multistage dividend discount model. He divides his investment horizon into two periods—explicit forecast period (where he forecasts the company dividends for each year) from year 2012–16 and terminal period (beyond Year 2016) for which he decides to use Gordon growth model. To estimate the required return, Sahil decides to use the Capital Asset Pricing Model (CAPM). Sahil's forecast of dividends per share for Quickheal (for next 5 years) and inputs for CAPM model are provided below:

Year	*Quickheal company future dividends per share*
2012E	8
2013E	10
2014E	13
2015E	14.5
2016E	16.5

*E refers to expected

Return On Equity (ROE)	25%
Retention ratio	40%
Risk free rate	8%
Beta	1.25
Equity risk premium	6.00%

Using the above information, calculate the intrinsic value per share for Quickheal company Should Sahil purchase the stock based on multistage dividend valuation if Quickheal is currently trading at a price of INR 150?

7. Jayant, an equity analyst wants to estimate the value of McCain Ltd. using Free Cash Flow to Equity (FCFE) valuation approach. To estimate the current FCFE, he collects the following information from company's financials for the current year 2010:

Particulars (Year 2010)	*Amount (in crores)*
Net profit for the year	120
Depreciation	5
Capital expenditure	20
Increase in working capital for the year	3
Debt repayments for the year	9
New debt issued during the year	11

Jayant expects the current FCFE to grow at an annual rate of 8% for next 5 years (year 2011–15). Beyond year 2015 FCFE is expected to grow at a constant rate of 4%. If required rate of return is 11% and number of outstanding shares is 10 crores, calculate the intrinsic value per share of the stock using multistage FCFE model.

8. Shailesh, a retail investor decides to use the relative valuation methodology to identify whether RKB bank is under/overvalued. For this he identifies the following peer or comparison companies and collects the following data with regards to Earnings per share (EPS) and Book Value Per Share (BVPS):

Company	*Price*	*EPS for next year*	*BVPS for next year*	*Growth in earnings*
AKJ Bank	2,300	129	1,500	20%
Smithfield Bank	1,208	70	700	10%
IBP Bank	120	23	130	5%
MAT Financial	3,050	230	2,400	15%
Hallblack Bank	700	65	750	2%
RUJ Bank	140	20	100	6%

RKB is currently trading at a price of ₹230. Its next year EPS is ₹21 and the next year expected BVPS is ₹198. Expected growth in earnings for RKB bank is 15%.

Using the above information

(a) Calculate the mean and median multiple for peer companies using P/E and P/B price multiple. Also calculate the PEG multiple for all companies

(b) Determine whether RKB is under/overvalued on the basis of relative valuation methodology

CASE 1

Asian Paints Company -Valuation Using Multistage Dividend Discount Model

In September 2014, Kartik, an equity analyst with a brokerage firm based out of Bandra Kurla Complex, Mumbai was analyzing the financials of Asian Paints Limited, a market leader in decorative paints in India. Decorative paints account for over 75% of the overall paint market in India and include wall finishes for interior and exterior use, enamels, wood finishes and ancillary products such as primers, putties, etc. In 2013–14, the paint market in India witnessed a slowdown impacting the retail demand for decorative paints. However, Asian paints continued to grow in most parts of the country on account of healthy product mix and superior pricing power. Going forward, improving macro and lower commodity prices can have a positive impact on the demand conditions. This would provide a positive fillip to the company's share price which is currently trading at ₹645.

Kartik decided to value Asian paints using multistage dividend discount model. For this he decides to explicitly forecast the company's dividends for the next 10 years (till 2024). He considered the period beyond year 10 as terminal period and decides to value it using Gordon growth model (see Tables CS1.1 and CS1.2).

TABLE CS1.1

Asian Paints (In crores)	*FY 2014*	*FY 2013*
Total revenue	12,849	11,053
Cost of materials consumed	7,341	6,413
Gross profit	5,508	4,640
Employee and other expenses	3,376	2,794
Operating profit (EBITDA)	2,132	1,846
Finance costs	42	37
Depreciation	246	155
Profit before tax	1,844	1,655
Tax	572	496
Profit after tax	1,273	1,160
Weighted average number of equity shares outstanding (in crores)	96	96
Earnings per share (EPS)	13.27	12.09
Dividend per share	5.30	4.60

Source: https://www.asianpaints.com

TABLE CS1.2
Assumptions For Forecasting

Assumptions	*2015-2024*
Revenues	Increase of 30%
Cost of materials consumed	As % of Revenues similar to 2014
Employee and other expenses	As % of Revenues similar to 2014
Depreciation	As % of Revenues similar to 2014
Finance costs	Similar to 2014
Tax rate	30%
Dividend payout ratio	40%

Risk Free Rate	8%
ERP (Equity Risk Premium)	6.5%
Beta	0.70
$g_{Terminal}$	5%

Questions

1. Using multistage dividend discount model, find out the Intrinsic Equity Value per share of the Asian paints based on above data and assumptions.
2. Based on Intrinsic Equity Value per share calculated above, decide whether Kartik should invest in Asian paints stock.

CASE 2

Pidilite Industries-Valuation Using Free Cash Flow To Firm (Fcff)

On 31 August 2013, it was a late evening for Rajesh Sharma, senior research analyst at one of the prominent brokerage firm operating out of Gurgaon, Haryana. Rajesh, who headed the Indian consumer sector research team, was particularly examining the latest financial information from Pidilite Industries Ltd. (PIDI:IN), a consumer and specialities chemical company headquartered in Mumbai, India. Rajesh wondered whether Pidilite Industries Ltd. would be a good investment for any of his existing institutional clients who were looking to deploy funds in high growth companies. Pidilite dominant presence in niche, underpenetrated and high growth categories had ensured high margins and superior growth opportunities in past. To decide upon the same, Rajesh needed to value the company using the financial information he gathered. Rajesh decided to value Pidilite using multistage Free Cash Flow to Firm (FCFF) model. For this he decides to explicitly forecast the company's Free Cash Flows for the next 5 years (till 2018). He considered the period beyond year 5 as terminal period and decides to value it using Gordon growth model.

TABLE CS2.1

Pidilite (In Millions)	*FY 2013*	*FY 2012*
Total revenue	37,486	31,700
Cost of materials consumed	20,081	17,403
Gross profit	17,405	14,297
Employee and other expenses	10,710	9,026
Operating profit (EBITDA)	6,695	5,271
Finance costs	214	307
Depreciation	686	637
Profit before tax	5,795	4,327
Tax	1,595	1,100
Profit after tax	4,200	3,226
Weighted average number of equity shares outstanding (in millions)	510	521
Earnings per share (EPS)	8.24	6.20

TABLE CS2.2

Assumptions for Forecasting	*2014–2018*
Revenues	Increase of 20% over previous year
Cost of raw materials	As % of sales similar to 2013
Operating expenses	As % of sales similar to 2013
Depreciation	As % of sales similar to 2013
Tax rate	30%
Working capital increase (each year)	10 million
Capital expenditure	3% of revenues for each year

TABLE CS2.3

Risk free rate	7.0%
ERP (equity risk premium)	6%
Beta	0.9
Incremental cost of debt	11%
$g_{Terminal}$	5%
Debt	1,622
Equity	15,521
Cash	1,506

Questions

1. Using multi-stage Free Cash Flow to Firm (FCFF) model, find out the Enterprise Value of Pidilite Industries based on above data and assumptions.
2. Calculate the Intrinsic Equity Value per share of Pidilite Industries and suggest whether Rajesh should buy the stock for his clients if its current traded market price is ₹226?

PART IV

FINANCING AND DIVIDEND DECISION

CHAPTER

11

Cost of Capital

LEARNING OBJECTIVES

After studying this chapter, you should be able to:

- Understand the concept of cost of capital and its constituents.
- Understand and calculate the cost of debt and cost of equity.
- Understand and calculate the cost of preference shares.
- Understand the implication of taxation on components of cost of capital.
- Discuss various ways to assign weights to components of cost of capital.
- Discuss the use of WACC in evaluating capital budgeting projects.

11.1 Introduction

Companies issue bonds and common equity to finance their projects. The capital that is raised from the market has a cost associated with it, and this cost is dependent on the risk associated with the various projects of the firm. A firm may raise capital for a particular project through equity, but for some other projects in future, the firm may use debt or preference shares. Thus, the risk of the firm is a function of all the projects and is reflected in its average cost of capital. While taking a capital budgeting decision, a project can be undertaken if the return from the project is above a certain hurdle rate. If the return from the project is higher than the hurdle rate, it will add to firms' value. The generally acceptable hurdle rate for a project is the cost of capital for a firm when the project risk is similar to the risk of the firm. However, if the project risk is considerably different from the firm risk, then a different approach needs to be taken to calculate the cost of capital for the project. This chapter would discuss in detail the calculation of individual components of cost of capital, and also further discuss special cases and issues related to cost of capital.

11.2 Weighted Average Cost of Capital and Basic Definitions

WACC represents the weighted average of the cost or rate of returns required by the equity, debt and preference shares investors of a company

To fund long-term project and assets, firms generally raise capital through various sources such as equity, debt and preference shares. Each of these sources of capital has a different cost or required rate of return reflecting varying degree of risk attached to it. For example, in case of equity, the returns expected by the shareholders would act as the cost of equity or cost for the retained earnings. Similarly, cost of debt and cost of preference shares represents the returns expected by the bondholders and preference shareholders respectively. Weighted Average Cost of Capital (WACC) represents the weighted average of the cost or rate of returns required by the equity, debt and preference shares investors of a company, the weights being the proportion of equity, debt and preference shares in the total capital of the firm. The expression for weighted average cost of capital is given by:

$$\text{WACC} = w_e \times k_e + w_d \times k_d \times (1-t) + w_p \times k_p$$

where

k_e = Cost of common equity
k_d = Cost of debt
$k_d \times (1-t)$ = After tax cost of debt
k_p = Cost of preference shares
w_e, w_d, w_p = Proportion of equity, debt and preference shares respectively in the capital structure

EXAMPLE 11.1 Dhiraj Industries have the following costs for various components of cost of capital:

k_d = 6.2%
k_e = 12.5%
k_p = 9.5%

Weights of w_d, w_e, w_p, are 40%, 50% and 10%, respectively. The tax rate is 30%. Calculate WACC.

Solution: Here, we can use the WACC formula which is as given below:

$$\text{WACC} = w_e \times k_e + w_d \times k_d \times (1-t) + w_p \times k_p$$

$$\text{WACC} = 0.5 \times 12.5\% + 0.4 \times 6.2\% \ (1 - 0.3) + 0.1 \times 9.5\% = 8.94\%$$

11.2.1 Components of Weighted Average Cost of Capital (WACC)

Now that we have understood the concept of weighted average cost of capital (WACC), let us look at its various constituents or components, viz. cost of equity, cost of debt and cost of preference shares in detail.

Preference stock is a class of ownership in a firm which has higher preference or claims over the earnings and assets of the firm over the common stock

Cost of Debt

Though calculation of cost of debt (k_d) seems straightforward, there are certain complications attached to it. While it may seem that we would just need the return required by the debt holders for calculation of k_d, a firm may have received debt funds at different times and at different rates. Similarly, complications arise due to the fact that some of this debt may be at floating rate; some of this may be convertible and may have different times to maturity.

Suppose Dhiraj Industries is trying to estimate the cost of debt for the current year. How should the CFO go about this? The firm would be comfortable in issuing certain types of debt. So Dhiraj Industries may have been issuing 10 year semi-annual bond for the last couple of times. The bankers of this firm are willing to issue 10 year semi-annual coupon bonds now at 12.5% coupon rate. Thus, the pre-tax cost of debt for Dhiraj Industries is 12.5%. This is the marginal cost of debt or cost of debt for new issue. For evaluating a project, the future cost of issuing a debt would be more relevant. Historical cost of debt can be more relevant in cases where it is difficult to estimate the future cost of debt or when the debt is publicly traded and yield to maturity can be calculated from the market prices of the bonds.

The after tax cost of debt in this case when tax rate is 30% would be:

$$\text{After tax cost of debt} = k_d \times (1-t)$$
$$= 12.5\% \times (1-0.3) = 8.75\%$$

The interest payments by a firm are tax deductible, and hence, the cost of debt should be considered post-tax. An issue of a new debt instrument has flotation cost associated with it. This cost needs to be included in the calculations of cost of debt.

EXAMPLE 11.2 Dhiraj industries issues ₹1000, 10-year bond with annual coupon rate of 12.5% with coupons paid semi-annually. The flotation cost is 1% and the market value of the bond is ₹975, find the cost of debt?

Solution: From Chapter 9, we can see the generalized formula bond value is:

$$V_B = \sum_{i=1}^{n} \frac{C}{(1+k_d)^n} + \frac{FV}{(1+k_d)^n}$$

Here, we also have the flotation cost, so the expression in this case would be:

$$V_B(1-F) = \sum_{i=1}^{n} \frac{C}{(1+k_d)^n} + \frac{FV}{(1+k_d)^n}$$

here, F is the flotation cost.

$$975 \times (1-0.01) = \sum_{i=1}^{20} \frac{62.5}{(1+k_d)^i} + \frac{1000}{(1+k_d)^n}$$

Solving this, we get $k_d/2$ = 6.57%. Therefore, k_d = 13.14%. This is pre-tax cost of debt. Another way of considering flotation costs is to reduce the cash flows by an estimated equivalent amount of flotation cost.

Cost of Preference Stock

Preference stock is a class of ownership in a firm which has higher preference or claims over the earnings and assets of the firm over the common stock. Preference stocks have features which are common to both debt and equity. It resembles debt as it has fixed dividend payments every period, like a debt instrument. It resembles common stock as it gives ownership to the holders of the preference stocks.

A preference share has a fixed payment every period in the form of dividend. This is similar to a coupon payment in case of a debt instrument. However, there is no maturity date and the dividend payment is till perpetuity. Thus, the valuation model for a preference stock can be generalized as follows:

$$V_{ps} = \frac{D_1}{(1+k_{ps})} + \frac{D_2}{(1+k_{ps})^2} + \cdots + \frac{D_\alpha}{(1+k_{ps})^\alpha}$$

The dividend paid is normally the same till perpetuity. The value of preference share with perpetual payment will thus have the following expression:

$$V_{ps} = \frac{D}{k_{ps}}$$

The cost of preference share would be

$$k_{ps} = \frac{D}{V_{ps}}$$

where D is the annual stated dividend and V_{ps} is the current market price of the preference share.

In case there is a flotation cost for the preferred stock, the expression for cost of preference share would be

$$k_{ps} = \frac{D}{V_{ps}(1-F)}$$

where, F is the flotation cost in percentage. In case of preference stock, dividend is calculated after the tax is paid. Hence, there is no tax benefit, and there is no tax deductibility or tax savings on preference stocks. Firms have tried to design financial instrument, which have characteristic similar to preference stocks but can also help the firm in getting tax benefits. Some of these instruments are Modified Income Preferred Securities (MIPS), Quarterly income debt securities, etc.

EXAMPLE 11.3 Dhiraj industries currently hold ₹100 preference shares which pay ₹14 as dividends. If it issues new preference shares, the cost of flotation would be 5%. What is cost of preference shares?

Solution: Here,

$$D = ₹14$$
$$V_{ps} = ₹100$$
$$F = 5\%$$

Thus,

$$k_{ps} = 14/(100 \times (1 - 0.05)) = 14.74\%$$

Cost of Common Stock

Cost of retained earnings is determined by the returns expected by the shareholders

Common equity can be raised either by issuing new equity or by utilizing the retained earnings of the firm. Retained earnings belong to the shareholders and the returns expected by the shareholders would be proxied as the cost of retained earnings.

When firms issue new equity, apart from the expected return by the shareholders', flotation costs represents an additional costs and hence raising new equity is generally considered costlier than utilizing retained earnings. As discussed in chapters 8 and 10, there are three different approaches to estimate cost of common stock.

CAPM Approach

As discussed in Chapter 8, the Capital Asset Pricing Method (CAPM) approach can be used to estimate cost of common stock. CAPM provides a framework to establish the relationship between the risk and the expected return for any risky asset.

To determine the required rate of return or cost of equity for equity shareholders, CAPM specifies the following equation:

$$\text{Cost of equity} = \text{Risk-free rate} + (\text{Equity risk premium}) \times \text{Beta}$$
$$k_e = R_F + (R_M - R_F) \times \beta$$

where k_e is cost of equity, R_M refers to market returns, R_F refers to risk-free rate and β represents the beta coefficient.

As discussed, in Chapter 8, beta coefficient measures the movement of the stock with respect to the movement of the market. A beta coefficient greater than one means the stock is riskier than the market and less than one signifies that the stock is less risky relative to the market.

EXAMPLE 11.4 Given R_F = 4%, β is 1.2 and risk premium is 6%. Calculate cost of equity.

Solution:

$$k_e = R_F + (R_M - R_F) \times \beta$$
$$k_e = 4\% + 6\% \times 1.2 = 11.2\%$$

Even though CAPM approach can be said to be a technically correct approach, there are certain disadvantages of using this approach. First, measurement of risk-free rates has controversy over whether to use long-term treasury rates or short-term treasury rates. For example, an investor using 1 year treasury rate as a proxy for risk-free rate would find his CAPM determined return much different from the investor using the 10 year treasury rate. This is because long-term treasury rates would be generally higher than short-term rates (assuming upward sloping yield curve). Secondly as discussed in Chapter 8, there are estimation issues with regards to equity risk premiums.

11.3 Bond Yield Plus Risk Premium Approach

Analysts, who are not comfortable with the CAPM approach, use an approximate method to measure cost of common stock. They charge a premium over the bond yield, which is based on their judgement of the risk of the stock. The premium charged is generally above the bond yield of the firm and is based on the risk of the concerned stock.

Bond Yield plus Risk Premium Approach add a risk premium over the bond yield to arrive at the cost of equity

$$k_e = \text{Bond yield} + \text{Risk premium}$$

Assume that the yield on a firm's bond is 7%. If the risk premium is 4%, then the expected return on the common stock using bond yield plus risk premium approach would be:

$$k_e = 7\% + 4\% = 11\%$$

Though this method is not a precise method, it gives a good estimate for measuring cost of common stock.

11.4 Dividend Discount Model (DDM) Approach

Investors should use target capital structures to arrive at the weights for the sources of funds

As discussed in Chapter 10, dividend discount model expresses the value of stock as a function of present value of an infinite stream of dividends discounted at the required rate of return.

$$P_0 = \frac{D_1}{(1+k)^1} + \frac{D_2}{(1+k)^2} + \cdots + \frac{D_n}{(1+k)^n} + \frac{P_n}{(1+k)^n}$$

This expression can be rewritten as:

$$P_0 = \frac{D_0(1+g)^1}{(1+k)^1} + \frac{D_0(1+g)^2}{(1+k)^2} + \cdots + \frac{D_0(1+g)^\infty}{(1+k)^\infty}$$

Further, it can be rewritten as:

$$P_0 = \frac{D_0(1+g)}{(k-g)}$$

OR

$$= \frac{D_1}{(k_e - g)}$$

where,

P_0 = The present or intrinsic value of the stock
D = Dividends per share
g = Constant growth rate in dividends
k or k_e = The required rate of return on the stock

This expression can be re-arranged to solve for k_e

$$k_e = \frac{D_1}{P_0} + g$$

Dividend yield can be estimated either using the past years data or by using analysts future estimates which are generally available on Bloomberg, Reuters etc. Growth in dividends or g can be estimated using the following function:

g = Return On Equity (ROE) × (1–Payout ratio)

or

g = Return On Equity (ROE) × (Retention ratio)

EXAMPLE 11.5 Rajesh imports stock is trading at a market price of ₹85. The firm paid dividends of ₹5 in the last year. If the payout ratio of firm is 50% and return on equity (ROE) is 16%, calculate the cost of equity for Rajesh imports.

Solution:

D_0 = ₹5

g = ROE × (1–payout ratio) = 16% × 50% = 8%

Thus, $D_1 = D_0 \times (1 + g) = 5 \times 1.08$ = ₹5.40

$$k_e = \frac{D_1}{P_0} + g$$

k_e = (5.4/85) + 8% = 14.35%

Thus, k_e = 14.35%

In case of cost of retained earnings, there would be no flotation costs. However, if a firm issues new equity, a substantial flotation cost is involved. This needs to be accounted in for the calculation of cost of equity when new equity is floated. Firms hire investment bankers to structure new equity, set terms for issue price and then sell it to investors. The fee for the bankers is the flotation cost and should be a part of the cost of equity.

While we have ignored the flotation costs in our calculations so far, it should generally be considered as it represents a substantial portion of the cost of new equity.

Flotation cost can be adjusted in the cost of equity calculations. The issuing company raises capital from new equity and a part of it goes to the investment bankers as fees. Thus, it is a cost which needs to be adjusted in the cost of equity calculations. The adjustment can be shown in calculations is as follows:

$$k_e = \frac{D_1}{P_0(1-F)} + g$$

where F is the flotation costs.

EXAMPLE 11.6 Rajesh imports stock is trading at a market price of ₹85. The firm paid dividends of ₹5 in the last year. If the payout ratio of firm is 50% and return on equity (ROE) is 16%, calculate the cost of equity for Rajesh imports. Assume flotation cost as 4%.

Solution:

$$D_0 = ₹5$$

$$g = \text{ROE} \times (1\text{–payout ratio}) = 16\% \times 50\% = 8\%$$

Thus, $D_1 = D_0 \times (1 + g) = 5 \times 1.08 = ₹5.40$

$$k_e = \frac{D_1}{P_0} + g$$

$$k_e = \frac{5.40}{85(1-0.04)} + 8\% = 14.6\%$$

Thus, $k_e = 14.60\%$

Even though flotation costs may seem higher, but if we consider flotation cost on a per project basis, it would be on the lower side. Equity issue as an activity is once in a decade activity and is done such that money is raised for all the projects for a period like next 10 years. Thus, per project cost of flotation would be low.

11.5 Deciding the Weights in WACC

In the equation for WACC, we have seen that there are weights assigned for each type of component of cost, i.e., equity, debt and preference shares. Using the historic capital structure to decide on the weights would not be appropriate as the future capital structure of the firm might be very different from the old one. So the question is how should investors decide on the weights for components of Weighted Average Cost of Capital (WACC)?

To maximize value in the long run, firms generally decide on their optimal or target capital structures. These firms would then raise capital based on their target capital structures and accordingly have the weights for the sources of funds, *viz.* equity, debt and preference share capital. Investors should ideally use these target proportions of debt, preferred stock and equity stock determined by the firm for calculating the

Weighted Average Cost of Capital (WACC).

Next there is generally a controversy regarding using of book value or the market value weights for the sources of funds. While logically market value weights are the true indicators of investor expectations and should be preferred over book value weights, in certain cases it may be difficult to obtain market value weights due to lack of data. For example, in case of unlisted firm, market value weight of equity would be unavailable. Similarly, market value weight of debt is generally unavailable as most of the debt securities do not get traded in the market. On account of the above problems, investors usually tend to use book value weights as the data is readily available.

11.6 WACC and Projects

Pure play approach can be used to calculate WACC in case of a new project

In evaluating projects, WACC is usually used as the discount rate for finding NPV or for comparison with the IRR of the project. But the question is whether is it correct to use the WACC as the hurdle rate? It might make sense when the project being considered has risks similar to that of the firm. For example, sales of a firm manufacturing luxury cars would be sensitive to the upcycle or downcycle in the economy. Consequently, the risk level for this firm would be very different from the firm which is into manufacturing of pens where demand is insensitive to the change in economic cycles. Thus if a firm manufacturing luxury cars diversifies into pen manufacturing, it would not be appropriate to use the WACC of the firm for this particular project as the new project would have lower risks compared to the WACC of the firm.

In such a case a different discount rate needs to be calculated for this new project. In such cases, a discount rate needs to be arrived at which recognizes the risk associated with this particular new project. This can be done using the pure play approach for finding out the WACC.

11.6.1 Pure Play Approach

When a firm decides to undertake a project which is completely different from the business activities of the firm, it is inappropriate to use the firms' WACC as the hurdle rate. In such a case, pure play approach can be applied to find the discount rate. The steps in pure play approach are as follows:

Step 1 Find a firm working in same or similar business as the new project the firm is venturing into. This would be called as the pure play firm.

Step 2 Calculate the beta of the pure play firm.

Step 3 The pure play firms' debt equity ratio would be different from the firm who is starting this new project. Hence, it would not be appropriate to use the pure play firms cost of capital. Hence, the pure play firm's beta is unlevered. This can be done by applying the Hamada's equation:

$$\beta_U = \frac{\beta_L}{\{1+(1-t)\times D/E\}}$$

where,

β_U = Beta of the unlevered firm

β_L = Beta of the levered firm or beta of the pure play firm.

t = Tax rate

D/E = Debt-equity ratio

Step 4 After the beta of the pure play firm has been unlevered, it is re-levered with the debt equity ratio of the firm whose project is being analyzed. This levered beta is used to calculate the cost of equity for the project of the firm and which can be further be used to calculate the WACC.

EXAMPLE 11.7 Sera Ltd., which is a steel manufacturing firm, is considering a dairy project for which it will be having a debt-equity ratio of 2:1 and pre-tax cost of debt of 16%. It has found a pure play firm in dairy which has a beta of 1.2 and debt equity ratio of 2.25. If the risk-free rate is 11%, expected return on market portfolio is 16%, calculate the required rate of return for the dairy project? Assume Tax rate as 30%.

Solution: First, we need to unlever the beta for the pure play firm.

$$\beta_U = \frac{\beta_L}{\{1+(1-t)\times D/E\}}$$

$$= \frac{1.2}{\{1+(1-0.3)\times 2.25\}} = 0.47$$

We need to re-lever the beta as per the debt equity ratio of Sera Ltd.

$$\beta_L = \beta_U \times \{1+(1-t)\times D/E\}$$

$$= 0.47\times\{1+(1-0.3)\times 2\} = 1.13$$

Cost of equity can be calculated as

$$k_e = R_F + (R_M - R_F) \times \beta$$

$$k_e = 11\% + 1.13 \times (16\% - 11\%) = 16.65\%$$

Now, we can calculate WACC

$$\text{WACC} = w_e \times k_e + w_d \times k_d \times (1-t) + w_p \times k_p$$

$$\text{WACC} = 0.33 \times 16.65\% + 0.67 \times 16\% \times (1 - 0.3) = 13\%$$

Thus, WACC = 13%

Researchable Issues

Faculty members, students and research scholars may like to consider the following selected issues for further research and case writing.

- Optimal Capital Structure and the Cost of Capital
- Determinants of Cost of Capital in India
- Cost of Capital for private firms in India
- Market value weights vs. Book Value weights for companies in India
- Target Capital Structures of BSE Sensex Companies in India

References

Diamond, D.W., and Verrecchia, R.E., "Disclosure, liquidity, and the cost of capital," *The Journal of Finance*, 46(4), 1325–1359, 1991.

Gebhardt, W.R., Lee, C.M., and Swaminathan, B., Toward an implied cost of capital," *Journal of Accounting Research*, 39(1), 135–176, 2001.

Modigliani, F., and Miller, M.H., Corporate income taxes and the cost of capital: A correction, *The American Economic Review*, 433–443, 1963.

Myers, S.C., Determinants of corporate borrowing, *Journal of Financial Economics*, 5(2), 147–175, 1977.

Points to Remember

- Cost of Capital is a weighted average of various components of cost of capital, i.e., debt, equity and preference shares.
- Cost of capital is the hurdle rate that is applied in evaluation of a project for capital budgeting decision.
- Cost of debt is the after-tax cost of debt which is found by multiplying new cost of debt with $(1 - t)$ where t is the marginal tax rate.
- Cost of preference share is calculated by taking the ratio of dividend paid to the price of preference share and is given by $k_p = D_p/V_p$.
- Cost of equity can be calculated by applying one of the three methods: (1) CAPM Approach, (2) Bond yield plus risk premium approach and (3) Dividend Discount Approach
- While issuing new equity, for calculating cost of equity, flotation cost should be considered in calculating the cost of equity.
- To maximize value, firms decide their optimal capital structures and weights are decided based on the optimal capital structure.
- Projects which have risks different from that of the firm cannot directly apply the WACC of the firm as the hurdle rate. In such cases, the pure play firm approach can be applied.

Questions

1. What is Weighted Average Cost of Capital and what is its significance.
2. Why does cost of debt require adjustment for taxes, whereas cost of equity does not have any such requirement?
3. If there is an increase in risk-free rate, would it affect cost of debt? Would it affect the cost of equity?
4. Why should one used market weights instead of book value weights? Explain.
5. Can a firm have a different risk than one of its project? Can we use firm WACC as the hurdle rate for the project? Explain.
6. What is levering and un-levering of beta? Explain.

Multiple Choice Questions

1. The components of a firm's cost of capital include:
   (a) Accounts receivable, equity and long-term debt
   (b) Preference share, accounts payable and equity
   (c) Preference share, equity and long-term debt
   (d) Common stock, short-term debt and inventory
2. Glenco Ltd. Beta is 0.9. If risk free free rate in the economy is 8% and equity risk premium is 5%, calculate the cost of equity for Glenco Ltd.
   (a) 15% (b) 12.5%
   (c) 9% (d) None of the above
3. Risk free rate for company ABC is 7%, market risk premium is 4% and beta is 1.2. Cost of debt for the company is 6% and tax rate is 30%. If Debt

component is twice that of equity in capital structure, calculate the WACC for the company

(a) 10% (b) 5.6% (c) 6.7% (d) 25%

4. The cost of common stock is 16% and the bond yield is 9% then the bond risk premium is

(a) 7% (b) 5% (c) 10% (d) 25%

5. If the retention ratio is 60% and return on equity (ROE) is 15%, calculate the growth rate of dividends (g)

(a) 10% (b) 6% (c) 9% (d) 8%

6. Which of the following methods uses peer companies with similar risk profile to calculate risk of the project

(a) Pure play method (b) Same play method
(c) CAPM method (d) Book value method

7. Bond risk premium is added to bond yield to calculate

(a) Cost of preference stock
(b) Cost of common stock
(c) Cost of debt
(d) Cost of derivative

8. Risk free rate for Arvind Ltd. is 9%, market risk premium is 6% and beta is 0.8. Cost of debt for the company is 10% and tax rate is 35%. If debt to equity ratio is 1:1, calculate the WACC for the company

(a) 10.5% (b) 9.4%
(c) 12.3% (d) None of the above

Self-Test Questions

1. Sreeja Ltd. has 45% debt and 55% equity in its structure. Bond has a yield to maturity of 9%, tax rate is 40%. The WACC of the company has been found to be 9.5%. What is the cost of common equity?
2. Raj Industries can issue preferred stock for a price of ₹55 per share. The issue terms say that the firm would pay a dividend of ₹4.5 per share till perpetuity. What is the cost of preferred stock?
3. Chandni Fertilizers stock is selling for ₹75 per share. They have just paid a dividend of ₹5 per share and the dividend is expected to grow at a rate of 6% per annum. The company plans to issue new equity and the flotation cost are 4%. What are the cost of retained earnings and cost of new equity?
4. Ajanta Company's stock is selling for ₹50. Its last dividend was ₹5.50, and the firm is expected to grow at 7% till perpetuity. Flotation costs associated with the sale of common stock are 10% of the proceeds raised. Estimate Parrot's cost of retained earnings.
5. Ajay Industries are thinking of issuing ₹100 par preferred stock with 13% dividend. The flotation cost of issuing the share is 5% and the market price of the shares is ₹95. Calculate the cost of preferred stock?
6. Nayan Steel Company has only debt and equity in its structure. It can borrow at 10% interest rate if it maintains its target capital structure of 40% debt and 60% equity. Recently it paid a dividend of ₹5. Its expected growth rate is 5% and the market value of share is ₹35. Tax rate is 40%. Calculate the WACC.

7. Agarwal Sweets has found that its after-tax cost of debt is 7% for the first ₹10 lakh of the bonds that it issues, and 9% for bonds issued above ₹10 lakh. The cost of preferred stock is 10%. Cost of its internal equity is 13%, and that of external equity is 15%. Currently, the firm's capital structure has ₹60 lakh of debt, ₹10 lakh of preferred stock, and ₹30 lakh of common equity. Tax rate is 30% and the firm is currently making projections for next period and the firm believes that it should have ₹7.5 lakh available from retained earnings for investment. What is the firm's marginal cost of capital if the firm requires ₹28 lakh investment?
8. Seema Corporation wants to consider equity financing. Currently, the share of the firm is selling for ₹45 per share. The firm's plans to pay a dividend of ₹3.5 next year and the dividend would grow at an annual growth rate of 5.0% after that. If the firm issues new stock, the flotation costs would equal 15.0% of the stock's market price. Tax rate is 40%. What is the firm's cost of external equity?

Problems

1. Neeraj Industries is considering raising of ₹100 crores by issuing debt, preference capital, equity and retained earnings. The book value and market value are as given below:

(₹ in crore)

	Book value	*Market value*
Ordinary shares	20	50
Reserves	10	–
Preference shares	10	15
Debt	60	45

The tax rate is 30% and the information is about components of costs is as given below:

1. The firm can sell ₹100 debenture with 13% rate of interest and flotation cost of 3% of the market price.
2. ₹100 preference share with 11% dividend payment selling at ₹110 and flotation cost of ₹8.
3. The ordinary shares of the firm is selling for ₹180 and the firm is expected to pay a dividend of ₹15 and the dividend payment would grow at a rate of 5%. New ordinary shares can be sole for ₹195. Flotation cost on issue of new shares is ₹10.

Calculate the WACC using both book value and market value.

CASE

Britannia Industries—Cost of Capital Calculation

Nitin, a retail investor wants to calculate the cost of capital for one of his holdings, Britannia Industries Ltd., a leading food company in India with over 5,000 crores in revenues. Nitin has collected the following information for Britannia Industries to arrive at the cost of capital calculation.

Excerpts from Britannia Balance Sheet

Britannia (in crores)	*As at 31st March 2013*
Equity and Liabilities	
Shareholders' funds	
Share capital	24
Reserves and surplus	612
Non-current liabilities	
Long-term borrowings	0.41
Deferred tax liability (net)	14
Other long-term liabilities	210
Long-term provisions	138
Current liabilities	
Short-term borrowings	189
Trade payables	333
Other current liabilities	210
Short-term provisions	134

Source: http://britannia.co.in/

Other Details

Risk free rate	8.0%
ERP (Equity Risk Premium)	6.5%
Beta	0.6
Pre-tax cost of debt	8%
Tax rate	27%

Questions

On the basis of the above information, calculate:

(a) Cost of equity for Britannia Industries

(b) Weighted Average Cost of Capital for Britannia Industries for the year 2013

CHAPTER

12

Theories of Capital Structure

LEARNING OBJECTIVES

After studying this chapter, you should be able to:

- Discuss the pros and cons of debt and equity financing.
- Calculate the cost of debt, equity and WACC after taxes
- Discuss the main assumptions and conclusions of the net income approach, net operating income and the traditional approaches to capital structure.
- Explain the MM approach and show how the arbitrage works.
- Explain the pecking order theory and its signalling effects.
- Suggest the optimal capital structure on the basis of given relevant information.
- Calculate the levered and unlevered betas.

12.1 Introduction

The term capital structure refers to the manner in which a firm has financed its business operations by combining different sources of funds. The main sources of funds available to a company may be classified into equity and debt sources. Equity refers to ownership capital, including ordinary share capital and retained earnings, on which the company is not committed to pay any fixed or pre-decided return. On the other hand, debt or borrowed capital may take the form of bonds issued by the company or bank loans, on which the company is committed to pay periodical interest charges as well as repay the principal amount of debt as per the agreed terms. A third popular way of raising capital is by issuing preference shares which have several features common with debt capital (fixed rate of dividends and priority in repayment of capital in case of winding up of the company), and is usually combined with debt sources.

12.2 Debt and Equity Financing: Pros and Cons

The advantages of debt financing include lower cost, tax-shield and flexibility.

As compared to equity (ownership capital), debt financing has certain advantages that make it an attractive source of capital. The main advantages of debt financing claimed are as follows:

1. Lower cost of capital: The cost of debt is normally lower than the cost of equity capital. As investment in equity is more risky, investors would expect a higher return on such investments which makes it a costlier source of financing as compared to debt.

2. Tax advantage: Interest paid on loans is treated as a business expense for the purpose of calculating taxable income and the income tax liability. For example, if a firm's operating income (profit before interest and taxes) is ₹100000, interest on loans amounts to ₹50,000 and the applicable tax rate is 30%, the company's tax liability would be ₹15,000, i.e., 30% (1,00,000 – 50,000). However, if the firm had not taken any loans and did not incur the interest expense, its tax liability would be ₹30,000, i.e., 30% of ₹1,00,000. The tax-benefit (often referred to as tax-shield) on interest expense reduces the effective cost of debt.

3. Flexibility: Loans can be repaid when not required, thus reducing the company's financial charges. This gives the firm considerable flexibility, which is mostly not possible with equity capital. The equity capital once issued would normally remain with the company for permanent, and cannot be reduced easily.

Against these advantages, debt financing has certain disadvantages too:

1. Financial risk: The financial risk of the company increases as it resorts to more and more debt financing in relation to equity financing. Financial risk is the possibility that if there is a downturn in business, the firm might not earn enough to pay interest or repay loans in time. Such a situation could not only lead to loss of goodwill, the legal action taken by the lenders could even force the company into bankruptcy.

2. Penalty cost: When a company goes for excessive debt financing, the lenders start asking for higher and penal rate of interest as a compensation for the greater financial risk.

Disadvantages of debt financing include increase in financial risk, penalty clauses and reduced profits.

3. Effect on profits: More the debt, higher would be the cost of interest, which would reduce the amount of profits available to the shareholders. The interest payable on borrowed funds becomes a fixed cost that can be a real headache, especially in recessionary times when sales and profits may plunge, but interest cost would remain unchanged and high.

12.3 Effect of Financial Leverage: The Debate

A company making use of debt financing in its capital structure is known as a 'levered' company and the one not resorting to debt financing is called an 'unlevered' company. One of the most debated issues in corporate finance relates to whether changing the degree of financial leverage (debt financing in relation to equity) in the capital structure could change the company's cost of capital and add value to the firm and its equity shareholders. In other words, can a company enhance its total market value or lower its cost of capital by varying the proportion of debt used in relation to equity capital?

One group of experts claims that since debt is a cheaper source of funding, a firm can enhance its market value and lower its cost of capital by varying the proportion of debt used in relation to equity capital, particularly if debt is used judiciously. Thus, according to this school of thought, the value of the firm and its cost of capital can be managed by changing the financial leverage. If that was true, every firm should try to find out the 'optimal' capital structure that would maximize its market value and minimize the cost of capital.

However, the opposite camp of experts claims that the value of the firm is independent of the manner in which a business is financed; that in the market place a firm is valued on the basis of its 'operating earnings' irrespective of how the business is funded. Hence, according to this camp, capital structure would not affect the value of the firm or its cost of capital.

Since the debate between the two camps has been raging for the past several decades, it would be a learning experience to examine the main theories of capital structure propounded by these opposite camps. Our aim here would be to analyze the possible effect of a change in capital structure (and capital structure alone) on the value of the firm and its cost of capital and their implications for the shareholders.

12.4 Assumptions of the Capital Structure Theories

In order to segregate the relationship between financial leverage and value of the firm, we would assume that other things remain constant. More specifically, we make the following assumptions on which the theories of capital structure are based:

1. The debt to equity ratio can be changed instantly. In other words, the company can issue new equity to repurchase debt immediately, and vice-versa.
2. The company's operating earnings (earnings before interest and taxes) are assumed to remain constant in perpetuity. In other words, the annual operating earnings of the company would not grow.
3. The company pays out all of its earnings as dividends. Thus, earnings is equal to dividends. This would help us avoid the effect of dividend decision on the value of the firm.
4. There are no transaction or bankruptcy costs.
5. Business risk of the firm is constant. In other words, the business of the firm continues in a stable manner to earn constant operating profits each year.
6. All investors are rational and have same expectations about the company's future operating profits.
7. Initially, we also assume there are no income taxes (corporate as well as personal). Later this assumption would be changed.

Capital structure theories assume that • the debt- equity ratio can be changed instantly, • operating earnings remain constant in perpetuity, and • the earnings = dividends.

12.4.1 Meanings and Definitions

In addition to the above assumptions, we would also assume that the company uses perpetual bonds for debt financing (and hence, pays out a constant amount of interest each year on the amount of debt outstanding). This along with the assumption that the company's operating earnings would remain constant in perpetuity would help us in keeping our calculations simple by using the perpetuity formula to determine the present value of future stream of annuity in perpetuity. You would recall from our discussion in the chapter on 'time value of money' that the present value of an amount receivable (or payable) in perpetuity = Amount receivable per annum ÷ Discount rate expressed as a proportion. Thus, the present value of an amount of ₹10,000 receivable each year in perpetuity if the rate of interest is 10%, would be equal to 10,000 ÷ 0.10 = ₹1,00,000.

As we set out to study the theories of capital structure, we would be frequently using the following definitions:

1. $k_e = \frac{P}{E} = \frac{\text{Profits available to equity shareholders}}{\text{Market value of equity shares outstanding}}$

   where, 'k_e' is the cost of equity capital. To illustrate, assume the company has issued 100 equity shares which have a current market value of ₹50 per share. If the firm's total earnings available to equity shareholders amount to ₹1,000 per annum, then k_e = 1,000 ÷ 5,000 = 0.20 or 20%. k_e is also called the required rate of return on equity investment because if the investors are currently willing to pay a price of ₹50 per share for getting an income of ₹10 per share per annum, then it means they are satisfied with getting a 20% return.

   Note that between k_e, P and E, if we are given any two, it should be possible to calculate the third variable. For example, if P is ₹1,000 and k_e (also called equity capitalization rate) is 0.20, the market value of equity (E) would be:

2. $E = \frac{P}{k_e} = \frac{\text{Profits available to equity shareholders}}{\text{Cost of equity capital}}$

   = ₹1000/0.20 = ₹5,000.

   Turning to cost of debt:

3. $k_d = \frac{I}{D} = \frac{\text{Annual interest expense}}{\text{Market value of debt outstanding}}$

   where, 'k_d' is the cost of debt outstanding. For example, if the company has issued 5 perpetual bonds which have a current market value of ₹1,000 per bond, and the company pays an interest of ₹120 per bond per annum (total interest payment of ₹120 × 5 = 600 per annum), then k_d = 600 ÷ 5,000 = 0.12 or 12%.

   Note that (assuming perpetual debt for simplicity) between k_d, I and D, if we are given any two, it should be possible to calculate the third variable. For example, if 'I' is ₹600 and k_d is 0.12, the market value of debt (D) would be:

4. $D = \frac{I}{k_d} = \frac{\text{Annual interest expense}}{\text{Cost of debt capital}}$

   = ₹600/0.12 = ₹5,000.

   Now we can turn our attention to the overall cost of capital:

5. $k_o = \frac{O}{V} = \frac{\text{Annual operating earnings}}{\text{Market value of the firm}}$

   where, k_o is the overall cost of capital of the firm. The market value of the firm (V) is made up of market value of debt (D) and equity (E). Thus, if the annual operating earnings amount to ₹1600, market value of equity and debt is ₹5,000 each (so that $V = 5{,}000 + 5{,}000 = 10{,}000$), we have:

$$k_o = \frac{O}{V} = \frac{1600}{10000} = 0.16 \text{ or } 16\%.$$

The k_o is also called the weighted average cost of capital, where the proportions of funding raised by individual sources act as the weights, so that k_o can be calculated as follows:

6. $k_o = k_d\left(\frac{D}{D+E}\right) + k_e\left(\frac{E}{D+E}\right)$

Thus, using the above examples, we get

$$k_o = 12\%\left(\frac{5000}{5000+5000}\right) + 20\%\left(\frac{5000}{5000+5000}\right)$$

$$= 12\%\ (0.50) + 20\%\ (0.50) = 16\%.$$

k_o is also known as the overall 'capitalization' rate for the firm because if we know the annual operating earnings of the firm and its k_o, we can determine the total market value of the firm:

7. $V = \frac{O}{k_o} = \frac{\text{Annual operating earnings}}{\text{Overall cost of capital of the firm}}$

Continuing with the above example, total operating earnings of the firm would amount to ₹1,000 + 600 = 1,600, and given the k_o of 16%, we have

$$V = \frac{1600}{0.16} = ₹10{,}000$$

We are now ready to examine the different theories of capital structure. We begin with the Net Income Approach as it would give us a good starting point.

Net Income Approach

The Net Income Approach is based on the following assumptions:

- Cost of equity (k_e) is assumed to remain constant at all levels of debt/equity ratio.
- Cost of debt (k_d) remains constant at all levels of debt/equity ratio and any amount of debt is available at the same interest rate.
- Income taxes are assumed to be nil.
- Debt/equity ratio can be changed instantly; that is, equity can be replaced by debt and vice-versa.

If these assumptions hold good, the optimal capital structure will be the one that uses maximum of debt and least amount of equity because that you go on increasing the proportion of cheaper debt with less and less of costly equity, the overall cost of capital k_o will decline and the market value of the firm would increase.

To illustrate, assume the firm's Net Operating Income (NOI) = ₹1,00,000, cost of equity k_e = 15% and the cost of debt k_d = 10%. With these assumptions, the value of the firm and the overall cost of capital at different levels of debt-equity would be as given in Table 12.1.

Net Income Approach assumes constant cost of equity and debt at all levels of D/E, and no income taxes. The optimal capital structure will be at point of maximum debt.

TABLE 12.1
Net Income Approach

	Particulars	*Debt* = 0	*D* = 2,50,000	*D* = 5,00,000
O	Net operating income	1,00,000	1,00,000	1,00,000
I	Annual interest	0	25,000	50,000
P	Profits for equity holders	1,00,000	75,000	50,000
k_e	Cost of equity capital k_e	0.15	0.15	0.15
E	Market value of equity [P/k_e]	6,66,666.67	5,00,000.00	3,33,333.33
D	Value of debt	0.00	2,50,000.00	5,00,000.00
V	Market value of firm [*D*+*E*]	6,66,666.67	7,50,000.00	8,33,333.33
	Implied k_o [*O*/*V*]	0.15	0.133	0.120

As the calculations show, the value of the firm increases and the overall cost of capital declines with every increase in the debt-equity ratio. This can be shown graphically in Figure 12.1.

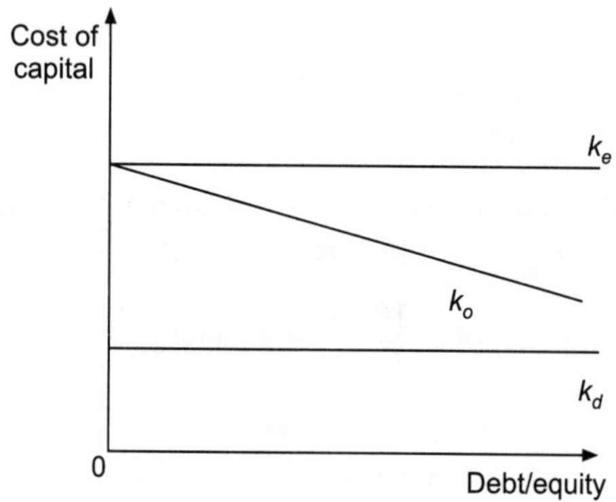

FIGURE 12.1
Behaviour of k_e, k_d and k_o under net income approach.

The x-axis shows the increasing debt/equity ratio while the y-axis shows the cost of capital in percentage. If the assumptions of the net income approach hold good, the k_o would be declining towards the k_d as the debt/equity ratio increases.

The assumption that cost of equity and debt would remain constant at all degrees of debt/equity ratio is not practical in real life.

The net income approach assumes the cost of equity as well as the cost of debt would remain constant at all degrees of debt/equity ratio which is not a practical proposition under the current scenario. However, there might have been times in the history of nations when possibly there was an over abundant supply of capital so that a reputed firm could avail any amount of funding within a large range without raising the cost of debt or equity capital. A somewhat similar opportunity was provided by the 'quantitative easing' policy of injecting huge liquidity into the system adopted by the USA and certain European countries in the aftermath of international financial crisis of 2008, to the extent that the rates of interest plummeted to near-zero levels in some European countries during 2009–11.

However, such a situation cannot be expected to prevail for long periods and the cost of equity or debt cannot be expected to remain unchanged at all degrees of debt/equity. This is because as the proportion of debt increases in relation to equity, the equity holders would get alarmed at the increasing financial risk and demand higher risk premiums thereby raising the required rate of return or the cost of equity capital. The cost of debt may also follow suit at high degrees of financial leverage.

Net Operating Income Approach

Net Operating Income (NOI) theory assumes that the market value of a firm is based on its earning capacity and is not affected by the changing debt/equity ratio.

Net Operating Income (NOI) approach is based on the following assumptions:

- The overall cost of capital (k_o) is assumed to remain constant at all levels of debt/equity ratio.
- Cost of debt (k_d) remains constant at all levels of debt/equity ratio. Further, any amount of debt would be available at the same rate of interest.
- Income taxes: assumed to be nil.

If these assumptions hold good, any capital structure will be as good as any other. As the debt/equity ratio increases, any advantage of cheaper debt is offset by a corresponding rise in k_e because at higher levels of debt/equity ratio, investors would require higher risk premium to invest in equity.

To illustrate, assume a company has Net Operating Income (NOI) of ₹1,00,000; k_o is 12.5%, and any amount of loan is available at 10% interest per annum. In such a situation, the value of the firm and the cost of equity capital at different levels of debt-equity would be as given in Table 12.2.

TABLE 12.2
Net operating income approach.

	Debt	*Debt*	*Debt*
	Nil	**2,50,000**	**5,00,000**
Net operating income	1,00,000	1,00,000	1,00,000
Overall cost of capital k_o	0.125	0.125	0.125
Market value of firm (*V*)	8,00,000	8,00,000	8,00,000
Less: Debt (*D*)	0	2,50,000	5,00,000
Market value of equity ($E = V - D$)	8,00,000	5,50,000	3,00,000
Profits for equity holders (*P*)	1,00,000	75,000	50,000
Implied k_e [=P/E]	0.1250	0.1364	0.1667

The overall cost of capital k_o is assumed to remain the same no matter whether the debt amounts to zero, ₹2,50,000 or even ₹5,00,000. As the calculations show, the value of the firm is determined by capitalizing the operating earnings at the overall cost of capital (k_o), so the total value of the firm remains stable at ₹8,00,000 at all levels of debt/equity ratio. However, with every increase in the proportion of debt financing, the k_e rises in such a way so as to offset any advantage of cheaper debt. This can be shown graphically in Figure 12.2:

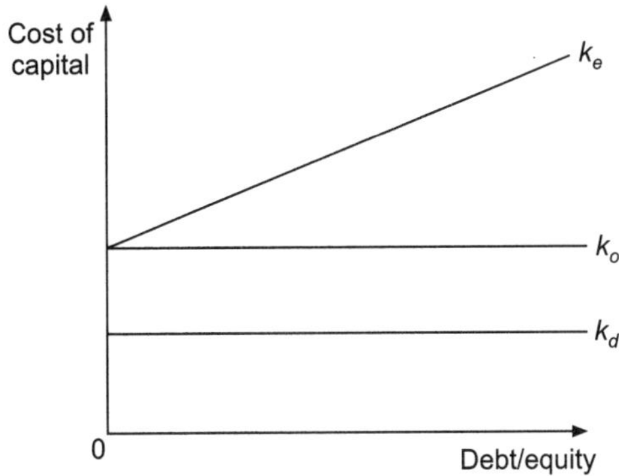

FIGURE 12.2
Behaviour of k_e, k_d and k_o under the net operating income approach.

In Figure 12.2, the x-axis shows the increasing debt/equity ratio while the y-axis shows the cost of capital in percentage. If the assumptions of the net operating income approach hold good, the k_o would remain unchanged and would not be affected by changes in the debt/equity ratio.

As per NOI approach, k_o remains constant at all degrees of D/E, because as the proportion of debt rises, the k_e would increase to offset any advantage of cheaper debt.

A critical assumption of the Net Operating Income (NOI) theory is that the market would put a valuation on the firm on the basis of its earning capacity and would not be affected by the changing debt/equity ratio. The change in debt/equity ratio is seen as a matter of distributing the financial risk between the debt holders and equity holders, so that if the proportion of debt rises, the resulting rise in the financial risk would increase the cost of equity in such a way so as to remove any advantage of the cheaper debt financing.

Several experts lead by Modigliani–Miller have advocated the Net Operating Income (NOI) approach. Modigliani–Miller strongly proposed that the cost of capital of a firm would be independent of the company's capital structure. Before we discuss the MM approach to capital structure, let us review another approach called the traditional theory of capital structure.

12.5 Traditional Theory of Capital Structure

The traditional approach says that a firm can increase its total market value through judicious mix of debt and equity funds. It implies that the cost of capital is not independent of the capital structure and there is an optimal structure.

12.5.1 Illustration of Traditional Approach

Assume the following information is available about a company:

- Cost of equity, k_e = 13% if debt = Nil; k_e = 14% when debt ₹2,50,000; k_e rises to 18% when debt = 5,00,000.
- Cost of debt, k_d = 10% if debt up to ₹2,50,000; above that level of debt k_d = 12%.
- Net Operating Income (NOI) = ₹1,00,000. Income taxes assumed to be nil.
- Debt/equity ratio can be changed instantly, that is equity can be replaced by debt and vice-versa.

If these assumptions hold good, the optimal capital structure will be the one that gives minimum k_o and maximizes the value of firm. The value of the firm and the overall cost of capital at different levels of debt-equity would be as given in Table 12.3.

TABLE 12.3 The traditional approach

	Debt Nil	*10% Debt 2,50,000*	*12% Debt 5,00,000*
Net operating income	1,00,000	1,00,000	1,00,000
Interest	0	25,000	60,000
Profits for equityholders [*P*]	100,000	75,000	40,000
Cost of equity capital [k_e]	0.13	0.14	0.18
Market value of equity [P/k_e]	7,69,231	5,35,714	2,22,222
Market value of debt	0	2,50,000	5,00,000
Market value of firm [*V*]	7,69,231	7,85,714	7,22,222
Implied k_o[NOI/*V*]	0.1300	0.1273	0.1385

The traditional approach implies that at moderate levels of debt, the total value of the firm would increase and the overall cost of capital k_o decreases.

The traditional approach implies that as the firm becomes more risky with leverage, although investors raise the equity capitalization rate, k_e, the increase in k_e initially would not completely offset the benefit of using cheaper debt funding. As a result, at moderate levels of debt, the total valuation and share prices increase and the overall cost of capital k_o decreases.

However, as the proportion of debt increases, beyond some point k_e rises at an increasing rate with leverage. Moreover, k_d also may rise beyond some point. The optimal capital structure is the point at which k_o is the minimum. This can be shown pictorially in Figure 12.3.

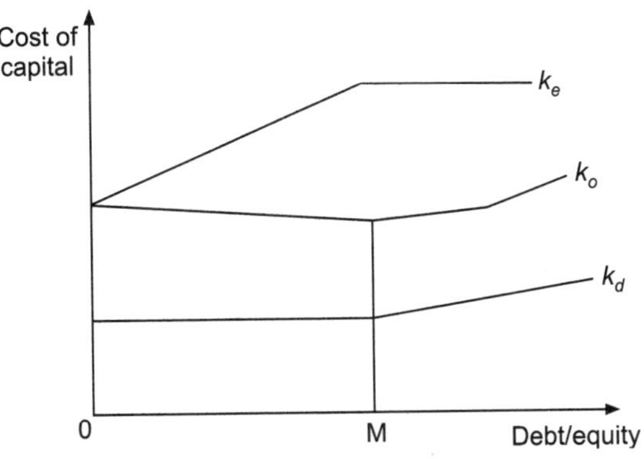

FIGURE 12.3 Behaviour of k_e, k_d and k_o under the traditional appraoch.

The horizontal x-axis shows the increasing debt/equity ratio while the y-axis shows the cost of capital in percentage. Point 'M' indicates the optimal capital structure. As the graph shows, as long as the firm has a low to moderate proportion of debt financing relative to equity in its capital structure, the advantages could exceed the disadvantages and the firm may be able to reduce the overall cost of capital. However, if the firm goes on increasing the proportion of debt financing relative to equity, the disadvantages would outweigh the advantages and the overall cost of capital starts rising.

At very high levels of leverage, the perceived high financial risk alarms the equity investors as well as debt providers who demand higher risk premium, thus raising the k_e, k_d and k_o.

At very high levels of leverage, the perceived high financial risk alarms the equity investors who would penalize the stock by either selling off (thereby putting a pressure on market values) or demanding higher risk premium to remain invested; k_e would rise steeply in such a situation. Beyond a reasonable limit, even the debt suppliers may ask for penalty interest rates on existing and additional borrowings by the company, so k_d too rises beyond a point. As a result of the rising cost of equity as well as debt beyond point 'M' on the graph, the overall cost of capital k_o also starts rising. Thus, firms should try to avoid this type of debt trap and adopt a judicious mix of debt and equity funds to keep its overall cost of capital low and maximize the value of the firm.

12.6 The Modigliani–Miller Approach

MM approach is the most debated theory of capital structure. MM advocate the net operating income approach and offer behavioral justification to prove why the overall cost of capital (k_o) would remain constant at all degrees of leverage.

MM make the following assumptions:

1. Capital markets are perfect and information is readily available.
2. There are no transaction costs, and all securities are infinitely divisible.
3. Both the firm as well as individual investors can borrow at the same interest rate
4. Investors have similar expectations and behave rationally.
5. There are no income taxes.

Using the Net Operating Income approach, MM draw three main conclusions:

1. The total market value of a firm is determined by capitalizing the expected stream of 'operating earnings' at a discount rate appropriate for the business risk of the firm. The capital structure is irrelevant to the valuation of the firm, and hence, the market value of the firm and its cost of capital are independent of its capital structure.
2. If the firm uses debt capital, the k_e increases in a way to exactly offset the use of cheaper debt funds.

MM assumptions include perfect capital markets, no transaction costs, rational investors and no income taxes.

3. The cut-off rate for investment purpose is completely independent of the way in which an investment is financed. In other words, the required rate of return used for evaluating investment projects would be determined by the business risk of the firm and would not be affected by the capital structure used.

MM argue that the total risk for all security holders (the debt holders *plus* equity holders) is not altered by change in its capital structure. Therefore, the total value of the firm must be the same regardless of its financing-mix.

12.6.1 Arbitrage Support of MM Theory

Arbitrage acts in a way to preclude two shares that are perfect substitutes from selling at different prices in the same market.

The critical support for MM's hypothesis is the presence of arbitrage in the capital market. Arbitrage refers to trading in shares in order to make a profit from differences in prices of the same share in two different markets or two similar shares in the same market. Arbitrage acts in a way to preclude two shares that are perfect substitutes from selling at different prices in the same market.

Assume two firms A and B have same net operating income of ₹50,000, and are similar to each other in all respects except that firm A does not have any debt while firm B has ₹2,50,000 of debt @8% interest. Traditional approach would give the results as in Table 12.4, assuming k_e for firm A is 12% and that for firm B is 13%.

TABLE 12.4
Financial leverage and value of the firm

	Firm A	*Firm B*
	Debt Nil	***Debt 2,50,000***
Net Operating Income [O]	50,000	50,000
Interest @ 8%	0	20,000
Profits for Equityholders [P]	50,000	30,000
Cost of equity, k_e	0.12	0.13
Market value of equity [$E = P/k_e$]	4,16,667	2,30,769
Market value of debt	0	2,50,000
Market value of firm ($D + E$)	4,16,667	4,80,769
Implied k_o [$O \div (D+E)$]	0.1200	0.1040

Thus, according to the traditional theory, the levered firm B (with debt) would have a higher market value and a lower overall cost of capital than firm A (without debt). This position, according to MM, cannot continue for long, because arbitrage will set in to drive the total value of the two firms equal to each other.

MM approach assumes that both the firm as well as individual investors can borrow at the same interest rate. To illustrate how arbitrage works, assume investor X owns 1% equity shares of firm B. He sells his equity for ₹2,307.69 (1% of ₹2,30,769), and takes a personal loan equal to 1% of firm B's loan that is 2,500.

Thus, the total amount available with him would now be ₹2,307.69 + 2,500 = 4,807.69.

Out of this amount he uses ₹4,166.67 to buy 1% equity of firm A that would entitle him to get a return of ₹500 (1% of ₹50,000, the operating income of firm A). Out of his income of ₹500, he must pay the interest on loan taken by him = 8% × 2,500 = 200 leaving him with a net return of ₹300 which he was getting in firm B. So what is his gain from the arbitrage?

His gain from arbitrage can be seen in two alternate ways:

(i) He is able to get the same income as before but on a smaller investment base. Out of ₹4,807.69 available with him, he invested ₹4,166.67 in firm A; so he has a surplus fund of ₹641.02 which he can spend anyway he likes. He can invest this amount to get an additional income.

(ii) If he had invested the entire amount of ₹4,807.69 in shares of firm A, he would get more than 1% shareholding and obviously stands to gain.

In other words, by substituting corporate leverage by personal leverage, the investor is able to get same return on lower investment (or higher return by investing the entire amount). So he would like to sell off 'B' shares and invest in 'A' shares.

When all investors follow the move to sell firm B shares and buy firm A shares, the share price of firm A will rise and 'B' share will fall until there is equilibrium so that the value of the two firms is equal and no more arbitrage would be possible.

12.6.2 Assessment of the MM Approach

Modigliani and Miller theory on capital structure is based on several assumptions, which limit its application in real life. They explore the relationship between capital structure, cost of capital and the value of the firm in the context of perfect capital markets having no income taxes, no transaction costs, perfect availability of information and availability of debt at same cost to both the company and the individual investors so that, when necessary, the individual investors can substitute corporate leverage with personal leverage.

The MM theory implies that there is no optimal capital structure. However, later they agreed that the income tax benefit on interest cost can reduce k_o and increase value of firm.

On the basis on these assumptions, the MM theory states that in a perfect capital market, as a firm uses more of cheaper debt, the increase in financial risk would cause a corresponding increase in the cost of equity exactly to completely wipe out any advantage of cheaper debt; therefore, the overall cost of capital remains constant at all degrees of leverage. The MM theory, thus, implies that there is no optimal capital structure; the market values the Net Operating Earnings of the firm, and how a firm is financed would be irrelevant to its overall cost of capital as well as the firm's value.

12.6.3 Tax-Shield and MM's Modification

In the revised version of their proposition, MM agreed that the income tax benefit on interest expenses may have some positive impact on the firm's value. MM conceded that when income taxes are involved, the after-tax cost of debt could become substantially lower and k_o can also decline with an increase in financial leverage or gearing.

Other assumptions of MM have also been criticized as unrealistic, but the debate continues.

12.7 The Pecking Order Theory

The Pecking order theory proposed by Donaldson suggests that in real life, managers might follow a priority order of financing sources which might be based more on factors such as floatation costs, signalling effect and the management's dislike of interference by suppliers of capital, rather than seeking an optimal capital structure that would maximize the value of the firm. In other words, managements may prefer such funding sources that can be raised with least floatation costs and would have least scrutiny by suppliers of capital regarding how and why the company invested the capital the way it did.

Thus, as far as possible, managers might prefer to finance investment projects with such sources that have least floatation costs and minimum possibility of being a threat to the existing management. Accordingly, first preference would be to finance projects using internal sources like retained earnings. For this purpose, management would consider the company's long-term investment plans and set such a dividend-payout policy that leaves maximum internal funds for reinvestment.

In real life, managers might prefer sources of finance with least floatation costs, least interference in management and which convey right signals.

When internally generated funds are inadequate to finance all investment plans and the company must resort to external sources, the company would prefer debt as compared to equity financing. Even while considering debt financing, managers might prefer plain vanilla debt rather than convertible securities (such as convertible bonds) that could later become equity capital. Debt is preferred because it has low floatation costs as compared to issuing new equity shares, and debt suppliers usually are least interfering in the management of the company as long as the company services the debt by timely payment of interest and repays the loan as per the agreed terms.

Next to debt financing in the pecking order would be preference share capital. It was pointed out in an earlier section that preference share capital has several features similar to debt financing, including fixed rate of preference dividend (similar to payment of interest) and redemption of preference share capital (similar to repayment of loans). Due to these similarities, preference share capital would be preferred over equity financing.

As per the pecking order theory, equity shares would be the least preferred source of financing a project because of the higher floatation costs of issuing equity shares, and also because, from the management's perspective, equity holders may be considered as the most demanding and intrusive. Hence, issuing new equity capital may be taken as a source of last resort.

Thus, the pecking order hypothesis seems to imply that companies do not always aim to achieve an optimal capital structure and instead are motivated by other factors in their choice of the financing sources.

The pecking order theory adds new insights to the capital structure decision making. However, a shortcoming of the pecking order theory is that it does not give due importance to the objective of maximizing the market value of the firm or minimizing the cost of capital of the firm.

12.8 The Trade-off Theory

The trade-off theory takes a cue from the MM approach and says that the firm should consider the effect of possible implicit costs attached to debt financing in addition to the explicit cost of interest. The implicit costs of debt financing are the legal and administrative costs associated with possible financial distress and bankruptcy proceedings if the company is unable to service its debt properly. In addition, there are the agency costs that arise due to the debt covenants which the firm is obliged to honor as per the loan agreements.

12.8.1 Costs of Financial Distress

The implicit costs of debt financing include costs of possible financial distress and agency costs.

As we stated in a previous section, the interest payable on borrowed funds becomes a fixed cost that can be a real headache especially in times of recession or downturn in business when product demand, sales and profits plunge but the interest cost would remain unchanged and high. It might become difficult for the firm to service its debt under such circumstances, which would result in loss of goodwill and could lead to legal proceedings by lenders for recovery of loans and accumulated interest.

Several large companies from power, infrastructure and other sectors in India defaulted in debt servicing during 2013–15. Such occurrences are neither pleasant for the defaulting companies nor for the lenders.

It must be mentioned here that in India, there are strict RBI rules that force commercial banks and NBFCs to treat a corporate loan as an NPA (Non-Performing Asset) if the company defaults in regular payment of interest beyond certain time limits. If the default continues for a prolonged period, the bank or other lenders would be forced to move the courts and even confiscate the property, machinery and other assets that were mortgaged as security for the loans taken. Court cases typically may take years to settle during which the company could suffer in a number of ways including the following:

1. **Loss of management time and organizational morale:** The managers who should be busy with strategic planning issues would waste time answering media queries and attending to legal proceedings. The employee morale would also be adversely affected leading to increased staff turnover.

2. **Impounding of productive assets:** Lenders may take possession of the assets that were mortgaged as security for the loans taken, thereby disrupting the company's business.

3. **Losses on distress sale of assets:** A real estate company had to dispose off a prime property worth over a hundred million dollars at almost half the price to settle an over-due loan repayment. Under such circumstances, even selling off the mortgaged assets may not be easy as it would require permission of the court and the lenders.

4. **Legal costs:** The company would incur legal and administrative costs associated with financial distress and bankruptcy proceedings.

12.8.2 Agency Costs

In addition to the cost of interest, debt providers including banks force certain other costs on the borrowers which are known as the agency costs. Such agency costs may be related to loan processing charges, up-front fees, administrative costs or caused by debt covenants.

To protect themselves, banks and other lenders insert certain covenants in the loan agreements that may put operational restrictions on the company.

There exists an agency relationship between the borrowing company and the banks/lenders that provide external financing to the company. Commercial banks are financial intermediaries that use the money belonging to their account holders and depositors to extend corporate loans. In order to protect themselves against unscrupulous borrowers, commercial banks and other lenders insert certain covenants in the loan agreements that may put operational restrictions on the company management. Such covenants may include restrictions on working capital, sale of assets or part of a business, declaration of dividends, appointment of directors and periodical reporting of financial performance.

Such restrictions on the executive actions might adversely affect the managerial efficiency. In addition, the cost of monitoring the usage of the loans and periodical checking/reporting to enforce implementation of the loan covenants are invariably passed on to the borrowers either by enhancing the interest rate payable on the amount of debt or charged separately. Such agency costs increase the effective cost of debt.

Agency costs might be relatively insignificant at lower levels of debt financing as the lenders may not see the need for extensive monitoring of the loan usage. However, at higher levels of financial leverage, the lenders would insist on extensive monitoring that would substantially raise the monitoring and other agency costs and could have a negative effect of the market value of the firm.

12.8.3 Value of the Firm, Taxes and Distress Costs

The value of the levered firm would increase due to the tax-shield on interest charges, but suffer from the possible costs of financial distress and agency costs as follows:

Value of the levered firm = Value of the unlevered firm + Tax-shield on debt financing
– Costs related to financial distress and agency costs

The tax-shield on debt financing would be higher and the cost related to financial distress and agency costs would be lower at low to moderate degree of financial leverage. On the contrary, at extremely high degrees of financial leverage, the costs related to financial distress and agency costs would far exceed the tax advantages on debt financing. Therefore, the firm should try to find that optimal financial leverage which would maintain a balance between the two and maximize the value of the firm.

12.9 The Signalling Theory

The signalling theory suggests that when there is information asymmetry between the company management and outside investors, changes in the capital structure by the management are seen by outsiders as signals about the firm's future prospects. Information asymmetry means that the management has more information about the future profitability and risk of the firm than outside investors. Therefore, investors try to see through corporate actions to get signals about the future prospects of the company.

Signalling theory suggests that financing of new projects by debt sources may be taken as a positive signal, and tapping equity as bad news by investors.

For example, when a company decides to finance a new project by debt sources, it may have a positive 'signalling' effect. Investors believe that management would not issue securities that are under-valued in the existing market conditions. Thus, when a company uses debt sources to finance new investment projects, investors would get a signal that the management considers equity shares to be under-valued currently and that is why the company is going for debt financing rather than issuing new equity shares at prices lower than their intrinsic value.

Another reason why debt financing is taken as a positive signal of better future prospects is the financial discipline that debt financing would impose on the management. Debt funding implies commitment to fixed financial charges, which can be smoothly met only if the project is successful. So when management decides to fund a new project by using debt sources, it is a signal to the investors that the management must be sure of the project success, that is why they have decided to fund it with debt sources, committing themselves to fixed financial charges.

The market might positively react to such signals and the share prices might go up, thereby increasing the market value of the firm. However, it should be noted that often unscrupulous managements may misuse the signal theory and deliberately send false signals to raise the market share prices in the short term, so that they can dispose-off their shareholding at higher prices before the public realizes the hoax signal. Therefore, investors should take such signals seriously only if they come from managements with long history of good governance and credibility.

To conclude, it is highly desirable that companies should consider all relevant factors before finalizing their capital structure.

12.10 Target Capital Structure and Recapitalization

The different theories of capital structure discussed so far assumed that the company was able to change its debt/equity ratio instantly. Such recapitalization in real life would, of course, have to go through certain steps. Suppose the company decided to replace some equity with more debt, then the required steps would be: (i) Decide how much more debt should be raised; (ii) Determine the effect of additional debt on the total value of the firm and the overall cost of capital (WACC), (iii) Since the amount of additional debt raised would be utilized to repurchase equity shares, we must determine the price at which the company should offer to repurchase shares and the number of shares that can be repurchased, and finally (iv) Determine the post-repurchase market value of equity, debt and the total value of the firm.

12.10.1 Target Capital Structure

Before the company goes for any recapitalization (that is, replacing debt with equity or replacing equity with debt), it would like to examine the effect of different degrees of debt/equity (or capital structures) on the value of the firm and overall cost of capital. The capital structure that promises to maximize the value of the firm and minimize the overall cost of capital would be preferred as the target capital structure.

Before we illustrate the recapitalization, it would be better to bring in the effect of taxes on the cost of capital. Modigliani–Miller also agreed that the tax-shield on interest payments could substantially reduce the after tax cost of debt that can help in bringing down the overall cost of capital. Considering taxes, the overall cost of capital k_o (commonly called WACC) can be calculated as follows:

$$k_o = k_d \left(\frac{D}{D+E}\right)(1 - t) + k_e\left(\frac{E}{D+E}\right)$$

Assume a company has issued debt of ₹5,000, equity capital of ₹5,000, its cost of equity is 20%, cost of debt (pre-tax) is 15% and the income tax rate is 40%, then the overall or Weighted Average Cost of Capital (WACC) would be:

Considering taxes, the overall cost of capital k_o can be calculated as follows:

$$k_o = k_d\left(\frac{D}{D+E}\right)(1 - t) + k_e\left(\frac{E}{D+E}\right)$$

$$k_o = 15\%\left(\frac{5000}{5000+5000}\right)(1-0.4) + 20\%\left(\frac{5000}{5000+5000}\right)$$
$$= 15\%\ (0.50)\ 0.6 + 20\%\ (0.50) = 14.50\%$$

The process of recapitalization and the relationship between capital structure, value of the firm and the weighted average cost of capital is explained with the help of the following example:

EXAMPLE 12.1 Recapitalization and Change in D/E

The following information is available for Infinity Company:

Existing situation before recapitalization:

Net operating income (EBIT)	: ₹90,000
Equity shares	: 10,000
Market price per equity share	₹40
Current debt at 10% interest (before tax)	: ₹100,000
Cost of equity	: 14%
Income tax rate	: 30%

After considering the WACC at different degrees of debt/equity ratio, the management has determined that a capital structure of 60% debt and 40% equity would yield the lowest overall Weighted Average Cost of Capital (WACC) and has accepted the same as the target debt/equity ratio. Therefore the company has decided to issue perpetual bonds to raise an amount required to repurchase equity shares in such a way that after the recapitalization, the debt/equity ratio should remain equal to the target ratio of 60% debt and 40% equity. At the new ratio of debt/equity, the cost of entire debt would rise to 11% (before tax) per annum and the cost of equity would increase to 16.2% due to increased leverage. Assume the company does not expect any growth in its annual earnings, which are expected to remain constant per annum, and all earnings are distributed as dividends.

(a) Calculate the current market value of the firm.
(b) Calculate the current (i) after tax cost of debt, and (ii) after tax WACC.
(c) Determine the additional amount of debt to be issued.
(d) Compute the repurchase price per share and determine the number of shares to be repurchased.
(e) How many shares would remain outstanding after the recapitalization?
(f) What would be the market value of the debt, equity and the firm after the above recapitalization has been achieved?

Solution:

(a) **Calculate the current market value of the firm.**

	Current Position
Net Operating Income	90,000
Interest @10%	10,000
Profit before Taxes	80,000
Taxes 30%	24,000
Profits for Equityholders [*P*]	56,000
Cost of equity capital, k_e	0.14
Market value of equity [P/k_e] [10,000 shares @ ₹40 per share]	4,00,000
Market value of debt	1,00,000
Market value of firm [*V*]	5,00,000

As the table shows:

- Value of debt = ₹1,00,000.
- Value of equity = ₹40 × 10,000 = 4,00,000.
- Value of equity can also be checked as = P/k_e = 56,000/0.14 = 4,00,000.
- Value of the firm when there is no growth = Value of debt + Value of equity = ₹1,00,000 + 4,00,000 = 5,00,000.
- The firm's current capital structure is: 20% Debt (1,00,000 ÷ 5,00,000) and 80% equity (4,00,000 ÷ 5,00,000).

(b) **Calculate the current (i) after tax cost of debt, and (ii) after tax WACC.**

Particulars	*Details*	*Cost %*
Interest before tax	10,000	
Debt (*D*)	1,00,000	
Before tax cost of debt	(10,000/1,00,000) × 100 =	10%
After tax cost of debt (k_d)	10% × (1 – 0.3) =	7%
Profit available for equity holders after tax	56,000	
Market value of equity (*E*)	4,00,000	
Cost of equity (after tax) (k_e)	56,000/4,00,000	0.14
Market value of firm (*D* + *E*)	1,00,000 + 4,00,000 = 5,00,000	
Proportion of debt [w_d]	1,00,000/5,00,000 =	0.20
Proportion of equity [w_e]	4,00,000/5,00,000 =	0.80
WACC = (w_d × k_d) + (w_e × k_e)	(0.20 × 7%) + (0.80 × 0.14)	12.6%
Before tax overall cost*	90,000/5,00,000 =	18.00%

Note: *Before tax overall cost can also be computed as = 12.6% × 100/(100 – 30) = 12.6% × 100/70 = 18%.

(c) **Determine the additional amount of debt to be issued.**

To compute the additional amount of debt to be issued, we need to take the following steps:

(i) Calculate the new WACC before tax:

$$\text{WACC after tax, } k_o = k_d\left(\frac{D}{D+E}\right)(1 - t) + k_e\left(\frac{E}{D+E}\right)$$

$$= (11\% \times 0.7 \times 0.6) + (16.2\% \times 0.4)$$

$$= 4.62\ \% + 6.48\% = 11.1\%$$

WACC before tax = 11.1 × 100/70 = 15.857%

(ii) Value of the firm at the new WACC:

V = NOI/WACC before tax = 90,000/0.15857 = ₹5,67,567.57

(iii) If the new value of the firm is ₹5,67,567.57, and the new debt has to be 60% of the value of the firm, then:
Total debt required = ₹5,67,567.57 × 60% = 3,40,540.54
Less: Old debt = ₹1,00,000
Hence, new additional debt required = 3,40,540.54 – 1,00,000 = 2,40,540.54.
Note that this additional amount of ₹2,40,540.54 debt raised will be used to repurchase equity shares. But what would be the repurchase price and how many shares would be repurchased?

(d) **Compute the repurchase price per share and determine the number of shares to be repurchased.**

New value of the firm	= 5,67,568
Less: Old debt	= –1,00,000
New value of equity before repurchase	= 4,67,568
Number of existing shares	= 10,000
New equity price per share =4,67,568/10,000	= 46.7568

Since the total amount available for repurchase of shares is ₹2,40,540.54, and the repurchase price to be offered is ₹46.7568, the number of shares that can be repurchased = ₹2,40,540.54 ÷ ₹46.7568 = 5,144.50 shares (assuming a fraction of share is allowed.)

(e) **How many shares would remain outstanding after the recapitalization?**
Number of shares remaining outstanding after the recapitalization = 10,000 – 5,144.50 = 4,855.50 shares.

(f) **What would be the market value of the debt, equity and the firm after the above recapitalization has been achieved?**
Presenting all computations together, we get the following picture before and after the recapitalization:

	***Prior* Debt = 20%**	***Post* Debt = 60%**
Net Operating Income	90,000	90,000
Interest	10,000	37,459.49
Profit before tax	80,000	52,540.51
Taxes 30%	24,000	15,762.15
Profits for Equity holders [p]	56,000	36,778.36
Cost of equity capital, k_e	0.14	0.162
Market value of equity [P/k_e]	4,00,000.00	2,27,027.20
Market value of debt	1,00,000.00	3,40,540.80
Market value of firm [V]	5,00,000.00	5,67,568.00
Implied k_o % [NOI/V] [before tax]	18.000	15.857

	After tax	**Before tax**
$k_o = [k_d \times D/(D+E)] + k_e \times E/(D + E)$		
Existing k_o = (10% × 0.7 × 0.2) + 14% × 0.8	0.12600	0.18000
After change in D/E ratio:		
k_o = (11% × 0.7 × 0.6) + (16.2% × 0.4)	0.11100	0.15857

The market values of debt, equity and the firm after the above recapitalization would be as follows:

- Market value of the debt: ₹3,40,540.80
- Market value of the equity: ₹2,27,027.20 [= 4,855.50 shares @ ₹46.7568]
- Market value of the firm: ₹5,67,568.00.

Thus, in this case, we find that the recapitalization or a change in the financial leverage has enhanced the value of equity and the value of the firm, as well as reduced the weighted average cost of capital.

12.11 CAPM, Capital Structure and Cost of Capital

In this section, we intend to discuss the relationship between optimal capital structure, CAPM (Capital Asset Pricing Model) and the overall cost of capital of the firm. The CAPM model was covered in a separate chapter, and it would be appropriate here to review the same before we proceed to explore its relationship with financial leverage.

12.11.1 Review of CAPM, BETA and the Cost of Capital

We discussed in the chapter on CAPM (Capital Asset Pricing Model) that, if certain assumptions hold good, the investors' expected rate of return on investment in a specific share 'x' could be estimated as follows:

$$R_x = R_F + (R_M - R_F)\beta_x$$

where,

- R_x is the expected rate of return on investment in share-x.
- R_F is the risk-free rate of return (such as the return on Government securities);
- R_M is the expected return on the market portfolio of equity shares during a period, say one year. The 'market portfolio of equity shares' in India could be represented by the NSE 50 share index or the BSE 30 share index; and
- β_x is the beta coefficient (or beta factor) for share-x. The Beta measures the sensitivity of the returns on investment in share-x to the returns on the market portfolio of equity shares. A beta equal to one would mean that the investment in specific share-x is only as risky as the market portfolio as a whole, while a beta greater than one would signify that investment in individual share-x is more risky than the investment in the market portfolio of shares, and hence the investor would expect a higher risk premium to motivate him to put his money in share-x. The opposite would be true if the beta of a specific share was lower than one.

CAPM revision: the investors' expected rate of return on investment in a specific share 'x' could be estimated as follows: $R_x = R_F + (R_M - R_F)\beta_x$

To illustrate, assume 'x' share's beta is 1.30, the risk-free rate of return (R_F) is 7.0% and the expected overall return on the market portfolio during a year is 16%, then:

$$R_x = R_F + (R_M - R_F)\beta_x$$
$$= 7\% + (16\% - 7\%)\ 1.30 = 18.7\ \%$$

Accordingly, investors would expect a return of 18.7% for investing in share-x as against 16% return for investing in the market portfolio of shares, because share-x is more risky as reflected by a beta of greater than one.

The Premium for Market Risk (Pmr)

Note that the $R_M–R_F$ expresses the 'premium for market risk (Pmr)', the premium or excess return an investor would require for investing in the market portfolio of shares rather than investing in the 'risk-free' Government securities. Therefore, the above equation of expected return on share-x can be written as follows:

$$R_x = R_F + (\text{Pmr})\beta_x$$

where, Pmr = $(R_M - R_F)$. Using the previous example, we can calculate the expected return on share-x as follows:

The CAPM equation of expected return on share-x can be written as: $R_x = R_F + (Pmr)b_x$, where $Pmr = (R_M - R_F)$.

Step 1 Pmr = $(R_M - R_F)$ = 16% – 7% = 9%.

Step 2 $R_x = R_F + (\text{Pmr})\beta_x$

= 7% + (9%) 1.30 = 18.7%

Expected Return Versus Cost of Equity

The expected return on share investments from the investor's perspective would be the cost of equity from the company's point-of-view, because it is the company that would be expected to earn such profits from business operations that would satisfy the investors, failing which the share prices would fall and shareholders' wealth would be adversely affected.

Cost of Equity Versus Cost of Capital

Once the cost of equity has been determined using the CAPM model, the Weighted Average Cost of Capital (WACC) can be computed as explained in a previous section. Note that the cost of equity is mostly stated on after-tax basis, but the cost of debt may be given on pre-tax basis, and should be adjusted for the tax-shield on interest before calculating the WACC (Weighted Average Cost of Capital) as follows:

$$\text{WACC after tax} = k_d\left(\frac{D}{D+E}\right)(1 - t) + k_e\left(\frac{E}{D+E}\right)$$

Continuing with the previous example where we determined the k_e = 18.7% using CAPM, assume the company's debt:equity ratio is 60:40, cost of debt (pre-tax) is 10%, and the applicable income tax rate is 30%, the overall cost of capital would be:

$$\text{WACC} = 10\% \ (1 - 0.3)(0.60) + 18.7\ (0.40)$$
$$= 4.2 + 7.48 = 11.68\%.$$

We are now ready to discuss the relationship between CAPM and the financial leverage.

12.11.2 Levered and Unlevered Beta (β)

Investors in levered firms (using debt financing) have to suffer from more risk as compared to firms that are unlevered and do not have debt financing in their capital structure.

Total risk may be classified into business risk and financial risk. The business risk relates to the success or failure of the firm's products in the market place and arises due to factors such as the variability in demand for the firm's products and market competition. On the other hand, financial risk relates to the possibility that in adverse business conditions, the firm may not be able to service its fixed interest payments or repay loans timely, which may lead to possible insolvency.

Since investors in levered firms suffer from more risk as compared to unlevered firms, the levered beta would be greater than unlevered beta.

We have seen that as per the CAPM model, the beta (β) factor indicates a specific share's riskiness in relation to the market as a whole. In other words, the greater the beta (β) factor, more risky would be the share concerned.

Relating the beta (β) factor to financial leverage, the beta of the levered firm (called the levered beta, β_L) would be greater than the beta of the unlevered firm (called the unlevered beta, β_U). This is because, as explained above, the levered firm is more risky than the unlevered firm. In general, higher the degree of debt proportion in the capital structure, greater would be the firm's beta factor (also called beta coefficient).

The relationship between levered and unlevered beta: $\beta_L = \beta_U [1 + (1 - t)(D/E)]$ where, b_L is levered beta, β_U is unlevered beta.

The relationship between levered and unlevered beta may be expressed as follows:

$$\beta_L = \beta_U[1+ (1-t)\ (D/E)]$$

where, β_L is levered beta, β_U is unlevered beta, 't' is the income tax rate applicable to the firm, 'D' is the market value of debt outstanding and 'E' is the market value of equity capital.

Conversely, if levered beta β_L is known, the unlevered beta β_U can be computed as follows;

$$\beta_U = \beta_L \div [1 + (1 - t)\ (D/E)]$$

The above equations were first introduced by Robert S. Hamada (1969) and are accordingly referred to as the Hamada equations.

EXAMPLE 12.2 Assume Zen Company's current capital structure comprises of 10% debt and 90% equity capital and the firm's beta is 1.30. Income tax rate applicable to the firm is 30%.

(a) What would be the unlevered beta of the firm?
(b) Estimate the firm's beta at debt levels of 20%, 40%, 60% and 80% of the market value of the firm.

Solution:

(a) Unlevered beta calculation:

$$\beta_U = \beta_L \div [1 + (1 - t)(D/E)]$$
$$= 1.30 \div [1 + (0.7)\ (10/90)]$$
$$= 1.30 \div [1 + (0.7)\ (0.1111)]$$
$$= 1.30 \div 1.0778 = 1.2062$$

(b) (i) **Levered beta at 20% debt financing:**

$$\beta_L = \beta_U[1+(1 - t)(D/E)]$$
$$= 1.2062[1 + (1-0.3)\ (20/80)]$$
$$= 1.2062\ (1.175) = 1.417$$

(ii) **Levered beta at 40% debt financing:**

$$= 1.2062[1 + (1-0.3)\ (40/60)]$$
$$= 1.2062(1.4667) = 1.769$$

The table below shows calculation of the levered beta (and its components) at different levels of debt financing in the firm's capital structure:

	Percentage of Value of the Firm					
Debt %	0	10	20	40	60	80
Equity %	100	90	80	60	40	20
Debt ÷ Equity	0	0.111	0.250	0.667	1.500	4.000
(D/E) (1 – 0.3)	0	0.078	0.175	0.467	1.050	2.800
1+[(D/E)(1 – 0.3)]	1	1.078	1.175	1.467	2.050	3.800
Unlevered beta β_U	1.2062					
Levered beta $\beta_L = \beta_U[1 + (1-t)(D/E)]$		1.300	1.417	1.769	2.473	4.584

As the table shows, the levered beta β_L will be 2.473 if debt forms 60% of the firm and could rise to as high as 4.584 at debt level of 80% in the firm's capital structure.

12.11.3 Financial Leverage and Overall Cost of Capital

As the beta of a levered firm increases, the cost of equity capital of the firm would also go up because investors would want additional risk premium for the increased risk.

Table 12.5 shows the cost of equity at different levels of debt financing in the firm:

TABLE 12.5 Levered Beta and k_e

	Percentage of Value of the Firm					
Debt Portion %	0	10	20	30	40	60
Equity Portion %	100	90	80	70	60	40
Debt ÷ Equity	0	0.111	0.250	0.429	0.667	1.500
(D/E) (1 – 0.3)	0	0.078	0.175	0.300	0.467	1.050
$1+[(D/E)(1-0.3)]$	1	1.078	1.175	1.300	1.467	2.050
Unlevered beta β_U	1.2062					
$\beta_L = \beta_U[1 + (1-t)(D/E)]$		1.300	1.417	1.568	1.769	2.473
$k_e = 7\% + 9(\beta_L)$	17.856	18.700	19.756	21.113	22.922	29.257

As the table shows, due to increasing value of the beta, cost of equity k_e rises sharply to 29.25 % as debt level rises to 60% of the value of the firm.

The rate of interest on debt funding might also increase at higher proportions of debt financing in relation to equity. As lenders perceive higher possibility of default in servicing the debt, they would penalize the firm by raising the required return on debt funding provided to the firm.

Assume our illustrative firm Zen Company finds that interest rates would be as given in Table 12.6 (at different levels of debt financing).

TABLE 12.6 Zen Company Interest Rates

	Percentage of Value of the Firm					
Debt %	0	10	20	30	40	60
Cost of Debt (k_d)	0	10	10.25	10.5	11	14

Putting all available information together, we find the overall cost of capital at different debt-equity ratio would behave as shown by Table 12.7.

TABLE 12.7 Debt-equity Ratio

	Percentage of Value of the Firm					
Debt %	0	10	20	30	40	60
Equity %	100	90	80	70	60	40
Debt ÷ Equity	0	0.111	0.250	0.429	0.667	1.500
(D/E) (1 – 0.3)	0	0.078	0.175	0.300	0.467	1.050
$1+[(D/E)(1-0.3)]$	1	1.078	1.175	1.300	1.467	2.050
Unlevered beta β_U	1.2062					
$\beta_L = \beta_U[1 + (1-t)(D/E)]$		1.300	1.417	1.568	1.769	2.473
$k_e = 7\% + 9(\beta_L)$	17.8558	18.7001	19.7556	21.1125	22.9218	29.2544
Cost of debt, k_d	0	10	10.25	10.5	11	14
k_d after tax	0	7	7.175	7.35	7.7	9.8
$k_o = k_e(w_e) + k_d(w_d)$*	17.86	17.53	17.24	16.98	16.83	17.58

* 'w_d' is the relative weight (proportion) of debt, and 'w_e' is the relative weight (proportion) of equity in the capital structure.

The computations indicate that the overall cost of capital WACC would decline with initial introduction of debt financing, reaching a lowest point at a debt level of 40%, but after that would start rising again. Therefore, under the given situation, the optimal capital structure would be at a debt portion of 40% as it would minimize the overall cost of capital.

You may like to answer the following question yourself before checking with the suggested answer.

EXAMPLE 12.3 Younger Company's current capital structure comprises of 20% debt and 80% equity capital and the current beta on its shares is 1.25. The risk free rate of return is 7%, the market risk premium is 6% and the income tax rate applicable to the firm is 30%. The company is considering changing its capital structure to finance 50% with debt and 50% with equity.

(a) Calculate the company's current cost of equity.
(b) Calculate the company's unlevered beta.
(c) Calculate the new beta at 50% debt level, and
(d) Determine the company's new cost of equity.

Solution:

(a) **Calculating the company's current cost of equity using CAPM model:**

$$R_x = R_F + (\text{Pmr})\beta_x$$
$$= 7\% + (6)(1.25)$$
$$= 14.5\%$$

The current beta is levered beta of 1.25 when the firm is levered with 20% debt financing.

(b) **Calculating the company's unlevered beta:**

$$\beta_U = \beta_L \div [1 + (1-t)\ (D/E)]$$
$$= 1.25 \div [1 + (0.7)\ (20/80)]$$
$$= 1.25 \div [1 + (0.7)\ (0.25)]$$
$$= 1.25 \div 1.175 = 1.064$$

(c) **Calculating the new beta at 50% debt level:**

$$\beta_L = \beta_U[1 + (1-t)\ (D/E)]$$
$$= 1.064\ [1 + (1 - 0.3)\ (50/50)]$$
$$= 1.064\ (1.70) = 1.809$$

(d) **Determining the company's new cost of equity using the CAPM model:**

$$R_x = R_f + (\text{Pmr})\beta_x$$
$$= 7\% + (6)(1.809)$$
$$= 17.85\%$$

Thus, if the company raises debt financing to 50%, its cost of equity would rise to 17.85%. The table below summarizes the calculated unlevered beta, levered beta at 50% debt level, and the cost of equity:

	Percentage of Value of the Firm		
Debt %	0	20	50
Equity %	100	80	50
Debt ÷ Equity	0	0.250	1.000
(D/E) (1 – 0.3)	0	0.175	0.700
1+[(D/E)(1 – 0.3)]	1	1.175	1.700
Unlevered beta β_U	1.064		
$\beta_L = \beta_U[1+(1-t)(D/E)]$		1.250	1.809
$k_e = 7\% + 6(\beta_L)$	13.384	14.50	17.85

Researchable Issues

Faculty members, students and research scholars may like to consider the following selected issues for further research and case writing.

- Capital structure practices and share prices: evidence from the Indian markets.
- Capital structure practices and corporate governance.
- Signalling theory and investor exploitation.
- Capital structure, dividend policy and value of the firm.
- The irrelevance of MM approach: Evidence from an emerging market.

References

Brealey, Richard A., Myers, Stewart C., Allen, Franklin, *Principles of Corporate Finance*, 10th ed., 2011, McGraw-Hill/Irwin, New York.

Gitman, Lawrence J., *Principles of Managerial Finance*, 11th ed., Pearson, Addison Wesley, Boston, 2006.

Hamada, Robert S., "Portfolio Analysis, Market Equilibrium, and Corporate Finance", *Journal of Finance*, March 1969, pp. 13–31.

Horne, Van, James, C., *Financial Management and Policy*, 12th ed., Prentice-Hall of India, Delhi, 2005.

Levy, H. and Sarnat M., *Capital Investment and Financial Decisions*, Prentice Hall.

Modigliani, Franco and Miller, Merton H., "Corporate Income Taxes and the Cost of Capital: A Correction", *American Economic Review*, Vol. 63, June 1963, pp. 433–42.

Modigliani, Franco and Miller, Merton H., "The Cost of Capital, Corporation Finance and the Theory of Investment", *American Economic Review*, Vol. 48, June 1958, pp. 261–97.

Myers, Stewart C. and Majluf, Nicholas S., "Corporate Financing and Investment Decisions When Firms Have Information That Investor Do Not Have", *Journal of Financial Economics*, Vol. 13, June 1984, pp. 187–222.

Points to Remember

Capital structure: The term capital structure refers to the manner in which a firm has financed its business operations by combining different sources of funds.

Assumptions: The theories of capital structure are based on several assumptions including (i) the debt to equity ratio can be changed instantly, (ii) the company's operating earnings remain constant in perpetuity, and (iii) the company pays out all of its earnings as dividends.

Net Income Approach is based on the following assumptions (i) Cost of equity (k_e) is assumed remains constant at all levels of debt/equity ratio, (ii) Cost of debt (k_d) remains constant at all levels of debt/equity ratio, (iii) any amount of debt is available at the same interest rate, and (iv) no income taxes. Then the optimal capital structure will be the one that uses maximum of debt and least amount of equity.

Net Operating Income Approach assumes that the overall cost of capital (k_o) and cost of debt (k_d) would remain constant at all levels of debt/equity ratio. It says that any capital structure will be as good as any other because any advantage of cheaper debt is exactly offset by an equivalent rise in k_e.

The Traditional Approach says that a firm can increase its total market value through judicious mix of debt and equity funds, and the optimal capital structure will be the one that minimizes k_o and maximizes the value of firm.

M-M advocate the Net Operating Income approach and argue that arbitrage would force the overall cost of capital (k_o) to remain constant at all degrees of leverage. Arbitrage acts in a way to preclude two shares that are perfect substitutes from selling at different prices in the same market.

The Pecking order theory suggests that in real life, managers might prefer to finance investment projects with such sources that have least floatation costs and cause least interference in the management. Accordingly, first preference would be to finance projects using internal sources like retained earnings.

The Trade-off theory says that the firm should consider the effect of possible implicit costs attached to debt financing such as the legal and administrative costs associated with possible financial distress and bankruptcy proceedings if the company is unable to service its debt properly. In addition, there are the agency costs that arise due to the debt covenants which the firm is obliged to honour as per the loan agreements.

Target capital structure: Before the company decides on its capital structure, it would like to examine the effect of different degrees of debt/equity on the value of the firm and overall cost of capital. The capital structure that promises to maximize the value of the firm and minimize the cost of capital would be chosen as the target capital structure.

Levered and unlevered beta: The beta of a firm with debt financing (called the levered beta, β_L) would be greater than the beta of a firm without debt financing (called the unlevered beta, β_U). This is because the levered firm is more risky than the unlevered firm. In general, higher the degree of debt proportion in the capital structure, greater would be the firm's beta.

Questions

1. Discuss the pros and cons of debt and equity financing.
2. Explain the formula to calculate the cost of debt, equity and WACC after taxes. Illustrate their calculations using suitable numerical examples.
3. Discuss the main assumptions, conclusions and weaknesses of the net income approach to capital structure.
4. Critically examine the assumptions and conclusions of the MM approach to capital structure. Using a suitable numerical example show how the arbitrage works.
5. Explain the pecking order theory and discuss its advantages and disadvantages.
6. Explain the meaning of optimal capital structure. Discuss and illustrate the main theory that advocates the idea of optimal capital structure.
7. Differentiate between levered and unlevered betas, and illustrate their calculations using suitable numerical examples.
8. Discuss the main assumptions, conclusions and weaknesses of the net operating income approach to capital structure.
9. Discuss the main assumptions and conclusions of the traditional approach to capital structure.
10. With reference to the trade-off theory, explain the costs of distress and agency costs. What are the implications of the trade off theory for an optimal capital structure?

Multiple Choice Questions

1. The Net Operating Income (NOI) approach to capital structure assumes that:
   (a) The cost of debt and equity remain constant at all degrees of leverage.
   (b) The overall cost of capital remains constant at all degrees of leverage.
   (c) The dividends per share grow at a constant rate per annum.
   (d) None of the above.
2. ABC has a Net Operating Income of ₹10,000, and any amount of debt is available at 10%. Cost of equity is constant at 15%. What would be the total value of the firm at a debt level of ₹25,000?
   (a) ₹75,000 (b) ₹55,000
   (c) ₹40,000 (d) None of the above
3. According to the traditional theory of capital structure, the overall cost of capital might decrease to a low level as the firm _______ debt financing in proportion to equity. At some point beyond the optimal level, the overall cost of capital increases as the amount of debt _______.
   (a) Decreases; Increases. (b) Decreases; Decreases.
   (c) Increases; Increases. (d) Increases; Decreases.
4. Which of the following approaches to capital structure do Modigliani–Miller advocate?
   (a) The Net Income approach (b) The Traditional approach
   (c) The net operating income approach (d) None of the above.
5. According to the Pecking order theory, managers are likely to follow the following priority order of financing sources:
   (a) First debt, second retained earnings and lastly equity.
   (b) First retained earnings, second debt and lastly equity.
   (c) First equity, second debt and lastly retained earnings.
   (d) All sources in equal proportions.
6. A firm's current capital structure comprises of 20% debt and 80% equity capital and the income tax rate applicable to the firm is 30%. If the firm's current beta is 1.30 what would be the unlevered beta of the firm?
   (a) 1.106 (b) 1.175
   (c) 1.307 (d) None of the above
7. A firm's current capital structure comprises of zero debt and 100% equity capital and the income tax rate applicable to the firm is 30%. If the firm's current beta is 1.12 what would be the levered beta of the firm at a capital structure of 60% debt and 40% equity?
   (a) 1.129 (b) 2.031
   (c) 2.296 (d) None of the above

Self-Test Questions

1. **Net Income Approach:** The following information is available about a firm:
   - The firm's annual net operating income (NOI) is ₹1,00,000.
   - Its cost of equity (k_e) is 15%, and it remains constant at all degrees of debt/equity.
   - Its cost of debt (k_d) is 10% and any amount of debt is available at the same interest rate. Income taxes are assumed to be nil.

Using the net income approach:

(a) what would be the value of firm and its overall cost of capital (k_o), if its capital structure included
(i) debt = nil, (ii) debt = ₹2,50,000 and (iii) debt = ₹5,00,000.

(b) What would be the optimal capital structure that would maximize the value of firm and minimize the overall cost of capital k_o.

2. **Net Operating Income Approach:** The following information is available about a firm: the firm's annual Net Operating Income (NOI) is ₹1,00,000, its overall cost of capital (k_o) is 12.5% and it remains constant at all degrees of debt/equity. Its cost of debt (k_d) is 10% and any amount of debt is available at the same interest rate. Income taxes are assumed to be nil.

   Using the Net Operating Income approach:

   (a) what would be the value of firm and its cost of equity capital (k_e), if its capital structure included
   (i) Debt = nil, (ii) Debt = ₹3,00,000 and (iii) Debt = ₹6,00,000?

   (b) How would you explain the change in k_e at different debt levels?

   (c) What would be the optimal capital structure?

3. **The Traditional Approach:** The following information is available about the Spice Company:
   - Estimated cost of equity k_e = 12% if Debt = Nil; k_e = 13% when debt ₹2,50,000; k_e rises to 18% when debt is increased to ₹5,00,000.
   - Cost of debt k_d: 8% if debt up to ₹2,50,000; above that k_d = 10%.
   - Net Operating Income (NOI): ₹1,00,000 per annum.
   - Income taxes: Nil.

   Using the traditional approach:

   (a) What would be the value of firm and its overall cost of capital (k_o), if its capital structure included
   (i) Debt = nil, (ii) Debt = ₹2,50,000 and (iii) Debt = ₹5,00,000.

   (b) What would be the optimal capital structure that would maximize the value of firm and minimize the overall cost of capital k_o.

4. **MM Theory and Arbitrage:** Assume two firms A and B have same net operating income of ₹80,000 and are similar to each other in all respects except that firm A does not have any debt while firm B has ₹4,00,000 of debt. Cost of equity k_e = 12% for all-equity firm, k_e = 14% for the levered firm. Cost of debt k_d: 6%. Both the firm as well as individual investor can borrow at the same interest rate.

   (a) Using the traditional approach, calculate the value of each firm and its overall cost of capital (k_o),

   (b) Show how arbitrage will work and what would be its effect on the value of the two firms?

5. **Recapitalization and Change in *D/E***

   The following information is available for Vision Company:
   Existing situation before recapitalization:

Net operating income (EBIT)	: ₹66,000
Equity shares	: 10,000
Market price per equity share	: ₹24
Current debt at 10% interest (before tax)	: ₹60,000
Cost of equity	: 15%
Income tax rate	: 40%

After considering the WACC at various degrees of debt/equity ratio, the management has determined that a capital structure of 50% debt and 50% equity would yield the lowest overall (Weighted Average) Cost of Capital (WACC) and has decided this as the target debt/equity ratio. Therefore, the company has decided to issue perpetual bonds to raise an amount required to repurchase equity shares in such a way that after the recapitalization, the debt/equity ratio should remain equal to the target ratio of 50% debt and 50% equity. At the new ratio of debt/equity, the cost of entire debt would rise to 11% (before tax) per annum and the cost of equity would increase to 17% due to increased leverage. Assume the company does not expect any growth in its annual earnings which are expected to remain constant per annum, and all earnings are distributed as dividends.

(a) Calculate the current market value of the firm.
(b) Calculate the current (i) after tax cost of debt, and (ii) after tax WACC.
(c) Determine the additional amount of debt to be issued.
(d) Compute the repurchase price per share and determine the number of shares to be repurchased.
(e) How many shares would remain outstanding after the recapitalization?
(f) What would be the market value of the debt, equity and the firm after the above recapitalization has been achieved?

Problems

1. **Net Income Approach:** The following information is available about a firm:
   - The firm's annual net operating income (NOI) is ₹60,000,
   - Its cost of equity (k_e) is 14% and it remains constant at all degrees of Debt/equity.
   - Its cost of debt (k_d) is 8% and any amount of debt is available at the same interest rate. Income taxes are assumed to be nil.

   Using the Net Income Approach:

   (a) What would be the value of firm and its overall cost of capital (k_o), if its capital structure included (i) Debt = Nil, (ii) Debt = ₹1,50,000 and (iii) Debt = ₹3,00,000.
   (b) What would be the optimal capital structure that would maximize the value of firm and minimize the overall cost of capital k_o.
2. **Net Operating Income Approach:** The following information is available about a firm: the firm's annual net operating income (NOI) is ₹60,000, its overall cost of capital (k_o) is 12% and it remains constant at all degrees of debt/equity. Its cost of debt (k_d) is 8% and any amount of debt is available at the same interest rate. Income taxes are assumed to be nil.

   Using the Net Operating Income approach:

   (a) What would be the value of firm and its cost of equity capital (k_e), if its capital structure included (i) Debt = Nil, (ii) Debt = ₹1,50,000 and (iii) Debt = ₹3,00,000?
   (b) How would you explain the change in k_e at different debt levels?
   (c) What would be the optimal capital structure?
3. **The Traditional Approach:** The following information is available about the Kapri Company:
   - Estimated cost of equity k_e = 12% if Debt = Nil; k_e = 13% when debt ₹1,50,000; k_e rises to 20% when debt is increased to ₹3,00,000.

- Cost of debt k_d: 6% if debt up to ₹1,50,000; above that k_d = 11%.
- Net operating income (NOI): ₹60,000 per annum.
- Income taxes: Nil.

Using the traditional approach:

(a) What would be the value of firm and its overall cost of capital (k_o), if its capital structure included (a) Debt = Nil, (b) Debt = ₹1,50,000 and (c) Debt = ₹3,00,000.

(b) What would be the optimal capital structure that would maximize the value of firm and minimize the overall cost of capital k_o.

4. **MM Theory and Arbitrage:** Assume two firms A and B have same net operating income of ₹60,000 and are similar to each other in all respects except that firm A does not have any debt while firm B has ₹2,50,000 of debt. Cost of equity k_e = 14% for all-equity firm, k_e = 16% for the levered firm. Cost of debt k_d: 8%. Both the firm as well as individual investor can borrow at the same interest rate.
   (a) Using the traditional approach, calculate the value of each firm and its overall cost of capital (k_o),
   (b) Show how arbitrage will work and what would be its effect on the value of the two firms?

5. **Recapitalization and Change in D/E**

   The following information is available for Paragliding Company:
   Existing situation before recapitalization:

Net operating income (EBIT)	: ₹74,000
Equity shares	: 10,000
Market price per equity share	: ₹34
Current debt at 10% interest (before tax)	: ₹60,000
Cost of equity	: 14%
Income tax rate	: 30%

   After considering the WACC at various degrees of debt/equity ratio, the management has determined that a capital structure of 50% debt and 50% equity would yield the lowest overall (Weighted Average) Cost of Capital (WACC) and has decided this as the target debt/equity ratio. Therefore, the company has decided to issue perpetual bonds to raise an amount required to repurchase equity shares in such a way that after the recapitalization, the debt/equity ratio should remain equal to the target ratio of 50% debt and 50% equity. At the new ratio of debt/equity, the cost of entire debt (before tax) would rise to 11% per annum and the cost of equity would increase to 15% due to increased leverage. Assume the company does not expect any growth in its annual earnings which are expected to remain constant per annum, and all earnings are distributed as dividends.
   (a) Calculate the current market value of the firm.
   (b) Calculate the current (i) after tax cost of debt, and (ii) after tax WACC.
   (c) Determine the additional amount of debt to be issued.
   (d) Compute the repurchase price per share and determine the number of shares to be repurchased.
   (e) How many shares would remain outstanding after the recapitalization?
   (f) What would be the market value of the debt, equity and the firm after the above recapitalization has been achieved?

6. The Harvest Company's current capital structure comprises of 25% debt and 75% equity capital and the firm's current beta is 1.40. Income tax rate applicable to the firm is 30%.

(a) What would be the unlevered beta of the firm?
(b) Estimate the firm's beta at debt levels of 50% and 75% of the firm's market value.

7. Missionary Company's current capital structure comprises 25% debt and 75% equity capital and the current beta on its shares is 1.36. The risk free rate of return is 6%, the market risk premium is 8%, and the income tax rate applicable to the firm is 30%. The company is now considering changing its capital structure to finance 60% with debt and 40% with equity.
   (a) Calculate the company's current cost of equity.
   (b) Calculate the company's unlevered beta.
   (c) Calculate the new beta at 60% debt level, and
   (d) Determine the company's new cost of equity.
8. NCR Company's current capital structure comprises 100% equity and zero debt, and its current beta is 1.05. The new CFO feels that the company can benefit by introducing some debt financing in its capital structure due to lower cost of debt and the tax-shield benefit. He has collected information about the interest rates the company would have to pay at different levels of debt financing as shown below:

Debt Percentage in the Firm and Interest Cost				
Debt % in Capital Structure	20	40	60	80
Rate of Interest before Tax	10	10.5	13.5	18

   The company uses the CAPM model to estimate the cost of equity capital. The risk free rate of return is 6%, the market risk premium is 8% and the income tax rate applicable to the firm is 30%.

   Calculate the WACC at different levels of debt financing, and suggest an optimal capital structure for the firm.

CASE

Kingfisher Airline Debt Woes

Many were surprised when in September 2014, the state owned United Bank of India declared the heavily indebted Kingfisher Airlines and its promoter Vijay Mallya as wilful defaulters. Their declaration as wilful defaulters can be predicted to have serious direct and indirect consequences. Not only they would be disqualified to borrow from the bank in future, it could also adversely affect Vijay Mallya's position as a Director in several companies. Besides, criminal proceedings could also be instituted against the wilful defaulters.

Kingfisher Airlines, a part of the large United Breweries group, started its operations in May 2005. Kingfisher Airlines introduced several innovative features, such as world-class in-flight service, mouth-watering cuisine, a 'welcome kit' with gifts, in-flight entertainment system and more importantly, treating passengers as 'guests' rather than mere customers. As a result of these attractive features, the airline received an encouraging response from customers, and it not only captured one-fifth of the market share, but also received several awards for innovation and customer service.

Later however, the company started facing financial problems. Particularly from 2011, the company had difficulty in serving its huge debt burden. Most of the company's acquisitions of aircrafts were financed with debt. A huge debt burden coupled with high operating cost and low margins resulted in a liquidity crunch, and the company defaulted in loan payments as well as payment of taxes and staff salaries. Following the non-payment of taxes and/or other dues, the tax authorities ordered freezing of the company's bank accounts, the International agency IATA suspended it from the clearing house facility and oil companies stopped the supply of jet fuel to the airline.

The liquidity crunch the company was facing can be estimated from the extremely poor financial charges ratio for years 2009 to 2013 as follows:

	Mar '13	*Mar '12*	*Mar '11*	*Mar '10*	*Mar '09*
Financial charges coverage ratio	–1.83	–1.43	0.48	0.17	0.02
Fin. charges coverage ratio (post tax)	–1.83	–0.55	0.66	0.36	0.29

Source: Adapted from BSE data KFA Group

The acute liquidity crunch resulted in frequent cancellations of flights and customers started avoiding the airline. The airline pilots went on strike for non-payment of salaries which resulted in cancellation of more flights and further depleted the airline's customer base. The company was making losses and its net worth had been eroded. The company was also suspected of using questionable accounting practices. The airline suspended its operations in October 2012.

Kingfisher Airlines owed about ₹7,500 crore to a consortium of 17 banks, out of which the amount due to United Bank was ₹400 crore loan plus interest. Following the declaration of the airline and Mallya as wilful defaulters by United Bank of India, other consortium banks like IDBI were also said to be contemplating similar actions against them.

The initial response of Mallya, who was well-known for a flamboyant and luxurious living style, was to strike back at the bank claiming that the bank had declared him a wilful defaulter without giving him an opportunity to represent his case and daring the bank to prove it in the court of law.

"However, corporate lawyers, bankers and corporate governance experts said that after UBI's declaration, Mallya can end up ceding control of the large cash-generator United Breweries Limited (UBL) and the profit-making Mangalore Chemicals & Fertilizers (MCF). His minority stake in United Spirits (USL) and many real estate assets in India are also potential targets for lenders. Mallya's status as a company director—he's the chairman of USL, UBL and MCF—is also under threat as he may not meet the criterion of 'fit and proper' as understood in the Companies Act. That puts a big question mark on his continuance on the boards of these companies." [Economic Times, Aug. 12, 2014]

In April 2015, the Board of Directors of United Spirits Ltd. demanded that promoter and Chairman Vijay Mallya should resign from the Board. Their demand was based on the findings of an internal enquiry, which had indicated that Mallya might have been involved in certain financial irregularities and legal violations. "Among other issues, the internal inquiry looked at inter-company loans between United Spirits and UB Group entities that were used to prop up the now defunct Kingfisher Airlines. The inquiry also covered some agreements allegedly entered into by United Spirits with a Kingfisher Airlines creditor and certain claims made by United Spirits debtors, some of whom later refused to repay the company." [Livemint, April 25, 2015]

Out of the outstanding amount of ₹7,500 crore (excluding penal interest), the consortium of lenders were able to realize about ₹1,000 crore by selling the shares pledged as collateral for the loans.

In spite of declaring Kingfisher and Mallya as wilful defaulters, United Bank of India was not hopeful of recovering the outstanding loan any time soon, as he explained to the BSE. "The Exchange had sought clarification from United Bank of India with respect to news appearing on Financial Chronicle on 25 May 2015, titled; 'United Bank says lost hope of recovering loan to Kingfisher'. United Bank of India replied stating "The bank continues to fight the legal battles for recovery of dues through the consortia.

It is also individually fighting legal battles in connections with the declaration of the promoters and directors of the borrower company as well as the borrower Company as Wilful Defaulters and winding-up of the corporate guarantor. Through these measures, Bank feels that recovery is possible in the long run. Considering the long-drawn nature of these legal entanglements, claims raised by other statutory/regulatory authorities in view of the defaults committed by the borrower under other statutes and regulations and the amounts recovered so far, the Bank feels that the possibility of any immediate major break through in the account is difficult for the present." [BSE India, 25 May 2015] Bad loans were not a problem for United Bank alone, but had become a persistent headache for majority of the PSU banks. At the time of writing this, in June 2015, the Reserve Bank was considering a new harsh rule in consultation with other banks and SEBI. According to the proposed new rule, if a borrower failed to repay debts even after the management had been given a second chance and its loans had been restructured, the lender banks would automatically get control of 51% of the equity capital of the defaulting companies.

Richard Branson had once said, "The quickest way to become a millionaire is to start as a billionaire and invest in an airline". In 2012, when an NDTV anchor asked Branson to comment on Kingfisher airline and Vijay Mallya, he replied as follows: "He (Mallya) used his own money to set up what was a very good airline and took a big risk and lost a lot of money. I don't think anybody can criticise him for that. His lifestyle, people can criticise somebody for that. I think, generally, people who have been successful and entrepreneurs ought to be careful and get the balance right in their lifestyle. You don't need the biggest cars or the biggest this or the biggest that. I think people gain respect from using their money to construct, to make people's lives better." When the TV anchor further asked if he would be "brave enough to invest in a bleeding airline at this point", Branson quipped, "we wouldn't want to do anything foolish". [NDTV 27 October 2012]

Questions:

1. With reference to the Kingfisher loan default, identify the costs of distress and the agency costs that could arise due to high financial leverage.
2. Do you think the trade-off theory is relevant to emerging markets such as India?
3. In view of the experience of Kingfisher airlines, if you were a CFO empowered to decide on the company's capital structure, would you follow the MM approach or the traditional theory? Why?

CHAPTER

13

The Capital Structure Decision

Excessive leverage by banks is widely believed to have contributed to the global financial crisis.

—Katia D'Hulster, World Bank

LEARNING OBJECTIVES

After studying this chapter, you should be able to:

- Discuss the pros and cons of debt and equity financing.
- Carry out the EBIT-EPS analysis.
- Compute and explain the EBIT indifference point.
- Explain the operating, financial and combined leverage.
- Discuss the effect of positive and negative financial leverage on EPS.
- Identify main factors that should be considered while deciding the capital structure policy.

13.1 Introduction

Having discussed the main theories of capital structure in the previous chapter, we now turn our attention to the capital structure decision making in practice, keeping in mind the financial objectives of the business. Throughout this book we have maintained that the main financial objective of the firm is to maximize the wealth of the shareholders (assuming the company form of business). The shareholders' wealth equals the number of shares outstanding multiplied by the market price per share. The Modigliani–Miller approach as well as the traditional theory clearly emphasize that investors value equity shares on the basis of the earnings available to equityholders. The Price-Earning (*P*/*E*) ratio is a popular method of estimating the market value of a share. For example, if a *P*/*E* ratio of 10.0 is considered appropriate to value a firm's equity shares, and the earnings per equity share is ₹6, then the market value of the equity shares in equilibrium would be equal to (*P*/*E* ratio × EPS =10 × 6 =) ₹60 per share. Later, if the earnings increase from ₹6 per share to ₹8 per share, market value would be expected to rise from to 10 × 8 = 80. If a shareholder 'S' held 1000 shares in the company, his wealth would increase to ₹1000 × 80 = 80,000 from the previous value of ₹60,000.

Applying this to the capital structure decision would imply that a company should adopt such a financing plan that would maximize the earnings per share left for the equityholders after paying for interest on borrowed capital, preference dividends and taxes, as applicable. Indeed a frequently applied technique to decide the capital structure is called EBIT-EPS analysis. However, in addition to the impact on the EPS, the firm should also consider several other factors before arriving at a final decision on the capital structure. Such factors would include the financial and operating leverage and availability of cash flow to service the debt obligations.

> A company should adopt such a financing plan that would maximize the earnings per equity share.

We begin with the EBIT-EPS analysis in the next section and later consider other relevant aspects.

13.2 EBIT-EPS Analysis

An EBIT-EPS analysis highlights the effect of different financing plans on the Earning Per Share (EPS) for a given amount of Earnings Before Interest and Taxes (EBIT) of the firm. Since the financial objective of the company is to maximize the wealth of equityholders, the firm should select the financing alternative that maximizes the EPS to equityholders.

The steps required for carrying out the EBIT-EPS analysis are as follows:

1. Identify the alternative financing plans that are available to the company, or the alternative sources of funds that the company would consider for financing a project. The major sources of financing a project would be equity capital, debt and preference share capital.
2. The company should determine the amount of new annual 'earnings before interest and taxes' that it would be earning after taking up the new project.
3. Collect information on the rate of interest (pre-tax) payable on debt, fixed preference dividend payable and the rate of income taxes as applicable to the firm.
4. For each financing alternative, start with the 'earnings before interest and taxes', make adjustments for the interest payable, preference dividend and taxes payable and determine the total earnings that would be available to equityholders.
5. Divide the total earnings available to equityholders by the number of equity shares outstanding as per the specific financing plan being considered to calculate the Earnings Per (equity) Share (EPS).
6. Select the financing alternative that promises highest earnings per share.

> EBIT-EPS analysis highlights the effect of different financing plans on the Earning Per Share (EPS).

Note that the EBIT-EPS analysis begins with earnings before interest and taxes (EBIT). The EBIT is the annual net operating income of the company that can be determined by deducting all operating costs (such as material cost, labour cost and overheads related to manufacturing and selling the products) except interest and corporate (income) taxes.

Before taking up an example of EBIT-EPS analysis, it would be necessary to understand the difference between treatment of interest on debt and preference dividends for income-taxes. For the purpose of income taxes, interest on debt is considered a business expense and is deducted from the EBIT 'before' determining the company's taxable income and the tax liability thereon. On the other hand, dividends—both on preference share capital and equity share capital—are regarded as 'distribution of profits', and hence paid out of after-tax profits of the company. In other words, while the company gets some tax-shield (tax savings) on the interest charges paid on debt capital, there is no such tax advantage on payment of dividends on either preference or equity share capital.

Consider the following illustration on EBIT-EPS analysis.

EXAMPLE 13.1 The Sporty Company at present has an all equity capital structure of 10,000 shares of ₹10 each. To finance its new investment project, it now wants to raise an additional ₹1,00,000 for which it has identified three alternative funding sources as follows:

1. Additional 10,000 shares of ₹10 each;
2. Debt at 15% interest;
3. Preference capital at 15% dividend.

The present EBIT of the company is ₹50,000 per annum, but with the new project, the EBIT will rise to ₹80,000 per annum. Income tax rate is 30%.

Using the EBIT-EPS analysis, decide which financing alternative should be accepted.

Solution: The existing all equity capital structure consists of 10,000 shares of ₹10 each, or a total equity capital of ₹1,00,000. After raising the planned additional capital, total funds raised would rise to ₹2,00,000. If the new funds required are raised by issuing new equity shares, the total number of equity shares would rise to 10,000 + 10,000 = 20,000. Instead, if the company uses either debt or preference share capital sources for the additional funding, the number of equity shares outstanding would remain constant. With this understanding, we can proceed to prepare the EBIT-EPS analysis as follows:

	Financing Options Amount in ₹		
	All equity	***Debt***	***Preference***
EBIT per annum (with new project)	80,000	80,000	80,000
Annual Interest (1,00,000 × 15%)	0	(15,000)	0
Earnings Before Taxes (EBT)	80,000	65,000	80,000
Tax @ 30%	*(24,000)	(19,500)	(24,000)
Earnings After Taxes (EAT)	56,000	45,500	56,000
Preference dividend	0	0	(15,000)
Earnings for equityholders	56,000	45,500	41,000
Number of Equity shares**	20,000	10,000	10,000
Earnings Per Share (EPS) ₹	2.8	4.55	4.1

*Figures in brackets indicate deduction.

** The number of equity shares under the 'all equity' funding option would rise to 20,000 shares. In the financing options of debt and preference capital, the number of equity shares would remain unchanged at 10,000 because the company would not need to issue any new equity share.

Explanation: Under the all-equity option, the earnings before taxes are the same as EBIT because the company does not have any interest expenses. The entire EBIT is taxed at the applicable rate and the remaining after-tax income is divided by total number of equity shares outstanding (old plus new) to calculate the EPS. Under the debt option, first deduct the interest charges on debt to calculate the earnings before taxes on which income taxes would be payable. The after-tax income is divided by the existing number of equity shares to calculate the EPS, because no new equity shares would be issued.

Similar to the all-equity option, under the preference capital alternative the entire EBIT is taxed at the applicable rate because the company does not have any interest expenses (so, EBIT = EBT). Out of the remaining after-tax income, we must first pay up the preference dividend before determining the net profits available to equityholders. The amount of net profits available to equityholders is divided by the existing number of equity shares to calculate the EPS because no new equity shares would be issued.

Have you noted that even though the rate of interest on debt is same 15% as the fixed dividend on preference capital, the net earnings per share under the debt option is higher than the earnings per share under the preference capital option? The difference is due to the tax-shield on interest payments which is not available on the payment of preference dividends. Thus, the debt option with tax-shield leaves more net earnings for the equityholders, which in turn, provides higher EPS than would be the case under the preference capital option.

Conclusion: A comparison of the EPS under the three alternative financing plans shows that the EPS would be highest under the debt financing plan. Therefore, other things being equal, the company should go for the debt alternative to finance the new project.

13.2.1 The Equation Method to Calculate EPS

The EPS under different financing options can be computed by using the following equation:

$$\text{EPS} = \frac{(\text{EBIT} - I)(1 - t) - P_d}{N}$$

where,

EBIT = Earnings before interest and taxes
I = Annual pre-tax interest on debt (existing + new)
t = Rate of income tax applicable to the company
P_d = Fixed dividend payable on preference capital
N = Total number of equity shares (existing plus proposed)

Let us calculate the EPS under the three financing options given in the previous illustration as follows (ignore the items that are not relevant to a specific financing option):

(a) **EPS under the all equity option:**

$$\text{EPS} = \frac{(\text{EBIT} - I)(1 - t) - P_d}{N}$$

Since there are no interest or preference dividends payable, we are left with:

$$\text{EPS} = \frac{(\text{EBIT})(1 - t)}{N}$$

Note that N = Existing shares plus new shares 10,000 + 10,000 = 20,000.

$$\text{EPS} = (80{,}000)\ (1 - 0.3)/20{,}000$$
$$= 56{,}000/20{,}000 = ₹2.8$$

(b) EPS under the equity + Debt option:

$$\text{EPS} = \frac{(\text{EBIT} - I)(1 - t) - P_d}{N}$$

Since there is no preference dividend payable, we are left with:

$$\text{EPS} = \frac{(\text{EBIT} - I)(1 - t)}{N}$$

Note that N = 10,000 existing shares only as no new equity shares would be issued under this financing option.

$$= [(80{,}000 - 15{,}000)\ (1 - 0.3)] \div 10{,}000$$
$$= [(65{,}000)\ (0.7)] \div 10{,}000$$
$$= ₹4.55$$

(c) **EPS under the equity + Preference option:**

$$\text{EPS} = \frac{(\text{EBIT} - I)(1 - t) - P_d}{N}$$

Since there is no interest payable, we are left with:

$$\text{EPS} = \frac{(\text{EBIT})(1 - t) - P_d}{N}$$

Note that N = 10,000 existing shares only as no new equity shares would be issued.

$$\text{EPS} = [(80{,}000)\ (1 - 0.3) - 15{,}000] \div 10{,}000$$
$$= [(56{,}000 - 15{,}000)] \div 10{,}000$$
$$= ₹4.10$$

Given a choice, some managers might prefer the tabular presentation as it makes things simple and presents all details neatly.

Earning per share $= \frac{(\text{EBIT} - I)(1 - t) - P_d}{N}$

where,
EBIT = Earnings before interest and taxes
I = Interest,
T = Income tax rate,
P_d = Preference dividend,
N = Number of shares.

13.2.2 EBIT Indifference Point

While comparing equity financing with either debt or preference capital, we can determine an EBIT indifference or break-even point, which is defined as that level of EBIT at which the EPS would be the same whether the company goes for one source of funding or the other. In other words, at the EBIT indifference point, the company would be indifferent or neutral between the two sources of financing the project.

Using the equation method explained above, the EBIT indifference point between two financing plans '*a*' and '*b*' can be determined by solving the following equation for the value of *X*:

$$\frac{(X - I_a)(1 - t) - P_{da}}{N_a} = \frac{(X - I_b)(1 - t) - P_{db}}{N_b}$$

where

X = EBIT indifference point between the two financing options.

I_a, I_b = Annual interest expenses before taxes under financing plans '*a*' and '*b*', respectively.

t = Income tax rate applicable to the company

P_{da}, P_{db} = Annual preference dividend payable under plan '*a*' and '*b*' respectively

N_a, N_b = The number of equity shares outstanding under financing plans '*a*' and '*b*' respectively.

For the Sporty Company illustration, EBIT indifference point between equity (plan '*a*') and debt financing (plan '*b*') would be as follows:

$$\frac{(X - Ia)(1-t) - P_{da}}{N_a} = \frac{(X - I_b)(1-t) - P_{db}}{N_b}$$

Financing the project with equity capital (plan '*a*') means the company would not have to pay any fixed financial charges of interest or preference dividends. On the other hand, if it goes for debt financing it would have to pay the fixed cost of interest. Neither plan has any preference dividend obligation. Thus, the above equation can be simplified as follows:

$$\frac{(X)(1-t)}{N_a} = \frac{(X - I_b)(1-t)}{N_b}$$

Inserting given values, we get:

$$\frac{(X)(1-0.3)}{20{,}000} = \frac{(X-15000)(1-0.3)}{10{,}000}$$

$$\frac{(0.7X)}{20{,}000} = \frac{(X-15000)(0.7)}{10{,}000}$$

$$\frac{(0.7X)}{20{,}000} = \frac{(0.7X-10500)}{10{,}000}$$

By rearranging, we get:

$$(0.7X)\ 10{,}000 = (0.7X - 10{,}500)\ 20{,}000$$
$$7{,}000X = 14{,}000X - 21{,}00{,}00{,}000$$
$$14{,}000X - 7{,}000X = 21{,}00{,}00{,}000$$
$$X = 21{,}00{,}00{,}000/7{,}000$$
$$X = 30{,}000$$

Accordingly, an EBIT level of ₹30,000 would be the indifference point. This calculation can be cross-checked as given in Table 13.1.

TABLE 13.1
Cros-checking the indifference point

	Financing Options	
	All Equity	***Debt***
EBIT	30,000	30,000
Interest	0	15,000
Taxable Earnings	30,000	15,000
Less: Taxes @ 30%	9,000	4,500
Earnings after taxes	21,000	10,500
Less: Preference Dividends	0	0
Earnings available to Equityholders	21,000	10,500
Number of equity shares	20,000	10,000
EPS	1.05	1.05

EBIT indifference point is that level of EBIT at which EPS would be the same whether the company goes for one source of funding or the other.

13.2.3 Graphical Presentation of EBIT Indifference Point

The EBIT indifference point for Sporty Company can be presented graphically by taking EBIT on horizontal axis and EPS on the vertical axis as in Figure 13.1.

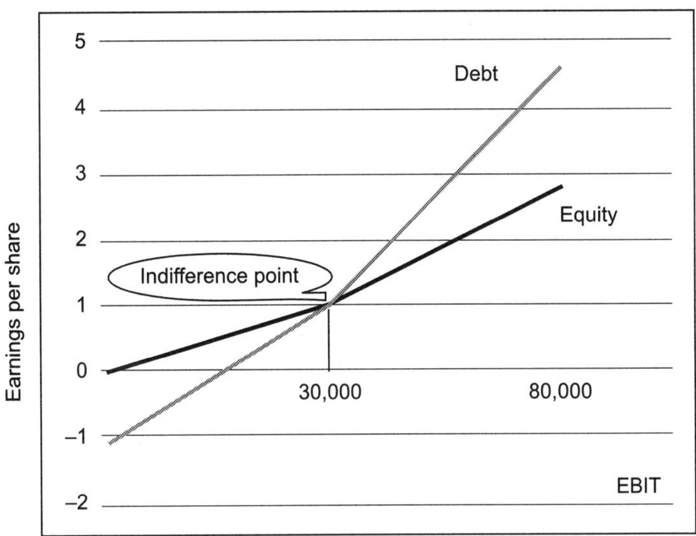

FIGURE 13.1
EBIT indifference point of a Sporty company.

The equity line starts from the point '0' depicting that EPS under this option would be zero if EBIT is zero. However, the debt line intercepts the horizontal axis at an EBIT level of ₹15,000 indicating that under the debt financing scheme, the company must earn this much EBIT to keep EPS at zero. If the EBIT is less than ₹15,000 and the company goes for debt option, the company's EPS would turn negative (less than zero). The possibility of negative EPS at EBIT levels less than ₹15,000 shows the disadvantage of debt financing. If the EBIT declines to zero, the EPS under the debt option would be negative ₹–1.05 [= (0 – 15,000) 0.7 ÷ 10,000].

The graph shows the indifference point at an EBIT level of ₹30,000 at which the EPS would be the same under equity as well as debt option. At any EBIT level higher than the indifference point, debt option would provide a greater EPS than the equity option. On the other hand, at any EBIT level lower than the indifference point, equity option would provide a greater EPS than the debt option. For example, we have seen that at EBIT level of ₹80,000, debt option yields a much higher EPS of ₹4.55 as compared to a lower EPS of 2.80 under the equity option.

What is the implication of this indifference point for financing strategy? If the management is confident of achieving an EBIT of more than ₹30,000 under all circumstances, it would prefer to finance the new project with debt, so that the company can get the advantage of financial leverage and increase EPS on equity shares. In fact, higher the EBIT above the indifference point, more attractive the debt option. In other words, using debt financing or financial leverage brings increased earnings to equity shareholders as long as the EBIT level remains higher than the indifference point.

At any EBIT level higher than the indifference point, the financing option with leverage would provide a greater EPS than the equity option, and vice-versa.

The above conclusion is not surprising because it is sheer common sense that a firm should borrow funds only when it can deploy those funds in a way to earn more profit than the cost of interest. The surplus profit earned over and above the cost of debt would add to the earnings available to equityholders.

13.2.4 EBIT Indifference Point between Equity and Preference Capital

Similar to the computation of the indifference point between equity and debt financing, we can determine the indifference point between equity and preference capital. Using equity capital means the company would not have to pay any fixed financial charges while if it goes for preference capital there would be the fixed financial charge of preference dividends. The EBIT indifference level between equity and preference financing alternatives would be that level of EBIT which yields the same EPS so that the firm would be indifferent between the two financing options.

To illustrate, let us continue with the Sporty Company situation. Assume the company is considering two alternative financing plans: equity financing plan '*a*' and preference capital plan '*b*' and wishes to determine the indifference point between the two. Mathematically, it can be done by solving the following equation for the value of *X*:

$$\frac{(X-I_a)(1-t)-P_{da}}{N_a}=\frac{(X-I_b)(1-t)-P_{db}}{N_b}$$

Note that in the given situation of Sporty Company, the equity option would not have any interest cost or preference dividends; similarly in the preference capital option, there is no interest cost. Considering these factors, the above equation can be simplified as follows:

$$\frac{(X)(1-t)}{N_a}=\frac{(X)(1-t)-P_{db}}{N_b}$$

For Sporty Company, the equation would be:

$$\frac{(0.7X)}{20{,}000}=\frac{(0.7X)-15{,}000}{10{,}000}$$

Rrranging, we have:

$$(0.7X)\ 10{,}000 = (0.7X - 15{,}000)\ 20{,}000$$
$$7{,}000X = 14{,}000X - 30{,}00{,}00{,}000$$
$$14{,}000X - 7{,}000X = 30{,}00{,}00{,}000$$
$$X = 30{,}00{,}00{,}000/7{,}000$$
$$X = 42{,}857.14$$

The indifference point EBIT level of ₹42,857.14 should give the same EPS under equity and preference options, as shown in Table 13.2.

TABLE 13.2
Indifference Point EBIT Level

	All equity	***Preference***
EBIT per annum (with new project)	42,857.14	42,857.14
Annual Interest	0	0
Earnings Before Taxes (EBT)	42,857.14	42,857.14
Tax @ 30%	12,857.14	12,857.142
Earnings After Taxes (EAT)	30,000	30,000
Preference Dividend	0	15,000
Earnings for Equityholders	30,000	15,000
Number of Equity shares*	20,000	10,000
Earnings Per Share (EPS) ₹	1.5	1.5

* The number of equity shares under the 'all equity' option would be existing 10,000 + new 10,000 = total 20,000. In the financing option of preference capital, the number of equity shares would remain unchanged at 10,000 because the company would not need to issue any new equity shares.

The above indifference point indicates that at any EBIT levels of more than ₹42,857.14 the preference capital financing will provide higher EPS. If the EBIT can drop to any level below ₹42,857.14, then it would be better for the company to go for equity financing because at EBIT levels below this, equity option would yield higher EPS.

The above indifference point between equity and preference can be shown graphically as in Figure 13.2.

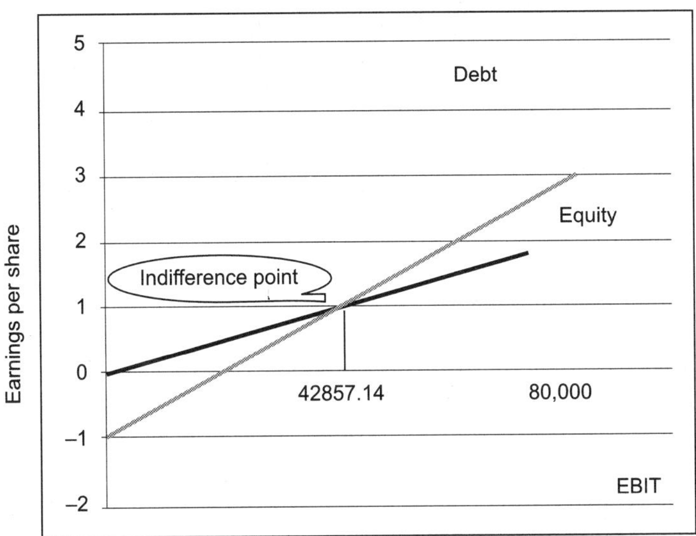

FIGURE 13.2
Indifference point between equity and preference.

An interesting question at this stage would be to ask whether the preference dividends are legally as binding as the interest payments on debt. The answer is no, the payment of preference dividends are not as binding as the interest on debt. The Companies Act provides that preference dividends should be paid 'before' any dividends are paid to equity shareholders, but it does not say that preference dividends 'must' be paid under all conditions. Therefore, if the company makes losses in a year and does not want to pay equity dividends, it would not be under any obligation to pay preference dividends that year. On the other hand, payment of interest on debt is legally binding irrespective of whether the company is making profits or losses.

In spite of the fact that preference dividends are not as binding as the payment of interest on debt, all well-meaning companies would want to pay preference dividends as stated at the time of issuing the preference shares, and hence, it is a good practice to provide for such dividends in the EBIT-EPS analysis.

13.2.5 A Variation of EBIT-EPS Analysis

While planning for the future, companies in cyclical and highly competitive industries often face uncertainty regarding the EBIT levels they would expect to achieve in coming periods. Often they might find it easier to estimate a 'range' of EBIT rather than an exact single value with certainty. In such circumstances, a company may estimate the earnings per share that would be available to equity shareholders under different scenarios or assumptions regarding EBIT levels such as high, average and low. This way the company would be able to analyze the impact of a change in EBIT on the EPS. Such an EBIT-EPS analysis can help in understanding how sensitive is the EPS to changes in EBIT. Consider the following example.

EXAMPLE 13.2 Robin Company, at present, has an all-equity capital structure of 40,000 shares of ₹10 each. For its new expansion project, the company proposes to raise ₹4,00,000 either by additional equity or by taking debt. New equity shares can be issued at ₹12.5 per share. Debt financing is available at 14% interest per annum. The company is not certain about the EBIT level and has estimated the Earnings Before Interest and Taxes (EBIT) under different scenarios as follows:

Scenario	*EBIT Estimate*
Recession	₹1,00,000
Normal/Expected	₹1,80,000
Boom	₹2,40,000

The rate of income tax applicable to the company is 30%.

(a) Determine the Earning Per Share (EPS) of the company under the three scenarios if the new project is funded by equity.
(b) Determine the earning per share of the company under the three scenarios if the new project is funded by debt.
(c) What will be the EBIT indifference (break-even) point between debt and equity financing?

Solution:

(a) **EPS of the company under the three scenarios if the new project is funded by equity.**

	Equity Option		
	Recession	*Normal*	*Boom*
EBIT per annum	1,00,000	1,80,000	2,40,000
Interest	0	0	0
Earnings Before Taxes (EBT)	1,00,000	1,80,000	2,40,000
Tax @ 30%	30,000	54,000	72,000
Earnings After Taxes (EAT)	70,000	1,26,000	1,68,000
Preference dividend	0	0	0
Earnings for equityholders	70,000	1,26,000	1,68,000
Number of Equity shares*	72,000	72,000	72,000
Earnings Per Share (EPS) ₹	0.97	1.75	2.33

*New shares issued at ₹12.5 per share = ₹4,00,000 ÷ 12.5 = 32,000; therefore total number of shares outstanding under the equity option = 40,000 existing + 32,000; new = 72,000.

(b) **EPS of the company under the three scenarios if the new project is funded by debt.**

	Debt Option		
	Recession	*Normal*	*Boom*
EBIT per annum	1,00,000	1,80,000	2,40,000
Interest (4,00,000 × 14%)	56,000	56,000	56,000
Earnings Before Taxes (EBT)	44,000	1,24,000	1,84,000
Tax	13,200	37,200	55,200
Earnings After Taxes (EAT)	30,800	86,800	1,28,800
Preference dividend	0	0	0
Earnings for equityholders	30,800	86,800	1,28,800
Number of Equity shares*	40,000	40,000	40,000
Earnings Per Share (EPS) ₹	0.77	2.17	3.22

*No new shares would be issued in the debt option, so the number of shares outstanding would remain the same is 40,000.

Analysis

The EPS in the scenario of recession is higher in the equity option, but in other scenarios the debt option provides higher EPS. The management should consider the probability of recession vis-à-vis normal and boom conditions before deciding on the capital structure. If there is a strong probability of recession prevailing in the industry for the next several years, it would be better to finance the new project by issuing equity shares. Debt option should be preferred if there is high probability of either normal or boom conditions.

(c) **EBIT indifference point (break-even) between debt and equity financing.**

Financing the project with equity capital (let us call it plan '*a*') means the company would not have to pay any fixed financial charges of interest or preference dividends. On the other hand, if it goes for debt financing (plan '*b*') it would have to pay the fixed cost of interest. Neither plan has any preference dividend obligation. Thus, the indifference point equation (covered in a previous section) can be simply stated as follows:

$$\frac{(X)(1-t)}{N_a} = \frac{(X - I_b)(1-t)}{N_b}$$

$$\frac{(X)(1-0.3)}{72{,}000} = \frac{(X-56{,}000)(1-0.3)}{40{,}000}$$

$$\frac{(0.7X)}{72{,}000} = \frac{(X-56{,}000)(0.7)}{40{,}000}$$

$$\frac{(0.7X)}{72{,}000} = \frac{(0.7X-39{,}200)}{40{,}000}$$

By rearranging, we get:

$$(0.7X)\ 40{,}000 = (0.7X - 39{,}200)\ 72{,}000$$

$$28{,}000X = 50{,}400X - 2{,}82{,}24{,}00{,}000$$

$$28{,}000X - 50{,}400X = 2{,}82{,}24{,}00{,}000$$

$$X = 2{,}82{,}24{,}00{,}000/22{,}400$$

$$X = 1{,}26{,}000.$$

Accordingly, an EBIT level of ₹1,26,000 would be the indifference point. This calculation can be cross-checked as follows:

	Equity	*Debt*
EBIT per annum (with new project)	1,26,000	1,26,000
Interest (4,00,000 × 14%)	0	56,000
Earnings Before Taxes (EBT)	1,26,000	70,000
Tax	37,800	21,000
Earnings After Taxes (EAT)	88,200	49,000
Preference dividend	0	0
Earnings for equityholders	88,200	49,000
Number of Equity shares	72,000	40,000
Earnings Per Share (EPS) ₹	1.23	1.23

The above indifference point between equity and preference can be shown graphically as follows:

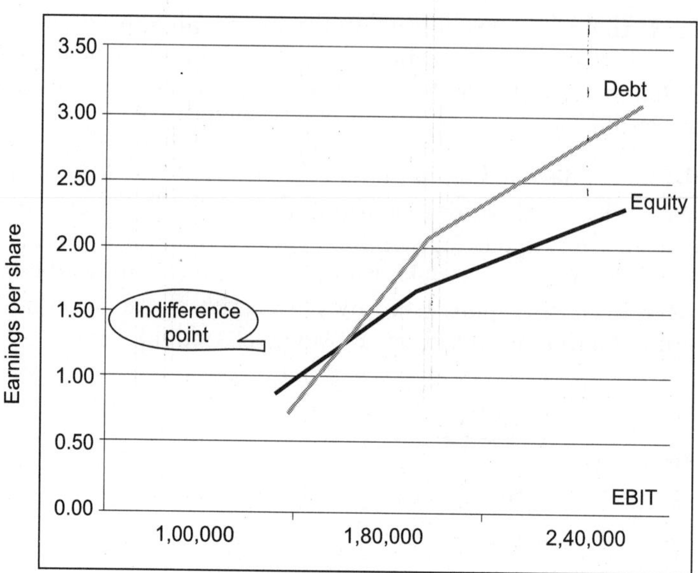

FIGURE 13.3

13.2.6 Pros and Cons of the EBIT-EPS Analysis

Management would like to adopt such financing options or mix of debt, preference and equity sources that would maximize the EPS. Since investors value equity shares on the basis of the earnings per share, maximizing EPS should lead to maximization of shareholders' wealth. In this process, the EBIT-EPS analysis can play an important role by examining the effect of different financing alternatives on the earnings per share. It can also be used to analyse how sensitive is the EPS to changes in levels of EBIT by determining the EPS at different levels of EBIT. It is therefore, a helpful tool in determining the capital structure.

A limitation of the EBIT-EPS analysis is that it does not consider the degree of financial risk that would arise at different levels of financial leverage. Common sense would dictate that a firm should not go for extremely high financial leverage even if it seems to promise greater EPS. Though the EBIT-EPS analysis is helpful in comparing the alternative financing options, the degree of leverage cannot be ignored while deciding on the capital structure. Leverage is discussed in detail in the next section.

13.3 Operating and Financial Leverage

Leverage refers to the existence of fixed costs in the cost structure of a firm. Fixed costs may be related to operating activities or financing activities.

Leverage refers to the existence of fixed costs in the cost structure of a firm. Fixed costs may be related to operating activities (production and sale of products) of the firm or its financing activities. Examples of operating fixed costs may be factory rent, fixed staff salaries, annual insurance premium, annual maintenance charges, etc. An example of financial fixed cost is the interest payable on the amount of loans taken.

By definition, a fixed cost would remain constant in total amount incurred during a period over a wide range of output. While variable costs (such as material cost, electricity consumption, packaging, etc.) rise or fall proportionately to the level of production and sales, fixed costs are committed 'period' costs that must be paid per period irrespective of the level of sales or operating activity.

In recession, when a firm's sales are down, fixed costs would have to be paid for in full, thus increasing the 'average' per unit fixed cost. On the contrary, when sales increase, the same fixed cost would get spread over a larger number of sales units due to which profits would rise more than proportionately than increase in the volume of sales.

Accordingly, the presence of fixed costs creates a leverage effect that profits would decline more than proportionately with every fall in sales and rise more than proportionately with every increase in sales. Thus, leverage has a magnifying effect on profits.

Leverage has a magnifying effect on profits so that profits would decline more than proportionately with every fall in sales and rise more than proportionately with every increase in sales.

Before we illustrate the effect of leverage, let us understand that all costs whether fixed or variable, must be covered from the sales revenue before a firm can report profits, as shown in the simplified in Table 13.3.

TABLE 13.3
ABC Company

Item	(₹)
Sales revenue (Number of units sold × price)	1,000
Less: Variable operating costs (Material, labour cost and variable expenses)	400
Contribution = Sales revenue – Variable operating costs	600
Less: Fixed operating cost	250
Earnings Before Interest and Taxes (EBIT)	350
Less: Interest or other financial charges	150
Earnings (or profit) Before Taxes	200

Fixed costs related to operating activities create the operating leverage and fixed costs related to financing activities lead to the financial leverage. Thus total leverage of a firm consists of the operating leverage and the financial leverage. The calculation of operating, financial and total leverage is explained as follows:

1. **Operating leverage:** Operating leverage is created by the existence of fixed costs in the operating cost structure of the firm. The operating leverage can be computed with reference to a specific level of sales in terms of units sold (or sales revenue). Assuming a firm's current level of sales is '*X*' units, the operating leverage (L_o) for this level of sales may be calculated below:

Operating Leverage (L_o):

$$= \frac{\text{Sales revenue at } X \text{ units} - \text{Total variable cost}}{\text{Sales revenue at } X \text{ units} - \text{Total variable cost} - \text{Fixed operating cost}}$$

$$= \frac{\text{Total contribution at } X \text{ units}}{\text{EBIT at } X \text{ units}}$$

2. **Financial leverage:** Similar to the operating leverage, financial leverage at '*X*' units of sales may be calculated as follows:

$$\text{Financial Leverage } (L_f) = \frac{\text{EBIT at } X \text{ units}}{\text{EBIT at } X \text{ units} - \text{Annual interest}}$$

$$= \frac{\text{EBIT at } X \text{ units}}{\text{Earnings before Tax}}$$

EXAMPLE 13.3 From the following information provided about Lotus Company, calculate the operating and financial leverage:

Annual sales volume = 10,000 units
Selling price = ₹10 per unit
Variable operating cost = ₹5 per unit
Annual fixed operating cost = ₹30,000
Annual interest cost = ₹5,000

Solution: Presenting the information in the format presented above (see ABC Company example):

Item	(₹)
Sales revenue (10,000 × 10)	1,00,000
Less: Variable operating costs (10,000 × 5)	50,000
Contribution (Sales revenue – Variable cost)	50,000
Less: Fixed operating cost	30,000
Earnings Before Interest and Taxes (EBIT)	20,000
Less: Interest charges	5,000
Earnings (or profit) before taxes	15,000

$$\text{Operating Leverage } (L_o) = \frac{\text{Total contribution}}{\text{EBIT}}$$

$$= \frac{50,000}{20,000}$$

$$= 2.5 \text{ times.}$$

An operating leverage of 2.5 means that for every change of one per cent in sales (from the given sales level of 10,000 units), the EBIT would change by 2.5 per cent. For example, if sales decline by 10% from the current level, the EBIT would fall by 10% × 2.5 = 25%.

$$\text{Financial Leverage } (L_f) = \frac{\text{EBIT}}{\text{Earnings before tax}}$$

$$= \frac{20,000}{15,000}$$

$$= 1.333$$

A financial leverage of 1.333 means that for every change of one per cent in EBIT, the Earnings Before Taxes (EBT) would change by 1.333%. For example, if EBIT decline by 25% from the current level, the EBT would decline by 25% × 1.333 = 33.33%.

3. **Total leverage:** The total leverage may be calculated as follows:

$$\text{Total Leverage } (L_t) = L_o \times L_f$$

$$= (2.5)\ (1.333) = 3.333$$

13.3.1 Interpretation of Leverage

A combined leverage of 3.333 times means that for every one per cent change in sales (from the given sales level of 10,000 units), the profits before taxes would change by 3.333%. For example, if sales decline by 10% from the current level, profit before taxes would decline by 10% × 3.333 = 33.33%. Let us cross check it.

EXAMPLE 13.4 Same data about cost and prices as the previous illustration of Lotus Company, but assume the sales decline by 10% to 9,000 units. Calculate the new profit before taxes.

Solution: Presenting the information:

Item	(₹)
Sales revenue (9,000 × 10)	90,000
Less: Variable operating costs (9,000 × 5)	45,000
Contribution (Sales revenue – Variable cost)	45,000
Less: Fixed operating cost	30,000
Earnings Before Interest and Taxes (EBIT)	15,000
Less: Interest or other financial charges	5,000
Profit before taxes	10,000

Comparing with the original situation, we have:

Change in profit before taxes = ₹10,000 – 15,000 = ₹–5,000.

$$\% \text{ Change in profits} = \frac{-5000}{15,000} \times 100 = -33.33\%.$$

It was mentioned in a previous section that leverage has a magnifying effect on profits, which we can see working here: sales declined by 10% but profits before taxes fell by a disproportionate 33.33%. Note that this magnifying effect works both ways: when sales decline as well as when sales rise. Consider the following example.

EXAMPLE 13.5 Same data about cost and prices as the previous illustration of Lotus Company, but assume that sales rise by 20% (from base level of 10,000 units) to 12,000 units. Calculate the new profit before taxes.

Solution: Presenting the new information:

Item	(₹)
Sales revenue (12,000 × 10)	1,20,000
Less: Variable operating costs (12,000 × 5)	60,000
Contribution (Sales revenue – Variable cost)	60,000
Less: Fixed operating cost	30,000
Earnings Before Interest and Taxes (EBIT)	30,000
Less: Interest charges	5,000
Earnings (or profit) before taxes	25,000

Change in profit before taxes = ₹25,000 – 15,000 = ₹10,000.

$$\% \text{ change in profits} = \frac{10,000}{15,000} \times 100 = 66.66\%.$$

Once again we see the magnifying effect of leverage on profits. Even though rise in sales was only 20%, profits increased by as much as 66.66% as a result of the combined operating and financial leverage.

13.3.2 Calculating Leverage from Comparative Data

When comparative data is available for two (or more) levels of sales, costs and profits, the degree of leverage may be computed by using the following formulas:

$$\text{Operating Leverage } (L_o) = \frac{\% \text{ change in EBIT}}{\% \text{ change in the sales volume}}$$

$$\text{Financial Leverage } (L_f) = \frac{\% \text{ change in EBT}}{\% \text{ change in EBIT}}$$

where EBT = Earnings before taxes available to equity holders

EBIT is also called the operating profits. Using data relating to the previous example of Lotus Company at annual sales volume of 10,000 units and 9,000 units, we can compute the operating and financial leverage as given in Table 13.4.

TABLE 13.4 Operating and financial leverage

Units sold	10,000	9,000	
	₹	₹	*Change*
Sales revenue (@ ₹10)	1,00,000	90,000	10%
Less: Variable operating costs (@ ₹5)	50,000	45,000	
Contribution (Sales revenue – Variable cost)	50,000	45,000	
Less: Fixed operating cost	30,000	30,000	
Earnings Before Interest and Taxes (EBIT)	20,000	15,000	25%
Less: Interest charges	5,000	5,000	
Earnings (or profit) Before Taxes	15,000	10,000	33.33%

$$\text{Operating leverage } (L_o) = \frac{\text{\% change in EBIT}}{\text{\% change in the sales volume}} = \frac{25}{10} = 2.5$$

$$\text{Financial leverage } (L_f) = \frac{\text{\% change in EBT}}{\text{\% change in EBIT}} = \frac{33.33}{25} = 1.333$$

$$\text{Combined or total leverage} = 2.5 \times 1.333 = 3.333$$

13.3.3 Margin of Safety and Point of Zero EPS

The margin of safety may be defined as the difference between a given level of EBIT and the level of EBIT at which EPS would be equal to zero. The margin of safety may be computed as the inverse of the combined leverage as follows:

$$\text{Margin of safety} = \frac{1}{\text{Combined leverage}} \times 100$$

Applying this to the Sporty Company combined leverage of 3.333 computed above, the margin of safety for Sporty Company would be:

$$\text{Margin of safety} = \frac{1}{3.333} \times 100 = 30\% \text{ (approximately)}$$

This indicates that the maximum decline the company can tolerate without running into the zone of negative EPS is 30% decline in sales from the base level (10,000 units). This can be cross checked by computing the EPS at 10,000 – 30% = 7,000 units of sales as follows:

TABLE 13.5 Sporty Company

Item	(₹)
Sales revenue (7,000 × 10)	70,000
Less: Variable operating costs (7,000 × 5)	35,000
Contribution (Sales revenue – Variable cost)	35,000
Less: Fixed operating cost	30,000
Earnings Before Interest and Taxes (EBIT)	5,000
Less: Interest charges	5,000
Earnings (or profit) before taxes	Nil

In other words, with the given fixed operating and fixed interest costs in the cost structure of the firm, if sales decline below 7,000 units, the firm would be running into losses and earning a negative EPS. Thus the absolute margin of safety available in the situation of Sporty Company is 3,000 units of sales. Such analysis helps the firm in understanding the risk involved with respect to the financial leverage being considered.

13.3.4 Positive and Negative Financial Leverage

Financial leverage could be positive or negative depending on whether the funds raised from debt sources were deployed in a way to earn higher returns than the cost of interest. Assume a firm has raised ₹10,000 by debt at an interest rate of 10% per annum and used this amount in an investment project. Three situations may arise in this respect:

1. **Return on investment is more than cost of interest:** If the firm was able to deploy funds to earn a return of say 25% while the cost of interest is 10%, the firm is earning a surplus return over the interest cost. This type of situation represents a positive financial leverage and the use of debt funding would be desirable and well-justified. Positive leverage would lead to higher EPS for equity shareholders.

2. **Return on investment is less than the cost of interest:** If the firm was able to deploy funds to earn a return of only 8% while the cost of interest is 10%, the firm is not even earning enough to meet the interest cost. This type of situation represents a negative financial leverage and the use of debt funding would not be justified as it would reduce the EPS available to equityholders.

3. **Return on investment is equal to the cost of interest:** If the firm was able to deploy funds to earn a return of 10% while the cost of interest is also 10%, the firm is just earning enough to meet the interest cost, but no surplus gain for the shareholders. This type of situation would not be considered favourable unless some other strategic reasons are present to justify the use of debt financing.

Financial leverage can be positive or negative depending on whether the funds raised by debt were deployed in a way to earn higher returns than the cost of interest.

EXAMPLE 13.6 To illustrate the effect of positive and negative leverage, assume four companies R, S, T and U are from the same industry and identical in all respects except their capital structure. Each company has assets of ₹1,00,000 each on which each company earns a return on investment (that is, EBIT) of 15%. Company R is financed entirely by equity while the remaining three companies have 50% debt and 50% equity financing. Assume further that Company S pays 12% interest on debt; Company T pays 15% interest while Company U pays 18% interest. The rate of income tax is 30% and the face value of equity shares is ₹10 each.

(a) Calculate the EPS for each company,
(b) Comment on the effect of leverage on the firm's profitability.

Solution: Comparison of four companies with different financial leverage:

	R	*S*	*T*	*U*
Assets (₹)	1,00,000	1,00,000	1,00,000	1,00,000
ROI	0.15	0.15	0.15	0.15
EBIT per annum	15,000	15,000	15,000	15,000
Interest payment	0	6,000	7,500	9,000
Earnings Before Taxes (EBT)	15,000	9,000	7,500	6,000
Income Tax (30%)	4,500	2,700	2,250	1,800
Earnings After Taxes (EAT)	10,500	6,300	5,250	4,200
Preference dividend	0	0	0	0
Earnings for equityholders	10,500	6,300	5,250	4,200
Number of equity shares	10,000	5,000	5,000	5,000
Earnings Per Share (EPS) ₹	1.05	1.26	1.05	0.84

The above table shows the effect of financial leverage on the EPS of the four companies. Companies R and T have same EPS even though R is all equity financed company while T has 50% debt funding. Since company T earns same 15% return on investment as the rate of interest it pays, there is no positive effect of financial leverage on the company's EPS. Unless there are some strategic reasons to justify the use of debt financing, the company could avoid debt.

In comparison, Company S was able to deploy funds to earn a return higher than the cost of interest it pays. Accordingly, Company S is earning a surplus return over the interest cost which has resulted in a higher EPS for equity shareholders. This situation represents a positive financial leverage and the use of debt funding would be well justified.

Company U has fared the worst among the four companies. Company U was able to deploy funds to earn a return less than the cost of interest; in other words, it is not even earning enough to meet the interest cost. As a result, the EPS available to equityholders has declined as compared to what it would have been without debt financing. Clearly, this situation represents a negative financial leverage and the use of debt funding in Company U is not justified.

13.3.5 Financial Leverage with Preference Capital

We have said above that the return on investment (that is, EBIT) should be more than cost of interest for the firm to have a positive financial leverage so that the use of debt funding can be justified. If instead of debt, the firm is considering use of preference capital to finance the new project and wants to compute the minimum ROI that should be earned to make the financial leverage positive, the above formula would need to be adjusted for the effect of income taxes. Note that interest charges on debt are paid out of EBIT, but preference dividends are paid out of the profits after taxes.

Therefore, the ROI on preference capital should cover not only the fixed dividend promised to the investors (in preference shares) but also the income taxes that have to be paid before paying the preference dividends. In other words, the actual ROI should be greater than the break-even ROI computed as follows:

$$\text{Break-even ROI} = \text{Rate of fixed preference dividend} \div [1 - \text{Tax rate}]$$

Thus, if the rate of preference dividend is 10% and the income tax rate applicable to the firm is 30%, then the break-even ROI would be:

$$\text{Break-even ROI} = 10\% \div [1 - 0.3]$$
$$= 10\% \div 0.7 = 14.29\%$$

Therefore in this situation, the firm must earn ROI of more than 14.29% to have positive leverage with preference capital and justify its use to finance the project.

EXAMPLE 13.7 A company is considering using 12% preference capital to finance a project. If the rate of income taxes applicable to the firm is 40%, what would be the minimum ROI that would give the firm a positive financial leverage?

Solution: The Return on Investment (ROI) should be greater than the sum of income taxes plus dividend rate:

$$\text{ROI} > \text{Rate of fixed preference dividend} \div [1 - \text{Tax rate}]$$
$$\text{ROI} > 12\% \div [1 - 0.4] = 12\% \div 0.6 = 20\%$$

Accordingly, in the given situation, the firm must earn ROI of more than 20% to have favourable financial leverage with preference capital.

13.3.6 Leverage and the Financing Strategy

Leverage is a double-edged weapon: in good times it can increase profits much faster than the rate of increase in sales, but in times of declining sales it would dampen profits sharply. The financing strategy of a firm must ensure that the combined or total leverage remains within reasonable and tolerable limits. For example, for a firm having high operating leverage it could be suicidal to have a high financial leverage too. This is because, in times of recession, when sales and profits are down, the combined weight of operating fixed cost and financial charges burden might put the firm in financial distress and it could default in servicing its debt obligations.

The financing strategy of a firm must ensure that the combined or total leverage remains within reasonable and tolerable limits.

By studying the past trends and taking into account the future forecasts of business prospects, the firm should estimate the extent to which sales can be adversely affected. These limits can be used to decide tolerable operating and financial leverages.

The product life cycle should also be kept in mind. For example, the financial leverage can be increased during the growth phase of the product and should be reduced when the firm approaches the stage of stable operations and the declining phase.

Between operating and financial leverages, operating leverage could potentially be more serious since for many firms the operating fixed charges are much higher than the financial fixed charges. Also, often it is very difficult to get rid of fixed operating costs. Relatively, the fixed financial charges can be avoided by repaying debts, but to do so, the firm must have adequate cash flows. The ability of the firm to generate steady operating cash flows to meet timely interest payments and repay debt is the ultimate determinant of the capital structure. This aspect is taken up for discussion in the next section.

13.4 Financial Ratios

The importance of operating cash flows in servicing debt cannot be overstated. It is out of the operating cash flows that a firm would pay for the interest charges on loans, preference dividends and any other fixed financial obligations such as lease payments. Larger and more stable the cash flows, greater would be the debt taking capacity of the firm. The relationship between operating cash flows and fixed financial charges including interest on debt are often analyzed both by managers and external experts to examine how reasonable and diligent is the capital structure policy of the firm.

13.4.1 Interest Coverage Ratio

This ratio measures the company's ability to service debt out of its operating earnings (that is, EBIT). A high interest coverage ratio indicates that the firm would be able to pay timely interest on debt comfortably even in recessionary conditions when sales and operating income tend to decline.

Interest Coverage = Profit before interest and taxes/Annual interest expense

Assuming a company has annual Earnings Before Interest and Taxes (EBIT) of ₹2,50,000 and its annual interest cost is ₹50,000, then the interest coverage ratio would be 5.0. An interest coverage ratio of 4 to 5 times may be considered desirable, but what would be a satisfactory ratio would also depend on the nature of the industry and stability of the firm's operating cash flows. Utility firms which usually have stable cash flows may find a somewhat lower interest coverage ratio satisfactory as compared to other firms whose sales and cash flows are subject to wide fluctuations.

A high interest coverage ratio indicates that the firm would be able to pay timely interest comfortably even in recessionary conditions.

A variation of the 'interest coverage' ratio is to compute a 'fixed financial charges' coverage ratio that would cover interest as well as other fixed financial charges (such as lease payments, if applicable) out of the operating income.

Higher the ratio better would be the assurance of timely payment of interest and other fixed financial charges. A ratio close to one would increase the chances of a default and financial distress.

A limitation of the interest coverage (and fixed financial charges coverage) ratio is that it does not take into account the repayment of the principal amount of debt. Many experts would favour using the debt service coverage ratio discussed below instead of the ratio that covers only the interest part of a loan.

13.4.2 Debt Service Coverage Ratio (DSCR)

The debt service coverage ratio, as the name implies, considers servicing both the interest as well as the annual debt repayment instalments since both of them should be met out of the operating earnings of the firm. The DSCR ratio is computed by relating the operating earnings (EBIT) to the sum total of annual interest charges plus the loan repayment instalment:

$$\text{DSCR} = \frac{\text{Earnings before interest and taxes}}{\text{Interest charges} + \dfrac{\text{Loan repayment}}{1-t}}$$

where, 't' is the income tax rate applicable to the firm. Note that the principal amount of the loan is repaid out of 'after-tax' profits, because of which the loan instalment due annually would be adjusted for the tax effect. Continuing with the same example as the interest coverage ratio (EBIT of ₹2,50,000 and its annual interest cost is ₹50,000), if the annual repayment instalment is ₹25,000 and the income tax rate is 40%, the DSCR would be:

$$\text{DSCR} = \frac{2{,}50{,}000}{50{,}000 + \dfrac{25{,}000}{1-0.4}}$$

$$\text{DSCR} = \frac{2{,}50{,}000}{50{,}000+41{,}667} = \frac{2{,}50{,}000}{91{,}667}$$

$$= 2.73 \text{ times}$$

Higher the ratio better would be the assurance of timely payment of interest and repayment of the principal amount of debt. A ratio close to one would increase the chances of a default and financial distress.

13.4.3 EBIT versus Free Cash Flow

Some experts argue that instead of using EBIT as the numerator, it would be better to use earnings before interest, taxes, depreciation and amortization (EBITDA) for calculation of the interest coverage and debt services coverage ratios. Their argument is that EBITDA is a better measure of the cash flow that would be required to service financial charges and to repay loans. Their argument may hold good to some extent provided the funds represented by depreciation and amortization are not needed by the firm to replace or upgrade fixed assets such as plant and machinery. To the extent such funds would be required to carry out essential replacement or up-gradation of fixed assets, they cannot be called 'free cash flows', and hence, would not be available to meet financial charges or to repay loans. Secondly, knowing that debt financing can be risky, the firm must leave spare cash to meet contingencies and must not count every penny in their pursuit of debt financing. Due to these reasons, a conservative estimation of operating cash flow, as represented by EBIT may be appropriate for calculation of the ratios.

13.5 Credit Rating, Timing and Reserve Debt Capacity

The credit rating agencies may downgrade a firm with aggressive debt ratios, conveying an increased possibility of default by the firm. This, in turn, would raise the cost of capital as debt suppliers would seek a higher risk premium. The reverse may happen when a firm has a low debt ratio in its capital structure.

As Gordon Donaldson suggests, firms should commit only so much cash flow to servicing debt obligations as they are sure to earn during the most adverse circumstances, such as a recession. It would therefore be desirable for a firm to keep adequate reserve debt capacity to fall back on during tough times.

13.6 Timing and Repayment Schedule

Timing is a crucial part of capital structure planning. Funds planning should indicate when and how much funding would be required for each phase of the project being executed. If funds are raised much before the time they are required, the interest meter would start ticking long before the funds are actually utilized. Equally important is that the funding plan should also specify when and how the project would generate cash flows to repay the loans as soon as possible so that over time the interest cost can be reduced. Timely execution of the project and control over cash outflows and cash inflows is absolutely necessary.

13.7 The Ten Commandments of Capital Structure

In this and the previous chapter, we have discussed a number of factors that have a bearing on the capital structure decision. To revise, here is a list of ten most critical factors—like the Ten Commandments—that should be considered while deciding on the firm's capital structure policy.

1. Operating income and cash flows: They should be estimated as carefully and accurately as possible because they define the debt capacity of the firm.

2. Cost of capital: The relative cost of debt and equity should be analyzed and the firm should go for debt only if debt is substantially cheaper so that induction of debt would significantly lower the overall cost of capital.

3. Income tax rates: One of the most talked about advantage of debt financing is the tax-shield available on interest expense. The tax advantage should be evaluated against the financial risk.

4. Debt-equity ratios: Help the firm keep a check on the proportion of debt in the capital structure in tune with industry norms.

5. Trade-offs: The possibility of failure to service the debt and distress costs should be weighed against the advantages claimed for debt financing.

6. Degree of leverage: The operating, financing and combined leverage should be analyzed before finalizing the capital structure strategy. Debt should be used only when the leverage is positive.

7. Debt covenants: The debt agreement may include some clauses that place restrictions on executive actions. Their effect on the functioning of the firm must be studied and debt covenants should be carefully negotiated with the lenders.

8. Market conditions and the legal framework: Debt funding becomes more compelling when equity markets are down and the firm is not getting the right price for equity issues. Also, which sources of debt funding are permitted by the regulatory authorities would surely impact the financing decision. For example, restrictive eligibility conditions for raising debt from international markets might constraint a firm's capital structure decision.

9. Impact on EPS and value of the firm: The main reason for debt financing is to use borrowed capital to boost the earnings per share for the equityholders.

10. Corporate governance and miscellaneous: Debt financing requires high degree of corporate governance, transparency and discipline on the part of the management so that it can maintain a high degree of credibility in the market.

Researchable Issues

Faculty members, students and research scholars may like to consider the following selected issues for further research and case writing.

- Capital structure practices and share prices: evidence from the Indian markets.
- Capital structure practices and corporate governance.
- Signalling theory and investor exploitation.
- Capital structure, dividend policy and the value of the firm.
- Capital structure practices in the services sector.
- A critical appraisal of capital structure practices in real estate and infrastructure sectors.

References

Gitman Lawrence J., *Principles of Managerial Finance*, 11th ed., Pearson Addison Wesley, Boston, 2006.

Hamada, Robert S., "Portfolio Analysis, Market Equilibrium, and Corporate Finance", *Journal of Finance*, March 1969, pp. 13–31.

Horne Van, James C., *Financial Management and Policy*, 12th ed., Prentice Hall of India, Delhi, 2005.

Katia D'hulster, 'The leverage ratio—a new binding limit on banks, Note Number-II, December 2009, International Finance Corporation, World Bank, www.worldbank.org/financialcrisis/pdf/leverage-ratio-web.pdf

Levy, H. and Sarnat M., *Capital Investment and Financial Decisions*, Prentice Hall, New Jersey, 1978.

Modigliani, Franco and Miller, Merton H., "Corporate Income Taxes and the Cost of Capital: A Correction", *American Economic Review*, **63**, June 1963, pp. 433–442.

Richard A. Brealey, Stewart C. Myers, and Franklin Allen, *Principles of Corporate Finance*, 10th ed., McGraw-Hill, Irwin, New York, 2011.

Stewart C. Myers and Nicholas S. Majluf, "Corporate Financing and Investment Decisions When Firms Have Information That Investor Do Not Have", *Journal of Financial Economics*, **13**, June 1984, pp. 187–222.

Points to Remember

- **Investors value** equity shares on the basis of the earnings available to equityholders. Accordingly a firm should adopt such a financing plan that would maximize the earnings per share left for the equityholders after paying for interest on borrowed capital, preference dividends and taxes.

- **EBIT-EPS analysis** highlights the effect of different financing plans on the Earning Per Share (EPS) for a given amount of 'earnings before interest and taxes' (EBIT) of the firm. Since the financial objective of the company is to maximize the wealth of equityholders, the firm should select the financing alternative that maximizes the EPS to equityholders.
- **Equation method:** The EPS under different financing options can be computed by using the equation: $\text{EPS} = \dfrac{(\text{EBIT} - I)(1-t) - P_d}{N}$ where EBIT = Earnings before interest and taxes, I = Annual pre-tax interest on debt, t = Rate of income tax applicable to the company, P_d = Fixed dividend payable on preference capital, and N = Total number of equity shares.
- **EBIT indifference point** is that level of EBIT at which the company would be neutral between the two sources of financing the project. The EPS at the EBIT indifference point would be the same whether the company goes for one source of funding or the other.
- **Leverage** arises due to the existence of fixed costs in the cost structure of a firm. Fixed costs related to operating activities of the firm create operating leverage and fixed costs related to financing activities create financing leverage. As a result of the leverage effect, profits would decline more than proportionately with every fall in sales and rise more than proportionately with every increase in sales. Thus leverage has a magnifying effect on profits.
- **Positive financial leverage** occurs when a firm is able to deploy debt funds to earn a return higher than the cost of interest it pays so that the firm will earn a surplus return which would result in higher EPS for equity shareholders.
- **Financial ratios**, such as interest coverage ratio and debt service coverage ratio are helpful in analyzing a firm's preparedness in servicing the debt obligations. While the interest coverage ratio shows whether the firm would be able to pay timely interest out of its operating income, debt service coverage ratio indicates the firm's ability to service debt including payment of interest and repay the loans comfortably.

Questions

1. Discuss the pros and cons of debt and equity financing.
2. Explain the meaning and purpose of EBIT-EPS analysis and illustrate the same using a suitable numerical example.
3. Explain the meaning and use of EBIT indifference point. Using a suitable numerical example show how to compute the indifferent point by equation method, and present the same graphically.
4. Differentiate between operating and financial leverage and explain how they arise. Using a suitable numerical example show how an understanding of the combined leverage can help in capital structure decision making.
5. What is positive financial leverage and when does it arise? Using a suitable numerical example show the effect of positive and negative financial leverage on EPS.
6. Differentiate between interest coverage ratio and debt service coverage ratio. Using suitable numerical examples, explain their computation and use in deciding the capital structure.
7. Discuss and illustrate the main factors that should be considered while deciding on the capital structure policy.

Multiple Choice Questions

1. In order to keep the total leverage within reasonable and tolerable limits:
   (a) A firm having high operating leverage should avoid a high financial leverage.
   (b) A firm having high operating leverage should also have a high financial leverage.
   (c) A firm's operating leverage should be equal to the financial leverage.
   (d) None of the above.
2. Relating financing strategy to the product life cycle:
   (a) The financial leverage should be reduced during the growth phase and can be increased during the declining phase.
   (b) The financial leverage can be increased during the growth phase and should be reduced during the declining phase.
   (c) The financial leverage should neither be increased during the growth phase nor can it be reduced during the declining phase.
   (d) None of the above.
3. What would be the operating and financial leverage of a firm with following particulars?

   Sales volume = 1,000 units
   Selling price per unit = ₹10
   Variable cost per unit = ₹6
   Fixed operating cost = ₹2,500
   Interest = ₹900

   (a) Operating leverage 2.67, financial leverage 2.78
   (b) Operating leverage 4.00, financial leverage 2.78
   (c) Operating leverage 2.67, financial leverage 2.50
   (d) None of the above.
4. What would be the combined leverage of a firm with following particulars?

   Sales volume = 1,000 units
   Selling price per unit = ₹ 10
   Variable cost per unit = ₹ 6
   Fixed operating cost = ₹ 2,500
   Interest = ₹ 900

   (a) 6.67 (b) 7.42
   (c) 11.12 (d) None of the above.
5. A firm has provided the following details about its planned performance for a year:

Sales	2,50,000
Less: variable cost	1,50,000
Contribution	1,00,000
Less: Fixed cost	40,000
EBIT	60,000
Interest	12,000
EBT	48,000

   What would be the approximate percentage change in EBT if its actual sales increased by 10%?
   (a) Increase by 10.42% (b) Decrease by 20.83%
   (c) Increase by 20.83% (d) None of the above

6. A firm has provided the following details about its planned performance for a year:

Sales	2,50,000
Less: Variable cost	1,50,000
Contribution	1,00,000
Less: Fixed cost	40,000
EBIT	60,000
Interest	12,000
EBT	48,000

What would be the approximate percentage change in EBT if its actual sales declined by 20%?

(a) Decrease by 32.72% (b) Decrease by 41.67%
(c) Increase by 41.67% (d) None of the above

7. Lower financial leverage results from use of more ________.

(a) Debt capital (b) Equity capital
(c) Debt and preference capital (d) None of the above

8. Assume a firm has annual sales of ₹30,00,000 and its variable cost of goods sold is 80%. Its fixed operating costs amount of ₹2,00,000 and it has debt of ₹20,00,000 that costs 12% interest per annum. What would be the combined (total) leverage of the firm?

(a) 3.75 (b) 2.50
(c) 1.50 (d) None of the above

Self-Test Questions

1. Swan Company at present has an all equity capital structure of 20,000 shares of ₹10 each. To finance its new investment project, it now wants to raise an additional ₹1,50,000 for which it has identified three alternative funding sources as follows:
   1. Additional 10,000 shares at ₹15 per share;
   2. Debt at 15% interest;
   3. Preference capital at 14% dividend.

   The present EBIT of the company is ₹75,000 per annum but with the new project, the EBIT will rise to ₹1,20,000 per annum. Income tax rate is 30%.

   Using the EBIT-EPS analysis, decide which financing alternative should be accepted.

2. Using the same data as in Q1, calculate the EBIT indifference point between equity and debt financing plans using the equation method.

3. From the following information provided about Grapes Company, calculate the operating and financial leverage:

   Annual sales volume = 25,000 units
   Selling price = ₹24 per unit
   Variable operating cost = ₹10 per unit
   Annual fixed operating cost = ₹1,50,000
   Annual interest = ₹80,000

4. Four companies J, K, L and M are from the same industry and identical in all respects except their capital structure. Each company has assets of ₹2,00,000 each and each company earns a return on investment (that is, EBIT) of 14%. Company J is financed entirely by equity while the remaining three companies have 50%

debt and 50% equity financing. Assume that Company K pays 10% interest on debt; Company L pays 14% interest while Company M pays 17% interest. The rate of income tax is 30% and the face value of equity shares is ₹10 each.
(a) Calculate the EPS for each company, and
(b) Comment on the effect of leverage on each company's profitability.

Problems

1. Apple Company at present has an all equity capital structure of 20,000 shares of ₹10 each. To finance its new investment project, it now wants to raise an additional ₹2,00,000 for which it has identified three alternative funding sources as follows:
   1. Additional 20,000 shares of ₹10 each;
   2. Debt at 14% interest;
   3. Preference capital at 12% dividend.

   The present EBIT of the company is ₹60,000 per annum but with the new project, the EBIT will rise to ₹1,40,000 per annum. Tax rate is 30%.

   Using the EBIT-EPS analysis, decide which financing alternative should be accepted.
2. Using the same data as in Q1, calculate the EPS under different financing options by the equation method.
3. Using the same data as in Q1, calculate the EBIT indifference point between equity and preference capital financing plans using the equation method.
4. From the following information provided about Grapes Company, calculate the operating and financial leverage:

   Annual sales volume = 6,000 units
   Selling price = ₹80 per unit
   Variable operating cost = ₹30 per unit
   Annual fixed operating cost = ₹1,50,000
   Annual interest = ₹50,000
5. Four companies V, X, Y and Z are from the same industry and identical in all respects except their capital structure. Each company has assets of ₹4,00,000 each and each company earns a return on investment (that is, EBIT) of 16%. Company V is financed entirely by equity while the remaining three companies have 50% debt and 50% equity financing. Company X pays 12% interest on debt; Company Y pays 16% interest while Company M pays 18% interest. The rate of income tax is 30% and the face value of equity shares is ₹10 each.
   (a) Calculate the EPS for each company
   (b) Comment on the effect of leverage on each company's profitability.

CASE

Maruti Suzuki India Limited—Long Term Financing Strategy
An emerging market subsidiary of an MNC is looking for the Best ways to finance its huge expansion program

The Abstract

Experts on capital structure claim that a business could reduce its overall cost of capital by using more of debt financing in proportion to shareholder funds. This in turn would make its products more competitive and improve its profitability, particularly in a cost-conscious emerging market like India. Yet, quite contrary to what the financial logic would apparently dictate, the passenger car industry leader Maruti Suzuki, a subsidiary of the Suzuki Motors Corporation, Japan, has been consistently avoiding debt as far as possible. All financial ratios point out to a great scope for enhancing shareholder value by using more of debt than at present. The Maruti financing policy is in contrast with the more venturesome financing policy followed by some of its competitors.

Why is Maruti management shy of the financial risk? What is the rationale behind its conservative financing policy? What are the determinants of the financing mix and how does the company integrate its financing strategy with its overall business strategy? Would the company change its financing policy in favour of debt financing for the next phase of the expansion? These are some of the aspects covered in the present case.

Key Words: Capital structure, debt-equity ratio, EBIT (earnings before interest and taxes), interest coverage ratio, financial risk, Crore (10 million or 100 Lac), ₹(Indian Rupee).

The Case

"You finance guys have a knack of making a mountain out of a mole," shouted Raghunath in the management committee meeting that had been called to discuss the long term financing strategy of Maruti Suzuki, "Now look at this financing situation that according to you is a big problem. I do not see the problem at all! Okay we need funds for the expansion plans, and yes, it is a huge amount, but then all the sources of funding available to our competitors are available to us too, isn't it?", he glared at the finance manager through his thick glasses before continuing, "so why don't you guys decide to mix the financing in the same proportions of debt and equity funding that others are doing? It is as simple as that and the issue is closed."

The Company

The Maruti Suzuki India Limited (MSIL, formerly known as MarutiUdyog Limited) is a subsidiary of Suzuki Motor Corporation, Japan. It was established in 1981 at a time when an overhaul of the Indian passenger car industry was overdue and the car buyers craved for fuel efficient cars backed by modern technology. Before the entry of Suzuki, the Indian passenger car market had been dominated by two major car makers Premier Automobiles and Hindustan Motors for over three decades. Maruti's first model M-800 introduced in December 1983 [source:www.marutisuzuki.com/about-us] became an instant hit and the company enjoyed a near monopoly in the market until mid-1990s. But the industry started getting crowded when the liberalization of the Indian economy and de-licensing of the passenger car industry in 1990s led to the entry of global players like Hyundai, Ford and General Motors as well as domestic giants such as Tata Motors. The intense competition that followed adversely affected Maruti's market share as well as profit margins resulting in a substantial downturn in the company's fortunes. The company that earned profits of ₹977 crore in FY1998 went down to incur a loss of ₹269 crore in FY2001. [Source: www.plus.capitaline.com]

The jolted company launched an aggressive drive to innovate and revamp operations, fighting on many fronts including product design, quality control, localization of high value components that were previously imported and other areas of cost reduction in order to revive its profitability and gain a position of sustainable competitiveness. These efforts showed salutary results reflected in a decline in the 'materials cost to net sales' ratio from a high of 90.9% in 2001 to 76.6% in 2005, thus improving profit margins. Similarly, the cost of debt was lowered by repaying a substantial part of borrowed capital between 2001 and 2005. Company's debt that previously stood at ₹1,112 crore was brought down to ₹308 crore during the period. [Source: The Company annual Reports FY2002 to FY2006]

Bullish on the Future

As a result of these efforts, the company was able to make a spectacular come-back and its profit rose to ₹770 crore in FY2004 and further to ₹1,305 crore in FY2005. During the same period, the company ploughed back profits by restricting dividend payout, as well as made a public issue of equity in 2003 which together raised the shareholders' funds (including reserves) from ₹2,643 crore in 2001 to ₹4,379 crore in 2005 [source: The Company annual reports FY2002 to 2006]. Since then, the company never looked back and progressed from strength to strength. It has been the market leader for close to three decades and cumulatively, "Maruti Suzuki is the only Indian Company to have crossed the 10 million sales mark since its inception. In 2011–12, the company sold over 1.13 million vehicles including 1,27,379 units of exports". [Source: The Company annual report 2011–12]. Now in early 2013 the company was very bullish on the future of the industry in the country. Though the car demand had witnessed some sluggishness in recent months [Exhibit-4], the company regarded it as a passing phase that did not need to be taken seriously. It had planned huge investments [source: Technology-corbee, 2012] aimed at modernizing its main plants, setting up a brand new diesel engine plant, double its capacity in the next five years, and build new research and development, as well as testing facilities. Overall, an aggregate investment of ₹15,000 crore (about USD 2.5 billion) was planned for which the company would need financing.

The Financing Options

Sharman the finance manager had spent considerable time studying the financing pattern used by Maruti as well as its main competitors particularly Tata Motors. Tata Motors operated both in commercial vehicles as well as passenger car segments and its total annual sales revenue was significantly higher than Maruti. Sharman had noted with interest that Tata Motors adopted considerable debt financing [see Exhibit-2A and 2B]. His own plan of action for the management committee meeting was to first highlight how important was the financing decision for the company, then present main alternatives of debt and equity financing and finally sum up with his recommendations on the best source of financing for the next phase of investment.

Sharman had barely started when Raghunath had interrupted. There seemed a lot of weight in what Raghu had said and Sharman felt stumped for an instant. He thought for a minute and replied, "I think our financing scheme should represent the company's own strategy and not merely copy what others are doing."

Atul the CEO normally reserved his comments, but thought he must intervene, "I think Sharman has a point. If all we are doing is to copy others, why would the company need us? Whether it is product innovation, marketing channels or financing, we have to consider our own objectives, mission, risks and opportunities and decide what is uniquely best for us; even this meeting is in that direction. The company does not pay us fat salaries just to use a herding approach which can be very dangerous in a competitive market." Then he turned to Sharman, "Have you considered how much external financing the company would require, and secondly, what would you propose for the financing method?"

Sharman was glad to get some support from the CEO and said, "Yes, of course," and looked around. The management committee comprised of several senior managers in addition to the CEO. There was Raghu with a technical background, Saney the marketing chief, Hayato the planning manager, Chanda the CSR manager and a couple of other senior managers. Sharman had recently joined the company and was not senior enough to be a member of the management committee but as the CFO, also a member, was travelling, Sharman was asked to take charge of the presentation. He was very keen to make an impression as a senior finance position was likely to become vacant and he wanted to establish himself as the perfect choice for the same.

Debt Financing: Pros and Cons

He fixed up his laptop projecting company data on the LCD board and said, "As you know the company has been following a conservative approach with regards to paying dividends, so it has impressive annual retained earnings. In the year 2011–12, the company reported retained earnings of ₹1,383 crore. Assuming retained earnings continue at this pace for the next five years, the company would have ₹6,915 crore, leaving a balance of ₹8,085 crore to be raised from external sources."

Hayato was a short and slim person from Japan and many regarded him as a confidante of the foreign shareholders. He showed his concern, "You know, when we deal with the future, it is not good to count every penny. Often there are ups and downs, so taking the contingencies into account I would think that we should not count on more than ₹5,000 crores to come by from internal sources. He turned to the CEO, 'what do you say, Atul'?"

Atul knew that the Board of Directors was under pressure to increase dividends and some other pending decisions would also use up part of the retained earnings. The annual royalty payable to the parent company also required considerable cash outflow. In a related development, the British FMCG major Unilever had recently hiked the royalty rates chargeable from its highly successful Indian subsidiary Hindustan Unilever; Atul was sure this development would not escape the attention of his own parent company which might also decide to increase the royalty payable by the Indian operations. Without revealing any of these, he replied, "Yes, the figure Mr. Hayato gave is a good basis to proceed."

Sharman noted the point and continued, "I may add here that we have not included the cash flow made available from the annual depreciation charged, because such funds would be required to meet the routine replacement of plant in order to maintain the physical capital of the company." He paused for a second before continuing, "I have made a thorough analysis of the debt-equity ratios of our company as well its competitor Tata Motors and have come to the conclusion that the best way to raise the external funds required would be through debt financing. It would help the company in reducing its overall cost of capital and increase the returns available to equity holders."

Raghu again interrupted him, "Well I do not know about the depreciation, but I totally disagree when you say the whole lot should come from loans. Debt funds do not come cheap, and would mean a financial burden for the company." Hayato immediately echoed, "Yes, and debt would increase the financial risk too. I think Maruti-Suzuki should be a debt-free company."

Atul said to Sharman, "Can you elaborate on the effect of debt financing on the overall cost of capital?"

Sharman was prepared for this, "As equity investments are more risky, shareholders require a risk premium, and hence a higher return on their investment—that makes the equity capital more expensive than debt. If we mix the two sources—costly equity and cheaper debt—the result would obviously be a lower weighted average cost. Let us assume the cost of equity capital is 20% and the gross cost of interest is 10%. Interest payment on loans is a tax-deductible expense and gets the company a tax-shield, so that if the corporate tax rate is 30%, the net cost of debt would work out to only 7.0% [i.e. 10 × (1 – 0.30)]. Now, if debt and equity are combined in equal proportions by maintaining a debt-equity ratio of 50:50, the overall cost of capital would be just 13.50% [1/2 × 20 + 1/2 × 7.0] as compared to 20% if the company went for an all-equity financing."

Raghu was on his feet again, "Do you realize how contradictory your own suggestions are? You just said that equity investments are risky because of which such investors would require a higher return on their investment. Obviously, you are referring to the business or operating risk. Now if we add the burden of debt financing and - as Mr. Hayato just said – increased financial risk, it would only worsen the equity investors' risk perception which means they would penalize the company by demanding a correspondingly higher return on their investment. The higher cost of equity would in turn wipe out any advantage in cost of capital that you claim from debt financing, thus making the whole issue of financing mix ridiculously invalid."

He looked around the room to make sure everyone paid attention as he continued, "In fact, I recall having read an article which showed that in perfect capital markets, how a business firm is financed would be irrelevant to its value [Ross, 2012] ; the market values a firm by its earning capacity and not how the firm is financed. That is why I said we could mix financing the way our competitors are doing, or any other way because it would not really make a difference to the value of the firm or the overall cost of capital."

Sharman felt he was losing ground but knew there had to be an explanation if the concept of optimum capital structure was to hold good. Putting his thoughts together, he patiently explained, "Of course, there is a trade-off between risk and return; 'no pain-no gain' is a simple rule of life. You rightly emphasized on the words "perfect capital markets", but the question is where would you find them? In the imperfect world we live in, we must take calculated risks to meet the corporate objectives. In principle we could say that debt increases the financial risk and I can understand your concern about debt financing since it creates fixed interest liability that must be paid regularly whether we sink or sail. But in reality it would become risky only at higher levels of debt financing relative to the equity. As you can see from the company's brief financial statements (Exhibit 1A and 1B), the current debt level is so low that even if all of the next phase of investments are funded through debt, we would not have a worrisome financial risk."

"And do not forget the tax advantage on interest cost that would surely act to bring down the overall cost of capital. Another big advantage of the debt option is the flexibility to repay debt when it is no longer required; such flexibility is usually not available in the equity option. All considered, I am confident the debt option should be preferable."

Impact on the Shareholders' Return

Hayato asked, "Did you say debt has a favourable impact on the returns available to equity holders? How is that?"

Even before Sharman could answer, Chanda who had been quiet so far said, "If we raised debt, I would be worried about the terms and conditions that banks typically insist on. The loan covenants could be very rigid and stifle our normal operations. Debt is after all a liability and no lender could be totally benign. I remember the Shakespeare play where the lender literally takes a pound of flesh off the borrower when the latter could not service his debt in time."

Sharman tried to defend boldly, "Well first things first. Clearly, when we invest in profitable projects, the company would earn more on the borrowed capital than the cost of interest. The surplus earned in this way would go to enhance the earnings available to equity holders and the earnings per share (EPS). It would have a positive effect on the share price too because investors normally use a price-earnings (P/E) ratio to value stock. You would be glad to know that the new investments planned are likely to increase the company's earnings before interest and taxes (EBIT) by an additional ₹4,075 crore per annum." Then, trying to hide his irritation, he turned to Chanda, "Please, can we leave such stories where they belong - novels or other works of fiction! This is modern business we are talking about where the lenders need the borrowers as much as the other way round. In the real world we live in, all entities including individuals, firms, even nations borrow and lend."

Hayato politely said, "My friend, all this is fine, but I think as far as possible Maruti-Suzuki should be a debt-free company. Debt financing in my view is like a fair-weather friend. I have seen companies which thrived on debt financing when the business was on a high, but during recession when sales and profits went down, they could not even earn enough to pay for their interest dues and virtually collapsed. Therefore, the financing strategy we choose should ensure that our capacity to meet fixed interest charges is never compromised and always remains beyond doubt."

Corporate Objectives and Financing

Atul was listening to the ongoing discussion and knew that the financing decision must be integrated with the overall objectives of the company. Maruti Suzuki's corporate objectives were to remain market leaders in the passenger car segment, increase its market share, and create entry barriers for competitors by ensuring maximum customer satisfaction by providing highly efficient cars at affordable prices and low maintenance cost throughout the life of the car, while simultaneously enhancing shareholder welfare in terms of share values and payment of dividends.

He said, "It is important that we should not lose sight of our corporate objectives. In the early years, Maruti had to rely on debt capital due to modest availability of equity capital. The debt to equity ratio at that time was close to 1:1; that is, debt and equity mixed in equal proportions. However, as the company grows and has internal accruals of funds through retained earnings, don't you think the dependence on borrowed capital should reduce? Particularly at a time when the interest rates are so high, perhaps we should prefer the equity option for the external funding required."

Sharman smiled, "I have to both agree and disagree with the points you have raised. I agree with you that for cash rich and well established companies like us, priority should be given to internal sources of financing. However, I wish to differ with you regarding the choice between debt and equity for the remaining part of funding required when internal sources have been exhausted. Research findings show that companies use a 'pecking-order' of financing sources [Brealey, 2012], according to which after depleting internal sources, companies prefer debt over equity when they need external financing. Equity financing would then be used as a source of last resort, if debt is not available at reasonable terms."

Sharman felt more at ease while addressing the CEO than either Raghu or Hayato. Knowing that he had made a point, he continued, "Regarding the interest rates, yes, it is true that average interest rates have been pretty high at 14-15% per annum in recent months, particularly because the Reserve Bank of India, the country's central bank, has been following a tough monetary policy. But that need not directly apply to our company. Because of the company's impeccable market standing, banks would be happy to lend us at minimum interest rate which at present is 10.50% [source: banknetindia.com]. I have checked with the country's leading banks and you can take it confirmed."

Equity and Preference Capital

Maruti Suzuki was established as a result of the joint collaboration between Suzuki of Japan and the Government of India. Since then, Suzuki had purchased a considerable part of the Government's stake in the company and now held over 54% shareholding in the company. The share capital of Maruti-Suzuki in 2012 was made up of 28.89 crore equity shares of the par value of Rs. 5 each [source: MSIL annual report 2011–12]. The company equity shares were listed on both the national level stock exchanges: the Bombay Stock Exchange (BSE) and the National Stock Exchange (NSE).

Saney asked, "If the company goes for the equity route, what is the projected price per share we could get? I am asking this because I am myself a shareholder and have observed that the stock exchange values are subject to huge volatility. During the past one year, the minimum and maximum Maruti share prices quoted on the BSE and the NSE have ranged between ₹1428 on the higher side and ₹900 on the lower [Exhibit -3]. So can we hope to sell fresh shares at approximately the average of these two prices?"

Hayato seemed to have come alive, "My friends, again, no doubt the higher the share price we get the better it would be but I would go for a conservative approach here. I have observed several public issues. As soon as information goes out that the company would be making a fresh issue of shares, market analysts start advising investors to sell out, simply because the additional availability of shares post-issue would put pressure on the market price which would likely decline. Investors are well informed today. That is why most companies offer their 'rights' issues at a hefty discount which might range up to 20% of the pre-issue market price. This is particularly relevant because ours would be a pretty large public issue." He looked at his papers before continuing, "In our situation, I have been advised by an investment banker that we could be confident of a successful issue at an issue price of ₹800 per share for the additional public issue."

Sharman was impressed with Hayato's meticulous home work because even his own discrete enquiries with some broking houses had indicated a similar range. At the same time, he felt it was his duty to caution the group, "But the big question in case of the equity financing option is whether the foreign shareholders of Maruti-Suzuki, that is the parent company, would be willing and capable of subscribing to their part of the proportionate additional shares issued? If that is not possible, their effective post-issue relative equity holding would decline which I am sure they would not like."

Chanda offered a way out, "A few years ago, I had invested in the preference shares of another company, which has been paying me fixed rates of dividends ever since. So if the equity route is not feasible, may be the company could explore issuing preference shares. I have noted that Maruti-Suzuki does not have any preference share capital so far."

Sharman seemed happy at the mention of preference share capital, "Thanks Chanda; I may add here that going by market trends, the cost of preference share capital in terms of the fixed dividend payable to investors would likely be same as the Base interest rate of 10.50% per annum I said earlier."

Hayato looked surprised, "What is preference share capital? Could it be similar to what is called the 'second capital' in some countries? Anyways, with regard to the willingness and ability of the parent company to subscribe to the additional shares, yes, to the best of my information and belief, the parent company would be able to do so, provided the future profitability and earnings per share looked promising. I am somewhat concerned that the company's reported net profit has continuously declined during the past three years."

Atul looked at his note book and said, "Well, no doubt our industry suffers from its share of volatility in market conditions but we are confident about the brighter future prospects. In fact I can add here that Sharman's figure of the incremental 'earnings before interest and taxes' (EBIT) of ₹4,075 crore per annum from the new projects is a reasonably conservative estimate; we might actually end up doing better than that if the business environment turns more favourable. Still Mr. Hayato's point about the company's capacity to service debt during the downturns is very valid. Therefore, I think we should make our analysis with three sets of assumptions regarding the estimated level of EBIT: (i) Base-case scenario where the new EBIT would consist of the current earnings from continuing operations plus Sharman's figure as given above; (ii) A worst-case scenario of the aggregate EBIT downturn by 20%, and finally (iii) A boom-case scenario with the aggregate EBIT going up by 20% as compared to the level under scenario (i)."

As Hayato and others nodded agreement, he asked Sharman, "Can you brief us on the current 'corporate income tax rate' as well as the Dividend Distribution Tax (DDT) in our country?" Sharman was ready, "Sorry I forgot. Taxation is a complicated issue, but simply stated, the corporate net incomes are taxed at an effective rate of 32.445%. All dividends received are tax-free in the hands of the shareholders but the company paying the dividends has to pay the DDT on the total amount of dividends distributed. The effective DDT rate currently is 16.225%. We can assume these rates to be valid for our calculations."

Atul was happy as well as confused; happy at the quality of discussion and confused as to what he was finally going to recommend to the Board? To conclude the meeting he said, "Thank you all for making it convenient to participate. Sharman, if you can pass on the financial data along with your analysis and the ratios you have calculated, I will like to go through it all again before I write to the Board."

Questions

1. Briefly explain the following and discuss their implications for the optimal capital structure: MM theory, the traditional approach and the pecking order theory.
2. Identify the factors that companies in competitive industries in general and MSIL in particular should take into account while deciding their capital structure.
3. Using data provided in Exhibits 1 and 2, calculate: (a) the debt-equity ratios and (b) interest coverage ratios for Maruti Suzuki and compare them with those of Tata Motors. Summarize your main findings.
4. Briefly discuss the main features of financing strategy of MSIL in recent years. In your opinion, what should be the objectives of the future financing strategy?
5. Using relevant quantitative information provided in the case, carry out an EBIT-EPS analysis on an annual basis under (i) equity, (ii) debt and (iii) preference capital financing options for each of the three EBIT-scenarios mentioned in the case. [Ignore the time value of money.]
6. How would your analysis in the previous question change if the CEO gives you the feedback that the Board is ready to consider any suitable capital structure provided it satisfies the following targets ratios: (a) debt to equity ratio not to exceed 1:2, that is, debt should not be more than half of the equity (share capital plus reserves), and (b) a minimum interest coverage ratio of 5.00 under all scenarios.
7. In your opinion, how should Maruti-Suzuki finance its expansion investments? Why?

   Note: The case is based on secondary sources of information and may contain certain assumptions and estimates. The names used in the case are hypothetical and it is prepared solely for the academic purpose of facilitating class-room discussion.

EXHIBIT 13.1A

Maruti-Suzuki Profit & Loss account
[Income Statement for year ended...]

(₹ in crore)

	March 2012	*March* 2011	*March* 2010	*March* 2009	*March* 2008
Income					
Operating income	35,558	36,562	29,318	20,729	18,067
Expenses					
Material consumed	28,171	28,807	22,435	16,340	13,622
Manufacturing expenses	2,086	2,160	1,278	910	671
Personnel expenses	844	704	546	471	356
Selling expenses	996	960	916	738	560
Administrative expenses	641	614	405	389	326
Expenses capitalised	–43	–26	–	–22	–20
Cost of sales	32,694	33,218	25,580	18,826	15,516
Operating profit	2,865	3,343	3,738	1,904	2,551
Other recurring income	474	746	618	548	456
Adjusted PBDIT	3,338	4,089	4,356	2,451	3,007
Financial expenses	55	24	34	51	60
Depreciation	1,138	1,014	825	707	568
Other write offs	–	–	–	–	–
Adjusted PBT	2,144	3,051	3,497	1,694	2,380
Tax charges	511	820	1,095	457	763
Adjusted PAT	1,633	2,231	2,402	1,237	1,616
Non recurring items	–107	39	44	–56	38
Other non cash adjustments	109	19	51	38	77
Reported net profit	1,635	2,289	2,498	1,219	1,731
Earnings before appropriation	13,493	12,339	10,502	8,244	7,368
Equity dividend	217	217	173	101	145
Preference dividend	–	–	–	–	–
Dividend tax	35	35	29	17	25
Retained earnings	13,241	12,087	10,300	8,126	7,199
Reported Net Profit Less Dividend and Dividend Tax	1,383	2,037	2,296	1,100	1,562

EXHIBIT 13.1B

Maruti-Suzuki Balnance Sheet

(₹ in crore)

	March 2012	*March* 2011	*March* 2010	*March* 2009	*March* 2008
Sources of funds					
Owner's fund					
Equity share capital	145	145	145	145	145
Share application money	–	–	–	–	–
Preference share capital	–	–	–	–	–
Reserves and surplus	15,043	13,723	11,691	9,200	8,271
Loan funds					
Secured loans	–	31	27	0	0
Unsecured loans	1,078	278	795	699	900
Total	16,266	14,177	12,657	10,044	9,316
Fixed assets					
Gross block	14,735	11,738	10,407	8,721	7,285
Less: Revaluation reserve	–	–	–	–	–
Less: Accumulated depreciation	7,214	6,208	5,382	4,650	3,989
Net block	7,521	5,529	5,025	4,071	3,297
Capital work-in-progress	1,406	1,429	388	861	736
Investments	6,147	5,107	7,177	3,173	5,181
Net current assets					
Current assets, loans and advances	7,310	6,443	3,856	5,570	3,191
Less: Current liabilities and provisions	6,119	4,331	3,788	3,632	3,088
Total net current assets	1,191	2,112	68	1,938	102
Miscellaneous expenses not written	–	–	–	–	–
Total	16,266	14,177	12,657	10,044	9,316
Notes:					
Number of equity shares outstanding (crores)	28.89	28.89	28.89	28.89	28.89

EXHIBIT 13.2A

Tata Motors Profit & Loss Account

(₹ in crore)

	March 2012	*March* 2011	*March* 2010	*March* 2009	*March* 2008
Income					
Operating income	54,217	47,957	35,373	25,661	28,768
Expenses					
Material consumed	40,458	34,693	24,759	19,039	20,932
Manufacturing expenses	2,938	2,225	1,652	1,172	1,230
Personnel expenses	2,691	2,294	1,836	1,551	1,545
Selling expenses	2,370	2,289	1,583	1,224	1,179
Administrative expenses	2,489	2,569	2,250	1,867	1,983
Expenses capitalised	–907	–818	–741	–916	–1,131
Cost of sales	50,040	43,252	31,340	23,938	25,737
Operating profit	4,178	4,706	4,033	1,723	3,031
Other recurring income	574	421	402	842	359
Adjusted PBDIT	4,752	5,126	4,435	2,565	3,390
Financial expenses	1,219	1,384	1,246	705	472
Depreciation	1,607	1,361	1,034	875	652
Other write offs	–	106	144	51	64
Adjusted PBT	1,926	2,276	2,011	934	2,202
Tax charges	99	385	589	13	548
Adjusted PAT	1,827	1,891	1,421	922	1,654
Non-recurring items	–585	–79	819	80	375
Other non-cash adjustments	–	–	–	15	–
Reported net profit	1,242	1,812	2,240	1,017	2,029
Earnings before appropriation	3,321	3,746	3,926	2,400	3,043
Equity dividend	1,281	1,274	859	312	578
Preference dividend	–	–	–	–	–
Dividend tax	182	193	133	34	81
Retained earnings	1,859	2,279	2,934	2,054	2,383

EXHIBIT 13.2B

Tata Motors Balance sheet

(₹ in crore)

	March 2012	*March* 2011	*March* 2010	*March* 2009	*March* 2008
Sources of funds					
Owner's fund					
Equity share capital	634.75	634.65	570.6	514.05	385.54
Share application money	–	3.06	–	–	–
Preference share capital	–	–	–	–	–
Reserves and surplus	18,709.16	19,351.40	14,208.55	11,855.15	7,428.45
Loan funds					
Secured loans	6,915.77	7,766.05	7,742.60	5,251.65	2,461.99
Unsecured loans	4,095.86	8,132.70	8,883.31	7,913.91	3,818.53
Total	30,355.54	35,887.86	31,405.06	25,534.76	14,094.51
Uses of funds					
Fixed assets					
Gross block	27,111.76	21,883.32	18,416.81	13,905.17	10,830.83
Less: Revaluation reserve	23.75	24.19	24.63	25.07	25.51
Less: Accumulated depreciation	9,965.87	8,466.25	7,212.92	6,259.90	5,443.52
Net block	17,122.14	13,392.88	11,179.26	7,620.20	5,361.80
Capital work-in-progress	2,073.96	4,058.56	5,232.15	6,954.04	5,064.96
Investments	20,493.55	22,624.21	22,336.90	12,968.13	4,910.27
Net current assets					
Current assets, loans and advances	15,538.16	14,775.61	12,329.48	10,836.58	10,781.23
Less: Current liabilities and provisions	24,872.27	18,963.40	19,672.73	12,846.21	12,029.80
Total net current assets	–9,334.11	–4,187.79	–7,343.25	–2,009.63	–1,248.57
Miscellaneous expenses not written	–	–	–	2.02	6.05
Total	30,355.54	35,887.86	31,405.06	25,534.76	14,094.51
Notes:					
Number of equity Shares outstanding (Lakh)	31,735.47	6,346.14	5,705.58	5,140.08	3,855.04

EXHIBIT 13.3

Stock market data: Monthly high and low prices of the Company's equity shares on BSE and NSE for the year 2011–2012.

Month	*Bombay Stock Exchange*		*National Stock Exchange*	
	High (₹)	*Low* (₹)	*High* (₹)	*Low* (₹)
April 11	1,335	1,217	1,335	1,214
May 11	1,334	1,189	1,334	1,190
June 11	1,259	1,087	1,255	1,086
July 11	1,225	1,130	1,225	1,130
August 11	1,287	1,048	1,283	1,048
September 11	1,161	1,045	1,162	1,041
October 11	1,178	1,010	1,185	1,010
November 11	1,152	910	1,153	907
December 11	1,016	906	1,015	900
January 12	1,225	917	1,226	917
February 12	1,375	1,182	1,375	1,183
March 12	1,428	1,250	1,429	1,248

[*Source:* MSIL Annual report 2011–2012, Table 10, page 51]

EXHIBIT 13.4

MSIL sales and profits–Financial Year 2011–2012

	2011–2012	**2010–2011**	***% change***
	(₹ *in million*)		
Net Sales	3,47,059	3,58,490	Down by 3.2%
Net Profit	16,351	22,887	Down by 28.6%
Total Volume	11,33,695 nos	12,71,005 nos	Down by 10.8%
Domestic	10,06,316 nos	11,32,739 nos	Down by 11.2%
Exports	1,27,379 nos	1,38,266 nos	Down by 7.9%

"For the year, the Company's bottom-line was impacted by adverse currency movement and increased commodity prices. The overall slowdown in the car market, including the skew towards diesel cars, also affected performance."

[*Source:* www.marutisuzuki.com/Maruti-Suzuki-financial-results-2011–12.]

CASE REFERENCES

Maruti Suzuki Annual Reports for FY 1995 to FY 2012.

www.banknetindia.com/banking/intplrd.htm, Accessed January 2013

www.moneycontrol.com [Accessed January 2013]

www.marutisuzuki.com/Maruti-Suzuki-financial-results-2011–12 [Accessed January 2013]

www.technology.corbee.in/2012/03/maruti-suzuki-plans-heavy-investments. [Accessed Oct. 2012].

www.marutisuzuki.com/about-us.aspx. [Accessed September 2012]

http://money.rediff.com/companies/maruti-suzuki-india/balance-sheet.

CHAPTER

14

Dividend Decision, Share Buybacks and Bonus Issues

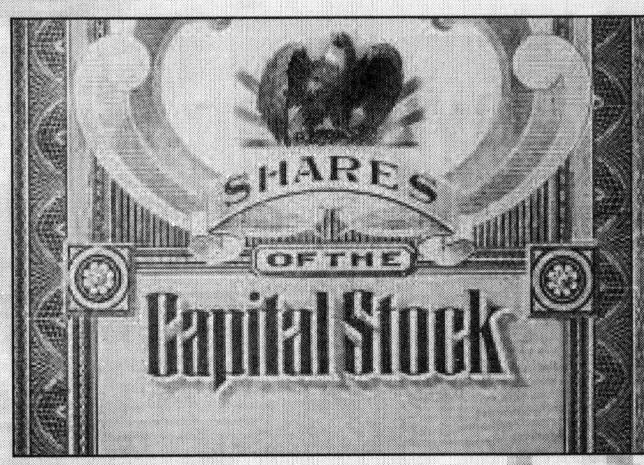

LEARNING OBJECTIVES

After studying this chapter, you should be able to:

- Understand the relationship between dividends and financing decisions.
- Discuss the Modigliani–Miller theory of irrelevance of dividends.
- Explain the arguments favouring relevance of the dividend policy.
- Discuss the practical aspects that companies have to consider while deciding on their dividend policy.
- Determine the optimum dividend policy using dividend growth model.
- Explain the meaning of buyback of shares and the reasons why a company would want to repurchase its own shares.
- Distinguish between bonus shares and share-splits, and discuss their effect of shareholders' wealth.

14.1 Introduction

Investment, financing and dividend decisions are regarded as the three most important decisions ever made by the management. Having devoted several chapters to the discussion of investment and financing decisions, we now turn our attention to the dividend decision in this chapter. After all, a firm raises funds and invests them in business projects to earn returns for the business owners, who are the equity shareholders in the case of companies. The most common way of providing returns to the shareholders out of the earnings of the company is by paying cash dividends. Indeed many shareholders keenly await declaration and payment of cash dividends at the end of each quarter or financial year.

However, in recent times, share buyback has emerged as an important alternative to payment of cash dividends. It is claimed that under certain circumstances, the share buyback method of returning cash to the shareholders may be more advantageous than merely distributing the earnings by paying cash dividends. Another way of rewarding shareholders is by paying stock-dividends (bonus shares) which are additional shares issued to existing shareholders free of cost.

A critical question here would be to ask 'what should be the basis on which to decide the most suitable form of distributing cash (or providing returns out of earnings) to the shareholders'. There are theoretical and practical perspectives on the issue under consideration. Theoretically, following the objective of shareholder wealth maximization, the company should use such a form of providing returns to shareholders that maximizes the value of the firm. However, from a practical perspective, companies have also to consider the managerial, legal and tax aspects that can play an important role in deciding the form of providing returns to the shareholders. The presence of information asymmetry and uncertainty only add more complexity to the situation.

All these aspects are examined in this chapter one by one. We begin with dividend decision and then cover share buyback and other related aspects.

14.2 The Dividend Decision

There is a relationship between the dividends and financing decisions because a company can utilize its earnings either to pay cash dividends to the shareholders or retain the same for financing investment projects. To the extent the company can internally finance the investment projects out of retained earnings, it would not have to depend on external financing. Companies that pay out all or most of their earnings as cash dividends have to depend on external sources of funds to undertake new projects.

Equity investors expect that they would be getting cash dividends from the company in which they have invested their hard-earned money

In a sense the cash dividends (including a terminal dividend on the winding up of the company) are the only way in which the equity investors can get cash returns on their investments. For now, we ignore the other alternatives of distributing cash to shareholders by repurchasing shares, because the buyback program may not appeal to many shareholders and they may decide not to participate in the same. That explains the importance of cash dividends, and it is a reasonable expectation of equity investors that they would be getting cash dividends from the company in which they have invested their hard-earned money.

Does that mean they would not invest in a company where there is no hope of getting cash dividends in the foreseeable future? Consider the following example:

The initial public offer prospectus (2002) of the Bharti Tele-Ventures Limited (Airtel) stated as under:

"We have not declared or paid any cash dividends on our equity shares since inception and do not expect to pay any cash dividends for the foreseeable future.... Investors seeking cash dividends should not purchase our shares."

Do you think the above statement of dividend policy would have adversely affected the investors' interest in the equity IPO and it would have failed? Before we discuss what happened to the IPO, let us examine what the theories of dividend decision have to say. The main issue at stake is: does the dividend decision have any impact on the value of the firm; because if dividend policy does not have any effect on the value of the firm, then it would not matter whether or not the company pays the dividends.

14.3 Modigliani–Miller (MM) Theory of Irrelevance

According to some experts led by Modigliani–Miller, the investors value a firm only on the basis of its earning capacity and how the earnings are split between payment of dividends and retained earnings is immaterial. They suggest that investors are indifferent about how a company uses its earnings, and that the decision to distribute earnings by paying dividends or retaining them for financing investment projects would not have any impact on the value of the firm.

According to Modigliani–Miller, the investors value a firm on the basis of its earning capacity and not how the earnings are split between cash dividends and retained earnings.

Since as per the MM approach, the value of the firm depends on its earnings (and earnings alone), the firm must first focus on utilizing its earnings for reinvestment in projects that would further increase the future earnings and the value of the firm. Thus, under this approach, the dividend decision becomes a passive or residual policy: the preferred use of the earnings being to finance the investment projects.

The Residual Dividend Policy

Following this approach, every year the company should consider its investment needs and as long as it has 'acceptable' projects to undertake, it would utilize its earnings to finance the same. Only when, and to the extent, it has surplus cash—not required for investment—it would declare and pay cash dividends on its equity shares. Consider the following example.

EXAMPLE 14.1 The Sultan Company has projected the next five years' net profits and investment (capital expenditure) requirements as follows:

Year	*Net profit* [₹ '000]	*Planned investment* [₹ '000]
1	4,000	3,000
2	4,000	4,000
3	5,000	4,000
4	5,000	2,500
5	5,000	6,000

The Company has 1 million shares outstanding and has been paying out a cash dividend of ₹2 per share.

Determine the dividend per share and the amount of external financing required each year if the company adopts the 'residual decision' approach to dividend policy.

Solution:

Year	*Net profit* (₹ '000)	*Planned investment* (₹ '000)	*Profits available for dividend* (₹ '000)	*Dividend per share* (₹)	*External financing* (₹ '000)
1	4,000	3,000	1,000	1	0
2	4,000	4,000	0	0	0
3	5,000	4,000	1,000	1	0
4	5,000	2,500	2,500	2.5	0
5	5,000	6,000	0	0	1,000
Total	**23,000**	**19,500**	**4,500**		**1,000**

The residual policy would lead to minimum cash dividends per share as well as least external financing requirement since the company would be financing projects with internal financing as far as possible. As a result, dividends payout could fluctuate from year to year, depending on the availability of earnings after setting aside funds required to undertake new projects.

Assumptions: The Modigliani–Miller suggestion of residual dividend policy is based on the following assumptions which are similar to the ones we discussed in the chapter on capital structure:

- Capital markets are perfect and information is readily available.
- There are no transaction costs, and all securities are infinitely divisible.
- Investors have similar expectations and behave rationally.
- No floatation costs and no income taxes.
- The firm has a definite investment plan and all shareholders have perfect knowledge of the same.
- The equity holding is widely spread out and no investor is large enough to influence the market.

Shareholders' Indifference

On the basis of these assumption, Modigliani–Miller conclude that equity shareholders should be indifferent between getting cash dividends and reinvestment of the earnings, because both these alternatives would result in enhancing their wealth. If the company distributes the earnings as cash dividends, shareholders can reinvest the amount on their own; and if earnings are retained, the company would reinvest the same on behalf of the shareholders. As long as the company reinvests the earnings in acceptable projects that would yield a return higher than the required rate of return, the earnings of the company and share prices would go on increasing and so would the shareholders' wealth. The capital appreciation by way of increase in the share prices would compensate shareholders for non-payment of cash dividends leaving the shareholders indifferent between the two options. Given the assumptions stated above and because investors are assumed to behave rationally, the M–M conclusions of dividend irrelevance and residual policy seem convincing.

Residual Policy and Investors' Need for Cash

But if there are no or inadequate cash dividends, how would shareholders meet their requirements of cash? There might be shareholders who depend on payment of cash dividends to meet their household expenses. Shareholders may include retired people and other groups who depend on cash dividends to make their ends meet. The supporters of the residual dividend policy argue that such shareholders can sell-off a fraction of their shareholding periodically to get the desired cash when dividends paid by the company are absent or lower than expected. On the contrary, when the company pays out higher than expected dividends (due to lack of new investment opportunities), the investors could use surplus cash (after meeting their household needs) to buy more of the company's shares. In this way, shareholders are able to substitute their 'self-made' dividends for company paid dividends.

Dividends versus Shareholders' Wealth

M–M argue that if the company decides to distribute its earnings as cash dividends, it would have to finance new investment projects by raising fresh equivalent funds from external sources (say, by issuing new equity shares). The cost of capital (returns provided) on new external funds would reduce the share market prices to an extent that would be exactly equal to the amount of dividends paid. In other words:

Decline in value of existing shares = Dividends paid

According to MM, the current market price of a share would be equal to the present value of the dividend receivable at the end of a period plus the present value of the share market price as at the end of the period, both discounted at the equity investors' required rate of return. Thus,

$$P_0 = \frac{1}{1+r}(D_1 + P_1)$$

where P_0 is the present market price of the share; 'r' is the equity investors' required rate of return, D_1 is the dividend per share receivable at the end of one year, and P_1 is the share market price as at the end of one year. Consider the following example.

EXAMPLE 14.2 The present market price of Honeybee Company's equity shares is ₹25 per share. The company is expected to pay a dividend of ₹3.00 per share at the end of one year. Investors' required rate of return on equity is 20%. Assume there are no taxes.

Assume Xavier has 1000 shares of the company. Using Modigliani–Miller theory:

(a) Assuming the company pays out a dividend of ₹3 per share, calculate the expected price per share and Xavier's wealth (from his shareholding) at the end of one year;

(b) Assuming no dividends are paid out, calculate the expected price per share and Xavier's wealth (from his shareholding) at the end of one year.

(c) Comment on the results in relation to the MM theory of irrelevance of dividend policy.

Solution:

We know that: $P_0 = \frac{1}{1+r}(D_1 + P_1)$

Turning the equation around, we get the value of P_1.

Thus, $$P_1 = P_0(1 + r) - D_1$$

where, r is the required rate of return. Then, for the given situation:

P_0 = ₹25 per share

Required return r = 20%

D_1 = ₹3 per share

Substituting the values:

(a) P_1 with dividend = ₹25 (1.20) – 3
= ₹27 per share

(b) P_1 without dividend = ₹25 (1.20) – 0
= ₹30 per share

Comparing Xavier's wealth at end of one year:
With dividend = (1,000 × ₹27) + (1,000 × 3)
= ₹27,000 + 3,000 = ₹30,000
Without dividend = (1,000 × ₹30) + (1,000 × 0)
= ₹30,000

(c) In both cases, the wealth of shareholder would be same ₹30 per share or a total of ₹30,000.

Hence, in a world of no taxes, perfect information and no transaction costs, the existing shareholders should be neutral between receiving cash dividends and capital gains as a result of retained earnings.

ILLUSTRATION 14.1 THE BHARTI TELE-VENTURES LIMITED (AIRTEL) IPO PROSPECTUS OF 2002

You might be wondering as to what happened to the initial public offer (IPO) (2002) of the Bharti Tele-Ventures Limited (Airtel) which had stated the following dividend policy in its prospectus: "*We ... do not expect to pay any cash dividends for the foreseeable future... Investors seeking cash dividends should not purchase our shares.*"

The above statement of dividend policy did not seem to deter investors and the issue, which opened on January 28, 2002 for a total of 18.5 crore equity shares at a base price INR 45 per share (i.e., face value ₹10 per share and premium of ₹35 per share) was over-subscribed 2.5 times. Investors seemed to attach more weight to the tremendous growth potential as stated in the IPO prospectus, "the company seeks to capitalize on the growth opportunities that it believes is available in the Indian telecommunications market and consolidate its position to be the leading integrated telecommunications services provider in key markets in India, with a focus on providing cellular services." [www.airtel.in]

This example goes to prove that while dividends might be an important consideration for investors, they would also consider the future investment opportunities available to the company and would be happy with the company retaining all or a large proportion of the earnings as long as the retained earnings were invested in projects with a positive NPV.

Incidentally, the statement in the company IPO prospectus that "*We do not expect to pay any cash dividends for the foreseeable future*" should not be interpreted to mean that the company would never pay dividends. Sooner or later every profitable company should and would pay cash dividends; so the statement only meant to convey that for the time being the company did not plan to pay cash dividends as it expected to reinvest all of its profits back in to the growing business.

In this respect, even the Modigliani–Miller approach should not be taken to mean that a company could permanently abstain from paying dividends. Of course, shareholder would expect to get dividends but can sacrifice current dividends in the hope of getting higher dividends in the future if the company has good investment projects to undertake. In that sense, they would not mind if the company retained profits now to pay higher dividends at a future point of time.

14.4 The Clientele Theory

Clientele Theory says the company should target its share issues to such investors whose needs for cash dividends and capital gains go well with the company's dividend policy.

The Airtel experience is a reminder that while some investors could be more interested in getting current income by way of cash dividends, there would be others who would be keen to invest for long-term prosperity. This group of investors would want the company to postpone paying dividends for the foreseeable future and reinvest all its earnings for greater capital appreciation in medium to long term. The important point to note is that a company does not necessarily have to cater to the investment needs of all types of investors in the world. As long as there is a clientele or group of investors who would go along with the stated dividend policy of the company, the company's issue of shares would be successful. The company would therefore do well to identify the right clientele or segment of investors to target for the issue of shares and try to satisfy their investment needs.

14.5 Relevance of Dividend Policy

There are several arguments that can be given against the MM's irrelevance of dividend policy and in favour of the relevance of the dividend policy. These arguments negate the residual dividend approach of Modigliani and Miller and suggest that the company should carefully design its dividend policy keeping in view the shareholders' requirements and other considerations. Shareholders can have strong preferences either for cash dividends or capital gains, and if the company does not satisfy this need of the investors, they could lose interest in the company's shares, which would result in a decline in the share prices and the wealth of the shareholders.

Shareholders can have strong preferences either for cash dividends or capital gains which the company should consider while framing dividend policy.

Arguments in favour of the relevance of dividend decision are briefly discussed as follows:

1. Resolution of uncertainty: Given the uncertain future, shareholders would tend to prefer cash dividends against possible future capital gains. There have been several instances where things did not turn out the way management has forecasted or announced, either due to managerial fraud or a change in the Government policy or business environment. A case like Satyam Computers fraud can shake the confidence of shareholders, and they would want cash dividends to prove that the company is actually profitable.

2. Shareholders' need for current income: If majority of the company's shareholders constitute individual investors or groups who rely on cash dividends for meeting their living expenses or other recurring needs, the company would better choose to distribute at least a good proportion of its earnings as cash dividends to keep the shareholders satisfied. While it is not necessary to have a 100% dividend payout ratio, stability of dividends from year to year would be particularly valued by such shareholders so that they can do their own financial planning in advance.

3. Transactions cost: In real life where investors have to pay transaction costs on buying and selling shares, shareholders would prefer getting cash dividends straight from the company instead of having to sell a part of their shareholding to meet current expenditure.

Shareholders may prefer cash dividends due to future uncertainty, need for current income, transaction costs and income taxes.

4. Impact of taxes: If there is a difference in the rates of taxes applicable to cash dividends as against taxes on capital gains, there can be a preference either in favour of or against distribution of earnings as cash dividends. The Indian law and rules regarding taxes on dividends and capital gains are covered in a later section.

14.5.1 Formulating Dividend Policy: Practical Aspects

In practice, companies have to consider several aspects while deciding on their dividend policy. For example, this message was clearly conveyed by Essar Shipping Limited in its Information Memorandum for Listing of Equity Shares in November 2011:

"The declaration and payment of dividend will be recommended by the Board of Directors and approved by its Shareholders, at their discretion, and will depend on a number of factors, including, but not limited to, its profits, capital requirements and overall financial condition." [www.essar.com]

To take another example, I-Flex Solutions Limited conveyed a similar message to its prospective investors in its IPO Prospectus (June 2002) as follows:

"The declaration and payment of dividend will be recommended by the Board of Directors, in its discretion, and will depend on a number of factors, including but limited, to our earnings, capital requirements and overall financial condition." [I-Flex Solutions]

The practical aspects that a company should consider while deciding on its dividend policy are briefly discussed as follows:

Future Investment Opportunities

Perhaps the most important determinant of the dividend policy are the growth prospects in the industry and the availability of acceptable investment projects. If a company has reached a stage in its life-cycle where no further investment would be financially viable,

Practical aspects of dividend decision include investment opportunities, control and shareholders preferences.

it would be better to distribute the available cash to the shareholders so that they can invest the same on their own. Indeed, cash rich companies such as Infosys which have huge cash and equivalents on their balance sheets have often been questioned to explain why they should not pay higher cash dividends when they are not investing the retained earnings in new projects.

Shareholders' Preferences

The objective of maximizing shareholders' wealth would be best served if the company follows a dividend policy that is in tune with the shareholder preferences with respect to cash dividends versus future capital gains. Of course, it is equally important that the management strikes a balance between the shareholders preference for cash dividends and capital expenditure requirements to ensure the company's growth and competitive sustainability.

Control

If a company has distributed its profits to pay dividends and needs additional funds to undertake new projects, the majority shareholders must subscribe for at least the same proportion of the new issue as their existing shareholding, otherwise their percentage holding of the company's equity capital would decline and they might lose control over the company.

Liquidity Position

Payment of cash dividends obviously means a drain on the cash and liquid resources of the company. Accordingly, the company can declare and pay dividends only if its liquidity condition is good.

Access to Capital Markets

Other relevant factors could be: liquidity position, control, market conditions, legal and taxation aspects.

Companies would find it convenient to pay dividends when the capital markets are doing well and raising external capital is easier. Also, as compared to large blue-chip companies, smaller organizations may find it difficult to tap capital markets. For such companies, internal funding from retained earnings is an important and more reliable source of funding; accordingly, such organizations could opt for larger retention of profits.

Cost of Raising Equity Externally

Making a fresh equity issue requires an elaborate arrangement and could be relatively a time consuming and costly affair. This factor alone may deter many companies to keep their dividends low, and retain more of the profits to finance new projects.

Applicable Taxes and Other Legal Aspects

These will be discussed in a separate section later.

Stability of Dividends

Equity investors attach importance to stability of dividends, which can be viewed in two ways: (a) Stability of dividends per share, and (b) Stability of dividend payout ratio.

Several investors, who depend on cash dividends to meet their household or other planned expenses, would want the company to at least maintain, if not increase, the dividends so that their financial plans would not go haywire. Erratic dividend policy may not be preferred as it would not help investors plan their finances.

Incidentally, stability of dividends can be viewed by companies in two ways: (a) Stability of dividends per share, and (b) Stability of percentage of profits distributed as cash dividends. In the latter case, the total amount distributed as cash dividends year after year would be a constant proportion of the profits, but would fluctuate year to year in dividends per share. Consider the following example.

EXAMPLE 14.3 [To facilitate comparison of results with the 'residual dividend' policy discussed earlier, we use the Sultan Company data again here.]

The Sultan Company has projected the next five years' net profits and investment (capital expenditure) requirements as follows:

Year	*Net profit* [₹ '000]	*Planned investment* [₹ '000]
1	4,000	3,000
2	4,000	4,000
3	5,000	4,000
4	5,000	2,500
5	5,000	6,000

It has 1 million shares outstanding and has been paying out a cash dividend of ₹2 per share.

(a) Determine the dividend per share and the amount of external financing required each year if the company decides to follow a stable dividend payout ratio of 50%.
(b) Calculate the amount of external financing required each year if the company decides to pay stable dividend of ₹2 per share.

Solution:

(a) **If the company follows a stable dividend payout ratio of 50%**

Year	*Net profit* [₹ '000]	*Amount of 50% payout* [₹ '000]	*Dividend per share* [₹]	*Amount available for investment* [₹ '000]	*Planned investment* [₹ '000]	*External financing* [₹ '000]
1	4,000	2,000	2	2,000	3,000	1,000
2	4,000	2,000	2	2,000	4,000	2,000
3	5,000	2,500	2.5	2,500	4,000	1,500
4	5,000	2,500	2.5	2,500	2,500	0
5	5,000	2,500	2.5	2,500	6,000	3,500
Total	23,000	11,500		11,500	19,500	8,000

(b) **If the company pays a stable dividend of ₹2 per share**

Year	*Profit* [₹ '000]	*DPS* [₹]	*Profits used for dividend* [₹ '000]	*Profits available for investment* [₹ '000]	*Planned investment* [₹ '000]	*External financing* [₹ '000]
1	4,000	2	2,000	2,000	3,000	1,000
2	4,000	2	2,000	2,000	4,000	2,000
3	5,000	2	2,000	3,000	4,000	1,000
4	5,000	2	2,000	3,000	2,500	–500
5	5,000	2	2,000	3,000	6,000	3,000
Total	23,000		10,000	13,000	19,500	6,500

As we can see from the above tables, the total amount paid out as dividends as well as the total amount of external financing for the period would be different depending on how 'stability' of dividends is interpreted. The distribution of cash as dividends would be higher under both these options as compared to the 'residual dividends approach' illustrated earlier using the same data.

14.5.2 Signalling Effect of Dividend Policy

Though in theory, we sometimes assume the existence of perfect capital markets and full availability of information related to the company's future plans to all investors, in reality the situation may be very different. The company management would be much better informed about the future plans and prospects of the company than outside investors. In view of this asymmetric information, investors often try to get 'signals' about the future prospects of the company from changes in the company's dividend policy. Management is also aware of this signaling effect and may deliberately maneouver the dividends policy in a way that would give the desired signals to the investors.

Shareholders usually expect that the company would either maintain the same level of dividends as last year or increase the same. In this scenario, a cut in dividends may be taken as a signal that the future prospects of the company are not good. An increase in dividends would convey a positive message about the future prospects.

If the company's annual profits decline, but the company pays out the same dividend per share as the previous year, the shareholder might get the signal that the management feels confident about the company's future prospects, and the decline in profits is only a passing blip.

The proportion of profits distributed as cash dividends are also carefully watched by investors and financial analysts. Financial analysts often recommend their clients to avoid or reduce investments in companies which are distributing most or all of their profits as cash dividends, because such a dividend policy would not leave much to reinvest in the growth of the business, and hence, future prospects of the company would look bleak.

The step-ladder increase in dividends

A step-ladder dividends policy would be preferred by shareholders who depend on dividend income to meet their current expenses.

In view of the shareholders' expectation that the company would either maintain or increase the level of dividends, companies would be advised to tread cautiously and raise dividends only when they would be confident of maintaining dividends at the increased new level in the future. A frequent increase and cut in dividends would not be advisable, particularly if the shareholders are of the types who depend on dividend income to meet their household and other recurring expenses.

Accordingly, it is felt that if the company is experiencing a continuous rise in its earnings, cash dividends should be increased with a time lag in a step-ladder fashion as given in Figure 14.1.

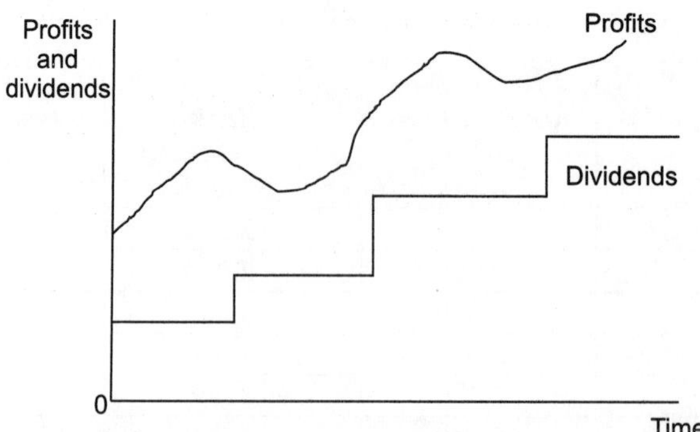

FIGURE 14.1
Step-ladder increase.

As the figure shows, instead of rushing to increase dividends with every small rise in profits, the company should let the profits stabilize at the new higher level, and raise dividends when the new high level of dividends becomes sustainable.

Illustration 14.2 Dividend Policy of ITC Limited

A company whose dividend policy comes closer to the text book prescription is ITC Limited, one of India's most reputed companies from the FMCG (fast moving consumer goods) industry. The table below presents the earnings per share and dividends per share performance of ITC Limited for the period 2011 to 2015:

	2011	2012	2013	2014	2015
Reported EPS (₹)	6.45	7.88	9.39	11.05	11.99
Dividend per share	4.45	4.5	5.25	6	6.25
Dividend Payout Ratio	68.99	57.11	55.91	54.30	52.13

The graphical presentation of ITC Limited's reported EPS and dividend per share for the period 2011 to 2015 would appear as follows:

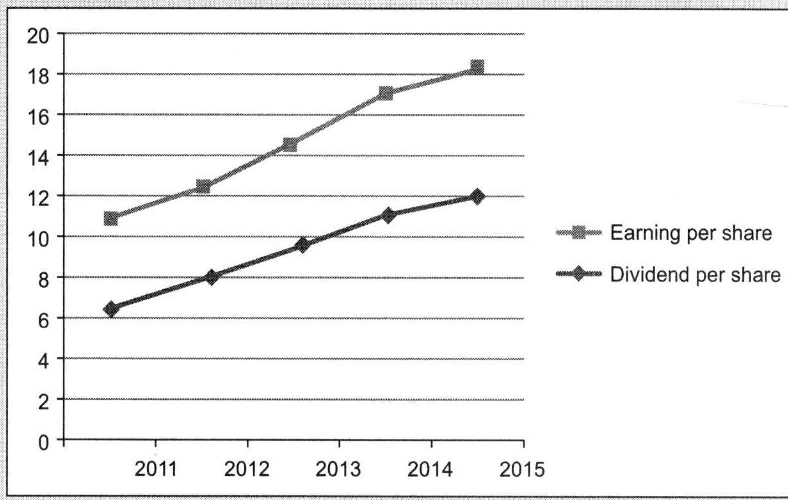

Analysis of ITC dividend policy: From the above data and graphical presentation, we can conclude the following about the dividend policy of ITC Ltd: (i) the company paid at least the same dividend in any year as the previous year. This helps the investor to project his income from dividends; (ii) As earnings increased, the dividend per share has also been increased slowly and steadily, which again would help in building investor confidence; (iii) The dividend payment ratio has declined over the period from 68.99% in 2011 to 52.13% in 2015, indicating that the company wants to retain a greater percentage of earnings for reinvestment that should further increase the future earnings and dividends. Thus, the company wants to finance more new projects from internal resources, yet keeping a balance between the company's needs for reinvestment and the investors' need for cash dividends.

14.5.3 Deciding the Optimum Dividend Policy Using Dividend Growth Model

We can use the dividend growth model, which was discussed in an earlier chapter, to design an optimum dividend and retention policy of a company. The dividend growth model can take into account the current dividend policy of the company, the percentage of the earnings retained, the cost of equity as well as the return available on new investments. Let us first briefly review the dividend growth model and then consider how to use the same for deciding on an optimal dividend policy for the company.

Review of the Dividend Growth Model

The dividend valuation model is used to determine the estimated market value of a share. If the dividend per share could be assumed to remain constant year after year with zero growth rate, then

$$P_0 = \frac{D}{ke}$$

The dividend growth model can be used to design an optimum dividend and retention policy of a company.

where P_0 is the ex-dividend current market price of a share, D is dividend per share assumed to remain constant year after year with zero growth rate, and k_e is the equity investors' required rate of return. For example, if a company is expected to pay a constant dividend of ₹6 per share annually for the foreseeable future, and the investors expect a return of 15%, then the estimated market price of the share would be ₹6 ÷ 0.15 = ₹40 per share.

However, if the dividend per share is expected to grow at a constant growth rate of say g per annum, then the ex-dividend expected market price can be estimated by the following formula:

$$P_0 = \frac{D_0(1+g)}{ke-g}$$

where P_0 is the current ex-dividend market price of a share, D_0 is current dividend per share assumed to continuously grow annually at g growth rate, and k_e is the equity investors' required rate of return. For example, if a company's current dividend is ₹6 per share which is expected to grow at a constant growth rate of 5% annually for the foreseeable future, and the investors expect a return of 15%, then the estimated ex-dividend market price of the share would be as follows:

$$P_0 = \frac{D_0(1+g)}{ke-g}$$

$$P_0 = \frac{6(1+0.05)}{0.15-0.05}$$

$$= ₹63 \text{ per share}$$

Ex-dividend and Cum-dividend Market Prices

Remember that the above formula was to estimate the ex-dividend share price. The cum-dividend price (which is more relevant when the dividend payment is imminent) would be estimated as follows:

$$P_0 = \frac{D_0(1+g)}{ke-g} + D_0$$

In the above example, the cum-dividend share price would be:

$$P_0 = \frac{6(1+0.05)}{0.15-0.05} + 6$$

$$= ₹63 + 6 = ₹69 \text{ per share.}$$

Optimal Dividend Policy

Relating the above concepts to dividend decision, if we know D_0, and can estimate g and k_e at different rates of retention of earnings, we can determine the optimum dividend policy. Note that our objective is to maximize shareholders wealth, which would be represented by the cum-dividend market values (because dividend will be paid soon after a decision is made about the amount of earnings to be retained). As the dividend amount would vary between different rates of retention of profits, we should compare the cum-dividend market values to decide the optimum retention and dividend policy.

Consider the following example:

EXAMPLE 14.4 Barby Company has 1,00,000 shares outstanding and has earned a profit of ₹5,00,000 in the year just concluded. The company is wondering as to what retention or dividend policy would best serve to maximize the shareholders' wealth. The company plans to finance all new investment projects exclusively out of the retained earnings.

If the company pays out all profits as dividends and does not reinvest, its earnings will stagnate at the current level of ₹5,00,000 per annum. It has attractive investment opportunities which will result in future growth in earnings and dividends. However, if the company retains the earnings for re-investment, the equity investors' perceived risk, and hence, the required rate of return would rise due to the risk and uncertainty related to new projects.

The following table sums up the expected growth rate and the equity investors' required rate of return at different levels of retained earnings:

Alternative plans	*% of earnings retained*	*Growth rate in earnings and dividends*	*Required return**
A	0	0%	15%
B	25	6%	16%
C	50	9%	18%
	*Shareholders' required rate of return on all investments		

Once a decision is made about the percentage of earnings to be retained, the balance profits will be distributed immediately as dividends for this year.

According to the dividend growth model, what would be the optimum retention policy for the company?

Solution: We know that:

$$P_0 = \frac{D_0(1+g)}{ke-g}$$

where, P_0 is the current 'ex-dividend' market price of a share. However, since dividend for this year is about to be paid soon, it is the 'cum-dividend' value that will be more relevant.

$$\text{Cum-dividend, } P_0 = \frac{D_0(1+g)}{ke-g} + D_0$$

Remember that our objective is to maximize shareholders wealth, which is represented by the cum-dividend market values in this situation. As the dividend amount varies between different alternatives, we should compare the cum-dividend market values to decide the optimum retention policy.

We can now compare the estimated market share values under different options of retention of earnings.

- **Plan A:** The cum-div Market Value (MV) if retention is 0%, i.e., 100% earnings are paid out as dividends:

$$\begin{aligned}\text{MV cum-div} &= [D_0(1 + g) \div (k_e - g)] + D_0\\ &= [5,00,000\ (1.0) \div (0.15 - 0)] + 5,00,000\\ &= 5,00,000 \div 0.15 + 5,00,000\\ &= 33,33,333 + 5,00,000 = 38,33,333 \text{ [Total market value]}\end{aligned}$$

Number of shares = 1,00,000

MV cum-div per share = 3,833,333 ÷ 1,00,000 = ₹38.33 per share

- **Plan B:** The cum-dividend market value if retention is 25%, i.e., 75% earnings are paid out as dividends:

MV cum-div = $[D_0 (1 + g) \div (k_e - g)] + D_0$

$g = 6\%$

$= 3,75,000 \times 1.06 \div (0.16 - 0.06)] + 3,75,000$

$= 39,75,000 + 3,75,000 = 43,50,000$ [Total market value]

$= 43,50,000 \div 1,00,000$ shares = ₹43.50 per share

- **Plan C:** The cum-div market value if retention is 50%, i.e., 50% earnings are paid out as dividends:

  MV cum-div = $[D_0(1 + g) \div (k_e - g)] + D_0$

  $g = 9\%$

  $= [(2,50,000 \times 1.09) \div (0.16 - 0.09)] + 2,50,000$

  $= 38,92,857 + 2,50,000 = 41,42,857$ [Total market value]

  $= 41,42,857 \div 1,00,000$ shares = ₹41.42 per share

Hence, out of the three alternatives, the best retention/dividend policy would be to retain 25% and payout 75% as dividend.

14.5.4 Estimating the Growth Rate '*G*'

In Example 14.4, the dividends growth rate was directly given. Where it is not directly given, it can be estimated as follows:

$$g = rb$$

where

g = The annual growth rate in dividends,
r = Rate of return on the company's new investments, and
b = Proportion of profits that is retained.

Assuming Company ABC pays out 30% of its profits as cash dividends and retains the remaining 70% which it can invest in new projects yielding a return of 20%, the growth rate g will be approximately $70\% \times 0.20 = 14\%$.

To take another example, if XYZ Company pays out 60% of its profits as cash dividends and retains the remaining 40% which it can invest in new projects yielding a return of 25%, the growth rate g will be approximately $40\% \times 0.25 = 10\%$.

14.5.5 Legal Aspects of Paying Dividends

In addition to the managerial considerations in deciding the dividend policy of a company, it is necessary to abide by the legal requirements. The legal requirements related to the declaration and payment of dividends by companies in India are covered under Section 123 of the Companies Act, 2013. The main provisions related to sources of funds for dividends, transfer to or from reserves and form of cash dividends are as follows:

Sources of Paying Dividend

A company can declare and pay dividends for any financial year only out of the following:

1. Profits of the company for that year after providing for depreciation;
2. Profits of any previous year (after providing for depreciation) remaining undistributed;
3. Out of both (1) and (2); or
4. Funds provided by the Central or State Government "for the payment of dividend by the company in pursuance of a guarantee given by that Government" (Section 123).

Transfer to Reserves

Before declaring dividends, the company may transfer such a percentage of the profits to reserves as it deems appropriate.

Mainly, a company can pay dividends out of: (i) Profits for current year, (ii) Retained profits of any previous year and (iii) Out of both (i) and (ii).

Dividends Out of Past Profits

Where the current year's profits are either absent or inadequate and the company wants to declare dividends from its "accumulated profits earned by it in previous years and transferred by the company to the reserves", such dividends can be declared or paid only out of 'free reserves'. Free reserves mean such reserves that are available for distribution as dividends as per the latest balance sheet of the company. Reserves resulting from unrealized gains, notional gains or revaluation surplus are not treated as free reserves.

Further, if the company wants to declare dividends from its "accumulated profits earned by it in previous years and transferred by the company to the reserves", it must satisfy the rules that have been prescribed in the Companies (Declaration and Payment of Dividend) Rules, 2014 (as amended up to date). These rules include the following:

1. "The rate of dividend declared shall not exceed the average of the rates at which dividend was declared by it in the three years immediately preceding that year;
2. The total amount to be drawn from such accumulated profits shall not exceed one-tenth of the sum of its paid-up share capital and free reserves as appearing in the latest audited financial statement.
3. The amount so drawn shall first be utilized to set off the losses incurred in the financial year in which dividend is declared before any dividend in respect of equity shares is declared.
4. The balance of reserves after such withdrawal shall not fall below fifteen per cent of its paid-up share capital as appearing in the latest audited financial statement.
5. No company shall declare dividend unless carried over previous losses and depreciation not provided in previous year are set off against profit of the company of the current year." [Chapter VIII—Companies (Declaration and Payment of Dividend) Rules, 2014]

Interim Dividends

Interim dividends may be "declared out of the surplus in the profit and loss account and out of profits of the financial year in which such interim dividend is sought to be declared" [123(3)]. However, if the company has made a loss in the financial year up to the end of the quarter immediately preceding the declaration of the interim dividends, the interim dividend should not exceed the average dividend of the immediately preceding three years.

Mode of Payment

Any cash dividend "may be paid by cheque or warrant or in any electronic mode to the shareholder entitled to the payment of the dividend" [123(5)].

14.5.6 Taxation and Dividend Policy

The applicable dividend distribution tax and capital gains tax are briefly discussed as follows:

Dividend Distribution Tax (DDT)

Dividends paid by an Indian company are exempted from income taxes in the hands of the shareholders, but the company paying out the dividend has to pay a tax called the Dividend Distribution Tax (DDT) as per the provisions of Section 115-O of the Income Tax Act. Accordingly, for every ₹100 dividend paid to the shareholders, the company must earn more than ₹100 so that after payment of the DDT, it is still left with ₹100 to pay to the shareholders.

For the assessment year 2016–2017, the rates of DDT for Companies are as follows:

Basic rate = 17.647%

Effective rate = 20.358%

The effective rate given above is inclusive of surcharge of 12% and education-cess of 3%. The dividend distribution tax in a sense amounts to double taxation of the corporate profits: corporate profits being first taxed when they are earned, and then taxed again when the same profits are distributed as dividends. DDT might discourage companies from paying cash dividends which would mean greater retention of profits. Thus, DDT can have a major influence on the dividend policy.

Capital Gains Tax on Shares

If the company does not pay cash dividends, and instead chooses to retain profits, the retained profits would be reinvested in new projects that will increase future earnings and share prices. When the shareholder sells the shares after holding them for some time, the profits or gains made by him on the sale of shares would be taxable as per the provisions of the Income Tax Act related to tax on capital gains.

Capital gains are classified as short-term and long-term. In respect of shares which are listed on a recognised stock exchange in India, where the investor sells the shares after holding them for a period of more than 12 months and the Securities Transaction Tax (STT) has been paid on the sale transaction, such capital gains would be classified as long-term capital gains and are currently tax-exempt under Section 10(38) of the Income Tax Act. The tax-exempt nature of long-term capital gains (subject to certain conditions as discussed above) would further motivate companies to retain more profits rather than pay them out as cash dividends.

14.5.7 Procedure of Declaring and Paying Dividends

Essar Shipping Limited in its Information Memorandum for Listing of Equity Shares in November 2011 briefly summed up the procedure for declaring and paying dividends as follows:

"The process and rules governing declaration and payment of dividends is governed by the Companies Act. As prescribed by the Companies Act, an Indian company can declare dividends only upon recommendation by the Board of Directors and approval of the recommendation by the shareholders. The shareholders only have the power to decrease the amount recommended by the Board of Directors. Under the Companies Act, dividends may be paid out of profits of a company in the year in which the dividend is declared or out of the undistributed profits or reserves of previous years or out of both."

14.6 Buyback (Repurchase) of Shares

In February 2012, Reliance Industries, one of India's most-valued firms, announced a share buyback programme worth a massive ₹10,440 crore. The share buyback offer started from 1 February 2012, and closed on 19 January 2013. This was the largest such buyback program till date known in the history of the Indian capital market.

Buyback of shares refers to the repurchase of a company's own outstanding shares using the surplus cash in the company's balance sheet. The repurchase of its own shares by a company would result in reduction in the number of shares remaining in the market. Assuming the profits of the company remain unchanged, reduction in the number of outstanding shares (as a result of the buyback) would result in higher earnings per share in future that can have a positive effect on the share prices.

In this connection, it would be pertinent to ask why a company would buyback its own shares, what the legal aspects are and how to determine the price at which a company should offer to buyback its own shares. These issues shall be discussed below, but first let us have a brief look at the history of buyback of shares in India.

The buyback or repurchase of own shares by Indian companies is a relatively recent development. Sections 77A, 77AA and 77B of the Companies Act, 1956 which were inserted by the Companies (Amendment) Act, 1999 first time allowed companies to buyback their own shares. On the basis of these amendments, the Securities and Exchange Board of India (SEBI) framed the rules for buyback of securities (Buyback of Securities Regulations, 1999). Similarly, the Department of Company Affairs framed the related rules for Private Limited Companies and Unlisted Public companies.

Buyback of shares refers to the repurchase of a company's own outstanding shares using the surplus cash in the company's balance sheet.

In some countries led by the USA, companies have for long been allowed to repurchase their own shares as a means of capital restructuring. According to one source, "Companies in the S&P 500 spent $564.7 billion on share repurchases (in 2014–2015), which was a year-over-year increase of 18%. Apple was the largest spender on buybacks in the S&P 500 during the fourth quarter. The company spent $6.1 billion on share repurchases during the quarter."

In India too, the scenario concerning repurchase of own shares by companies has been warming up. However, the response of the shareholders to buyback offers by companies has been a mixed one and the buyback offers announced by several companies have not been successful. For example, Table 14.1 shows the size of the buyback offers, actually repurchased amount and the percentage success of the buyback programs announced in India during 2008–2009 to 2012–2013.

TABLE 14.1 Buyback programmes in India

Year	*Number of offers*	*Offer amount (₹ in crore)*	*Acquired amount (₹ in crore)*	*Percentage*
2008–2009	46	4,218	1,662	39
2009–2010	20	824	328	40
2010–2011	20	4,295	4,149	97
2011–2012	31	13,765	4,853	35
2012–2013	21	1,694	1,107	65

During 2013–2014, reportedly "31 buyback offers were concluded in 2013–2014 with a total acquired amount of ₹4,425 crore. The total amount on offer was ₹5,704 crore."

Source: Prime Database

14.6.1 Objectives of Share Buyback

There may be a number of reasons why a company would want to repurchase its own shares. These are discussed as follows:

Distribute Surplus Cash

Consider a company with a huge pile of cash on its balance sheet which it does not need for reinvestment. In such a situation it might want to distribute the same among its shareholders but at the same time would want to reduce its share capital too so that it has to service a lower base of share capital in future. This is one of the most significant reasons why companies go for share buybacks.

Increase Earnings Per Share

When a proportion of the shares have been repurchased, there will be lesser number of shares outstanding after the repurchase, and assuming the company's earnings remain stable, the earnings per share would boost.

Support Share Prices

In bear-phase of the stock market, the increase in earnings per share resulting from the share buyback should lead to higher share prices.

Prevent Takeover Bids

Reasons why a company would repurchase its own shares include distribution of surplus cash, increase Earnings Per Share (EPS) and support share prices in bear-phase of the market.

Share buybacks have also been prompted by the need to prevent possible takeover bids. Particularly in a bear market, when the share prices may considerably decline, it might encourage competitors or market predators to acquire shares from the market at cheaper rates than their intrinsic value. In 2015, many shares were trading at their 52 week-lows that sparked takeover rumours of the respective companies. Aware of such a likely effect, a company may go for share buyback to support share prices in a bear market with the objective of preventing a takeover bid on the company.

Increase Promoters Holding

If the promoters do not participate in the buyback program and keep the number of shares they held before the buyback, naturally their percentage shareholding in the company would rise, thus giving them a better control over the company.

Positive Tax Effect

Share buybacks by the company result in capital gains for the shareholders. Due to the lower rates of income taxes on capital gains (subject to certain conditions) versus cash dividends (see dividend distribution tax covered in a previous section), many companies might find buybacks to be more beneficial from the perspective of income taxes. Reportedly the management of JK Lakshmi cement (February 2012) preferred the buyback route as it was more tax effective as compared to payment of cash dividends.

Eventual Delisting

Other reasons for buyback may include attempt to prevent take-over bid, positive tax effect, increase promoters' shareholding and eventual delisting.

Some companies may engage in buyback of shares with the ultimate objective of delisting their shares from the stock exchanges. For this purpose they may repurchase shares in a series of smaller lots (say 5–10% of the outstanding shares) at a time with the eventual objective of delisting of shares.

14.6.2 Determining The Repurchase Price

When a share buyback offer is made, shareholders are more likely to accept the offer if they get a price equal to or more than the intrinsic value of the shares. Shareholders are aware that after the company has repurchased a part of its shares, lesser number of shares would remain outstanding which would lead to higher earnings per share and dividends (assuming stability of the company's profits). This would result in higher market price of shares, providing greater returns to investors after the buyback. The existing shareholders who offer their shares for buyback would like to be compensated for the loss of future benefits that they would suffer by accepting the buyback offer. For this purpose, the buyback price offered by profitable companies should be higher than the current market price of the shares.

The money spent on buyback comes from the distributable profits of the company, which could have been paid out as cash dividends instead of financing the buyback program. Assuming no income taxes and nil transaction costs, the two options of dividends and repurchase of shares should theoretically not make a difference to the shareholders wealth.

The buyback price should be such that balances the interests of the two groups of shareholders: one offering shares for buyback and the other not offering their shares.

The buyback price should be decided keeping in view the interests of the two groups of shareholders: one offering shares for buyback and the other not offering their shares. The company would like to offer such a price to buyback its shares that would leave investors who render shares in a buyback exercise not worse off that those not offering their shares for sale. Such a theoretical equilibrium price can be estimated as follows:

$$R_P = \frac{S(P_0)}{S-N}$$

Where R_P is the share repurchase price, P_0 is the current market price per share, S is the number of shares outstanding prior to the buyback, and N is the number of shares to be purchased.

Buyback price $= \frac{S\,(P_0)}{S-N}$ where P_0 is the current share price, S is the number of shares outstanding before buyback, and N is the number of shares to be repurchased.

Consider the following example.

EXAMPLE 14.5 Tower Telecom Limited witnessed rapid growth for the past several years, but now its business is not expected to grow fast. It has substantial amount of surplus funds which it is considering to disburse among shareholders through a share repurchase instead of cash dividend. Out of its present 3,00,000 shares outstanding, it plans to repurchase 10% or 30,000 shares. The current market price is ₹400 per share. [*Note:* The current market price is cum-dividend]

Ignoring taxes and transaction costs, determine the following:

(a) The price at which the company should offer to repurchase shares?
(b) The total amount of money the company would be distributing through share re-purchase?

Solution:

(a) Calculation of the repurchase price:
Existing shares number S = 3,00,000
Shares to repurchase N = 30,000
Current price: P_0 = 400
[*Note:* P_0 is cum-dividend]

Repurchase price: $R_P = \frac{S(P_0)}{S-N}$
= 3,00,000(400)/(3,00,000 – 30,000)
= ₹444.4

(b) Total funds required for repurchase program:

= 30,000 × 444.4 = ₹1,33,33,333.33

The equilibrium repurchase price of ₹444.4 would balance the interests of the shareholders who offer their shares for buyback and others who do not. If the actual repurchase price is fixed at say ₹500, those offering their shares for repurchase would get disproportionate advantage at the cost of others who do not participate in the repurchase programme. On the other hand, if the actual repurchase price is fixed at say ₹400, those who do not participate in the repurchase programme would get disproportionate advantage at the cost of others who offer their shares for repurchase.

14.6.3 Legal and Procedural Aspects of Buybacks

Sections 68(1) and 68(2) of the Companies Act, 2013 provide a framework with regard to the eligibility and funding of the buybacks. The salient provisions are discussed below.

When Can a Company Buyback

A company must satisfy certain conditions before it would be eligible to buyback its own equity shares. Some of the main eligibility conditions are as follows:

- The company should be authorized by its Articles of Association to buyback its own shares.
- Buyback shares should be fully paid.
- The buyback should be authorized by a Board resolution if the company wants to repurchase shares (or other securities) to the extent of 10% or less of the paid up equity capital and free reserves of the company.
- A special resolution should have been passed at the general meeting of the company if the company wants to buyback equity shares up to 25% of the paid up equity capital in that financial year. [Section 68(c)]
- There should be a gap of at least one year between the closing of one buyback offer and the beginning of the next.
- The debt to equity ratio should not be more than 2:1 after the buyback. For the purpose of calculating this ratio, debt would include both secured and unsecured debt and equity would include paid up equity share capital and free reserves of the company.
- For shares listed on a recognized stock exchange, the buyback programme should follow the rules framed by SEBI for this purpose.
- The company should file a declaration with the Registrar certifying that the company is capable of meeting its liabilities and will not become insolvent within one year of the buyback of shares.

Some Other Important Provisions

- If the company has repurchased shares out of the free reserves or share premium account, "a sum equal to the nominal value of the shares so purchased shall be transferred to the capital redemption reserve account." [Section 69]. The capital redemption reserve account may be used by the company for issuing bonus shares.
- The company should not have defaulted in repayment of deposits (accepted from public either before or after the buyback), servicing its debt (payment of interest or repayment of loans) or preference shares [Section 70].

How to Fund a Buyback Programme

A Company can repurchase its own shares out of the following sources:

- Retained profits and free reserves.
- Share (or other securities) premium account. or
- Proceeds of any shares or other specified securities. However, "no buyback of any kind of shares or other specified securities shall be made out of the proceeds of an earlier issue of the same kind of shares or same kind of other specified securities." [Section 68]

14.6.4 Methods of Buyback

The two popular methods used by companies to repurchase their shares are: (i) the tender method and (ii) purchasing shares from the open market.

The Tender Method

In this method, the company sends an offer letter to the existing shareholders to buyback shares on a proportionate basis. The offer letter would include a tender/offer form that the shareholders would fill up and follow the instructions if they are interested in participating in the repurchase offer. The company could consider the theoretical 'repurchase price' we discussed in an earlier section along with other factors to decide the repurchase price to be offered to shareholders.

Popular methods used by companies to repurchase their shares are (i) the tender method and (ii) purchasing shares from the open market.

Open Market Method

As the name suggests, this method involves repurchasing shares from the open market at the prevailing market price either through the book building process or the stock exchange. An example of this method is provided by the Cairn India buyback of shares that commenced in January 2014. Selected excerpts from the 'Public Announcement' made by the company in relation to the procedure and methodology used to buyback shares are given in the Illustration.

ILLUSTRATION 14.3

CAIRN INDIA LIMITED

[Selected Excerpts]

Public Announcement

For the attention of the shareholders/beneficial owners of the equity shares of Cairn India Limited

Offer for Buyback of equity shares from the open market through the stock exchanges....

Process and Methodology to be Adopted for the Buyback:

1. The buyback offer is open to all shareholders holding equity shares in physical form ("Physical Shares") and beneficial owners holding equity shares in dematerialized form ("Demat Shares"), save and except the promoters or the persons in control.
2. The buyback offer will be implemented by the company by way of open market purchases through the stock exchanges, as provided under the buyback regulations.
3. The buyback offer will be implemented using the nationwide trading terminals of the stock exchanges only through the order matching mechanism except "all or none" order matching system.
4. For the implementation of the buyback offer, the company has presently appointed Standard Chartered Securities (India) Limited, Morgan Stanley India Company Private Limited and Axis Capital Limited as the registered brokers ("Company's Brokers") through whom the purchases and settlements on account of the buyback offer would be made by the company.

The company shall, commencing from 23rd January 2014 (i.e. the date of opening of the buyback offer), place "buy" orders on the BSE and/or NSE at least once in every week on the normal trading segment to buyback the equity shares through one or more of the company's brokers in such quantity and at such price, not exceeding the maximum buyback price of ₹335 (Rupees three hundred and thirty five) per equity share, as it may deem fit, depending upon the prevailing quotations of the equity shares on the stock exchanges.

[*Source:* www.cairnindia.com/investors/buy-back; clause 2.4]

14.7 Bonus Issues and Share-Splits

Bonus shares refer to the additional fully-paid shares issued by a company free of cost to its existing shareholders in proportion to their current shareholding. Issue of bonus shares does not involve any cash transaction since they are issued free of cost to the company's existing shareholders. The purpose of bonus issue is not to raise new funds; rather the objective may be to issue additional shares by converting reserves and retained earnings into share capital.

Bonus shares are additional shares issued by a company free of cost to its existing shareholders in proportion to their current shareholding.

For example, if a company issues bonus shares in the ratio of 1:1, it means that the shareholder would get one free additional share for every share held by him. Bonus issues are also called stock dividends as they may be considered a way of rewarding shareholders particularly where the company has been retaining large proportions of its profits and has in the process built huge reserves. Bonus issues are also known as capitalization issues because they are funded by capitalization of reserves and retained earnings.

Bonus issues have become popular over time. Table 14.2 gives examples of bonus issues made by selected companies recently.

TABLE 14.2
Bonus issues by select companies

Company	*Bonus ratio*	*Date*		
		Announcement	*Record*	*Ex-bonus*
Motherson Sumi	1:2	10-06-2015	–	23-07-2015
Aurobindo Pharma	1:1	28-05-2015	21-07-2015	20-07-2015
Federal Bank	1:1	16-05-2015	09-07-2015	08-07-2015
Kotak Mahindra	1:1	05-05-2015	09-07-2015	08-07-2015
Relaxo Footwear	1:1	11-05-2015	02-07-2015	01-07-2015
Infosys	1:1	24-04-2015	–	15-06-2015

[*Source:* Moneycontrol.com]

In the table, the bonus ratio shows the number of additional shares you would get for every share you hold; record date is the date by which you should have the shares in your demat account to make you eligible for getting the bonus shares; and ex-bonus date is the date on which stock exchanges adjust the market price of the share for the bonus issue. On the ex-bonus date, the stock exchange would reduce the market price according to the ratio of bonus issue. If the share price before the bonus issue was ₹100 and the company made a 1:1 bonus issue, the stock exchange would reduce the share price to ₹50 on the ex-bonus date, because for every single share held previously the shareholder would now hold two shares.

The above example shows that as far as immediate benefits are concerned, the shareholder gets no advantage when the company makes a bonus shares. Assume an investor originally held 10 shares of the above company with the market price of ₹100 per share, the total value of his shareholding being ₹100 × 10 = ₹1,000. The value of his shares would still be the same immediately after the bonus issue: ₹50 × 20 = ₹1,000. Thus, on the ex-bonus date, the number of shares held by him would proportionately increase and the share price would proportionately decline to leave him neutral. But that is only for the immediate benefits.

Typically bonus issues have a signaling effect; investors try to get signals about the future prospects of the company from the bonus issue announcements. Assuming a 1:1 bonus issue, the number of shares would double which means the company would have to serve a larger base of equity share capital in future. The company would have to earn more in future years in order to pay the same dividends as in the past. Looking at it from the investors' perspective, such a bonus issue would convey the signal or message that the company's future is bright and the management is confident of serving a larger base of equity share capital. Particularly with regards to companies with a long history (such as Tata Steel or Reliance or Infosys), a bonus issue could send a positive signal and may push up the share price over time.

Signaling effect: Investors try to get signals about the company's future prospects from the bonus issues. A large bonus issue would convey bright future prospects.

In addition to rewarding shareholders, another common reason why companies go for bonus issues is to reduce the share market price to more affordable levels, making it convenient for small investors to invest in the shares.

Several Indian companies have issued bonus shares at regular intervals. The Indian IT conglomerate Infosys has rewarded its shareholders with a number of bonus issues during the past twenty years, as shown in Table 14.3.

Infosys Ltd.			
Year	***Month***	***Ratio***	***Ex bonus date***
2015	April	1:1	15/06/2015
2014	October	1:1	02/12/2014
2006	April	1:1	13/07/2006
2004	April	3:1	01/07/2004
1999	January	1:1	08/02/1999
1997	June	1:1	19/08/1997
1994	June	1:1	19/08/1994

[*Source:* money.rediff.com]

TABLE 14.3
Bonus Announcements: 1994 to 2015

The table shows that if an investor held one share of Infosys before the bonus issue in 1994, and did not sell his shares, he would have a staggering 192 shares (for each share held in 1994) after the 2015 bonus issue. At the same time, the market price of the Infosys shares has also been rising over time, thus giving the investors outstanding returns during this period, making many shareholders billionaires in the process.

Let us consider the following example to understand the effect of a bonus issue.

EXAMPLE 14.6 Shareholders' equity of Biggs Company appears as follows:

	(₹)
Equity share capital (shares of ₹5 each)	10,00,000
Share premium account	12,00,000
Retained earnings	18,00,000
Total shareholders' equity	40,00,000

(a) Determine the total number of shares outstanding, and show how the equity account would change, if the company goes for a 50% bonus issue by capitalizing retained earnings equal to the nominal (par) value of the additional shares issued.

(b) If the share price before the bonus issue was ₹50 per share, ignoring any signaling effect, what would be the share price immediately after the 50% bonus issue?

Solution:

(a) **Effect of Bonus Issue on Shareholders' Equity**

Existing number of shares (₹10,00,000 ÷ 5) = 200,000
Bonus shares (50% × 2,00,000) = 1,00,000
Retained earnings capitalized = 1,00,000 shares × ₹5 each
= ₹5,00,000

Equity share capital would increase and retained earnings would decrease by ₹5,00,000. Shareholders' equity account after the bonus issue:

	(₹)
Equity share capital (3,00,000 shares of ₹5 each)	15,00,000
Share premium account	12,00,000
Retained earnings	13,00,000
Shareholders' equity	40,00,000

(b) **Share Price After the Bonus Issue**

Total market value before bonus shares = 2,00,000 shares @ ₹50 = ₹1,00,00,000
Number of shares after bonus issue = 3,00,000
Expected price after bonus issue = ₹1,00,00,000 ÷ 3,00,000 shares
= ₹33.33 per share.

14.7.1 Legal Aspects of Bonus Issues

Section 63 of the Companies Act, 2013 specifies the sources of funding bonus issues and the eligibility conditions. These are briefly discussed below.

A company can fund bonus issues out of its retained earnings, free reserves, share premium account and capital redemption reserve (except revaluation reserve).

Sources of Funding Bonus Issues

A company can issue fully paid bonus shares out of its retained earnings, free reserves, share premium account and capital redemption reserve. However, "no issue of bonus shares shall be made by capitalizing reserves created by the revaluation of assets" [Section 63(1)]. The reason for not allowing the use of revaluation reserve to finance bonus share issues is that revaluation reserves do not represent realized gains.

Eligibility to Issue Bonus Shares

To be eligible to issue bonus shares: (i) the company should be authorized by its Articles of association, (ii) the Board should recommend and the shareholders should approve the same in the general meeting, and (iii) the company should not have defaulted in servicing its debt or in payment of statutory payments to employees such as contribution to provident fund and gratuity. Also, "the bonus shares shall not be issued in lieu of dividend." [Section 63(1)]

14.7.2 Stock Splits

In a stock split, the par-value of a share is split over two or more shares. It is done to increase the number of shares and reduce the share's market price.

A stock split happens when a share of say ₹10 par-value is split into two shares of ₹5 each. The main purpose of the stock splits may be to increase the number of shares in the market and to make shares cheaper to enhance their affordability. During the past few years, several organizations including ONGC, ICICI bank and SBI have opted for stock splits. There are many ₹10 par value shares being traded at thousands of rupees per share. It can be argued that higher the market price, less affordable the share would be to small investors. Accordingly, we might see many more companies going to split their ₹10 shares into two or more shares of lesser value.

Similar to bonus issues, the stock splits also have an immediate effect of increasing the number of shares in the market. However, while the par value remains the same in bonus issues, stock splits effectively reduce the par value according to the split ratio. Another difference between bonus share issue and stock split is that while 'equity share capital' remains the same in stock splits, bonus issues increase the equity share capital by capitalizing retained earnings and free reserves.

Sometimes companies may go for **reverse-stock-split** which refers to consolidation of two or more shares into one share by proportionately increasing the par value of the share.

Consider the following example to understand the effect of a stock split.

EXAMPLE 14.7 Using the data of previous question (Biggs Company), show how the equity account would change if instead of a bonus issue, the company goes for a (a) 5-for-1 stock split and (b) a 1-for-2 reverse stock split.

Solution:

(a) *Effect of stock split:* The number of shares would increase five times and par value would decline to ₹1 per share:

	(₹)
Equity share capital (10,00,000 shares of ₹1 each)	10,00,000
Share premium account	12,00,000
Retained earnings	18,00,000
Shareholders' equity	40,00,000

(b) **Effect of a 1-for-2 reverse stock split**

	(₹)
Equity share capital (1,00,000 shares of ₹10 each)	10,00,000
Share premium account	12,00,000
Retained earnings	18,00,000
Shareholders' equity	40,00,000

Researchable Issues

Faculty members, students and research scholars may like to consider the following selected issues for further research and case writing.

- Dividend policy and shareholders' wealth
- Dividend practices in the Indian banking sector: Private sector banks versus PSBs.
- Dividend policy, capital structure and shareholders' wealth: A case study of Indian automobile industry.
- Dividend practices of MNCs operating in India.
- Dividend practices and corporate governance in real estate and infrastructure sectors.
- Dividend policy, signaling effect and investor exploitation.
- Bonus issues and shareholders' wealth: Evidence from an emerging market.

References

Desai, Mihir A., Foley, C. Fritz, Hines Jr., James R., Dividend Policy inside the Firm, NBER Working Paper No. 8698, Issued in January 2002, www.nber.org/papers/w8698.

Levy, H. and Sarnat M., *Capital Investment and Financial Decisions*, Prentice Hall, New Jersey, 1978.

Modigliani, Franco and Miller, Merton H., "The Cost of Capital, Corporation Finance and the Theory of Investment", *American Economic Review*, **48**, June 1958, pp. 261–97.

Websites

www.icai.org/post.html?Post_id=10511

www.incometaxindia.gov.in/tutorials/14-%20stcg.pdf

Chapter VIII—Companies (Declaration and Payment of Dividend) Rules, 2014.

Www.essar.com/upload/pdf/essarshipping_IM_2011_11.pdf.

John Butters, www.factset.com/websitefiles/pdfs/buyback_3.16.15 dated 16 March 2015.

www.primedatabasegroup.com/newsroom/PR-287.pdf. Prime databasepress Release dated 15th May, 2014.

www.moneycontrol.com/stocks/marketinfo/bonus.

Companies Act, 2013

http://money.rediff.com/companies/Infosys-Ltd/13020007/bonus?

www.mca.gov.in/ministryv2/companiesact.html.

http://taxguru.in/income-tax/income-tax-slab-financial-year-201516.html.

www.airtel.in/about-bharti/media-centre/bharti-airtel-news/corporate/bharti-tele-ventures-announces-rs.-45-as-the-floor-price-for-its-ipo;

Points to Remember

- **Relationship:** There is a relationship between the dividends and financing decisions because a company can utilize its earnings either to pay cash dividends to the shareholders or retain the same for financing investment projects.
- **Modigliani–Miller approach:** According to Modigliani–Miller, the investors value a firm only on the basis of its earning capacity; how the earnings are split between payment of dividends and retained earnings is immaterial. On the basis of certain assumptions they argue that dividend decision is irrelevant. Under the MM approach, the dividend decision becomes a passive or residual policy.
- **Clientele theory:** Different investors have diverse needs when it comes to cash dividends versus capital gains. As long as there is a clientele or group of investors who would go along with the stated dividend policy of the company, the company's issue of shares would be successful.
- **The relevance of dividend policy:** There are several arguments that can be given against the MM's irrelevance of dividend policy and in favour of the relevance of the dividend policy. These factors include: resolution of uncertainty, investors' need for current income, effect of taxes and transaction costs, etc.
- **In practice**, companies have to consider several aspects while deciding on their dividend policy including future investment opportunities, shareholders preferences, liquidity position, applicable taxes and other legal aspects.
- **Signaling theory** suggests that in view of asymmetric information, investors often try to get 'signals' about the future prospects of the company from the changes in the company's dividend policy.
- **Financing dividends:** A company can declare and pay dividends for any financial year out of the following: (i) Profits of the company for that year after providing for depreciation; (ii) Profits of any previous year remaining undistributed; and (iii) Out of both (i) and (ii).
- **Buyback** of shares refers to the repurchase of a company's own outstanding shares using the surplus cash in the company's balance sheet. The objectives of buybacks include distribution of surplus cash, increase earnings per share, support share prices in bear-phase, positive tax effect and eventual delisting.
- Theoretically, the company should offer such a price to buyback its shares that would leave investors not offering shares for sale not poorer than the ones who render shares in a buyback exercise. Methods that companies can use to repurchase their shares include (i) the tender method and (ii) purchasing shares from the open market.
- **Bonus shares** refer to the additional fully paid shares issued by a company free of cost to its existing shareholders in proportion to their current shareholding. A company can issue fully paid bonus shares out of its retained earnings and free reserves, share premium account and capital redemption reserve.

Questions

1. Explain the relationship between the dividends decision and financing policy.
2. Discuss the assumptions and conclusions of the Modigliani–Miller theory of irrelevance of dividends.
3. Enumerate the main arguments favouring relevance of the dividend policy. Between theories of relevance and irrelevance of dividends, which one do you support and why?

4. Discuss the practical aspects that companies have to consider while deciding on their dividend policy. Give real-life examples where possible.
5. Explain the meaning of buyback of shares and the reasons why a company would want to repurchase its own shares.
6. Explain the sources that a company can use to finance its share buy-back program. Briefly discuss the main legal aspects that a company has to follow in India for repurchasing its own shares.
7. Distinguish between bonus shares and stock-splits, and discuss their effect on the company's balance sheet as well as shareholders' wealth.
8. Briefly discuss the main Indian legal aspects that companies have to follow for issuing bonus shares and for stock-splits.
9. For each of the companies described below, choose the most appropriate dividend policy and explain the reason for doing so:

Company information	*Dividend payout ratio (tick one)*	*Explain the rationale for your choice*
High growth company with many acceptable investment proposals	High [ ] Low [ ]	
A closely held company having rich individuals as shareholders	High [ ] Low [ ]	
A PSU company with high liquidity majorly owned by Government which is facing a resource crunch	High [ ] Low [ ]	
A company which has aggressively financed projects through FCCBs coming up soon for redemption	High [ ] Low [ ]	

Multiple Choice Questions

1. According to the Modigliani–Miller approach to dividend policy, the value of a firm:
   (a) Would be maximized when a firm retains more of its earnings and distribute less as dividends.
   (b) Would be maximized when a firm distributes more of its earnings as dividends and retains less.
   (c) Depends solely on the firm's earnings power and is not influenced by the manner in which its earnings are split between dividends and retained earnings.
   (d) None of the above.

2. All of the following could be arguments in favour of the relevance of dividend decision in corporate finance, except:
   (a) Resolution of uncertainty for investors
   (b) Shareholders' need for current income
   (c) Possible future unwise investments by the company
   (d) All of the above could be arguments in favour of the relevance of dividend decision.

3. The Satan Company has projected next three years' net profits and capital expenditure requirements as follows:

Year	*Net profit*	*Capital expenditure*
1	30,000	40,000
2	40,000	40,000
3	60,000	30,000

Assuming the company has 10,000 shares outstanding, what would be the aggregate external financing over the three year period if each year the company follows a dividend payout ratio of 50%?

(a) ₹45,000 (b) ₹60,000
(c) ₹75,000 (d) None of the above.

4. The Satan Company has projected next three years' net profits and capital expenditure requirements as follows:

Year	*Net profit*	*Capital expenditure*
1	30,000	40,000
2	40,000	40,000
3	60,000	30,000

Assuming the company has 10,000 shares outstanding, what would be the aggregate amount of dividends paid over the three year period if each year the company follows a dividend payout ratio of 50%?

(a) ₹45,000 (b) ₹55,000
(c) ₹65,000 (d) None of the above.

5. The Satan Company has projected next three years' net profits and capital expenditure requirements as follows:

Year	*Net profit*	*Capital expenditure*
1	30,000	40,000
2	40,000	40,000
3	50,000	30,000

Assuming the company has 10,000 shares outstanding, what would be the aggregate external financing over the three year period if each year the company pays a constant dividend of ₹2 per share?

(a) ₹45,000 (b) ₹50,000
(c) ₹55,000 (d) None of the above.

6. Each of the following could be an objective of a company's shares buyback programme, except:
   (a) Distribute surplus cash
   (b) Increase earnings per share
   (c) Increase promoters holding
   (d) All of the above could be objectives of a buyback programme.
7. A company has 3,00,000 shares outstanding, out of which it plans to repurchase 15% shares at a fair price that should leave shareholders who offer their shares for buyback no-worse-off than other shareholders. If the current cum-dividend market price is ₹50 per share, what would be the fair price at which the company should offer to repurchase shares?

(a) ₹45.22 (b) ₹52.50
(c) ₹58.82 (d) None of the above.

8. A company has 3,00,000 shares outstanding, out of which it plans to repurchase 15% shares at a fair price that should leave shareholders who offer their shares for buyback no-worse-off than other shareholders. If the current cum-dividend market price is ₹50 per share, how much cash would the company need for its buyback program?
(a) ₹22.50 million (b) ₹26.47 million
(c) ₹30.64 million (d) None of the above.

Self-Test Questions

1. The League Company has projected the next five years' net profits and investment (capital expenditure) requirements as follows:

Year	*Net profit* [₹]	*Planned investment* [₹]
1	2,00,000	1,20,000
2	2,50,000	2,00,000
3	3,00,000	3,00,000
4	3,50,000	2,50,000
5	4,00,000	5,00,000

The Company has 10,000 shares outstanding.

Determine the dividend per share and the amount of external financing required each year if the company adopts the 'residual decision' approach to dividend policy.

2. Use the same data as in 1 (League Company). Further, the Company has 10,000 shares outstanding and has been paying out a cash dividend of ₹10 per share.
(a) Determine the dividend per share and the amount of external financing required each year if the company decides to follow a stable dividend payout ratio of 50%.
(b) Calculate the amount of external financing required each year if the company decides to pay stable dividend of ₹10 per share during each of the next five years.

3. The present market price of Green Company's equity shares is ₹40 per share. The company is expected to pay a dividend of ₹5.00 per share at the end of one year. Investors' required rate of return on equity is 25%. Assume there are no taxes.

Assume Charlie has 1000 shares of the company. Using Modigliani-Miller theory:
(a) Assuming the company pays out a dividend of ₹5 per share, calculate the expected price per share and Charlie's wealth (from his shareholding) at the end of one year;
(b) Assuming no dividends are paid out, calculate the expected price per share and Charlie's wealth (from his shareholding) at the end of one year.
(c) Comment on the results in relation to the MM theory of irrelevance of dividend policy.

Problems

1. The Surge Company has projected the next five years' net profits and investment (capital expenditure) requirements as follows:

Year	*Net profit* [₹]	*Planned investment* [₹]
1	3,00,000	2,50,000
2	4,00,000	3,00,000
3	5,00,000	4,50,000
4	6,00,000	5,00,000
5	6,00,000	8,00,000

The Company has 10,000 shares outstanding.

Determine the dividend per share and the amount of external financing required each year if the company adopts the 'residual decision' approach to dividend policy.

2. The current market price of Rosy Company's equity shares is ₹150 per share. Investors' required rate of return on equity is 18%. The company is expected to pay a dividend of ₹10.00 per share at the end of one year. Assume there are no taxes.

Assume Guru has 1,000 shares of the company. Using Modigliani–Miller theory:

(a) Assuming the company pays out a dividend of ₹10 per share, calculate the expected price per share and Guru's wealth (from his shareholding) at the end of one year;

(b) Assuming no dividends are paid out, calculate the expected price per share and Guru's wealth (from his shareholding) at the end of one year.

(c) Comment on the results in relation to the MM theory of irrelevance of dividend policy.

3. The Sterling Company has projected the next five years' net profits and investment (capital expenditure) requirements as follows:

Year	*Net profit* [₹]	*Planned investment* [₹]
1	70,000	60,000
2	60,000	70,000
3	50,000	80,000
4	80,000	60,000
5	90,000	50,000

The Company has 10,000 shares outstanding, and has been paying out a cash dividend of ₹4 per share.

(a) Determine the dividend per share and the amount of external financing required each year if the company decides to follow a stable dividend payout ratio of 50%.

(b) Calculate the amount of external financing required each year if the company decides to pay stable dividend of ₹4 per share during each of the next five years.

4. Diplomat Company has 10,000 shares outstanding and has earned a profit of ₹60,000 in the year just concluded. The company is wondering as to what retention or dividend policy would best serve to maximize the shareholders' wealth. The company plans to finance all new investment projects exclusively out of the retained earnings.

   If the company pays out all profits as dividends and does not reinvest, its earnings will stagnate at the current level of ₹60,000 per annum. It has attractive investment opportunities which, if undertaken, will result in future growth in earnings and dividends. However, if the company retains the earnings for re-investment, the equity investors' perceived risk, and hence, the required rate of return would rise due to the risk and uncertainty related to new projects.

   The following table sums up the expected growth rate and the equity investors' required rate of return at different levels of retained earnings:

Alternative plans	*% of earnings retained*	*Growth rate in earnings and dividends*	*Required return**
A	0	0%	12%
B	25	6%	14%
C	50	11%	16%
D	75	13%	22
*Shareholders' required rate of return on all investments			

   Once a decision is made about the percentage of earnings to be retained, the balance profits will be distributed immediately as dividends for this year.

   According to the dividend growth model, what would be the optimum retention policy for the company?

5. Skyline Company witnessed rapid growth for the past several years, but now its business is not expected to grow fast. It has substantial amount of surplus funds which it is contemplating to disburse among shareholders through a share repurchase instead of cash dividend. Out of its present 2,00,000 shares outstanding, it plans to repurchase 20% or 40,000 shares. The current cum-dividend market price is ₹80 per share. The company wouldlike to offer such a price for the repurchase of its shares that would leave investors not offering shares for sale no poorer than the ones who render shares for buyback.

   Ignoring taxes and transaction costs, determine the following:

   (a) Calculate the price at which the company should offer to repurchase shares?

   (b) Determine the total amount of money the company would be distributing through share re-purchase?

6. Shareholders' equity account of Alpine Company appears as follows:

	(₹)
Equity share capital (10,00,000 shares of ₹1 each)	1,20,000
Share premium account	30,000
Retained earnings	1,50,000
Shareholders' equity	3,00,000

   (a) Show how the equity account would changeifthe company goes for a 100% bonus issue by capitalizing retained earnings equal to the nominal (par) value of the additional shares issued.

   (b) If the share price before the bonus issue was ₹90 per share, ignoring any signaling effect, what should be the share price after the 100% bonus issue?

   (c) Show how the equity account would change if instead of a bonus issue, the company goes for a 2-for-1 stock split.

SHORT-CASE

Unitech's Dividend Fiasco

In a rare instance, the Unitech Board of Directors' proposal to pay a dividend was rejected by a majority of the shareholders in the Company's 40th Annual General Meeting held on 29 September 2011. The Board had recommended a dividend payment equal to 5% of the Unitech share's par value, totalling approximately ₹30 crore, for the financial year 2010–2011 subject to the shareholders' approval. In the AGM, majority of the shareholders felt that given the current high interest rate regime prevailing in the country, the company should better utilize the available funds for business rather than spend the same as cash dividends.

While some analysts hailed the incidence as a sign of maturing of the shareholders, some minority shareholders said that dividend recommended by the board was too little as compared to the company's reported net profit of ₹567 crore for the year and that is why they decided to reject the same. Indeed the company desperately needed cash to complete its held up projects and to service its huge debt.

Unitech Limited was established in 1972 as a soil testing firm which later entered into real estate business. The business progressed rapidly and the company went for a stock market listing of its shares in 1986. Despite ups and downs due to the cyclical nature of the industry, the company performed well, but its high point came in 2005 when the Government allowed Foreign Direct Investment (FDI) in construction activities. Foreign investors started taking keen interest in Unitech which was India's second largest real estate developer.

As a result, Unitech's share prices and market capitalization shot up at a speed that was fast and furious. On 30 May 2006, "The Company's share price rose to ₹13,422.80, taking its market cap to ₹16,765.08 crore. Unitech's share price has jumped more than 30 times from its 52-week low of ₹428 hit on 21 June 2005" [ET]. Buoyed by fast rising market capitalization and good future business prospects, the company in June 2006 decided to issue bonus shares in the ratio of 12:1 and also to split each ₹10 share into 5 shares of ₹2 each. Same year the company also raised fresh capital amounting to ₹3,000 crore on the UK's Alternative Investment Market. In August 2007, the company made another 1:1 bonus issue, thereby substantially increasing the equity base.

During the next two-three years, the company (through its approximately 350 subsidiaries) went on a land acquisition spree, taking its land bank to over 14,500 acres. Given the company's reputation at the time, it could have raised fresh equity funding to finance the land acquisition but instead chose to go for debt funding.

In 2007–2008, the company applied for the 2G telecom licences. The company wanted to diversify in to a new business to reduce the risk of over dependence on the cyclical real estate business. The company succeeded in getting the license at a substantial cost, but later got involved in legal problems when the 2G scam came to light and the CBI investigated the allocation of licences by the then telecom minister.

The company's business performance had been good so far and the company sold seven million square-feet of space during 2007–2008. Things however, dramatically changed after the collapse of Lehman Brothers in September 2008 and the eruption of the global financial crisis. The company could sell less than two million square feet of space during 2008–2009 giving a deadly blow to the cash inflows. The cash commitment and liabilities however did not decline and servicing debt and meeting other liabilities became a problem.

Debt level on the company's balance sheet was steadily rising. As on 31 March 2008, the company's debt stood at ₹8,117.53 crore in addition to current liabilities and provisions of ₹7,065.30 crore. Current assets at that time amounted to ₹8,749.16 which should be adequate to provide cover against current liabilities, but a major chunk of the company's current assets consisted of "loans and advances" which remained uncollected year after year. The loans and advances further rose to ₹13,717.68 crore at the end of year 2013–2014. In their report for the year 2013–2014, the statutory auditors 'qualified' their report about these loans and advances, casting a doubt over their recoverability. The company's financial data for the selected period is given in the Appendix.

The company in 2008 made several attempts to raise fresh equity by private placement of shares with Qualified Institutional Buyers (QIBs) but did not succeed, partly because the market sentiment had turned negative and partly because the company promoters expected a higher price per share than the QIBs were willing to pay. The shares that used to trade between ₹400–600 per share during 2006–2007 (after the bonus issues) touched a low of ₹21.90 per share by the end of FY2008.

Since 2009, the company had taken several steps to improve its cash flow, including exiting telecom operations (possibly incurring a loss), raising fresh funds, launching of affordable housing schemes and selling away of its headquarters and some other prime properties. To some extent the problems had been mitigated but cash flow challenges continued to daunt the company.

Despite fluctuating fortunes, the company had continuously paid dividend between years 2000 to 2010, though the percentage of dividends varied between a high of 40% in 2005 to a low of 5% in 2009. However, the Board did not recommend any dividend after the shareholders rejected the proposed dividend as stated in the beginning.

Between 2009 and 2014, the company made serious efforts to reduce its debt as a result of which by March 2014, the company's "total debt" had reduced to ₹2,731.68 crore from ₹8,117.53 crore in March 2008. However the company's reputation and investor confidence had been shaken due to its name being associated with the alleged 2G scam. The company shares were quoted on NSE at ₹7.80 at close of trading hours on 7th August 2015.

Case Questions

1. Was the Board justified in recommending the payment of dividend? Why?
2. Were the shareholders justified in rejecting the directors' proposal to pay dividend? Why?
3. Identify pros and cons of the dividend, bonus issue and financing policies adopted by the company and be prepared to defend your answer.

Annexure

1. Balance Sheet of Unitech

[₹ in crore]

	March 2014	*March 2012*	*March 2010*	*March 2008*	*March 2006*
Sources of funds					
Total share capital	523.26	523.26	487.76	324.68	12.49
Equity share capital	523.26	523.26	487.76	324.68	12.49
Share application money	0	0	225.2	0	0
Reserves	9,346.56	9,115.73	7,415.47	1,819.14	212.05
Networth	9,869.82	9,638.99	8,128.43	2,143.82	224.54
Secured loans	1,656.44	1,240.82	3,907.54	5,506.45	632.57
Unsecured loans	1,075.24	1,275.03	1,016.02	2,611.08	54.2
Total debt	2,731.68	2,515.85	4,923.56	8,117.53	686.77
Total liabilities	12,601.50	12,154.84	13,051.99	10,261.35	911.31

Application of funds					
Gross block	135.77	113.91	151.09	132.05	83.17
Less: Accum. Depn.	59	50.25	44.03	35.96	28.44
Net block	76.77	63.66	107.06	96.09	54.73
Capital WIP	25.3	24.97	9,666.03	7,083.41	1,824.66
Investments	3,242.95	2,424.81	1,654.15	1,397.99	282.39
Inventories	963.68	1,170.20	5.74	13.66	32.26
Sundry debtors	930.91	1,648.29	1,007.74	739.74	76.54
Cash and bank	88.76	158.1	135.7	236.01	74.73
Total current assets	1,983.35	2,976.59	1,149.18	989.41	183.53
Loans and advances	13,717.68	11,290.49	7,427.76	7,624.58	866.97
Fixed deposits	0	0	73.73	135.17	85.9
Total CA, loans and advances	15,701.03	14,267.08	8,650.67	8,749.16	1,136.40
Current liabilities	6,417.97	4,502.22	6,895.87	6,316.27	2,314.33
Provisions	26.58	123.46	130.07	749.03	72.55
Total CL and provisions	6,444.55	4,625.68	7,025.94	7,065.30	2,386.88
Net current assets	9,256.48	9,641.40	1,624.73	1,683.86	–1,250.48
Total assets	12,601.50	12,154.84	13,051.97	10,261.35	911.3
Contingent liabilities	8,246.86	12,751.24	1,649.94	2,325.69	434.87
Book value (₹)	37.72	36.84	32.41	13.21	179.81

Source: Dion Global Solutions Limited, c/o www.moneycontrol.com

2. Unitech Bonus Announcements

Year	*Month*	*Ratio*	*Ex Bonus Date*
2007	May	1:1	30/08/2007
2006	May	12:1	23/06/2006

3. Unitech Dividend Record

Year	*Month*	*Dividend (%)*
2010	May	10
2009	June	5
2008	June	13
2007	May	25
2006	June	10
2005	June	40
2004	July	30
2003	August	20
2002	July	20
2001	July	20
2000	August	30

[*Source:* money.rediff.com/companies/Unitech-Ltd]

Note: The case is based on secondary sources of information and is prepared with the sole academic purpose of facilitating class room discussion.

PART V

FINANCIAL RATIOS AND ANALYSIS

CHAPTER

15

Financial Ratio and Analysis

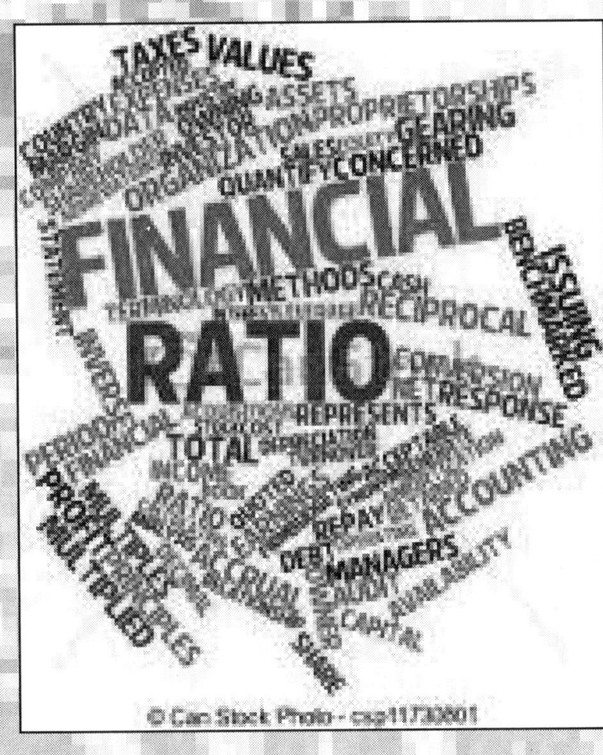

LEARNING OBJECTIVES

After studying this chapter, you should be able to:

- Understand the various types of financial ratios
- Discuss and calculate liquidity ratios
- Discuss and calculate working capital ratios
- Explain and calculate profitability ratios
- Discuss the purpose of turnover ratios and calculate main ratios
- Discuss and calculate capital structure ratios
- Understand and calculate return on investment ratios
- Understand the meaning and importance of the horizontal and common-size analysis
- Identify the steps involved in preparation of horizontal and common-size financial statements

15.1 Introduction

The primary objective of financial statements (Profit & Loss Account, Balance Sheet and Cash flow) is to provide information that is useful to existing and potential investors, lenders and other creditors in making investment decisions about the firm. While investors use the information embedded in financial statements to forecast the future earnings and cash flows of the firm, lenders use it to assess the creditworthiness or debt paying capacity. In either case, it becomes important that the users understand and interpret the large amount of data that these financial statements contain. This chapter discusses the various financial ratios that can help users in evaluating the financial performance of the firm and take rationale investment decisions.

15.2 Financial Ratios

The process of analyzing the firm using financial ratios begins with the collection of financial data from the annual reports of the companies. Generally users look at three types of financial statements namely *Profit & Loss Account, Balance Sheet and Cash flow* to analyze the financial performance of the firm. Financial ratios use information from these financial statements to provide a useful insight into the various aspects of a firm's performance including liquidity, working capital, profitability, efficiency and financial risk. Primarily, financial ratios can be grouped into the following six categories:

- Liquidity ratios
- Working capital ratios
- Profitability ratios
- Capital structure ratios
- Turnover ratios
- Return on investment ratios

15.2.1 Liquidity Ratios

Liquidity refers to the ability of the company to meet its short-term obligation in the normal course of business. At any given point of time, the short-term obligations (current liabilities) of the firm should be adequately covered by its current assets to ensure solvency. Liquidity ratios help investors in assessing the firm's ability to meet its short-term obligations in time and maintain solvency. The various liquidity ratios used by analysts to measure the liquidity position of a firm are current ratio and the quick (or acid test) ratio.

Current Ratio

Current ratio, one of the frequently used ratios to measure the short-term liquidity of a company, compares the amount of current assets as a multiple (or times) of current liabilities

Current ratio = Current Assets/Current Liabilities

Current assets generally includes cash & cash equivalents, trade receivables (debtors), inventories, short-term loans & advances or any other current assets that are expected to be realized in, or is intended for sale or consumption in, the company's normal operating cycle. Current liabilities includes short-term borrowings, trade payables (creditors), short-term provisions or any other current liabilities that is expected to be settled in the company's normal operating cycle. Table 15.1 shows the balance sheet of Pidilite Industries.

TABLE 15.1
Pidilite Industries Balance Sheet

(in millions)	*As at 31st March 2013*	*As at 31st March 2012*
Equity and Liabilities		
Shareholders' funds		
Share capital	513	508
Reserves and surplus	16,812	13,209
Non-current liabilities		
Long-term borrowings	–	923
Deferred tax liability (net)	484	454
Long-term provisions	143	101
Current liabilities		
Trade payables	2,071	1,702
Other current liabilities	3,728	4,929
Short-term provisions	1,634	1,179
Total	**25,384**	**23,006**
Assets		
Non-current assets		
Fixed assets (Net)		
Tangible assets	5,120	4,717
Intangible assets	217	242
Capital work-in-progress	4,087	3,713
Non-current investments	2,623	2,419
Long-term loans and advances	242	250
Other non-current assets	–	1.37
Current assets		
Current investments	2,846	909
Inventories	4,512	3,963
Trade receivables	3,668	3,261
Cash and bank balances	1,368	2,577
Short-term loans and advances	594	860
Other current assets	107	93
Total	**25,384**	**23,006**

For Pidilite Industries, Current ratio for the years 2012 and 2013 is:

Year 2012 = 11,663.36/7,810.38 = 1.49

Year 2013 = 13,094.65/7,433.40 = 1.76

Pidilite Industries current ratio indicates that the amount of its current assets is 1.49 times of the current liabilities in year 2012 and 1.76 times of its current liabilities in the year 2013. Generally, a high current ratio (>1) indicates that the firm has adequate resources to cover up its current liabilities, and there is little risk of default in settling its dues on time. However, while a higher current ratio is desirable from the solvency point-of-view, excessive investments in current assets may sometimes be an indication of inefficient financial management. For example, a very high current ratio (>2) would reduce the overall return on investment in the firm as excessive cash gets tied up in inventories and trade receivables which could have been used up for more productive purposes. While textbooks sometime suggest that an ideal current ratio should be equal to 2.0, in practice it would depend on the nature of the business and cash flows and the firm should look to balance both solvency and return efficiency.

Current ratio measures the short-term liquidity of a company by comparing the amount of current assets as a multiple (or times) of current liabilities.

Quick Ratio or Acid-Test Ratio

While current ratio is an important indicator of the liquidity position of the firm, it includes inventory among the liquid resources, which is generally regarded as the least liquid among the current assets. Consequently, efficacy of current ratio is sometimes questioned as an appropriate measure of liquidity because inventory may not be readily saleable in the event of adversity. In essence, a company with a high proportion of current assets in the form of cash and trade receivables would be regarded as more liquid than a company whose current assets consist primarily of inventories. Quick or acid-test ratio excludes inventories while comparing the amount of current assets as a multiple (or times) of current liabilities.

Quick ratio = (Current Assets–Inventories)/Current Liabilities

For Pidilite Industries, Quick ratio for the years 2012 and 2013 is:

Year 2012 = (11,663 – 3,963)/7,810.38 = 0.99

Year 2013 = (13,095 – 4,512)/7,433.40 = 1.15

Quick ratio excludes inventories while comparing the amount of current assets as a multiple (or times) of current liabilities.

In addition to inventories, items, such as hire-purchase debtors, loans and advances made to employees or associate companies, and pre-paid expenses which cannot be readily converted to cash should also be generally excluded while calculating the quick ratio.

15.2.2 Working Capital Ratios

Working capital ratios analyze a firm's performance in managing the individual items of working capital, i.e., trade receivables, inventories and trade payables.

Debtor collection period measures the average number of days taken to collect payment from debtors.

Trade Receivables or Debtor Collection Period

Trade receivables or debtor collection period measures the average number of days taken to collect payment from debtors. In essence it represents the average number of days taken to convert trade receivables or debtors into cash.

Debtor collection period = Trade receivables × 365/Annual credit sales

TABLE 15.2 Pidilite Industries Income Statement

Pidilite (in millions)	*Year 2013*	*Year 2012*
Sales	33,316	28,163
Other income	659	427
Cost of goods sold	18,135	15,674
Gross profit	15,840	12,917
Employee and other expenses	9,049	7,624
Operating profit (EBITDA)	6,791	5,293
Finance costs	121	245
Depreciation	532	479
Profit before tax	6,138	4,569
Tax	1,589	1,096
Profit after tax	4,549	3,473

For Pidilite Industries, Debtor Collection period for the years 2012 and 2013 is:

Year 2012 = 365 × 3,261/28,163 = 42

Year 2013 = 365 × 3,668/33,316 = 40

In the above calculation, since the breakup between cash and credit sales is not available, we have assumed total sales as credit sales (Table 15.2). Lower the Debtor Collection period, better it is as it indicates efficient management of debtors and shorter working capital cycles. A high debtors' collection period indicates slackness in debtors' control, which in turn, could lead to excessive investment in debtors and longer working capital cycles.

Inventory Holding Period or Inventory Days

Inventory holding period measures the average time an item of inventory remains in stock before it is sold or used up in the normal course of business. In other words, it measures the number of days taken to convert inventory into sales.

Inventory Holding period = Inventory × 365/Annual cost of goods sold

The 'inventory' in the above ratio should ideally be 'average inventory' held by a firm during a period. When data is available about the inventory levels at the beginning and close of the year, an estimate of the average inventory may be obtained by adding the beginning and closing balances of stock and then dividing the sum total by two.

Average inventory = (Opening stock + Closing stock)/2

However, if the figure of 'average inventory' is not available, we can use the year-end figure of inventory.

Inventory collection period measures the average time an item of inventory remains in stock before it is sold or used up in the normal course of business

For Pidilite Industries, Inventory holding period for the years 2012 and 2013 is

Year 2012 = 365 × 3,963/15,674 = 92

Year 2013 = 365 × 4,512/18,135 = 91

Lower the Inventory Holding period, better it is as it indicates lower cash being tied up in working capital.

Trade Payables or Creditor Days

Trade payables or creditor days measures the average number of days a firm takes to pay its creditors or suppliers.

Creditor days = Trade payables × 365/Annual credit purchases

In the above ratio, if the 'credit purchases' figure is not known, we can use 'total purchases'. If data on purchases is not available, an alternative may be to use the cost of goods sold as the basis.

Creditor days measures the average number of days a firm takes to pay its creditors or suppliers

For Pidilite Industries, creditor days for the years 2012 and 2013 are:

Year 2012 = 365 × 1,702/15,674 = 39.6

Year 2013 = 365 × 2,071/18,135 = 41.7

Higher the creditor days, better it is as it indicates shortened working capital cycle and cost-free source of financing.

15.2.3 Profitability Ratios

To generate value for the shareholders, it is imperative that the firm generates sufficient profitability from its business after providing for expenses. It has been observed that firms with sustainable profit margins generally tend to outperform in the market in terms of share price value. Consequently, analysis of profitability of the firm becomes an important metric for existing and potential investors, lenders and other creditors in making rationale investment decisions about the firm.

Profitability ratios basically measure the performance of the firm by relating the profits earned during a period to sales. Profits at the firm level can be measured at four different levels, sometimes called multi-step profit margins, as shown below:

Gross profit Level = Sales – Cost of goods sold

Operating profit or Earnings Before Interest and Taxes (EBIT) Level
= Gross profit – All Operating expenses except interest and taxes

Profit Before Taxes (PBT) Level = Operating profit – Interest expense

Net Profit After Taxes (PAT) Level = Profit before taxes – Taxes

Some analysts also tend to use Earnings before Interest, Taxes, Depreciation and Amortization (EBITDA) as a measure of operating profitability instead of Earnings before Interest and Taxes (EBIT). In that case, the Operating profit would be defined as:

Profitability ratios basically measure the performance of the firm by relating the profits earned during a period to sales

Operating profit or earnings before interest, taxes, depreciation and amortization (EBITDA) level = Gross profit – All Operating expenses except interest, taxes and depreciation/amortization

All the above measures of profit would be taken as a percentage of sales for calculating the profitability ratios.

For Pidilite Industries, profitability ratios for the year 2012 and 2013 are given in Table 15.3.

TABLE 15.3
Profitability ratio of Pidilite Industry

	Year 2013	*Year 2012*
Gross profit ratio	47.5%	45.9%
Operating profit ratio	18.8%	17.1%
Profit before taxes ratio	18.4%	16.2%
Net profit after taxes ratio	13.7%	12.3%

For calculating operating profitability, we have used the measure of Earnings before Interest and Taxes (EBIT).

15.2.4 Capital Structure Ratios

While many investors focus on the assets side of the balance sheet to assess the future performance of the firm, analysis of liabilities side is an equally important task given the possible implications of sources of finance for long-term liquidity, profitability and solvency of the company. Although an ideal capital structure (mix of debt and equity) can vary across industries depending upon the nature of businesses and cash flows, an evaluation of capital structure ratios can help investors in assessing the future earnings, cash flows and creditworthiness of the firm. The various capital structure ratios used by analysts are enumerated below:

Long Term Debt to Equity Ratio

Long term debt to equity ratio is the ratio of long term debt to shareholder's equity. Current liabilities are not included in the debt for this ratio.

Long-term debt to equity ratio = Long-term debt/Shareholders' funds

where,

Long-term debt = Long-term borrowings + Long-term provisions

Shareholder's funds can be computed from the assets side as well as liabilities side. Shareholder's funds from liabilities side:

Shareholders' funds = Paid up share capital + Reserves and surplus

Shareholder's funds from assets side:

Shareholders' funds = Non-current assets + Working capital – Non-current liabilities

where,

Working capital = Current assets – Current liabilities

For Pidilite Industries, Long-term debt to equity ratio for the years 2012 and 2013 is

Year 2012 = (923 + 101)/(508 + 13,209) = 0.075

Year 2013 = (0 + 143)/(513 + 16,812) = 0.008

Total Debt to Equity Ratio

Total debt to equity ratio is the ratio of total debt (long term debt + current liabilities) to shareholder's equity. Unlike the previous ratio (long term debt to equity), this ratio takes into account the current liabilities in addition to long term debt in the numerator.

Total debt to equity ratio = Total debt/Shareholders' funds

where,

Total debt = Long-term borrowings + Long-term provisions + Current liabilities

Total debt to equity ratio is the ratio of total debt (long term debt + current liabilities) to shareholder's equity

For Pidilite Industries, Total debt to equity ratio for the years 2012 and 2013 is:

Year 2012 = (923 + 101 + 7,810)/(508 + 13,209) = 0.64

Year 2013 = (0 + 143 + 7,433)/(513 + 16,812) = 0.44

Interest Coverage Ratio

This ratio measures the ability of the company to service debt out of its operating earnings. It is defined as a ratio of Earnings Before Interest and Taxes (EBIT) to annual interest expense. Generally higher the ratio, better it is as it signifies that the firm would be able to service its debt comfortably even in recessionary conditions when sales and profitability tends to decline.

Interest coverage ratio = Earnings before interest and taxes (EBIT)/Annual interest expense

Interest Coverage ratio measures the ability of the company to service debt out of its operating earnings

For Pidilite Industries, Interest Coverage ratio for the years 2012 and 2013 is

Year 2012 = 4,814/245 = 20 times

Year 2013 = 6,259/121= 52 times

While Pidilite has a very healthy interest coverage ratio, companies with coverage ratios of less than 2 times run a risk of default.

15.2.5 Turnover Ratios

Turnover ratios measure the efficiency with which the company utilizes its resources or assets to generate sales revenue. The turnover ratios commonly used by analysts to evaluate efficiency are:

Turnover ratios measure the efficiency with which the company utilizes its resources or assets to generate sales revenue

Asset Turnover Ratio

Asset turnover ratio measures how efficiently firm's assets are being utilized to generate the period's sales. The ratio is calculated as follows:

Total assets turnover ratio = Annual sales revenue/Total assets

where,

Total assets = Net fixed assets + Current assets

For Pidilite industries, total assets turnover ratio for the years 2012 and 2013 is:

Year 2012 = (28,163)/(8,673 + 11,663) = 1.38

Year 2013 = (33,316)/(9,424 + 13,095) = 1.48

Fixed Assets Turnover Ratio

Fixed asset turnover ratio measures how efficiently firm's fixed assets are being utilized to generate the period's sales. The ratio is calculated as follows:

Total fixed assets turnover ratio = Annual sales revenue/Fixed assets

For Pidilite Industries, Total fixed assets turnover ratio for the years 2012 and 2013 is:

Year 2012 = (28,163)/(8,673) = 3.25

Year 2013 = (33,316)/(9,424) = 3.54

While fixed assets turnover ratio for Pidilite industries is >3, total assets turnover ratio is <1.5. This indicates the over-investment in current assets is pulling down the overall efficiency or turnover ratio.

15.2.6 Return on Investment Ratios

Return on Investment Ratios analyze a firm's performance in relation to the stakeholders' investment in the business. The Return on Investment ratios commonly used by analysts are:

Return on Capital Employed

Return on capital employed measures the return earned by stakeholders on total capital employed in the business. The ratio is calculated as follows:

Return on capital employed = Earnings before Interest and Taxes (EBIT)/Total capital employed

Return on capital employed measures the return earned by stakeholders on total capital employed in the business

where

Total capital employed = Shareholder's fund + Non-current liabilities

For Pidilite Industries, Return on capital employed for the year 2012 and 2013 is:

Year 2012 = (5,292 – 479)/(508 + 13,209 + 923 + 454 + 101) = 32%

Year 2013 = (6,791 – 532)/(513 + 16,812 + 0 + 484 + 143) = 35%

Return on Net Worth (RONW)

Return on net worth measures the return from the point-of-view of shareholders or equityholders and is calculated by dividing the net profit available to ordinary shareholders by the shareholders' funds or net worth.

Return on net worth = (Profit after tax – preference dividends)/Shareholder's fund or net worth

where,

Shareholders' funds or net worth = Paid up share capital + Reserves and surplus

Note: While calculating shareholders' fund or net worth, reserves created out of revaluation of assets, write-back of depreciation and amalgamation are not be taken into account.

For Pidilite Industries, Return on net worth for the years 2012 and 2013 is:

Year 2012 = (3,473)/(508+13,209) = 25%

Year 2013 = (4,549)/(513+16,812) =26%

Return on net worth measures the return from the point of view of shareholders or equityholders

Du-Pont Return on Networth (RONW) Model

This model, which was first used by DuPont Company of U.S.A., explains that the return on Net Worth is the combined result of three separate ratios or components: *Net profit margin, total assets turnover ratio and the ratio of total assets to net worth (Leverage).*

RONW = Net profit margin × Asset turnover × Leverage

RONW = (Net profit/Sales) × (Sales/Total assets) × (Total assets/Net worth)

For Pidilite Industries, Du-Pont analysis for the years 2012 and 2013 is given in Table 15.4.

TABLE 15.4
Du-Pont analysis of pidilite.

	Year 2013	*Year 2012*
Net profit margin	13.7%	12.3%
Asset turnover ratio	1.48	1.38
Leverage	1.30	1.48
RONW	**26%**	**25%**

Du-pont analysis provides investors with a useful insight into the different components of RONW. It helps investors in assessing whether increase in RONW is being contributed by increasing margins or improving asset efficiency or is it the result of aggressive financing mix of using more debt. If the increase in RONW is coming from improving net profit margins, it reflects the superior pricing power of the company within the industry or sector. Similarly, increase on account of rising asset turnover ratio implies better utilization or efficiency of resources. Finally, increase in RONW on account of rising leverage imply taking on higher financial risk to improve returns which may not be a good sign.

15.3 Horizontal and Common-Size Analysis

The techniques, such as horizontal analysis and common-size analysis are generally used to analyze changes or trends in the financial performance of the firm either over time or in comparison to other competing firms.

Horizontal analysis involves comparing the same entity's financial statements (Profit & Loss account and the Balance Sheet) of two (or more) periods to analyze changes that have taken place over the period. While a comparison of items in the profit & loss account would reveal increase or decrease in incomes and expenses, analysis of balance sheet items would reveal the changes in assets, capital and liabilities that have taken place in the current period as compared to the previous one. Under horizontal analysis, changes between the two periods may be calculated in absolute amounts as well as in percentages.

Horizontal analysis involves comparing the same entity's financial of two (or more) periods to analyze changes that have taken place over the period

Horizontal Analysis of financial statements of Pidilite Industries for the years 2012 and 2013 is given in Table 15.5.

TABLE 15.5
Balance Sheet

(in millions)	*As at*	*As at*	*Horizontal analysis*	
	31st March 2013	*31st March 2012*	*Absolute change*	*Percentage change*
Equity and Liabilities				
Shareholders' funds				
Share capital	513	508	5	0.98%
Reserves and surplus	16,812	13,209	3,603	27.28%
Non–current liabilities				
Long-term borrowings	0	923	–923	–100.00%
Deferred tax liability (net)	484	454	30	6.61%
Long–term provisions	143	101	42	41.58%
Current liabilities				
Trade payables	2,071	1,702	369	21.68%
Other current liabilities	3,728	4,929	–1,201	–24.37%
Short–term provisions	1,634	1,179	455	38.59%
Total	**25,384**	**23,006**	**2,378**	**10.34%**
Assets				
Non–current assets				
Fixed assets (Net)				
Tangible assets	5,120	4,717	403	8.54%
Intangible assets	217	242	–25	–10.33%
Capital work–in–progress	4,087	3,713	374	10.07%
Non–current investments	2,623	2,419	204	8.43%
Long–term loans and advances	242	250	–8	–3.20%
Other non–current assets	0	1.37	–1	–100.00%
Current assets				
Current investments	2,846	909	1,937	213.09%
Inventories	4,512	3,963	549	13.85%
Trade receivables	3,668	3,261	407	12.48%
Cash and bank balances	1,368	2,577	–1,209	–46.92%
Short–term loans and advances	594	860	–266	–30.93%
Other current assets	107	93	14	15.05%
Total	**25,384**	**23,006**	**2,378**	**10.34%**

INCOME STATEMENT

(in millions)	Year 2013	Year 2012	Horizontal analysis	
			Absolute change	Percentage change
Sales	33,316	28,163	5,153	18.3%
Other income	659	427	232	54.3%
Cost of materials consumed	18,135	15,674	2,461	15.7%
Gross profit	15,181	12,489	2,692	21.6%
Employee and other expenses	9,049	7,624	1,425	18.7%
Operating profit (EBITDA)	6,132	4,865	1,267	26.0%
Finance costs	121	245	–124	–50.6%
Depreciation	532	479	53	11.1%
Profit before tax	5,479	4,141	1,338	32.3%
Tax	1,589	1,096	493	45.0%
Profit after tax	3,890	3,045	845	27.8%

15.4 Common-Size Analysis

Common-size analysis or vertical analysis involves a comparative analysis of two firms over the same period or of two periods for the same firm. Common-size analysis is done by expressing each line item in the financial statements as a percentage of a total value. For example, in a common-size Profit & Loss Account, each line item can be expressed as a percentage of total sales. Similarly, in a common-size balance sheet, each line item can be expressed as a percentage of the total assets.

Common-size analysis involves a comparative analysis of two firms over the same period or of two periods for the same firm

Common-Size Analysis of financial statements of Pidilite Industries for the years 2012 and 2013 is given in Table 15.6.

TABLE 15.6 Common-size analysis of Pidilite Industries

(in Millions)	*As at*	*As at*	*Common-size analysis (As % of Total Assets)*	
	31st March **2013**	*31st March* **2012**	*31st March* **2013**	*31st March* **2012**
Equity and Liabilities				
Shareholders' funds				
Share capital	513	508	2.02%	2.21%
Reserves and surplus	16,812	13,209	66.23%	57.42%
Non-current liabilities				
Long-term borrowings	0	923	0.00%	4.01%
Deferred tax liability (net)	484	454	1.91%	1.97%
Long-term provisions	143	101	0.56%	0.44%
Current liabilities				
Trade payables	2,071	1,702	8.16%	7.40%
Other current liabilities	3,728	4,929	14.69%	21.42%
Short-term provisions	1,634	1,179	6.44%	5.12%
Total	**25,384**	**23,006**	**100.00%**	**100.00%**
				(Contd.)

(in Millions)	*As at*	*As at*	*Common-size analysis (As % of total assets)*	
	31st March 2013	**31st March 2012**	**31st March 2013**	**31st March 2012**
Assets				
Non-current assets				
Fixed assets (Net)				
Tangible assets	5,120	4,717	20.17%	20.50%
Intangible assets	217	242	0.85%	1.05%
Capital work-in-progress	4,087	3,713	16.10%	16.14%
Non-current investments	2,623	2,419	10.33%	10.51%
Long-term loans and advances	242	250	0.95%	1.09%
Other non-current assets	0	1.37	0.00%	0.01%
Current assets				
Current investments	2,846	909	11.21%	3.95%
Inventories	4,512	3,963	17.77%	17.23%
Trade receivables	3,668	3,261	14.45%	14.17%
Cash and bank balances	1,368	2,577	5.39%	11.20%
Short-term loans and advances	594	860	2.34%	3.74%
Other current assets	107	93	0.42%	0.40%
Total	**25,384**	**23,006**	**100.00%**	**100.00%**

			Common-size analysis (as % of sales)	
Pidilite (in millions)	*Year 2013*	*Year 2012*	*Year 2013*	*Year 2012*
Sales	33,316	28,163	100%	100.0%
Other income	659	427	2%	1.5%
Cost of materials consumed	18,135	15,674	54%	55.7%
Gross profit	15,840	12,916	48%	45.9%
Employee and other expenses	9,049	7,624	27%	27.1%
Operating profit (EBITDA)	6,791	5,292	20%	18.8%
Finance costs	121	245	0%	0.9%
Depreciation	532	479	2%	1.7%
Profit before tax	6,138	4,568	18%	16.2%
Tax	1,589	1,096	5%	3.9%
Profit after tax	4,549	3,472	14%	12.3%

Researchable Issues

Faculty members, students and research scholars may like to consider the following selected issues for further research and case writing.

- Sectoral Ratio Analysis in India
- Capital Structure Ratios of Indian Companies vs Developed Market Companies

- Profitability Ratios of Large Companies vs Small Cap Companies in India
- Liquidity Ratios for Large Companies vs Small Cap Companies in India
- Working Capital ratios of FMCG Companies vs Commodity Companies in India

References

Altman, E.I., Financial ratios, discriminant analysis and the prediction of corporate bankruptcy. *The Journal of Finance*, Vol. 23, No. 4, 1968, pp. 589–609.

Beaver, W.H., Financial ratios as predictors of failure, *Journal of Accounting Research*, 1966, pp. 71–111.

Edmister, R.O., An empirical test of financial ratio analysis for small business failure prediction. *Journal of Financial and Quantitative analysis*, Vol. 7, No. 2, 1972, pp. 1477–1493.

Horrigan, J.O., Some empirical bases of financial ratio analysis, *Accounting Review*, 1965, pp. 558–568.

Points to Remember

- Primary objective of financial statements (Profit & Loss Account, Balance Sheet and Cash flow) is to provide information that is useful to existing and potential investors, lenders and other creditors in making investment decisions about the firm.
- Financial ratios use information from these financial statements to provide a useful insight into the various aspects of a firm's performance including liquidity, working capital, profitability, efficiency and financial risk.
- Liquidity ratios help investors in assessing the firm's ability to meet its short-term obligations in time and maintain solvency.
- Current ratio compares the amount of current assets as multiple (or times) of current liabilities. Quick or Acid-test ratio excludes inventories while comparing the amount of current assets as multiple (or times) of current liabilities.
- Accounts Receivables or Debtor Collection period measures the average number of days taken to collect payment from trade debtors. Inventory holding period measures the average time an item of inventory remains in stock before it is sold or used up in the normal course of business. Accounts Payables or Creditor days measures the average number of days a firm takes to pay its creditors or suppliers.
- Profitability ratios basically measure the performance of the firm by relating the profits earned during a period to sales.
- Total debt to equity ratio is the ratio of total debt (long term debt + current liabilities) to shareholder's equity.
- Interest Coverage Ratio measures the ability of the company to service debt out of its operating earnings. It is defined as a ratio of earnings before interest and taxes (EBIT) to interest. Generally higher the ratio, better it is as it signifies that the firm would be able to service its debt comfortably.
- Turnover ratios measure the efficiency with which the company utilizes its resources or assets to generate sales revenue.
- Returns on Investment Ratios analyze a firm's performance in relation to the stakeholders' investment in the business.
- Return on capital employed measures the return earned by stakeholders on total capital employed in the business. Return on net worth measures the return

from the point of view of shareholders or equity holders and is calculated by dividing the net profit available to ordinary shareholders by the shareholders' funds or net worth.

- Du-pont explains that the return on Net Worth is the combined result of three separate ratios or components: net profit margin, total assets turnover ratio and the ratio of total assets to net worth (Leverage).
- Horizontal analysis involves comparing the same entity's financial statements (profit & loss account and the balance sheet) of two (or more) periods to analyze changes that have taken place over the period.
- Common-size analysis or vertical analysis involves a comparative analysis of two firms over the same period or of two periods for the same firm.

Questions

1. Discuss various types of ratios used for financial analysis of the company.
2. Discuss the use and relevance of turnover ratios.
3. Discuss various capital structure ratios and their use in financial analysis.
4. Differentiate between horizontal and common-size analysis.
5. Discuss return on net worth ratio and Du-pont model.

Multiple Choice Questions

1. Seiko company's current assets and current liabilities are ₹1,800 crores and ₹700 crores respectively. If inventories are ₹300 crores, calculate the quick or acid test ratio for Seiko Ltd.

(a) 3.17 (b) 2.14
(c) 2.57 (d) None of the above

2. Trade receivables (Debtors) for company SDF Ltd. are ₹5,000 crores. If credit sales for SDF Ltd. are ₹20,000 crores, calculate the Accounts Receivables or Debtor Collection period for the company.

(a) 65 days (b) 73 days
(c) 91 days (d) 102 days

3. Trade payables (Creditors) for company AKM Ltd. are ₹1,000 crores. If cost of goods sold for AKM Ltd. is ₹12,000, calculate the accounts payables or creditor days for the company.

(a) 33.9 days (b) 47.1 days
(c) 30.4 days (d) 64.5 days

4. Inventories for company Zia Ltd are ₹700 crore. If cost of goods sold for Zia Ltd. is ₹6,000 crore, calculate the Inventory days for the company

(a) 85.7 days (b) 42.5 days
(c) 31.2 days (d) 76.8 days

5. EBITDA for company Solan Ltd. is ₹4,000 crore. If depreciation cost and interest expense are ₹200 crore and ₹150 crore respectively, calculate the interest coverage ratio for Solan Ltd.

(a) 6 times (b) 32 times
(c) 25 times (d) None of the above

6. Which of the following reserves shall be taken into calculation for net worth or shareholder's fund?
   (a) Revaluation reserves
   (b) Reserves created from write-back of depreciation
   (c) General reserve
   (d) None of the above
7. Sales of company Agro Ltd is ₹3,500 crore. If total assets of the company are INR 1,500 crore, calculate the asset turnover ratio for the company.
   (a) 1.6 (b) 2.3 (c) 0.9 (d) 0.42

Self-Test Questions

Balance Sheet of REI Company

REI Company (in millions)	*As at*
	31st *March* 2012
Equity and Liabilities	
Shareholders' funds	
Share capital	200
Reserves and surplus	10,000
Non-current liabilities	
Long-term borrowings	5000
Long-term provisions	200
Current liabilities	
Trade payables	1,500
Other current liabilities	2,000
Short-term provisions	700
Total	**19,600**
Assets	
Non-current assets	
Fixed assets (Net)	
Tangible assets	12,000
Intangible assets	200
Non-current investments	1,000
Long-term loans and advances	500
Other non-current assets	100
Current assets	
Current investments	2,440
Inventories	1,500
Trade receivables	800
Cash and bank balances	300
Short-term loans and advances	200
Other current assets	560
Total	**19,600**

Income Statement of REI Company

REI Company (in millions)	*Year* **2012**
Sales	19,000
Cost of goods sold	7,000
Gross profit	**12,000**
Employee and other expenses	5,000
Operating profit (EBITDA)	**7,000**
Finance costs	900
Depreciation	500
Profit before tax	**5,600**
Tax	1,680
Profit after tax	**3,920**

1. From the above information of REI Company, calculate the Liquidity Ratios for the Year 2012.
2. For REI Company, calculate the working capital ratios namely—(a) Accounts Receivables or Debtor Collection period, (b) Inventory Days, (c) Accounts Payable or Creditor Days for the year 2012.
3. Calculate the multi-step profit margins for REI company and calculate the various types of profitability ratios.
4. Calculate the following capital structure ratios for REI Company. (a) Long-term debt to equity ratio, (b) Total debt to equity ratio, (c) Interest coverage ratio.
5. Calculate the Return on Capital Employed (ROCE) and Return on Net Worth (RONW) for REI company. Further conduct a Du-pont analysis for separating RONW into various components.

CASE

TTK Prestige Ltd. and Hawkins Cooker Ltd.—Financial Ratio Analysis

In August 2013, Rajiv a credit analyst with a top rating agency based out of Mumbai was looking at the financial statements of TTK Prestige Company and Hawkins Ltd. Both TTK prestige and Hawkins are leaders in Kitchen appliances category with well-known brands. Rajiv wanted to do a financial performance comparison of both the companies and assess the liquidity position, profitability metrics, working capital days, asset turnover efficiency and solvency among other things. In addition to this, he plans to conduct a Du-pont analysis for both the companies to analyze its various components. He collects the following financial data from the annual reports of TTK Prestige Company and Hawkins Ltd.

TTK Prestige (in lakhs)	*As at* 31*st March* 2013	*As at* 31*st March* 2012
Equity and Liabilities		
Shareholders' funds		
Share capital	1,135	1,135
Reserves and surplus	38,411	27,394
		(*Contd.*)

TTK Prestige (in lakhs)	*As at* *31st March* 2013	*As at* *31st March* 2012
Non-current liabilities		
Long-term borrowings	96	1,459
Deferred tax liability (net)	1,012	681
Other long-term liabilities	500	500
Long-term provisions	782	953
Current liabilities		
Trade payables	12,333	2,161
Other current liabilities	9,188	8,161
Short-term borrowings	11,355	12,498
Short-term provisions	4,261	2,270
Total	**79,072**	**57,213**
Assets		
Non-current assets		
Fixed assets (Net)		
Tangible assets	16,584	15,077
Intangible assets	225	0
Capital work-in-progress	14,008	7,937
Non-current investments	2	2
Long-term loans and advances	2,245	969
Current assets		
Inventories	23,553	17,490
Trade receivables	14,321	10,604
Cash and cash equivalents	3,255	2,276
Short-term loans and advances	4,729	2,814
Other current assets	150	45
Total	**79,072**	**57,213**

TTK Prestige Company (in lakhs)	*Year* 2013	*Year* 2012
Sales	1,35,848	1,10,343
Other income	473	448
Cost of goods sold	77,657	61,789
Gross profit	58,665	49,002
Employee and other expenses	37,819	31,409
Operating profit (EBITDA)	20,846	17,593
Finance costs	1426.53	641
Depreciation	899.02	625
Profit before tax	18,520	16,327
Tax	5,212	4,988
Profit after tax	13,309	11,339

Hawkins (in lakhs)	*As at* 31*st March* 2013	*As at* 31*st March* 2012
Equity and Liabilities		
Shareholders' funds		
Share capital	529	529
Reserves and surplus	4,947	4,630
Non-current liabilities		
Long-term borrowings	1,101	1,220
Deferred tax liability (net)	102	95
Long-term provisions	212	204
Current liabilities		
Trade payables	2,861	2,729
Other current liabilities	4,059	3,727
Short-term borrowings	0	0
Short-term provisions	3,142	2,502
Total	**16,952**	**15,635**
Assets		
Non-current assets		
Fixed assets (Net)		
Tangible assets	2,037	1,983
Intangible assets	0	0
Capital work-in-progress	64	106
Non-current investments	8	10
Long-term loans and advances	437	271
Current assets		
Inventories	4,753	4,761
Trade receivables	4,124	3,119
Cash and cash equivalents	5,123	5,121
Short-term loans and advances	405	265
Total	**16,952**	**15,635**

Hawkins (in lakhs)	*Year 2013*	*Year 2012*
Sales	42,472	36,754
Other income	478	376
Cost of goods sold	18,058	15,791
Gross profit	24,892	21,339
Employee and other expenses	19,342	16,377
Operating profit (EBITDA)	5,550	4,963
Finance costs	300.98	288
Depreciation	242.53	219
Profit before tax	5,006	4,456
Tax	1,596	1,448
Profit after tax	**3,410**	**3,008**

1. For the Financial year 2012 and 2013, calculate the following ratios for TTK Prestige and Hawkins—(a) Liquidity ratios, (b) Working Capital Ratios, (c) Profitability Ratios, (d) Turnover ratios, (e) Capital Structure Ratios.
2. Calculate the Return on Capital Employed (ROCE) and Return on Net Worth (RONW) for TTK Prestige and Hawkins for the financial year 2012 and 2013. Conduct a Du-pont analysis for both the companies separating RONW into various components and comment on the same.
3. Analyze the changes or trends in the financial performance of TTK Prestige and Hawkins by doing a Horizontal as well as common-size analysis.

PART VI

WORKING CAPITAL MANAGEMENT

CHAPTER

16

Working Capital Management–1: Operating Cycle and Financing Aspects

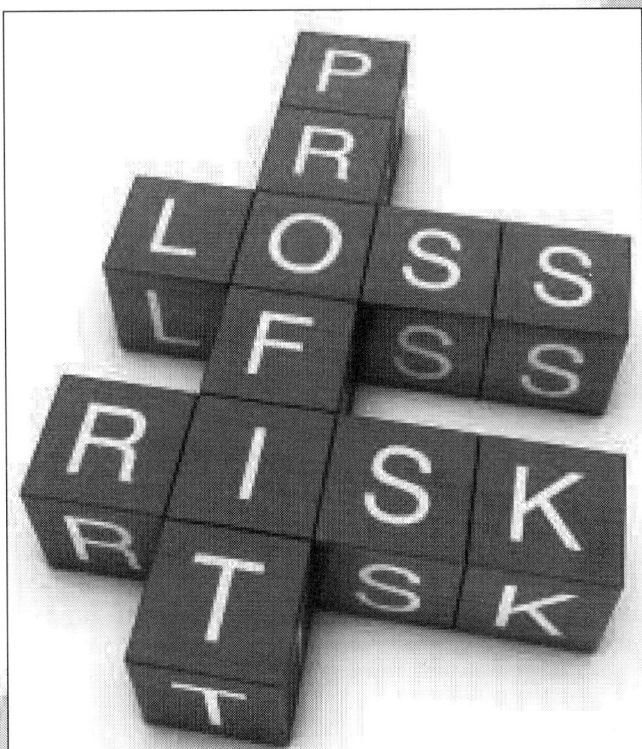

LEARNING OBJECTIVES

After studying this chapter, you should be able to:

- Understand the meaning and importance of working capital.
- Discuss the relationship between liquidity position and working capital and calculate the current ratio and quick ratio.
- Discuss the meaning and importance of the operating cycle concept.
- Compute the operating cycle and its elements.
- Identify the main factors that determine the working capital requirements.
- Explain the main forms of fund-based and non-fund bank assistance for working capital.
- Calculate the maximum permissible bank finance.

16.1 Introduction

Working capital refers to the funds invested in inventories, debtors and cash to ensure smooth daytoday functioning of the business.

The total investment in a project may be classified into two categories: investment in fixed assets and working capital investment. Fixed assets are long life assets such as plant, equipment, buildings and furniture which provide the basic infrastructure to facilitate production and sale of goods. However once plant, machinery and other fixed assets are in place, additional funds would be required to buy and stock up raw materials, to remunerate workers, to be able to sell on credit and to meet day to day expenses necessary to carry on the manufacturing and selling activities.

Working capital thus refers to the funds invested in liquid assets such as raw material stocks (inventories), debtors arising on account of credit sales made to customers and certain amount of cash and bank balances maintained to ensure smooth functioning of the business. Main function of working capital is thus to support the operating activities of the firm.

Raw material stocks, debtors, cash and bank balances are called liquid assets, because they are either already in the form of usable cash/bank balances or can be quickly converted into cash in a short period without incurring loss of value. If you compare debtors on one hand, and a fixed asset such as plant and machinery on the other, it is easy to understand that debtors would be more quickly converted into cash because the firm has already sold goods to customers who would now soon pay for the same. In comparison, realizing cash from the sale of plant and machinery would be very time consuming and might involve heavy losses in value if the firm wants to sell such fixed assets in distress.

Inventories, debtors, cash and bank balances are also called 'current' assets in accounting terminology. Current assets are defined as those assets that would be converted into cash (or equivalents) in a short period not exceeding twelve months in the normal course of business. In certain industries such as ship-building where it takes more than one year to complete a single operating cycle (from buying raw materials to delivering the product and receiving cash for sales), current assets may be defined to cover one full operating cycle.

The importance of working capital lies in the fact that in the absence of current assets, the investment in fixed assets might be rendered unproductive and unutilized simply because the firm cannot produce and sell goods without the required investment in raw material stocks, debtors, cash and bank balances. That is why often working capital is referred to as the life blood of a business.

16.2 Gross and Net Working Capital

Working capital investment may be considered either in terms of 'gross' working capital or 'net' working capital. Gross working capital refers to the total investment required in current assets while 'net' working capital refers to the total of current assets *minus* current liabilities.

16.2.1 Current Assets

Gross working capital equals current assets while net working capital = Total of current assets minus current liabilities.

Current assets represent short-term deployment of funds. In addition to inventories, debtors and cash/bank balances, current assets may also include short-term investment in marketable securities (such as Government securities, corporate bonds or mutual fund investments) which can be disposed off at short notice when the firm needs additional cash. Thus, such short-term investments are meant to provide additional working capital support in times of seasonal growth of business. During lean seasons when the firm would have surplus cash, the firm may again reinvest some of its surplus cash in short-term marketable securities to earn a return rather than keeping cash idle. For example, Maruti-Suzuki and many other firms regularly invest in marketable short-term securities as a contingent measure for managing working capital.

16.2.2 Current Liabilities

Current liabilities are defined as those financial obligations that would be payable in a short period not exceeding twelve months in the normal course of business. In addition to trade creditors for goods and services, current liabilities may also include advance payment received against orders, short-term borrowings such as inter-corporate deposits, lease rentals and installments of long-term loans repayable within 12 months as well as accrued expenses of salaries, interest and provision for taxation.

To the extent a firm can get credit facilities from the suppliers of raw materials, other inputs and services, it would not need to invest its own funds in the working capital and thus its net working capital investment would be reduced. Consider the following example.

EXAMPLE 16.1 A firm has annual sales of ₹30,00,000 with gross profit margin of 40% (that is, the cost of goods sold is 60%). An amount equal to two months' sales remains invested in debtors and inventories on an average.

(a) Determine the required working capital investment assuming the firm does not get any credit facility from suppliers of raw materials.

(b) What would be the net investment in working capital if the firm can arrange its suppliers to allow two months credit.

Solution:

(a) Required working capital investment assuming no credit facility from suppliers:

= ₹30,00,000 × 2/12 = ₹5,00,000.

(b) Net investment in working capital assuming two months credit from raw material suppliers:

= Current assets – creditors
= ₹(30,00,000 × 2/12) – (30,00,000 × 60% × 2/12)
= ₹5,00,000 – 3,00,000 = ₹2,00,000.

16.3 Issues Concerning Working Capital

The main issues that arise with respect to working capital management are:

1. How can a firm monitor its investment in working capital using financial ratios?
2. How much should a firm invest in working capital?
3. How should the firm finance its requirements of working capital?
4. What specific techniques can be used to manage different components of working capital more efficiently?

While the first three questions are answered in this chapter, the last question will be taken up in detail in the next chapter. We begin with financial ratios as our starting point. Most probably, you would already be familiar with some of these ratios, but it is important to cover them here because of two reasons: (i) these ratios are very useful in monitoring investment in the working capital and (ii) all banks and other lenders/creditors insist that the firm should supply these ratios as a part of the firm's loan/credit application.

16.3.1 Working Capital Ratios

The firm should maintain a balance between liquidity position and efficient management of working capital.

The working capital ratios are also called liquidity ratios. Liquidity refers to a firm's ability to comfortably meet its short-term obligations in the normal course of business. Liquidity ratios measure the short-term solvency of a company and focus on the size and relationship of current assets and current liabilities. The financial position of a company would not be considered sound if its short-term obligations (current liabilities) are not well covered by the current assets available to meet these obligations. Commonly used ratios to analyze the liquidity position of a firm are the current ratio and the quick (or acid test) ratio. These ratios would be illustrated with the help of the following example of Delight Retail Company.

EXAMPLE 16.2 The CEO of Delight Retails has been concerned about the company's working capital performance vis-à-vis other competitors in the industry. He has asked you to compare the company's liquidity ratios with the industry averages and suggest areas where there is scope for improving working capital management. Selected data from the company's profit & loss account and the balance sheet for the just concluded year are given in the table below:

Delight Retail Stores Limited
Excerpts from Profit and Loss Statement
For the year ended 31 December 20X1

			(₹)
Sales revenue			5,00,000
Purchases of stock in trade		3,80,000	
Add: Opening inventory	1,40,000		
Less: Closing inventory	1,70,000		
Change in inventories		(30,000)	
Cost of goods sold			(3,50,000)
Gross profit			1,50,000
Less expenses:			(85,000)
Operating profit (Profit before interest & taxes)			65,000
Finance cost (interest)			(35,000)
Profit before tax			30,000
Tax expense			(10,000)
Net Profit for the period			20,000

Delight Retail Stores Limited
Excerpts from Balance Sheet as on 31 December 20X1

	(₹)
Current assets:	
Inventories	1,70,000
Trade receivables	1,40,000
Cash & cash equivalents	5,000
	3,15,000
Current liabilities:	
Trade payables (creditors)	88,000
Other current liabilities	12,000
	1,00,000
Net working capital	**2,15,000**

Delight Retail Stores maintains large stocks and the widest range of items in its line of products to provide maximum choice and variety to customers. Most of its sales are credit sales.

The following information on the industry average ratios is available:

Ratio	*Industry average*
Current ratio	1.8 times
Quick ratio	1.0 time

Using liquidity ratios analyze the working capital performance of Delight Retail Stores and discuss the areas of improvement.

Solution: The liquidity ratios are explained below and illustrated using the data of Delight Retails.

The Current Ratio

One of the most frequently used ratios to measure the short-term liquidity of a company is the current ratio which is calculated as follows:

$$\text{Current ratio} = \text{Current assets} \div \text{Current liabilities}$$

The current assets normally include cash, bank balances, debtors, inventories, short-term marketable investments and other current assets that can be converted into spendable cash at short notice to meet the current liabilities. The current ratio is important for the creditors and other short term lenders who are concerned about whether the firm would have adequate liquid resources to discharge its dues without any hassles.

For Delight Retails, the ratio would be

$$= 3{,}15{,}000 \div 1{,}00{,}000$$
$$= 3.15 \text{ times}$$

The current ratio indicates the firm's capacity to comfortably discharge its current liabilities from its current assets.

The current ratio shows the amount of current assets as multiple (or times) of current liabilities and thus indicates the firm's capacity to comfortably discharge its current liabilities from its current assets. Delight Retails' current ratio of 3.15 times means that the amount of its current assets was as high as 3.15 times of the current liabilities, while the average current ratio for the industry is only 1.8 times.

What does a high current ratio mean? A high current ratio shows that the firm had adequate liquid resources to pay up its current liabilities, indicating little risk of default in settling its dues on time. From creditors' point-of-view, the higher the current ratio more secure they would feel because the firm has more than adequate liquid resources to settle their dues.

However, from the viewpoint of efficient financial management of a business, a very high current ratio might not be regarded beneficial, as it might signify an excessive investment in inventories, debtors and other current assets. An excessive and unnecessary investment in inventories and debtors would act to reduce the overall return on investment in the firm, because the unproductive funds blocked here could have been invested elsewhere to earn a return. A high current ratio might also result from an under-utilization of the trade credit available from suppliers of raw materials, which is normally a cost-free source of short-term funding. In the case of Delight Retails, if rest of the industry could manage well with a current ratio of 1.80, a ratio of 3.15 for Delight would surely look too high, and might indicate the need for reducing investment in inventory and debtors.

A very high current ratio indicates unnecessary blocking of investment in working capital.

While a very high current ratio is considered undesirable as it indicates an excessive blocking of investment in current assets, a very low current ratio would be equally undesirable as it would increase the financial risk of the firm with possible bankruptcy if it cannot meet its financial obligations. A current ratio of less than 1 would indicate that the firm at that point of time did not have liquid resources to pay up its current liabilities and would not be considered healthy.

Therefore, the current ratio should neither be too low nor should it be too high. Text books sometime suggest that an ideal current ratio should be equal to 2.0, but in practice it would depend on the nature of business and its cash flows. Many successful firms manage their liquidity well with a current ratio of 1.25 to 1.50.

The Quick (or Acid Test) Ratio

As an indicator of the liquidity position of the firm, the current ratio is often criticized for including inventories among the liquid resources. Inventories are regarded as the least liquid among the current assets. Inventories held by a firm might consist of raw materials, work-in-progress (semi-finished goods) and finished goods. Raw materials and semi-finished goods are not considered liquid as they would be essential for the smooth running of the business and are not meant for sale in their present condition. Finished goods that are ready to be sold might not have a ready market, and even when sold would probably take some more time before the customers would finally pay up.

Inventories are regarded as least liquid among current assets and are therefore excluded in the calculation of quick assets.

In such circumstances, a company with a high proportion of current assets in the form of cash and debtors would be regarded as more liquid than a company whose current assets consisted primarily of inventories. Hence, the acid-test or real confirmation of good liquidity position of a firm is said to be when it has adequate liquid assets even without considering inventories. The difference between the 'current' and 'quick' assets is the speed with which these assets can be converted into cash. Among current assets, inventories are regarded as the least liquid, and are therefore, excluded in the calculation of quick assets.

$$\text{Acid-test ratio} = (\text{Current assets} - \text{Inventories}) \div \text{Current liabilities}$$

For Delight Retails, the ratio would be

$$= (3{,}15{,}000 - 1{,}70{,}000) \div 1{,}00{,}000$$
$$= 1.45 \text{ times}$$

An acid-test ratio of 1.45 times for Delight Retails is higher than the industry average of 1.0 time. The quick ratio is regarded by some as a better guide to short-term liquidity than the current ratio. Similar to inventories, items such as hire–purchase debtors, loans and advances made to employees or associate companies, and pre-paid expenses which cannot be converted into cash at short notice should also be excluded in the calculation of quick ratio.

Liquidity ratios are important for commercial banks. A leading bank gives working capital loans only to those firms which have a minimum current ratio of 1.25.

In addition to creditors, liquidity ratios are important for lenders such as commercial banks. Many commercial banks in India specify the minimum current and quick ratios that should be maintained by companies to be eligible for bank working capital loans. For example, a leading bank has a policy that loans would be advanced to only those industrial units which maintain a minimum current ratio of 1.25 and a quick or acid-test ratio of 1.00.

16.4 Operating Cycle Of Working Capital

Unlike fixed assets which are meant to remain with the firm for a long time, the working capital items follow an investment–disinvestment–reinvestment cycle called the 'operating cycle' on a regular basis. The operating cycle period is the number of days a firm would take from buying inventories right up to the time it collects cash from customers after selling the inventories. In other words, the operating cycle measures the number of days taken to complete a full cash-to-cash cycle of operating activities.

The operating cycle of manufacturing firms would be expected to be longer than the trading firms, the main difference being that trading firms would not have inventories of raw materials and semi-finished goods while these are necessary for manufacturing firms. Except for this difference, other elements of the operating cycle for a manufacturing firm would be similar to that of a trading firm as explained below.

16.4.1 The Operating Cycle of a Manufacturing Firm

The operating cycle of working capital for a manufacturing firm is illustrated in Figure 16.1.

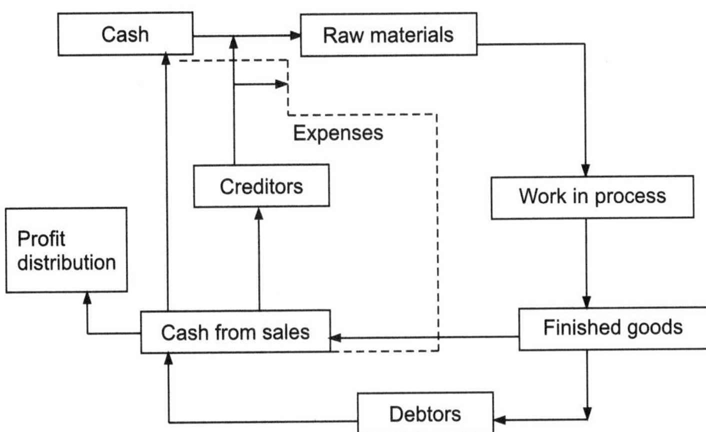

FIGURE 16.1
The Operating Cycle of Working Capital for a Manufacturing Firm..

For a manufacturing firm, the operating cycle begins with the purchase of raw materials meant to be converted into finished goods for sale. Materials are often purchased in bulk quantities (to economize on transportation costs) which means that each day a fraction of the quantity purchased would enter the production process while the rest of materials would remain in the store-room. Even after the goods have been produced, they may have to remain in stock until they are delivered to customers. Finally, when the produced goods are sold, some of them may be sold on cash basis and the balance on credit which means that the firm has to wait for some more time before the cash from credit sales would be realized. When cash from sales is realized, part of it is reinvested into the operating cycle, and the balance may be used for settling the creditors' dues and paying dividends, taxes, etc.

As shown in Figure 16.1, part of the raw materials and other services may be available on credit so that the firm does not have to pay cash for them immediately.

Operating Cycle Stages for Manufacturing Firms

Thus, for a manufacturing firm every rupee invested in the working capital passes through four main stages before being converted back into cash again. These four stages are:

1. The raw material storage period: This is the average period for which each unit of raw material remains in the store-room (warehouse) waiting to enter the production process. The raw material storage period can be estimated as follows:

Raw material storage period = Average raw material inventory
÷ Per day raw material consumption

2. The conversion (production) period: This is the average period required to convert raw materials into finished goods ready for sale. The conversion period would depend on the nature of product and the manufacturing technology used. It can be estimated as follows:

Conversion period = Average work in process inventory ÷ Per day cost of production

The cost of production would not only include the raw materials cost but also the cost of labour and manufacturing overhead expenses.

3. The finished goods storage period: Even after manufacturing, goods may not be sold immediately. They may have to be first transported to far-off markets where customers are located. For example, Tata Steel produces steel in Jamshedpur, but the company's customers exist in all corners of the country. Thus, the company's steel products manufactured in Jamshedpur have to be transported to different parts of the country before they could be sold; this could take a week on the average, sometimes more. Accordingly, the money invested in working capital would take so much longer before it is recovered in the form of cash. In other situations, such as fashion or luxury goods, the firm may produce goods in anticipation of demand so that the goods would have to remain in warehouse, and money would remain stuck until sales take place. The finished goods storage period can be estimated as follows:

Finished goods storage period = Average finished goods inventory ÷ Per day cost of goods sold

The cost of goods sold (or cost of sales) would include the cost of production and any other overheads, such as administrative, selling and distribution overheads.

4. The debtors' collection period: Where goods have been sold on credit, the customers would pay according to the terms of sales or may even take longer than the agreed credit period. Thus, there would be a time gap between sales and receipt of cash from customers. Only when cash has been realized from debtors does one operating cycle complete. The debtors collection period can be estimated as follows:

Debtors' collection period = Average debtors outstanding ÷ Per day credit sales

The suppliers' credit period: As already stated, the net investment in working capital would be reduced to the extent of credit facilities negotiated with suppliers of goods and services. The suppliers credit period can be estimated as follows:

Suppliers' credit period = Average creditors outstanding ÷ Per day credit purchases

To illustrate, if the average raw materials storage time in a firm is 40 days, conversion period is 20 days, finished goods storage time is 30 days and it takes 50 days to collect cash from debtors, the **total (gross) operating cycle** period for the firm would be 140 days. If a credit period of 30 days is available on the raw materials and services bought, the firm's **cash cycle or net operating cycle** will be 110 days.

The firm can improve the efficiency of its working capital management by reducing the operating cycle period. The following example shows the steps required to calculate the operating cycle and its elements for a manufacturing firm.

EXAMPLE 16.3 Following data has been taken from the financial statements of a cement company:

		(₹) Million
Total (credit) sales	=	7,318
Raw material consumed	=	933
Cost of production (Note-1)	=	5,363

Cost of goods sold (Note-2)	=	6,710
Opening raw material inventory: 1 January	=	253
Closing raw material inventory: 31 December	=	344
Opening work-in-process inventory	=	642
Closing work-in-process inventory	=	548
Opening finished goods inventory	=	79
Closing finished goods inventory	=	446
Opening debtors	=	77
Closing debtors	=	361
Other information:		
Credit period allowed by suppliers	=	60 days
Present investment in net working capital	=	₹3,055 Million

Notes:

1. Cost of production = Raw materials + Labour + Production overheads
2. Cost of goods sold = Cost of production + Other overheads

Assuming 360 days per annum:

(a) Determine the operating cycle period and its elements.

(b) Using the operating cycle calculated above, determine the net working capital required to support the given level of operations.

(c) Comment on whether there is scope to improve the management of working capital in the firm.

Solution: Calculation of average inventory & debtors

[(₹) Million]

	Opening balance	*Closing balance*	*Average**
Raw material inventory	253	344	298.5
Semi finished goods inventory	642	548	595
Finished goods inventory	79	446	262.5
Sundry debtors	77	361	219

*Average = (Opening balance + Closing balance) ÷ 2

(a) **Calculation of operating cycle and its elements (assuming 360 days per year):** The four stages or elements of the operating cycle of a manufacturing firm can be computed as follows:

(i) ***The raw material storage period***

= Average raw material inventory ÷ Per day raw material consumption

= (Average raw material inventory × 360) ÷ Annual cost of raw materials

= (298.5 million × 360) ÷ 933 million

= 115.18 days

(ii) ***The conversion period***

= Average work in process inventory ÷ Per day cost of production

= (Average work in process inventory × 360) ÷ Annual cost of production

= (595 million × 360) ÷ 5,363 million

= 39.94 days

(iii) ***The finished goods storage stage***

= Average finished goods inventory ÷ Per day cost of goods sold

= (Average finished goods inventory × 360) ÷ Annual cost of goods sold

= (262.5 million × 360) ÷ 6,710 million

= 14.08 days

(iv) ***Debtors collection period***
= Average debtors outstanding ÷ Per day credit sales
= (Average debtors outstanding × 360) ÷ Annual credit sales
= (219 million × 360) ÷ 7,318 million
= 10.77 days

Putting together the four operating cycle stages calculated above, we have:

S.No.	*Operating cycle stage*	*Days*
1	Raw material storage period	115.18
2	Conversion period	39.94
3	Finished goods inventory period	14.08
4	Debtors collection period	10.77
	Total gross operating cycle (approximately)	180 days

Operating cycle versus cash cycle period: It is given that the firm is able to get a credit period of 60 days from suppliers of material and other inputs. Accordingly, the firm's own investment will be blocked in the cash (or net) operating cycle for 120 days:

Gross operating cycle period = 180 days
Less: Suppliers' credit period = –60 days
Cash or net operating cycle = 120 days

(b) **Estimate the amount of working capital investment required:** To estimate the amount of working capital investment required, take the following steps:

Step 1 Calculate the turnover rate or the number of operating cycles completed per year by each rupee invested in the working capital:

Number of operating cycles completed annually;
= Number of days per year ÷ Days per net operating cycle
= 360 ÷ 120 = 3 operating cycles

Graphically, this can be seen as follows:

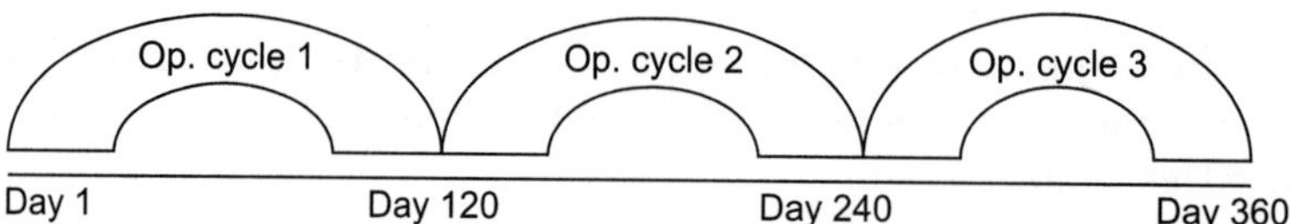

The graph shows that an amount of money invested in working capital on day-1 would complete a full operating cycle in 120 days and is then reinvested to support another round of operating activities, this time returning in the form of cash on day 240. On day 240, the same amount is again reinvested into the business and completes third cycle on day 360 of the year. [Note that we assume here the firm works for 360 days a year. In exam questions also, you may be asked to assume 360 days/year for ease of calculation. If no such assumption is given, use 365 days/year.]

Step 2 Required working capital:
= Annual cost of goods sold ÷ Number of operating cycles per annum
= ₹6,710 million ÷ 3 = 2,237 million

Step 3 As compared to a required working capital investment of ₹2,237 million, presently the company's investment in net working capital stands at ₹3,055 million which is far in excess of the required amount. Hence there is a considerable scope of improving the management of working capital.

16.4.2 The Operating Cycle of a Trading Firm

The operating cycle of working capital for a trading firm would be simpler than that of a manufacturing firm because trading firms have only one type of inventory: stock in trade for resale. We can illustrate the calculation of the operating cycle period for a trading firm by continuing with the example of Delight Retail Stores discussed in an earlier section.

EXAMPLE 16.4 Continuing with the example of Delight Retail stores, calculate the operating cycle of the firm and compare the same with the average operating cycle period of the industry.

Industry average operating cycle stages are as follows:

(a) Inventory holding period = 45 days
(b) Debtors collection period = 12 days
(c) Suppliers' credit period = 30 days

Solution:

(a) **Inventory Holding Period (IHP):** Inventory holding period measures the average time an item of inventory remains in stock before it is sold or used up in the normal course of business.

The desirable inventory levels and the holding period would differ from industry to industry. Inventory holding period:

$$\text{IHP} = \text{Average inventory} \times 365 \div \text{Annual cost of goods sold}$$

Inventory holding period = (Average inventory × 365) ÷ Annual cost of goods sold.

The 'inventory' in the above calculation should ideally be 'average inventory' held by a firm during a period. However, if the figure of 'average inventory' is not available, we can use the year-end figure of inventory. Also, since the 'average' may be calculated in a number of ways (average of opening and closing stock or average of monthly inventory), sometimes the year-end figure of inventory might be preferred, particularly if it is considered fairly representative of the normal inventory levels in the firm. Again, where the 'annual cost of goods sold' is not available, we can calculate the ratio by using the annual sales.

For Delight Retails the opening and closing inventory figures are given in the profit and loss statement.

$$\text{Average inventory} = (\text{Opening stock} + \text{Closing stock}) \div 2$$
$$= (1{,}40{,}000 + 1{,}70{,}000) \div 2 = ₹1{,}55{,}000.$$

Using the average inventory and cost of goods sold, the Inventory Holding Period (IHP) would be:

$$\text{IHP} = 1{,}55{,}000 \times 365 \div 3{,}50{,}000 = 161.6 \text{ days}$$

As compared to the industry average of just 45 days, the average inventory holding period of 161.6 days for Delight Retails is obviously too high, and may indicate poor inventory management. It again reinforces our earlier finding from liquidity ratios that the firm's investment in current assets is on the higher side.

(b) **Debtors' Collection Period (DCP):** Debtors' collection period measures the average number of days taken to collect payment from trade debtors (credit customers). The credit period allowed to customers should remain as small as possible and within the industry norms.

$$\text{DCP} = \text{Average trade debtors} \times 365 \div \text{Annual credit sales}$$

In the above calculation, if the figure of credit annual sales is not known, we can instead use 'total annual sales'. In case of Delight Retails, it is given that most of the sales were on credit. Relating year-end receivables of ₹1,40,000 and annual sales which is ₹5,00,000, we calculate the DCP as follows:

= 1,40,000 × 365 ÷ 5,00,000
= 102.20 days

Slackness in debtors' control leads to excessive investment in debtors, bad debts as well as higher interest cost on funds invested in debtors.

As compared to the industry average of just 12 days, Delight Retails seems to be taking too long to collect its debtors. This indicates slackness in debtors' control which in turn could lead to excessive investment in debtors, higher bad debts as well as higher interest cost on funds invested in debtors. A very high debtors' collection period is another indication that Delight Retails is not managing its current assets well.

It could be equally harmful to put a total ban on credit sales or reduce the credit period allowed to customers too much as compared to industry norms because an extreme tightening of the credit may have an adverse effect on sales.

(c) **Suppliers' Credit Period (SCP):** The credit facility available from suppliers of goods and services is a cost-free source of financing. Suppliers' credit period:

SCP = Average creditors × 365 ÷ Annual credit purchases

In the above calculation, if the 'credit purchases' figure is not known, we can use 'total purchases'. If data on purchases is not available, an alternative may be to use the cost of goods sold as the basis.

Delight Retails' purchases of ₹3,80,000 are given in the profit and loss statement while trade payables (creditors) of ₹88,000 are stated in the balance sheet. Using this data, the SCP would be

= 88,000 × 365 ÷ 3,80,000 = 84.5 days

Delight Retails is getting much longer credit period from suppliers as compared to the industry average of 30 days. However, since it is allowing a far longer credit period (102.2 days) to its own customers, it is suffering from a negative net credit period which it can try to avoid as far as possible.

Comparison:

Delight Retails' operating cycle = IHP + DCP – SCP
= 161.6 + 102.20 – 84.5 days
= 179.30 days.
Industry average operating cycle = 45 + 12 – 30 = 27 days

Delight Retails is aggressive in using suppliers' credit for a much longer period than the industry average. In spite of this, its net operating cycle period is much higher than the industry average, which means its investment in working capital would be far greater than required as per industry standards.

16.4.3 Limitations of the Operating Cycle Concept

The operating cycle as discussed above does not include any provision for the cash and bank balance that would be required for smooth running of the business. In addition to investment in inventories and debtors, etc., certain amount of cash would be needed. Since the model presented above does not provide for it, it should be separately added to the estimated required working capital. Second, the model only provides an approximation of the working capital requirements that should be refined as the firm gets more experienced with practical issues affecting working capital management. Of course, the aim should always be to keep working capital investment trim and reasonable.

16.5 Factors That Determine Working Capital

How much investment would be required for working capital in a business firm would depend on a number of factors discussed below:

1. Nature of business: The nature of business that a firm is engaged in is the most important factor that influences the working capital requirements. Typically manufacturing firms would require more working capital than trading and service oriented firms. For example, a consultancy organization may not require much investment in inventories but a manufacturing firm must have raw materials inventories, work-in-process inventories and finished goods inventories. Accordingly, the operating cycle in manufacturing firms is longer which increases the need for working capital.

2. Manufacturing technology: Manufacturing technology can significantly change the working capital requirement. Firms that have gone for automatic integrated technology are able to cut the production or raw material conversion time, thus reducing the operating cycle period and working capital needs. For example, in recent decades the steel and automotive industries have upgraded their manufacturing technology to reduce the manufacturing time per unit.

3. Production-sales supply chain: A car manufacturing company used to produce and store up large number of cars so that it could offer wide choice to customers and instantly deliver the car selected by the customer. In the process, the finished goods inventories would pile up as cars produced waited for customers to turn up, leading to huge increase in the working capital. Also, this process led to substantial production-sales mismatch because at times the company would produce say more black colour cars while the customer wanted grey or white colour. Over time, the company changed its policy from 'produce-to-sell' to 'sell-to-produce'. In the new system, the company keeps ready just one sample car of each colour in its showrooms; the customer makes his choice of the colour and pays up the booking amount. The company would take steps to assemble the car and inform the customer when his booked car would be ready for delivery. When the car is ready, the customer pays up the balance price and takes home his new car. This reversal of supply-chain has substantially reduced the need for investment in working capital.

Several factors including the nature of business, operating cycle, seasonal fluctuations, credit policy and technology determine the working capital needed.

4. Credit policy: As already stated, the credit policy extended to customers and credit facilities availed from suppliers of raw materials and services would obviously affect the net working capital requirements. Specific techniques of managing trade receivables are covered in the next chapter.

5. Price level changes: Changes in prices of the firm's raw materials and other inputs have a direct effect on working capital requirements. During inflationary periods, the firm would need more cash to buy the same quantity of inputs and vice-versa. During 2015–16, the declining prices of commodities including crude oil, iron ore and coal played an important role in reducing the working capital needs and improving profit margins of many firms.

6. Seasonal business fluctuations: A large number of firms dealing in items such as agricultural products, refrigerators and air-conditioners face seasonal variations in business which also affects their working capital requirements. Careful planning of seasonal needs of working capital can help the firm in arranging extra funds (from banks loans or other sources) for working capital in high-activity seasons and return the same during lean seasons. Financing of the seasonal fluctuations in working capital is discussed in detail in a later section.

16.6 Over-Capitalization and Over Trading

As already noted, the volume of current assets required would depend on the nature of a company's business. However, an understanding of the operating cycle discussed above can help a firm avoid over-capitalization and over-trading.

Over-capitalization

While over-capitalization pulls down the return on investment, over-trading can cause liquidity crunch, frequent stock-outs and loss of business.

Too much investment in excessive holding of stocks, debtors and cash and too little use of trade creditors would pull down the overall return on investment in business. Over-capitalization results from ineffective and inefficient procedures or practices regarding inventories, debtors or cash. The specific techniques for managing individual items of working capital discussed in next chapter can go a long way in keeping investment in these items trim and efficient.

Over-trading

Over-trading or trying to support too large a volume of trade with too little working capital should be equally avoided. Over-trading may result from a rapid increase in sales without corresponding increase in working capital. Over-trading can result in loss of credibility in the market if the firm frequently defaults in meeting payment deadlines to suppliers due to inadequate resources, and increase the risk of insolvency. Relating it to inventories, over-trading may result in frequent stock-outs that would cause loss of business to competitors and hence undesirable.

16.7 Financing Working Capital Requirements

A variety of long-term and short-term financing sources may be available to a firm including equity capital, medium and long-term loans, short-term bank financing, creditors and other current liabilities. The cost and other terms and conditions attached to these sources should be carefully analyzed to prepare a strategy for financing the acquisition of fixed assets and current assets. In particular, the following factors should be considered while deciding on the financing plan:

1. Maturity matching between assets and liabilities: As stated in the beginning of this chapter, total investment in a project may be classified into two categories: investment in fixed assets and investment in current assets. Fixed assets are long-life assets while current assets are short-term assets. Experts suggest that the financing plan should keep a balance between the life of the asset and the funding sources. Accordingly, the acquisition of fixed assets should be funded out of long-term sources.

2. Fluctuating and permanent current assets: In practice, while a part of the working capital needs may fluctuate with seasonal changes in level of business activity (as explained in a previous section), there would be a minimum level of current assets that would always be required as long as the firm is in business. For example, there would always be some inventories, certain amount of cash balance and some trade debtors arising from credit sales. Such minimum level of current assets that are always needed by the firm are called 'permanent' or base level of current assets.

3. Business growth and working capital: Over time, as the firm's business grows, so would be its working capital requirements to support the increased level of business volume.

16.7.1 Long-term versus Short-term Sources

Considering the above factors, a firm could choose from a range of possible financing plans, some of which could be aggressive and others more conservative as explained below:

1. Option-1: Finance all fixed assets and permanent net current assets from long-term sources; only the fluctuating current assets are financed from short-term sources (Figure 16.2):

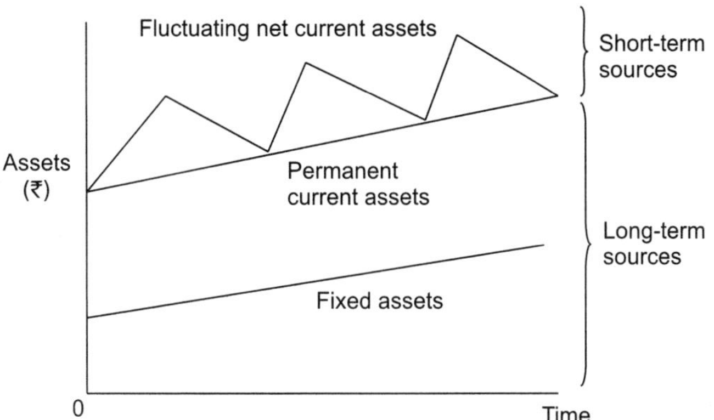

FIGURE 16.2 Option 1.

Such an approach may be considered conservative and less risky as it aims to match the maturity of assets and liabilities.

2. Option-2: Finance all fixed assets and a part of the permanent net current assets from long-term sources; the balance (part of the permanent current assets and entire fluctuating current assets) from short-term sources:

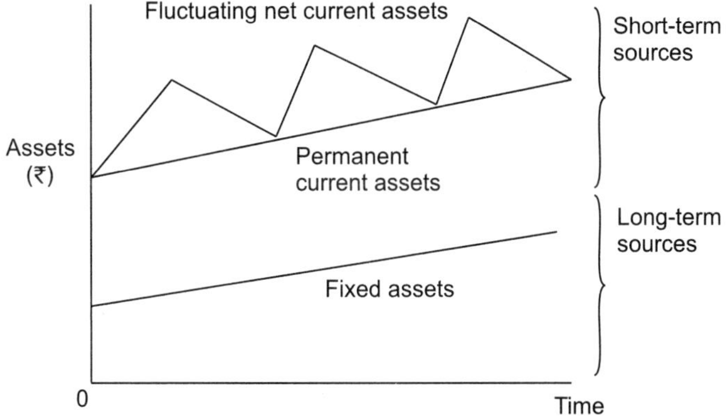

FIGURE 16.3 Option 2.

Such an approach may be considered moderately risky, but manageable because if a situation of liquidity crunch arises, a part of the permanent current assets may be relatively easily converted into cash to meet short-term obligations.

3. Option-3: Using short-term funding sources not only to finance all fluctuating current assets, all permanent net current assets but also some of the fixed assets. Only the balance (a part of the fixed assets) would be funded out of long-term sources.

This type of funding would be considered very risky as it creates a serious maturity mismatch between assets and liabilities. In option-3, the firm has raised funds on short-term basis, but invested them in acquisition of permanent current assets and even long-term assets on the assumption that short-term loans can be 'rolled' over again and again, and thus, would not have to be paid-up in the short-to medium-term. But this

Financing fixed assets from short-term sources would be risky as it creates a maturity mismatch between assets and liabilities.

assumption could be proved wrong. Indeed, there have been times when the lending banks have refused to extend the short-term loans any further and asked for their immediate repayment. Thus, in such a financing plan there would be a constant danger of the company not being able to meet its obligations and bills as they become due.

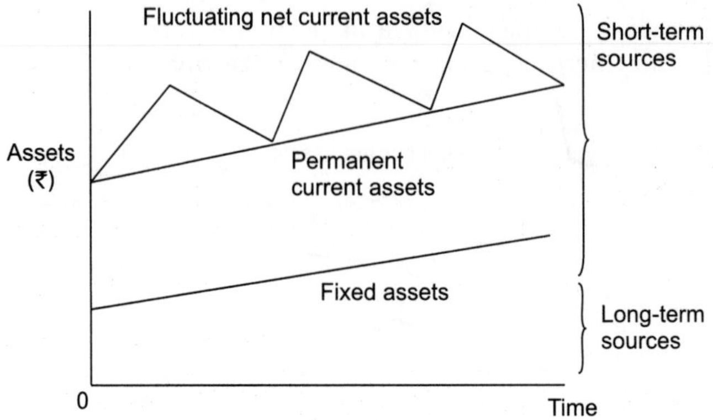

FIGURE 16.4
Option 2.

Trade creditors or current liabilities as sources of funding are apparently cost free sources. As a result, some firms may be tempted to excessively use this source in order to keep their own working capital investment low. However, this objective should be balanced against the possibility of losing credibility in the market or in extreme case even bankruptcy. Also, when a buyer firm starts asking for longer and longer credit facilities, the seller firm would start including the interest cost in the product prices so that effectively such sources would no longer be cost-free.

Fixed assets as well as permanent current assets should be financed from long-term sources.

In general, it is only prudent that acquisition of fixed assets should be financed from long term sources such as equity and long term debt. Again, it is considered safer that permanent current assets should also be financed from long-term sources, while the balance may be financed from short-term sources such as bank loans.

The long-term sources of funds were explained in the chapter of capital structure. Many firms depend on bank loans for financing their working capital requirements.

16.8 Bank Financing of Working Capital

Traditionally, banks have been the major external source of financing working capital needs of the industry. Several Indian banks have an impeccable record of serving the industry for decades and centuries. For example, the State Bank of India has completed more than two hundred years of existence, during which it has been providing valuable financing services to the industry.

Lending for working capital suits commercial banks because it helps them match the maturity of their assets and liabilities.

Providing working capital finance comes naturally to commercial banks, because it helps them in matching the maturity of their assets and liabilities. Majority of a commercial bank's liabilities (current and saving bank account deposits) are short-term in nature which the depositors can withdraw at any time. Accordingly, the bulk of a bank's investments must be in short-term assets (loans) that may be converted into cash at a short notice. If a bank uses the short-term (current and saving bank accounts) deposits to provide long-term loans, it would create a serious liquidity problem due to a maturity mismatch between its assets and liabilities. Historically, several banks have failed and were declared bankrupt due to liquidity crunch. Thus, working capital financing is a good way for banks to earn a return on their funds as well as maintain their own liquidity ratios at a satisfactory level.

Different aspects of bank financing of working capital are discussed below.

16.8.1 Bank Appraisal of Loan Applications

Bank loan applicants must satisfy the minimum criteria of '3Cs': Character, Capital and Collateral.

While banks would like to meet the financing needs of the industry, they have also to ensure that their money remains safe and they earn a satisfactory return for their shareholders. Accordingly, banks must lend only to such firms or entrepreneurs who satisfy a minimum criteria of '3Cs': Character, Capital and Collateral. These three words highlight that a good borrower is one who is a man of character (well-meaning honest person), has a significant stake in business (has invested his own capital) and can provide adequate collateral (security for loan). These and other important factors considered by banks in appraisal of loan applications are explained below:

1. Purpose of loans: A bank would prefer to lend for productive purposes that will generate cash flows for the firm, out of which it can pay regular interest and repay the loans as per agreed terms. In addition banks also lend for personal needs, such as buying a car or a house, where it is assured of the repaying capacity of the borrower.

2. Length of the firm's operating cycle: As has been highlighted in previous sections, the length of the operating cycle has a significant effect on working capital needs. The lending bank would compare the operating cycle of the firm with the operating cycle of other firms in the industry to check if the client firm is managing its working capital efficiently.

3. Past record of the customer if the customer has previously borrowed from the bank: Otherwise, the bank would like to get a reference from another bank from which the customer had borrowed previously.

4. Financial position as shown by the borrower firm's financial statements: The bank would be particularly interested in analyzing the debt-equity, profitability and liquidity ratios to ensure that the firm is not already over-laden with debt, has a profitable business and maintains good liquidity.

Banks also consider the purpose of loan, length of operating cycle and credit rating of the firm.

5. Security or collateral for the loan: Where a borrower firm takes working capital loan against the security of inventories (stock of goods) or other movable property, usually the security provided is either in the form of hypothecation or a pledge. In **hypothecation**, the borrower retains possession of the goods provided as security, but if he defaults in paying the interest or repaying the loans, the bank can file a suit for selling the hypothecated goods to realize the outstanding loan and interest due to the bank. In a **pledge contract**, the possession of the goods is with the lender and if the borrower does not pay his dues to the bank, the bank has a right to sell the goods and realize its dues.

6. Credit rating of the customer: There are several credit rating agencies in India (such as CRISIL and ICRA) which allot a 'credit rating' to a firm taking into account its past record of meeting financial obligations in time, default cases (if any) and financial position of the firm. Such information would be invaluable to the bank in deciding whether to lend to the firm and if so, what should be the interest rate and other terms and conditions attached to the loan. The rate of interest charged from clients with high credit rating would be considerably lower than others.

In addition, banks have to follow the guidelines of the Reserve Bank of India as updated from time-to-time.

16.8.2 Forms of Bank Finance

The working capital assistance provided by commercial banks can be classified into two categories: fund-based and non-fund-based. Fund-based assistance (such as an overdraft or a loan) involves investment of the bank's funds. Non-fund-based assistance (such as a letter of credit or a bank guarantee) does not involve investment of the bank's funds.

The main forms of bank finance are explained as follows:

A cash credit or overdraft facility gives flexibility to the firm to overdraw up to a maximum agreed limit and interest is charged only on the portion actually utilized.

1. Cash credit or overdraft facility: A cash credit or overdraft is an arrangement where a bank allows a firm to overdraw on its bank account up to a maximum agreed limit. Assume that State Bank of India has allowed an overdraft facility of ₹100 million to a firm. The firm can withdraw cash or issue cheques of any amount up to the allowed limit. The firm also has the flexibility to deposit amounts back in to the account to reduce the amount of overdraft. The main advantage of an overdraft facility is that the bank would charge interest only on the amount of overdraft facility utilized, and for the period it is used.

However, the interest rate charged on such overdraft accounts may be somewhat higher than bank loans (explained below). Also, in addition to the interest charged, there may be a fixed amount of 'commitment' fee charged on the overdraft limit sanctioned because from the bank's perspective, the bank has earmarked funds and is committed to provide this facility whether the client fully uses it or not.

Loan amount is credited to borrower's account and the bank charges interest on entire amount of loan whether the client utilizes it fully or not.

2. Loans: In a loan agreement, the bank credits the fixed agreed amount of the loan to the current account of the borrower, or can pay the loan amount by cheque to the borrower. The loan is given for a specific agreed period and the bank would charge interest on the entire amount of the loan sanctioned whether the client utilizes it fully or not. The advantage of a loan over an overdraft is that overdraft facility may be withdrawn by the bank at very short notice that can create liquidity problems for the borrower firm. The rate of interest charged on the loan is lower than the overdraft.

3. Bills financing: It involves discounting bills of exchange with banks. A bill of exchange is a negotiable instrument drawn by the seller of goods and accepted by purchaser or his bank or both. The rate of discount (i.e. financing cost) depends on the quality of the bill.

16.8.3 Non-fund-based Assistance

Two of the popular ways of providing non-fund-based bank assistance are the letter of credit and the bank guarantee:

Letter of Credit

A letter of credit assures the seller that buyer's bank will release the agreed price on presentation of necessary documents confirming delivery of goods.

Often a seller of goods may get an order from a new customer who is not known to the seller and the seller may be worried about the timely receipt of the sales price after he has supplied the goods. In such a situation, the buyer may ask his bank to issue a letter of credit in favour of the seller of goods on his (buyer's) behalf. A letter of credit is an undertaking given by a bank (called issuing bank) to pay to the seller (called beneficiary) a certain sum of money on behalf of the buyer. The issuing bank will pay the amount to the seller only on presentation of the necessary documents confirming that goods have been supplied by the seller. The documents to be presented as proof of delivery of goods are specified in the letter of credit and may include a commercial invoice, a transport document such as a bill of lading and an insurance document.

Letters of credit are popular in export–import business. For example, if an Indian firm is exporting goods to an importer from Germany for the first time, it would insist on a letter of credit from the German importer's bank before supplying the goods. The buyer would deposit the invoice amount with his bank in advance or arrange for a bank loan so that payment for the goods supplied can be made to the supplier immediately on production of necessary documentary proof of the goods delivered.

Bank Guarantee

At times, a bank may stand a guarantee that if the buyer of goods does not honour his commitment to make timely payment, then the bank would pay on behalf of the buyer. In this case, bank's liability to pay arises only if the buyer defaults, not otherwise.

16.8.4 Maximum Permissible Bank Finance (MPBF)

This method was introduced by the RBI in 1970s on the recommendations of the Tandon Committee. The Tandon Committee had systematically studied the operating cycle periods of several industries, including steel, textiles and cement after which it suggested three formulas for calculation of Maximum Permissible Bank Finance (MPBF) discussed as follows:

The first method recommended by the Tandon Committee was most liberal and allowed bank financing up to 75% of the working capital gap.

1. Method 1: Under this method, the Maximum Permissible Bank Finance (MPBF) would be 75% of the working capital gap (calculated as per laid down norms). The working capital gap would be equal to current assets less current liabilities. The balance 25% of the working capital gap must be financed by the borrower as his margin:

$$\text{MPBF} = 0.75\ (\text{CA} - \text{CL})$$

where,

CA = Current assets as per norms laid down;
CL = Current liabilities as per norms laid down;

2. Method 2: Under this method, the borrower firm's margin should be at least equal to 25% of the current assets calculated as per the norms.

$$\text{MPBF} = 0.75\ (\text{CA}) - \text{CL}$$

3. Method 3: Under this method, the current assets of the borrower firm would be classified into (i) core current assets and (ii) other current assets. Core current assets are the minimum amount of inventory, debtors and cash that would be required for smooth functioning of the business. The borrower firm should finance all of the core current assets and 25% of the remaining current assets as margin. Out of the remaining gap, the bank will finance the part that is not funded by current liabilities.

$$\text{MPBF} = 0.75\ (\text{CA} - \text{CCA}) - \text{CL}$$

where,

CA = Current assets as per norms laid down;
CL = Current liabilities as per norms laid down;
CCA = Core current assets.

Many banks in India continue to use the methodology recommended by the Tandon committee to assess the working capital needs of the corporate sector. However, Method-3 suggested by the Tandon Committee was not implemented.

EXAMPLE 16.5 Pawan Industries has current assets amounting to ₹10 crore, out of which core current assets (CCA) are ₹3 crore. Its current liabilities amount to ₹5 crore. Calculate the Maximum Permissible Bank Finance as per the three methods suggested by Tandon Committee.

Solution: Maximum Permissible Bank Finance (MPBF) under the three methods:

- Method 1: MPBF = 0.75 (10 crore – 5 crore) = ₹3.75 crore
- Method 2: MPBF = 0.75 (10 crore) – 5 crore = ₹2.5 crore
- Method 3: MPBF = 0.75 (10 crore – 3 crore) – 5 crore = ₹0.25 crore

As is evident, bank credit available for financing working capital would be much lower under method-3 than in other methods. Method-3 was never implemented.

16.8.5 Percentage of Sales or Turnover Method

This method was introduced by Reserve Bank of India in 1993 on the recommendations of the Nayak Committee. The method was specially meant to improve the flow of bank finance to small scale industries, merchants and exporters that would require working capital financing of up to ₹50 million. The Nayak Committee recommendations are based on an operating cycle period of 90 days for the borrowing firm.

Under the turnover method, the bank can provide working capital financing up to a maximum of 20% of the annual sales value.

Under this simplified method, the working capital requirements are estimated at 25% of the borrowing firm's projected gross sales turnover. Out of this, the promoter's contribution should be at least 5% of the projected annual sales and the bank can provide working capital financing up to a maximum of 20% of the annual sales value. An additional condition under this method is that the borrowing firm should maintain a current ratio of at least 1.25.

Several banks were reportedly using this method particularly for financing the working capital needs of smaller size firms. While appraising loan applications under this method, the bank should carefully analyze the reasonableness of the projected annual sales turnover in view of the firm's past performance, future order book and other information available.

EXAMPLE 16.6 Assuming a firm's projected annual sales turnover is ₹300 million, calculate the maximum permissible bank finance (MPBF) under the percentage of sales (turnover) method.

Solution:

$$\text{MPBF} = 25\% \times 300 \text{ million} - 5\% \times 300 \text{ million}$$
$$= ₹60 \text{ million.}$$

Researchable Issues

Faculty members, students and research scholars may like to consider the following selected issues for further research and case writing.

- Working capital management: trends and issues.
- Working capital problems of small industry.
- Working capital challenges in power sector.
- Technology, operating cycle and working capital management.
- Working capital in infrastructure sector: trends, issues and the roadmap for future.
- Working capital in MNCs: management and financing challenges.

Points to Remember

- **Gross and net working capital:** Managing both gross and net working capital is important. Gross working capital refers to the total investment required in current assets while 'net' working capital refers to the total of current assets *minus* current liabilities.

- **Liquidity and working capital:** Liquidity refers to a firm's ability to comfortably meet its short-term obligations in the normal course of business. Current ratio and quick ratio help in monitoring the liquidity position of a firm. While liquidity is important, a very high current ratio may indicate over investment in working capital that can pull down the return on investment.
- **Operating cycle:** The operating cycle period is the number of days a firm would take from buying stocks right up to the time it collects cash from customers after selling the goods. The firm can improve the efficiency of its working capital management by reducing the operating cycle period.
- **Determinants of working capital:** A number of factors determine the investment required in working capital. These factors include the nature of business, length of the operating cycle, seasonal fluctuations, credit policy and manufacturing technology. The firm should avoid over-capitalization and over-trading.
- **Long-term vs. short-term sources:** Prudence requires that acquisition of fixed assets as well as permanent current assets should be financed from long-term sources, while the fluctuating working capital needs may be financed from short-term sources. However firms differ in their approach to financing fixed assets and working capital needs.
- **Bank appraisal of loan applications:** Banks consider a number of factors in appraising loan applications, including the purpose of the loan, character of borrowers, debt-equity ratio, security provided and credit rating of the firm.
- **Forms of bank assistance:** Bank assistance for working capital can be fund based or non-fund-based. Fund-based assistance includes an overdraft or a loan. Non-fund-based assistance includes letter of credit and bank guarantee.
- **Maximum Permissible Bank Finance:** The Tandon Committee in 1970s suggested three formulas for calculation of Maximum Permissible Bank Finance (MPBF). The first method allowed bank financing up to 75% of the working capital gap. The MPBF under method-2 and method-3 would be smaller, requiring more margins from the borrowing firm.

Questions

1. Explain the meaning and importance of gross and net working capital.
2. Discuss the relationship between liquidity and working capital management. Using suitable numerical examples show how to calculate and interpret the current ratio and quick ratio.
3. Discuss the meaning and importance of the operating cycle concept. Using suitable numerical examples show how to compute the operating cycle and its different stages for a trading firm.
4. Discuss the main factors that determine the working capital requirements in a manufacturing firm.
5. Explain the main forms of fund-based and non-fund-based bank assistance for working capital.

Multiple Choice Questions

1. If the annual sales turnover of a company is ₹12,00,000, its profit margin is 25% of sales, and on average debtors take 3 months before payment, how much of the company's investment is blocked in debtors?

(a) ₹ 1,10,000 (b) ₹ 2,25,000
(c) ₹ 3,00,000 (d) None of the above

2. The following data relate to ABC, a manufacturing company:

Sales turnover for the year	₹12,00,000
Costs as percentage of sales	%
Direct material	30
Direct labour	25
Variable production overheads	10
Fixed production overheads	15
Selling and distribution	5

On average, work-in-progress represents two months' worth of half-produced goods (100% material cost is incurred in the beginning of the manufacturing process). If work-in-progress is valued at material, labour and variable production overheads, find the value of company's work-in-progress.

(a) ₹72,000 (b) ₹95,000
(c) ₹1,20,000 (d) None of the above

The following information relates to next two questions:

Rimjhim Company has current assets amounting to ₹20 million, and current liabilities amounting to ₹12 million.

3. What would be the MPBF for Rimjhim Company as per Method-1 suggested by the Tandon Committee?
(a) ₹3 million (b) ₹4 million
(c) ₹6 million (d) None of the above

4. What would be the MPBF for Rimjhim Company as per Method-2 suggested by the Tandon Committee?
(a) ₹3 million (b) ₹4 million
(c) ₹6 million (d) None of the above

Self-Test Questions

1. The following data relate to Esteem Snacks, a manufacturing company:

Sales turnover for the year	₹15,00,000
Costs as percentage of sales	%
Direct material	30
Direct labour	25
Variable production overheads	10
Fixed production overheads	15
Selling and distribution expenses	5
Profit margin	15

On average:
(a) Debtors take 2.5 months before payment;
(b) Raw materials are in stock for three months;
(c) Work-in-progress represents two months' worth of half-produced goods (100% material cost is incurred in the beginning of the manufacturing process);
(d) Finished goods represents one month's production;
(e) Credit period allowed by suppliers is as follows:

(i) Direct materials	2 months
(ii) Direct labour	0.25 months

(iii) Variable production overhead	1 month
(iv) Fixed production overhead	1 month
(v) Selling and distribution expenses	0.5 month

Work-in-progress and finished goods are valued at material, labour and variable production overheads. In addition to the above, the firm would need to maintain a cash balance of ₹25,000 on a regular basis to ensure smooth running of the business.

Compute the working capital requirements of Esteem Snacks Company.

2. Crown Company has current assets amounting to ₹200 million, out of which Core Current Assets (CCA) are ₹50 million. Its current liabilities amount to ₹80 million. Calculate the Maximum Permissible Bank Finance as per the three methods suggested by Tandon Committee.

Problems

1. The following data relates to Global trading company:

   Annual sales revenue = ₹1,440 million
   Annual cost of goods sold = ₹1,080 million
   Inventory = ₹225 million
   Trade debtors = ₹360 million
   Trade creditors = ₹90 million

   Following information is available about the industry average:

   Inventory holding period = 40 days
   Trade debtors collection period = 50 days
   Trade creditors payment period = 45 days

   (a) Calculate the following for Global trading company:
      (i) Inventory holding period
      (ii) Average collection period
      (iii) Average creditors payment period
   (b) Using the calculations in (a) above, compute the cash cycle of the firm and estimate the required working capital investment to support the annual sales.
   (c) If the company could achieve the industry norms for inventory, debtors and creditors, how much of working capital investment can be reduced?

   Note: Assume a 360 days/year.

2. Solar Company has provided the following particulars for two years:

	Year-1	*Year-2*
Sales revenue	45,000	50,000
Cost of sales	36,000	40,000
Average inventories	9,000	12,500
Average trade receivables	6,000	8,000
Average trade payables	12,000	8,000

   Assuming 360 days/year for calculations:
   (a) Calculate the gross and cash operating cycle for year-1.
   (b) Calculate the gross and cash operating cycle for year-1.
   (c) Comment on the change in cash operating cycle over the period.

3. Assuming Capri Company's projected annual sales turnover is ₹750 million, calculate the maximum permissible bank finance (MPBF) under the percentage of sales (turnover) method.
4. Gravity Company has current assets amounting to ₹400 million, out of which core current assets (CCA) are ₹60 million. Its current liabilities amount to ₹240 million. Calculate the Maximum Permissible Bank Finance as per the three methods suggested by Tandon Committee.

CASE

Dabur India: Working Capital and Operating Cycle Analysis

After running as a family business for over 100 years, the management of Dabur India was handed over to a team of professional managers in late 1990s. The new management faced a gigantic task of improving performance in several critical areas. In particular, the new management suspected working capital management as one area that required urgent attention.

The Company

The story of Dabur began in 1880s with a visionary endeavour by Dr. S.K. Burman to provide effective and affordable natural cures for the killer diseases of those days, like cholera, malaria and plague for ordinary people in far-flung villages in Bengal. Soon 'Daktar' (Doctor) Burman became popular for his effective cures, and that is how his venture Dabur got its name—derived from the Devanagri rendition of Daktar Burman. Dr. Burman set up Dabur in 1884 to produce and dispense Ayurvedic medicines, with the vision of good health for all.

More than a century later, by 1990s Dabur had grown manifold. Over the years, the family had understood the need for incorporating a professional management team that would be able to launch Dabur onto a high growth path in the emerging competitive environment. Therefore, in 1998–99 the Burman family started handing over the management of the company to professionals and down-scaled its direct involvement in day-to-day operations.

In early years of the new millennium, Dabur India had emerged as a leading nature-based health and family care products company with 8 manufacturing units, 5000 distributors and over 1.5 million retail outlets spread all over India and abroad. Dabur crossed a turnover of ₹1,000 crores in year 2000–01, and further ₹1,300 crore in 2004–05 thereby establishing its market leadership in its line of activity. Its main product lines included:

- **Hair-care:** *Vatika, Dabur Amla Hair Oil*
- **Health supplements:** *Glocose-D, Dabur Honey, Chyawanprash, Real*
- **Digestives and confectionaries:** *Hajmola, Anardana Churan*
- **Oral care:** *Dabur Lal Dant Manjan, Dabur Red Toothpaste*
- **Baby and skin care:** Dabur Tel, Gulabari, etc.

The new management team which took charge in 1998–99 made important changes in several areas including the organizational structure, supply-chain, sales, marketing and purchase/procurement of materials with the objective of improving efficiency and to induce competency in all functional areas.

One area the new management considered as full of potential was the management of working capital. A lot of investment seemed blocked in inventories and debtors, which could be pulling down the overall Return On Capital Employed (ROCE). When the management tried to tighten the systems for better control over inventories, debtors and creditors, there was stiff resistance from people within and outside the company who were opposed to any change in the system. In spite of the initial opposition, a number of initiatives were taken by the company during the period 1999 to 2004 to make the management of different components of working capital more efficient.

Inventory Management

Given the large variety of products that were manufactured and marketed and hundreds of different raw materials used by the company, accurate forecasting of inventory was very important for effective working capital management. A wrong forecast could lead to piles of inventory, thus blocking unnecessary investment and increasing storage cost as well as the risk of damage associated with perishable items.

After the new management took over, an inventory management system was instituted involving all related departments, like procurement, manufacturing, marketing, sales and supply chain. The finance department was involved throughout the process and helped in linking all operations and controlling flow of information through various departments.

The annual planning process began in November–December each year with the objective of finalizing the company's annual budget before the start of the next accounting year from April. The sales targets for the forthcoming period were decided by the Management Committee (which comprised of the heads of sales, marketing, human resources, commercial, supply chain, production and finance) taking into consideration the company's product-packaging-mix of about one thousand SKU's (Stock Keeping Units). The sales targets took into account the sales trends and special promotion schemes.

On the basis of sales targets set for the forthcoming period, the sales department established product-wise requirements of the finished goods. This information was used by the production department to prepare a rolling production plan and establish the quantity of each type of raw material required for meeting the production targets. The information on raw material requirements was then communicated to the purchase/procurement department.

As the production department itself established the requirements of raw materials to be purchased, it prevented excess purchases and helped in reducing the storage cost as well as the cost of funds blocked in inventories. For each item purchased a safety stock was identified and maintained to take care of any fluctuations in lead-time and usage of raw materials before fresh supplies would arrive. Suitable safety stocks were maintained for finished goods too.

Raw materials were classified on the basis of value, quantity required and location of procurement. While purchases of more valuable items were handled by the central procurement unit, low-value and/or low-number items could be locally purchased on a decentralized basis. The main aim was to minimize the cost of the raw materials including the transportation cost. Specialized professionals (called Category Managers) were appointed to look after the procurement of different types of raw materials.

As far as possible, the company procured materials on back-to-back basis following the Just-in-Time (JIT) approach. However, JIT inventory system was not applicable for all inputs. Many of the company's inputs were agricultural products that were available at cheaper prices seasonally when fresh crops arrived into the market. If the annual requirement of raw materials was not purchased/tied-up during this period, the company would have to pay much higher prices that could rise by as much as 50% to 75% in the off-season months. As a result, the company must procure such raw materials within the period of their seasonal abundance (typically just 45-65 days) and preserve them for later use. Often, enough stocks are procured to partly use them in the current year (40%) and partly (60%) next year.

Fortunately, with the coming up of the Commodities Exchange in India, the company had an alternative way of managing raw material cost, and that was by taking a position in the derivatives (futures and options) market. For example, suppose the company could buy a call option for 1 million kg of material X at an exercise price of ₹15 per kg with a maturity of 3 months. The call option gave the company a right (but not obligation) to buy the stated quantity of X material at the agreed exercise price. To buy a call option the company would have to pay a cost, called premium (say ₹0.50 per kg), but at the same time the call option would hedge it against possible losses if the market price of X rose beyond the exercise price before the maturity of the option. For example, if the price of X increased to ₹18 per kg, the company would find it advantageous to exercise its option to buy the material at ₹15.

Usually, the company entered into futures and options contracts for periods ranging from 3 to 9 months. Hedging combined with e-procurement significantly helped the company in cost control and reduction. According to the CFO, "We managed to cut costs through our e-procurement system. We as a company may or may not have control over commodity prices, but our marketing and purchase guys are taking futuristic positions and even though this practice constitutes a business risk it is beginning to show results."

Another significant tool of cost reduction used by Dabur India was 'value engineering' to identify and develop more cost-effective materials. For example, this has resulted in reducing the cost of packaging for several of the company products. Research and development activities also helped in reducing the time of processing, which increased productivity.

Debtors Management

The company had mainly three types of customers: stockists, institutions and international/export customers. The company did not have a standard credit policy that could be applied to all customers. Instead, distinct credit terms were offered to each group depending on various factors, such as the product, place, price, demand and competition.

Stockists

The credit terms to the stockists varied from 1–10 days depending on factors stated above as well as their locations vis-à-vis the depot towns. Depot towns were mostly the state capitals or other commercial towns/cities where the company had its own sales depots operating.

1. Stockists in Town Depots: 70% of the company's stockists were located in or around the 'depot towns'. At these places, the company used the Cash Management System (CMS) offered by banks; stockists' cheques collected till the end of a day would be deposited next morning into the company's local bank account from where the funds were transferred to the corporate bank account.

Earlier these stockists used to enjoy 5–10 days credit period but now the company decreased the time frame to 1 day. For new stockists, sales were normally made on demand-draft basis. If a stockist's cheque bounced, the stockist would have to make payment only by demand-draft. If a party defaulted on payment (or a party's cheques bounced) more than once, then for all its transactions with Dabur India in the coming year the party would be required to make payments only by demand-draft.

2. Stockists in remote areas: The rest 30% of the turnover with stockists took place at remote places away from depot towns with no easy access to banks so that the 'anywhere cheque' system was logistically not possible. Such stockists might be allowed a credit period of up to 10 days. On the average, the money was credited in company's bank account in 3–7 days.

Institutions

Institutions like Canteen Stores Department (CSD), large stores, hotels and modern malls were offered softer payment terms that could range from 15 to 90 days. Though such institutions were slower in making payments, the higher profit margins on such sales more than made up the cost of extended credit.

International Customers

Similarly, credit terms negotiated with export customers would depend on the international competition and product pricing, etc.

Where longer credit terms must be offered as a part of the marketing strategy, the company often resorted to 'factoring' as a means of financing debtors. The factoring arrangements were made with banks or specialized factoring companies. In such cases, the company ensured that profit margins from such sales were high enough to cover the cost of factoring.

Cash Management

As stated above, the company maintained bank accounts at all depots towns. Cheques/drafts received from customers in nearby places were sent for local clearing to initially collect funds in these bank accounts. This step reduced the average collection period (as compared to the time it would take if customer cheques were first received at head-office and then sent for out-station clearing) thereby increasing the velocity of cash inflows. Funds so collected at the depot towns were each day transferred to the company's head-office (or corporate) bank account. The company had a 'sweeping arrangement' with the bank at head-office by which any funds transferred from the depot towns were automatically applied towards settling the company's cash credit loan from the bank and reducing its debit balance. These steps resulted in reducing and controlling the financing cost of working capital.

When the company has surplus funds, the company invested the same in short-term investments or instruments, like mutual funds and governement securities.

Suppliers of Raw Materials

The company had more than 1000 suppliers inclusive of service providers like advertisement companies. Out of these, 100–150 were regular suppliers. Most suppliers were small business units with annual trading volume of ₹2–3 crore with Dabur India.

The Company enjoyed credit periods ranging from 7 to 90 days from the creditors, which at times could be extended up to 120 days. The suppliers used the bills discounting to avail bank financing against their receivables from Dabur India and would bear the bank charges as well. However, if the credit period was extended beyond 120 days, the bills discounting charges would be paid by Dabur India.

Financing Working Capital

The Company made an aggressive use of all ethical means to increase the velocity of cash inflows from customers and tried to slow down the cash outflows to creditors. Credit facilities from suppliers of raw materials, other goods and services, were therefore, the main sources of financing working capital. However, it had not been easy for the company to negotiate favourable terms with its debtors and creditors. The Dabur management spent considerable time and effort to train debtors and suppliers in modern ways of financing, such as factoring or bills discounting, and helped them by bank introductions. When a policy change in credit terms seemed necessary, it was first negotiated with the big creditors and debtors before being implemented for all suppliers and customers.

Discussions with suppliers took place in a highly transparent manner. Among the methods used to control credit were techniques, such as regression, progression, slap or standardized terms. The management identified and bridged the communication gaps by educating the suppliers.

Dabur India's journey in the management of working capital for the period 2000 to 2015 is reflected in relevant excerpts from the company's balance sheets and profit and loss accounts given in Tables CS1.1 and CS1.2 below. Year 2000 data would be more representative of the traditional working capital management, while year 2005 data reflects the effect of new management initiatives (described above) to tighten the management of working capital.

TABLE CS1.1 Balance Sheet of Dabur India

[(₹) Crore]

	Mar '15	*Mar '10*	*Mar '05*	*Mar '00*
Inventories	550.6	298.44	128.03	144.29
Sundry debtors	338.79	130.48	49.28	118.18
Cash and bank balance	123.94	48.8	10.27	14.9
Total current assets	1,013.33	477.72	187.58	277.37
Loans and advances	202.12	348.94	65.39	80.65
Fixed deposits	0	115.11	0.38	54.21
Total CA, loans and advances	1,215.45	941.77	253.35	412.23
Current liabilities	977.21	471.73	245.78	93.04
Provisions	245.83	440.1	89.39	21.6
Total CL and provisions	1,223.04	911.83	335.17	114.64
Net current assets	–7.59	29.94	–81.82	297.59

TABLE CS1.2 Profit and Loss Account of Dabur India

[(₹) Crore]

	Mar '15	*Mar '10*	*Mar '05*	*Mar'00*
Net sales	5,431.28	2,867.42	1,231.09	1,004.05
Stock adjustments	32.25	9.68	7.96	12.15
Expenditure				
Raw materials	2,875.72	1,393.97	554.68	540.83
Power and fuel cost	50.61	35.43	21.69	15.49
Employee cost	392.99	212.34	82.09	63.14
Other manufacturing expenses	0	22.74	0.75	1.67
Selling and admin expenses	0	557.26	363.15	271.99
Miscellaneous expenses	1,205.71	103.84	35.37	23.19
Total expenses	4,525.03	2,325.58	1,057.73	916.13

Source: Adapted from Dion Global Solutions Limited.

Questions

1. Using the data in Table CS1.1 and CS1.2, calculate the necessary working capital ratios and the net operating cycle for the company.
2. Comment on the trends in working capital management in the company during the periods: (i) 2000 to 2005, and (ii) 2005 to 2015.
3. Enumerate and discuss the importance of the company's initiatives during 1999 to 2005 in improving the management of working capital.
4. What are the future challenges and risks that the company might face in the area of working capital management?

CHAPTER

17

Working Capital Management – 2: Inventory, Debtors and Cash Management

LEARNING OBJECTIVES

After studying this chapter, you should be able to:

- Understand the importance of efficient management of inventories, debtors, creditors and cash.
- Calculate economic order quantity and explain its importance.
- Identify the main factors that determine investment in receivables and how a firm can protect its receivables against loss.
- Explain and distinguish between concentration banking and lock-box system to reduce the float.
- Discuss the pros and cons of factoring and distinguish between factoring 'with recourse' or 'without recourse'.
- Discuss ways to deal with cash deficits and surplus.
- Prepare cash budget and identify magnitude and periods of cash deficit and surplus.

17.1 Introduction

The previous chapter dealt with overall estimation and monitoring of the working capital investment using the operating cycle concept, as well as financing aspects. In this chapter, we turn our focus on specific techniques that can be used to effectively manage investment in individual items of working capital: stocks (inventory), debtors, creditors and cash management. The techniques discussed in this chapter would have a positive effect on the financial performance of the firm in several ways. Firstly, an efficient management of inventories, debtors and creditors would help in reducing the cash operating cycle of the firm leading to a reduction in the net working capital requirements. Secondly, a prudent management of cash and short-term investments using the methods explored here would yield better returns, thus further augmenting the firm's financial performance. We begin our discussion with inventory or stocks control before taking up other items.

17.2 Inventory or Stock Control

An effective stock control would necessitate a perfect coordination between the sales, production and purchase departments of the firm. Before a firm starts purchasing materials, it should plan about the total quantity of each material it would require in a period, the optimum quantity to order at a time and the minimum and maximum stock levels that should be maintained for each material.

The main objectives of stock control are to:

1. Avoid excessive stocks: Holding of unnecessary high stocks adds to the storage and interest costs in addition to encouraging pilferage and wastage of materials.

2. Minimize the risk of shortages: Adequate stock levels would be required to ensure smooth functioning of the firm. Frequent disruption in the production activity due to shortage of raw materials can only result in a sub-optimal performance of the firm.

3. Manage investment in stocks: As investment in stocks increases, so would the cost of financing as the firm would have to pay interest charges on the working capital loans. High interest cost has a direct adverse effect on the rate of return in the firm.

4. Management by exception: The stock control system should be such that once established it can be operated by junior staff, and would not require the continuous attention and involvement of senior executives on a day-to-day basis. However, senior executives must periodically check the efficacy of the stock control systems and take immediate corrective measures whenever the trends indicate that investment in stocks is going out of order, or a critical stock item has been in short supply.

The main techniques of stock control are explained as follows:

17.2.1 Economic Order Quantity: How Much to Order

The economic order quantity answers the question: how much to order at a time? Materials can be purchased in smaller or larger lots. If a firm purchases the required materials in smaller lots, it would need lesser warehouse space and incur lower interest cost, but would also be ordering more frequently that would increase its transport and ordering costs. Thus, buying materials in smaller quantities could be a smart move if the suppliers are located next door, but could work out extremely expensive if the suppliers of the materials are located far away, particularly if the firm is buying from suppliers located in other cities or abroad.

Two main types of costs associated with materials purchases are the inventory carrying (or holding) costs and the material ordering costs:

1. Carrying or holding costs: It includes the warehouse rent, material handling and interest costs. The total carrying costs incurred during a year would tend to rise as we increase the quantity per order, because if we buy a huge quantity in one order as compared to the firm's daily requirement of the material, the average materials holding period would increase and so would the associated costs of warehousing, material handling and interest charges on bank loans taken to finance the acquisition of inventories.

Carrying costs are assumed to be variable costs and may be expressed as an amount incurred per annum per unit of stock held; for example, a firm's carrying cost for a material may be ₹50 per annum per unit of the material held.

2. Ordering costs: Ordering costs, as the name suggests, are associated with placing the orders for and receiving the required materials. Each time an order is to be placed the firm would invite quotations from material vendors, spend executive time in analyzing the same, place the purchase order, follow up and incur transportation or shipping expenses. The total ordering costs incurred during a year would tend to reduce if the order size is increased and vice-versa. For example, if the firm buys all of its annual requirements of a material in a single order, it would incur the ordering costs only once per annum. Larger the number of orders placed in a year, higher would be the annual ordering costs. An ordering cost is assumed to be a fixed cost payable per order.

The Economic Order Quantity (EOQ) is that order quantity of the material which would minimize the aggregate annual cost of ordering and carrying stocks. Consider the following example.

EXAMPLE 17.1 The Green Company requires 1800 units of material N2907 per annum. It can purchase the material in the following lots:

The entire 1800 units in a single lot, or
Two lots of 900 units each; or
Three lots of 600 units each; or
Four lots of 450 units each; or
Five lots of 360 units each; or
Six lots of 300 units each.

A fixed cost of ₹10,000 per order is incurred on administration and transport. The storage, interest and other carrying costs amount to ₹100 per annum per unit of the stock held.

Calculate the economic order quantity.

Solution: The following table summarizes the related costs of ordering and holding inventories on an annual basis. The ordering cost is found by multiplying the number of orders placed in a year with the fixed cost of placing each order.

The holding or carrying cost is calculated by multiplying the average-stock-held (taken as 1/2 of the quantity ordered) by the holding costs per unit per annum. The average-stock-held is taken as 1/2 of the quantity ordered on the assumption that materials purchased would be consumed at a constant rate. Graphically, it can be shown as follows:

As shown in the graph, the firm buys OQ (order quantity) units at time-1 which gets used up over the period reaching level-0 at the beginning of time-2 when the next delivery of OQ quantity is received. Assuming that the inventories are consumed at a constant rate, the average quantity at hand will be OQ/2 as shown in the graph.

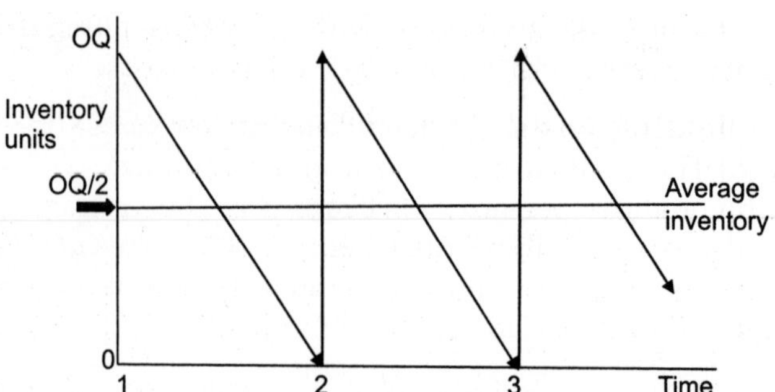

To take an example, if we buy 100 units of a material and consume the same at the constant rate of 10 units per day, the entire quantity would be consumed by the end of day-10. The average stock held could then be found by taking the average of the quantity at the beginning and end of the period = (100 + 0)/2 = 50, or simply 1/2 of the quantity ordered.

As stated above the EOQ is that order size which gives the lowest aggregate annual cost of ordering and holding stocks as calculated below:

Orders per year	*Units per order*	*Ordering cost (₹)*	*Holding cost (₹)*	*Total cost (₹)*
1	1,800	10,000	90,000	1,00,000
2	900	20,000	45,000	65,000
3	600	30,000	30,000	60,000
4	450	40,000	22,500	62,500
5	360	50,000	18,000	68,000
6	300	60,000	15,000	75,000

Note: Costs calculated above are on annual basis. Annual ordering cost = ₹10,000 × number of orders placed in a year. For example, if the firm buys the entire quantity required in a single order, the annual ordering cost would be = 1 order × ₹10,000 = ₹10,000. Holding cost equals average inventory × ₹100. For example, if the firm buys the entire quantity of 1800 units in a single order, average quantity would be 1800/2 = 900 units and the annual inventory holding cost = 900 units × ₹100 = ₹90,000.

It is clear that the total annual cost of ordering and holding stocks would be lowest if the order quantity is 600 units per order; the firm would thus order 600 units, three times in a year.

The EOQ can be graphically shown as follows:

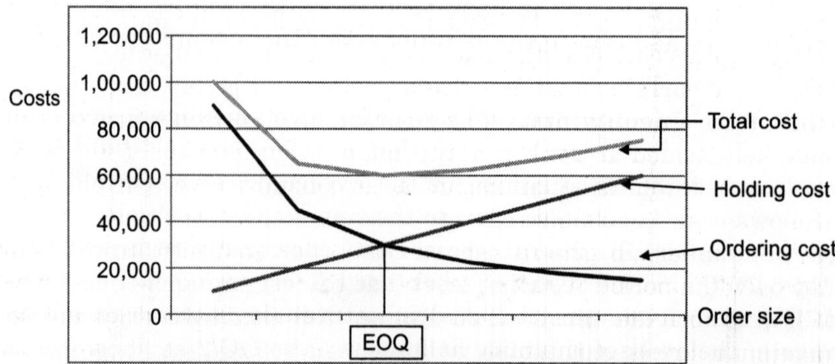

As the graph shows, EOQ would be the order quantity at which the total of annual carrying and ordering costs are minimized.

The economic order quantity (EOQ) by mathematical formula:

The EOQ can also be calculated by the following formula:

$$\text{EOQ} = \sqrt{(2 \times C_o \times D)} \div C_c$$

where,

C_o = Ordering cost per order
D = Demand (or consumption) of the material per period
C_c = Carrying cost per unit, per-period

For the Green Company example:

$$\text{EOQ} = \sqrt{2 \times 10{,}000 \times 1{,}800} \div 100$$
$$= 600 \text{ units}$$

Practical considerations: In practice, in addition to the ordering and carrying costs, a firm should also take into account the cost of stock-outs (if adequate stocks are not maintained) in terms of the loss of profits and the adverse effect on company's goodwill.

17.2.2 Order Level and Safety Stock

The decision on when to place the next order should be based on a number of factors including the daily consumption of the materials, transportation cost and the lead time required to get delivery of materials after an order has been placed. Firms usually adopt a periodic review system or fix a stock level at which a fresh order should be placed with the vendors for additional purchases.

Periodic Review System

In periodic review system, orders for purchase of materials are placed at fixed intervals of time, say each month. The quantity to be ordered at any time would be decided after a review of the trend of demand or usage of the materials concerned.

Some buffer or safety stocks are normally held to meet unexpected fluctuations in demand.

Reorder Level System

In this system, a level of stock-in-hand is decided, at which a new purchase order should be placed with the vendors. Materials are often purchased in bulk quantities to economize on transportation costs, which means that each day a fraction of the quantity purchased would be used or consumed while the rest of materials would remain in the store-room. When the stock in hand reduces to the re-order level, a fixed quantity (EOQ) is ordered. In addition to the re-order level, the maximum and minimum levels to be maintained are also decided.

Safety Stock and Uncertainty: The re-order level, maximum and minimum stock levels should be decided in such a way that a safety stock is built in to deal with uncertainty and possible fluctuations in the expected lead time and the demand or usage of the material. Lead time refers to the time gap between placing of a new order and receipt of supplies. In general, greater the uncertainty regarding these variables more would be the amount of safety stock needed.

The following formulas may be used in determining the re-order level, minimum and the maximum levels of the materials.

(i) **Reorder level** = Maximum Lead Time × Maximum Usage per period. Note that if the maximum expected lead time is given in number of weeks, maximum usage should also be taken on weekly basis.

(ii) **Minimum level** = Reorder level – (Average lead time × Average usage)

(iii) **Maximum level** = Reorder level + reorder quantity – (Minimum lead time × Minimum usage)

EXAMPLE 17.2 Two materials X and Y are used in a firm on a regular basis, as follows:

Minimum usage per week:	50 units
Maximum usage per week:	150 units
Average usage per week:	100 units
Reorder quantity for X:	600 units
Reorder quantity for Y:	1,000 units
Lead time for X:	4 to 6 weeks
Lead time for Y:	2 to 4 weeks

For each material calculate the (a) Reorder level, (b) Minimum level, and (c) Maximum level.

Solution:

(a) Reorder Level = X: 6 × 150 = 900 units
Y: 4 × 150 = 600 units

(b) Minimum Level = X: 900 – (100 × 5) = 400 units
Y: 600 – (100 × 3) = 300 units

(c) Maximum Level = X: 900 + 600 – (50 × 4) = 1,300 units
Y: 600 + 1,000 – (50 × 2) = 1,500 units

ABC Analysis

The ABC analysis emphasizes that the relative value of different materials would vary from each other, and therefore they would require different degree of control and supervision. Taking into account both unit prices and quantities of materials used, materials are classified into A, B and C categories.

'A' category would represent the most valuable and critical items that should be subjected to a greater degree of control because any inefficiency in management of such materials would cost the firm a lot. Typically, some costly materials may account for only 10–15% of the volume or number of units in stock but due to high unit prices they may constitute up to 70% of the total value of inventory in hand. Such items would be classified as 'A' category items.

On the other hand, some low-cost items may account for 50–60% of the volume or number of units of inventory but their aggregate value may be just 10–15% of the total value of inventory in hand. Such items would be classified as 'C' category items. Obviously items outside these ranges would go to the 'B' category of materials. Accordingly, in relation to the 'A' category materials, items in 'B' and 'C' categories would be less valuable and critical to the functioning of the firm and need not be subjected to the same degree of close supervision and control as the 'A' category items.

Functional value versus cost: The relative cost of different materials should not be the only criteria to classify items into A, B and C categories. Often some items of relatively insignificant cost may be critical to the smooth functioning of a business. For example, in a tailoring unit making shirts and suits, the cost of thread may be relatively insignificant but all the same the stitching of the shirt or suit would not be possible in the absence of thread. The shortage of some essential machinery spare parts can hold up the entire production process in a factory even if their cost is next to nothing. Thus the functional criticality of different materials should be embedded in the inventory control systems. For this purpose, some firms use a different classification (called XYZ) system to categorize materials according to their functional value.

Just in Time Inventory System

The just in time inventory system aims at reducing costs related to storage and carrying of inventories. As far as possible, materials should be purchased in time they are required for usage. In pursuit of this objective, many large firms encourage their material suppliers to set up plants in close vicinity of the buyer firm's location. Once this is done, the supplier would be provided with a time schedule when materials would be required, according to which deliveries should be made. Such a system practically does away with the need to have a warehouse on the buyer firm's premises.

However, JIT system would be difficult to apply to agricultural items that are available at lower prices only during certain periods of the year, or goods requiring long lead times.

17.3 Receivables (Debtors) Management

Trade receivables or debtors arise from credit sales. There is an interrelationship between the sales performance and extension of credit to customers. Therefore, the establishment of the receivables policy should be a top management decision. The purpose of having receivables is to increase sales and profits. If a firm could have the same volume of sales without having receivables, there would be no point in selling on credit.

While every organization would want to sell on strictly 'cash' terms, several factors discussed below can force a firm to sell on credit basis.

17.3.1 Factors Affecting the Level of Receivables

1. The type of product or service sold: For some types of goods or services one seldom expects a credit facility; this category may include train or bus tickets. On the other hand, credit facility may be routinely expected from vendors of intermediate goods and raw materials that would be used to manufacture some other products for sale.

2. The customs of an industry: The competition and set customs may force a firm to fall in line with the industry practice of allowing certain credit facility to customers.

3. The stages of the business cycle: Receivable may increase in prosperous times when new customers are added and old customers increase their purchases.

4. The cash position of a firm and the size of a firm, etc.

17.3.2 How to Keep Receivables Moving Towards Cash

Whether a firm is in manufacturing, wholesale or retail business, the accounts receivables must be collected promptly if the firm is to have a steady inflow of funds. Customer-wise receivables must be closely monitored on a regular basis.

The following precautions can help a firm in protecting the receivables against loss:

1. Precaution Before the sales is made

- It would be wiser not to extend credit facilities to unknown new customers without a letter of credit or a guarantee for payment.
- Credit worthiness of customers should be assessed before extending any credit facility. Obtain reports on the financial position and integrity of the buyers.

2. Precautions after the sales is made

- Use commercial credit insurance where available.
- Ask the customer to pledge collateral.
- Closely monitor the debtors' behaviour and take necessary steps to protect the accounts against loss.
- Consider offering discounts for early payments.

3. Monitoring the credit system: Management will require information on a regular basis to evaluate the impact of credit allowed on working capital investment and to take corrective action where necessary. The following reports can help the management perform this analysis:

1. ***Age analysis of outstanding debts:*** A suitable classification of total outstanding debtors into categories such as: (i) debtors outstanding less than 30 days, (ii) debtors outstanding for 31 to 60 days, (iii) debtors outstanding for 61 to 90 days, and (iv) debtors outstanding for more than 90 days, help the management understand the payment habits of the customers.
2. Often there is a difference between the credit period "allowed" to customers and the credit period "availed" by them. Some customers would deliberately delay the payment even after the permitted credit period is over and would release payments only after reminders. A regular comparison of the 'allowed' and 'availed' credit periods would indicate the effectiveness of the debtors collection team.
3. ***Financial ratios:*** Financial ratios when compared with the previous periods or the 'target' credit period can indicate trends in credit levels and the incidence of overdue and bad debts.
4. ***Statistical data analysis:*** It can assist in identifying causes of default and the incidence of bad debts among different classes of customers.

17.3.3 Concentration Banking and Lock-Box System

Concentration banking and lock-box system are techniques to reduce the "float" and speed up collections from customers. The float refers to the time delay between writing of a cheque by a customer and receipt of the funds in the seller's bank account when it can be used for business.

Many companies from FMCG and other sectors have millions of customers spread across the country who would insist on making payments by cheques. Assume Dabur India with its head-office in Delhi/NCR region has to receive certain amount of money from a customer located in Tamil Nadu. In the traditional method, the customer would write a cheque for the amount payable to Dabur and mail it to the company at its Delhi/NCR head-office. The cheque may reach the company in 3–4 days. Once the cheque is received at company's head-office in Delhi/NCR, the staff would process it and deposit the same in the company's bank account, say next day. The company's bank would send the cheque for collection through the outstation clearing system, which may again take several days; the reason for the delay being that the cheque must be presented to the buyer's bank where the latter would release funds only after verifying the issuer's signatures. The whole process may take a week (or more) and the cost of this delay may become very significant if there are thousands and lakhs of cheques stuck in the collection process.

Some companies may have a **central billing system.** Sales information from all regional offices in the country would pour into a centralized billing office at the head-office which in turn would send the sales invoices to customers. Such centralized billing systems only add to the 'float' and might render the cash management system inefficient. Float can be cut down by a decentralized billing system in which the invoices would be instantly raised at the sales point itself.

Concentration Banking

In this method the company opens regional bank accounts at places close to where its customers are located. Customers would be instructed to send the payments to the regional office of the company or the local bank account (and not to the company's head-office). All cheques received at regional offices are deposited into local bank accounts for faster bank clearing. Local banks are instructed to transfer all surplus funds (beyond a certain minimum balance required) each day to the company's central bank account where it can be used for business. The main purpose of concentration banking is to cut the dispatch time and make cash management more efficient.

A good example of concentration banking is the way Dabur India reportedly managed to speed up its sales collections from different parts of the country. 'The company maintained bank accounts at all depots towns. Cheques/drafts received from customers in nearby places were sent for local clearing to initially collect funds in these bank accounts. This step reduced the average collection period (as compared to the time it would take if customer cheques were first received at head-office and then sent for out-station clearing) thereby increasing the velocity of cash inflows. Funds so collected at the depot towns were each day transferred to the company's head-office (or corporate) bank account. The company had a 'sweeping arrangement' with the bank at head-office by which any funds transferred from the depot towns were automatically applied towards settling the company's cash credit loan from the bank and reducing its debit balance. These steps resulted in controlling and reducing the financing cost of working capital.' [Refer Dabur case in Chapter 16]

Lock Box System

In this method, customers are advised to mail their payments to special local post-office boxes hired by the company. The post-office box key is handed over to the bank which arranges to collect cheques from the lock box each day and send for local clearing immediately. The bank would also send details of the cheques received to the firm for accounting purposes. The lock box system can considerably increase the velocity of cash collections, thereby making cash available for business use faster than it would be possible otherwise.

The firm would have to incur certain costs to operate both concentration banking and lock box system. A cost-benefit analysis should be carried out before deciding on whether or not it would be worthwhile to use either of them.

EXAMPLE 17.3 A firm currently has a centralized billing cum collection system which results in considerable delay in collecting dues from the customers. It is estimated that by instituting a lock-box system the collection delay can be reduced by five days. The lock-box system would cost ₹6,00,000 per annum to operate. If the average collection of the firm is ₹2.5 million per day and the firm can earn a return of 12% per annum on its investments, what would be the net cost or benefit of using the lock-box system?

Solution: Amount of cash released by the lock-box system = ₹2.5 million × 5 days = ₹12.5 million. The cost-benefit analysis would then be as follows:

Savings from the lock-box system = 12% × 1,25,00,000 = ₹15,00,000
Less: Cost of operating lock-box system = ₹6,00,000
Net savings = ₹15,00,000 – 6,00,000 = ₹9,00,000.
Due to significant savings, the firm should go for the lock-box system.

Electronic Fund Transfer

Though electronic fund transfer techniques have dramatically cut down the float, and increased the velocity of cash collections, the method can work only where the customer is willing to cooperate and modern banking facilities are available at locations where the customers are located. Wherever possible, firm selling the goods must insist on electronic fund transfers.

17.3.4 Analyzing the Effect of a Change in Credit Policy

A change in credit policy can have a significant influence on sales. To assess the profitability of a changed credit policy (say, a more liberal extension of credit), the firm can make a cost-benefit analysis considering all relevant factors such as the added demand for products arising from the relaxed credit terms, profitability of additional sales, the change in the average collection period (which may increase due to slower collection), and the required rate of return on investment.

Relevant Cost-benefit Analysis

The cost-benefit analysis should be carried out on an 'incremental' basis, so that only such costs are included in the analysis that are affected by the change in credit policy. For example, if an extended credit period is allowed to customers, investment in the debtors would increase. Such investment should be measured at cost and not the sale price of products because the profit margin included in the sale price is not a part of the firm's investment.

Also, some fixed costs (such as rent and staff salaries) might not be affected by the change in credit policy. To the extent a fixed cost remains unchanged due to a change in credit policy it should not be included in the cost-benefit analysis. Accordingly, assuming no change in fixed costs, the increased investment (due to an extended credit period) would be measured at the variable cost of the credit sales. However, if there is a change in fixed costs of the firm due to the change in credit policy, the effect of such change should be included in the cost-benefit analysis. Consider the following example.

EXAMPLE 17.4 Amber Paints company is considering a change in credit policy that will result in an increase in the average collection period from one to two months. The relaxation in credit is expected to produce an increase in sales in each year amounting to 25% of the current sales volume.

Selling price per unit = ₹10.00
Variable cost per unit = ₹8.50
Current annual sales = ₹24,00,000

Assume that the 25% increase in sales would result in additional stocks of ₹1,00,000 and additional creditors of ₹20,000. The company's required rate of return on investments is 20%.

Advise the company on whether or not to extend the credit period offered to customers if:

(a) All customers take the longer credit of two months;
(b) Existing customers do not change their payment habits, and only the new customers take a full two months' credit.

Note: The Company measures its debtors' investment at variable cost.

Solution: Amber Paints Company:

(a) Increase in sales ₹24,00,000 × 25% = ₹6,00,000
Contribution from increase in sales = ₹6,00,000 × 0.15 = 90,000

Additional investment if all customers take 2 months:	
Debtors on existing sales (old policy)	2,00,000
Debtors on existing sales (new policy)	4,00,000
Increase in debtors on existing sales	= 2,00,000
New debtors on additional sales (6,00,000 × 2/12)	= 1,00,000
Total increase in debtors	= 3,00,000
Variable* cost of investment in debtors @85%	= 2,55,000
Add increased investment in stocks	= 1,00,000
Less: increase in creditors	= –20,000
Net investment due to change in credit policy	= 3,35,000
Required return = 3,35,000 × 20%	= –67,000
Net gain (Contribution ₹90,000 – required return 67,000)	= 23,000

Note: *Profit margin is excluded to calculate the firm's investment in debtors.

The change in credit policy is acceptable because the additional contribution is greater than the required return and there is a net gain of ₹23,000.

Alternative method: An alternative way to analyze the profitability of change in credit policy would be to relate profits (contribution) from additional sales (₹90,000) with the additional investment required (₹3,35,000) as follows:

Return on investment = (90,000 ÷ 3,35,000) × 100 = 26.87%

Since the actual return of 26.87% is greater than the required return of 20%, the change in credit policy is acceptable.

(b) **Additional investment if only new customers take 2 months:**

New Debtors (6,00,000 × 2/12)	1,00,000
Variable cost of investment in debtors @85%	85,000
Add: increase in stocks	1,00,000
Less: increase in creditors	–20,000
Net investment due to change	1,65,000

Comparison:

Contribution from additional sales = 6,00,000 × 15%	= ₹90,000
Required return = ₹1,65,000 × 20%	= –33,000
Net gain	57,000

Thus, the change in credit policy is acceptable.

17.3.5 Factoring

Factoring became popular in America in the 19th century when a fast increasing population resulted in a huge demand for European textiles and other goods. Factors were employed by the European exporters to receive the consignments in America, store the goods, find customers, sell the goods and remit the sales proceeds to the European exporters. The factors would charge a commission for their services and remit the sales proceeds after deducting their commission.

In the modern context, factoring is an agreement in which a firm that has sold goods or services on credit and thus has outstanding receivable, sells its receivables to the 'factor'. A factor is a financial intermediary who takes over the responsibility for all credit control, sales accounting and debt collection from the buyer(s). Factoring can be 'with recourse' or 'without recourse'. When it is 'with recourse', the firm selling the goods or services on credit has to bear the bad debt losses that might arise if any of the credit customers fails to pay the dues as a result of his bankruptcy. In 'non-course' or 'without recourse' factoring, the factor has to bear the losses if any of the debtors fails to pay the dues.

Functions of a Factor

Depending on the type of factoring agreement, the main functions of a factor can be as follows:

1. Administration of the sale ledger: The factor can take over the responsibility of recording sales, making and dispatching timely sales invoices to the credit customers. The seller firm would thus save on the administrative time and cost because in the absence of the factor, the firm would have to hire staff to perform these important functions.

2. Collection of accounts receivables: The factor would follow up with the credit customers and collect money from them when due. This allows the firm to focus on its main activities of producing and selling goods rather than worrying about chasing customers to pay up their dues. It would also save on the cost of running a collection department.

3. Financing facility: The factor can also advance funds against the firm's debtors to ensure smooth functioning of the firm's business without waiting for the customers to pay up. The firm's advantage is that it would not have to take bank loans to finance debtors. Banks usually have lengthy and tedious appraisal procedures and need considerable documentation. In comparison the factors act swiftly and may advance funds within hours of the sales taking place.

The factor may advance up to 70–80% of the value of credit sales immediately on selling the goods and release the balance after deducting his commission as well as interest on the amount of money paid in advance. The interest rate charged by the factor would likely be higher than the rate of interest charged by the bank, because the factors themselves borrow from the banks to lend to the firms.

4. Take over the credit risk: As stated earlier, factoring can be 'with recourse' or 'without recourse'. In 'non-course' or 'without recourse' factoring, the factor has to absorb the losses if any of the debtors fails to pay the dues.

5. Advisory services: In addition to the above, factors can also provide valuable advisory services such as credit worthiness of new clients.

Financial Evaluation of Factoring

For financial evaluation of factoring, we would need information on the costs of receivables management with and without the factoring services. Consider the following example.

EXAMPLE 17.5 The Expo Company's terms for sales are "2/10, net 40" which means that the customer can deduct 2% discount if the invoice is paid within 10 days, otherwise full invoice amount without discount would be due within 40 days.

The past experience of the company has been that on an average 40% of the customers avail of the discount, while the balance of the receivables are collected on an average 70 days after the invoice date. 3% of the sales turnover currently results into bad debts.

The firm is currently financing its receivables through a mix of equity (50%) and bank loans (50%). The cost of equity is 24% and the effective interest rate on bank loans is 16% per annum. The projected sales for the next year are ₹600 lakh.

A proposal to use 'non-recourse' factoring service is under consideration of the management as an alternative to in-house management of receivables collection and credit monitoring which at present costs the company an administrative overheads of ₹2.80 lakh per annum.

According to the factoring proposal, the factor would offer guaranteed payment in 40 days and take over the work related to sales ledger administration and credit monitoring. The factor would charge a commission @4% on the annual sales turnover. The factor would advance 80% of sales value (net of factoring commission) immediately; the balance would be financed by the company through equity. The factor's discount/interest charge on the funds advanced would be 18 per cent per annum.

Using the above information, analyze the costs and benefits of factoring to the company. Should the company accept the factoring service? [Assume there are 360 days in a year, and that bad debts are not considered for calculation of the average collection period. Ignore taxes.]

Solution: The Expo Company Factoring Analysis

Cost of in-house management of debtors: Let us first calculate the weighted average cost of its present funding of debtors as follows: Weighted average cost = (0.50 × 24%) + (0.5 × 16%) = 20% per annum. We can now proceed with the decision analysis.

	Relevant costs	*Amount (₹ lakh)*
1.	Cash discount (600 × 0.40 × 0.02)	4.80
2.	Cost of receivables investment (see Note below)	15.33
3.	Bad debt losses (600 × 0.03)	18.00
4.	Avoidable administrative overheads	2.80
	Total	**40.93**

Note: Cost of funds invested in receivables:

Average collection period = (10 days × 0.40) + (70 days × 0.60)
= 46 days

Cost of funding receivables = ₹600 × 46/360 × 0.20 = ₹15.33 lakh

Cost of non-recourse factoring:

	Relevant costs	*Amount (₹lakh)*
1.	Factoring commission (₹600 × 0.04)	24.00
2.	Interest to the factor (Note-1)	9.22
3.	Cost of equity funds (Note-2)	3.71
	Total	**36.93**

***Note*-1:**

Eligible amount of advance = 0.80 × ₹ (600 – 24)
= ₹460.8 lakh

Discount (interest charge) = ₹460.8 × 0.18 × 40/360
= ₹9.22 lakh

***Note*-2:** Cost of equity finance:

Amount of receivables financed by equity
= ₹(600 – 460.8) = ₹139.2 lakh

Discount (interest) charge = ₹139.2 × 0.24 × 40/360
= ₹3.71 lakh

Decision Analysis: Cost-benefit of non-recourse factoring

	(₹ lakh)
Benefits	40.93
Costs	–36.93
Net benefit of factoring	4.00

Factoring versus Forfaiting

Forfaiting is similar to factoring, and is used as a method of financing receivables pertaining to export–import business. Forfaiting involves purchase of receivables arising out of international trade including purchasing credit instruments such as bills of exchange or other negotiable instruments on a "non-recourse" basis. Forfaiting is always on a non-recourse basis while factoring may be 'with recourse' or 'non-recourse'.

Illustration 17.1 SBI GLOBAL FACTORS

SBI Global Factors Limited (SBIGFL) is the major provider of international factoring, import factoring, domestic factoring and forfaiting services under one roof in India. It has established itself as a market leader in international factoring providing improved value added services to its clients. [http://www.sbiglobal.in]

17.4 Creditors Management

As already stated, it is important that both gross and net working capital should be carefully planned and controlled. The firm's net working capital requirements can substantially go down if it can take advantage of suppliers' credit. Smart businessmen try to keep the terms of trade favourable to them; they bargain credit terms with their customers and suppliers in such a way that credit period allowed to them by suppliers is always more than the credit period they would allow to their own customers. This way they can keep their own working capital investment as low as possible.

In general, large firms may have greater capacity to effectively negotiate with the input suppliers for better credit facilities but smaller firms may often suffer from both sides: while their customers demand more and more credit facilities (thus increasing investment in debtors), they may not have adequate credibility in the market to be able to buy on credit. Over time, however, they should try to build a market reputation of settling the suppliers' dues on time so that the suppliers' confidence in them grows and they can buy on credit. Business firms should also try to make their working capital management more efficient by using the concepts discussed in this and the previous chapter.

Evaluating Cash Discount Offers

Suppliers may often offer cash discount on early settlement of invoices. Such cash discount offers by suppliers should be availed if the rate of interest implicit in the offer gives an acceptable rate of return to the firm. For example, assume a supplier's terms of sales are "2.5/7, net 30" which means the buying firm can deduct 2.5% discount if the invoice is paid within 7 days, otherwise full invoice amount without discount must be paid within 30 days. In other words, assuming the invoice amount is ₹100 the buyer firm can either pay ₹97.5 on the 7th day or use this ₹97.5 for a period of 30 – 7 = 23 days and pay ₹100 on the 30th day. This amounts to an implicit annual rate of interest as calculated below:

$$\text{Annual rate of interest} = \left(\frac{2.5}{97.5} \times \frac{365}{23}\right) 100 = 40.69\%$$

Thus, the buying firm would be sacrificing a return of 40.69% per annum by not accepting the cash discount offer. Where there are no cash discounts offered by the suppliers, the buying firm should avail of the full credit period offered and the payment should be made on the last day permissible as per the invoice.

17.5 Cash Management

Importance of adequate cash (including bank balances) cannot be overstated as cash is always required; there would never be a time in the life of a business when the firm would not need some cash resources. However, keeping too much idle cash would be unproductive and can reduce the firm's return on investment. Efficient management of cash is therefore an important treasury function in any organization.

An efficient cash management system would not only allow each rupee to earn more income through profitable investment, but also reduce the company's dependence on outside sources of finances.

17.5.1 Cash Management Functions

Cash management covers the following aspects:

1. Speeding up inflows: Speeding up the inflows of cash from sales by proper management of debtors. Where a firm has a large number of outstation customers, the firm can avail of real-time funds transfer services offered by banks to speed up the collections from outstation customers into a central bank account.

2. Slowing down outflows: Firms try to achieve this by adopting a centralized payment system and settling invoices on the last day of the credit period allowed by creditors.

3. Cash planning: Proper cash budgeting is necessary to forecast and plan the timing of cash inflows and outflows. Cash budget is discussed in a separate section.

4. Meeting shortages: Bank overdraft facilities or short-term loans may be used to meet temporary shortages of cash.

5. Short-term investments: There would be times when there is surplus cash with the firm that would not be required for some time. Instead of keeping it idle, it would be advisable to invest the same in short-term financial instruments such as Government securities to earn a return.

17.5.2 Reasons of Cash Problems

Failure to manage liquidity and resolve cash problems would adversely affect a firm's performance. It is therefore important to understand how do these problems arise and how to resolve them. Cash problems may arise on account of the following:

1. Losses from business operations.
2. Inflation may increase the cost of materials and other inputs, forcing the firm to invest more cash.
3. Fast growth in business without adequate arrangement of additional working capital.
4. Seasonal increase in sales.
5. Purchase of fixed assets such as plant and machinery without tying up separate long-term sources for financing them.
6. The repayment of loans without arranging to raise further borrowings.

17.5.3 Managing Cash Deficits

The treasurer of the firm must have a system of forecasting in advance the timing and magnitude of cash shortages that are likely to arise and be prepared with an array of well thought after ways to resolve the shortages. Methods used by corporate treasurers to meet short-term cash shortages include the following:

1. Postponing less important capital expenditure.
2. Accelerating cash inflows which would otherwise be expected in a later period by offering cash discounts and pressing customers for early payments.
3. Sale of assets, such as marketable securities or even some fixed assets in extreme case of cash shortage.
4. Negotiating a reduction in cash outflows so as to postpone or reduce payments. For example, this may involve (i) asking suppliers to allow longer credit period (ii) rescheduling of loan repayments with a bank and (iii) reducing dividend payments.
5. Raise funds through short-term bank loans, over draft or by issuing short-term securities such as commercial paper (explained later).
6. A centralized cash management system with cash pooling is also helpful in cash management. Often one division of a company may have surplus cash while another division may be facing cash shortage (and incurring interest expense by borrowing from a bank to meet the shortage). Centralized cash management with pooling services offered by some banks can be utilized to manage corporate cash more efficiently.

17.5.4 Ways to Utilize Short-term Surplus Cash

As a part of cash planning, the treasurer of the firm must have a system of forecasting in advance the timing and magnitude of cash surpluses that are likely to arise and be prepared with an array of well-planned ways to invest the surplus cash that would not be required for some time. Methods used by corporate treasurers to invest short-term surplus cash include the following:

1. Repay bank loans
2. Advance payments to raw material suppliers
3. Extend better credit terms to win over some important customers.
4. Short-term investments.

17.5.5 Short-term Investments

Short-term investments play an important role in financial management. They provide added liquidity because they can be disposed off and converted into spendable cash at short notice. By augmenting liquidity, short-term investments help in matching the timing of cash inflows and outflows. They also avoid undesirable use of cash when the firm is flooded with funds.

Considerations for Short-Term Investments

Short-term investments should be carefully planned and executed after considering various aspects as follows:

1. Return on investment: The firm would have to strike a balance between return and risk considerations. Corporate securities, such as commercial paper or corporate bonds may yield better returns than Government securities but may be more risky.

2. Safety of investment: Government securities provide high safety of investment though the return may be lower than some other investments.

3. Liquidity: Since the very purpose of short-term investments is to augment liquidity, the firm should invest in securities that can be offloaded at short notice and without loss of value. Investments requiring a **lock-in period** should be avoided.

4. Other considerations: Transaction cost, tax considerations and stamp duty or other legal payments would also need to be considered.

Forms or Instruments of Short-Term Investments

A number of possible investment avenues may be available to choose from, which should be carefully analyzed against the risk, return and safety considerations so that the investment objectives are achieved. The main short-term investment options are discussed below.

1. Commercial paper: A Commercial Paper (CP) is an unsecured promissory note issued by companies to raise short-term funds. Commercial papers usually have a maturity period of up to 270 days, but the issuing company may roll over the maturity for an extended period. Commercial papers are issued at a discount and redeemed at face value. For example, a commercial paper with a face value of ₹100 may be issued at ₹90, the difference of ₹10 representing the return to the investor.

The Reserve Bank of India has issued detailed guidelines regarding the eligibility, form, tenure and other conditions for issuing CPs. Some of the relevant rules may be noted here:

(a) "CP shall be issued in denominations of ₹5 lakh and multiples thereof. The amount invested by a single investor should not be less than ₹5 lakh (face value).

(b) CP shall be issued at a discount to face value as may be determined by the issuer.

(c) No issuer shall have the issue of CP underwritten or co-accepted.

(d) Options (call/put) are not permitted on CP.

(e) CP shall be issued for maturities between a minimum of 7 days and a maximum of up to one year from the date of issue."

Commercial paper has certain advantages for the issuing company as well as the investors. For the issuing company, it can be a cheap and flexible source of short-term funds, particularly for the highly rated companies. For investors, commercial paper is an attractive short-term investment as compared to bank deposits.

However, small investors may not be able to participate in commercial papers because of the required minimum investment of ₹5,00,000 (face value) as per RBI rules. Also, the secondary market for commercial paper in India is not very active. CP investors mainly include money market funds, insurance companies, pension funds and other financial institutions with short-term cash surplus.

2. Certificate of Deposit (CD): The certificate of deposit is a negotiable instrument that certifies a term deposit with a bank. CD is a marketable instrument unlike a traditional bank deposit. The certificates of deposit can be sold or purchased in the secondary market. However, the secondary market is not very active.

3. Government securities: Treasury bills and other Government securities provide high safety of investment. Though return on such investments may be lower than some other investments, there is an active market and they have high liquidity value.

4. Other short-term investments: Other short-term investments may include bank time deposits, inter-corporate loans, shares or debentures of other companies and mutual funds. Each such investment would have its own distinctive risk-return profile and other features that should be carefully analyzed before investing.

Calculating Yield on Short-Term Investments

The short-term investments may be mostly in fixed income securities, such as bonds, treasury bills or commercial paper of maturities less than one year. The yield on such investments would consist of the interest income plus any capital appreciation. While detailed concepts of calculating the yield to maturity were discussed in an earlier chapter, it would be appropriate here to consider a simple situation of short-term investment in pure-discount securities such as T-bills or commercial paper issued at a discounted price and redeemed at face value on maturity.

The simple (non-compounded) percentage yield per annum on short-term investments in treasury-bills or commercial papers issued as pure-discount instruments can be calculated by the following formula:

$$\text{Yield} = \left(\frac{\text{Face value} - \text{Price}}{\text{Price}} \times \frac{365}{N}\right)100$$

where, 'N' = the days to maturity

For example, assume a company regularly invests in 91-day treasury bills. If it invested ₹9,750 and received ₹10,000 on maturity after 91 days, the approximate annualized yield can be determined as follows (assuming 365 days in the year):

$$\text{Yield} = \left(\frac{\text{Face value} - \text{Price}}{\text{Price}} \times \frac{365}{N}\right)100$$

$$= \left(\frac{250}{9{,}750} \times \frac{365}{91}\right)100$$

$$= 10.28\%$$

EXAMPLE 17.6 Apple Company regularly invests in 182-day commercial paper. If it invested ₹4,72,500 and received ₹5,00,000 on maturity after 182 days, what would be the approximate annualized yield? [Assume 365 days in the year.]

Solution:

$$\text{Yield} = \left(\frac{\text{Face value} - \text{Price}}{\text{Price}} \times \frac{365}{N}\right)100$$

Substituting the values, we get:

$$\text{Yield} = \left(\frac{27{,}500}{4{,}72{,}500} \times \frac{365}{182}\right)100$$

$$= 11.67\%$$

Problem of Fixed Minimum Investment Size

It was stated above that as per RBI rules, commercial papers should be issued in denominations of ₹5 lakh and multiples thereof; also the amount invested by a single investor should not be less than ₹5 lakh. Like commercial papers, other money market instruments or short-term investments may also be available in fixed minimum sizes which may not match with the size of surplus funds available with a firm for investing. To take a specific example, assume the investible amount available with a firm is ₹3,50,000. It would like to invest in a commercial paper which offers a yield (return) of 11% per annum against the bank short-term deposit interest rate of 6% per annum. However, the minimum size of investment required to buy a commercial paper is ₹5,00,000. The firm can borrow the deficit amount of ₹1,50,000 from a bank but the rate of interest payable on bank loan is 14% per annum. What should the firm do?

The situation can be converted into finding a break-even point of surplus cash, so that if the actual investible amount available with the firm is more than the break-even point, it should borrow money to invest in the commercial paper. On the other hand, if the actual investible amount available with the firm is less than the break-even point it should be contented with depositing the investible amount in a bank short-term deposit. The following formula can be used to find the break-even point of surplus cash:

$$SC^* = CP[(BI - CPI) \div (BI - DI)]$$

where,

SC* = Break-even surplus cash required for investment
CP = Minimum investment required in a commercial paper
BI = Rate of interest payable on borrowings
CPI = Rate of interest receivable on the commercial paper
DI = Rate of interest available on short-term bank deposit

Decision rule: If the actual surplus cash available for investment with the firm exceeds the 'SC*' calculated above, it would be advantageous for the firm to borrow the balance amount required to buy a commercial paper. However, if the actual surplus cash available for investment with the firm is less than the 'SC*' calculated above, it would be better to invest the amount in a bank term deposit instead of borrowing more funds to buy the commercial paper.

Calculating the 'SC*' in the given situation, we find:

$$\begin{aligned} SC^* &= CP[(BI - CPI) \div (BI - DI)] \\ &= 5{,}00{,}000(0.14 - 0.11) \div (0.14 - 0.06) \\ &= 5{,}00{,}000 \times 0.375 \\ &= ₹1{,}87{,}500. \end{aligned}$$

Since in the given situation, the actual funds available for investment exceed the break-even surplus cash, it would be preferable for the firm to borrow the balance ₹1,50,000 from a bank to buy a commercial paper.

Same formulae can be applied to evaluate investment opportunities in any other money market instrument with a minimum limit of investment required.

17.6 The Cash Budget

A cash budget shows the timing and amount of expected future cash inflows and outflows over various time intervals. The expected cash receipts and payments are tabulated in a way so as to forecast the cash balance of a business at defined time intervals, say at the end of each month.

All cash receipts and payments whether related to normal operating activities or one-off items (like purchase of fixed assets) are included in the cash budget. Monthly cash budgets are more common, though a cash budget may be prepared for other time intervals such as a week or a quarter.

17.6.1 Preparation of a Cash Budget

The preparation of a cash budget requires forecasting of the cash receipts and payments during each period covered by the cash budget.

Estimating Future Cash Receipts

The sources of expected cash receipts may include the following:

1. **Cash sales:** Cash sales result in instant receipt of the sales proceeds, and therefore, there is no time lag between sales and receipts of cash.

2. **Credit sales:** In case of credit sales, there is a time lag between sales and the receipt of cash from such sales. The time lag depends on the credit period allowed to customers and the efficiency of the collection department. Based on a firm's past experience, this time lag should be estimated, and used in preparing the cash budget.

For example, the firm's experience may be that 50% of the receivables from credit sales are collected one month from the date of sale and the balance 50% receivables are collected two months from the date of sale. If the January credit sales amounted to ₹10,000, cash from these sales would be received as follows: ₹5,000 in February and ₹5,000 in March.

3. Other receipts: In addition to sales collections, cash receipts may arise from sale of assets, issues of new shares and debentures, refund of taxes, income on investments or other sources. The cash receipts expected from such sources should be included in the cash budget in the period of their expected receipt.

In practice, the most difficult part of preparing a cash budget may be to arrive at a reliable forecast of sales. Other receipts are mostly planned in advance and may be more easily predictable

Estimating Future Cash Payments

1. Estimates of the payments: Estimates of payments for materials, labour and other services can be made on the basis of the sales forecasts and production schedules for the relevant period.

2. Time-lag: Just as with sales collections, there may be a time-lag between purchase of materials or other services and actual cash payments for the same. Thus, if the suppliers of materials allow a credit period of one month, cash payment for purchases made in January would be expected in February. Some expenses, such as wages might be paid for in the same period in which the related services have been utilized.

3. Miscellaneous expenditures: The amount and timing of payments for capital expenditure, dividends, taxes or repayment of long-term debt should also be reflected in the cash budget.

For the purpose of cash budget, 'cash' does not mean cash-in-hand or currency notes. In fact most companies do not keep any cash-in-hand and all receipts and payments are affected through bank accounts. Cash sales are also deposited into the bank account. Thus, for preparing cash budget, no distinction is made between strictly 'cash' transactions and bank transactions.

For preparing a cash budget, plan to have a column for each period covered by the cash-budget and two additional columns: one for entering details and the other for the 'total amount'.

EXAMPLE 17.7 From the following information relating to Modern Fashions, prepare a month-by-month cash budget for the four months: July to October. Also add brief comments that might be helpful to management.

(a) The company is expected to have a balance of ₹10,000 in the bank account at the end of June.

(b) The company's only product, a trendy shirt, sells at ₹100 per unit and has a variable cost of ₹70 made up of material cost ₹40, labour cost ₹20 and variable overhead of ₹10 per unit.

(c) Fixed overheads of ₹15,000 per month are paid on the 25th of each month.

(d) Cash sales are expected to average 200 units per month. A discount of 5% is allowed on all cash sales.

(e) Credit sales in units are estimated as follows:

June	July	August	September	October
700	900	1200	1500	1000

Credit customers settle their accounts after one month following sales.

(f) Production in units is planned as follows:

June	July	August	September	October
1000	1500	1200	1000	1000

Suppliers of materials are paid one month after the material is used in production.

(g) Wages are paid for in the same month as they are incurred. 50% of the variable overhead is paid in the month of production, the balance in the following month.

(h) Income tax of ₹13,000 is to be paid in September.

(i) An estimated ₹5,000 will be realized from the sale of an old delivery vehicle in July. A new delivery vehicle costing ₹35,000 will be purchased at the same time, the payment for which is to be made in August.

(j) Dividends amounting to ₹16,000 are to be paid in September.

Solution:

Modern Fashions Company
Monthly Cash Budget for the Period
1st July to 31st October

	July	*August*	*September*	*October*	*Total*
Receipts from: Cash sales	19,000	19,000	19,000	19,000	76,000
Credit sales	70,000	90,000	1,20,000	1,50,000	4,30,000
Sale of vehicle	5,000	–	–	–	5,000
Total receipts	94,000	1,09,000	1,39,000	1,69,000	5,11,000
Payments for: Materials	40,000	60,000	48,000	40,000	1,88,000
Labour	30,000	24,000	20,000	20,000	94,000
Variable O'head (see Note-1)	12,500	13,500	11,000	10,000	47,000
Fixed costs	15,000	15,000	15,000	15,000	60,000
Income tax	–	–	13,000	–	13,000
New vehicle	–	35,000	–	–	35,000
Dividend			16,000		16,000
Total payments	97,500	1,47,500	1,23,000	85,000	4,53,000
Receipts-payments	(3,500)	(38,500)	16,000	84,000	58,000
Opening cash balance (Note-2)	10,000	6,500	(32,000)	(16,000)	10,000
Closing cash balance	6,500	(32,000)	(16,000)	68,000	68,000

***Note*-1:** Variable overhead

	June (₹)	*July* (₹)	*August* (₹)	*September* (₹)	*October* (₹)
Variable OH incurred	10,000	15,000	12,000	10,000	10,000
50% paid in same month	5,000	7,500	6,000	5,000	5,000
50% in following month		5,000	7,500	6,000	5,000
Total paid in the month		12,500	13,500	11,000	10,000

***Note*-2:** The closing cash balance of a month becomes the opening balance of the next month.

Comments:

1. The cash-budget shows that there will be a cash deficit at the end of August and September. The management may try to avoid the cash deficit by postponing the purchase of (or payment for) the new vehicle and/or delay payments to suppliers, postpone payment of dividends, reduce purchases of materials or reduce the production volume during August and September.
2. If none of the above courses of action is possible, the company should negotiate overdraft facilities with the bank in time to avoid a liquidity problem.
3. The cash deficit is only temporary and the company will have a comfortable surplus by the end of October. The management should plan in advance to use this cash surplus.

Limitations of the Cash Budget

Though the cash budget is very helpful in short-term period-wise planning of cash receipts and payments, it does not show how these cash flows would cumulatively impact the firm's financial position as shown by its balance sheet. Also, the cash budget should not be confused with the profit and loss statement; in particular, there would be some non-cash items (such as depreciation) that would not impact the cash budget, but must be included in the profit and loss statement.

Accordingly, it would be a good practice to periodically prepare a pro-forma profit and loss account and a pro-forma balance sheet incorporating the expected changes in cash balances as shown by the cash budget. The pro-forma profit and loss statement would show the projected or forecast net income of a future period and the pro-forma balance sheet would reflect the projected or forecast financial position of the firm as on a future date. Together they would be a great help in financial planning. For example, if the pro-forma balance sheet shows that six months later, the firm's net working capital would be negative (indicating poor liquidity position), the firm should take corrective steps right now to avoid such a situation.

You are encouraged to analyze the Kohinoor Handicrafts case given at the end of the chapter. The case integrates preparation of cash budget with the pro-forma financial statements.

17.6.2 Cash Management Models

We have discussed above that firms would like to keep just a minimum amount of cash balance and invest the balance in bank term deposits or marketable securities. The purpose of investing funds in marketable securities or bank term accounts is to augment the liquidity position of the firm so that when the firm needs more cash, it could withdraw from the bank term deposit or sell marketable securities. On the contrary, if there is surplus cash in hand, the same should be invested back in marketable securities or deposited in bank term deposit.

This process of managing liquidity by depositing (investing) surplus cash and withdrawing cash (from bank term deposit or by selling marketable securities) to meet cash deficits would involve certain costs. Some of these costs may be fixed costs while others may be variable in nature. An example of a fixed cost in case of marketable securities may be the fixed brokerage that is payable per transaction irrespective of the size of the transaction. Other fixed costs may be the executive time and administrative overheads incurred per transaction. An example of the variable costs would be the opportunity cost of carrying or holding cash balances (loss of interest or return the firm would have earned if the amount had been invested); such variable costs would increase with the increase in average amount of cash balance held.

The question then is how to manage cash balances in a way that would minimize the total annual costs associated with holding cash balances. Several models have been proposed for management of cash balances. Out of these, the Miller-Orr model is regarded as being more sophisticated.

The Miller–Orr Model

The Miller–Orr model recognizes that there would be some uncertainty regarding both the cash receipts and cash payments, due to which the cash balance in hand would fluctuate from day to day. In such circumstances, the firm after considering relevant factors should determine three levels: an 'upper level', a 'lower level' and a 'point of return' (normal or expected level). Given these three levels, the model works as follows: (i) whenever the cash holding touches the upper level, the firm should invest an amount equal to the difference between upper level and the point of return so that the cash balance with the firm comes down to the normal or expected level; and (ii) whenever the cash holding touches the lower level, the firm should sell marketable securities (or withdraw from the bank term deposit) worth an amount equal to the difference between lower level and the point of return so that the cash balance with the firm increases to the normal or expected level.

The Miller–Orr model can be explained with reference to Figure 17.1.

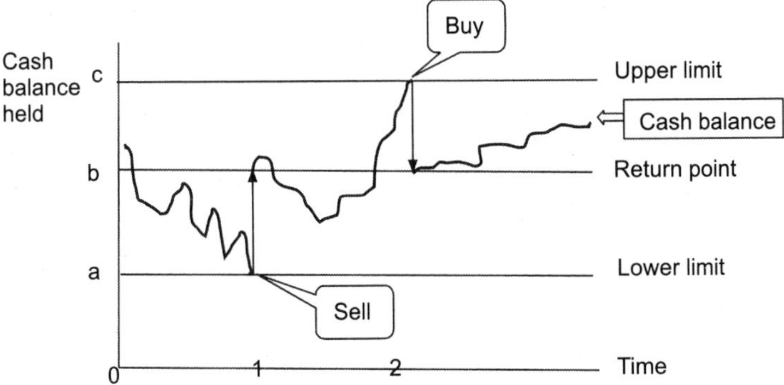

FIGURE 17.1
Miller–Orr Model

In the diagram, 'Buy' means the firm should invest surplus funds to reduce cash balance in hand; 'Sell' means the firm should sell investments to increase cash balance.

As can be seen from the graph, the cash balance is allowed to fluctuate between the specified limits. However, if on any day (at point-1) the cash balance touches the lower limit, the firm must act to either sell marketable securities or withdraw from the bank term deposits to augment its liquidity position and bring the cash balance back to the point of return. The value of investments to sell (or withdraw from the bank term deposit) would be equal to b–a.

On the contrary, if on any day (at point-2) the cash balance touches the upper limit, the firm must act to either buy marketable securities or deposit cash into the bank term deposits to reduce excess liquidity and bring the cash balance back to the point of return. The amount of cash to invest would be equal to c–b.

Determination of Upper, Lower and Return Point

The upper limit and the return point are calculated as per the Miller–Orr model while the lower limit has to be decided by the firm. The upper limit and the return point are calculated by the model keeping in view the variance of cash flows, the brokerage and holding costs.

The upper limit and return point can be calculated using the Miller–Orr model as follows:

$$\text{Return point} = 3\sqrt{[3B\sigma^2 \div 4Y]} + \text{LL}$$

$$\text{Upper limit} = 3\text{RP} - 2\text{LL}$$

where,

B = Fixed brokerage cost per transaction,
σ^2 = Variance of cash flows,
Y = Yield on investments,
LL = Lower limit as decided by the firm
RP = Return point

EXAMPLE 17.8 A firm earns an annual yield of 21.6% on its investment in marketable securities. For each sale or purchase transaction in marketable securities the firm incurs a fixed cost of ₹2,000 per transaction. The firm's management wants to maintain a minimum cash balance of ₹14,000 and the standard deviation of the change in daily cash balance is ₹4,000. Assuming 360 days in a year, determine the return point and the upper limit of cash balance by the Miller–Orr model.

Solution: Return on marketable securities per day = 21.6/360 = 0.06.

$$\text{Then, Return Point} = 3\sqrt{[3B\sigma^2 \div 4Y]} + \text{LL}$$

$$= 3\sqrt{[(3 \times 2{,}000 \times 4{,}000 \times 4{,}000) \div 4 \times 0.06)]} + 14{,}000$$

Workings:

3 × 2,000 × 4,000 × 4,000	=	96,00,00,00,000
4 × 0.06	=	0.24
96,00,00,00,000/0.24	=	4,00,00,00,00,000
$3\sqrt{4{,}00{,}00{,}00{,}00{,}000}$	=	7,368 (approximately)
Lower limit	=	14,000
Thus, Return point	=	$3\sqrt{[3 \times 2{,}000 \times 4{,}000 \times 4{,}000) \div 4 \times 0.06]} + 14{,}000$
	=	7,368 + 14,000
	=	₹21,368 approx.
Upper limit	=	3RP – 2LL
	=	3 × 21,368 – 2 × 14,000
	=	₹36,104

A limitation of the model is its assumption that the firm's cash flows are normally distributed, which may or may not be true in real life. Otherwise, the model could give the firm a good starting point to find an efficient way to manage its cash balances and short-term investments. As the firm gains experience in using the model, it can make any adjustment that may be required to improve the efficiency of cash management.

Researchable Issues

Faculty members, students and research scholars may like to consider the following selected issues for further research and case writing.

- Inventory management and the operating cycle.
- Measurement and management of corporate liquidity.
- Evaluating investment in inventory and receivables.
- Technology, debtors and cash management.
- Comparative analysis of credit policies in the FMCG industry.
- Comparative analysis of credit screening methods.
- Determination of cash balances: theory and evidence.

References

Bhattacharya Hrishikesh, *Working Capital Management: Strategies and Techniques*, PHI Learning, Delhi, 2004.

Bana, Abuzayed, "Working capital management and firms' performance in emerging markets: the case of Jordan", *International Journal of Managerial Finance*, Vol. 8, No. 2, Bingley, United Kingdom, pp. 155–179, 2012.
Websites:
www.rbi.org.in/Scripts/BS_ViewMasCirculardetails.aspx?id=9034.
www.fibafaktoring.com.tr/en/a-brief-history-of-factoring
www.sbiglobal.in

Freeman Tom, "Transforming the Finance Function for the New Millennium", *Corporate Controller*, 11, May 1998, pp. 23–29, 1998.

Mehta, Dileep, "The Formulation of Credit Policy Models", Management Science, 15, October 1968, pp. 30–50.

Miller, Merton H. and Daniel, Orr, "A Model of the Demand for Money by Firms", *Quarterly Journal of Economics*, 80, August 1966, pp. 413–35.

Sagner, James, *Essentials of Working Capital Management*, Wiley, 2010.

Points to Remember

- **Importance:** The quality of financial management in a firm greatly depends on the efficiency with which inventories, debtors, cash and creditors are managed.
- **Economic order quantity** (EOQ) is that order size of a material which would minimize the total annual carrying and ordering costs associated with material purchases. In addition to the EOQ, the firm should also determine the re-order level, the maximum and minimum levels to be maintained for efficient inventory control.
- **ABC inventory control system** takes into account unit prices and quantities of materials used to classify different materials into A, B and C categories.
- The **Just In Time (JIT)** inventory system emphasizes that as far as possible, materials should be purchased in time they are required for usage so that the costs associated with holding inventories could be minimized.
- **Factors affecting receivables:** A number of factors affect the investment in receivable including the type of product or service, customs of an industry, the stages of the business cycle and the cash position of a firm.
- In **concentration banking**, the company opens regional bank accounts and customers are asked to send payments to the regional offices/banks rather than head-office. In **lock box system** customers are advised to mail their payments to special local post-office boxes hired by the company. Decision to use these methods should be based on a cost-benefit analysis.
- **Factoring** involves outsourcing of debtors' collection and bad debt risk to an external agency. Factor can also advance funding against debtors for which they would charge interest.
- **Creditors:** The terms of trade should be negotiated with customers and creditors in such a way that as far as possible, credit period allowed by suppliers should cover the credit period the firm has to allow to its own customers. The firm should also try to avail the cash discount offered by creditors if it implies a return more than the firm's cut-off rate of return.

- **Cash management** covers a number of important aspects including speeding up the cash inflows, slowing down outflows, cash planning, meeting shortages and investing surplus cash.
- **Short-term investments:** The decisions regarding short-term investments are mainly based on considerations of return on investment, safety of investment and liquidity. Often, the safety of investment and liquidity may be given priority over return because the main purpose of short-term investments is to provide added liquidity to support the firm's business.
- A detailed **cash budget** can help in identifying the period and magnitude of cash deficits and surpluses in time to enable the firm to be ready with strategies to effectively deal with them.
- **The Miller–Orr model** involves setting up three levels of cash balances: the return point (normal cash balance), an upper limit and a lower limit. When cash balance rises to touch the upper limit, the firm should buy marketable securities to reduce cash to the return point. On the contrary, when the cash balance falls to touch the lower limit, the firm should sell marketable securities to restore the cash balance back to the return point.

Questions

1. "Inventories are necessary evils". In the light of this statement, explain the importance and objectives of efficient management of inventories.
2. What is economic order quantity and how is it influenced by carrying and ordering costs? Taking a suitable numerical example, show the EOQ calculation.
3. Discuss the main factors that determine the investment in receivables and explain the precautions that a firm should take to protect its receivables against loss.
4. Distinguish between concentration banking and lock-box system to reduce the float.
5. What is factoring? Distinguish between factoring 'with recourse' or 'without recourse' and explain the variables that a firm should consider to financially evaluate a factoring proposal.
6. Explain the functions of cash management. Discuss two main ways to deal with (i) cash deficits and (ii) cash surplus.
7. Explain the main considerations in evaluating short-term investments. Using suitable numerical examples show (i) how to calculate the yield on short-term investments and (ii) how to deal with the problem of fixed minimum investment size?
8. Explain the Miller–Orr cash management model with the help of a diagram. Using a suitable numerical example, show how to determine the Return Point and the Upper Limit of cash balance by the Miller–Orr model.

Multiple Choice Questions

1. A firm is considering a change in credit policy to boost sales that will result in an increase in gross profit by ₹3,00,000. The increase in sales would result in additional investment of ₹6,00,000 in debtors and ₹4,00,000 in inventories and the creditors will rise by ₹2,00,000. If the company's required rate of return on investments is 20%, what would be the net profit or loss from the change in the credit policy?

(a) Profit of ₹1,40,000
(b) Loss of ₹1,50,000
(c) Profit of ₹1,50,000
(d) None of the above

2. A firm is currently financing its receivables through a mix of equity and bank loans at an overall cost of capital of 10%. If the annual credit sales amount to ₹6.0 million and the average collection period is 30 days, what is the annual cost of financing receivables? [Assume 360 days in a year].
(a) ₹40,000 (b) ₹50,000
(c) ₹60,000 (d) None of the above

3. If 40% of a company's credit customers take 40 days to pay while the remaining take 60 days, what would the average debtors' collection period for the firm?
(a) 42 days (b) 47 days
(c) 52 days (d) None of the above

4. Which of the following would not be a method of easing cash shortages in a business?
(a) Purchase of fixed assets (b) Sale of fixed assets
(c) Short-term bank loans (d) Postponing dividends.

5. Alpha Company is considering a change in credit policy to boost sales that will result in an increase in the company's gross profit by ₹2,00,000. The increase in sales would result in additional investment of ₹4,00,000 in debtors and ₹2,00,000 in inventories, and the creditors will rise by ₹1,00,000. If the company's required rate of return on investments is 20%, what would be the net profit or loss from the change in the credit policy?
(a) Loss of ₹50,000 (b) Profit of ₹1,00,000
(c) Profit of ₹1,50,000 (d) None of the above

6. In a 'with-recourse' factoring agreement, the risk of bad-debts is borne by:
(a) The factor
(b) The firm selling goods on credit
(c) The firm's competitors
(d) None of the above

7. If a company makes credit annual sales of ₹40,00,000 on terms of '2/10, net 30' and 60% of its customers avail of the discount offered on early settlement, what would be the annual cost of discounts?
(a) ₹42,000 (b) ₹48,000
(c) ₹56,000 (d) None of the above

8. According to a factoring agreement, the factor has assured payment in 60 days, and has also agreed to advance 80% of the amount immediately. If the annual credit sales amount to ₹3 million and the factor charges interest of 15% per annum on the amount advanced by him, how much would be estimated amount of interest payable to the factor per annum? [Assume 360 days in a year.]
(a) ₹52,000 (b) ₹56,000
(c) ₹60,000 (d) None of the above

9. A Company regularly invests in 91-day T-bills. If it invested ₹19,700 and received ₹20,000 on maturity after 91 days, what would be the approximate annualized yield? [Assume 365 days in the year.]
(a) 8.28% (b) 7.18%
(c) 6.11% (d) None of the above

Self-Test Questions

1. Indo Nylon Company has been purchasing a material RM3 in lots of 16000 units which equals the six monthly usage of this material. The cost of the material is ₹100 per unit, ordering cost is ₹1,000 per order and the annual per unit carrying cost is 25% of the material price.

   Calculate the EOQ and determine how much can Indo Nylon save per year by buying the material in the most economical quantity.

2. Pizza Company regularly invests in 270-day commercial paper. If it invested ₹4,63,000 and received ₹5,00,000 on maturity after 270 days, what would be the approximate annualized yield? [Assume 365 days in the year.]

Problems

1. Global Fashions Limited is considering a change in credit policy that will result in an increase in average collection period from one to two months. The relaxation in credit is expected to produce an increase in sales in each year amounting to 20% of the current sales volume.

   Selling price per unit ₹100.00
   Variable cost per unit ₹80.00
   Current annual sales ₹48,00,000

   The required rate of return on investments is 25%. Assume that the 20% increase in sales would result in additional stocks of ₹5,00,000 and additional creditors of ₹2,00,000.

   Advise the company on whether or not to extend the credit period offered to customers, if

   (a) All customers take the longer credit of two months;
   (b) Existing customers do not change their payment habits, and only the new customers take a full two months' credit.

   Show calculations to support your advice. [Assume 360 days in a year].

2. A firm earns an annual yield of 18% on marketable securities. Dealing in marketable securities involves a fixed cost of ₹1,000 per transaction. The firm's management wants to maintain a minimum cash balance of ₹8,000 and the standard deviation of the change in daily cash balance is ₹1,200. Assuming 360 days in a year, determine the Return Point and the Upper Limit of cash balance by the Miller–Orr model.

3. Cake Company has surplus cash of ₹3,20,000 which it would like to invest in a commercial paper which offers a yield (return) of 12% per annum against the bank short-term deposit interest rate of 8% per annum. However, the minimum size of investment required to buy a commercial paper is ₹5,00,000. The firm can borrow the deficit amount of ₹1,80,000 from a bank but the rate of interest payable on bank loan is 15% per annum. Advise the firm whether (i) to borrow and buy a commercial paper, or (ii) to invest the surplus cash in bank term deposit?

4. From the following details related to Small-Grocers, prepare a cash budget for the months of January to April 20X8 and offer comments that would be helpful in cash management.

Item	Month	Amount
Actual sales	Dec 20X7 (Current year)	₹70,000
Expected sales	Jan 20X8 (Next year)	₹80,000
	Feb 20X8	₹1,20,000
	Mar 20X8	₹1,20,000
	Apr 20X8	₹80,000
	May 20X8	₹60,000

Sales are typically realized as follows: 50% in the month of sales and 50% in the following month.

Raw material cost amounts to 60% of the sales value. Raw materials are purchased and paid for in the month prior to the month of sales.

Labour costs amount to ₹2,000 per month and administration expenses amount to ₹1,000 per month. Sales commission is paid @10% of sales. Labour and administration expenses are paid in the month in which they are incurred but sales commission is payable in the month following the month of sales.

The cash balance on 31st Dec. 20X7 was ₹3,000.

CASE

Kohinoor Handicrafts Company

Kohinoor Handicrafts Company (KHC) purchased custom-made items from a number of artisans by providing product, quality, colour and design specifications. The cost of materials (handicrafts) purchased included the labour cost. The company fixed product prices in such a way that the Cost of Goods Sold, which consisted mainly of material costs and was fully variable, would be 70% of sales. The company had been consistently profitable in the past years, and was expected to continue that trend in 20X2 (Next year) too. However, a specific profit forecast had not yet been prepared and a meeting of the finance committee had been called in late December 20X1 (Current year) to consider various issues.

Among the main issues was the suggestion made by the new sales manager to increase the credit period to customers from the existing 30 days to 60 days from January 20X2. The competition in the firm's major product lines had been increasing which made it necessary to extend more liberal credit terms to achieve sales targets in 20X2. The finance committee was asked to consider the implications of the proposal on the company's funds requirements and prepare a forecast of bank financing requirements in the coming months.

The December 31, 20X1 Balance Sheet for KHC had just been audited and showed that the current cash balance was ₹2,50,000 which was much higher than firm's minimum operating cash needs of ₹1,50,000. The expected monthly sales from January to June 20X2 with credit terms of 60 days were as follows:

	(₹)
January	2,00,000
February	6,00,000
March	9,00,000
April	11,00,000
May	7,00,000
June	5,00,000

All sales were made on credit. Experience had shown that customer payments for 30 days credit sales were all received in the month following the month of sale. The sales manager had projected that under 60 days credit terms, only one-half of a given month's sales were likely to be paid for in the following month, and the remainder would be deferred for one additional month. This projection was to be incorporated in the cash budget.

On the payments side, KHC's payments for materials purchased were typically made during the month following the month in which purchases were made. The expected monthly purchases of materials during January–June 20X2 were:

	(₹)
January	2,50,000
February	5,00,000
March	10,00,000
April	6,00,000
May	4,00,000
June	2,00,000

General and administration expenses were estimated at a fixed amount of ₹60,000 per month and were paid for in cash at the same rate as the material costs. Depreciation charges amounted to ₹20,000 per month. Miscellaneous cash expenses also amounted to ₹20,000 per month. The level of 'miscellaneous accruals' was expected to remain unchanged in the firm's balance sheet over the next six months. Income tax payments of ₹1,00,000 each (for taxes accrued in 20 × 1) would be necessary in March and June. A new piece of machinery would be bought and installed in early March for which the payment of ₹3,00,000 was to be made in April. The machinery would add ₹10,000 per month to KHC's total depreciation charges, beginning March. Further a piece of old machinery which had originally cost ₹1,00,000 and which was fully depreciated was to be written off during April.

KHC's Board was planning to pay an aggregate dividend of ₹1,20,000 to the shareholders in mid-May and the committee was asked to include an expected cash payment for the same.

EXHIBIT 17.1

KHC BALANCE SHEET ON 31 DECEMBER 20X1

Assets		
Plant & Equipment-Gross	17,50,000	
Less: Accum. Depreciation	(5,20,000)	12,30,000
Inventory		5,00,000
Debtors		3,20,000
Cash		2,50,000
		23,00,000
Liabilities and Net Worth		
Share capital	7,00,000	
Retained Earnings	11,30,000	18,30,000
Creditors for materials*		1,50,000
Tax Accrual		2,00,000
Miscellaneous Accruals		1,20,000
		23,00,000

* Includes payables for materials (₹90,000) and general expenses (₹60,000)

1. Prepare a pro-forma Income Statement for KHC for the full period from 1st January to 30th June 20X2.
2. Prepare a pro-forma Balance Sheet as at the end of June, and identify the bank financing needs of the company at that point of time.
3. Prepare a cash budget the full period from 1st January to 30th June (monthly cash budget not required).

PART VII

NON-PROFIT ORGANIZATIONS

CHAPTER

18 Financial Management in Non-Profit Organizations

LEARNING OBJECTIVES

After studying this chapter, you should be able to:

- Difference between profit making and Non-Profit Organizations (NPOs)
- Understand the different forms of Non-profit firms
- Understand the concept of fund capital and debt for non-profit organizations
- Understand capital structure and capital budgeting decision for non-profit organizations

18.1 Introduction

Non-profit organizations are firms which are exempt from paying taxes and their objective is to serve the society.

In all the previous chapters, we have seen financial management from the perspective of profit oriented organizations. There is another class of firms which are known as Non-Profit Organizations (NPOs). NPOs are firms which are exempt from paying taxes and their objective is to serve the society. These organizations can serve for providing charitable activities, provide and promote education, support literary activities, etc. Examples of NPOs include voluntary organizations, like *Pratham*, *Care India*, etc. Most of the educational institutions in India are registered under the societies act and fall under the category of NPOs.

There are around 3.1 million voluntary organizations registered as societies in India. These organizations require financial management skills and differ in various aspects compared to for-profit organization. Thus, there is a need to understand the financial management in these organizations.

18.2 Firm Objective and Non-Profit Organization

The objective of a Non-Profit Organization is to maximize value for its stakeholders.

The objective of a profit-oriented firm is to maximize the shareholders wealth. What should be the objective of firms which do not fall in the criteria of profit making firms? The objective of an NPO should be to maximize or minimize certain decision variable. Researchers have pondered over this questions and the one objective that makes most sense for a Non-Profit Organization is to create value for the marginalized sections of the society who are the main stakeholders. The objective of some of the NPOs is enumerated as follows:

1. Care India: Empowerment of women and girls from poor and marginalized communities.

2. Pratham: Provide pre-school education to children in slums.

We can see that the objective of the above given NPOs is to support one or other marginalized sections of the society.

The performance for a for-profit organization can be measured by looking at the appreciation in share prices and the various financial ratios. What would be the performance measure for the NPO? Performance cannot be measured using financial ratios or the financial performance of the firm. It can be measured with the social impact of the programmes implemented or the grants received and utilized. Thus, there is considerable difference in the way we look at for-profit firms and NPOs.

18.3 Forms of Non-Profit Organizations

Legal framework divides NPOs into five types of entities. These are:

- Society registered under the Societies Registration Act of 1860
- Trust registered under the Indian Trust Act of 1882
- Cooperative registered under the Cooperatives Act of 1904
- Trade Union registered under the Trade Union Act of 1926
- Company registered under section 8 of the Companies Act of 2013

18.3.1 Society Registered under the Societies Registration Act of 1860

The aim of the Societies Registration Act of 1860 was to register literary, scientific and charitable societies. Amendments were made to this by various states to include other type of organization under this like educational, healthcare, etc. According to this act, seven persons can register a society by subscribing a Memorandum of Association. The society needs to file rules and regulations governing the society with the registrar of societies. The society has membership and a person can become a member by paying the membership fee. Societies are flexible organization with flexibility of making amendments to the rules and regulations.

18.3.2 Trust Registered under the Indian Trust Act of 1882

Trust can be either public or private and can be religious, charitable, communal or educational. A trust deed is enshrined to form a trust, which has the minimum and maximum number of trustees, the aims and objectives of the trust and the governance of the trust is spelled. The trust deed is executed on a non-judicial stamp paper. The trustees manage the trust, and are liable to breach of trust and the property of a trustee can be confiscated to recover losses. Trusts are flexible with minimum government interference. A trustee cannot enjoy any benefit from the trust and it is difficult to remove an appointed member.

18.3.3 Cooperative Registered under the Cooperatives Act of 1904

Cooperative act of 1904 has been modified by several states, and the institutes in the states need to abide by the laws of the state. Cooperatives have stringent laws and registrar yields a lot of control owing to rules which allow him to conduct elections, audit accounts and other such controls. Principles of cooperatives as per the cooperative act are voluntary memberships, democratic system, limited interest, etc. 10 members can form a cooperative and the general body is the final authority in managing the cooperative. Various committees are elected in a democratic manner.

18.3.4 Trade Union Registered under the Trade Union Act of 1926

A trade union is an institution formed to regulate the relations mainly between the workers and employers. Under the Trade Union Act, seven persons can register a trade union with a copy of rules and regulation and after the formation; it is required to submit an annual incomes and expenditures statement, any change in by-laws, etc. A trade union mainly functions for collective bargaining for the workers and yield some influence over wage and other requirements of the workers.

18.3.5 Company Registered under Section 8 of the Companies Act of 2013

Under the old Companies Act of 1956, the registration was as per section 25. However, in the new Companies' Act of 2013, the section which governs a non-profit making entity is governed under section 8. A Section 8 company requires a minimum of two trustees and there is no upper limit. Governance requires a board of governance or managing committee. The memorandum of association makes it expressly Non-Profit with the firm promoting charitable objectives with members not getting any benefit from the company. The directors in these firms act as trustees who can be reimbursed for management but cannot accept remuneration or share profits.

18.4 Cost of Fund Capital

For-Profit firms raise capital by debt, equity or preference shares. NPOs can raise capital either by issuing debt or by raising fund capital. Fund capital for the NPO is similar to what would be equity for a for-profit organization. Fund capital can be raised by the NPO through retaining profits from its operations, through grants from funding organizations or through donations from individuals or institutions. Besides this, NPOs can also raise fund capital from its members and trustees.

How can the cost of fund capital be measured? Fund capital is raised for activities, which will benefit the society, and hence, are funded by governments and other development organizations. Thus, it may seem there is no cost of fund capital as it is received for utilizing it in programs or projects which shall benefit a section of the society. However, if the fund is not utilized, it will be kept in a bank account or invested in some securities. It can also buy some real asset which can have appreciation in future and also be utilized for some constructive purpose. For example, the NPO can utilize funds to buy land and built a training centre. This land would appreciate in future and can also generate revenues by lending the facility to other organizations when not in use. Thus, if the money is utilized for some other purpose, it can have an opportunity cost. The cost of fund capital can be calculated from the perspective of the opportunity cost.

Fund Capital is mainly represented by the grants received by the NPOs and can be utilized in projects for the benefit of the society.

Various cooperatives return the profits to its members. For example, a milk cooperative distributes its profit to the members who sell milk to the cooperative and are also the member. Thus, the fund cost for a cooperative would be the returns expected by the members. Some grants are received for a very specific project, and cannot be utilized for any other purpose. In such cases, there will not be any opportunity cost and at the maximum, it could be the return the NPO can receive by keeping the funds in a bank account.

18.5 Cost of Debt in NPOs

NPOs might invest in projects which can be profitable and require large funds. For example, a sugar cooperative may want to raise funds to set up an integrated power plant. This will require large funds and one of the ways is by issuing bonds. NPOs can issue bonds to its board members in India. In other countries like USA, NPOs can issue tax-free bonds and these issues are mainly by NPOs working in infrastructure development. Some form of NPOs can also issue bonds in the public domain. For example, Indian Farmers Fertilizers Cooperatives Ltd. in India has issued bonds which have tax exemptions. The cost of debt would be coupon rate for the bonds selling at par.

NPOs can also raise funds through bank loans and loans from individuals or institutions which have a close link with the NPO and cost of debt would be the interest paid on the loans. This can be classified as non-market debt. Bond issues would classify as market-debt and it is overall very low in the NPO domain.

18.6 Capital Structure Decisions in NPOs

As we have studied earlier, the major factor in deciding whether to go for equity or bond is the tax benefit a for-profit firm would get. NPOs are normally exempt from taxes; hence there is no scope of getting tax benefit. However, if the NPO issues bond, it would be tax exempt and hence the benefit accrues. Secondly, fund cost for a firm will have opportunity cost in a similar risk project. Thus, the opportunity cost for fund capital would increase with increase in debt which is similar to a for-profit firm. Thus, there would be a trade-off and cost of financial distress would be similar to a for-profit firm. Fund capital for an NPO is similar to equity capital for a for-profit organization. Fund capital is not easily available for the NPO. NPOs mainly raise fund capital by grants and donations. It is not a market which is as easily accessible as the equity market and hence may force firms to have more debt than the optimal debt required in the capital structure. Thus, the ability to get fund capital is the major competency for NPOs.

NPOs operate in a market which is not complete and the capital is restricted and this is one of the major reasons why Modigliani–Miller model has not been applied to the NPOs. It is very difficult to argue on arbitrage conditions for the NPO. Even if the debt market is complete, it is not possible for an NPO to sell a donation received from someone who can be similar to an investor. Trade-off theory works by trading off the benefit of tax shield against bankruptcy cost. There is no tax shield for an NPO and bankruptcy costs are high. Thus, there is no possibility of a trade-off and the reason a firm would go for debt instead of fund capital is to fill gap of non-availability of fund capital. From the pecking order theory perspective, the pecking order would be: Internal equity > grant funds > debt. Firms would first try to utilize internal equity, then try to raise grant funds and lastly go for debt.

18.7 Capital Budgeting Decisions in NPOs

The main objective of the NPO is to provide service to the society. If the projects chosen are viable and if the firm is able to choose the right projects, the impact of the service on the people would be higher. It will also lead to more credibility and value for the NPO. Thus, capital budgeting decision is important for long-term viability of a non-profit firm.

The capital budgeting decision can be for a project or it can also be equivalent annual cost/benefit decision. Equivalent annual cost or benefit methods can be used for deciding an optimal replacement policy for some particular machinery. A non-profit organization would normally raise fund capital and utilize it for social benefit of the society. So, majority of the projects in NPOs domain would have an analysis of options where we need to look at minimizing the costs.

EXAMPLE 18.1 Gagan, an NGO, plans to start a project whereby they will supply fertilizers to small farmers for free under the "Kisan Vikas Yojna". Gagan needs to invest in a mini-truck to supply the farmers. They have two options: Truck X and Truck Y. Details are given below:

	X	*Y*
Initial cost	₹8,00,000	₹5,00,000
Salvage value	0	0
Life of the vehicle	5 years	4 years
Operating cost	₹20,000 per year	₹26,000 per year

Discount rate is 8%. Which alternative will Gagan choose?

Solution: This problem has the involvement of only costs and we can take a decision by looking at the option which has minimum cost. However, the life of the first option is 5 years and that of second option is 4 years. Thus, we can apply the equivalent annual cost method to make the decision.

The first step in this method is to calculate the present value of costs for project x.

$$\text{PV of cost} = 8{,}00{,}000 + \frac{20{,}000}{1.08} + \frac{20{,}000}{1.08^2} + \cdots + \frac{20{,}000}{1.08^5} = ₹8{,}79{,}854.20$$

This is the present value of costs for truck x. This cost can be converted into a annual cost by using the below given expression:

$$8{,}79{,}854 = \frac{x}{1.08} + \frac{x}{1.08^2} + \frac{x}{1.08^3} + \frac{x}{1.08^4} + \frac{x}{1.08^5}$$

$$8{,}79{,}854 = x * PVA_{8\%, 5\,years}$$

We can look for $PVA_{8\%, 5\,years}$ in the present value table to get:

$$8{,}79{,}854 = x * 3.993$$

Thus, x = ₹2,20,349.
This is the equivalent annual cost for machine x.

Similarly, we can find the equivalent annual cost for machine y which comes out to:

$$y = ₹1{,}76{,}960$$

Thus, the equivalent annual cost for truck y is lower, and hence, truck y should be selected.

The main advantage of equivalent annual cost method is that it has brought the comparison to a yearly level and thus making it comparable.

Researchable Issues

Faculty members, students and research scholars may like to consider the following selected issues for further research and case writing.

- Social Impact Bonds: Would it work in India?
- Evaluation of Fund Costs in Indian Non-profit organizations
- Financing Issues in Farmer Producer Organizations in India

References

Hansmann, H., Economic theories of nonprofit organization, *The nonprofit sector: A research handbook*, Yale University Press: New Haven, CT, 1, 1987, pp. 27–42.

Kaplan, R.S., Strategic performance measurement and management in non-profit organizations. *Nonprofit management and Leadership*, Vol. 11, No. 3, 2001, pp. 353–370.

Sloan, F.A., Not-for-profit ownership and hospital behavior. *Handbook of health economics*, 1, Elsevier: Amsterdam, 2000, pp. 1141–1174.

Young, D.R., *If Not For Profit, For What?*, Lexington Books, Lexington, MA, 2013.

Points to Remember

- Non-profit organizations perform to serve for charity, education, health, literary and religious activities.
- The objective of a for-profit organization is to maximize shareholders' wealth, whereas a non-profit organization is to maximize value for the marginalized sections of the society who are the stakeholder of the non-profit organization.
- From a legal perspective there are five forms of non-profit organizations: Society registered under the Societies Registration Act of 1860, Trust registered under the Indian Trust Act of 1882, Cooperative registered under the Cooperatives Act of 1904, Trade Union registered under the Trade Union Act of 1926, Company registered under Section 8 of the Companies Act of 2013.
- Fund capital for a non-profit organization is like equity capital for a for-profit organization. Fund capital is raised by grants from government and

other institutions, by profits of previous years or by individual or institutional donations.

- Non-profit organizations prefer fund capital over debt and ability to arrange for fund capital is an important competitive ability for an NPO.

Questions

1. Define a Non-Profit Organization.
2. Does the financial management for an NPO differ from a for-profit organization? Explain.
3. What is the objective of an NPO, and how is it different from a for-profit organization?
4. Explain the different forms of non-profit organization. Give example of each form of NPO.
5. What is fund capital and why is it preferred by NPOs over debt?

Multiple Choice Questions

1. The objective of a non-profit organization is:
   (a) Maximize shareholders' wealth
   (b) Maximize bondholders' wealth
   (c) Maximize value for marginalized section of the society
   (d) Minimize value for marginalized section of the society

2. Grant received from government and large organizations is:
   (a) Equity
   (b) Debt
   (c) Fund capital
   (d) Social capital

3. Which of the following statements is true:
   (a) An NPO would prefer equity over debt
   (b) An NPO would prefer fund capital over debt
   (c) An NPO would prefer debt over fund capital
   (d) None of the above

4. An NGO needs to decide whether to buy Xerox x-ray machine, which has a life of 5 years or Panasonic x-ray machine, which has a life of 7 years. Which is the appropriate technique to make the decision?
   (a) Net present value method
   (b) Payback period method
   (c) Internal Rate of return method
   (d) Equivalent annual cost method

Self-Test Questions

1. Kitchen for poor, an NGO, needs commercial stoves to run its kitchen. A new stove costs ₹1,20,000 and has 6 years of commercial life, generating ₹40,000 cash flow per year. The firm can also sell the stove at the end of each year (1–6). Following are the cash flows from sale of the machine:

End of year	*Net cash flow from sale*
1	1,00,000
2	85,000
3	75,000
4	60,000
5	30,000
6	0

What is the optimum replacement policy at a discount rate of 12%.

2. An NGO has received a credit of ₹10 million from a National Development Finance Body. The funds are to be used for financing to needy, deserving people to enable them to engage in some self-sustaining ventures. The credit carries a nominal annual interest rate of 10% and has to be repaid by the NGO in 5 half yearly installments. The NGO, in turn, would finance ₹20,000 to each of 500 beneficiaries who have already been identified. The beneficiaries would also have to repay the amount to the NGO in 5 equal half yearly installments but they would be charged a nominal annual interest rate of 12% per annum.

Answer the following questions:

1. What would be the half yearly installment that the NGO has to pay to the National Development Finance Body?
2. What would be the half yearly installment that each beneficiary has to pay to the NGO?

CASE

Farmers' Co-operative: A Case on Capital Budgeting

A Producer's Co-operative has been set up in a city to procure and market, a wide range of Agri produce of the farmers in neighbouring areas. The procured produce would be brought to a Central Storage (CS) to be set up in the city and sold through 200 retail shops – both belonging to the Co-operative. The CS would be a very sophisticated facility consisting of sorting and grading lines and cold stores with temperature and humidity controls. The co-operative has made estimates of project costs, likely activity levels and sales and revenues which are as follows:

(i) Cost of CS and associate facilities ₹30 crores
(ii) Cost of retail shops ₹6 crores
} to be fully incurred in the year before operations, i.e. Year 0

(iii) Projected activity levels

Year	1	2	3	4	5
Quantity of agri-produce to be sold (tons)	80,000	1,00,000	1,10,000	1,21,000	1,21,000
Weighted average variable cost/ ton (₹) excluding interest	7,000	7,000	7,000	7,000	7,000
Weighted average selling price/ ton (₹)	8,500	8,500	8,500	8,500	8,500

(iv) Fixed costs (₹) (other than interest and depreciation) 2 crores 2 crores 2 crores 2 crores 2 crores

(v) *Working Capital Requirement:* It has been found that the working capital requirement for each year consists of a minimum (permanent component) and a fluctuating part. Both the minimum component and the fluctuating part increase directly in proportion to the quantity being sold in the year. Management has decided to meet 50% of the minimum (permanent) component through retained earnings/equity infusions and 50% through medium term loan and the fluctuating component would be met through short-term bank borrowings at an interest rate of 12% per annum. The month-wise working capital computation for the first year is as follows:

April	3 crores
May	3 crores
June	4 crores
July	5 crores
August	6 crores
September	5 crores
October	5 crores
November	4 crores
December	4 crores
January	3 crores
February	3 crores
March	3 crores

(vi) Depreciation for tax purposes 25% on written down value

(vii) Tax rate 50%

(viii) Salvage value of CS and retail shops ₹9 crores (Ignore capital gains tax)

(ix) *CS, Retail shops and permanent working capital:* 50% through members' equity and 50% medium term loan. The loan carries an interest of 12% per annum. The principal of each medium term loan would be repayable in equal annual installments, along with interest on opening balance, such that all the respective loans are fully repaid by the end of the fifth year. The members expect a minimum return of 14% on equity.

(x) *Fluctuating Working Capital:* Short-term bank borrowings at an interest of 12% per annum.

Prepare the relevant project cash flows and find the NPV and IRR of the project to decide whether this project should be selected.

Appendix A

Table 1 Future Value of \$1 at the end of n periods (FVIF)

Table 2 Present Value of \$1 due at the end of n periods (PVIF)

Table 3 Future Value of an Annuity Interest Factor (FVIFA): \$1 per period at i% for n periods

Table 4 Present Value of an Annuity Interest Factor (PVIFA): \$1 per period at i% for n periods

Table 1 Future Value of $1 at the end of *n* periods (FVIF)

n	1%	2%	3%	4%	5%	6%	7%	8%	9%	10%	11%	12%	13%	14%	15%	16%	17%	18%
1	1.0100	1.0200	1.0300	1.0400	1.0500	1.0600	1.0700	1.0800	1.0900	1.1000	1.1100	1.1200	1.1300	1.1400	1.1500	1.1600	1.1700	1.1800
2	1.0201	1.0404	1.0609	1.0816	1.1025	1.1236	1.1449	1.1664	1.1881	1.2100	1.2321	1.2544	1.2769	1.2996	1.3225	1.3456	1.3689	1.3924
3	1.0303	1.0612	1.0927	1.1249	1.1576	1.1910	1.2250	1.2597	1.2950	1.3310	1.3676	1.4049	1.4429	1.4815	1.5209	1.5609	1.6016	1.6430
4	1.0406	1.0824	1.1255	1.1699	1.2155	1.2625	1.3108	1.3605	1.4116	1.4641	1.5181	1.5735	1.6305	1.6890	1.7490	1.8106	1.8739	1.9388
5	1.0510	1.1041	1.1593	1.2167	1.2763	1.3382	1.4026	1.4693	1.5386	1.6105	1.6851	1.7623	1.8424	1.9254	2.0114	2.1003	2.1924	2.2878
6	1.0615	1.1262	1.1941	1.2653	1.3401	1.4185	1.5007	1.5869	1.6771	1.7716	1.8704	1.9738	2.0820	2.1950	2.3131	2.4364	2.5652	2.6996
7	1.0721	1.1487	1.2299	1.3159	1.4071	1.5036	1.6058	1.7138	1.8280	1.9487	2.0762	2.2107	2.3526	2.5023	2.6600	2.8262	3.0012	3.1855
8	1.0829	1.1717	1.2668	1.3686	1.4775	1.5938	1.7182	1.8509	1.9926	2.1436	2.3045	2.4760	2.6584	2.8526	3.0590	3.2784	3.5115	3.7589
9	1.0937	1.1951	1.3048	1.4233	1.5513	1.6895	1.8385	1.9990	2.1719	2.3579	2.5580	2.7731	3.0040	3.2519	3.5179	3.8030	4.1084	4.4355
10	1.1046	1.2190	1.3439	1.4802	1.6289	1.7908	1.9672	2.1589	2.3674	2.5937	2.8394	3.1058	3.3946	3.7072	4.0456	4.4114	4.8068	5.2338
11	1.1157	1.2434	1.3842	1.5395	1.7103	1.8983	2.1049	2.3316	2.5804	2.8531	3.1518	3.4785	3.8359	4.2262	4.6524	5.1173	5.6240	6.1759
12	1.1268	1.2682	1.4258	1.6010	1.7959	2.0122	2.2522	2.5182	2.8127	3.1384	3.4985	3.8960	4.3345	4.8179	5.3503	5.9360	6.5801	7.2876
13	1.1381	1.2936	1.4685	1.6651	1.8856	2.1329	2.4098	2.7196	3.0658	3.4523	3.8833	4.3635	4.8980	5.4924	6.1528	6.8858	7.6987	8.5994
14	1.1495	1.3195	1.5126	1.7317	1.9799	2.2609	2.5785	2.9372	3.3417	3.7975	4.3104	4.8871	5.5348	6.2613	7.0757	7.9875	9.0075	10.1472
15	1.1610	1.3459	1.5580	1.8009	2.0789	2.3966	2.7590	3.1722	3.6425	4.1772	4.7846	5.4736	6.2543	7.1379	8.1371	9.2655	10.5387	11.9737
16	1.1726	1.3728	1.6047	1.8730	2.1829	2.5404	2.9522	3.4259	3.9703	4.5950	5.3109	6.1304	7.0673	8.1372	9.3576	10.7480	12.3303	14.1290
17	1.1843	1.4002	1.6528	1.9479	2.2920	2.6928	3.1588	3.7000	4.3276	5.0545	5.8951	6.8660	7.9861	9.2765	10.7613	12.4677	14.4265	16.6722
18	1.1961	1.4282	1.7024	2.0258	2.4066	2.8543	3.3799	3.9960	4.7171	5.5599	6.5436	7.6900	9.0243	10.5752	12.3755	14.4625	16.8790	19.6733
19	1.2081	1.4568	1.7535	2.1068	2.5270	3.0256	3.6165	4.3157	5.1417	6.1159	7.2633	8.6128	10.1974	12.0557	14.2318	16.7765	19.7484	23.2144
20	1.2202	1.4859	1.8061	2.1911	2.6533	3.2071	3.8697	4.6610	5.6044	6.7275	8.0623	9.6463	11.5231	13.7435	16.3665	19.4608	23.1056	27.3930
21	1.2324	1.5157	1.8603	2.2788	2.7860	3.3996	4.1406	5.0338	6.1088	7.4002	8.9492	10.8038	13.0211	15.6676	18.8215	22.5745	27.0336	32.3238
22	1.2447	1.5460	1.9161	2.3699	2.9253	3.6035	4.4304	5.4365	6.6586	8.1403	9.9336	12.1003	14.7138	17.8610	21.6447	26.1864	31.6293	38.1421
23	1.2572	1.5769	1.9736	2.4647	3.0715	3.8197	4.7405	5.8715	7.2579	8.9543	11.0263	13.5523	16.6266	20.3616	24.8915	30.3762	37.0062	45.0076
24	1.2697	1.6084	2.0328	2.5633	3.2251	4.0489	5.0724	6.3412	7.9111	9.8497	12.2392	15.1786	18.7881	23.2122	28.6252	35.2364	43.2973	53.1090
25	1.2824	1.6406	2.0938	2.6658	3.3864	4.2919	5.4274	6.8485	8.6231	10.8347	13.5855	17.0001	21.2305	26.4619	32.9190	40.8742	50.6578	62.6686
26	1.2953	1.6734	2.1566	2.7725	3.5557	4.5494	5.8074	7.3964	9.3992	11.9182	15.0799	19.0401	23.9905	30.1666	37.8568	47.4141	59.2697	73.9490
27	1.3082	1.7069	2.2213	2.8834	3.7335	4.8223	6.2139	7.9881	10.2451	13.1100	16.7386	21.3249	27.1093	34.3899	43.5353	55.0004	69.3455	87.2598
28	1.3213	1.7410	2.2879	2.9987	3.9201	5.1117	6.6488	8.6271	11.1671	14.4210	18.5799	23.8839	30.6335	39.2045	50.0656	63.8004	81.1342	102.9666
29	1.3345	1.7758	2.3566	3.1187	4.1161	5.4184	7.1143	9.3173	12.1722	15.8631	20.6237	26.7499	34.6158	44.6931	57.5755	74.0085	94.9271	121.5005
30	1.3478	1.8114	2.4273	3.2434	4.3219	5.7435	7.6123	10.0627	13.2677	17.4494	22.8923	29.9599	39.1159	50.9502	66.2118	85.8499	111.0647	143.3706

(Contd.)

Table 1 Future Value of $1 at the end of *n* periods (FVIF) (Contd.)

n	19%	20%	21%	22%	23%	24%	25%	26%	27%	28%	29%	30%	31%	32%	33%	34%	35%	36%
1	1.1900	1.2000	1.2100	1.2200	1.2300	1.2400	1.2500	1.2600	1.2700	1.2800	1.2900	1.3000	1.3100	1.3200	1.3300	1.3400	1.3500	1.3600
2	1.4161	1.4400	1.4641	1.4884	1.5129	1.5376	1.5625	1.5876	1.6129	1.6384	1.6641	1.6900	1.7161	1.7424	1.7689	1.7956	1.8225	1.8496
3	1.6852	1.7280	1.7716	1.8158	1.8609	1.9066	1.9531	2.0004	2.0484	2.0972	2.1467	2.1970	2.2481	2.3000	2.3526	2.4061	2.4604	2.5155
4	2.0053	2.0736	2.1436	2.2153	2.2889	2.3642	2.4414	2.5205	2.6014	2.6844	2.7692	2.8561	2.9450	3.0360	3.1290	3.2242	3.3215	3.4210
5	2.3864	2.4883	2.5937	2.7027	2.8153	2.9316	3.0518	3.1758	3.3038	3.4360	3.5723	3.7129	3.8579	4.0075	4.1616	4.3204	4.4840	4.6526
6	2.8398	2.9860	3.1384	3.2973	3.4628	3.6352	3.8147	4.0015	4.1959	4.3980	4.6083	4.8268	5.0539	5.2899	5.5349	5.7893	6.0534	6.3275
7	3.3793	3.5832	3.7975	4.0227	4.2593	4.5077	4.7684	5.0419	5.3288	5.6295	5.9447	6.2749	6.6206	6.9826	7.3614	7.7577	8.1722	8.6054
8	4.0214	4.2998	4.5950	4.9077	5.2389	5.5895	5.9605	6.3528	6.7675	7.2058	7.6686	8.1573	8.6730	9.2170	9.7907	10.3953	11.0324	11.7034
9	4.7854	5.1598	5.5599	5.9874	6.4439	6.9310	7.4506	8.0045	8.5948	9.2234	9.8925	10.6045	11.3617	12.1665	13.0216	13.9297	14.8937	15.9166
10	5.6947	6.1917	6.7275	7.3046	7.9259	8.5944	9.3132	10.0857	10.9153	11.8059	12.7614	13.7858	14.8838	16.0598	17.3187	18.6659	20.1066	21.6466
11	6.7767	7.4301	8.1403	8.9117	9.7489	10.6571	11.6415	12.7080	13.8625	15.1116	16.4622	17.9216	19.4977	21.1989	23.0339	25.0123	27.1439	29.4393
12	8.0642	8.9161	9.8497	10.8722	11.9912	13.2148	14.5519	16.0120	17.6053	19.3428	21.2362	23.2981	25.5420	27.9825	30.6351	33.5164	36.6442	40.0375
13	9.5964	10.6993	11.9182	13.2641	14.7491	16.3863	18.1899	20.1752	22.3588	24.7588	27.3947	30.2875	33.4601	36.9370	40.7447	44.9120	49.4697	54.4510
14	11.4198	12.8392	14.4210	16.1822	18.1414	20.3191	22.7374	25.4207	28.3957	31.6913	35.3391	39.3738	43.8327	48.7568	54.1905	60.1821	66.7841	74.0534
15	13.5895	15.4070	17.4494	19.7423	22.3140	25.1956	28.4217	32.0301	36.0625	40.5648	45.5875	51.1859	57.4208	64.3590	72.0733	80.6440	90.1585	100.7126
16	16.1715	18.4884	21.1138	24.0856	27.4462	31.2426	35.5271	40.3579	45.7994	51.9230	58.8079	66.5417	75.2213	84.9538	95.8575	108.0629	121.7139	136.9691
17	19.2441	22.1861	25.5477	29.3844	33.7588	38.7408	44.4089	50.8510	58.1652	66.4614	75.8621	86.5042	98.5399	112.1390	127.4905	144.8043	164.3138	186.2779
18	22.9005	26.6233	30.9127	35.8490	41.5233	48.0386	55.5112	64.0722	73.8698	85.0706	97.8622	112.4554	129.0872	148.0235	169.5624	194.0378	221.8236	253.3380
19	27.2516	31.9480	37.4043	43.7358	51.0737	59.5679	69.3889	80.7310	93.8147	108.8904	126.2422	146.1920	169.1043	195.3911	225.5180	260.0107	299.4619	344.5397
20	32.4294	38.3376	45.2593	53.3576	62.8206	73.8641	86.7362	101.7211	119.1446	139.3797	162.8524	190.0496	221.5266	257.9162	299.9389	348.4143	404.2736	468.5740
21	38.5910	46.0051	54.7637	65.0963	77.2694	91.5915	108.4202	128.1685	151.3137	178.4060	210.0796	247.0645	290.1999	340.4494	398.9188	466.8752	545.7693	637.2606
22	45.9233	55.2061	66.2641	79.4175	95.0413	113.5735	135.5253	161.4924	192.1683	228.3596	271.0027	321.1839	380.1618	449.3932	530.5620	625.6127	736.7886	866.6744
23	54.6487	66.2474	80.1795	96.8894	116.9008	140.8312	169.4066	203.4804	244.0538	292.3003	349.5935	417.5391	498.0120	593.1990	705.6474	838.3210	994.6646	1178.6772
24	65.0320	79.4968	97.0172	118.2050	143.7880	174.6306	211.7582	256.3853	309.9483	374.1444	450.9756	542.8008	652.3957	783.0227	938.5110	1123.3502	1342.7973	1603.0010
25	77.3881	95.3962	117.3909	144.2101	176.8593	216.5420	264.6978	323.0454	393.6344	478.9049	581.7585	705.6410	854.6384	1033.5900	1248.2197	1505.2892	1812.7763	2180.0814
26	92.0918	114.4755	142.0429	175.9364	217.5369	268.5121	330.8722	407.0373	499.9157	612.9982	750.4685	917.3333	1119.5763	1364.3387	1660.1322	2017.0876	2447.2480	2964.9107
27	109.5893	137.3706	171.8719	214.6424	267.5704	332.9550	413.5903	512.8670	634.8929	784.6377	968.1044	1192.5333	1466.6449	1800.9271	2207.9758	2702.8974	3303.7848	4032.2786
28	130.4112	164.8447	207.9651	261.8637	329.1115	412.8642	516.9879	646.2124	806.3140	1004.3363	1248.8546	1550.2933	1921.3048	2377.2238	2936.6078	3621.8825	4460.1095	5483.8988
29	155.1893	197.8136	251.6377	319.4737	404.8072	511.9516	646.2349	814.2276	1024.0187	1285.5504	1611.0225	2015.3813	2516.9093	3137.9354	3905.6884	4853.3225	6021.1478	7458.1024
30	184.6753	237.3763	304.4816	389.7579	497.9129	634.8199	807.7936	1025.9267	1300.5038	1645.5046	2078.2190	2619.9956	3297.1512	4142.0748	5194.5655	6503.4522	8128.5495	10143.0193

Table 2 Present Value of $1 due at the end of *n* periods (PVIF)

n	1%	2%	3%	4%	5%	6%	7%	8%	9%	10%	11%	12%	13%	14%	15%	16%	17%	18%
1	0.9901	0.9804	0.9709	0.9615	0.9524	0.9434	0.9346	0.9259	0.9174	0.9091	0.9009	0.8929	0.8850	0.8772	0.8696	0.8621	0.8547	0.8475
2	0.9803	0.9612	0.9426	0.9246	0.9070	0.8900	0.8734	0.8573	0.8417	0.8264	0.8116	0.7972	0.7831	0.7695	0.7561	0.7432	0.7305	0.7182
3	0.9706	0.9423	0.9151	0.8890	0.8638	0.8396	0.8163	0.7938	0.7722	0.7513	0.7312	0.7118	0.6931	0.6750	0.6575	0.6407	0.6244	0.6086
4	0.9610	0.9238	0.8885	0.8548	0.8227	0.7921	0.7629	0.7350	0.7084	0.6830	0.6587	0.6355	0.6133	0.5921	0.5718	0.5523	0.5337	0.5158
5	0.9515	0.9057	0.8626	0.8219	0.7835	0.7473	0.7130	0.6806	0.6499	0.6209	0.5935	0.5674	0.5428	0.5194	0.4972	0.4761	0.4561	0.4371
6	0.9420	0.8880	0.8375	0.7903	0.7462	0.7050	0.6663	0.6302	0.5963	0.5645	0.5346	0.5066	0.4803	0.4556	0.4323	0.4104	0.3898	0.3704
7	0.9327	0.8706	0.8131	0.7599	0.7107	0.6651	0.6227	0.5835	0.5470	0.5132	0.4817	0.4523	0.4251	0.3996	0.3759	0.3538	0.3332	0.3139
8	0.9235	0.8535	0.7894	0.7307	0.6768	0.6274	0.5820	0.5403	0.5019	0.4665	0.4339	0.4039	0.3762	0.3506	0.3269	0.3050	0.2848	0.2660
9	0.9143	0.8368	0.7664	0.7026	0.6446	0.5919	0.5439	0.5002	0.4604	0.4241	0.3909	0.3606	0.3329	0.3075	0.2843	0.2630	0.2434	0.2255
10	0.9053	0.8203	0.7441	0.6756	0.6139	0.5584	0.5083	0.4632	0.4224	0.3855	0.3522	0.3220	0.2946	0.2697	0.2472	0.2267	0.2080	0.1911
11	0.8963	0.8043	0.7224	0.6496	0.5847	0.5268	0.4751	0.4289	0.3875	0.3505	0.3173	0.2875	0.2607	0.2366	0.2149	0.1954	0.1778	0.1619
12	0.8874	0.7885	0.7014	0.6246	0.5568	0.4970	0.4440	0.3971	0.3555	0.3186	0.2858	0.2567	0.2307	0.2076	0.1869	0.1685	0.1520	0.1372
13	0.8787	0.7730	0.6810	0.6006	0.5303	0.4688	0.4150	0.3677	0.3262	0.2897	0.2575	0.2292	0.2042	0.1821	0.1625	0.1452	0.1299	0.1163
14	0.8700	0.7579	0.6611	0.5775	0.5051	0.4423	0.3878	0.3405	0.2992	0.2633	0.2320	0.2046	0.1807	0.1597	0.1413	0.1252	0.1110	0.0985
15	0.8613	0.7430	0.6419	0.5553	0.4810	0.4173	0.3624	0.3152	0.2745	0.2394	0.2090	0.1827	0.1599	0.1401	0.1229	0.1079	0.0949	0.0835
16	0.8528	0.7284	0.6232	0.5339	0.4581	0.3936	0.3387	0.2919	0.2519	0.2176	0.1883	0.1631	0.1415	0.1229	0.1069	0.0930	0.0811	0.0708
17	0.8444	0.7142	0.6050	0.5134	0.4363	0.3714	0.3166	0.2703	0.2311	0.1978	0.1696	0.1456	0.1252	0.1078	0.0929	0.0802	0.0693	0.0600
18	0.8360	0.7002	0.5874	0.4936	0.4155	0.3503	0.2959	0.2502	0.2120	0.1799	0.1528	0.1300	0.1108	0.0946	0.0808	0.0691	0.0592	0.0508
19	0.8277	0.6864	0.5703	0.4746	0.3957	0.3305	0.2765	0.2317	0.1945	0.1635	0.1377	0.1161	0.0981	0.0829	0.0703	0.0596	0.0506	0.0431
20	0.8195	0.6730	0.5537	0.4564	0.3769	0.3118	0.2584	0.2145	0.1784	0.1486	0.1240	0.1037	0.0868	0.0728	0.0611	0.0514	0.0433	0.0365
21	0.8114	0.6598	0.5375	0.4388	0.3589	0.2942	0.2415	0.1987	0.1637	0.1351	0.1117	0.0926	0.0768	0.0638	0.0531	0.0443	0.0370	0.0309
22	0.8034	0.6468	0.5219	0.4220	0.3418	0.2775	0.2257	0.1839	0.1502	0.1228	0.1007	0.0826	0.0680	0.0560	0.0462	0.0382	0.0316	0.0262
23	0.7954	0.6342	0.5067	0.4057	0.3256	0.2618	0.2109	0.1703	0.1378	0.1117	0.0907	0.0738	0.0601	0.0491	0.0402	0.0329	0.0270	0.0222
24	0.7876	0.6217	0.4919	0.3901	0.3101	0.2470	0.1971	0.1577	0.1264	0.1015	0.0817	0.0659	0.0532	0.0431	0.0349	0.0284	0.0231	0.0188
25	0.7798	0.6095	0.4776	0.3751	0.2953	0.2330	0.1842	0.1460	0.1160	0.0923	0.0736	0.0588	0.0471	0.0378	0.0304	0.0245	0.0197	0.0160
26	0.7720	0.5976	0.4637	0.3607	0.2812	0.2198	0.1722	0.1352	0.1064	0.0839	0.0663	0.0525	0.0417	0.0331	0.0264	0.0211	0.0169	0.0135
27	0.7644	0.5859	0.4502	0.3468	0.2678	0.2074	0.1609	0.1252	0.0976	0.0763	0.0597	0.0469	0.0369	0.0291	0.0230	0.0182	0.0144	0.0115
28	0.7568	0.5744	0.4371	0.3335	0.2551	0.1956	0.1504	0.1159	0.0895	0.0693	0.0538	0.0419	0.0326	0.0255	0.0200	0.0157	0.0123	0.0097
29	0.7493	0.5631	0.4243	0.3207	0.2429	0.1846	0.1406	0.1073	0.0822	0.0630	0.0485	0.0374	0.0289	0.0224	0.0174	0.0135	0.0105	0.0082
30	0.7419	0.5521	0.4120	0.3083	0.2314	0.1741	0.1314	0.0994	0.0754	0.0573	0.0437	0.0334	0.0256	0.0196	0.0151	0.0116	0.0090	0.0070

(Contd.)

Table 2 Present Value of $1 due at the end of *n* periods (PVIF) (Contd.)

n	19%	20%	21%	22%	23%	24%	25%	26%	27%	28%	29%	30%	31%	32%	33%	34%	35%	36%
1	0.8403	0.8333	0.8264	0.8197	0.8130	0.8065	0.8000	0.7937	0.7874	0.7813	0.7752	0.7692	0.7634	0.7576	0.7519	0.7463	0.7407	0.7353
2	0.7062	0.6944	0.6830	0.6719	0.6610	0.6504	0.6400	0.6299	0.6200	0.6104	0.6009	0.5917	0.5827	0.5739	0.5653	0.5569	0.5487	0.5407
3	0.5934	0.5787	0.5645	0.5507	0.5374	0.5245	0.5120	0.4999	0.4882	0.4768	0.4658	0.4552	0.4448	0.4348	0.4251	0.4156	0.4064	0.3975
4	0.4987	0.4823	0.4665	0.4514	0.4369	0.4230	0.4096	0.3968	0.3844	0.3725	0.3611	0.3501	0.3396	0.3294	0.3196	0.3102	0.3011	0.2923
5	0.4190	0.4019	0.3855	0.3700	0.3552	0.3411	0.3277	0.3149	0.3027	0.2910	0.2799	0.2693	0.2592	0.2495	0.2403	0.2315	0.2230	0.2149
6	0.3521	0.3349	0.3186	0.3033	0.2888	0.2751	0.2621	0.2499	0.2383	0.2274	0.2170	0.2072	0.1979	0.1890	0.1807	0.1727	0.1652	0.1580
7	0.2959	0.2791	0.2633	0.2486	0.2348	0.2218	0.2097	0.1983	0.1877	0.1776	0.1682	0.1594	0.1510	0.1432	0.1358	0.1289	0.1224	0.1162
8	0.2487	0.2326	0.2176	0.2038	0.1909	0.1789	0.1678	0.1574	0.1478	0.1388	0.1304	0.1226	0.1153	0.1085	0.1021	0.0962	0.0906	0.0854
9	0.2090	0.1938	0.1799	0.1670	0.1552	0.1443	0.1342	0.1249	0.1164	0.1084	0.1011	0.0943	0.0880	0.0822	0.0768	0.0718	0.0671	0.0628
10	0.1756	0.1615	0.1486	0.1369	0.1262	0.1164	0.1074	0.0992	0.0916	0.0847	0.0784	0.0725	0.0672	0.0623	0.0577	0.0536	0.0497	0.0462
11	0.1476	0.1346	0.1228	0.1122	0.1026	0.0938	0.0859	0.0787	0.0721	0.0662	0.0607	0.0558	0.0513	0.0472	0.0434	0.0400	0.0368	0.0340
12	0.1240	0.1122	0.1015	0.0920	0.0834	0.0757	0.0687	0.0625	0.0568	0.0517	0.0471	0.0429	0.0392	0.0357	0.0326	0.0298	0.0273	0.0250
13	0.1042	0.0935	0.0839	0.0754	0.0678	0.0610	0.0550	0.0496	0.0447	0.0404	0.0365	0.0330	0.0299	0.0271	0.0245	0.0223	0.0202	0.0184
14	0.0876	0.0779	0.0693	0.0618	0.0551	0.0492	0.0440	0.0393	0.0352	0.0316	0.0283	0.0254	0.0228	0.0205	0.0185	0.0166	0.0150	0.0135
15	0.0736	0.0649	0.0573	0.0507	0.0448	0.0397	0.0352	0.0312	0.0277	0.0247	0.0219	0.0195	0.0174	0.0155	0.0139	0.0124	0.0111	0.0099
16	0.0618	0.0541	0.0474	0.0415	0.0364	0.0320	0.0281	0.0248	0.0218	0.0193	0.0170	0.0150	0.0133	0.0118	0.0104	0.0093	0.0082	0.0073
17	0.0520	0.0451	0.0391	0.0340	0.0296	0.0258	0.0225	0.0197	0.0172	0.0150	0.0132	0.0116	0.0101	0.0089	0.0078	0.0069	0.0061	0.0054
18	0.0437	0.0376	0.0323	0.0279	0.0241	0.0208	0.0180	0.0156	0.0135	0.0118	0.0102	0.0089	0.0077	0.0068	0.0059	0.0052	0.0045	0.0039
19	0.0367	0.0313	0.0267	0.0229	0.0196	0.0168	0.0144	0.0124	0.0107	0.0092	0.0079	0.0068	0.0059	0.0051	0.0044	0.0038	0.0033	0.0029
20	0.0308	0.0261	0.0221	0.0187	0.0159	0.0135	0.0115	0.0098	0.0084	0.0072	0.0061	0.0053	0.0045	0.0039	0.0033	0.0029	0.0025	0.0021
21	0.0259	0.0217	0.0183	0.0154	0.0129	0.0109	0.0092	0.0078	0.0066	0.0056	0.0048	0.0040	0.0034	0.0029	0.0025	0.0021	0.0018	0.0016
22	0.0218	0.0181	0.0151	0.0126	0.0105	0.0088	0.0074	0.0062	0.0052	0.0044	0.0037	0.0031	0.0026	0.0022	0.0019	0.0016	0.0014	0.0012
23	0.0183	0.0151	0.0125	0.0103	0.0086	0.0071	0.0059	0.0049	0.0041	0.0034	0.0029	0.0024	0.0020	0.0017	0.0014	0.0012	0.0010	0.0008
24	0.0154	0.0126	0.0103	0.0085	0.0070	0.0057	0.0047	0.0039	0.0032	0.0027	0.0022	0.0018	0.0015	0.0013	0.0011	0.0009	0.0007	0.0006
25	0.0129	0.0105	0.0085	0.0069	0.0057	0.0046	0.0038	0.0031	0.0025	0.0021	0.0017	0.0014	0.0012	0.0010	0.0008	0.0007	0.0006	0.0005
26	0.0109	0.0087	0.0070	0.0057	0.0046	0.0037	0.0030	0.0025	0.0020	0.0016	0.0013	0.0011	0.0009	0.0007	0.0006	0.0005	0.0004	0.0003
27	0.0091	0.0073	0.0058	0.0047	0.0037	0.0030	0.0024	0.0019	0.0016	0.0013	0.0010	0.0008	0.0007	0.0006	0.0005	0.0004	0.0003	0.0002
28	0.0077	0.0061	0.0048	0.0038	0.0030	0.0024	0.0019	0.0015	0.0012	0.0010	0.0008	0.0006	0.0005	0.0004	0.0003	0.0003	0.0002	0.0002
29	0.0064	0.0051	0.0040	0.0031	0.0025	0.0020	0.0015	0.0012	0.0010	0.0008	0.0006	0.0005	0.0004	0.0003	0.0003	0.0002	0.0002	0.0001
30	0.0054	0.0042	0.0033	0.0026	0.0020	0.0016	0.0012	0.0010	0.0008	0.0006	0.0005	0.0004	0.0003	0.0002	0.0002	0.0002	0.0001	0.0001

Table 3 Future Value of an Annuity Interest Factor (FVIFA): $1 per period at *i*% for *n* periods

n	1%	2%	3%	4%	5%	6%	7%	8%	9%	10%	11%	12%	13%	14%	15%	16%	17%	18%
1	1.0000	1.0000	1.0000	1.0000	1.0000	1.0000	1.0000	1.0000	1.0000	1.0000	1.0000	1.0000	1.0000	1.0000	1.0000	1.0000	1.0000	1.0000
2	2.0100	2.0200	2.0300	2.0400	2.0500	2.0600	2.0700	2.0800	2.0900	2.1000	2.1100	2.1200	2.1300	2.1400	2.1500	2.1600	2.1700	2.1800
3	3.0301	3.0604	3.0909	3.1216	3.1525	3.1836	3.2149	3.2464	3.2781	3.3100	3.3421	3.3744	3.4069	3.4396	3.4725	3.5056	3.5389	3.5724
4	4.0604	4.1216	4.1836	4.2465	4.3101	4.3746	4.4399	4.5061	4.5731	4.6410	4.7097	4.7793	4.8498	4.9211	4.9934	5.0665	5.1405	5.2154
5	5.1010	5.2040	5.3091	5.4163	5.5256	5.6371	5.7507	5.8666	5.9847	6.1051	6.2278	6.3528	6.4803	6.6101	6.7424	6.8771	7.0144	7.1542
6	6.1520	6.3081	6.4684	6.6330	6.8019	6.9753	7.1533	7.3359	7.5233	7.7156	7.9129	8.1152	8.3227	8.5355	8.7537	8.9775	9.2068	9.4420
7	7.2135	7.4343	7.6625	7.8983	8.1420	8.3938	8.6540	8.9228	9.2004	9.4872	9.7833	10.0890	10.4047	10.7305	11.0668	11.4139	11.7720	12.1415
8	8.2857	8.5830	8.8923	9.2142	9.5491	9.8975	10.2598	10.6366	11.0285	11.4359	11.8594	12.2997	12.7573	13.2328	13.7268	14.2401	14.7733	15.3270
9	9.3685	9.7546	10.1591	10.5828	11.0266	11.4913	11.9780	12.4876	13.0210	13.5795	14.1640	14.7757	15.4157	16.0853	16.7858	17.5185	18.2847	19.0859
10	10.4622	10.9497	11.4639	12.0061	12.5779	13.1808	13.8164	14.4866	15.1929	15.9374	16.7220	17.5487	18.4197	19.3373	20.3037	21.3215	22.3931	23.5213
11	11.5668	12.1687	12.8078	13.4864	14.2068	14.9716	15.7836	16.6455	17.5603	18.5312	19.5614	20.6546	21.8143	23.0445	24.3493	25.7329	27.1999	28.7551
12	12.6825	13.4121	14.1920	15.0258	15.9171	16.8699	17.8885	18.9771	20.1407	21.3843	22.7132	24.1331	25.6502	27.2707	29.0017	30.8502	32.8239	34.9311
13	13.8093	14.6803	15.6178	16.6268	17.7130	18.8821	20.1406	21.4953	22.9534	24.5227	26.2116	28.0291	29.9847	32.0887	34.3519	36.7862	39.4040	42.2187
14	14.9474	15.9739	17.0863	18.2919	19.5986	21.0151	22.5505	24.2149	26.0192	27.9750	30.0949	32.3926	34.8827	37.5811	40.5047	43.6720	47.1027	50.8180
15	16.0969	17.2934	18.5989	20.0236	21.5786	23.2760	25.1290	27.1521	29.3609	31.7725	34.4054	37.2797	40.4175	43.8424	47.5804	51.6595	56.1101	60.9653
16	17.2579	18.6393	20.1569	21.8245	23.6575	25.6725	27.8881	30.3243	33.0034	35.9497	39.1899	42.7533	46.6717	50.9804	55.7175	60.9250	66.6488	72.9390
17	18.4304	20.0121	21.7616	23.6975	25.8404	28.2129	30.8402	33.7502	36.9737	40.5447	44.5008	48.8837	53.7391	59.1176	65.0751	71.6730	78.9792	87.0680
18	19.6147	21.4123	23.4144	25.6454	28.1324	30.9057	33.9990	37.4502	41.3013	45.5992	50.3959	55.7497	61.7251	68.3941	75.8364	84.1407	93.4056	103.7403
19	20.8109	22.8406	25.1169	27.6712	30.5390	33.7600	37.3790	41.4463	46.0185	51.1591	56.9395	63.4397	70.7494	78.9692	88.2118	98.6032	110.2846	123.4135
20	22.0190	24.2974	26.8704	29.7781	33.0660	36.7856	40.9955	45.7620	51.1601	57.2750	64.2028	72.0524	80.9468	91.0249	102.4436	115.3797	130.0329	146.6280
21	23.2392	25.7833	28.6765	31.9692	35.7193	39.9927	44.8652	50.4229	56.7645	64.0025	72.2651	81.6987	92.4699	104.7684	118.8101	134.8405	153.1385	174.0210
22	24.4716	27.2990	30.5368	34.2480	38.5052	43.3923	49.0057	55.4568	62.8733	71.4027	81.2143	92.5026	105.4910	120.4360	137.6316	157.4150	180.1721	206.3448
23	25.7163	28.8450	32.4529	36.6179	41.4305	46.9958	53.4361	60.8933	69.5319	79.5430	91.1479	104.6029	120.2048	138.2970	159.2764	183.6014	211.8013	244.4868
24	26.9735	30.4219	34.4265	39.0826	44.5020	50.8156	58.1767	66.7648	76.7898	88.4973	102.1742	118.1552	136.8315	158.6586	184.1678	213.9776	248.8076	289.4945
25	28.2432	32.0303	36.4593	41.6459	47.7271	54.8645	63.2490	73.1059	84.7009	98.3471	114.4133	133.3339	155.6196	181.8708	212.7930	249.2140	292.1049	342.6035
26	29.5256	33.6709	38.5530	44.3117	51.1135	59.1564	68.6765	79.9544	93.3240	109.1818	127.9988	150.3339	176.8501	208.3327	245.7120	290.0883	342.7627	405.2721
27	30.8209	35.3443	40.7096	47.0842	54.6691	63.7058	74.4838	87.3508	102.7231	121.0999	143.0786	169.3740	200.8406	238.4993	283.5688	337.5024	402.0323	479.2211
28	32.1291	37.0512	42.9309	49.9676	58.4026	68.5281	80.6977	95.3388	112.9682	134.2099	159.8173	190.6989	227.9499	272.8892	327.1041	392.5028	471.3778	566.4809
29	33.4504	38.7922	45.2189	52.9663	62.3227	73.6398	87.3465	103.9659	124.1354	148.6309	178.3972	214.5828	258.5834	312.0937	377.1697	456.3032	552.5121	669.4475
30	34.7849	40.5681	47.5754	56.0849	66.4388	79.0582	94.4608	113.2832	136.3075	164.4940	199.0209	241.3327	293.1992	356.7868	434.7451	530.3117	647.4391	790.9480

(Contd.)

Table 3 Future Value of an Annuity Interest Factor (FVIFA): $1 per period at *i*% for *n* periods (Contd.)

n	19%	20%	21%	22%	23%	24%	25%	26%	27%	28%	29%	30%	31%	32%	33%	34%	35%	36%
1	1.0000	1.0000	1.0000	1.0000	1.0000	1.0000	1.0000	1.0000	1.0000	1.0000	1.0000	1.0000	1.0000	1.0000	1.0000	1.0000	1.0000	1.0000
2	2.1900	2.2000	2.2100	2.2200	2.2300	2.2400	2.2500	2.2600	2.2700	2.2800	2.2900	2.3000	2.3100	2.3200	2.3300	2.3400	2.3500	2.3600
3	3.6061	3.6400	3.6741	3.7084	3.7429	3.7776	3.8125	3.8476	3.8829	3.9184	3.9541	3.9900	4.0261	4.0624	4.0989	4.1356	4.1725	4.2096
4	5.2913	5.3680	5.4457	5.5242	5.6038	5.6842	5.7656	5.8480	5.9313	6.0156	6.1008	6.1870	6.2742	6.3624	6.4515	6.5417	6.6329	6.7251
5	7.2966	7.4416	7.5892	7.7396	7.8926	8.0484	8.2070	8.3684	8.5327	8.6999	8.8700	9.0431	9.2192	9.3983	9.5805	9.7659	9.9544	10.1461
6	9.6830	9.9299	10.1830	10.4423	10.7079	10.9801	11.2588	11.5442	11.8366	12.1359	12.4423	12.7560	13.0771	13.4058	13.7421	14.0863	14.4384	14.7987
7	12.5227	12.9159	13.3214	13.7396	14.1708	14.6153	15.0735	15.5458	16.0324	16.5339	17.0506	17.5828	18.1311	18.6956	19.2770	19.8756	20.4919	21.1262
8	15.9020	16.4991	17.1189	17.7623	18.4300	19.1229	19.8419	20.5876	21.3612	22.1634	22.9953	23.8577	24.7517	25.6782	26.6384	27.6333	28.6640	29.7316
9	19.9234	20.7989	21.7139	22.6700	23.6690	24.7125	25.8023	26.9404	28.1287	29.3692	30.6639	32.0150	33.4247	34.8953	36.4291	38.0287	39.6964	41.4350
10	24.7089	25.9587	27.2738	28.6574	30.1128	31.6434	33.2529	34.9449	36.7235	38.5926	40.5564	42.6195	44.7864	47.0618	49.4507	51.9584	54.5902	57.3516
11	30.4035	32.1504	34.0013	35.9620	38.0388	40.2379	42.5661	45.0306	47.6388	50.3985	53.3178	56.4053	59.6701	63.1215	66.7695	70.6243	74.6967	78.9982
12	37.1802	39.5805	42.1416	44.8737	47.7877	50.8950	54.2077	57.7386	61.5013	65.5100	69.7800	74.3270	79.1679	84.3204	89.8034	95.6365	101.8406	108.4375
13	45.2445	48.4966	51.9913	55.7459	59.7788	64.1097	68.7596	73.7506	79.1066	84.8529	91.0161	97.6250	104.7099	112.3030	120.4385	129.1529	138.4848	148.4750
14	54.8409	59.1959	63.9095	69.0100	74.5280	80.4961	86.9495	93.9258	101.4654	109.6117	118.4108	127.9125	138.1700	149.2399	161.1833	174.0649	187.9544	202.9260
15	66.2607	72.0351	78.3305	85.1922	92.6694	100.8151	109.6868	119.3465	129.8611	141.3029	153.7500	167.2863	182.0027	197.9967	215.3737	234.2470	254.7385	276.9793
16	79.8502	87.4421	95.7799	104.9345	114.9834	126.0108	138.1085	151.3766	165.9236	181.8677	199.3374	218.4722	239.4235	262.3557	287.4471	314.8910	344.8970	377.6919
17	96.0218	105.9306	116.8937	129.0201	142.4295	157.2534	173.6357	191.7345	211.7230	233.7907	258.1453	285.0139	314.6448	347.3095	383.3046	422.9539	466.6109	514.6610
18	115.2659	128.1167	142.4413	158.4045	176.1883	195.9942	218.0446	242.5855	269.8882	300.2521	334.0074	371.5180	413.1847	459.4485	510.7951	567.7583	630.9247	700.9389
19	138.1664	154.7400	173.3540	194.2535	217.7116	244.0328	273.5558	306.6577	343.7580	385.3227	431.8696	483.9734	542.2719	607.4721	680.3575	761.7961	852.7483	954.2769
20	165.4180	186.6880	210.7584	237.9893	268.7853	303.6006	342.9447	387.3887	437.5726	494.2131	558.1118	630.1655	711.3762	802.8631	905.8755	1021.8068	1152.2103	1298.8166
21	197.8474	225.0256	256.0176	291.3469	331.6059	377.4648	429.6809	489.1098	556.7173	633.5927	720.9642	820.2151	932.9028	1060.7793	1205.8144	1370.2211	1556.4838	1767.3906
22	236.4385	271.0307	310.7813	356.4432	408.8753	469.0563	538.1011	617.2783	708.0309	811.9987	931.0438	1067.2796	1223.1027	1401.2287	1604.7332	1837.0962	2102.2532	2404.6512
23	282.3618	326.2369	377.0454	435.8607	503.9166	582.6298	673.6264	778.7707	900.1993	1040.3583	1202.0465	1388.4635	1603.2645	1850.6219	2135.2951	2462.7089	2839.0418	3271.3256
24	337.0105	392.4842	457.2249	532.7501	620.8174	723.4610	843.0329	982.2511	1144.2531	1332.6586	1551.6400	1806.0026	2101.2765	2443.8209	2840.9425	3301.0300	3833.7064	4450.0029
25	402.0425	471.9811	554.2422	650.9551	764.6054	898.0916	1054.7912	1238.6363	1454.2014	1706.8031	2002.6156	2348.8033	2753.6722	3226.8436	3779.4536	4424.3801	5176.5037	6053.0039
26	479.4306	567.3773	671.6330	795.1653	941.4647	1114.6336	1319.4890	1561.6818	1847.8358	2185.7079	2584.3741	3054.4443	3608.3106	4260.4336	5027.6732	5929.6694	6989.2800	8233.0853
27	571.5224	681.8528	813.6759	971.1016	1159.0016	1383.1457	1650.3612	1968.7191	2347.7515	2798.7061	3334.8426	3971.7776	4727.8868	5624.7723	6687.8054	7946.7570	9436.5280	11197.9960
28	681.1116	819.2233	985.5479	1185.7440	1426.5719	1716.1007	2063.9515	2481.5860	2982.6443	3583.3438	4302.9470	5164.3109	6194.5318	7425.6994	8895.7812	10649.6543	12740.3128	15230.2745
29	811.5228	984.0680	1193.5129	1447.6077	1755.6835	2128.9648	2580.9394	3127.7984	3788.9583	4587.6801	5551.8016	6714.6042	8115.8366	9802.9233	11832.3890	14271.5368	17200.4222	20714.1734
30	966.7122	1181.8816	1445.1507	1767.0813	2160.4907	2640.9164	3227.1743	3942.0260	4812.9771	5873.2306	7162.8241	8729.9855	10632.7460	12940.8587	15738.0774	19124.8593	23221.5700	28172.2758

Table 4 Present Value of an Annuity Interest Factor (PVIFA): $1 per period at i% for n periods

n	1%	2%	3%	4%	5%	6%	7%	8%	9%	10%	11%	12%	13%	14%	15%	16%	17%	18%
1	0.9901	0.9804	0.9709	0.9615	0.9524	0.9434	0.9346	0.9259	0.9174	0.9091	0.9009	0.8929	0.8850	0.8772	0.8696	0.8621	0.8547	0.8475
2	1.9704	1.9416	1.9135	1.8861	1.8594	1.8334	1.8080	1.7833	1.7591	1.7355	1.7125	1.6901	1.6681	1.6467	1.6257	1.6052	1.5852	1.5656
3	2.9410	2.8839	2.8286	2.7751	2.7232	2.6730	2.6243	2.5771	2.5313	2.4869	2.4437	2.4018	2.3612	2.3216	2.2832	2.2459	2.2096	2.1743
4	3.9020	3.8077	3.7171	3.6299	3.5460	3.4651	3.3872	3.3121	3.2397	3.1699	3.1024	3.0373	2.9745	2.9137	2.8550	2.7982	2.7432	2.6901
5	4.8534	4.7135	4.5797	4.4518	4.3295	4.2124	4.1002	3.9927	3.8897	3.7908	3.6959	3.6048	3.5172	3.4331	3.3522	3.2743	3.1993	3.1272
6	5.7955	5.6014	5.4172	5.2421	5.0757	4.9173	4.7665	4.6229	4.4859	4.3553	4.2305	4.1114	3.9975	3.8887	3.7845	3.6847	3.5892	3.4976
7	6.7282	6.4720	6.2303	6.0021	5.7864	5.5824	5.3893	5.2064	5.0330	4.8684	4.7122	4.5638	4.4226	4.2883	4.1604	4.0386	3.9224	3.8115
8	7.6517	7.3255	7.0197	6.7327	6.4632	6.2098	5.9713	5.7466	5.5348	5.3349	5.1461	4.9676	4.7988	4.6389	4.4873	4.3436	4.2072	4.0776
9	8.5660	8.1622	7.7861	7.4353	7.1078	6.8017	6.5152	6.2469	5.9952	5.7590	5.5370	5.3282	5.1317	4.9464	4.7716	4.6065	4.4506	4.3030
10	9.4713	8.9826	8.5302	8.1109	7.7217	7.3601	7.0236	6.7101	6.4177	6.1446	5.8892	5.6502	5.4262	5.2161	5.0188	4.8332	4.6586	4.4941
11	10.3676	9.7868	9.2526	8.7605	8.3064	7.8869	7.4987	7.1390	6.8052	6.4951	6.2065	5.9377	5.6869	5.4527	5.2337	5.0286	4.8364	4.6560
12	11.2551	10.5753	9.9540	9.3851	8.8633	8.3838	7.9427	7.5361	7.1607	6.8137	6.4924	6.1944	5.9176	5.6603	5.4206	5.1971	4.9884	4.7932
13	12.1337	11.3484	10.6350	9.9856	9.3936	8.8527	8.3577	7.9038	7.4869	7.1034	6.7499	6.4235	6.1218	5.8424	5.5831	5.3423	5.1183	4.9095
14	13.0037	12.1062	11.2961	10.5631	9.8986	9.2950	8.7455	8.2442	7.7862	7.3667	6.9819	6.6282	6.3025	6.0021	5.7245	5.4675	5.2293	5.0081
15	13.8651	12.8493	11.9379	11.1184	10.3797	9.7122	9.1079	8.5595	8.0607	7.6061	7.1909	6.8109	6.4624	6.1422	5.8474	5.5755	5.3242	5.0916
16	14.7179	13.5777	12.5611	11.6523	10.8378	10.1059	9.4466	8.8514	8.3126	7.8237	7.3792	6.9740	6.6039	6.2651	5.9542	5.6685	5.4053	5.1624
17	15.5623	14.2919	13.1661	12.1657	11.2741	10.4773	9.7632	9.1216	8.5436	8.0216	7.5488	7.1196	6.7291	6.3729	6.0472	5.7487	5.4746	5.2223
18	16.3983	14.9920	13.7535	12.6593	11.6896	10.8276	10.0591	9.3719	8.7556	8.2014	7.7016	7.2497	6.8399	6.4674	6.1280	5.8178	5.5339	5.2732
19	17.2260	15.6785	14.3238	13.1339	12.0853	11.1581	10.3356	9.6036	8.9501	8.3649	7.8393	7.3658	6.9380	6.5504	6.1982	5.8775	5.5845	5.3162
20	18.0456	16.3514	14.8775	13.5903	12.4622	11.4699	10.5940	9.8181	9.1285	8.5136	7.9633	7.4694	7.0248	6.6231	6.2593	5.9288	5.6278	5.3527
21	18.8570	17.0112	15.4150	14.0292	12.8212	11.7641	10.8355	10.0168	9.2922	8.6487	8.0751	7.5620	7.1016	6.6870	6.3125	5.9731	5.6648	5.3837
22	19.6604	17.6580	15.9369	14.4511	13.1630	12.0416	11.0612	10.2007	9.4424	8.7715	8.1757	7.6446	7.1695	6.7429	6.3587	6.0113	5.6964	5.4099
23	20.4558	18.2922	16.4436	14.8568	13.4886	12.3034	11.2722	10.3711	9.5802	8.8832	8.2664	7.7184	7.2297	6.7921	6.3988	6.0442	5.7234	5.4321
24	21.2434	18.9139	16.9355	15.2470	13.7986	12.5504	11.4693	10.5288	9.7066	8.9847	8.3481	7.7843	7.2829	6.8351	6.4338	6.0726	5.7465	5.4509
25	22.0232	19.5235	17.4131	15.6221	14.0939	12.7834	11.6536	10.6748	9.8226	9.0770	8.4217	7.8431	7.3300	6.8729	6.4641	6.0971	5.7662	5.4669
26	22.7952	20.1210	17.8768	15.9828	14.3752	13.0032	11.8258	10.8100	9.9290	9.1609	8.4881	7.8957	7.3717	6.9061	6.4906	6.1182	5.7831	5.4804
27	23.5596	20.7069	18.3270	16.3296	14.6430	13.2105	11.9867	10.9352	10.0266	9.2372	8.5478	7.9426	7.4086	6.9352	6.5135	6.1364	5.7975	5.4919
28	24.3164	21.2813	18.7641	16.6631	14.8981	13.4062	12.1371	11.0511	10.1161	9.3066	8.6016	7.9844	7.4412	6.9607	6.5335	6.1520	5.8099	5.5016
29	25.0658	21.8444	19.1885	16.9837	15.1411	13.5907	12.2777	11.1584	10.1983	9.3696	8.6501	8.0218	7.4701	6.9830	6.5509	6.1656	5.8204	5.5098
30	25.8077	22.3965	19.6004	17.2920	15.3725	13.7648	12.4090	11.2578	10.2737	9.4269	8.6938	8.0552	7.4957	7.0027	6.5660	6.1772	5.8294	5.5168

(Contd.)

Table 4 Present Value of an Annuity Interest Factor (PVIFA): $1 per period at *i*% for *n* periods (Contd.)

n	19%	20%	21%	22%	23%	24%	25%	26%	27%	28%	29%	30%	31%	32%	33%	34%	35%	36%
1	0.8403	0.8333	0.8264	0.8197	0.8130	0.8065	0.8000	0.7937	0.7874	0.7813	0.7752	0.7692	0.7634	0.7576	0.7519	0.7463	0.7407	0.7353
2	1.5465	1.5278	1.5095	1.4915	1.4740	1.4568	1.4400	1.4235	1.4074	1.3916	1.3761	1.3609	1.3461	1.3315	1.3172	1.3032	1.2894	1.2760
3	2.1399	2.1065	2.0739	2.0422	2.0114	1.9813	1.9520	1.9234	1.8956	1.8684	1.8420	1.8161	1.7909	1.7663	1.7423	1.7188	1.6959	1.6735
4	2.6386	2.5887	2.5404	2.4936	2.4483	2.4043	2.3616	2.3202	2.2800	2.2410	2.2031	2.1662	2.1305	2.0957	2.0618	2.0290	1.9969	1.9658
5	3.0576	2.9906	2.9260	2.8636	2.8035	2.7454	2.6893	2.6351	2.5827	2.5320	2.4830	2.4356	2.3897	2.3452	2.3021	2.2604	2.2200	2.1807
6	3.4098	3.3255	3.2446	3.1669	3.0923	3.0205	2.9514	2.8850	2.8210	2.7594	2.7000	2.6427	2.5875	2.5342	2.4828	2.4331	2.3852	2.3388
7	3.7057	3.6046	3.5079	3.4155	3.3270	3.2423	3.1611	3.0833	3.0087	2.9370	2.8682	2.8021	2.7386	2.6775	2.6187	2.5620	2.5075	2.4550
8	3.9544	3.8372	3.7256	3.6193	3.5179	3.4212	3.3289	3.2407	3.1564	3.0758	2.9986	2.9247	2.8539	2.7860	2.7208	2.6582	2.5982	2.5404
9	4.1633	4.0310	3.9054	3.7863	3.6731	3.5655	3.4631	3.3657	3.2728	3.1842	3.0997	3.0190	2.9419	2.8681	2.7976	2.7300	2.6653	2.6033
10	4.3389	4.1925	4.0541	3.9232	3.7993	3.6819	3.5705	3.4648	3.3644	3.2689	3.1781	3.0915	3.0091	2.9304	2.8553	2.7836	2.7150	2.6495
11	4.4865	4.3271	4.1769	4.0354	3.9018	3.7757	3.6564	3.5435	3.4365	3.3351	3.2388	3.1473	3.0604	2.9776	2.8987	2.8236	2.7519	2.6834
12	4.6105	4.4392	4.2784	4.1274	3.9852	3.8514	3.7251	3.6059	3.4933	3.3868	3.2859	3.1903	3.0995	3.0133	2.9314	2.8534	2.7792	2.7084
13	4.7147	4.5327	4.3624	4.2028	4.0530	3.9124	3.7801	3.6555	3.5381	3.4272	3.3224	3.2233	3.1294	3.0404	2.9559	2.8757	2.7994	2.7268
14	4.8023	4.6106	4.4317	4.2646	4.1082	3.9616	3.8241	3.6949	3.5733	3.4587	3.3507	3.2487	3.1522	3.0609	2.9744	2.8923	2.8144	2.7403
15	4.8759	4.6755	4.4890	4.3152	4.1530	4.0013	3.8593	3.7261	3.6010	3.4834	3.3726	3.2682	3.1696	3.0764	2.9883	2.9047	2.8255	2.7502
16	4.9377	4.7296	4.5364	4.3567	4.1894	4.0333	3.8874	3.7509	3.6228	3.5026	3.3896	3.2832	3.1829	3.0882	2.9987	2.9140	2.8337	2.7575
17	4.9897	4.7746	4.5755	4.3908	4.2190	4.0591	3.9099	3.7705	3.6400	3.5177	3.4028	3.2948	3.1931	3.0971	3.0065	2.9209	2.8398	2.7629
18	5.0333	4.8122	4.6079	4.4187	4.2431	4.0799	3.9279	3.7861	3.6536	3.5294	3.4130	3.3037	3.2008	3.1039	3.0124	2.9260	2.8443	2.7668
19	5.0700	4.8435	4.6346	4.4415	4.2627	4.0967	3.9424	3.7985	3.6642	3.5386	3.4210	3.3105	3.2067	3.1090	3.0169	2.9299	2.8476	2.7697
20	5.1009	4.8696	4.6567	4.4603	4.2786	4.1103	3.9539	3.8083	3.6726	3.5458	3.4271	3.3158	3.2112	3.1129	3.0202	2.9327	2.8501	2.7718
21	5.1268	4.8913	4.6750	4.4756	4.2916	4.1212	3.9631	3.8161	3.6792	3.5514	3.4319	3.3198	3.2147	3.1158	3.0227	2.9349	2.8519	2.7734
22	5.1486	4.9094	4.6900	4.4882	4.3021	4.1300	3.9705	3.8223	3.6844	3.5558	3.4356	3.3230	3.2173	3.1180	3.0246	2.9365	2.8533	2.7746
23	5.1668	4.9245	4.7025	4.4985	4.3106	4.1371	3.9764	3.8273	3.6885	3.5592	3.4384	3.3254	3.2193	3.1197	3.0260	2.9377	2.8543	2.7754
24	5.1822	4.9371	4.7128	4.5070	4.3176	4.1428	3.9811	3.8312	3.6918	3.5619	3.4406	3.3272	3.2209	3.1210	3.0271	2.9386	2.8550	2.7760
25	5.1951	4.9476	4.7213	4.5139	4.3232	4.1474	3.9849	3.8342	3.6943	3.5640	3.4423	3.3286	3.2220	3.1220	3.0279	2.9392	2.8556	2.7765
26	5.2060	4.9563	4.7284	4.5196	4.3278	4.1511	3.9879	3.8367	3.6963	3.5656	3.4437	3.3297	3.2229	3.1227	3.0285	2.9397	2.8560	2.7768
27	5.2151	4.9636	4.7342	4.5243	4.3316	4.1542	3.9903	3.8387	3.6979	3.5669	3.4447	3.3305	3.2236	3.1233	3.0289	2.9401	2.8563	2.7771
28	5.2228	4.9697	4.7390	4.5281	4.3346	4.1566	3.9923	3.8402	3.6991	3.5679	3.4455	3.3312	3.2241	3.1237	3.0293	2.9404	2.8565	2.7773
29	5.2292	4.9747	4.7430	4.5312	4.3371	4.1585	3.9938	3.8414	3.7001	3.5687	3.4461	3.3317	3.2245	3.1240	3.0295	2.9406	2.8567	2.7774
30	5.2347	4.9789	4.7463	4.5338	4.3391	4.1601	3.9950	3.8424	3.7009	3.5693	3.4466	3.3321	3.2248	3.1242	3.0297	2.9407	2.8568	2.7775

Appendix

B Answers to Multiple Choice Questions

Chapter 1

1. (c) **2.** (c) **3.** (b) **4.** (a) **5.** (b)

Chapter 2

1. (c) ₹2756.25 **2.** (b) ₹7938.32 **3.** (c) ₹14876.03 **4.** (a) ₹7972

Chapter 3

1. (a) **2.** (b) **3.** (c) **4.** (c) **5.** (a) **6.** (c) **7.** (a)

Chapter 4

1. (a) **2.** (c) **3.** (b) **4.** (a) **5.** (c) **6.** (a) **7.** (b)

Chapter 5

1. (a) Risk is quantifiable while uncertainty is not quantifiable.
2. (c) NPV would decline by 30%
3. (c) Increase of 20% in initial investment
4. (b) ₹1,18,000
5. (a) 1.24
6. (c) Both of the above
7. (b) Increase the risk of the proposed project

Chapter 6

1. (c) The profitability index
2. (b) 1.33
3. (b) Project 5 (full) + project 3 (full) + project 2 (50%)
4. (a) ₹38,500
5. (c) 15.5%
6. (b) 8.57%
7. (c) ₹70,000

Chapter 7

1. (b) 2. (b) 3. (b) 4. (c) 5. (d) 6. (b) 7. (b) 8. (a) 9. (c) 10. (b)

Chapter 8

1. (d) 2. (c) 3. (c) 4. (a) 5. (b) 6. (c) 7. (b) 8. (b)

Chapter 9

1. (b) 2. (c) 3. (a) 4. (b) 5. (c) 6. (a) 7. (b) 8. (c) 9. (c) 10. (a)

Chapter 10

1. (d) 2. (c) 3. (b) 4. (c) 5. (b) 6. (b) 7. (c) 8. (a) 9. (b) 10. (b)

Chapter 11

1. (c) 2. (b) 3. (c) 4. (a) 5. (c) 6. (a) 7. (b) 8. (a)

Chapter 12

1. (b) 2. (a) 3. (c) 4. (c) 5. (b) 6. (a) 7. (c)

Chapter 13

1. (a) 2. (b) 3. (c) 4. (a) 5. (c) 6. (b) 7. (b) 8. (a)

Chapter 14

1. (c) 2. (d) 3. (a) 4. (c) 5. (b) 6. (d) 7. (c) 8. (b)

Chapter 15

1. (b) 2. (c) 3. (c) 4. (b) 5. (c) 6. (c) 7. (b)

Chapter 16

1. (b) ₹2,25,000 2. (b) ₹95,000 3. (c) ₹6 million 4. (a) ₹3 million

Chapter 17

1. (a) 2. (b) 3. (c) 4. (a) 5. (b) 6. (b) 7. (b) 8. (c) 9. (c)

Chapter 18

1. (c) 2. (c) 3. (b) 4. (d)

Appendix C

Answers to Self-Test Questions

CHAPTER 2

1. Ans.

$$TV = P(1 + r)^n$$

where,

TV = Terminal value or the amount accumulated

P = Principal amount initially deposited

r = Interest rate per annum (expressed as a decimal)

n = Number of years of the term deposit

Substituting the values:

(i) Terminal value at the end of one year:

$$= ₹40,000 \times (1.07) = ₹42,800$$

(ii) Terminal value at the end of two years:

$$= ₹40,000 \times 1.07 \times 1.07$$
$$= ₹40,000 \times 1.1449$$
$$= ₹45,796$$

(iii) Terminal value at the end of three years:

$$= ₹40,000 \times 1.07 \times 1.07 \times 1.07$$
$$= ₹40,000 \times (1.07)^3$$
$$= ₹40,000 \times 1.225043$$
$$= ₹49,001.72$$

(iv) Terminal value at the end of five years:

$$= ₹40,000 \times (1.07)^5$$
$$= ₹40,000 \times 1.402552$$
$$= ₹56,102.08$$

2. Ans.

The principal amount (P):

$$P = TV \div (1 + r)^n$$

Substituting the values:

(i) If a terminal value of ₹5,00,000 is required at the end of three years, the principal amount (P) of deposit now should be:

$$P = ₹5,00,000 \div (1.07)^3 = ₹4,08,148.94$$

(ii) If a terminal value of ₹5,00,000 is required at the end of four years, the principal amount (P) of deposit now should be:

$$P = ₹5,00,000 \div (1.07)^4 = ₹3,81,447.6$$

(iii) If a terminal value of ₹5,00,000 is required at the end of five years, the principal amount (P) of deposit now should be:

$$P = 5,00,000 \div (1.07)^5 = ₹3,56,493.1$$

3. **Ans.** To calculate the present values using the PV tables, it would be helpful to draw a table with columns as shown below:

Finding Present Values Using PV Tables

S. No.	*Future Value*	Years 'N'	Rate 'R'	*PVF (For Given 'n' And 'r')*	*Present Value*
1	25,000	1	0.11	0.90090	22,522.50
2	30,000	3	0.1	0.75131	22,539.30
3	35,000	5	0.09	0.64993	22,747.55
4	40,000	10	0.08	0.46319	18,527.60

The present values in the last column are obtained by multiplying the amount receivable (future value) by the respective 'PVF'.

CHAPTER 3

1. **Ans. Ronny Company**

(a) **Calculation of accounting rate of return** (ARR) based on 'average' investment:

Annual average profit after taxes = 40,000/5 = 8,000

Average investment = 60,000/2 = 30,000.

$$\text{ARR} = \frac{8,000}{30,000} \times 100 = 26.67\%$$

(b) **Calculation of payback period:** To calculate the payback period, we must first convert accounting profits into cash flows by adding back depreciation charged to accounting profits, as shown below.

[₹ '000]

Year >>>	1	2	3	4	5
PAT as given	20,000	20,000	10,000	–5,000	–5,000
Add back depreciation	12,000	12,000	12,000	12,000	12,000
Net cash flow	32,000	32,000	22,000	7,000	7,000

Payback period: Considering the stream of cash flows, ₹32,000 out of the total initial investment of ₹60,000 was recovered in first year. The balance investment of ₹28,000 would be recovered in approximately 28,000/32,000 = 0.88 of the second year. Hence the payback period is 1.88 years.

Conclusion: Since the project earns an ARR higher than the cut-off rate, and because the Payback period is also within the acceptable range, the company should undertake the project.

2. **Arrow Company: Calculation of ARR**

Step 1 Calculate the increase in annual profit (due to cost savings):

	(₹)
Incremental cost savings (or Profit Before Depreciation & Taxes) per annum	40,000
Less: Depreciation [(120 – 20)/5]	20,000
Earnings before taxes (EBT)	20,000
Less: Income Tax (25% × EBT)	5,000
Profit after taxes (PAT) per annum	15,000

Step 2 Average investment = [Initial Investment + Closing balance] ÷ 2

Step 3 The Accounting Rate of Return would be =

$$\frac{\text{Average annual profit after taxes}}{\frac{1}{2}\text{ of }(1{,}20{,}000+20{,}000)}=\frac{15{,}000}{70{,}000}=21.43\%$$

Conclusion: The ARR calculated above indicates that the project is acceptable.

CHAPTER 4

1. **Calculation of NPV:** To calculate payback period and NPV, we must first convert accounting profits into cash flows.

Calculation of cash flows from given profits/(losses) after depreciation and taxes:

Year >>>	1	2	3	4	5
PAT as given	30,000	30,000	20,000	–10,000	–10,000
Add back depreciation	15,000	15,000	15,000	15,000	15,000
Net cash flow	45,000	45,000	35,000	5,000	5,000
PVF at 15%	0.8696	0.7561	0.6575	0.5718	0.4972
PV of CFs	39,132	34,024.5	23,012.5	2,859	2,486

Total PV of future CFs = ₹1,01,514

NPV = PV of future CFs – Initial Investment

= ₹1,01,514 – 75,000 = +26,514.

The proposal is acceptable as its NPV is positive.

2.

Saaz Company investment proposal

Years	0	1	2	3	4
Initial investment	–2,00,000	0	0	0	0
Profit after tax given		40,000	40,000	40,000	–20,000
Add back depreciation charged		35,000	35,000	35,000	35,000
Working capital recovered		0	0	0	60,000
Net cash flow	–2,00,000	75,000	75,000	75,000	75,000
Annuity PV factor [n = 1 to 4, r = 16%]	2.7982				
Total PV of CFs [75,000 × 2.7982]	2,09,865				
Less: Initial investment	2,00,000				
NPV @ 16%	9,865				

As the NPV is positive, the proposal is acceptable. However, as the NPV is quite small, there is not much margin of error. Therefore, the company should analyze the proposal's risk profile and undertake it carefully to avoid or minimize risk.

3. **Ans.**

Grace Company—ARR and NPV

Years	0	1	2	3	4	5
Savings or Profit before depreciation & taxes	–1,00,000	30,000	30,000	30,000	30,000	30,000
Less: Depreciation [(100 – 10)/5	0	18,000	18,000	18,000	18,000	18,000
Earnings before taxes (EBT)	0	12,000	12,000	12,000	12,000	12,000
Less: Income Tax (25% × EBT)	0	3,000	3,000	3,000	3,000	3,000
Profit after taxes (PAT)	0	9,000	9,000	9,000	9,000	9,000
Add back depreciation	0	18,000	18,000	18,000	18,000	18,000
Cash flow from operations	0	27,000	27,000	27,000	27,000	27,000
Add salvage value	0	0	0	0	0	10,000
Net cash flow	–1,00,000	27,000	27,000	27,000	27,000	37,000
PV factor @ 12%	1.0000	0.8929	0.7972	0.7118	0.6355	0.5674
Present value of cash flows	–1,00,000	24,108.3	21,524.4	19,218.6	17,158.5	20,993.8

(a) **The ARR is** = $\dfrac{\text{Average annual profit after taxes}}{\frac{1}{2}\text{ of }(1{,}00{,}000+10{,}000)} = \dfrac{9{,}000}{55{,}000} = 16.37\%$

(b) **Net Present Value** = Total PV of Cash Flows – Initial Investment = **₹3,003.6**

Conclusion: Both ARR and NPV indicate acceptance of the proposal even though between ARR and NPV methods, NPV is certainly more reliable. Since the NPV of the proposed project is positive, it is acceptable. However, the margin of error is very thin due to a small amount of NPV. Hence, the project should be undertaken carefully to avoid risk.

CHAPTER 5

1. **Ans.** Safex Company

(a) **Calculation of the Project's NPV:** Note that since there are no income taxes involved, there is no need to consider the depreciation. Therefore, we can use the cash flows as given to calculate the NPV as follows:

NPV calculation: Safex company

Year	*Item*	*Cash flow* (₹)	*PVF @ 15%*	*Present value* (₹)
0	Plant and equip	–2,50,000	1.0000	–2,50,000
1 to 3	Revenue	4,00,000	2.2832	9,13,280
1 to 3	Variable cost	–2,40,000	2.2832	–5,47,968
1 to 3	Fixed cost	–40,000	2.2832	–91,328
3	Scrap value	50,000	0.6575	32,875
				Net Present Value = 56,859

(b) **Percentage change required in the initial investment for the investment decision to change:** In order to change the investment decision, the entire NPV should be eroded. That will happen when the initial investment increases by an amount greater than ₹56,859. In percentage, therefore, the initial investment would need to increase by more than:

$$\%\text{Increase in Initial Investment} = \frac{\text{NPV}}{\text{Initial Investment}} \times 100$$

$$= \frac{56{,}859}{2{,}50{,}000} \times 100 = 22.74\%$$

Thus the initial investment would need to increase by more than 22.74% for the decision to change.

(c) **Percentage change required in variable cost for the investment decision to change:** In order to change the investment decision, the NPV should decline by ₹56,859. That will happen when the 'present value' of variable cost increases by an amount greater than ₹56,859. In percentage terms, therefore, the 'present value' of variable cost increase would need to rise by more than:

$$= \frac{\text{NPV}}{\text{Present Value of annual variable cost}} \times 100$$

$$= \frac{56{,}859}{5{,}47{,}968} \times 100 = 10.38\%$$

(d) **Percentage change required in fixed cost for the investment decision to change:** In order to change the investment decision, the NPV should decline by ₹56,859. That will happen when the 'present value' of the annual fixed cost increases by an amount greater than ₹56,859. In percentage terms, therefore, the 'present value' of fixed cost would need to rise by more than:

$$= \frac{\text{NPV}}{\text{Present Value of annual fixed cost}} \times 100$$

$$= \frac{56{,}859}{91{,}328} \times 100 = 62.26\%$$

Conclusion: Presenting the percentage changes in the three estimates that would be required for the investment decision to change:

S.No.	*Variable*	*% Change in estimate needed to change decision*
1	Initial investment	22.74%
3	Variable cost	10.38%
4	Fixed cost	62.26%

From the above it is clear that, among the three items considered, the calculated NPV is most vulnerable to changes in the variable cost: the margin of safety being just 10.38%. Similarly, the initial investment required is also a crucial factor though the margin of safety here is better than variable cost. The management should manage these items carefully and take precautions to ensure minimum variability in these items.

2. **Ans. Gardenia Company**

Three Level Estimates: Gardenia Company

Year	*PVF @*	*Optimistic*		*Most likely*		*Pessimistic*	
	12%	*Cash flow*	*PV*	*Cash flow*	*PV*	*Cash flow*	*PV*
0	1.0000	–2,25,000	–2,25,000	–2,50,000	–2,50,000	–2,75,000	–2,75,000
1	0.8929	1,40,000	1,25,006	1,30,000	1,16,077	1,20,000	1,07,148
2	0.7972	1,30,000	1,03,636	1,20,000	95,664	1,10,000	87,692
3	0.7118	1,10,000	78,298	1,00,000	71,180	90,000	64,062
	NPV		81,940		32,921		–16,098

Summary of the results

Type of estimate	*NPV*
Optimistic	81,940
Most likely	32,921
Pessimistic	–16,098

The NPV is positive in the most likely (normal) scenario and much higher in the optimistic scenario, which indicates that the project should be undertaken. However, considering the range of NPVs makes it clear that a downside is possible in the pessimistic scenario. Given this additional information, the management should proceed with the project only if it is not risk-averse. Also, the management should work on contingency plans and all efforts should be made to ensure that the pessimistic scenario can be avoided.

3. **Ans. Rose Company**

(a) **Determine the expected values of cash flows:** The expected value of cash flow is the probability-weighted average of all possible cash flows.

	Worst case	*Likely*	*Best case*	*Expected*
Year	*Scenario probability × cash flow*			*Value of CF*
0	0.25(–2,50,000)	0.5(–2,50,000)	0.25(–2,50,000)	–2,50,000
1	0.25(60,000)	0.5(80,000)	0.25(1,00,000)	80,000
2	0.25(60,000)	0.5(80,000)	0.25(1,00,000)	80,000
3	0.25(60,000)	0.5(80,000)	0.25(1,00,000)	80,000
4	0.25(60,000)	0.5(80,000)	0.25(1,00,000)	80,000
4	0.25(40,000)	0.5(60,000)	0.25(80,000)	60,000

(b) **Calculation of expected net present value**

Year	*Cash flow*	*PVF@12%*	*Present Value*
0	–2,50,000	1.0000	–2,50,000
1	80,000	0.8929	71,432
2	80,000	0.7972	63,776
3	80,000	0.7118	56,944
4	80,000	0.6355	50,840
4	60,000	0.6355	381,30
			NPV = 31,122

The positive expected NPV indicates that the project is acceptable.

(c) **Calculation of best case NPV**

Year	*Cash flow*	*PVF@12%*	*Present Value*
0	–2,50,000	1.0000	–2,50,000
1	1,00,000	0.8929	89,290
2	1,00,000	0.7972	79,720
3	1,00,000	0.7118	71,180
4	1,00,000	0.6355	63,550
4	80,000	0.6355	50,840
			NPV = 1,04,580

(d) **Calculation of worst case NPV**

Year	*Cash flow*	*PVF@12%*	*Present Value*
0	–2,50,000	1.0000	–2,50,000
1	60,000	0.8929	53,574
2	60,000	0.7972	47,832
3	60,000	0.7118	42,708
4	60,000	0.6355	38,130
4	40,000	0.6355	25,420
			NPV = –42,336

(e) **NPV in most likely scenario**

Year	*Cash flow*	*PVF@12%*	*Present Value*
0	–2,50,000	1.0000	–2,50,000
1	80,000	0.8929	71,432
2	80,000	0.7972	63,776
3	80,000	0.7118	56,944
4	80,000	0.6355	50,840
4	60,000	0.6355	38,130
			NPV = 31122

Presenting the results of three scenarios:

Scenario	*NPV*	*Probability*
Best-case	1,04,580	0.25
Most likely	31,122	0.50
Worst-case	–42,336	0.25

The expected NPV can also be calculated by extending the above table, as follows:

Scenario	*NPV*	*Probability*	*Product*
Best-case	1,04,580	0.25	26,145
Most likely	31,122	0.50	15,561
Worst-case	–42,336	0.25	–10,584
			NPV = 31,122

Standard deviation of the NPV: The following statistical formula can be used to compute the standard deviation of the NPV:

$$\sigma\text{NPV} = \sqrt{\sum_{i=1}^{n} \text{Pi}(\text{NPVi} - \text{Expected NPV})^2}$$

Using the scenario NPVs and their probabilities, and the expected NPV of ₹31,122, we have:

$$\sigma\text{NPV} = \sqrt{[0.25(1{,}04{,}580 - 31{,}122)^2 + 0.50(31{,}122 - 31{,}122)^2 + 0.25(-42{,}336 - 31{,}122)^2]}$$
$$= 51{,}943$$

Coefficient of variation can be calculated as follows:

$$\text{CV of NPV} = \frac{\sigma\text{NPV}}{\text{EV of NPV}}$$
$$= \frac{51{,}943}{31{,}122}$$
$$= 1.67$$

To evaluate the relative riskiness of the proposed project, the calculated coefficient of variation of 1.67 for the proposed project would be compared with the average coefficient of variation of other projects undertaken by the firm. Assuming other projects have an average coefficient of variation of 1.0, the coefficient of variation of 1.70 would mean the proposed project is relatively risky.

Dependence of cash flows over time and the probability of getting the worst cash flows

If the cash flows are **perfectly correlated over time**, the probability of getting the worst case is 0.25 itself, because if the first year cash flows are low, the subsequent years' cash flows would also be low.

If the cash flows are **independent over time**, if the first year cash flows are low, yet the subsequent years' cash flows could be low or high. Then the probability of getting low cash flows in all years or getting the worst case is = 0.25 × 0.25 × 0.25 × 0.25 = 0.0039.

Conclusion: The standard deviation and coefficient of variation show the project is risky. However, motivated by the prospects of making a high positive NPV of ₹1,04,580 in the best-case scenario and because the probability of getting the worst-case scenario is less than 1% (assuming the cash flows are independent over time), the management may decide to embrace the higher risk and undertake the project. It should also put in place the strategies required to avoid the worst-case scenario as far as possible.

4. **Ans. Prohealth Company**

Prohealth Company Decision Tree (₹ in '000)

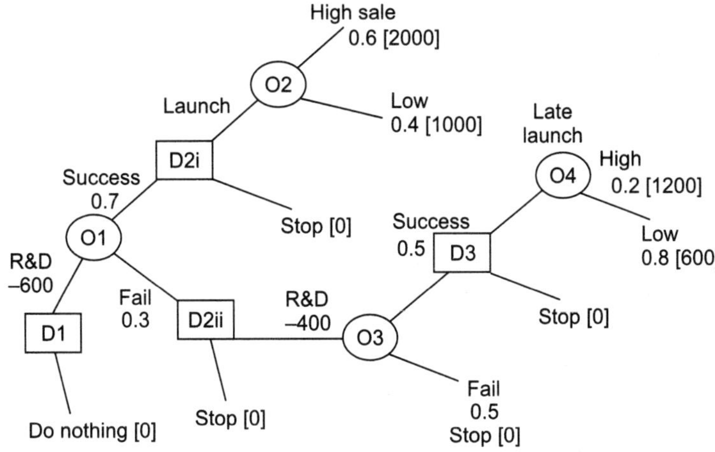

Note: Figures in brackets [ ] show cash flows.

Explanation:

- Decision boxes D1 to D3 show the points at which the firm has to choose between alternative courses of action.
- Outcome boxes 'O1 to O4' show the possible outcomes of the decisions taken along with probabilities.
- The (present values of) cash inflows have also been inserted with each possible outcome and its probability.

Now, we can take steps to analyze the investment decision using the expected values of possible outcomes. For this purpose, we use the roll-back technique starting calculations from right side of the tree and moving to the left side until we find the expected NPV at decision point D1.

(a) **Find the expected value at outcome point 'O2'** as follows:

Outcome of product launch	*Cash flow (₹)*	*Probability*	*Product [CF × prob]*
High sales	20,00,000	0.6	12,00,000
Low sales	10,00,000	0.4	4,00,000
Expected value			16,00,000

(b) **At decision point D2(i), the firm should decide** as follows:
Expected value if product launched = ₹16,00,000
Expected value if product Not launched= ₹Nil
Gain by launching the product = ₹16,00,000.

Hence, if the initial R&D is successful, the firm should launch the product because the expected value of launching (₹16,00,000) far exceeds the expected value of not launching (cash flow = nil).

(c) **Find the expected value at outcome point 'O4'** as follows:

Outcome of late launch	*Expected value of cash flow*	*Probability*	*Product [EV of CF × prob]*
High sale	12,00,000	0.2	2,40,000
Low sale	6,00,000	0.8	4,80,000
Expected value			7,20,000

(d) **At decision point D3, the firm should decide** as follows:
Expected value if product late-launched = ₹7,20,000
Expected value if product NOT launched = ₹Nil
Gain by launching the product = ₹7,20,000

Therefore, if the extended R&D is successful, it is better to market the product late than not launching it at all.

(e) **Find the expected value at outcome point 'O3'** as follows:

Outcome of extended R&D	*Expected value of cash flow*	*Probability*	*Product [EV of CF × prob]*
Success	7,20,000	0.5	3,60,000
Failure	0	0.5	0
Expected value			3,60,000

(f) **At decision point D(ii), the firm would decide** as follows:
Expected value if R&D successful = ₹3,60,000
Investment required for extended R&D = ₹–4,00,000
Net loss by extending the R&D = ₹–40,000

Therefore, if the initial R&D is a failure, the firm should abandon the project rather than investing a further ₹4,00,000 in extended R&D as it result in losses.

(g) **Find the expected value at outcome point 'O1'** as follows:

Outcome of initial R&D	*Cash flow (₹)*	*Probability*	*Product [CF × Prob]*
Success	16,00,000	0.7	11,20,000
Failure	0	0.3	0
Expected value			11,20,000

(h) **Finally, at decision point D1, the firm should decide** as follows:
Expected value if R&D launched = ₹11,20,000
Expected value if R&D Not launched = ₹Nil
Net cash inflow if R&D launched = ₹11,20,000
Less: Investment required to start R&D = ₹–6,00,000
Net Present Value of the project = ₹5,20,000

Conclusion: Since the NPV is positive, it is advised that the firm should undertake the initial R&D. The sequence of decisions should be to invest in the R&D project; if the initial R&D is successful, the firm should launch the product. If initial research fails, the project should be abandoned.

CHAPTER 6

1. **Ans.**

(a) **Calculate the NPV and profitability index of the proposals.**

The given cash inflows of years 1 and 2 form an annuity, so we can use the present value factor (PVF) of annuity at 15% to find out the present values of cash inflows before proceeding to compute the NPVs and PIs. Present Value factor for n = 2, r = 15% is 1.6257. [See present value tables in the Annexure at the end of the book.]

Project	*Initial outflow*	*Cash inflow per annum [year1-2]*	*Annuity PVF @15%*	*Present value of CF*	*NPV*	*PI*
1	80,000	59,000	1.6257	95,916	15,916	1.20
2	50,000	40,600	1.6257	66,003	16,003	1.32
3	60,000	53,500	1.6257	86,975	26,975	1.45
4	70,000	64,600	1.6257	1,05,020	35,020	1.50
5	40,000	32,000	1.6257	52,022	12,022	1.30
6	20,000	17,000	1.6257	27,637	7,637	1.38

(b) **Rank the proposals in descending order of the profitability index.**

Projects would be ranked on the descending order of PI as follows:

Project	*Initial outflow*	*NPV*	*PI*	*Rank*
1	80,000	15,916	1.20	6
2	50,000	16,003	1.32	4
3	60,000	26,975	1.45	2
4	70,000	35,020	1.50	1
5	40,000	12,022	1.30	5
6	20,000	7,637	1.38	3

(c) **Select the combination of projects that would maximize the NPV assuming all projects are divisible:** Assuming projects are divisible, the investment budget of ₹20,000 would be allocated as follows:

Project	*Initial outflow*	*NPV*	*PI*	*Rank*
4 [full]	70,000	35,020	1.50	1
3 [5/6]	50,000	22,479	1.45	2
Total	**1,20,000**	**57,499**		

Thus if projects are divisible, project number 4 would be taken up in full along with 5/6 of project 3 to fully utilize the investment budget and get a NPV of ₹57,499.

(d) **Select the combination of projects that would maximize the NPV assuming all projects are indivisible.**

Knowing that the projects are indivisible, the company would try out different combinations to exhaust the investment limit as well as maximize the collective NPV. Since the company can either take a project in entirety or leave it, the available combinations of full projects would be:

Projects combined	*Combined investment*	*Combined NPV*
1 + 5	1,20,000	27,938
3 + 5 + 6	1,20,000	46,634
2 + 4	1,20,000	51,023

Considering the possible combinations, it would be advisable for the company to undertake the projects 2 + 4 because this combination provides higher NPV than other combinations. This combination would exhaust the investment budget, though the aggregate NPV would not be as high as it would have been if the projects had been divisible.

2. **Ans.**

1. Calculate the NPV of the project using real cash flows and cost of capital.

The cash flows are already given in real terms without the effect of inflation. The given cost of capital is in money terms that can be converted into real cost of capital as follows:

$$(1 + r) = (1 + 0.14) \div (1 + 0.05555)$$
$$= 1.08$$

Then $r = 0.08$ or 8% approximately.

Using the real cost of capital of 8%, we calculate the project's NPV as follows:

Year	*Cash flow*	*PVF@8%*	*PV*
0	–60,000	1.0000	–60,000
1	20,000	0.9259	18,518
2	20,000	0.8573	17,146
3	20,000	0.7938	15,876
4	20,000	0.7350	14,700
			NPV = 6,240

2. Calculate the NPV of the project using money (nominal) cash flows and cost of capital.

In order to evaluate the project in terms of money (nominal) cash flows and cost of capital, the given 'real' cash flows will have to be first converted into nominal cash flows by increasing them at 5.555% annual compound rate to include the effect of inflation. Allowing for some approximation (due to rounding off), the net present value would be calculated as follows:

Year	*Cash flow*	*Nominal cash flows (increased @ 5.555% P.A.*	*PVF @14%*	*PV*
0	–60,000	–60,000	1.0000	–60,000
1	20,000	21,111	0.8772	18,517
2	20,000	22,284	0.7695	17,147
3	20,000	23,522	0.6750	15,876
4	20,000	24,828	0.5921	14,700
				NPV* = 6,240

Note * Small difference may arise due to rounding off.

As this example shows, the two approaches should give the same results provided the same rate of inflation is applied to all variables. Therefore, if the adjustment for inflation is made, it should be made for the cash flows as well the cost of capital. Otherwise, both these elements can be taken on 'real' terms for project evaluation.

3. **Ans.** For each machine, first calculate the present value of costs during the life-cycle of the machine and then divide the result by the appropriate annuity PV factor.

Machine—Alpha

Items	*Years*	*Cash flow* (₹)	*PVF @12%*	*Present Value* (₹)
Machine price	0	1,00,000	1.0000	1,00,000
Annual repairs	1–10	8,000	5.6502	45,202
Operating cost	1–10	10,000	5.6502	56,502
Trade-in value*	10	–15,000	0.3220	–4,830
				Total PV = 1,96,874
Annuity PV factor [n = 10, r = 12%]				5.6502
Annualized equivalent cost = 1,96,874/5.6502 =				34,844

To own and use Machine—Alpha will cost the company a sum of ₹34,844 per year.

Machine—Gamma

Items	*Years*	*Cash flow* (₹)	*PVF @ 2%*	*Present Value* (₹)
Machine price	0	60,000	1.0000	60,000
Annual repairs	1–5	12,000	3.6048	43,258
Operating cost	1–5	16,000	3.6048	57,677
Trade-in value*	5	–8,000	0.5674	–4,539
				Total PV = 1,56,395
Annuity PV factor [n = 10, r = 12%]				3.6048
Annualized equivalent cost = 1,56,395/3.6048 =				43,385

To own and use Machine—Gama will cost the company a sum of ₹43,385 per year. Therefore, Machine—Alpha should be preferred because it has lower equivalent annual cost of owning and running the machine.

4. **Ans.** For each replacement cycle, first calculate the present value of costs during a single cycle and then divide the result by the appropriate annuity PV factor, as follows:

Replace every two years

	Year 0	*Year 1*	*Year 2*
Price	–80,000		
Maintenance		–10,000	–10,000
Trade-in value			40,000
Net cash flows	–80,000	–10,000	30,000
PV factor @10%	1	0.9091	0.8264
Present value	–80,000	–9,091	24,792
			NPV = –64,299
Annuity PV factor (APVF)			1.7355
Equivalent annual cost = NPV/APVF			–37,049

To replace the air-conditioners every two years the company would have to set aside a sum of ₹37,049 per year.

Replace every three years

	Year 0	*Year 1*	*Year 2*	*Year 3*
Price	–80,000			
Maintenance		–10,000	–10,000	–10,000
Trade-in value				30,000
Net cash flows	–80,000	–10,000	–10,000	20,000
PV factor @10%	1	0.9091	0.9091	0.7513
Present Value	–80,000	–9,091	–9,091	15,026
				NPV = –82,329
Annuity PV factor (APVF)				2.4869
Equivalent annual cost = NPV/APVF				–33,105

To replace the air-conditioners every three years, the company would have to set aside a sum of ₹33,105 per year. Thus replacing the air-conditioners every three years is more economical than replacing them every two years.

Replace every four years

	Year 0	*Year 1*	*Year 2*	*Year 3*	*Year 4*
Price	–80,000				
Maintenance		–10,000	–10,000	–10,000	–10,000
Trade-in value					10,000
Overhaul/Servicing					–20,000
Net cash flows	–80,000	–10,000	–10,000	–10,000	–20,000
PV factor @ 10%	1	0.9091	0.9091	0.7531	0.683
Present Value	–80,000	–9,091	–9,091	–7531	–13,660
					NPV = –1,18,528
Annuity PV factor (APVF)					3.1699
Equivalent annual cost = NPV/APVF					–37,392

To replace the air-conditioners every four years, the company would have to set aside a sum of ₹37,392 per year. Thus, replacing the air-conditioners every four years is more expensive than replacing them every three years. Therefore, the optimal replacement period for air-conditioners would be every three years as this replacement cycle gives the company least equivalent annual cost.

5. **Ans.**

(a) **Calculate the NPV assuming it is an all equity funded project:**

Annual cash inflow in perpetuity = ₹59,000
Cost of equity = 0.20
Present value of the cash inflows = ₹59,000 ÷ 0.20 = 2,95,000.
Net present value = ₹2,95,000 – 3,00,000
= –₹5,000.

The project would be rejected if it was an all equity funded project due to a negative NPV. The high cost of equity is used as the discount rate that has heavily discounted the cash flows resulting in a negative NPV. However, the company plans to finance 50% of the initial investment by debt funding which will bring in some tax benefits as follows.

(b) **Calculate the present value of tax-shield on interest expense:**

Amount of debt funding in the project = ₹3,00,000 × 50% = 1,50,000
Rate of interest per annum = 13%
Annual interest payable = ₹19,500
Tax-shield on interest expense @30% = ₹19,500 × 30% = 5,850
Present value of tax-shield in perpetuity = 5,850 ÷ 0.13 = 45,000.

(c) **Adjusted Present Value (APV)**

= All equity NPV + PV of tax-shield
= –₹5,000 + 45,000
= ₹40,000.

Since the adjusted present value is positive, the project is acceptable.

CHAPTER 7

1. $E(R_i) = \sum_{i=1}^{n}$ (Probability of Return under each scenario) × (Estimated Return under each scenario)

$E(R)$ = 10% × 50% + 50% × 40% + (–40%) × 10% = 21%

Scenario	*Probability*	*Price*	*Return*
Normal	50%	330	10%
Boom	40%	450	50%
Recession	10%	180	–40%
Expected return			21%

2. $$\text{GMHPR} = \sqrt[N]{(1+\text{HPR}_1)\times(1+\text{HPR}_2)\times\cdots\times(1+\text{HPR}_n)} - 1$$

$$\text{AMHPR} = \frac{\text{HPR}_1 + \text{HPR}_2 + \cdots + \text{HPR}_n}{N}$$

Year	*Endowment portfolio yearly returns*	*Benchmark index yearly returns*
2010	14%	10%
2011	21%	25%
2012	–17%	–24%
2013	4%	1%
2014	–6%	–3%
AMHPR	3.2%	1.8%
GMHPR	2.3%	0.5%

3. $$\sigma^2 = \left[\frac{1}{N}\sum_{i=1}^{n}[\text{HPR}_i - \overline{\text{HPR}}]^2\right]$$

$$\sigma = \sqrt{\frac{1}{N}\sum_{i=1}^{n}[\text{HPR}_i - \overline{\text{HPR}}]^2}$$

Year	*ITC Ltd*	*Vijaya Bank*
2007	23%	–24%
2008	22%	40%
2009	–20%	–52%
2010	46%	59%
2011	23%	76%
Variance	4.54%	24.52%
Standard Deviation	21.30%	49.52%

Note: In excel spreadsheet, variance and standard deviation can also be directly calculated using function VARP() and STDEVP() respectively

4. **Portfolio Risk**

$$\sigma_P^2 = w_A^2 \times \sigma_A^2 + w_B^2 \times \sigma_B^2 + 2 \times w_A \times w_B \times \rho_{A,B} \times \sigma_A \times \sigma_B$$

$$\sigma_P^2 = (0.4)^2 \times 0.0106 + (0.6)^2 \times 0.0515 + 2 \times 0.6 \times 0.4 \times 0.1031 \times 0.2269 \times 0.98$$
$$= 0.0312 \text{ or } 3.12\%$$

5.

Scenario	*Investment A expected return*	*Prob.*	*Squared deviations*	*Prob. *Squared deviations*
Scenario 1	41%	0.2	6.605%	1.321%
Scenario 2	23%	0.1	0.593%	0.059%
Scenario 3	–10%	0.3	6.401%	1.920%
Scenario 4	–6%	0.1	4.537%	0.454%
Scenario 5	28%	0.3	1.613%	0.484%
Expected return		**15.3%**		
Variance				4.238%
Standard deviation				20.59%
CV				1.35

Scenario	*Investment B expected return*	*Prob.*	*Squared deviations*	*Prob. *Squared deviations*
Scenario 1	13%	0.2	0.578%	0.116%
Scenario 2	11%	0.1	0.314%	0.031%
Scenario 3	–10%	0.3	2.372%	0.711%
Scenario 4	–4%	0.1	0.884%	0.088%
Scenario 5	17%	0.3	1.346%	0.404%
Expected return		**5.4%**		
Variance				1.350%
Standard deviation				11.62%
CV				2.15

On the basis of CV, Investment A is better. Lower the CV, lower the risk per unit of return

6. **Portfolio return**

$$R_p = w_A \times R_A + w_B \times R_B$$
$$R_p = 0.3 \times 6\% + 0.7 \times 0.60\% = 2.22\%$$

Portfolio risk

$$\sigma_P^2 = w_A^2 \times \sigma_A^2 + w_B^2 \times \sigma_B^2 + 2 \times w_A \times w_B \times \rho_{A,B} \times \sigma_A \times \sigma_B$$

$$\sigma_P^2 = (0.3)^2 \times 0.1328 + (0.7)^2 \times 0.1645 + 2 \times 0.3 \times 0.7 \times 0.3645 \times 0.4056 \times 0.89 = 0.1475 \text{ or } 14.75\%$$

7.

Scenario	*GDP*	*Return of DLF stock*	*Probability*
Flat GDP Growth	7%	10%	25%
GDP growth is 3% Points above last year	10%	17.50%	35%
GDP growth is 2% Points below last year	5%	5%	40%
Expected return			**10.63%**

8. $$\sigma_P^2 = w_A^2 \times \sigma_A^2 + w_B^2 \times \sigma_B^2 + w_C^2 \times \sigma_C^2 + 2 \times w_A \times w_B \times \rho_{A,B} \times \sigma_A \times \sigma_B + 2 \times w_B \times w_C \times \rho_{B,C} \times \sigma_B \times \sigma_C + 2 \times w_C \times w_A \times \rho_{C,A} \times \sigma_C \times \sigma_A$$

$$\sigma_P^2 = (0.4)^2 \times 1.70\% + (0.35)^2 \times 0.68\% + (0.25)^2 \times 0.58\% + 2 \times 0.4 \times 0.35 \times (-0.52) \times 13.04\% \times 8.23\% + 2 \times 0.35 \times 0.25 \times (0.40) \times 8.23\% \times 7.60\% + 2 \times 0.25 \times 0.4 \times (-0.32) \times 13.04\% \times 7.60\% = 0.22\%$$

Similarly Portfolio Standard Deviation (σ) = $\sqrt{0.22\%}$ = 4.65%

CHAPTER 8

1.

Portfolio	*Returns*	*Standard deviation*
Risky securities portfolio	10%	8%
Risk Free Asset	7%	–

Portfolio Return = Weight of the risky assets × return of the risky assets + Weight of the risk-free asset × return of the risk-free asset

Portfolio risk on combining the risky assets with a risk-free asset can be determined as:

$$\sigma^2_{P(Risky,Risk\text{-}free)} = w^2_{Risky} \times \sigma^2_{Risky} + w^2_{Risk\text{-}free} \times \sigma^2_{Risk\text{-}free} + 2 \times w_{Risky} \times w_{Risk\text{-}free} \times \rho_{Risky,Risk\text{-}free} \times \sigma_{Risky} \times \sigma_{Risk\text{-}free}$$

Given that Variance (or Standard Deviation) for a risk-free security is zero,

$$\sigma^2_{P(Risky,Risk\text{-}free)} = w^2_{Risky} \times \sigma^2_{Risky}$$

Portfolio Standard Deviation = $\sigma_{P(Risky, Risk\text{-}free)} = w_{Risky} \times \sigma_{Risky}$

Portfolio Return = 0.70 × 10% + 0.30 × 7% = 9.1%

Portfolio Standard Deviation = 0.7 × 8% = 5.6%

2.

Month	Stock returns	Benchmark index returns
1	18%	12%
2	27%	12%
3	–12%	–28%
4	–4%	–1%
5	16%	5%
Variance (Market Returns)	Var()	2.75%
Covariance (Stock Returns, Market Returns)	COVAR()	1.92%

Beta = Covariance (Stock Returns, Market Returns)/Variance (Market Returns)
= 1.92%/2.75% = 0.70

3. Expected Return as per SML = Risk Free Rate + (Equity Risk Premium) × Beta
Expected Return = 7% + 5% × 1.2 = 13%

Since the analyst expected return of 18% is greater than the SML determined return, the stock lies above the Security market line and is undervalued.

4.

Month	BGS Stock returns	Benchmark index returns
1	12%	15%
2	17%	18%
3	32%	19%
4	–41%	–19%
5	–14%	–5%

Beta = Slope (Stock Returns, Benchmark Index Returns) = 1.68

Adjusted beta = Regressed Beta × 0.67 + Market Beta × 0.33

Adjusted beta = 1.68 × 0.67 + 1 × 0.33 = 1.45

CHAPTER 9

1. $C = 14$, FV = 100, $n = 3$ and $k_d = 12\%$
Value of bond is ₹104.80

$$V_B = \frac{14}{(1.12)^1} + \frac{14}{(1.12)^2} + \frac{14}{(1.12)^3} + \frac{100}{(1.12)^3} = ₹104.80$$

2. FV = 1,000, $C = 80$, $V_B = 970$, $n = 8$
YTM is 8.54%

$$\text{YTM} = \frac{C + (\text{FV} - V_B)/n}{(\text{FV} + 2 * V_B)/3} = \frac{80 + (1{,}000 - 970)/8}{(1{,}000 + 2 * 970)/3} = 8.54\%$$

3. (a) Value of bond is ₹925.9

$$V_B = \frac{1,000}{(1.08)^1} = ₹925.9$$

(b) 10.57%

4. (a) ₹1,113.0
(b) ₹10,000

5. (a) Annually

FV = 1,000, C = 120, n = 5 years, k_d = 10%
V_B = ₹1,075.82

(b) Semi-annually

FV = 1,000, C = 60, n = 10, k_d = 5%
V_B = ₹1,077.72

(c) Quarterly

FV = 1,000, C = 30, n = 20, K_d = 2.5%
V_B = ₹1,077.95

6. (a) Annual yield = 5/95 = 5.26%
(b) 5%
(c) 4.55%

7. We need to first find the value of the bond when it is not called. It is a semi-annual bond. Thus, we need to use the below given formula

$$V_B = \sum_{i=1}^{2n} \frac{C/2}{(1 + k_d/2)^{2n}} + \frac{FV}{(1 + k_d/2)^{2n}}$$

n = 20, Annual coupon = 100, FV = 1,000, k_d = 9.50% annual

$$V_B = \sum_{i=1}^{40} \frac{100/2}{(1 + 0.095/2)^i} + \frac{1,000}{(1 + 0.095/2)^{40}} = ₹1,044.4$$

If it is called in 12 years, we can find the YTC with the following information:

n = 12 × 2 = 24, C = 100/2 = 50, V_B = 1044.4 and call price = 1150

$$V_B = \sum_{i=1}^{n} \frac{C}{(1 + \text{YTC})^n} + \frac{\text{Call price}}{(1 + \text{YTC})^n}$$

$$1044.4 = \sum_{i=1}^{24} \frac{50}{(1 + \text{YTC})^i} + \frac{1,150}{(1 + \text{YTC})^{24}}$$

Solving for YTC, we get

YTC = 5.01%

8. Inflation = 1.23% – 0.80% = 0.53%

CHAPTER 10

1. According to Gordon Growth Model, intrinsic value of stock can be calculated as:

$$P_0 = \frac{D_0(1+g)}{(k-g)} \text{ OR } \frac{D_1}{(k-g)}$$

where

P_0 = The present or intrinsic value of the stock
D = Dividends per share
g = Constant growth rate in dividends
k = The required rate of return on the stock

Dividends = Earnings per share × Dividend payout ratio = 15 × 30% = 4.5

g can be determined using Return on Equity (ROE) and Retention ratio

Return on Equity = EPS/BVPS = 15/120 = 12.5%
Retention Ratio = 100% – Dividend Payout Ratio = 70%
g = 12.5% × 70% = 8.75%

Required Rate of Return or cost of equity (k) = Risk Free Rate + (Equity Risk Premium) × Beta

Required Rate of Return = 9% + 7% × 1.2 = 17.4%
P_0 = 4.5 × (1 + .0875)/(17.4% – 8.75%) = 12.57

2.

	(₹ *in crores*)
Net profit for the current year	2,000
Capital expenditure for the year	400
Increase in working capital	100
Debt issue	200
Debt repayment	100
Depreciation expense	50

FCFE = Net profit or Net income
+ Depreciation and amortization (non-cash charges)
–/+Investment in Non-Cash Working Capital
– Capital Expenditure (Investment in Long-term Assets)
+ Increase in Net debt (Issue of new debt-repayment of older debt)

FCFE = 2,000 + 50 – 100 – 400 + 200 – 100 = 1,650

3.

Company	*Price*	*EPS for past year*	*EPS for next year*	*Trailing P/E Ratio*	*Forward P/E Ratio*
Zylo Software	100	10	12	10.0x	8.3x
Nita Tech	290	80	95	3.6x	3.1x
Super Tech	12	1.5	2	8.0x	6.0x
Jeet Software	1,000	260	250	3.8x	4.0x
Amba Tech	650	120	150	5.4x	4.3x
Alfa Tech	24	5	8	4.8x	3.0x
Mean P/E Multiple				5.9x	4.8x
Median P/E Multiple				5.1x	4.2x

Company	*Price*	*EPS for past year*	*EPS for next year*	*Trailing P/E Ratio*	*Forward P/E Ratio*
Raj Software	150	22	25	6.8x	6.0x

As evident from the above table, Raj software trailing and forward P/E ratio is greater than the peerset companies or the sector. Assuming other things equal, Raj software is overvalued relative to the sector.

4. $P_0 = \dfrac{D_0(1+g)}{(k-g)}$ or $\dfrac{D_1}{(k-g)}$

P_0 = 2.50 × (1 + .05)/(15% – 5%) = 25

Given that the intrinsic value of Alok Industries is greater than the market traded price of ₹20, Rita should purchase the stock.

5. Intrinsic Value of Hindustan Systems using Multistage Dividend Discount Model:

		Year	*Dividends per Share*	*Dividend Growth*	*Present Value of Dividends*
***k* (Required rate of return)**	**12.0%**	Year 1	100.00		89.29
***g* (for terminal growth)**	6.00%	Year 2	115.00	15.00%	91.68
		Year 3	132.25	15.00%	94.13
		Year 4	152.09	15.00%	96.65
		Year 5	167.30	10.00%	94.93
		Year 6	184.03	10.00%	93.23
		Terminal value	**3,251**		
		Present value of terminal value	1,647		
		Present value of explicit forecast period	560		
		Intrinsic value of Hindustan Systems	2,207		

6. Intrinsic Value of Quicheal using Multistage Dividend Discount Model:

		Year	*Dividends per Share*	*Present value of Dividends*
Beta	1.25	2012E	8.00	6.93
Equity Risk Premium	6.0%	2013E	10.00	7.50
Risk Free	8.0%	2014E	13.00	8.44
k (CAPM)	15.5%	2015E	14.50	8.15
Retention ratio	40%	2016E	16.50	8.03
ROE	25%			
				(Contd.)

		Year	Dividends per Share	Present value of Dividends
g (for terminal growth)	10.00%			
		Terminal value	330	
		Present value of terminal value	161	
		Present value of explicit forecast period (2012–2016)	39	
		Intrinsic value of Quickheal	200	

Given that the intrinsic value of Quickheal (INR 200) is greater than the market traded price of INR 150, Sahil should purchase the stock.

7.

Particulars (Year 2010)	*Amount (₹in crores)*
Net profit for the year	120
Depreciation	5
Capital expenditure	20
Increase in working capital for the year	3
Debt Repayments for the year	9
New debt issued during the year	11

FCFE = Net profit or Net income
+ Depreciation and amortization (non-cash charges)
–/+Investment in Non-Cash Working Capital
– Capital Expenditure (Investment in Long-term Assets)
+ Increase in Net debt (Issue of new debt-repayment of older debt)

FCFE = 120 + 5 – 3 – 20 + 11 – 9 = 104

		Year	FCFE	FCFE growth	Present value of FCFE
k (Required Rate of Return)	11.0%	2010	104.00		
g (for terminal growth)	4.00%	2011	112.32	8%	101.19
		2012	121.31	8%	98.45
		2013	131.01	8%	95.79
		2014	141.49	8%	93.20
		2015	152.81	8%	90.69
		Terminal value	2,270.32		
		Present value of terminal value	1,347.33		
		Present value of explicit forecast period	479.33		
		Intrinsic value of McCain	1,826.65		
		Number of shares (in crores)	10.00		
		Intrinsic value per share of McCain	182.67		

8.

Company	*Price*	*EPS for next year*	*BVPS for next year*	*Growth in Earnings*	*Forward P/E Ratio*	*Forward P/B Ratio*	*PEG Ratio*
AKJ Bank	2,300	129	1,500	20%	17.8x	1.5x	0.89
Smithfield	1,208	70	700	10%	17.3x	1.7x	1.73
IBP	120	23	130	5%	5.2x	0.9x	1.04
MAT	3,050	230	2,400	15%	13.3x	1.3x	0.88
Hallblack	700	65	750	2%	10.8x	0.9x	5.38
RUJ Bank	140	20	100	6%	7.0x	1.4x	1.17
Mean P/E Multiple					11.9x	1.3x	1.8x
Median P/E Multiple					12.0x	1.3x	1.1x

Company	*Price*	*EPS for next year*	*BVPS for next year*	*Growth in Earnings*	*Forward P/E Ratio*	*Forward P/B Ratio*	*PEG Ratio*
RKB Bank	230	21	198	15%	11.0x	1.2x	0.73

As evident from the above table, RKB bank forward P/E and P/BV ratio is less than the peerset companies or the sector. PEG ratio for RKB bank is less than 1. Assuming other things equal, RKB bank is undervalued relative to the sector.

CHAPTER 11

1. $\text{WACC} = w_e * k_e + w_d * k_d * (1 - t)$

$w_e = 0.55$, $w_d = 0.45$, $k_d = 9\%$, $t = 40\%$ and WACC = 9.5%

Thus, $9.5\% = 0.55 \times k_e + 0.45 \times 9\% \times (1 - 0.4)$

Solving, $k_e = 12.85\%$

2. $k_p = 4.5/55 = 8.18\%$

3. $D_0 = ₹5$, $g = 6\%$, $P_0 = ₹75$
Thus, $D_1 = 5 \times (1 + 0.06) = ₹5.3$
Cost of retained earning,

$$k_{re} = \frac{D_1}{P_0} + g = \frac{5.3}{75} + 6\% = 13.06\%$$

Flotation cost, $F = 4\%$
Cost of new equity,

$$k_e = \frac{D_1}{P_0(1-F)} + g = \frac{5.3}{75(1-0.04)} + 6\% = 13.36\%$$

4. Cost of retained earnings,

$$k_{re} = \frac{D_1}{P_0} + g = \frac{5.5 * (1.07)}{50} + 7\% = 18.77\%$$

5. $k_{ps} = \frac{D}{V_{ps}(1-F)} = \frac{13}{95(1-0.05)} = 14.4\%$

6: k_d = 10%,

$$k_{re} = \frac{D_1}{P_0} + g = \frac{5(1.05)}{35} + 5\% = 20\%$$

$$\text{WACC} = 0.6 * 0.2 + 0.1 * 0.4 * (1-0.4) = 14.4\%$$

7. The firm's debt:equity:preferred stock = 60%:30%:10%
For 26 lakh investment, the firm would need:
Debt = 26 × 0.6 = ₹15.6 lakh
Preferred stock = ₹2.6 lakh
Equity = ₹7.8 lakh
Out of this, ₹7.5 lakh is from retained earnings and ₹0.3 lakh is from new equity
After tax cost of debt [$k_d(1-t)$] = 9%
Cost of preferred stock = 10%
Cost of retained earning = 13%
Cost of new equity = 15%
Thus,

$$\text{WACC} = \frac{15.6}{26} * 9\% + \frac{2.6}{26} * 10\% + \frac{7.8}{26} * 13\% + \frac{0.3}{26} * 15\% = 10.47\%$$

8. $k_e = \frac{D_1}{P_0(1-F)} + g = \frac{3.5}{45(1-0.15)} + 5\% = 14.15\%$

CHAPTER 12

1. **Ans.**

	Debt nil	**10% *Debt* 2,50,000**	**10% *Debt* 5,00,000**
Net Operating Income	1,00,000	1,00,000	1,00,000
Interest	0	25,000	50,000
Profits for Equityholders [*P*]	1,00,000	75,000	50,000
Cost of Equity Capital k_e	0.15	0.15	0.15
Market Value of Equity [P/k_e]	6,66,666.67	5,00,000.00	3,33,333.33
Market Value of Debt	0	2,50,000	5,00,000
Market Value of Firm [*V*]	6,66,666.67	7,50,000.00	8,33,333.33
Implied k_0 [NOI/*V*]	0.150	0.133	0.120
Implied k_0 %	15	13.33	12

[1] Using the net income approach:

[a] If Debt = Nil, then the value of firm and its overall cost of capital (k_0) would be ₹6,66,666.67 and 15%.

[b] If Debt = ₹2,50,000, then the value of firm and its overall cost of capital (k_o) would be ₹7,50,000 and 13.33%.

[c] If debt = ₹5,00,000, then the value of firm and its overall cost of capital (k_o) would be ₹8,33,333.33 and 12%.

[2] The optimal capital structure that would maximize the value of firm and minimize the overall cost of capital k_0 would be when debt level is ₹5,00,000.

2. **Ans.**

	***Debt* 0**	***Debt* 3,00,000**	***Debt* 6,00,000**
Net Operating Income	1,00,000	1,00,000	1,00,000
Overall Cost of Capital, k_0	0.125	0.125	0.125
Market Value of Firm	8,00,000	8,00,000	8,00,000
Less: Debt	0	3,00,000	6,00,000
Market Value of Equity (*E*)	8,00,000	5,00,000	2,00,000
Profits for Equityholders (*P*)	1,00,000	70,000	40,000
Implied k_e % [= *P*/*E*]	12.5	14	20

[1] Using the Net Operating Income approach:

[a] If Debt = Nil, value of firm and its cost of equity capital (k_e) would be ₹8,00,000 and 12.5%, respectively.

[b] If debt = ₹3,00,000, value of firm and its cost of equity capital (k_e) would be ₹8,00,000 and 14%, respectively.

[c] If debt = ₹6,00,000, value of firm and its cost of equity capital (k_e) would be ₹8,00,000 and 20%, respectively.

[2] The overall cost of capital k_0 is assumed to remain the same at all levels of debt financing. As the calculations show, the value of the firm is determined by capitalizing the operating earnings at the overall cost of capital (k_0), so the total value of the firm remains stable at ₹8,00,000 at all levels of debt/equity ratio. However, with every increase in the proportion of debt financing, the k_e rises in such a way so as to exactly offset any advantage of cheaper debt.

[3] Under the net operating approach, there is no optimal capital structure and any capital structure is as good as the other. This is because the total market value of the firm as well as the overall cost of capital (k_0) remain the same at all levels of debt/equity ratio.

3.

	***Debt* 0**	**8%*Debt* 2,50,000**	**10%*Debt* 5,00,000**
Net Operating Income	1,00,000	1,00,000	1,00,000
Interest	0	20,000	50,000
Profits for Equityholders [*P*]	1,00,000	80,000	50,000
Cost of Equity Capital k_e	0.12	0.13	0.18
Market Value of Equity [P/k_e]	8,33,333.33	6,15,384.62	2,77,777.78
Market Value of Debt	0	2,50,000	5,00,000
Market Value of Firm [*V*]	8,33,333.33	8,65,384.62	7,77,777.78
Implied k_0 % [NOI/V]	12.0	11.6	12.9

[1] Using the traditional approach:

[a] If Debt = Nil, the value of firm and its overall cost of capital (k_0) would be ₹8,33,333.33 and 12%, respectively.

[b] If debt = ₹2,50,000, the value of firm and its overall cost of capital (k_0) would be ₹8,65,384.62 and 11.6%, respectively.

[c] If debt = ₹5,00,000, the value of firm and its overall cost of capital (k_0) would be ₹7,77,777.78 and 12.9%, respectively.

[2] The optimal capital structure that would maximize the value of firm and minimize the overall cost of capital k_0:

The traditional approach implies that at low levels of debt financing, the increase in k_e does not completely offset the benefit of using cheaper debt funding. As a result, at moderate levels of debt, the total value of the firm increases and the overall cost of capital k_0 decreases. However as the proportion of debt increases beyond some point, k_e rises at an increasing rate with leverage. Moreover, k_d also may rise beyond some point. The optimal capital structure is the point at which k_0 is the minimum which in this case is a debt level of ₹2,50,000.

4. **Ans.**

[a] **Using the traditional approach, calculation of the value of each firm and its overall cost of capital (k_o):**

	A	*B*
	***Debt* = 0**	***Debt* = 4,00,000**
Net Operating Income	80,000	80,000
Interest	0	24,000
Profits for Equityholders [*P*]	80,000	56,000
Cost of Equity Capital k_e	0.12	0.14
Market Value of Equity [P/k_e]	6,66,666.67	4,00,000
Market Value of Debt	0	4,00,000
Market Value of Firm [*V*]	6,66,666.67	8,00,000
Implied k_o % [NOI/*V*]	12.00	10.00

As the above table shows, as per the traditional theory, the levered firm B (with debt) would have a higher market value and a lower overall cost of capital than firm A (without debt). This position, according to MM, cannot continue for long, because arbitrage will set in to drive the total value of the two firms equal to each other.

[b] **How arbitrage will work and what would be its effect on the value of the two firms?**

MM approach assumes that both the firm and individual investors can borrow at the same interest rate. To illustrate how arbitrage works, assume investor X owns 1% equity shares of firm B. He sells his equity for ₹4,000 (1% of ₹4,000), and takes a personal loan equal to 1% of firm B's loan = 4,000.

Thus, the total amount available with him would now be = ₹4,000 + 4,000 = 8,000. Out of this amount he uses ₹6,666.67 to buy 1% equity of firm A that would entitle him to get a return of ₹800 (1% of ₹80,000, the operating income of firm A). Out of his income of ₹800, he must pay the interest on loan taken by him = 6% × 4,000 = 240, leaving him with a net return of ₹560 which is the same as he was getting in firm B. By this arbitrage, he is able to get the same income as before but on a smaller investment base. He can invest the surplus amount to get an additional income.

In other words, by substituting corporate leverage by personal leverage, the investor is able to get same return on lower investment (or higher return by investing the entire amount). So he will prefer to sell off 'B' shares and invest in 'A' shares. When all investors follow the move to sell firm B shares and buy firm A shares, the share price of 'A' will rise and 'B' share will fall until there is equilibrium so that the value of the two firms is equal and no more arbitrage would be possible.

5. **Ans.**

(a) **Calculate the current market value of the firm.**

	Current
	10% *D* = 0.20
Net Operating Income	66,000.00
Interest	6,000.00
PBT	60,000.00
Taxes 40%	24,000.00
Profits for Equityholders [*P*]	36,000.00
Cost of Equity Capital k_e	0.15
Market Value of Equity [P/k_e]	2,40,000.00
Market Value of Debt	60,000.00
Market Value of Firm [*V*]	3,00,000.00
Implied k_o% [NOI/*V*] [Before Tax]	22.00

As the table shows:

- Value of debt = ₹60,000
- Value of equity = ₹24 × 10,000 = 2,40,000
  Value of equity can also be checked as = P/k_e = 36,000/0.15 = 2,40,000
- Value of the firm when there is no growth = Value of debt + Value of equity = ₹60,000 + 2,40,000 = 3,00,000.

(b) **Calculate the current (i) after tax cost of debt, and (ii) after tax WACC.**

Particulars	***Details***	***Cost %***
Interest Before Tax	6,000	
Debt (*D*)	60,000	
Before Tax Cost of Debt	(6,000/60,000) × 100 =	10%
After Tax Cost of Debt (k_d)	10% × (1 – 0.4) =	6%
Profit Avilable for Equityholders After Tax	36,000	
Market Value of Equity (*E*)	2,40,000	
Cost of Equity (After Tax) (k_e)	36,000/2,40,000	0.15
Market Value of Firm (*D* + *E*)	60,000 + 2,40,000 = 3,00,000	
Proportion of Debt [w_d]	60,000/3,00,000 =	0.20
Proportion of Equity [w_e]	2,40,000/3,00,000 =	0.80
WACC = ($w_d \times k_d$) + ($w_e \times k_e$)*	(0.20 × 6%) + (0.80 × 0.15)	13.2%
Before Tax Overall Cost (WACC)**	66,000/3,00,000 =	22.00%

Notes: w_d* is the relative weight (proportion) of debt, and w_e is the relative weight (proportion) of equity in the capital structure.

** Before tax overall cost can also be computed as = 13.2% × 100/(100 – 40) = 13.2% × 100/60 = 22%.

(c) **Determine the additional amount of debt to be issued.**

To compute the additional amount of debt to be issued, we need to take the following steps:

(i) **Calculate the new WACC before tax:**

$$\text{WACC after tax } k_o = k_d\left(\frac{D}{D+E}\right)(1-t) + k_e\left(\frac{E}{D+E}\right)$$

$$= (11\% * 0.5 * 0.6) + (17\% * 0.5)$$

$$= 0.118 = 11.8\%$$

$$\text{WACC before tax} = 11.8\% \times 100/60 = 19.67\%$$

(ii) Value of the firm at the new WACC:

V = NOI/WACC before tax = 66,000/0.1967 = ₹3,35,593.22

(iii) **If the new value of the firm is** ₹3,35,593.22, and the new debt has to be 50% of the value of the firm, then:

Total new debt = ₹3,35,593.22 × 50% = 1,67,796.61

Less: Old debt = ₹60,000

Hence, new additional debt required = 1,67,796.61 – 60,000 = 1,07,796.61.

Note that this additional amount of ₹1,07,796.61 debt raised will be used to repurchase equity shares. But what would be the repurchase price and how many shares would be repurchased?

(d) **Compute the repurchase price per share and determine the number of shares to be repurchased.**

New Value of the Firm	3,35,593.22
Less: Old Debt	60,000
New Value of the Equity Before Repurchase	2,75,593.22
Number of Existing Shares Outstanding	10,000
New Equity Price Per Share	27.56

Since the total amount available for repurchase of shares is ₹1,07,796.61, and the repurchase price to be offered is ₹27.56, the number of shares that can be repurchased = ₹1,07,796.61 ÷ ₹27.56 = 3,911.44 shares (assuming a fraction of share is allowed)

(e) **How many shares would remain outstanding after the recapitalization?**

Number of shares remaining outstanding after the recapitalization = 10,000 – 3,911.44 = 6,088.56 shares.

(f) **What would be the market value of the debt, equity and the firm after the above recapitalization has been achieved?**

Presenting all computations together, we get the following picture:

	Prior	***Post***
	10% D = *20%*	11% D = *50%*
Net Operating Income	66,000.00	66,000.00
Interest	6,000.00	18,457.63
PBT	60,000.00	47,542.37
Taxes 40%	24,000.00	19,016.95
Profits For Equityholders [P]	36,000.00	28,525.42
Cost of Equity Capital k_e	0.15	0.17
		(Contd.)

	Prior	*Post*
	10% D = 20%	*11% D = 50%*
Market Value of Equity [P/k_e]	2,40,000.00	1,67,796.61
Market Value of Debt	60,000.00	1,67,796.61
Market Value of Firm [V]	3,00,000.00	3,35,593.22
Implied k_o % [NOI/V] [Before Tax]	22.00	19.67

	k_o **After tax**	k_o **Before tax**
$k_o = [k_d \times D/(D + E)] + k_e \times E/(D + E)$		
Prior k_o = (10% * 0.6 * 0.2) + 15% * 0.8	0.132	0.2200
Post k_o = (11% * 0.6 * 0.5) + (17% * 0.5)	0.118	0.1967

The market values of debt, equity and the firm after the above recapitalization would be as follows:

- Market value of the debt: ₹1,67,796.61
- Market value of the equity: ₹1,67,796.61
- Market value of the firm: ₹3,35,593.22

Thus, in this case, we find that the recapitalization or a change in the financial leverage has enhanced the value of equity and the value of the firm, as well as reduced the weighted average cost of capital.

CHAPTER 13

1. **Ans.** The existing all equity capital structure consists of 20,000 shares of ₹10 each, or a total equity capital of ₹2,00,000. After raising the planned additional capital, total funds raised would rise to ₹3,50,000. If the additional funds required are raised by issuing new equity shares at a price of ₹15 per share (including share premium of ₹5 per share), the total number of equity shares would increase to 20,000 + 10,000 = 30,000. If the company chooses to raise the additional funding from either debt or preference share capital, the number of equity shares outstanding would remain constant. With this understanding, we can proceed to prepare the EBIT-EPS analysis as follows.

Amount in (₹)

	Financing Options		
	All equity	*Debt*	*Preference*
EBIT per annum (with new project)	1,20,000	1,20,000	1,20,000
Existing Interest	0	0	0
Additional Interest cost	0	22,500	0
Earnings Before Taxes (EBT)	1,20,000	97,500	1,20,000
Income tax	36,000	29,250	36,000
Earnings After Taxes (EAT)	84,000	68,250	84,000
Preference Dividend	0	0	21,000
Earnings for Equity holders	84,000	68,250	63,000
No of Equity shares*	30,000	20,000	20,000
Earnings Per Share (EPS) (₹)	2.80	3.41	3.15

*In equity option, the total number of equity shares = Existing 20,000 + New 10,000 = 30,000.

A comparison of the EPS under the three alternative financing plans shows that the EPS would be highest under the debt financing plan. In spite of issuing new equity shares at a premium, the EPS under the equity option falls way behind the EPS under debt option. The preference capital is cheaper than debt on a pre-tax basis, but due to the tax-shield on interest expense, the EPS under debt option is higher than the preference alternative. Therefore, other things being the same, the company can go for the debt alternative to finance the new project.

2. Ans. For the given situation, EBIT indifference point between equity (plan '*a*') and debt financing (plan '*b*') would be:

$$\frac{(X - Ia)(1-t)}{Na} = \frac{(X - Ib)(1-t)}{Nb}$$

where,

X = EBIT indifference point between the two financing plans.

Ia, Ib = Annual interest expenses before taxes under financing plans '*a*' and '*b*' respectively.

t = Income tax rate applicable to the company

Na, Nb = The number of equity shares outstanding under the financing plans '*a*' and '*b*' respectively.

Financing the project with equity capital (plan '*a*') means the company would not have to pay any fixed financial charges of interest. On the other hand, if it goes for debt financing it would have to pay the fixed cost of interest.

Substituting values for the given situation,

$$\frac{(X)(1-0.3)}{30{,}000} = \frac{(X - 22{,}500)(1-0.3)}{20{,}000}$$

$$\frac{(0.7X)}{30{,}000} = \frac{(X - 22{,}500)(0.7)}{20{,}000}$$

$$\frac{(0.7X)}{30{,}000} = \frac{(0.7X - 15{,}750)}{20{,}000}$$

By rearranging, we get:

$$(0.7X)\ 20{,}000 = (0.7X - 15{,}750)\ 30{,}000$$

$$14{,}000X = 21{,}000X - 47{,}25{,}00{,}000$$

$$21{,}000X - 14{,}000X = 47{,}25{,}00{,}000$$

$$X = 47{,}25{,}00{,}000/7{,}000$$

$$X = 67{,}500$$

Accordingly, an EBIT level of ₹67,500 would be the indifference point. This calculation can be cross-checked as follows:

	All equity	*Debt*
EBIT per annum (with new project)	67,500	67,500
Existing Interest cost	0	0
Additional Interest cost	0	22,500
Earnings Before Taxes (EBT)	67,500	45,000
Income tax	20,250	13,500
Earnings After Taxes (EAT)	47,250	31,500
Preference Dividend	0	0
Earnings for Equity holders	47,250	31,500
No of Equity shares*	30,000	20,000
Earnings Per Share (EPS) ₹	1.575	1.575

3. Ans. Presenting the information systematically:

Item	(₹)
Sales revenue (25,000 × 24)	6,00,000
Less: Variable operating costs (25,000 × 10)	2,50,000
Contribution (Sales revenue – variable cost)	3,50,000
Less: Fixed operating cost	1,50,000
Earnings before interest and taxes (EBIT)	2,00,000
Less: Interest charges	80,000
Earnings (or profit) before taxes	1,20,000

$$\text{Operating leverage } (L_o) = \frac{\text{Total contribution}}{\text{EBIT}} = \frac{3,50,000}{2,00,000} = 1.75$$

An operating leverage of 1.75 means that for every change of one percent in sales (from the base sales level), the EBIT would change by 1.75%.

$$\text{Financial leverage } (L_f) = \frac{\text{EBIT}}{\text{Earnings before Tax}} = \frac{2,00,000}{1,20,000} = 1.67$$

A financial leverage of 1.67 means that for every change of one percent in EBIT, the earnings before taxes (EBT) would change by 1.67%.

Total leverage: The total leverage may be calculated as follows:

$$\text{Total leverage } (L_t) = L_o \times L_f = (1.75)\ (1.67) = 2.92$$

4. Ans.

Step 1 First let us calculate the interest payable by each company:

	J	*K*	*L*	*M*
Assets	2,00,000	2,00,000	2,00,000	2,00,000
Debt = 50% of Assets	1,00,000	1,00,000	1,00,000	1,00,000
Interest Rate	0	10%	14%	17%
Interest Amount	0	10,000	14,000	17,000

Step 2 Comparison of four companies with different financial leverage:

	J	*K*	*L*	*M*
Assets	2,00,000	2,00,000	2,00,000	2,00,000
ROI	0.14	0.14	0.14	0.14
EBIT per annum	28,000	28,000	28,000	28,000
Interest	0	10,000	14,000	17,000
				(Contd.)

	J	*K*	*L*	*M*
Earnings Before Taxes (EBT)	28,000	18,000	14,000	11,000
Tax	8,400	5,400	4,200	3,300
Earnings After Taxes (EAT)	19,600	12,600	9,800	7,700
Preference Dividend	0	0	0	0
Earnings for Equity holders	19,600	12,600	9,800	7,700
No of Equity shares*	20,000	10,000	10,000	10,000
Earnings per share (EPS) ₹	0.98	1.26	0.98	0.77

Step III Effect of leverage on the firm's profitability:

The above table shows the effect of financial leverage on the EPS of the four companies. Companies J and L have same EPS even though J is all equity financed company while L has 50% debt funding. However, since company L earns same 14% return on investment as the rate of interest it pays, there is no positive effect of financial leverage on the company's EPS. Unless there are some strategic reasons to justify the use of debt financing, the company could avoid debt.

In comparison, Company K was able to deploy funds to earn a return higher than the cost of interest it pays. Due to this, the firm is earning a surplus return over the interest cost which has resulted in a higher EPS for equity shareholders. This situation represents a positive financial leverage and the use of debt funding would be well justified.

Company M has fared the worst among the four companies. Company M was able to deploy funds to earn a return less than the cost of interest; in other words, it is not even earning enough to meet the interest cost. As a result, the EPS available to equity holders has declined as compared to what it would have been without debt financing. Clearly, this situation represents a negative financial leverage and the use of debt funding in this situation is not justified.

CHAPTER 14

1. **Ans.** In the residual dividend policy, first priority is to retain and reinvest profits as much as required. Accordingly, the distribution of profits between cash dividends and retained earnings (reinvestment) will be as follows:

Year	*Net profit* (₹)	*Planned investment* (₹)	*Profits available for dividend* (₹)	*Dividend per share* (₹)	*External financing* (₹)
1	2,00,000	1,20,000	80,000	8	0
2	2,50,000	2,00,000	50,000	5	0
3	3,00,000	3,00,000	0	0	0
4	3,50,000	2,50,000	1,00,000	10	0
5	4,00,000	5,00,000	0	0	1,00,000
Total	15,00,000	13,70,000	2,30,000		1,00,000

Thus, the residual dividend policy would lead to minimum cash dividends per share as well as least external financing requirement. Also, dividends would fluctuate from year-to-year depending on the availability of earnings after setting aside funds required to undertake new projects.

2. **Ans.**

(a) **If the company follows a stable dividend payout ratio of 50%**

Year	*Net profit* (₹)	*50% payout* (₹)	*Dividend per share* (₹)	*Amount available for investment* (₹)	*Planned investment* (₹)	*External financing* (₹)
1	2,00,000	1,00,000	10	1,00,000	1,20,000	20,000
2	2,50,000	1,25,000	12.5	1,25,000	2,00,000	75,000
3	3,00,000	1,50,000	15	1,50,000	3,00,000	1,50,000
4	3,50,000	1,75,000	17.5	1,75,000	2,50,000	75,000
5	4,00,000	2,00,000	20	2,00,000	5,00,000	3,00,000
Total	15,00,000	7,50,000	7,50,000		13,70,000	6,20,000

(b) **If the company pays a stable dividend of ₹10 per share**

Year	*Profit* (₹)	*DPS* (₹)	*Profits used for dividend* (₹)	*Profits available for investment* (₹)	*Planned investment* (₹)	*External financing* (₹)
1	2,00,000	10	1,00,000	1,00,000	1,20,000	20,000
2	2,50,000	10	1,00,000	1,50,000	2,00,000	50,000
3	3,00,000	10	1,00,000	2,00,000	3,00,000	1,00,000
4	3,50,000	10	1,00,000	2,50,000	2,50,000	0
5	4,00,000	10	1,00,000	3,00,000	5,00,000	2,00,000
Total	15,00,000		5,00,000	10,00,000	13,70,000	3,70,000

As we can see from the above tables, the total amount paid out as dividends as well as the total amount of external financing for the period would be different depending on how 'stability' of dividends is interpreted. The distribution of cash as dividends would be higher under both these options as compared to the 'residual dividends approach' illustrated earlier using the same data.

3. **Ans.**

We know that: $P_0 = \frac{1}{1+r}(D_1 + P_1)$

Turning the equation around, we get the value of P_1.

Thus, $P_1 = P_0(1 + r) - D_1$

Where, r is the required rate of return. Then, for the given situation:

P_0	Current share price	40
'r'	Investors' required return	25%
D_1	Expected dividend at year end	₹5 per share

Substituting the values:

(a) P_1 with dividend = ₹40 (1.25) – 5

= ₹45 per share

(b) P_1 without dividend = ₹40 (1.25) – 0

= ₹50 per share

(c) Comparing Charlie's wealth at end of one year:
With dividend = (1,000 × ₹45) + (1,000 × 5)
= ₹45,000 + 5,000 = ₹50,000
Without dividend = (1,000 × ₹50) + (1,000 × 0)
= ₹50,000

In both cases, the wealth of shareholder would be same ₹50 per share or a total of ₹50,000. Hence in a world of no taxes, perfect information and no transaction costs, the existing shareholders should be neutral between receiving cash dividends and capital gains as a result of retained earnings. Thus, according to MM theory the dividend decision is irrelevant.

CHAPTER 15

1. Liquidity Position can be calculated through Current Ratio and Quick Ratio
Current ratio = Current Assets/Current Liabilities
Quick ratio = (Current Assets-Inventories)/Current Liabilities
For REI Company
Current ratio = 1.38
Quick ratio = 1.02
2. Debtors collection period = Trade Receivables × 365/Annual Credit sales
Inventory Holding period = Inventory × 365/Annual cost of goods sold
Creditor days = Trade Payables × 365/Annual Credit purchases

For REI Company

Debtors collection period = 15.37 days
Inventory Holding period = 41.71 days
Creditor days = 78.21 days
3. For REI Company, profitability ratios are:

	Year 2012
Gross profit Ratio	63%
Operating profit Ratio	37%
Profit before taxes Ratio	29%
Net profit after taxes Ratio	21%

4. Long-term Debt to Equity ratio = Long-term Debt/Shareholders' Funds
Total Debt to Equity ratio = Total Debt/Shareholders' Funds

Interest Coverage ratio = Earnings before interest and taxes (EBIT)/Annual Interest Expense
For REI Company
Long-term Debt to Equity ratio = 0.51
Total Debt to Equity ratio = 0.92
Interest Coverage ratio = 7.22
5. Return on capital employed = Earnings before Interest and Taxes (EBIT)/Total Capital Employed

Return on Net Worth = (Profit after Tax – Preference Dividends)/Shareholder's Fund or Net Worth

For REI Company
Return on capital employed = 42%
Return on Net Worth = 38%

Du-pont analysis	*Year 2012*
Net profit Margin	21.0%
Asset turnover Ratio	0.97
Leverage	1.92
RONW	**38%**

CHAPTER 16

1. **Ans.**

Step 1 Calculate the annual cost of various elements:

Cost item	*% of sales*	*Sales*	*Annual cost (₹)*
Direct materials	30	15,00,000	4,50,000
Direct labour	25	15,00,000	3,75,000
Variable production overhead	10	15,00,000	1,50,000
Fixed production overhead	15	15,00,000	2,25,000
Sales and distribution cost	5	15,00,000	75,000

The profit margin, 15% of sales in this example, should be excluded in estimation of the annual costs.

Step 2 Calculate the investment required in current assets

Current assets	*Calculation*	*Amount in (₹)*
(a) Debtors	15,00,000 × 0.85 × 2½/12	2,65,625
(b) Raw materials stock	4,50,000/4	1,12,500
(c) Work-in-progress	Material = 75,000 + Labour = 31,250 + Variable OH = 12,500	1,18,750
(d) Finished Goods	37,500 + 31,250 + 12,500	81,250
	Total current assets	**5,78,125**

Step 3 Determine financing available from creditors

Creditors for	*Calculation*	*Amount (₹)*
(i) Direct materials	2 months × 37,500	75,000.00
(ii) Direct labour	0.25 month × 31,250	7,812.50
(iii) Variable overhead	1 month × 12,500	12,500.00
(iv) Fixed overhead	1 month × 18,750	18,750.00
(v) Selling and distribution expenses	0.5 month × 6,250	3,125.00
	Total current liabilities	1,17,187.50

Step 4 Determine the net working capital required

Total current assets	5,78,125.00
Total current liabilities	1,17,187.50
Net working capital required	4,60,937.50
Add cash balance required	25,000.00
Total working capital requirement	4,85,937.50

The firm in this situation would need to arrange ₹4,85,937.50 for investing in working capital from sources other than creditors. If the debtors and inventory holding days can be reduced, or creditor days increased, then the investment in working capital can be further reduced.

2. **Ans.** Maximum Permissible Bank Finance (MPBF) under the three methods:

Method 1: MPBF = 0.75 (CA – CL)
= 0.75 (200 – 80) million
= ₹90 million

Method 2: MPBF = 0.75 (CA) – CL
= 0.75 (200 million) – 80 million
= ₹70 million

Method 3: MPBF = 0.75 (CA – CCA) – CL
= 0.75 (200 – 50) million – 80 million
= ₹32.5 million

CHAPTER 17

1. **Ans.** The annual quantity required is 16,000 × 2 = 32,000. Carrying or holding cost is ₹25 per unit per annum.
   (a) EOQ = $\sqrt{2 \times 32{,}000 \times 1{,}000/25}$ = 1,600 units
   (b) Ordering and holding costs if the company uses EOQ:
   Ordering cost = 1,000 × 32,000/1,600 = ₹20,000
   Holding cost = (1,600/2) × 25 = ₹20,000
   Total = ₹40,000
   (c) Ordering and holding costs at the order size of 16,000 units:
   Ordering cost = 1,000 × 32,000/16,000 = ₹2,000
   Holding cost = (16,000/2) × 25 = ₹2,00,000
   Total = ₹2,02,000
   Comparing the costs under (b) and (c) above, the company can save ₹2,02,000 – 40,000 = ₹1,62,000 by shifting to the EOQ system.
2. **Ans.**

$$\text{Yield} = \left(\frac{\text{Face value} - \text{Price}}{\text{Price}} \times \frac{365}{N}\right)100$$

Filling in the values, we get:

$$\text{Yield} = \left(\frac{37{,}000}{4{,}63{,}000} \times \frac{365}{270}\right) 100 = 10.80\%$$

CHAPTER 18

1. **Ans.** This problem can be solved by applying the equivalent annual benefit method. We find the equivalent annual benefit if the machine is replaced for all the possibilities and the one with maximum equivalent benefit would be the optimum replacement policy. This is as given below:

	Replacement year					
Cash Flows	**1**	**2**	**3**	**4**	**5**	**6**
0	–1,20,000	–1,20,000	–1,20,000	–1,20,000	–1,20,000	–1,20,000
1	1,40,000	40,000	40,000	40,000	40,000	40,000
2		1,25,000	40,000	40,000	40,000	40,000
3			1,15,000	40,000	40,000	40,000
4				1,00,000	40,000	40,000
5					70,000	40,000
6						40,000
Present value of cost	5,000.00	15,363.52	29,456.77	39,625.06	41,213.85	44,456.29
Equivalent annual benefit	₹1,387	₹4,262	₹8,172	₹10,992	₹11,433	₹10,812

In this table, we can see that maximum benefit is received if the machine is replaced in the fifth year. Thus, replacing the machine every 5 years would be the optimum replacement policy.

2. In the first problem, we need to find the half yearly payment to be made by the NGO. This can be calculated as given below:

$$10 = \frac{x}{1.05} + \frac{x}{1.05^2} + \frac{x}{1.05^3} + \frac{x}{1.05^4} + \frac{x}{1.05^5}$$

$$10 = x * PVA_{5\%,5}$$

Thus, solving for x, we get x = ₹2.31 million. Thus, half yearly payment is ₹2.31 million

3. We can solve in the same way and half yearly payment for a beneficiary receiving ₹20,000 would be ₹4,747.

Index